GLOBAL PRO BONO

The principle and practice of pro bono, or volunteer legal services for the poor and other marginalized groups, is an increasingly important feature of justice systems around the world. Pro bono initiatives now exist in more than eighty countries – including Colombia, Portugal, Nigeria, and Singapore – and the list keeps growing. Covering the spread of pro bono across five continents, this book provides a unique data set permitting the first-ever comparative analysis of pro bono's growing role in the access to justice movement. The contributors are leading experts from around the world, whose chapters examine both the internal roots of and global influences on pro bono in transnational context. Global Pro Bono explores the dramatically expanding geographical and political reach of pro bono: documenting its essential contribution to bringing more justice to those on the margins, while underscoring its complex and contested meaning in different parts of the world.

SCOTT L. CUMMINGS is the Robert Henigson Professor of Legal Ethics at the UCLA School of Law, where he teaches and writes about the legal profession, law and social change, and local government law. He is the faculty director of UCLA's Program on Legal Ethics and the Profession.

FABIO DE SA E SILVA is assistant professor of international studies and the Wick Cary Professor of Brazilian Studies at the University of Oklahoma. He is also an affiliated fellow at Harvard Law School's Center on the Legal Profession. He studies the social organization and the political impact of law and justice in Brazil and comparatively.

LOUISE G. TRUBEK is clinical professor of law emerita at the University of Wisconsin Law School, where she founded the Center for Public Representation. Louise is a graduate of the University of Wisconsin and the Yale Law School. An active scholar, she does research on public policy, public administration and human rights, and the legal profession.

CAMBRIDGE STUDIES IN LAW AND SOCIETY

Founded in 1997, Cambridge Studies in Law and Society is a hub for leading scholarship in socio-legal studies. Located at the intersection of law, the humanities, and the social sciences, it publishes empirically innovative and theoretically sophisticated work on law's manifestations in everyday life: from discourses to practices, and from institutions to cultures. The series editors have longstanding expertise in the interdisciplinary study of law, and welcome contributions that place legal phenomena in national, comparative, or international perspective. Series authors come from a range of disciplines, including anthropology, history, law, literature, political science, and sociology.

A list of books in the series can be found at the back of this book.

GLOBAL PRO BONO

Causes, Context, and Contestation

Edited by

Scott L. Cummings
University of California, Los Angeles

Fabio de Sa e Silva
University of Oklahoma

Louise G. Trubek
University of Wisconsin–Madison

CAMBRIDGE
UNIVERSITY PRESS

CAMBRIDGE
UNIVERSITY PRESS

Shaftesbury Road, Cambridge CB2 8EA, United Kingdom

One Liberty Plaza, 20th Floor, New York, NY 10006, USA

477 Williamstown Road, Port Melbourne, VIC 3207, Australia

314–321, 3rd Floor, Plot 3, Splendor Forum, Jasola District Centre, New Delhi – 110025, India

103 Penang Road, #05–06/07, Visioncrest Commercial, Singapore 238467

Cambridge University Press is part of Cambridge University Press & Assessment, a department of the University of Cambridge.

We share the University's mission to contribute to society through the pursuit of education, learning and research at the highest international levels of excellence.

www.cambridge.org
Information on this title: www.cambridge.org/9781108469920

DOI: 10.1017/9781108567251

First published 2022
First paperback edition 2025

A catalogue record for this publication is available from the British Library

Library of Congress Cataloging-in-Publication data
Names: Cummings, Scott L., 1969– editor. | Silva, Fabio de Sa e, 1980– editor. | Trubek, Louise G., 1937– editor.
Title: Global pro bono: causes, context, and contestation / Scott L. Cummings, UCLA; Fabio de Sa e Silva, University of Oklahoma; Louise G. Trubek, University of Wisconsin, Madison.
Description: Cambridge, United Kingdom; New York, NY, USA: Cambridge University Press, 2021. | Includes index.
Identifiers: LCCN 2020009234 (print) | LCCN 2020009235 (ebook) | ISBN 9781108476157 (hardback) | ISBN 9781108567251 (ebook)
Subjects: LCSH: Legal assistance to the poor. | Public interest law.
Classification: LCC K133 .G56 2020 (print) | LCC K133 (ebook) | DDC 344.03/258–dc23
LC record available at https://lccn.loc.gov/2020009234
LC ebook record available at https://lccn.loc.gov/2020009235

ISBN 978-1-108-47615-7 Hardback
ISBN 978-1-108-46992-0 Paperback

CONTENTS

CONTRIBUTORS

Alice L. Brown is an attorney based in Johannesburg who is a board member of the public interest law firm Section27 and a visiting research fellow with the African Centre for the Study of the US at the University of the Witwatersrand. Previously, she practiced law with the NAACP Legal Defense Fund in the United States and acted as the representative of the Ford Foundation Office for Southern Africa. She obtained her JD from New York University School of Law.

Andrew Boon has a PhD in law from the University of Westminster for a study of professionalism, ethics, and legal education. He is a professor of law at City, University of London.

Annette Olesen has a PhD in law from the University of Southern Denmark and studies access to justice, legal aid, and the voluntary sector. She is an associate professor at the Department of Sociology and Social Work, Aalborg University.

Arpita Gupta is an associate professor at the Jindal Global Law School, O.P. Jindal Global University, India. She holds an SJD from the University of Wisconsin Law School, and an LLM from the Catholic University of Portugal (UCP), Lisbon.

Avis Whyte holds an LLM in European and international trade law from Leicester University. A member of the Centre on the Legal Profession at the University of Westminster, London, Avis's research focuses on this field. She is an assistant course leader, senior researcher, and senior lecturer at Westminster.

Daniel Bonilla Maldonado is a full professor of law at Universidad de los Andes in Bogotá. He holds a doctorate and a Master of Laws from Yale Law School and a law degree from Universidad de los Andes.

Edwin Rekosh is co-founder and managing partner of Rights CoLab. He previously founded PILnet: The Global Network for Public Interest Law. He was a member of the adjunct faculty of Columbia Law School for twenty-one years and a visiting professor of law at

Cardozo Law School and Central European University. He holds a JD from Columbia Law School.

Fabio de Sa e Silva is assistant professor of international studies and the Wick Cary Professor of Brazilian Studies at the University of Oklahoma. He is also an affiliated fellow at Harvard Law School's Center on the Legal Profession. He studies the social organization and the political impact of law and justice in Brazil and comparatively.

Fiona Kay holds a PhD in sociology from the University of Toronto and studies gender and racial diversity in the legal profession, career pathways among notaries and lawyers in civil law jurisdictions, and the regulation of paralegals. She is a professor of sociology at Queen's University in Kingston, Canada.

Fiona McLeay is the regulator of lawyers in the state of Victoria, Australia. She was formerly the CEO of Justice Connect, Australia's leading pro bono access to justice nonprofit. She holds a BA (Hons) and an LLM from the University of Melbourne, an LLB from the University of New South Wales, and an LLM from New York University Law School.

Helena Whalen-Bridge is an associate professor at the National University of Singapore Faculty of Law. She holds an LLM from the National University of Singapore and a JD from the University of Connecticut. Her research on the legal profession focuses on regulation, legal ethics, and access to justice.

Jayanth K. Krishnan is the Milt and Judi Stewart Professor of Law and director of the Stewart Center on the Global Legal Profession at the Indiana University – Bloomington Maurer School of Law. He holds a PhD from the University of Wisconsin–Madison and a JD from Ohio State University.

Jeremy Perelman is an associate professor at the Sciences Po Law School. His research focuses on the intersection between human rights–based approaches to sustainable development, global economic governance, and social change advocacy in the Global South. He is also the faculty and executive director of the Sciences Po Law School Clinic.

Jin Dong holds a PhD in sociology from State University of New York at Buffalo. His main research interests include law, social change, and globalization. He is the author of several scholarly articles regarding lawyers' pro bono and the legal profession in the age of globalization.

John Bliss is an assistant professor at the University of Denver Sturm College of Law. He is also a faculty affiliate at the Harvard Law School Center on the Legal Profession. He holds a JD from Berkeley Law and a PhD from Berkeley's Jurisprudence and Social Policy program.

Jonathan Klaaren is a professor at the University of the Witwatersrand (Wits). He holds a PhD in sociology from Yale and law degrees from Columbia (JD) and Wits (LLB). He served as head/dean of the Wits Law School from 2010 to 2013.

Kunle Ajagbe is a partner at Aidan Partners Law Firm in Lagos, Nigeria. He was called to the bar in 1999 and has previously worked in some of Nigeria's leading commercial law firms. He is a graduate of the Nigerian Law School and holds an LLB from Obafemi Awolowo University.

Lamin Khadar is the pro bono manager for Europe at the international law firm, Dentons. He is also an adjunct global professor of law at New York University in Paris, where he runs a legal clinic. He completed his PhD at the European University Institute in 2019, which was awarded the Mauro Cappelletti Prize for best thesis in comparative law. He qualified as a lawyer in England in 2012.

Leire Larracoechea San Sebastián is co-founder and executive director of Fundación Pro Bono España. She is also an adjunct professor at IE Law School's legal clinic. Previously, Leire was the director of Pro Bono Partnerships at the Cyrus R. Vance Center for International Justice and an associate lawyer at Cuatrecasas. She holds an LLM from Harvard Law School and was awarded a Fulbright scholarship.

Louis Assier-Andrieu is a professor at Sciences Po, a research assistant with the laboratory of Claude Lévi-Strauss (Collège de France), a fellow at the Mario Einaudi Center for International Studies (Cornell) and the Cambridge Group for the History of Social Structure, and a senior adviser to the ministries of justice and foreign affairs (France). His areas of expertise include the cultural theory of law, the historical anthropology of Western law, legal norms and cultural norms, and the history and culture of the legal profession.

Louise G. Trubek is clinical professor of law emerita at the University of Wisconsin Law School, where she founded the Center for Public Representation. Louise is a graduate of the University of Wisconsin and the Yale Law School. An active scholar, she does research on public policy, public administration and human rights, and the legal profession.

Lucy Adams is the strategic advocacy and policy manager of Civil Justice at Victoria Legal Aid and was previously the head of Homeless Law and Advocacy at Justice Connect, Australia's leading pro bono access-to-justice nonprofit. She has a BA/LLB (Hons) from the University of Melbourne and was awarded a Churchill Fellowship to study the criminalization of homelessness and poverty.

Michelle Ha was a fellow at PILnet: The Global Network for Public Interest Law focusing on refugee assistance pro bono. She received a Harvard Sinclair-Kennedy Fellowship to conduct research on legal assistance for asylum seekers in Spain. She holds a JD from Harvard Law School, where she served as the president of the Harvard Immigration Project and director of the International Refugee Assistance Project.

Ole Hammerslev is a professor in sociology of law at the University of Southern Denmark. He holds a PhD in sociology and an LLM from the University of Copenhagen. His research focuses on the legal profession, access to justice, globalization, and state construction.

Qian Cheng is a venture capitalist in Silicon Valley. He holds a PhD in law from Wuhan University and an LLM in corporate governance and practice from Stanford Law School. His research has focused on venture capital financing, technology law, and lawyering for innovation.

Robert Granfield holds a PhD in sociology from Northeastern University and is a professor of sociology and the vice provost for faculty affairs at the University at Buffalo – The State University of New York. His research has focused on the socialization of law students, the social organization of the legal profession, drug policy, and addiction studies.

S. Todd Crider is an M&A and finance partner at Simpson Thacher & Bartlett LLP, New York, where he heads the Latin American practice. He was a founder of the Cyrus Vance Center for International Justice. His pro bono practice focuses on issues of access to justice, indigenous peoples' rights, and advocacy for justice and rule of law. He holds a JD from Columbia Law School.

Scott L. Cummings is the Robert Henigson Professor of Legal Ethics at the UCLA School of Law, where he teaches and writes about the legal profession, law and social change, and local government law. He is the faculty director of UCLA's Program on Legal Ethics and the Profession.

Steven A. Boutcher is the executive officer of the Law and Society Association and senior research fellow at the Institute of Social Science Research at the University of Massachusetts, Amherst. His research broadly focuses on the intersection of law, social movements, and organizations, with a particular focus on the institutionalization of pro bono in large US firms and its connection to social movement causes.

Susana Santos holds a PhD in sociology from ISCTE University Institute of Lisbon and a Master's Degree in communication, culture, and technology studies. She is a research fellow at the Centre of Studies in Sociology (CIES) and an adjunct professor in the Department of Sociology, ISCTE. Her research has focused on the socialization of lawyers, the effects of globalization on the legal profession and legal education, and the study of transnational elites, combining qualitative and quantitative methods.

Thabang M. Pooe is a practicing advocate with the Johannesburg Society of Advocates and in-house counsel at public interest law center, Section27. She holds an LLM (specializing in public interest law and policy) from the University of California, Los Angeles, and an LLB from the North West University.

CHAPTER ONE

WHAT IS GLOBAL ABOUT PRO BONO AND WHAT IS GLOBAL PRO BONO ABOUT?

Scott L. Cummings, Fabio de Sa e Silva, and Louise G. Trubek

INTRODUCTION

The principle and practice of pro bono – volunteer legal services for the poor and other marginalized groups – is an increasingly important feature of justice systems around the world.[1] A quarter century ago, organized pro bono programs were a rarity in the United States and virtually nonexistent elsewhere.[2] Now, in contrast, pro bono has become widely diffused and institutionally central in a growing number of countries throughout the Global North and Global South. In a sign of pro bono's increasing international profile, PILnet (the Network for Public Interest Law), a key sponsor of the global pro bono movement, has hosted Pro Bono Forums across continents (ten in Europe and five in Asia), bringing together law firm pro bono coordinators, civil society partners, and representatives from more than fifty pro bono organizations in countries as diverse as Indonesia and Italy. In 2013, the Global Pro Bono Network was founded as a consortium of pro bono intermediaries and now includes 52 organizations in 34 countries. A 2016 survey of large-firm pro bono, covering 64,500 lawyers from 130 law firms in 75 countries, showed lawyers contributed 2.5 million pro bono hours over a 12-month period, with an annual average of 39.2 hours per lawyer. Once confined to the professional margins, pro bono now occupies a central position in the global access-to-justice movement.

Yet, as pro bono spreads, it develops in diverse ways that reveal different approaches and unique understandings of the role that volunteer services should play in promoting professionalism and equal justice. In countries where it has a strong presence, pro bono yields important positive outcomes for underserved individuals and nongovernmental organizations (NGOs) that advocate on their behalf. But pro bono also invites controversy – often attacked by proponents of state-based legal aid as a vehicle of neoliberal privatization and resisted by solo and small-firm lawyers as unfair competition. Our book seeks to deepen understanding of pro bono as a double-edged sword: a means of redistributing legal resources to those who desperately need them, but also a tool of professional legitimation that can reinforce profound inequalities in the legal system – thus reflecting a core paradox of contemporary professionalism. Covering the advance of pro bono in over twenty countries across five continents, this book provides a unique comparative data set permitting the first-ever analysis of pro bono's contested role as a tool of access to justice and a feature of legal professionalism around the world.

In so doing, the book spotlights important issues at the heart of sociolegal study of globalization and its impact on legal practice and professional identity.[3] Although public service has long been considered an essential feature of legal professionalism,[4] the central question this book explores is *why* professions in different parts of the world adopt specific ideas and institutions in support of pro bono – actualized by private lawyers providing free legal services to poor individuals and underrepresented groups. Our approach is to examine this question comparatively,[5] exploring how the interaction between local and global factors shapes pro bono in specific national contexts – a process we call *hybridization*. Our analysis yields important new insights on processes of transnational diffusion, in which a core set of ideas and practices are emulated by professional entrepreneurs building organized pro bono programs around the world, yet result in significant institutional and ideological variation across countries and practice sites. To better understand hybridization, this book focuses empirically on a range of factors shaping how pro bono is translated from global norm to local practice: the independence of the legal profession and its relation to national government, the scale of large law firms and the power of global corporate clients, the interaction between market-based and state-based systems for providing legal services to the poor, the influence of the small-firm bar and law schools on professional standards and practices, the role of global funders, and the local nature of legal need. Evaluating how these factors play out in different national contexts leads us to an important conclusion: there is no singular understanding of pro bono but rather a set of contested meanings and practices shaped by global and local legal actors vying to advance their own professional priorities and embed distinctive visions of professional service.[6]

It is a critical moment to assess the increasing importance of pro bono as a pillar of national justice systems.[7] Recent surveys have identified organized pro bono efforts in more than eighty countries – from established programs in Australia and the United Kingdom to upstart initiatives in the Czech Republic, Georgia, Haiti, Malta, and Uganda – and the list keeps growing.[8] As the contributions to this book demonstrate, contemporary pro bono norms and practices develop from multiple sources. The roots of pro bono grow from indigenous traditions of public service, nurtured by local professional associations, which provide legitimacy and resources. Yet the nature and scope of pro bono is also influenced by a multitude of global actors, which promote information exchange through conferences and websites while providing models that are promoted and imitated on the ground. Around the world, the movement to build pro bono programs is supported by funders like the Open Society Foundations (OSF) and thought leaders like the Cyrus R. Vance Center for International Justice and the Global Pro Bono Bar Association. Simultaneously, pro bono models are transmitted through globe-trotting law practice, corporate social responsibility (CSR) programs, and transnational NGO activism. As this book shows, these local and global forces interact in context-specific ways as domestic traditions of professional service become linked to cosmopolitan notions of pro bono, influenced in many cases by US models, but building on and responding to national professional structures. Through this process of hybridization, the result is less a unifying vision of "global pro bono" than a proliferation of multiple, diverse local pro bono systems shaped by professional stratification, preexisting investments in legal aid, and North-South colonial legacies. In our analysis of hybridization, a consistent theme is the struggle over the very meaning of pro bono, who does it, and who benefits from it – revealing distinctive patterns of conflict and cooperation among different segments of the bar. Why hybridization happens, what it looks like, and what consequences it has for the people who need legal services are our main inquiries.

To address these inquiries, we present leading-edge work from a global network of researchers who came together around a common interest in studying pro bono's institutionalization and impact. The framework and chapters coalesced around a series of encounters,[9] culminating in a November 2017 meeting at the UCLA School of Law, sponsored by the US National Science Foundation. Through these encounters, contributors developed original studies of pro bono in the following countries (in the order they appear in the book): the United States, Canada, Brazil, Argentina, Chile, Colombia, England and Wales, France, Portugal, Spain, Denmark, Australia, South Africa, Nigeria, India, Singapore, and China. One team also produced a study of pro bono in Europe writ large. This introduction aims to set the theoretical and methodological framework for these studies, synthesize their findings, and draw lessons for pro bono theory and practice.

Global Pro Bono: A Working Definition

Whereas the term "pro bono" did not appear in the professional lexicon of lawyers in many places around the world at the turn of the millennium, it has now achieved commonplace status in the countries in this book and beyond. As we have argued, however, the meaning of this term varies from country to country – and even within countries, the ideal of pro bono often diverges from its practice. To address this variation, we started from the premise that pro bono – as a central element of legal service provision and professional identity – is a terrain of struggle, not a set of stable ideas or practices.[10] In this vein, we invited our contributors to take issue with the concept itself – to contest its meaning as a core aim of our project.

Nevertheless, to standardize inquiry, we set forth a definition of pro bono as legal services provided for free or at significantly below-market rates to individuals who cannot afford to pay or organizations that advocate on their behalf. On the basis of this definition, we expected contributors to focus attention on voluntary service provided by private lawyers outside of paying client work to assist indigent clients in issue areas of important legal need, such as health, housing, social welfare, and civil rights. We also expected our definition to include free legal representation provided to large classes of marginalized or subordinated people, NGOs serving disadvantaged communities, and even private enterprises with a social mission. Although we were primarily interested in pro bono work by private lawyers planned in advance, we anticipated variation in the form and scope of pro bono service in relation to lawyers' practice sites. For instance, based on research in the United States and elsewhere, we expected lawyers in small firms or solo practice to perform pro bono service differently than their large-firm counterparts: rather than planning to provide free services in advance, reducing fees retroactively for clients unable to pay.[11] Furthermore, we predicted that lawyers in government and NGO practice might also do pro bono, but rarely at the levels of (or in the same way as) their private sector counterparts.[12]

The "global" dimension of pro bono as used in this book is meant to illuminate two perspectives. One is comparative – investigating the origins, features, and impact of pro bono activity within individual nations, and then comparing those nations' similarities and differences. The second perspective is transnational – tracing the forces shaping the transmission of pro bono across nations. This perspective focuses primary attention on the role of transnational pro bono actors – foundations and other NGOs that sponsor international pro bono initiatives, as well as global law firms, which carry specific pro bono ideologies and practices into new markets. From this transnational point of view, we also see domestic lawyers working on behalf of clients or causes outside of their home country's borders,[13] although this type of cross-border pro bono is residual to the main body of data that appears in this book[14] – reflecting the ongoing importance of the nation-state as a site for law practice on behalf of those in need. Indeed, given the uniqueness of national legal cultures and institutions, and the geographically bounded nature of legal need, we hypothesize that the bulk of pro bono around the world will be undertaken within national jurisdictions, even if the pro bono model often counts on support and inspiration from foreign sources. However, as we note in conclusion, we suspect that current struggles against the spread of authoritarian populism within and beyond the countries covered in this book may provide more impetus to transnational efforts by progressive legal elites to protect the rule of law.

Theory and Method: The Study of Pro Bono within and across Countries

As a theoretical matter, we are interested in how professional norms of public service and access-to-justice traditions are converted into the concept of pro bono organized as free service to poor individuals and underrepresented groups; how that concept is codified in ethical rules and institutional support structures; and what pro bono looks like in terms of who provides it and who receives it. This process of conversion from general norm to specific practice – what we call hybridization – is mediated by the circulation of ideas in the global marketplace as well as the changing structure of national legal professions and their relationship to inequality.

Focusing on the process of hybridization raises critical questions about individual agency, political governance, and international power.[15] At the individual level are questions of motivation and activism. Who decides to promote pro bono, in what form, and why? There must be interest convergence between private firm lawyers who provide resources and advocates of the poor and other underserved groups in need of support. This convergence draws attention to the nature and purpose of public service and its relation to professional legitimation. At a structural level, the hybridization framework raises questions about the link between the legal profession and political governance more broadly, since pro bono resonates with a neoliberal vision of the state in which obligations to society, in the form of safety net and other redistributive programs, give way to deregulation that serves the private interests of corporations, whose success is equated with the public good. This book explores the degree to which government agencies and NGOs promoting pro bono – as a model of private charity set against state-based legal aid – are inspired by neoliberal philosophies that redefine the meaning of access to justice and the rule of law. Finally, to the extent that pro bono is viewed as an export of the Global North, it raises questions about power relations and US influence. Many pro bono entrepreneurs do, in fact, receive training at elite US law schools and obtain support from US-based foundations and NGOs. The pro bono programs of global law firms and corporate legal departments reach all over the world, spreading US-inspired pro bono concepts and organizational models. Yet influence is never entirely top down: as pro bono takes shape across different countries, it encounters alternative traditions of voluntary legal work, generating new exchanges and communities of practice in the Global South. It is this complex process of hybridization that we aim to illuminate.

Toward this end, our comparative project examines pro bono's development in seventeen individual countries plus Europe as a region. The countries in this book were selected for study based on criteria of geographic variation (we wanted to examine pro bono on all continents, with significant representation of countries in the Global South), organizational development (we wanted to look at countries that had achieved enough pro bono development to make investigation worthwhile), and institutional diversity (we wanted to compare countries with different types of legal systems and that had taken different approaches to organizing pro bono service). After reviewing publicly available sources of global pro bono organizations and speaking to experts in the field, we identified target countries with substantial pro bono programs and histories, and began recruiting researchers to execute country studies. In doing so, we were mindful of the need to mobilize researchers with appropriate country-specific expertise, which we did through existing scholarly networks and by holding open forums at conferences during the formative phase of the project. In the end, we succeeded in assembling research teams composed of leading scholars and practitioners, whose contributions cover a wide range of countries and provide an unprecedented data set of pro bono practices. With the team of researchers in place, we asked them to produce chapters organized around three central inquiries, which form the framework for the book and the foundation of our analysis in this opening chapter.

The book's first inquiry probes the *causes* of pro bono's emergence and development in the countries under review. What factors cause pro bono to be institutionalized – by which we mean to develop as a widely shared professional norm and set of common practices?[16] Who are the most important actors influencing pro bono domestically and globally? What stakes do they have in promoting or fighting against pro bono? What resources and networks of support do they mobilize? What accounts for their success or failure? This inquiry illuminates the process of hybridization by exploring how the scope, nature, and output of pro bono in individual countries are shaped by the interaction of local and global factors.[17] Local factors include the relative size and power of the large- and small-firm practice sectors; the scope and organization of state-funded legal aid; the existence and influence of legal NGOs engaged in cause-oriented advocacy; the breadth of government support structures for pro bono; the size and autonomy of the private bar; the nature of legal education; the existence of third-party monitors to collect and report pro bono data; and the presence of domestic pro bono entrepreneurs. Global factors include the influence of neoliberal values; the degree of penetration of transnational NGO intermediaries and global pro bono funders; the relationship between multinational corporations and transnational law firms; the interaction between CSR and pro bono culture; and the integration of technology. The resulting pro bono system in each country borrows aspects of global pro bono, while building on and adapting local institutions and traditions.

Our second inquiry investigates the *consequences* of pro bono's institutionalization from two perspectives. From the first perspective, we aim to understand the basic structure of pro bono: its organization and ethical codification. Here, we ask: What tools and protocols are created to deliver pro bono services inside law firms and throughout the wider bar? How do these tools and protocols promote the efficiency and integrity of pro bono services? How is pro bono encoded in ethical rules, if at all? What are the roles that clearinghouses and other legal services organizations play? From a second perspective, we are interested in the distributional consequences of pro bono: Who provides and receives pro bono and in what form? Which types of legal matters are valued and which devalued as pro bono becomes more organized? What type of support comes from the large- and small-firm practice sectors? Which lawyers promote pro bono and which view it as a threat? What impact does the development of pro bono have on other legal resources, particularly state-based legal aid, and in this sense, how much can pro bono be said to support neoliberalism or reduce the economic insecurity it produces? How does pro bono respond to the legal needs of the poor, other underrepresented groups, and social movements? Has pro bono ultimately increased access to justice and by what measure?

Our final inquiry explores the global *contestation* over the meaning of pro bono, mapping variation in how pro bono is understood and implemented within and across national contexts. As this inquiry reveals, conflict over pro bono's role in domestic professions is the rule, not the exception, and this conflict erupts around consistent themes. Is pro bono a homegrown practice or a foreign transplant? Does it complement or substitute for the state's commitment to provide free legal aid? And should pro bono be considered a strictly legal service, mobilizing lawyers' special expertise, or should it encompass broader charitable service, which may be provided by lawyers in discharging their public duties?

Our method of analysis is to derive the most important factors shaping pro bono based on systematic review of the book's chapters and to map those factors in relation to the country-specific evidence of pro bono's development. This mapping allows us to look for similarities and differences across cases, thus illuminating patterns of hybridization in comparative context. Our main goal is to outline lessons learned about the causes and consequences of global pro bono, while setting forth the main lines of conflict over its meaning. Based on this analysis, we offer explanations for the patterns we encounter, suggesting reasons for different approaches to pro bono across countries – and leading us to hypothesize about what the future of global pro bono might hold and how our research might help frame questions to guide its development.

From a theoretical perspective, one of our aims is to use our investigation of pro bono to deepen scholarship on the legal profession and its role in society at a moment when lawyers are increasingly participating in – and thus helping to constitute – a global arena of legal practices and institutions. Greater integration of previously closed economies and changes in philosophies and practices in economic development have posed new questions about legal globalization and lawyer professionalism not explored in the scholarly domain. What are the challenges and opportunities confronting lawyers in an era of globalization and how are they dealing with them? Are some kinds of legal practice gaining traction, while others are losing ground? Are legal practices and organizational forms from the Global North, especially the United States, being transplanted to the Global South, as much of the existing literature on globalization predicts? Although our book does not answer all these questions, we hope that the study of global pro bono offers insights into larger dynamics that shine greater light on these fundamental issues.

HYBRIDIZATION: CAUSES, CONSEQUENCES, AND CONTESTATION

This section synthesizes and organizes the book's main findings on pro bono's global development. We start from the premise that hybridization occurs when global pro bono values interact with country-specific conditions, producing distinctive varieties of pro bono in different national settings. This section provides a framework for understanding this variety, using evidence from individual cases to suggest broader dynamics and themes. Following our central lines of inquiry, we begin by identifying the causal factors that shape pro bono's hybridization, and then turn to evaluate pro bono's impact on access to justice and its contested meaning across countries.

Causes

What causes pro bono to institutionalize when and where it does, and what accounts for its distinctive format? As the chapters in this book show, the answer to this question is deeply contingent on the peculiar ways in which local and global factors interact in particular countries at specific moments in time. Here, our goal is to map the most significant factors, based on our reading of the record assembled in the country studies, and to highlight their impact by mobilizing relevant examples. In doing so, we proceed from the local to the global, not because we think the local is more important, but because pro bono as a global transplant must adapt to local structures and practices. We thus start by reviewing the domestic factors that have enabled or constrained pro bono's institutionalization, and then shift focus to highlight global factors flowing out of the spread of neoliberalism and the transnational pro bono movement. As this analysis reveals, there is no sealed boundary between the "local" and "global": many of the structures we identify as homegrown have in fact been deeply shaped by globalization, while global trends all emanate from local contexts. In this sense, the local–global division we offer is best understood as an analytical framework – providing bottom-up and town-down perspectives on hybridization – rather than demarcating separate domains of activity and influence.

Local Factors

Corporate Law Sector

In every country under review, we see that norms and practices of pro bono are historically embedded in the legal profession, and there are long-standing traditions of lawyers across private practice engaging in some "voluntary legal work."[18] It is in this sense that the roots of what we now think of as "pro bono" grow out of indigenous soil and that the concept of pro bono expresses locally derived ideals of what it means for lawyers to be part of a public profession. Since pro bono springs from the duty of private lawyers to give back to society, it is not surprising that the structure of the domestic private practice sector profoundly affects the development of pro bono. Because law practice around the world historically has been, and continues to be, primarily conducted by lawyers practicing in small units, the nature of pro bono bears the strong imprint of solo and small-firm lawyer volunteerism, which tends to be ad hoc and episodic. Moreover, as we will discuss, the structure of solo and small-firm practice – especially its reliance on individual clients and, in some places, its dependence on government funding – can mobilize lawyers in this sector against the arrival of globalized pro bono models associated with large corporate law firms, which pose a competitive threat.

One of the most striking and consistent findings from our country studies is that the rise of contemporary pro bono correlates strongly with the growth of the domestic corporate law firm sector, which appears across cases as an essential precondition to pro bono in its institutionalized form. We treat the development of the corporate law sector as one of the local factors shaping pro bono in light of its relation to other forms of domestic private practice and because of variation in how open domestic legal professions are to the entry of foreign law firms. Nonetheless, it is obvious that the growth of the corporate law sector is a global phenomenon powered by the expansion of global markets and the need for sophisticated legal advice by transnational corporations seeking to exploit economic opportunities around the world.[19] At the domestic level, growth in the corporate law sector – in terms of the number of such firms and, more crucially, their size – produces opportunities for pro bono to take root: both because law firm growth creates the excess capacity needed to permit lawyers to spend time on pro bono outside of billable work and because growth connects domestic firms to the global corporate law sector, facilitating the transmission of pro bono values and practices. For large law firms seeking to model success, market services, and recruit talent, performing pro bono becomes an essential part of what it means to play on the global stage and gain legitimacy with corporate clients and elite lawyers alike. (For this reason, the country studies suggest that corporate firms watch what their counterparts in other countries do: for example, Canadian firms report monitoring US pro bono practices, while Danish firms have drawn inspiration from the United Kingdom.)

Accordingly, an important theme in the development of pro bono is the evolution of "Big Law" – although what counts as "big" varies significantly by context. In the United States, corporate law firm growth in the 1980s and 1990s created the megafirms in which pro bono activity increased in amount, while becoming more organized and efficient. A similar trend occurred in the United Kingdom, where large solicitor firms grew to compete with incoming US giants, which brought pro bono practices in the 1990s that influenced their UK counterparts to hire pro bono coordinators and create policies to demonstrate their commitment to socially meaningful practice. The Anglo-American behemoths then expanded into continental Europe in the 1990s and 2000s, accelerating after European Union (EU) law changed to lift intraunion restrictions on law firm mergers. In Australia, once liberalization permitted the entry of US and UK firms, the corporate law sector expanded rapidly in the 2000s and firms restructured according to the global law firm model, which accelerated preexisting pro bono trends. A similar trajectory occurred in Canada, where law firms in large urban areas experienced rapid growth in the 1990s, followed by an increase in organized pro bono programs and activity in those firms.

In the Global South, where the corporate law sector is not as developed or powerful, it nonetheless plays a significant role in incubating pro bono practice. The positive relationship between corporate law growth and pro bono institutionalization is evident in "emerging economies," including some of the so-called BRIC countries (Brazil, Russia, India, and China) covered in this book. In Brazil, for example, the transition to democracy opened up a period of market liberalization that transformed the economy, leading to rapid law firm growth to meet new corporate legal demand. From 1990 to 2010, law firms grew in number (more than doubling) and size, with many exceeding 100 lawyers for the first time,[20] creating the foundation for the importation of pro bono programs in large firms organized around the US model. In India, home to 1.3 million lawyers, less than 0.1 percent practice in large law firms, and the definition of "large" is quite different than in the United States and Europe – with only 19 firms of more than 100 lawyers. However, with the impending opening of the domestic profession to foreign law firms, there has been significant growth among elite firms, which have begun to preemptively change practices, adding pro bono programs in a competitive bid to signal professionalism and trustworthiness to clients, and attract top law school talent. Chinese pro bono also developed after the government eased restrictions on internal consolidation and foreign partnerships in the 1990s, following a top-down "rule by law" initiative to adapt Western institutional forms to the Chinese political system. This effort resulted in the creation of megafirms in Shanghai and Beijing, which incorporated pro bono ideas from foreign partners, while encouraging significant pro bono service from Chinese lawyers as a way to meet new government demands for social responsibility.

Conversely, the dearth of a substantial corporate law presence impedes pro bono's institutionalization, as suggested by the fact that in countries with small corporate legal sectors – like Nigeria, where most lawyers are solos (and foreign firms are excluded), and South Africa, where there are only seventeen firms with more than fifty partners – organized pro bono is underdeveloped. However, it would be a mistake to presume that institutionalized pro bono follows inexorably from the growth of the corporate law sector. Indeed, research from South America suggests that public gestures of law firm commitment to pro bono are not always matched by the reality of service where there is limited support from the bar and national government, insufficient funding to facilitate client connections, and no external monitoring. In Argentina, Chile, and Colombia, despite the growth of corporate firms after liberalization and symbolic agreements by elite firm leaders to meet pro bono goals, the lack of financial incentives to do pro bono (like billable hour credit) and the absence of strong partnerships with client groups has led to weak pro bono, which has had little impact on overall access to justice. Neither has the reality of pro bono service by large law firms met the rhetoric of support in Brazil. While observers have attributed disappointing law firm pro bono performance there to restrictions imposed by the bar association limiting pro bono to NGO clients, even after those restrictions were struck down in 2015, law firm pro bono service to individual clients has continued to be low, and only two firms in São Paulo have taken serious steps to include needy individuals in their pro bono programs. As these experiences suggest, while the development of a strong corporate law sector may be a necessary condition for pro bono to institutionalize, it is by no means sufficient, and the extent of law firm pro bono participation depends heavily on internal leadership and incentives, as well as meaningful integration of the corporate law sector into the broader system of access to justice.

Legal Aid and NGO Sector

The trajectory of pro bono's development in a given country hinges on its relationship to government-sponsored legal aid and NGOs dedicated to serving poor clients and advancing social causes. We begin with the role of legal aid: state-funded programs providing legal services to low-income individuals (and, in some places, organizations that work on their behalf) in civil and (less frequently) criminal cases. A central finding from our country studies is that the structure and level of government investment in legal aid profoundly affects the breadth of professional support for pro bono, and the quantity and quality of pro bono service that lawyers deliver. In particular, because the structure of legal aid creates constituencies that mobilize for and against pro bono, it appears as a decisive factor influencing pro bono practice.

The dynamic between pro bono and legal aid must be understood in the context of neoliberal restructuring that has made pro bono both more necessary and deeply controversial.[21] In Canada, Europe, and the United States, the retrenchment of government funding for legal aid has been followed by the expansion of pro bono as a volunteer response to the decline of the welfare state. In those places, lawyers concerned about access to justice have raised warnings about the degree to which building pro bono – although important in the abstract – undermines political support for a legal aid system under siege. Similarly, in Brazil, the movement to institutionalize pro bono that took shape in the early 2000s was resisted by lawyers seeking to open public defender's offices (Brazil's equivalent of legal aid) as mandated by the Constitution. Those lawyers feared that more pro bono would mean less government investment in public defender's offices, even though the demand for legal services in the country could not feasibly be addressed by them.

In understanding the relationship between pro bono and legal aid, an essential element is whether legal aid is structured via staffed offices with full-time lawyers, paid for by the state (as in the United States), or whether legal aid is administered through a "judicare" model, in which private lawyers accept legal aid cases and are directly compensated by the state for their work. Many countries have a mixed system with some elements of both models. A crucial feature of the professional landscape in countries with a judicare model – Canada, the United Kingdom and other Western European countries (Denmark, France, Portugal, and Spain), Argentina, Brazil, Chile, and Colombia – is that a large portion of the private bar depends on state payments as a core part of their practice. In Western Europe, these lawyers constitute the "Social Bar" and rely on legal aid for their livelihood (in France and the Netherlands, nearly 50 percent of lawyers work on legal aid cases). As the country studies demonstrate, Social Bar lawyers systematically oppose pro bono (especially from large firms) as "unfair competition" since it directs free services to people who would otherwise seek assistance through the legal aid scheme (thereby reducing Social Bar lawyer income). Those countries with a robust judicare system report the most conflict between solo and small-firm lawyers, dependent on legal aid payments, and promoters of pro bono. In this book, country studies of Canada, Brazil, the United Kingdom, France, Spain, and Portugal all document the existence of "turf wars" between pro bono lawyers and those solo and small-firm lawyers providing legal aid.

The intensity of these turf wars depends on other features of the legal aid system. One key determinant is the amount of government subsidy for private lawyers performing judicare services and hence the degree to which lawyers in the private sector depend on legal aid to earn a living. In some countries, like India, the stipend is so paltry – described as "poverty wages" – that most lawyers do not organize their practice around state funding and hence local bar resistance to pro bono appears to be less significant. In China, which has a mixed system in which there are 6,600 lawyers staffing legal aid programs, the government has actively encouraged private lawyers to supplement staffed-office work through judicare; however, the stipend is so low that most lawyers view judicare service as a form of pro bono. Another important factor affecting the pro bono–legal aid relationship is the type of case covered by the legal aid system. For instance, in South Africa, 90 percent of legal aid cases are criminal cases, creating wide space for civil pro bono. Similarly, in Canada, legal aid is organized around criminal services, permitting pro bono promoters to strike a "compromise" by focusing on civil services – a theme we will return to later in this chapter.

In contrast to the conflict around judicare, in countries with robust NGO legal sectors (encompassing legal aid and public interest law) there tends to be a more symbiotic relationship with the pro bono system since NGOs depend on private firm personnel and financial resources. In the United States, which has staffed-office legal aid (which includes a significant portion of organizations not funded by the government) and robust public interest law, there is a strong pro bono culture promoted by legal NGOs dependent on law firm largesse. Similarly, in Australia, fully staffed community legal centers (outside of the legal aid scheme) funded by a mix of state and philanthropic sources have welcomed pro bono support and advocated for its expansion. A distinct symbiosis occurs in countries with a substantial number of public interest law NGOs, which generate the bulk of their resources from philanthropy and private bar support. In South Africa, public interest law groups established under apartheid skillfully mobilized pro bono support and, as they have expanded to play vanguard roles enforcing constitutional rights in the post-apartheid era, have been important supporters of pro bono's development. In Nigeria, military-era NGOs that defended citizens against state abuse, like the Civil Liberties Organization, converted after democratization to partner with private sector lawyers to build democratic institutions and represent clients in truth commissions. As these cases suggest, pro bono is most welcome in contexts in which well-developed NGOs gain advantage by leveraging private legal resources.

Government

As the discussion of legal aid illustrates, government policy can raise challenges for pro bono. But it can also serve as a spur. Indeed, our country studies provide a range of examples of how government often plays a supportive role in helping to build pro bono programs and stimulate private lawyer volunteerism. We see two primary mechanisms of government influence. First, government may channel pro bono into specific types of practice by issuing guidelines defining its scope and nudging lawyers to expand free legal service. An example of this occurred in the United Kingdom, where the attorney general issued a key 2002 protocol that defined pro bono as legal advice and representation of poor individuals and organizations that work on their behalf – thereby reclaiming pro bono from the more general "public service" logic of law firm social responsibility and marking an important turning point in the movement to direct solicitor legal resources to underserved communities. Second, government may increase pro bono activity by conditioning publicly conferred benefits on a demonstrated commitment – at either the individual or law firm level – to pro bono service. This is the case in Australia, where government contracting rules require firms doing business with the state to demonstrate their pro bono service. These rules have motivated firms with substantial government work to increase pro bono activity. In a similar vein, India's Ministry of Law and Justice promulgated a 2017 Pro Bono Legal Services Initiative exhorting private lawyers to undertake pro bono and making clear that pro bono service would be considered for government appointments, while India's Supreme Court (borrowing from Nigeria) requires demonstrated pro bono for admission to the elite status of senior advocate.

In other places, however, government rules have had a more ambiguous impact on pro bono. Although pro bono advocates in countries with constitutional provisions guaranteeing the right to counsel (Brazil, Western European nations, South Africa, and India) have sought to mobilize those provisions to support greater investment in pro bono programs, they are frequently met by opponents who insist the constitution requires increasing state funding for legal aid. Further, and in contrast to the UK protocol already discussed, there have been instances of policy making that appear to undermine the definition of pro bono as an inherently legal service. This has occurred most prominently in South Africa. There, in 2014, the legislature passed the Legal Practice Act, which in the course of consolidating lawyers into a unified professional category, mandated that all lawyers perform "community service" – a vague term that seems to encompass nonlegal services and has therefore sparked debate about whether lawyers should be allowed to discharge their public duties through broad charitable work. In countries without an independent legal profession, government rules may simultaneously encourage pro bono service and dictate its content. Thus, in China, where the bar is an extension of and controlled by government, pro bono depends on the active support of the Chinese Communist Party – or, at least, the lack of overt opposition. As this book's study of China highlights, the government's promotion of pro bono has led to its expansion, particularly at the large-firm level, with pro bono directed toward nonaggressive cases in which lawyers assist individuals in routine matters that do not challenge party policy or power.

Organized Bar

In each country in our book, the organized bar plays a crucial role in shaping pro bono – either to promote or hinder it. Our country studies provide examples of how, in some places, bar associations have nudged pro bono forward through a variety of means: organizing clearinghouses (the UK Bar Pro Bono Unit, Denmark's Lawyers on Call), sponsoring conferences (the UK Law Society, Law Society of South Australia, and various Latin America bar associations), and even providing direct funding (the Victoria Law Foundation in Australia). At the most active end of the spectrum, we see bar associations designing full-fledged pro bono programs to supplement legal aid. This occurred in Singapore, where the Law Society established the Criminal Legal Aid Scheme in 1985 to fill the void created by the state's inaction on criminal legal aid.

In contrast, the organized bar, responsive to solo and small-firm lawyer interests, can mobilize fierce opposition to pro bono. This was the case in Brazil, where the São Paulo bar passed a rule restricting the provision of pro bono to NGO clients, thereby protecting solo and small-firm practitioners dependent on legal aid and "low bono" cases on behalf of individuals. This rule placed significant constraints on pro bono's development in Brazilian law firms until it was abrogated by the national bar – revealing how divisions within the bar itself, structured vertically with national and local arms, can profoundly affect the status of pro bono in domestic legal systems.

Law Schools

In the United States, law schools have played an important role inculcating pro bono culture in students, with a majority of schools instituting mandatory or voluntary pro bono requirements.[22] Outside the United States, however, law schools do not appear to serve this broad function and none of the country studies document similar law school–based pro bono programs. Law schools have nevertheless advanced the pro bono cause by incubating pro bono think tanks and instilling professional values. The most prominent example of the incubation model is the Australian Pro Bono Centre, housed in and funded by the Sydney Law School, where it has emerged as an important repository of pro bono best practices, produced significant research on pro bono activity in the bar, and performed a significant network-building function. On the pedagogical side, many of the country studies stress the supportive role that law school clinical education has played in promoting a professional service ethic, which provides the seedbed from which pro bono grows. This role appears most vividly in the French case, where Louis Assier-Andrieu and Jeremy Perelman describe the innovative Science Po Corporate Social Responsibility Pro Bono Clinic, in which senior law firm lawyers supervise students on pro bono CSR cases around the globe. As the authors suggest, this version of pro bono clinical education – like pro bono itself – is double-edged: training students in sophisticated human rights methods, while building the law firms' reputation among elite law students and expanding markets for CSR-related practice. Other chapters (on China, Nigeria, Singapore, South Africa, and Spain) point to the power of clinical education in deepening student appreciation for law's impact on underserved groups in ways that help strengthen pro bono culture.

Monitors

Outside of established legal institutions such as law schools and the bar, empirical research suggests that oversight by third-party monitors with the power to confer external benefits and impose sanctions can be effective in motivating pro bono activity.[23] Ordinal ranking systems, in which law firms provide pro bono data to a third party that collates that data and uses it to place firms in a hierarchy based on established criteria, have proven to be a powerful pro bono stimulant. The impact of rankings has been most visible in the American profession, where the 1994 launch of the *American Lawyer* (*AmLaw*) pro bono rankings of large firms (measured by average hours per lawyer) transformed pro bono practice by creating competition for positional status that led firms to hire pro bono coordinators, institute formal pro bono policies, and push lawyers to ramp up pro bono service.[24] Although no other country reports the same type of rankings-induced growth, our country studies provide some evidence that rankings have influenced pro bono culture in other nations. For instance, *AmLaw*'s 2014 decision to change its algorithm to count pro bono hours of foreign office lawyers in its ranking of US firms appears to correlate with the expansion of pro bono policies and practices in European affiliates. Similarly, the studies of Argentina, Brazil, Colombia, and Chile suggest that the *Latin Lawyer* magazine's extensive coverage of firm pro bono activity and recognition of significant pro bono achievements have been important drivers of pro bono engagement by elite South American law firms (even though the magazine does not conduct a formal ranking).

Beyond rankings, our country studies reveal other roles for monitors in creating public benchmarks designed to strengthen law firm pro bono commitment and motivate lawyer behavior. In Argentina, Brazil, Chile, and Colombia, pro bono clearinghouse leaders persuaded elite firms to sign the Declaration for the Americas (modeled on the US Pro Bono Institute's Law Firm Challenge), pledging to devote 20 pro bono hours per lawyer each year, and to report to and be held accountable by the clearinghouses, which publicize firm compliance. Similarly, in 2007, the Australian Pro Bono Centre announced a National Pro Bono Target, inviting firms to publicly commit to an annual goal of 35 hours per lawyer and to report performance back to the Centre. According to the Australia country study, the target has been widely adopted by large law firms and has had a positive impact on pro bono participation: for those Australian firms that have committed to meet the target, the average pro bono hours per lawyer in 2016–2017 was 34.8 (more than double than for nonsignatories).

Entrepreneurs

A key insight from our book is the importance of interest convergence between local entrepreneurs, typically legal elites with global experience (foreign law degrees or fellowships), and transnational actors in building domestic pro bono culture.[25] This convergence is notable in multiple country studies, which provide distinctive accounts of domestic entrepreneurialism. In Brazil, for example, it was a US-educated lawyer (now dean of one of the country's most important law schools, FGV Direito SP) who was funded by Ford and OSF to conduct a study mission in the United States and invited US pro bono leaders (including the director of Los Angeles's Public Counsel) back to Brazil to help launch the Instituto Pro Bono. In Spain, a meeting between law firm leaders and Vance Center representatives in 2007 is cited as the spark that ignited the movement to build the first-ever Spanish pro bono clearinghouse. Portugal's Pro Bono Association was started by one law firm partner and one associate (who later became an intern at Public Counsel) inspired by the international model of pro bono advanced by PILnet to build a domestic pro bono network. In Australia, the key entrepreneur was a South African–born leader of the Public Interest Advocacy Centre, Andrea Durbach, who migrated to Australia after representing Black defendants accused of killing a police officer during apartheid in one of the most notorious political trials in South African history. Her experience in South Africa as a public interest lawyer working closely with the private bar contrasted sharply with the lack of private bar engagement with public interest groups in Australia; after her colleague spent a year in the United States studying pro bono organizations, Durbach began doing outreach to large Australian firms to convince them to contribute more pro bono service, and the first Australian pro bono clearinghouse was created in 1992.

As these stories suggest, entrepreneurial energy is critical to converting pro bono ideals into operating systems, providing external benefits to those in need of access to justice, while also conferring professional benefits on the entrepreneurs themselves, whose profiles are elevated on the domestic stage by virtue of their connection to global elites who offer resources and status as part of the transplant process. It is in this sense that pro bono entrepreneurs have "mixed motives": doing well by doing good in helping to build a domestic pro bono field linked to the global pro bono movement. Once again, actions at the "local" level are deeply intertwined with "global" institutions, which provide resources and prestige – while sometimes reinforcing neocolonial dynamics that make them controversial. The study of Argentina, Chile, and Colombia directly analyzes the controversy surrounding the entrepreneur's role in a neocolonial context. There, elite academics – all US-trained (including the author, Daniel Bonilla) – formed the vanguard spearheading a threefold process of transplanting pro bono. First, they defined a justice gap; second, they identified pro bono as a possible solution; and third, they brokered relationships with US actors, particularly leaders of the Vance Center, alongside other Global North NGOs and law firms, which provided pro bono policies and practices that formed the "mirror image" of those ultimately put into place. The study provides a cautionary tale: when pro bono is primarily a top-down project, advanced by elites without broad support from local bar representatives, NGOs, and client constituencies, it fails to take root and is only weakly institutionalized – with lip service paid by law firm leaders not matched by the contributions of lawyers on the ground.

Global Factors

Progressive Neoliberalism

As we have seen, in the process of pro bono's hybridization, there is no clear dividing line between the local and the global: domestic foundations of pro bono – from models of corporate law practice and legal aid, to the nature of government and bar policy, to the role of legal education and entrepreneurialism – are never hermetically sealed from external influence. Rather, local practices tend to develop in ways that reflect broader global trends and bear the imprint of powerful global actors. Here, we shift perspectives to directly spotlight those global trends and actors, beginning by tracing the impact of ideology, specifically, the rise of "progressive neoliberalism."[26]

With the fall of the Berlin Wall and the end of the Soviet Union, progressive neoliberalism emerged in the 1980s to offer a new and, many of its proponents believed, inevitable pathway for individual countries and the broader global order to develop. At its core, progressive neoliberalism involved an attempt to combine free trade with the promotion of fundamental human rights. As such, it entailed a contradiction that did not go unnoticed by its critics. To enable free trade, states had to lessen their role in the economy (via deregulation and privatization) and spending on social policy (via welfare reform). Such retreat of the state, in turn, put even the most basic human rights at risk. To manage this contradiction, advocates of progressive neoliberalism relied on a twin faith. First, they believed in a "trickle-down" model of economics, which predicted that the benefits from free trade would be more or less evenly distributed within and across countries.[27] Second, they believed that citizen engagement would fill, at least partially, the gaps left by the state's retreat in social policy. In particular, they imagined that NGOs and other civic groups would come in to support those in need.[28]

The case of the United States is paradigmatic and thus central to our understanding of how progressive neoliberalism has empowered pro bono in the contemporary era. As the US country study highlights, neoliberal austerity led directly to the institutionalization of American pro bono. Following the Reagan Revolution, severe cutbacks were imposed on legal aid funds, contributing to a massive "justice gap," in which millions of poor people were unable to access lawyers for their legal needs.[29] In response, government and bar leaders called upon private law firms to increase their commitment to provide free legal services to poor people and other disadvantaged groups through pro bono. The pro bono movement was encouraged by the American Bar Association (ABA), which made it an ethical aspiration for lawyers to devote at least 50 pro bono hours annually to poor clients or organizations that advocate on their behalf. The bar and key intermediary groups also fostered the growth of pro bono programs that provided training and evaluation, while matching pro bono supply and demand. These programs made pro bono a more solid and sustainable enterprise, while cementing the relationship between key stakeholders: large law firms, clients, legal aid offices, and public interest law organizations.[30] These transformations changed the landscape of both legal aid and private law practice in the United States, and by the late 2000s, a significant portion of civil legal services to the poor was provided pro bono by large law firms.[31]

Across countries with strong social welfare traditions, we notice that the global development of pro bono follows a similar script. Particularly in the Commonwealth (the United Kingdom, Australia, and Canada), continental Europe (Denmark, France, Portugal, and Spain), and South America (Argentina, Brazil, Chile, and Colombia), the first calls for pro bono coincided with fiscal crises and consequent attacks on the welfare state. These calls were met by the creation of structures designed to advance rule-of-law and access-to-justice principles by counteracting declining state support for legal aid with augmented pro bono from private lawyers. Furthermore, pro bono's growth in those countries relied on globalized organizational forms (propagated by transnational NGOs and foundations, as well as global firms and corporate clients making CSR pledges) and expert knowledge sources (entrepreneurial lawyers with foreign educational credentials and work experience). These global pro bono promoters embraced mobilization of professional charity as a foundational pillar of democratic governance – a principle heavily influenced by Third Way "new governance" approaches to neoliberalism developed in the North American context.[32]

As our hybridization framework makes clear, however, it would be wrong to think that the spread of pro bono as a feature of progressive neoliberalism has been an entirely top-down project and that countries represented in this book are simply conduits of models incubated in the United States. Foundational research on law and development and legal globalization shows that diffusion processes are inherently complex: relying on domestic actors who "buy into" foreign frameworks, while shaping them in response to local demands.[33] Variation across contexts is the norm for legal transplants. And the evidence presented in this book illustrates the deep challenges and resistance to US-style pro bono across jurisdictions where it is found today. Nevertheless, it would be equally wrong to deny the influence of the US pro bono model – both as an example to be emulated and a trap to be avoided – and its complicated relation to neoliberalism, which must be reckoned with as a motive force behind pro bono's diffusion in order to fully appreciate pro bono's emerging place in the global legal order.

Transnational NGOs

As the discussion of progressive neoliberalism suggests, pro bono has become a global export, part of the new law and development tool kit promoted by NGOs in the Global North, mostly from the United States. These transnational NGOs believe that pro bono provides an important way to strengthen the independence of the legal profession, access to justice, and therefore the rule of law in countries with liberal democratic traditions (now under threat from right-wing populism), emerging democracies, and even authoritarian states with weak legal institutions. A recurrent theme in the country studies is the power of these transnational actors to provide resources, global legitimacy to domestic legal elites, technical know-how, and networking opportunities. As we have noted in our discussion of entrepreneurs, pro bono does not spread on its own accord but requires enthusiastic backers who can demonstrate its claimed benefits, provide ready-made models and carefully articulated arguments in its favor, and offer access to global funders and prestige.

In this regard, a few transnational NGOs stand out for their pioneering, though sometimes controversial, roles in building the global pro bono field. US-based groups, in particular, have been key promoters. In Latin America (and to a lesser extent in Europe), the Vance Center (based in New York City) has played a leading role in "pro bono promotion," framed within a broader rule of law agenda aimed at advancing "global justice by engaging lawyers across borders to support civil society."[34] Subsidized and governed by New York's leading law firms, a "cornerstone" of the Vance Center's work is "the promotion of pro bono practice in legal markets in which pro bono culture is unknown or in development."[35] After sponsoring a 2000 conference that galvanized the pro bono movement in Latin America, the center's primary contribution has been to export and implement the Pro Bono Declaration, and to curate the Pro Bono Network, composed of more than a dozen clearinghouses. The US Pro Bono Institute, known for its vanguard role in leading the American pro bono movement, has also been a leading global pro bono proselytizer, disseminating critical lessons from the US experience. In a telling example, the institute's leader, Esther Lardent, traveled to Australia in 2003 to present at the second annual national pro bono conference, considered a watershed moment in the birth of the contemporary pro bono movement in that country. As a sign of its influence, we see other countries (for example, Brazil and Spain) establishing their own "Pro Bono Institutes" in efforts to model success.

Groups outside the United States have also led transnational pro bono initiatives. With funding from OSF, PILnet opened an office in Hungary in 1997. The organization has been a leading pro bono promoter in Europe, spearheading the annual Pro Bono Forum that helped to build the field of European pro bono leaders, while supporting national efforts to create "sister clearinghouses" in Spain, Portugal, and other countries. As the European chapter in this book recounts, PILnet was critical during the 2000s in connecting public interest organizations to funders that supported development of pro bono programs, making links between organizations and law firms, and orienting European pro bono toward NGO representation to avoid conflict with the Social Bar. Its 2012 Madrid Forum, by bringing together leaders from the Madrid Bar Association and elite Spanish firms, is noted as a catalyst for pro bono development in Spain. Other international NGOs have played less sweeping but no less important roles. For instance, in Singapore, the Joint International Pro Bono

Committee helped connect international community organizations to Singapore law firms, while the United Nations Development Program (UNDP) promoted pro bono in India as part of a broader package of civil justice reforms. The role of the UNDP, in particular, highlights the need for future inquiry into the role of supranational institutions in sponsoring pro bono as part of broader political reform missions.

Global Philanthropy

Although transnational knowledge is necessary to spread pro bono across borders, it is not sufficient: building networks that connect people and ideas, and establishing organized pro bono programs that coordinate supply and demand, require money. Accordingly, as we see across country studies, global philanthropic support for infrastructure is a crucial feature of pro bono's development. The question of how pro bono gets placed on the agenda of philanthropies with global reach and resources to remake civil society in their image is fundamental and largely left unexamined in the chapters ahead – thus inviting further research. And yet the role of major funding institutions appears systematically as a foundational cause of hybridization, even if their inner workings and motivations are hidden behind an opaque curtain of power.

In some instances, it is clear that pro bono promotion is consonant with philanthropic commitment to the politics of progressive neoliberalism, understood in terms of building liberal democracies in which free markets and robust civil society are conjoined. This has been the explicit agenda of OSF, which has left an indelible impact on the civil justice system in Europe, where it invested heavily in pro bono programs in the 2000s after withdrawing financial support from public interest law (which it also incubated after the demise of Soviet influence in Central and Eastern Europe). Other foundations have taken a more targeted approach, as demonstrated by the role of Taproot in Portugal, which has sought to connect lawyers from the burgeoning global in-house corporate legal sector to NGOs that could benefit from their expertise.

Our country studies provide additional examples of how global funders can spark but also destabilize pro bono development – on the one hand, providing seed funding that raises visibility and stimulates organizational growth, and on the other, investing insufficient resources (or withdrawing funding) in ways that undermine progress. In Africa, global funders are reported to have played a stimulus role:

with international donors entering Nigeria after the 1999 democratic transition to support fledging pro bono programs, while the Atlantic Foundation gifted crucial resources to initiate ProBono.Org in South Africa. In contrast, the lack of sustained philanthropic commitment is cited as a key barrier to pro bono's institutionalization in Argentina, Chile, and Colombia. As this suggests, interventions by global philanthropy can be a decisive force catapulting pro bono forward or holding it back. Why these interventions occur, and how they fit into the broader political missions funders seek to advance, are central issues that require more systematic scholarly investigation.

Corporate Social Responsibility

Also decisive in influencing the rise and shape of pro bono at the large-firm level is the advent of CSR:[36] a set of contested principles designed to hold transnational corporations to account to local communities, typically through voluntary commitments requiring sustainable production, disclosure of social impact, and charitable giving. How the CSR obligations of corporate *clients* influence the amount and type of pro bono provided by corporate *lawyers* is a central theme in studies of countries with highly developed corporate legal sectors.[37] Although criticized as a public relations tool used to resist legal liability and hide global depredation,[38] CSR has caused transnational corporations to invest in measures to ensure compliance with negotiated standards throughout their supply chains – including legal counsel. As a result, law firms eager to attract and retain global corporate clients have touted their pro bono service as an expression of CSR. There is a twofold benefit to this CSR framing: corporate clients may count law firms as ethical service providers, meeting the *clients'* CSR supply chain standards, while the law firms *themselves*, to the extent that they are also viewed as global commercial entities, can demonstrate their social responsibility and thus independently satisfy CSR demands directly applied to them. In both cases, firm lawyers engage in pro bono as a way to "create value" for their firms, part of the broader "business case" for pro bono in which firms do well (drawing in corporate clients, and recruiting and retaining top legal talent), while also doing good.

The study of US pro bono takes on this issue most directly, showing how large corporate law firms have started to promote local charity and larger social efforts by lawyers under the banner of CSR. As the study highlights, much of what these firms count as CSR work has a legal component but is not traditional legal representation, such as law-oriented educational programs for high school students. Beyond this, the US chapter traces how CSR motivates large firms to undertake "nonlegal community service activities" without any legal dimension whatsoever, for example, "scholarships, holiday parties, food banks, habitat for humanity," as well as green initiatives like recycling. The result, according to this study, is an increasing merger of professional and CSR "logics" for pro bono service, with 39 of the *AmLaw* 100 firms drawing on CSR frames in describing their pro bono work. This occurs as law firms attempt to gear their pro bono work to meet overlapping but not entirely coextensive professional and CSR standards. However, this strategy has potential trade-offs. In many cases, pro bono is no longer framed as a professional obligation but as a broader strategy to "improve communities," couched in the language of global citizenship, in which there is no intrinsic link between pro bono and legal expertise.

Other country studies document CSR's growing influence on pro bono practice. In Brazil, the emergence of CSR as a movement for stronger corporate accountability during the country's meteoric economic rise corresponds precisely with the development of the Instituto Pro Bono, and CSR is reported to be a driving force behind large-firm investment in pro bono – seen as a "tiebreaker" for corporations choosing among law firms. The study of Canadian firms also reveals how pro bono leaders there have sought to make the business case for pro bono to satisfy CSR requirements and attract clients. Similar trends are noted in the United Kingdom, France, and Portugal, while the Denmark chapter describes how firms there publish pro bono reports as part of CSR branding strategies. The European chapter argues that it is the drive to comply with CSR norms that has motivated European Big Law to engage in pro bono as a way to meet the expectations of corporate clients. In France, CSR is viewed as providing law firms a potential "competitive advantage" by allowing them to develop new areas of legal expertise relevant to fee-generating work and to attract new legal talent seeking to have a social impact beyond billing hours. As this suggests, the impact of these CSR trends is ambiguous. Overall, the CSR movement has clearly propelled large law firms competing for global business to make investments in pro bono policies and practices that help meet client CSR obligations. Yet how much of this is window dressing versus meaningful service is a contested question explored throughout the book. And, as the country studies suggest, by framing lawyers' public role in nonlegal terms, CSR potentially channels zero-sum volunteer energy out of meeting poor people's legal needs toward broader community service projects, undermining lawyers' special duty to use law for the public good.

Technology

The global diffusion of knowledge and practices requires communication across vast dimensions of time and space. As we have seen, to promote an idea like pro bono, there is often no substitute for face-to-face encounters – foreign study, site visits, and conferences figure prominently in this book's account of the global pro bono movement, permitting promoters to convey nuanced analyses, inspire action, and build relationships essential to sustain the difficult work of developing structures. But it is also true that the speed and scope with which an idea spreads can be accelerated and enhanced by the strategic use of technology, which disrupts the status quo by easing barriers to communication and permitting one-click access to massive amounts of data and best-practice material. In this sense, technology is an *enabling* force – lacking intrinsic content but permitting transnational actors and domestic entrepreneurs to connect more easily and frequently, while also linking lawyers and clients inside countries and across borders.

From our country studies, we identify two key ways in which technology helps to promote the transnational diffusion and domestic institutionalization of pro bono. First, technology enables *remote technical assistance*: permitting domestic pro bono organizations to identify and reach out to global pro bono promoters with experience and ready-made models, allowing promoters to efficiently conduct cross-border data exchange and host web-based repositories of forms and other information, and facilitating ongoing technical support and troubleshooting. This type of technological exchange is apparent in the case of pro bono's development in Argentina, Chile, and Colombia, where remote connection has been essential, with the Vance Center using its technological capacity to coordinate cyber-networks and compliance among law firm signatories to the Declaration for the Americas.

Second, technology enables *remote case intermediation*: providing web-based matchmaking platforms through which NGOs can request legal assistance from pro bono lawyers who establish profiles listing their credentials, expertise, and interests. Some of these platforms are transnational by design: iProbono, which aims to strengthen civil society "by providing wraparound legal support" and facilitating the representation of marginalized people, connects NGOs throughout South Asia (including India, Bangladesh, Sri Lanka, and Nepal) with lawyers in the region and in the United Kingdom. These lawyers engage in work such as providing transactional assistance to social enterprises and litigating for welfare benefits. TrustLaw Connect, created by legal publishing giant Thomson Reuters Foundation, similarly matches "high-impact NGOs working to create social and environmental change" (in India and elsewhere) with "the best law firms and corporate legal teams" around the globe. There are fledging country-specific versions of these platforms in Spain (probonos.net) and South Africa (ProBono.Org). While these cyber-intermediaries reduce transaction costs and thus make it easier for lawyers interested in pro bono to find cases that match their expertise and timing, there are important open questions about their organization and impact. How much do these sites curate pro bono matters in ways that privilege certain types of work (such as social enterprise) over others in order to cater to lawyer expertise and address restrictions on cross-border practice? How much vetting of pro bono lawyers is done and how much do site staff engage in monitoring and quality control in relation to managing volunteer work? Finally, is there any evidence that lawyers use sites to build connections and brands in order to create markets for fee-generating work? As these emergent technologies evolve, answering these questions will allow us to better evaluate the trade-offs of their role in advancing global access to justice.

Consequences

As we have argued, pro bono's hybridization involves the evolution of lawyer volunteerism from ad hoc charity to organized practice. In this evolution, local and global forces come together at the national and subnational level to produce a range of consequences that can be identified and evaluated. Drawing upon our country studies, in this section we look at the consequences of hybridization from two perspectives. First, we highlight how hybridization affects the *infrastructure* of pro bono service: through the creation of pro bono policies in law firms, pro bono rules designed by the bar, and pro bono intermediaries established in civil society. Second, we explore consequences in relation to the *distribution* of pro bono service: how many lawyers engage in pro bono, which sectors of the bar are most active, what types of clients receive support, and which legal matters are privileged. As the chapters of this book reveal, the nature and scope of these consequences differ dramatically by country – reflecting the unique ways in which the local and global factors canvassed above coalesce in specific contexts – ultimately producing a variegated map of who provides and who receives access to justice.

Infrastructure

Examining the development of pro bono infrastructure draws attention to the fact that successful institutionalization requires systemic change in professional practice, which simultaneously asserts pro bono as a normative priority and creates organizational vehicles for its execution. In this sense, infrastructure development is a consequence of the hybridization processes we have traced – a consequence that itself creates the conditions of possibility for pro bono's further growth. Here, we look at infrastructure development as an outcome of hybridization visible in policy codification – within firms and the bar more broadly – and organizational formation – creating spaces that consolidate resources, build leadership, and link lawyers and clients.

Law Firm Policies

Law firm policies on how to define and credit pro bono, as well as how to organize and distribute it, are important indicators of pro bono commitment – although the devil is always in the details. General exhortations to do pro bono mean little unless supported by firm leadership and staff, and backed by billable hour credit, which law firms in most countries still do not provide. Nevertheless, there is significant evidence that law firms have begun to formalize policies for vetting, allocating, and evaluating pro bono matters through the creation of committees, intake protocols, conflicts checking, and reporting systems. For proponents of pro bono, these are positive signs that law firms are taking seriously their service duty: establishing systems within bureaucratic firm structures to coordinate across practice groups and branch offices, while putting pro bono on a formal footing that elevates it as a legitimate goal worthy of lawyer time and resources. For skeptics, law firm policies can operate like smoke and mirrors: presenting an image of pro bono commitment that burnishes the profession's reputation, while obscuring the reality of inadequate implementation. Both of these visions are on display in the country studies and reflect the different degree to which pro bono, as a legal transplant, becomes institutionalized in professional culture.

On one side, the country-level data demonstrate pro bono's pervasive (albeit inconsistent) institutional development within large law firms. In addition to the United States, large firms in Asia, Australia, Canada, Europe, and South America report having formalized intake and conflicts policies, uniform standards of representation, and reporting systems. This internal law firm infrastructure is often explicitly based on the US model, which is disseminated directly by US firms and promoted as a suite of best practices by US intermediaries – although there is wide variation and important exceptions. For instance, among a small number of Singapore firms that require pro bono, none have formal policies, while law firm reporting requirements in China come from state mandates.

In one clear trend, firms across the globe are mimicking US practice by establishing pro bono committees and hiring coordinators to manage pro bono intake, assign cases to appropriate lawyers, track output, and report performance to relevant oversight bodies. The UK and European chapters detail the growth of pro bono coordinators in UK firms, spurred by the rise of CSR (which requires personnel devoted to compliance) and the increasing presence in London of law offices connected to the US corporate legal sector (which already embrace the coordinator role). Other European country studies show similar trends. Globally networked firms in France, mostly Parisian branches of Anglo-American firms, have hired dedicated pro bono officers, who organize and publicize lawyer pro bono activity. In Spain, elite firms supported by the Vance Center began organizing pro bono programs on the US model in the mid-2000s, accelerating their pace after the 2012 European Pro Bono Forum; Portuguese firms have set up pro bono committees headed by lawyers with power, who check conflicts, conduct intake, and seek publicity; while top Danish firms have also hired pro bono coordinators to perform such tasks. Similar developments can be seen in Australia, where it is reported that most firms had pro bono coordinators (and permitted lawyers to get billable credit for pro bono work) by the mid-2000s, and in Argentina, Chile, and Colombia, where the majority of large firms organized pro bono around a standard US-inspired tripartite format, overseen by a pro bono committee, partner, and coordinator. In other Global South countries, structure is still evolving, with some ambitious programs – for instance, Webber Wentzel and Cliffe Dekker Hofmeyr in South Africa both have dedicated pro bono practice groups with full-time lawyers providing service to individuals, NGOs, and government bodies on public interest and human rights matters – matched by ongoing informality and fledging organization.

On the other side, it is also clear that investment in pro bono infrastructure at law firms does not necessarily yield a consistent access-to-justice return. This case is made most forcefully in the chapter on Argentina, Chile, and Colombia, where it is argued that upgrading law firm pro bono programs has not led to significant pro bono output, primarily due to the lack of genuine incentives like billable hour credit, producing what sociologists call institutional decoupling: when the creation of formal rules does not match actual practice.[39] This happens when rules are meant to signal legitimacy to important actors in the external environment, rather than serving the interests of less powerful groups that are claimed to be beneficiaries. As the chapter shows, in Argentina, Chile, and Colombia, poor clients' interests are often ignored in the pro bono system because they are not significant stakeholders in its design and implementation. In this account, when firms hire dedicated pro bono personnel, such personnel serve a role unrelated to service provision: demonstrating civic virtue to clients and competitors, and thereby branding firms in ways that bolster reputation and promote bottom lines (although the chapter makes clear that firm branding is not part of a deliberate public relations strategy, as it is in other countries). This perspective cautions against equating law firm policies – by themselves – with the successful institutionalization of pro bono practice.

Bar Rules

As with law firm policies, ethical rules promulgated by domestic bar associations present a chicken-and-egg problem: Do such rules *lead* pro bono institutionalization (and thereby act more in a causal role) or do they *lag* behind (suggesting they are a consequence of processes pushed forward by other forces)? The evidence presented in this book is insufficient to answer this question, but it does show a lack of systematic correlation between codified pro bono rules and institutional development. Indeed, only a handful of country studies in this book identify local professional rules encouraging pro bono (the United States, Canada, India, South Africa, and China stand out) and their content is mixed. In the United States, the ABA first codified a voluntary pro bono standard in 1983 (amended to add a fifty-hour aspirational target in 1993), which preceded pro bono's institutionalization, and no doubt nudged it forward, although the most significant increase in pro bono at the large-firm level is commonly attributed to the advent of *AmLaw* rankings.

In other countries, ethical codification occurs at later points in pro bono's development. The Canadian Bar Association passed a resolution in favor of a voluntary fifty-hour standard in 1998, at the precise moment of significant organizational activity in support of pro bono in law firms and the wider bar. In India, bar rules have required lawyers to provide "free legal assistance to the indigent and oppressed" since 1975, but substantial institutional development did not begin until the 2017 Pro Bono Legal Services Initiative, launched by the Ministry of Justice, formally defined pro bono as a goal to be pursued by the legal profession and attached benefits (preference in government hiring) to its performance. The South African study reports that the country's ethical codification grew from the bottom up in 2003, with a mandatory pro bono rule set forth by the Cape Law Society that spread to other regions and was eventually adopted by the national Law Society. In contrast, the Chinese rule came from the top down, set in 2004 by the national bar, which directed local bar associations to promote lawyer public interest activities. In each of these cases, codification of ethical rules explicitly adopting pro bono goals appears to occur as part of a package of professional and political reforms designed to strengthen lawyer service, suggesting that codification is more an expression of institutional change than its cause.

Civil Society Intermediaries

In the countries examined in this book, we see the emergence of civil society organizations that promote pro bono as a central feature of institutional development – a marker of professional legitimacy that provides a vehicle for facilitating pro bono's further advance. These intermediaries are established with critical financial and leadership support from the domestic corporate law sector, typically working in tandem with philanthropic foundations and transnational NGOs that provide models and tools. These intermediaries play multiple roles, but in most cases focus on bridging client need and law firm supply (for this reason, they are also referred to as clearinghouses since they serve to clear the market for pro bono service). In this role, intermediaries operate to reduce transaction costs: encouraging law firms to participate in pro bono work by curating cases to meet firm lawyer expertise and taste, making it "easy" for busy corporate lawyers to take time out for pro bono work. Intermediaries also perform other backup services to facilitate representation. These include conducting trainings, troubleshooting cases with difficult clients (and lawyers), providing background research, and otherwise ensuring that lawyers and clients stay connected and follow through. In addition, intermediary leaders perform wider pro bono advocacy: pitching pro bono to law firm representatives (and sometimes leaders from other sectors, like small firms, government agencies, and in-house departments), conferring awards for outstanding service, and engaging in public relations and outreach that solidify pro bono within legal culture. Some intermediaries featured in this book are also seen conducting surveys and other research on access to justice, collaborating with law school clinics, serving as conduits for international exchange, and generally acting as thought leaders.

The proliferation of intermediaries highlights not only their symbolic and material importance as catalysts of pro bono, but also the powerful machinery of legal transplant behind their spread.[40] As mentioned above, the US Pro Bono Institute – although itself focused more on advocacy than case facilitation – has served as an inspiration for and (in many cases) a partner in the creation of clearinghouses around the globe. Aside from the state-based public interest law clearinghouses (PILCHs) in Australia – the first of which was started in 1992 after a study of the US scene – nearly all of the clearinghouses profiled in the country studies borrowed heavily from the US model promoted by the Pro Bono Institute and its partner organizations (as well as the Vance Center). These include Argentina (Pro Bono Commission, 2000), Chile (Pro Bono Foundation, 2000), Brazil (Instituto Pro Bono, 2001), Colombia (Pro Bono Foundation, 2009), Portugal (Pro Bono Association, 2014), France (Paris Bar Endowment Fund, 2015), India (ProBono India, 2016), and Spain (Fundación Pro Bono España, 2018). Although differing in size and scope, the central remit of each group is to build networks across the law firm and legal aid/NGO sectors, which requires speaking to different audiences about the multifaceted benefits of pro bono service: to firms about the social and psychic rewards of giving back and the potential financial return on enhanced professional reputation; to legal aid groups and NGOs on the value of augmented personnel resources and the attendant financial support that often flows with it; and to the broader public about the significance of client lives changed and social problems solved. In having these conversations and building bridges between private sector lawyers and public interest clients, there are serious questions about how clearinghouse leaders assess the state of legal need, select worthy cases, and identify partners to which pro bono resources are channeled. Commentators have noted that skillful intermediation requires that clearinghouses direct pro bono resources to legal need – rather than adapting need to private lawyer preferences simply to increase pro bono participation, which distorts access to justice rather than widening its path.[41] It is for this reason that we hear many of the authors in this book calling for close collaboration between clearinghouse leaders and other access-to-justice stakeholders in designing the overall system of legal services delivery and defining the specific role that pro bono should play.

Distribution

Distributional analysis focuses on who does pro bono, how much pro bono they do, and for which clients – what Andrew Boon and Avis Whyte refer to in their chapter as the "volumes and nature of work." Here, we assemble evidence and identify patterns of pro bono supply and demand: highlighting what our country studies teach about which lawyers are most likely to perform pro bono service, and what types of clients are most likely to benefit as a result.

Lawyers: Who Does Pro Bono?

There are two dimensions along which to evaluate the supply of pro bono service: the first tracks the degree to which pro bono is done by lawyers across different practice settings – the *stratification* dimension – and the second tracks the degree to which it is done by lawyers within the same kinds of firms – the *hierarchy* dimension.

In terms of stratification, there are a few central takeaways. Overall, across practice sites, it is safe to say that pro bono remains a marginal feature of professional practice around the world. Even in a country like the United States, with a highly developed and well-financed pro bono infrastructure, approximately half of lawyers report doing no pro bono at all.[42] Although many of this book's chapters find growing awareness of pro bono among lawyers (see, in particular, Denmark and Spain), as a matter of practice, pro bono remains the exception rather than the rule. Unsurprisingly, where pro bono activity does occur, it is concentrated in the private legal sector: lawyers in government practice and other areas of public service (including legal aid and education) are systematically less likely to engage in pro bono work. Further, within the private legal sector, in-house lawyers do less pro bono than outside counsel. Among private practice lawyers, it is clear that those in settings at the smaller end of the scale – solo and small-firm lawyers – tend to be the highest pro bono performers on average and tend to perform pro bono of a particular type: making ad hoc decisions to provide free representation or write down legal fees for those unable to pay.

Precisely because of domestic traditions of this sort of informal volunteerism, we see solo and small-firm lawyers in many countries where data is available taking a lead position in the distribution of pro bono service. For instance, in the province of Ontario – where the authors of the Canadian chapter collected survey data – less than 50 percent of the largest-firm lawyers reported pro bono work (performing the fewest hours per year on average), while 73 percent of solos engaged in pro bono (performing 88 hours of service on average), and nearly two-thirds of small-firm lawyers did pro bono. The importance of solo and small-firm pro bono is generally linked to the overall dominance of that form of practice (particularly in countries with very small large-firm sectors) and, in some places, its connection to legal aid. In the latter vein, the studies of China, Nigeria, and Portugal all report that solo practitioners, who struggle to earn a living and thus have little capacity for pure pro bono, tend to engage in pro bono work in connection with state-run legal aid programs – accepting meager state stipends as a form of what they understand to be pro bono service (for example, nearly one-fifth of Chinese pro bono cases in 2017 were legal aid cases designated by local governments).

For countries seeking to expand pro bono service in a more organized fashion, a crucial challenge is mobilizing support from larger law firms with excess capacity to provide pro bono and the prestige to lead further growth. Thus, we see that in countries with more developed pro bono systems, large-firm pro bono contributions are relatively high. In Australia, for example, where pro bono is considered "robust" – with a 2016 overall pro bono participation rate among firms of 50 or more lawyers of 57 percent (for an annual total of more than 400,000 pro bono hours) – the largest firms (over 450 lawyers) recorded the highest average pro bono hours per lawyer (40). Other countries, with dramatically diverse professions, report significant rates of large-firm pro bono participation: in France, elite Parisian firms perform the most pro bono service, as do the Big Five firms in South Africa, which have highly organized and high-performing pro bono programs. In contrast, where pro bono culture is weak, large firms underperform. This is true in Brazil, where only one firm in São Paulo has adopted an individual representation pro bono policy; in Argentina, Chile, and Colombia, where there is a lack of commitment by partners and a reluctance by law firms to invest in training and conflicts checking, correlating with a very low overall number of large-firm pro bono cases conducted through clearinghouses (fewer than 350 per year); and in Spain, which has some of the lowest overall pro bono numbers (11 annual hours per lawyer on average) in Europe.

In the United States, where the large-firm sector has been a leading force in pro bono's growth, the distribution of pro bono service follows a U-shaped pattern, with lawyers in the largest and smallest practice sites performing the most pro bono service on average. A 2016 survey by the ABA found that, overall, US lawyers performed an average of 37 hours of pro bono work per year; the annual average for solo lawyers was 45 hours, while for lawyers in big firms (300 or more) it was 73.[43] The US pattern reflects the broader problem of a "missing middle" – the relative paucity of pro bono in midsize law firms. This pattern is also apparent in France, where pro bono is "merely tolerated" and "ad hoc" in midsize firms, and in South Africa, which reports a pro bono "gap" in firms of ten to twenty lawyers.

One other interesting yet underappreciated aspect of pro bono service is how it varies between differently qualified lawyers – solicitors and barristers – in dual-license professional systems. Although the data in this book is largely limited to the studies of England and Wales and South Africa, they do suggest potential differences in participation rates and styles of pro bono activity, which flow from distinctive professional privileges and areas of expertise (with solicitors generally engaged in counseling and transactional work and barristers focused on advocacy). In England and Wales, solicitor pro bono participation has grown to about 40 percent (resulting in roughly 50 hours per year on average for those who do pro bono); although there is no comparable data on barrister pro bono, there is increasing barrister participation in pro bono programs, with a focus on criminal, personal injury, and international pro bono work. In South Africa (where the division was between advocates and attorneys until recent professional unification), although advocates were required to commit 20 hours per year to pro bono, the definition was so broad that many met the goal by counting work they already did, while attorneys often avoided pro bono in high-demand areas (such as family law and housing) on the ground that they lacked the relevant expertise.

In terms of the hierarchy dimension of pro bono – who is most responsible for distributing free services *within* firms – our country studies identify potential patterns worthy of further examination. One relates to the quantity and quality of pro bono participation by lawyers of different status, from senior partner to junior associate, in the law firm pyramid structure. All we can say at this point is that country-specific evidence points in different directions. Although the Canadian chapter finds that pro bono service correlates with lawyer decision-making power, suggesting that senior partners are most likely to engage in pro bono, in other countries, it appears that pro bono responsibility flows down to less experienced lawyers – who have little power to reject cases and see potential professional benefits (training and contacts) in pro bono work. The latter situation characterizes pro bono work in the United States, where law firm associates carry a disproportionate share, as well as in Portugal and South Africa. In contrast, in Argentina, Chile, and Colombia, it is reported that the pro bono burden falls most heavily on junior partners – those in the middle of the hierarchy, who are "victims" of the pro bono system, unable to refuse assignments by senior partners (who do very little pro bono), and not expected (like associates) to be singularly focused on billing hours. While younger English barristers appear more likely to engage in pro bono work, the proportion of partners in solicitor firms doing pro bono has rapidly expanded owing to the growth of pro bono infrastructure (and there is similar evidence of increasing partner participation in Spain). More research is needed into what explains differences in pro bono participation by status – particularly why in some places partners do more – and what the impact is on clients in countries where pro bono is primarily executed by less experienced lawyers often with little supervision.

The limited demographic data on pro bono presented in this book – how pro bono participation is affected by lawyers' race, gender, age, and other identity-based factors – are also suggestive of patterns that point toward future avenues of inquiry. Although the empirical evidence from Canada does not show that pro bono participation *rates* are affected by race or gender, lawyers who identify as persons of color and women are more likely to devote their pro bono time to particular *types* of pro bono work (community service) than their white male counterparts. As suggested above, age appears to be an important factor in pro bono participation, although the relationship is complex. In the United States, although law firms rely on junior lawyers to shoulder the pro bono burden, ABA data indicate that professionwide, older lawyers (aged 55–75) do more pro bono on average than their younger counterparts[44] – a pattern that suggests greater opportunity for economically secure senior US lawyers to give back as they transition to retirement. Pro bono by solo and small-firm lawyers in France is conducted primarily by semiretired lawyers, on one end of the age spectrum, and younger (often female lawyers), on the other.

An additional arena of demographic disparity is in pro bono leadership. In South America, although leaders of pro bono committees (typically equity partners) are uniformly men, pro bono coordinators (non-equity-track lawyers) are disproportionately female – a theme that reverberates in Portugal, where women are more visible in pro bono coordinator positions. The feminization of pro bono leadership within the law firm hierarchy raises serious questions about whether female lawyers opt into pro bono positions out of a stronger commitment to service or to achieve better work-family balance, or whether female overrepresentation in pro bono programs reflects discrimination against women excluded from more traditional power positions inside law firms.

Clients: Who Receives Pro Bono?

On the demand side of the distribution equation, the question is which types of clients are most likely to receive pro bono service and how the triage priorities of pro bono programs compare with other delivery systems. Pro bono lawyers do not simply respond to legal need. Instead, in a context in which demand overwhelms supply and thus allocative choices must be made, pro bono lawyers necessarily channel resources to some types of clients and causes over others based on multiple factors, including existing relationships with community groups, commercial client pressure, individual normative preferences, conflicts between lawyers in different segments of the bar, and claims of appropriate expertise. Out of the interplay of these factors, despite the absence of strict rules dictating how pro bono resources are to be deployed, we can begin to discern distributional patterns organized around two major areas of representational divergence: whether pro bono lawyers concentrate their efforts on *individual versus NGO clients*, and whether they focus on *civil versus criminal representation*. Although more work needs to be done investigating the reasons for these patterns, our conclusion is that they are largely driven by the degree of cooperation or conflict among lawyers in large-firm pro bono programs, legal aid and public interest law groups, and solo and small-firm practice – resulting in what we call *institutional compromises* around the distribution of free legal services across these domains as a way to manage turf wars. The precise nature of compromise in different contexts is also influenced by the relationship between pro bono case content and lawyer expertise, which varies across the corporate and individual service hemispheres of the bar.

Within this framework, as it turns out, the countries where pro bono is most targeted toward low-income individual clients in civil cases – the United States and Australia – are also the most anomalous. This is because of the unique relationship in these countries between the corporate law sector and legal aid, which developed (in different degrees) on a staffed-office model, in which full-time lawyers provide free assistance through NGOs, which ultimately have come to heavily depend upon pro bono support (although not without early controversy and ongoing tension). In the United States, as discussed earlier, it was the financial instability of government-subsidized legal aid in the wake of neoliberal austerity that cemented a pro bono partnership between corporate lawyers and legal aid in support of civil legal services. In the absence of significant judicare – and thus active opposition by solo and small-firm lawyers – this partnership evolved to profoundly shape the nature of US pro bono work. According to the ABA, four-fifths of pro bono service in 2016 went to individuals.[45] Demonstrating the interconnection with legal aid, family law (the most important area of legal aid practice) was by far the most popular area of pro bono service.[46] Similarly, the lack of judicare in Australia, coupled with the rise of an independent community legal center sector, created opportunities for a close partnership unencumbered by jurisdictional conflict over individual representation.

In both countries, channeling pro bono service – particularly from large-firm lawyers – into individual representation of low-income clients has meant redefining what it means for pro bono lawyers to have requisite expertise. Because large-firm lawyers steeped in areas like antitrust or intellectual property have little substantive knowledge to contribute to the modal pro bono case, those lawyers are instead valued for their specific procedural (being good at litigation) or general problem-solving skills, and are given backup substantive support by full-time experts in legal aid organizations. (Legal aid leaders are willing to make investments in backup support, in part, because they believe that financial donations from firms follow the pro bono participation of their lawyers.) This situation contrasts sharply with that in a country like India, where large-firm pro bono lawyers, citing expertise grounds, focus primarily on transactional legal services to NGOs, leaving individual service work to solo practitioners in a pro bono delivery system divided between the corporate and individual representation spheres. As this suggests, expertise is a contested concept that can be mobilized as a rationale to support quite different pro bono arrangements.

Indeed, targeting large-firm pro bono to NGO clients is the most prevalent distributional pattern in the countries studied in this book – a result flowing from the comparative expertise of corporate lawyers and also, more significantly, the institutional compromise between Big Law and the Social Bar. Specifically, in all countries where NGOs are the primary recipients of large-firm pro bono service – in addition to India, all the countries canvassed in Europe and South America – the defining feature is the existence of a mobilized constituency of Social Bar lawyers (solo and small-firm practitioners funded by the state to perform legal aid) resisting pro bono for low-income individuals as a form of turf protection (since pro bono for those clients creates the potential for less legal aid). As a result of institutional compromise, low-income individual client representation remains the domain of Social Bar lawyers, while large firms commit to directing their pro bono activity – in the form of transactional legal support, the preparation of research reports, legal training and advice, and other nonlitigation services – toward NGOs (and, to a lesser degree, social enterprises).

This compromise is evident throughout Europe, where Edwin Rekosh and Lamin Khadar report that nearly 85 percent of big firm pro bono goes to NGOs and social enterprises. As their chapter on Europe argues, this result is partly a product of Big Law expertise – European corporate lawyers, skilled in navigating regulatory compliance, are able to assist NGOs seeking to engage in complex policy processes – but the result also follows from explicit agreements by Big Law to avoid low-income client representation as a concession to national bar associations concerned about protecting Social Bar lawyers. This concession avoids conflict with the Social Bar while still allowing large national law firms to use pro bono as a marketing tool to attract clients and talent in the face of competition by US and other global firms. The studies of individual European countries buttress this finding. In France, although large-firm lawyers provide free consultations to individuals through access-to-justice intermediaries, they devote significant resources to the full-scale representation of NGOs. In Portugal and Spain, firms prefer to concentrate pro bono on NGOs and social enterprises, while in Demark, law firms tailor pro bono toward organizations at the expense of individuals (who, as in India, depend on pro bono lawyers from solo practice and small law offices). Again, this NGO orientation, fueled by turf wars, is reinforced by claims of relative expertise. For example, the structure of UK solicitor firms – which focus on corporate law – and the nature of their foreign office development on the European continent – which relies on lawyers engaged in global transactional work (with many not licensed to litigate in local jurisdictions) – render UK-firm lawyer expertise more compatible with representing NGOs and social enterprises on governance issues, conducting legal research, and building public–private partnerships.

The South American chapters tell a similar institutional compromise story. In Brazil, solo lawyers successfully lobbied the São Paulo bar to block pro bono to individual clients. It took a long and intense campaign by the pro bono movement to overturn this limitation, but ongoing turf wars with solo and small-firm lawyers, who wish to keep large firms out of individual representation, and with the public defender's office, which seeks to protect its jurisdiction over legal aid, have continued to make individual pro bono too costly for most firms to undertake. In Argentina, Chile, and Colombia, it is reported that, of the tiny number of large-firm pro bono cases, almost none involve litigation (which is too expensive) and of those characterized as in the public interest, most involve corporate-style advising for NGOs.

The second prominent type of institutional compromise emerging from our country studies – also driven by the relation between pro bono and legal aid – is organized around a civil–criminal case divide. Thus, in Canada, where (unlike most other jurisdictions) legal aid is concentrated on criminal cases, pro bono lawyers avoid criminal representation in favor of meeting civil legal needs in areas such as disability, civil rights, housing, and labor. In this regard, Canada joins the United States and Australia as countries in which pro bono is directed to individual representation in civil cases – although it arrives at this position via a distinct route. Moreover, while surveyed Canadian lawyers overall devote the largest share of their pro bono hours to low-income individual clients, there is a large–small firm split, with large-firm lawyers much less likely to devote their pro bono hours to helping the poor (directing roughly 10 percent of pro bono to low-income clients) than their small-firm counterparts (who devote close to one-third of pro bono to low-income clients). In this sense, Canadian large-firm lawyers share tendencies with their colleagues in Europe and

South America, in that they are more likely to devote pro bono time to transactional work for NGOs. A civil–criminal pro bono service division also exists in Singapore, although it is the mirror image of that in Canada. Specifically, because of widespread *civil* legal aid coverage, and the paucity of state-financed representation for indigent *criminal* defendants (who have been largely excluded from legal aid, outside of capital cases), pro bono lawyers focus on criminal representation (with a smaller portion also representing individuals with civil problems who do not meet legal aid cutoffs).

Finally, from a distributional perspective, it is important to highlight the robust relationship between pro bono and public interest law across a diverse range of countries. Unlike legal aid, which is centered on ordinary dispute resolution, public interest law seeks legal reform through courts and thus requires litigation resources and skill. In the United States, where public interest law organizations emerged around the same time as state-funded legal aid, they formed an alliance with elite firms eager to demonstrate civic virtue (and whose leaders often shared the substantive values of public interest law organizations),[47] permitting public interest groups to leverage firm money and pro bono resources for reform-oriented legal challenges. This alliance has largely persisted, as the US chapter underscores, and forms the basis for significant large-firm pro bono support for civil rights, environmental justice, women's rights, and other public interest litigation cases. There is an irony here insofar as public interest law organizations, which aspire to more radical change, come to rely on pro bono, which is a resource constrained by the inherently conservative (in the sense of supporting the status quo) orientation of corporate law firms. As political culture becomes more polarized, we might expect some law firm leaders to espouse more right-wing political views and thus to mobilize their firms' pro bono resources to support right-wing political causes.

In other countries with strong traditions of public interest law – particularly Australia, India, and South Africa – we see similar pro bono support for public interest law groups in need of sustained resources, although in India and South Africa, such support comes primarily from solo and small-firm lawyers aligned with social movements. An analogous pattern is visible in Nigeria, where human rights challenges to the military dictatorship relied on pro bono support from small-firm lawyers that translated into ongoing partnerships between such firms and public interest groups after democratization. As mentioned, China is an outlier because the profession is dominated by the state, channeling most pro bono into state-run legal aid programs. However, even there, because of long-standing struggles over human rights, we see some private lawyers – those in the "challenger" mode – providing pro bono service for litigants protesting state abuses of power to build the rule of law and extend liberal values.

Contestation

We have, thus far, synthesized evidence from our country studies to explore the first two elements of the tripartite framework around which this book is organized: probing the relationship between pro bono's *causes* and *consequences*. We have argued that, although the diffusion of pro bono is driven by globalized ideas and transnational networks, local institutions and actors profoundly shape the process by which the public character of lawyering and preexisting traditions of access to justice are transformed into "pro bono" – understood as the systematic provision of free legal services by private lawyers as an ethical duty. In making this argument, we have used the concept of hybridization as a way to illustrate how the alchemy of global and local factors in specific countries produces wide variation – but also discernible patterns – in terms of pro bono's organizational footprint and distributional output. In this section, we extend the discussion by turning to the third element of our analytical framework: exploring "global pro bono" as a terrain of inevitable and ongoing *contestation*. As we suggest, the conflicts over pro bono visible in this book are not simply about how to define its basic meaning (although that is one dimension), but more deeply reflect fundamental tensions around professional autonomy, the role of the state in redressing inequality, the duty of lawyers to promote justice, and the degree to which law is a profession or a business. Our precise aim here is to elevate the key pro bono debates around which these tensions manifest: erupting over claims of foreign intervention, interference with legal aid, lawyers backsliding in their commitment to access to justice, and law firms deploying pro bono toward profit-seeking ends.

Indigenous Tradition or Foreign Transplant?

A foundational debate cutting across the chapters of this book revolves around pro bono's origins and professional autonomy: Where does the idea of pro bono come from and who gets to decide its practical content and meaning? Although at first glance the question seems innocuous enough, embedded within it is an implicit concern about US hegemony and whether US-centric models are force-fed to countries in exchange for wider benefits of global integration – a concern resonant with overtones of neocolonialism, exacerbated when the line of pro bono's transmission crosses the Global North–Global South divide. For this reason, we find a resistance to strong claims of US (or more general "global") influence on the development of pro bono – the concept of pro bono as a foreign transplant – and instead see accounts that stress the domestic roots of pro bono as an indigenous tradition. In one example that captures this resistance, the chapter on Nigeria, while acknowledging the importance of the country's quest for global recognition in adopting its Pro Bono Declaration (patterned on those in South America), argues that the Declaration should be understood as an expression of an indigenous professional principle in support of legal aid for the disadvantaged.

Although our evidence is too spotty to draw strong conclusions, it is reasonable to presume that the intensity of the conflict over pro bono as a global transplant is inversely related to the depth of its domestic institutionalization. As we have seen, pro bono is most likely to become deeply embedded in domestic legal culture when it seamlessly builds upon traditional service norms and harmonizes with existing access-to-justice institutions. Putting the United States to one side (since the origins of institutionalized pro bono were internal to its system and hence there was never any conflict over foreign transplant), countries in this book with the strongest pro bono systems appear to be those in which internal constituencies use global templates and resources, but ultimately submerge pro bono's foreignness, instead leveraging the normative force of domestic professional service and assimilating pro bono to national values. Following this model, we see pro bono in Australia claiming a distinctive cultural position Down Under, developing from a partnership between the community legal center and large-firm sectors, with each viewing pro bono as a valuable asset: community legal centers seeking resource support, and firms seeking legitimacy in the profession and with clients, particularly those playing in the global arena and fixated on CSR.

In contrast, top-down pro bono projects disconnected from the lived realities of receiving communities, especially when undertaken across the North-South divide, appear unlikely to result in substantial institutionalization.[48] Particularly where the legal aid and public interest law sectors are not willing partners, it is difficult for indigenous promoters to frame pro bono in relation to domestic access-to-justice traditions, forcing them to fight against the image of pro bono as an unwelcome transplant that undermines domestic institutions. As the South American experience reveals, this fight plays out in a postcolonial context, where efforts at North–South transmission of pro bono trigger deeply felt suspicion toward US power – a suspicion that is mobilized against pro bono and limits the extent to which it becomes culturally embedded. In the end, who is able to control the narrative of pro bono's origin story – and whether that story is assigned local or transnational roots – helps to explain the degree of pro bono's professional assimilation.

Complement or Substitute?

In nearly every country studied in this book, a significant debate exists about the extent to which pro bono "complements" or "substitutes" for legal aid. Opponents of pro bono – both those who believe that the state owes a duty to its citizens to ensure access to justice and Social Bar lawyers with a self-interest in the state-funded system – make the argument that pro bono is a substitute that undermines the government's social welfare role. In so doing, they point to a variety of evidence ranging from explicit statements by government officials in support of pro bono as part of neoliberal austerity programs to the coincident timing of pro bono's rise and legal aid's decline. Promoters of pro bono, in contrast, make the argument in favor of complementarity – arguing that pro bono should only be used to fill gaps in the state system and that legal aid leaders should have the primary role in defining what gaps exist and how to best address them. Promoters also stress that pro bono lawyers in the corporate bar should be a leading voice defending state-based legal aid and advocating for its expansion. However, even in countries where efforts at complementarity are strong and sincere, there is an undercurrent of concern that the best-intentioned and well-designed pro bono systems can be used as a pretext for retrenchment on government commitment to legal aid.

The language of complementarity – and the underlying sensitivity about the perception of pro bono as private charity undercutting public support for the poor – is a thread that runs throughout the chapters. It is perhaps most prominent in the Australian context, where pro bono leaders have been vocal in making the case for the "best use" of pro bono to fill gaps in the existing access-to-justice system. More generally, we see the rhetoric of complementarity prominent in those countries where turf wars around legal aid have produced institutional compromise. These include Canada, where large law firms take on NGO clients and avoid criminal law cases to "complement" legal aid; France, where progressive large firms, also focused on NGO representation, have positioned their pro bono as a "complement" to state-funded judicare, dispensed to individual low-income clients under the program of *aide juridictionnelle*; Portugal and Spain, where the "complement" language is used to support pro bono clearinghouses that steer clear of state-funded legal aid services to individuals; and Singapore, where pro bono support for noncapital criminal cases "complements" the legal aid civil justice focus.

These movements to promote complementarity raise important questions that warrant further inquiry. Most significantly, they force consideration of the extent to which complementarity reflects a robust effort at thoughtful institutional design or a rhetorical strategy to mitigate interjurisdictional conflict. In this latter regard, it seems possible that well-intentioned advocates of complementarity may unwittingly authorize neoliberal agendas even as they forcefully advocate against them. Evidence for this possibility comes from the United Kingdom, where it is reported that the mantra of pro bono as "an adjunct to, not a substitute for, a proper system of publicly funded legal services" was proclaimed most loudly at the precise moment that legal aid was being significantly slashed. At the very least, the UK experience provides a cautionary tale of complementarity: revealing that the rise of pro bono, no matter how skillfully managed, creates space for powerful proponents of substitution to curtail legal aid despite best efforts to protect its legacy.

Legal or Public Service?

Another fundamental debate spanning diverse countries across the geography of global pro bono turns on the degree to which pro bono is defined as a quintessentially "legal" service or more broadly in terms of "public" service, understood in terms of nonlegal volunteerism and community engagement. This debate is far from academic. Indeed, it goes to the core of why lawyers are expected to "do good" in the first instance: a special duty to balance the scales of justice derived from the fact that lawyers have a monopoly over the provision of legal services, which makes them essential gatekeepers to the legal system. That duty (especially when paired with the ideal of complementarity discussed previously) militates in favor of a conception of pro bono targeted to those with legal needs excluded from the private legal marketplace on account of lack of resources. It is when lawyers are seen deviating from legal pro bono by providing nonlegal public service (and seeking professional credit for doing so) that critics rise up to ask: What good is a lawyer's duty to do good if it does not advance access to justice?

As we have seen, the tension between pro bono as a legal or public service has become more acute due to the interplay between large-firm pro bono and CSR – with firms at times seeking a double dividend by counting broad volunteer work in both categories. There are examples of this trend in places as distinct as the United States, where some law firms package pro bono under abstract CSR-informed social commitments (such as promoting "community," "inclusion," and "sustainability"), and Portugal, where it is reported that lawyers pursuing CSR credit engage in activities like planting trees, clearing forests, and painting walls (and calling all that pro bono). Such charitable activities, of course, are admirable. But they do not advance legal justice and thus squander lawyers' unique expertise by misallocating volunteer time to activities that could be undertaken by others. CSR is not the only influence, however, pulling pro bono away from its legal roots. In South Africa, the passage of national legislation unifying the profession and requiring broad "community service" for all lawyers has unleashed concern about the fate of legally oriented pro bono; while in China, the political sensitivity of rights activism – and the professional control exerted over lawyers by the Chinese Communist Party – has led most private lawyers to define pro bono broadly to include civic engagement, volunteer service for the public good, and Party activities.

In considering responses to the legal-public service dilemma, one can presume that lawyers, like all professionals, would prefer flexibility to define their own standards of conduct rather than having to act according to strict regulatory mandates. Furthermore, one can presume that flexibility would be exercised in favor of taking action that aligns with the interests of private lawyers' most important constituents: paying clients. In light of this reality, the research in this book teaches that financial incentives for lawyers to move away from legally oriented pro bono may be checked by countervailing pressure. In particular, in order to counteract such pro bono "drift," it is critical to have other institutional actors in place with power in the system – able to assert stricter pro bono definitions and empowered with oversight authority to enforce them. There are important models of such actors throughout the chapters that follow. In the United States, a trio of powerful professional and private groups has asserted a narrow definition of pro bono: the ABA, which promulgated the rule defining pro bono as "legal services without fee or expectation of fee to persons of limited means" or organizations "designed primarily to address the needs of persons of limited means"; the Pro Bono Institute, whose Law Firm Pro Bono Challenge holds signatory firms to the ABA standard; and the *American Lawyer* magazine, which also measures the amount of strictly legal services to individuals or organizations to rank large-firm pro bono activity. In the United Kingdom, as discussed, the 2002 attorney general protocol defining pro bono in legal terms rescued pro bono from being watered down by Big Law's pursuit of CSR. Similarly, the Australian Pro Bono Centre's survey of large firms uses a definition of pro bono confined to legal activities, while the Pro Bono Declaration for the Americas adopts the US standard by defining pro bono services as "those provided without a fee, or expectation of a fee, principally to benefit poor or underprivileged persons or communities or the organizations that assist them." Enforcement of these legally oriented standards occurs through public reporting mechanisms that enable the "naming and shaming" of firms that do not meet them.

Good for Society or Good for Business?

A final debate revolves around whether pro bono is aimed at improving society – a vehicle for lawyers to discharge their duty to serve the public good – or whether it is aimed at enhancing law firms' bottom lines. Is pro bono the expression of altruism – or lawyer "generosity" in Louis Assier-Andrieu and Jeremy Perleman's terms? Or is it a market strategy to recruit talent and clients by large-firm lawyers, who appropriate the halo of professional legitimacy as public servants while aggressively representing powerful companies intent upon using law as a tool of economic control? Or is it – can it be – both?

This debate flows inevitably from the vanguard role of large law firms in building pro bono systems and expresses deeper anxiety about whether lawyers form an elevated profession (fulfilling the "lawyer-statesman" ideal[49]) or are simply an economic guild intent on protecting and expanding the market for legal business.[50] This anxiety is perfectly captured in the paradoxical "business case for pro bono," which figures prominently in the public pronouncements and private discussions of pro bono leaders in countries where pro bono culture depends on institutionalization in Big Law. According to this business case, pro bono presents law firms with an opportunity for a "double bottom-line" return: good for society but also good for profits, insofar as it burnishes law firms' reputation with corporate clients eager to present a positive social image, while serving as a critical factor in the cutthroat competition to attract and retain lawyers who desire something more out of law practice than billing hours. Pro bono leaders in the United States pioneered the business case as a way to "sell" pro bono to law firms reluctant to incur the opportunity and infrastructure costs of building pro bono programs. As the US chapter highlights, the marketing function of pro bono is prominently displayed on flashy websites touting the transformative contributions of firm lawyers, which are geared toward an audience of aspiring associates and corporate CSR compliance officers. Indeed, as pro bono spreads globally, it is clear that CSR has become an increasingly important factor pushing firms to embrace the business case. In this regard, the Denmark chapter emphasizes that the merger of CSR and pro bono programs there has focused firms on linking "earnings, recruitment, branding and charity" as "interknitted elements" viewed through a "win-win perspective," in which firms draw in new clients and junior lawyers through legal voluntary work. Beyond CSR, we see law firms in some countries searching for more concrete ways to monetize pro bono. This comes through perhaps most vividly in the chapter on Portugal, where it is reported that some law firms pursue pro bono clients in Portuguese-speaking countries in Africa in order to strengthen ties between Portuguese firms and local elites – thereby mining new business opportunities.

Yet there are significant risks in touting the business case too loudly. Crass connection between law firm pro bono – with its aspiration to transcend commercialism to serve the public good – and market strategy feeds cynicism about the motives of those behind the pro bono movement, undercutting arguments in favor of complementarity and rankling supporters of legal aid, who view law firm self-interest in pro bono as further evidence of the perils of privatization. Moreover, to the degree that law firms evaluate their pro bono in relation to economic return, one would suspect their calculus to misallocate pro bono resources away from meeting genuine legal need toward achieving what is best for firm image and bringing the most satisfaction to firm lawyers. In this way, assimilating pro bono practice to market values threatens to undermine the very legitimacy of professionalism – rendering pro bono yet another tool of legal inequality rather than a vehicle to redress it.

PATTERNS OF PRO BONO DEVELOPMENT

In this section, we step back from our analytical framework – causes, consequences, and contestation – to make general observations about why pro bono appears to be more developed in some places than in others. These observations flow from our comparative approach, which focuses attention on questions of similarity and difference. Looking across the countries profiled in this book, what can be said about distinctive patterns of pro bono development? What are the most important factors – such as jurisdictional conflict between elite and nonelite private lawyers – that contribute to those patterns? Why, in some countries, do we see weak institutionalization or circumscribed domains of pro bono development, while in others there is a stronger commitment to pro bono as a professional value and broader distribution of pro bono service? In assessing institutionalization, timing is obviously important – countries with longer histories of organizing around pro bono have more developed norms and practices. Resources and the scale and diversity of private law practice are also significant. Here, we attempt to move beyond these basic factors to array the countries studied in this book along a spectrum of institutionalization and to offer some thoughts about why pro bono culture and practice appear more robust in different locations. We stress at the outset that there are an enormous number of important variables and the complexity of legal systems defies easy categorization. However, we offer the following overview as an invitation to further research.

As this chapter has highlighted, there are two key findings from our research that shape our analysis of pro bono patterns. First, the development of a substantial Big Law sector (even if not "big" by US standards) is an essential precondition to the institutionalization of pro bono. Only with large-firm resources and leadership does pro bono gain widespread legitimacy – tied to the elite profile of large firms striving to demonstrate their social utility and thus justify their status and power. In the absence of a large-firm sector with an incentive to perform professional service and the bureaucratic structure to allocate such service in an efficient manner, pro bono remains concentrated at the level of small-scale practice and generally ad hoc.

Our second critical finding is that the role pro bono plays within a country's access-to-justice system depends heavily on the nature of the existing legal aid and public interest law sectors. As suggested in our discussion of distributional consequences, pro bono culture appears to be most deeply embedded in countries in which legal aid is organized around staffed offices (not judicare) and/or when there is a significant non-state-based system for providing legal services to the poor and supporting public interest legal work – all of which depend on private philanthropic resources. In these settings, pro bono is a crucial supplement to underfunded legal aid and public interest law, and does not raise the specter of "unfair competition" with solo and small-firm lawyers who depend on government subsidies to perform legal aid. In some countries with a judicare model, pro bono has not encountered significant bar resistance because either the cutoff threshold for legal aid eligibility is so low or stipends are so paltry that local lawyers are not dependent on them (this appears to be the case in Singapore and China, for example). In contrast, in judicare countries throughout Europe and South America, a division of labor has developed based on institutional compromise.

On the basis of these core findings, we outline three general categories of institutional development. Again, we stress that these categories are ideal types that simplify reality and thus necessarily obscure complexity for the purposes of elementary comparison. Yet we believe that this comparison is helpful to illuminate important structural dynamics that shape pro bono and its relationship to broader economic and political arrangements.

The first category is one of *strong institutionalization*, characterized by the following features: high rates of pro bono participation across private practice settings (particularly at the large-firm and solo/small-firm practice levels); explicit and strong ethical incorporation of pro bono in bar rules; thought leadership and organizational formalization at the elite law firm level; strong and broad-based clearinghouses; support from the legal aid and public interest law sectors; and wide distribution of pro bono services across client categories (individual, NGO, and law reform). Here we put the United States and Australia – both highly developed countries in which neoliberalism has taken firm root. The keys to pro bono in these countries include, as we have highlighted, the strength and organization of the corporate bar and the minimization of conflict between legal aid and pro bono. In both countries, there are strong public interest law organizations, which invite law firm support for law reform litigation, which does not arouse opposition of private lawyers (though it can aggravate government targets). An additional factor in both countries is the crucial role of intermediaries (the US Pro Bono Institute and Australian PILCHs) that connect law firms and legal service providers, as well as outside monitoring agents (*AmLaw* and the Australian Pro Bono Centre), which report on pro bono activity and motivate compliance with aspirational standards by creating race-to-the-top competitions. The experiences of these two countries underscore the need for interest convergence between the public and private hemispheres of the profession to generate and sustain support for pro bono. In the United States and Australia, there is buy-in from elite firms (due to pressure from clients and the bar), buy-in from local NGOs (due to dependence on firms for financial and voluntary resources), and buy-in from governmental and philanthropic agencies committed to leveraging private involvement for the public good. In short, broad-based internal constituencies (corporate law firms, legal aid and public interest law groups, bar leaders, and government officials) have mobilized in favor of pro bono and encountered weak internal resistance.

The second category, which is the most common and spans the broadest range, we characterize as *mixed institutionalization*. Here, we see variable rates of pro bono participation across and within practice sites (with large firms underperforming relative to other sectors, often relying heavily on junior lawyers without strong participation by partners); inconsistent ethical codification, which often lags behind other indicia of institutional development; a disjuncture between the form and function of large-firm pro bono, with levels of service not matching formal organizational and rhetorical support; fledgling or otherwise limited-capacity intermediaries; resistance to pro bono led by solo and small-firm lawyers in the Social Bar and legal aid; and compartmentalized patterns of client service resulting from institutional compromise. It is quite difficult to confidently "locate" countries in this category, given the limits of our data set and because the category itself so broad – and thus we do so with circumspection. In the Global North, we include countries with substantial large-firm sectors, strong social welfare traditions, and moderate pro bono infrastructure: Canada, Denmark, England and Wales, and France. As discussed, in these countries, we see the diffusion of formal organizational policies at the large-firm level and general buy-in from large-firm leadership. This occurs within a framework of divided institutional responsibilities, in which pro bono lawyers in large firms take on cases that do not interfere with the legal aid system and Social Bar: representing NGOs as clients (in Western Europe) and avoiding criminal cases (in Canada). From the Global South, we include India and South Africa – democratic countries with strong constitutional rights, deep traditions of public interest law, developing intermediaries, and "emerging economies" with small but symbolically important large-firm sectors (opening to the entry of foreign law firms) that have played leadership roles around pro bono. We also include the two more authoritarian countries – China and Singapore – which have a substantial large-firm sector, strong bar and governmental leadership (with coordination between the two), and complex legal aid systems that shape distinctive types of institutional compromises around pro bono (with pro bono in China oriented toward government-sanctioned volunteerism and in Singapore toward criminal cases).

In the third category are countries with *weak institutionalization*. Here, we see relatively low pro bono participation across sectors, with anemic large-firm participation and typical patterns of ad hoc pro bono in solo and small-firm practice; the absence of ethical codification or weakly articulated ethical standards; timid leadership from the large-firm sector (which is relatively small) and limited firm investments in pro bono programs, which are often marginalized by assigning less powerful lawyers to be in charge; resistance to pro bono by legal aid and small-scale practitioners, and weak public interest law; no or low-capacity clearinghouses; and disorganized patterns of client representation. The countries in this category are also quite diverse and have pro bono systems shaped by distinct factors, including timing, lack of large-firm commitment and resources, and internal resistance to pro-bono-as-transplant. The latter factor appears most important in the South American countries (Argentina, Brazil, Chile, and Colombia), where Daniel Bonilla Maldonado and Fabio de Sa e Silva conclude that pro bono has been a failed legal transplant due to the lack of professional and grassroots buy-in, resistance by small-scale practitioners, and the disinclination of large-firm lawyers (despite public commitments to pro bono) to invest heavily in a strategy that has no clear economic payoff in the domestic market. Similar patterns of top-down pro bono incorporation met by internal resistance characterize the experiences so far in Spain and Portugal, which also have fledgling pro bono clearinghouses. Because of this, one might predict that the trajectory of pro bono in these two countries, over time, would align more closely with their European counterparts. Pro bono in Nigeria, at this early stage, is held back by the structure of the private bar, still dominated by solo and small-firm practice, as well as by paltry initial investments in pro bono systems – although, looking into the future of a country engaged in neoliberal reform as a condition of entry into the ranks of emerging economic powerhouses, one would expect the arc of pro bono development to trend sharply upward.

THE FUTURE OF GLOBAL PRO BONO

We conclude our introduction by considering the future trajectory of global pro bono – in all its diverse and conflictual forms. Futurology is inherently speculative – and therefore imprecise – but one can try to draw inferences based on current trends. As this book goes to press, however, confidence in our ability to predict any future, much less the future of pro bono, has been shaken to its core by a global pandemic that has crippled the economy and laid bare the massive deficiencies of neoliberal systems, particularly that of the United States, where decades of neoliberal restructuring left tens of millions without work and nowhere to turn for basic needs and security. This unprecedented crisis, combined with the eruption of worldwide protests in support of racial justice, has wiped away settled principles, and motivated calls for fundamental system redesign. Although the scale of the crisis has produced significant pro bono mobilization (to the extent that lawyers can play roles helping people access medical and economic benefits, maintain housing, and fight police abuse), it has also dramatically refocused attention on the critical role of government aid. Therefore, we begin by acknowledging that our attempts to extrapolate future trends based on the precrisis evidence presented in this book may ultimately land in a world transformed beyond recognition. With that in mind, we proceed forward nonetheless, offering a set of final reflections on the prospective role of illiberalism and transnationalism in any future global pro bono order.

Because the hybridization framework we have presented places development models at the center of pro bono's global diffusion, it seems plausible that pro bono's global future will be inextricably linked to the future of progressive neoliberalism itself – a future that appeared uncertain even before COVID-19. At one level, precrisis corporate capitalism demonstrated remarkable resilience. Although the beginning of the new millennium brought serious challenges to the established global order, jolted by financial crisis and confronted by sustained efforts to build viable alternatives,[51] capitalism appeared to emerge stronger than ever (although, as mentioned, the pandemic has shaken capitalism as the economic dislocation wrought by COVID-19 has surpassed that of the Great Recession by several orders of magnitude). If neoliberalism continues to hold sway, managing to reconsolidate on postcrisis ground, one could imagine that pro bono becomes more strongly assimilated to law firm commercial goals, undermining its value as a public good. This could, for example, cause the business dimension of pro bono work to eclipse the ethical and professional dimensions of it, or elevate generalized public service above specifically legal service.

Yet countervailing trends raise serious questions about the viability of progressive neoliberalism and hence its impact on the shape of pro bono to come. Future research should consider that the resilience and ultimate strength of the neoliberal project may not be able to rely on the prior alliance of deregulation and an egalitarian "politics of recognition." On the contrary, we have witnessed a powerful new linkage between capitalism and political illiberalism, from Trump and Brexit in the Global North to Bolsonaro in the Global South. Here, it is interesting to note that, although global pro bono is most visible in our volume as a liberal democratic project, it does have roots in more authoritarian regimes, like China, to the extent that the law firm sector there is globalized and pro bono has proven to be instrumental in the unique Chinese "rule by law" model. On the other hand, the advent of right-wing populism in the United States has stimulated an upsurge in pro bono around certain issues, like Trump's ban on Muslim immigration, which provoked a significant law firm pro bono mobilization at airports across the United States. Where this will ultimately lead pro bono – toward resurgence to defend the rule of law under threat or retreat in the face of capitalism unleashed – is a question with critical stakes going forward.

A related question involves the relevance and fate of transnational advocacy for human rights and social justice – the counterhegemonic global response to illiberalism witnessed in the outpouring of worldwide support for the Black Lives Matter movement. If lawyers are to play a significant role in countering illiberal forces and policies around the world, this will likely require some degree of cross-national collaboration. For example, public interest litigation in the EU could be a source of hope for countries like Hungary or Poland, whose democratic decline is dramatic.[52] In raising the potential benefits of transnational legal collaboration, however, we are aware that in some countries experiencing the expansion of pro bono, there has been significant local pushback against foreign influence and fears of foreign imposition. How can we balance the emphasis on the local with the need to avoid the trap of resurgent nationalism, one of the cards often played by authoritarian populists to attain and keep power? As Scott Cummings and Louise Trubek have noted in the context of public interest law,

> The delicacy of this cross-border engagement should not impede efforts by lawyers from the North and South to collaboratively advocate for social justice. Going forward, it is . . . crucial that lawyers across the North-South divide continue to frankly confront the history and current reality of US power, while also attempting to move beyond distrust in order to open up the possibility for transformative alliances across borders.[53]

Perhaps in the tensions around the meaning of global capitalism and the nature of global activism lie the most fertile ground for the development of global pro bono practice and scholarship in the years to come. Is pro bono going to become a terrain for the accommodation of an ultraliberal economic order, for the contestation of an illiberal political order, or both – if that is, at all, possible? Will this take place primarily within or across countries? More broadly, how might the patterns we identify in this book contribute to better-informed policy conversations about the role of pro bono, not just at the periphery but at the center of the legal profession? And how might legal professions do a better job balancing competing interests in designing an effective system for enhancing access to justice around the world? This book does not answer these questions, but we hope readers will find them valuable for their research and practice going forward.

OVERVIEW OF THE BOOK

This book is organized geographically. Part One begins with the Americas, starting with the evolution of pro bono in the Global North (the United States and Canada) and then turning to studies from the Global South (Brazil, Argentina, Chile, and Colombia). The US study is first, not because we believe that the American experience is the paradigm, but because the forces of institutionalization began there earliest; it is home to many of the most significant law firm and NGO pro bono promoters; it is the most studied country; and many of its ideas and structures have, in fact, been copied – and criticized – by those in other countries in which pro bono has evolved. The US case therefore operates as an inescapable focal point: as an example to be either emulated or distinguished.

In Chapter 2, John Bliss and Steven Boutcher examine the US experience, drawing on interviews with pro bono coordinators and a content analysis of pro bono statements from leading law firms to demonstrate conflicting professional and CSR rationales for American pro bono. As background, they trace the emergence of voluntary pro bono as a way of legitimizing professionalism, while highlighting the stratification of pro bono participation across different sectors of the bar. Their core focus is on the institutionalization of pro bono in large law firms and, in particular, the ways that emerging CSR trends have affected the conduct and presentation of pro bono. In terms of CSR, Bliss and Boutcher outline its broader conception of public service and document how firms have adopted different strategies for synchronizing pro bono and CSR, with some merging and others trying to differentiate the two. Their study reveals that big firms, operating under different monitoring frameworks, have to speak to different audiences. Although firms may try to speak with one voice, the different demands of pro bono and CSR constituencies often make that impossible. In conclusion, the authors suggest that the logic of CSR may pull pro bono away from its professional roots, grounded in legal service to the poor, and toward more diffuse business-oriented conceptions of charity – raising fundamental questions about what it means for law to be a public profession.

In Chapter 3, Robert Granfield and Fiona Kay examine the evolution of Canadian pro bono, tracing the rise of state-funded legal aid through the 1970s and the neoliberal "common sense revolution" that led to its decline – sparking greater investment in pro bono. In their account, pro bono development occurred through the leadership of the Canadian Bar Association and the support of emerging clearinghouses, which powered the rise of pro bono to a privileged position in the profession, with volunteer lawyers providing services in corporate and "people-oriented" law, such as family and employment. The authors stress that the proximity of Canadian urban centers to the United States has promoted incorporation of US models, since large-firm leaders in places like Toronto and Montreal monitor their US counterparts and adopt US policies and practices, often after having participated in US exchanges and trainings. Further, they observe that CSR has played a significant role in advancing pro bono, causing Canadian firms to engage in pro bono to attract large corporate clients, which can list firms as CSR-compliant providers in their supply chains. However, Granfield and Kay also note important distinctions between the US and Canadian models of pro bono. Most significantly, because of resistance by solo and small-firm lawyers who rely on legal aid funding to subsidize their practice, Canadian pro bono leaders have pledged to "complement" and not "replace" legal aid through a compromise strategy in which law firms avoid criminal representation, which is the bread and butter of the legal aid bar. The result is a bifurcated system in which legal aid lawyers provide criminal services while civil legal services are dispensed through pro bono. And within the pro bono system there is another division, with big firms focusing on transactional services to NGOs due to expertise and conflicts, while small-scale practitioners provide individual services. Overall, pro bono culture is relatively well-embedded in the Canadian profession, with law firms adopting consistent policies and lawyers in places with clearinghouses, like Ontario, reporting high pro bono participation rates, although pro bono remains stratified, with solos doing the most hours and large-firm lawyers doing the least.

Shifting to the Global South reveals similar processes of hybridization but also, in some cases, greater resistance to pro bono framed as a legal transplant. The case of Brazilian pro bono, presented in Chapter 4 by Fabio de Sa e Silva, charts a distinctive course that, like the Canadian case, raises the problem of "turf wars" between elite law firms and small-scale practitioners whose livelihood depends in part on government-subsidized legal aid. Sa e Silva focuses on the São Paulo bar, which in 2001 placed regulatory limits on pro bono work, excluding direct services to individuals. As he describes, the creation of pro bono in Brazil unfolded in large part as an elite project, in which US-trained lawyers established the Instituto Pro Bono in São Paulo in 2000. This project was supported by the emerging corporate law sector, which was turning to pro bono as a way to engage with the growing CSR movement and become a trustworthy partner for global corporate clients. Yet this project ran headlong into the reality of bar politics. The advent of pro bono mobilized the opposition of judicare lawyers – threatened by what they viewed as Big Law's undue invasion of their market niche – who won the São Paulo bar resolution limiting pro bono service to NGOs only. As the chapter recounts, although the national bar ultimately passed a rule permitting direct pro bono service to individuals, it has not been widely implemented by large firms, which are unwilling to incur the costs of training lawyers to develop expertise and do not want continued conflict with the local bar. To the extent that firms have made limited changes to their pro bono programs to serve needy individuals, this is largely due to the facilitation provided by intermediaries like Instituto Pro Bono and the idealism of some firm lawyers.

In Chapter 5, Daniel Bonilla Maldonado provides a critical analysis of pro bono in Argentina, Chile, and Colombia, describing an analogous process of flawed legal transplant, while also highlighting new dynamics. In Bonilla's account, pro bono in these countries has been an elite project: promoted by US-trained local academics who conceived of pro bono as a way to respond to the justice gap and coordinated with US law firm lawyers (seeking access to South American markets) and the Vance Center (together, the "Mandarins"), who helped draft the Pro Bono Declaration for the Americas and establish key clearinghouses. As a result, the framework of pro bono in Argentina, Chile, and Colombia does not reflect local culture, but rather copies the New York–centric approach advocated by the Vance Center, which promoted structures built around pro bono coordinators and formal policies. Under this framework, solo and small-firm lawyers, who dominate the legal market, are not incorporated into the pro bono system. The lack of institutionalization is also highlighted by the fact that firms have taken on a small number of cases with no mechanism for tracking and evaluation. Bonilla suggests that although pro bono entrepreneurs have changed legal culture, they have not had an impact on access to justice due to a lack of commitment by law firm partners, the absence of accountability systems (like rankings), and a dearth of significant professional and financial incentives to do pro bono (like billable credit). This has meant that pro bono in these countries is primarily conducted by junior lawyers under pressure to help firms comply with Declaration standards. The resulting landscape of large-firm pro bono focuses on corporate-style advising for NGOs that leverages law firm lawyer expertise.

Part Two shifts to pro bono in Europe, where its development also tracks professional and welfare state politics. This part begins, in Chapter 6, with an analysis of the spread of pro bono throughout Europe presented by Edwin Rekosh and Lamin Khadar. As in the United States and Canada, neoliberal austerity undermined the strength of legal aid beginning in the 1980s – a period that also saw the explosion of large-law-firm growth, both in number and size. However, the path of European pro bono has been different than in the United States for several reasons. In Western Europe, legal aid follows a judicare model, which has empowered the Social Bar; although austerity has led to its decline in many places, it remains strong in countries such as France and the Netherlands, where nearly half of all lawyers are engaged in legal aid work. In Central and Eastern Europe, legal aid developed after 2000 – promoted by OSF as a way to provide individual legal services and build nascent civil justice systems. As a result, Big Law pro bono throughout Europe has focused on NGO representation so as not to offend the entrenched Social Bar in Western Europe or the nascent legal aid systems in Central and Eastern Europe. The chapter also analyzes the role of transnational firms and NGOs in spreading pro bono. It notes how UK firms, competing with US counterparts, built pro bono programs that spread to the continent through law firm mergers, while US firms increased their European branch office pro bono activity after *AmLaw* rankings began tracking it in 2014. On the NGO side, PILnet played a strong role in the 2000s orienting Big Law pro bono toward NGO representation to steer clear of unfair competition claims by the Social Bar. Law firms themselves embraced NGO representation as a way of building on existing expertise and avoiding problems of local licensing for lawyers in foreign offices engaged in corporate work – thereby reinforcing European pro bono's emphasis on transactional lawyering and helping civil society actors navigate the complex EU process for law reform.

Andrew Boon and Avis Whyte, in Chapter 7, dig deeper into the UK experience with pro bono. Following the general trajectory of welfare state peak and decline, they locate pro bono's foundations in the creation of Poor Persons Committees, staffed by solicitors performing volunteer work on family law matters in the early twentieth century. After the 1949 legal aid legislation and the advent of social welfare as a distinct field of law, legal aid was provided through a judicare system. When austerity came in the 1980s, payment reductions to legal aid lawyers caused many solicitors to exit poverty law practice, although governmental costs still mounted because of the lack of funding caps for individual cases. The Labour Party, promoting Third Way politics, turned to pro bono to increase access to lawyers while reducing the costs of legal aid. Bar councils and law societies took up the challenge, creating pro bono referral units in the 1990s, at the same time that large solicitor firms began adopting CSR policies and building pro bono programs to compete in the global marketplace. These trends intertwined to expand pro bono culture. Referral units grew in size and importance, buttressed by the 2010 creation of the National Pro Bono Centre, which consolidated leadership. In this context, Boon and Whyte conclude that a 2002 attorney general protocol defining pro bono as advice to or representation of individuals or groups unable to afford legal services helped to solidify pro bono as a professional norm, leading to an increase in the proportion of UK lawyers performing pro bono.

Chapter 8 analyzes pro bono in France. There, Louis Assier-Andrieu and Jeremy Perelman argue that, from one perspective, pro bono has followed a typical US-inspired hybridization story. Legal aid, operated through cash payments to private lawyers, is massive in scale (involving 25,000 lawyers handling nearly 1 million cases per year), but also under neoliberal pressure. In response, the bar has organized pro bono intermediaries to coordinate pro bono service from private lawyers. Yet, as the authors report, lawyer pro bono participation varies significantly across practice sites. While large corporate law firms have developed pro bono programs, typically focused on free consultations to NGOs, in midsize firms, pro bono is tolerated but not well-supported, while solo and small-firm lawyers (who generally consider themselves cause lawyers) provide little pro bono. Following the hybridization framework, the chapter traces the influence of transnational NGOs, namely PILnet, in providing leadership (through the European Pro Bono Forum). It also analyzes the growth and impact of clearinghouses, such as the Paris Bar Endowment Fund; NGOs designed to connect lawyers to transnational human rights cases; and law school clinics, like the CSR Pro Bono Clinic at Science Po, which cultivates pro bono commitment, while exploring CSR as a way for firms to develop expertise and enhance "human capital loyalty" to attract new clients and talent. In this dynamic context, Assier-Andrieu and Perelman suggest that French pro bono has developed as a "complement" to legal aid and other models of access to justice, primarily owing to the strong national commitment to judicare. However, the authors resist identifying French pro bono as discontinuous with earlier traditions. To the contrary, they suggest that French pro bono is the current expression of a fundamental component of legal professionalism, which they term lawyers' "generosity," and argue that such generosity must continue to drive pro bono for the profession to carry out its democratic function.

In Chapter 9, Leire Larracoechea San Sebastián, Michelle Ha, and Todd Crider analyze Spain. Like other Western European countries, Spain's access-to-justice system was initially built on the foundation of a constitutionally guaranteed right to counsel and strong legal aid. However, beginning in the 1980s, legal aid suffered significant cuts, up to 40 percent in some regions after the Great Recession. Against the backdrop of fiscal constraint, the authors focus on clearinghouses as key actors in promoting pro bono to fill in service gaps and engage the private sector in fighting poverty. With Spanish lawyers among the worst pro bono performers in Europe, the key question the authors explore is how to strengthen pro bono in relation to the profession's traditional role as a protector of rights. To do so, they chart pro bono's tentative early growth, noting how it was shaped through a partnership of domestic entrepreneurs and leaders of the global pro bono movement. To spur greater private sector volunteerism after the new millennium, local law firm leaders, with guidance from US and European NGOs, began establishing pro bono programs. The top law firm, Cuatrecasas, launched a formal pro bono program in 2007 after a trip by its lawyers to New York coordinated by the Vance Center and the New York City Bar Association. As other firms followed, a "Group of Seven" organized around the idea of forming a clearinghouse to facilitate collaborative pro bono activity. At the same time, local bars and law schools launched initiatives promoting professional service. Pro bono's Spanish profile was raised by PILnet's decision to hold the 2012 European Pro Bono Forum in Madrid, followed by the creation of a web-based intermediary, probonos.net. As a result, the authors report that the average number of pro bono hours among Spanish lawyers doubled between 2015 and 2016. Planning for a pro bono clearinghouse accelerated when Vance Center representatives visited Spanish pro bono leaders in 2016, set up a working group, and developed a strategic plan for "pro bono assistance as a complement to state-funded agencies." Despite the fact that this process culminated in the creation of Fundación Pro Bono España, the authors argue that pro bono in Spain remains immature due to resistance by state-funded legal aid lawyers critical of large-firm pro bono competition, which has caused large firms to steer clear of individual cases in favor of NGO representation and strategic litigation on behalf of vulnerable groups like migrant youth.

In Chapter 10, Susana Santos provides an analysis of Portuguese pro bono. Like Spain, Portugal's Constitution grants the right to legal aid for all citizens, EU residents, and asylum seekers. Legal aid is funded by the state under a judicare model, but austerity combined with the rise of CSR in law firms motivated socially minded lawyers to start the Pro Bono Association in 2014 with the goal of bringing the practice of global pro bono (championed by PILnet) to Portugal. The association is a social solidarity organization that connects NGOs, law students, and individual lawyers. Despite its successful launch, its acceptance and growth have been stymied by a familiar combination of resistance from legal aid lawyers and distrust from corporate lawyers wary of the relevance of their expertise. As a result, Portuguese large-firm pro bono follows the European model of targeting NGOs, while ad hoc pro bono practice by small-scale lawyers continues to be an ongoing feature of the Portuguese scene.

Chapter 11 rounds out the European picture by turning north to Denmark, another stalwart social welfare state, with a judicare system under siege after austerity. Annette Olesen and Ole Hammerslev differentiate legal voluntary work, which all lawyers do, and pro bono, introduced in large law firms in the 2000s, after liberalization unleashed firm growth through mergers. The Danish large-firm pro bono movement builds on prior foundations of voluntary and university-supported legal work in the 1960s and 1970s, particularly the Lawyers on Call system, which provided basic legal advice by volunteers. However, voluntary programs were of limited importance throughout the twentieth century, as state legal aid remained the dominant system for providing free legal services to the poor. This began to change in the new millennium. In 2007, new federal restrictions precluded people with insurance from accessing legal aid and eliminated entire areas of legal aid eligibility (like administrative cases against the state), while public expenditure on legal aid was cut dramatically. In response, the government has actively encouraged pro bono as a new public-private partnership. The result, as the authors show, is a growing pro bono culture. A content analysis of legal periodicals reveals that pro bono became prominent in the early 2000s in Danish law firms, which drew inspiration from the US-UK model. As firms hired coordinators to track pro bono and make it efficient, pro bono levels increased. And yet significant challenges remain. Partly because of the influence of CSR, the meaning of pro bono is contested, as large firms mobilize different conceptions of pro bono as a strategy for branding and client recruitment, while directing representation to NGOs as a concession to local resistance by small-scale practitioners to individual client pro bono service.

Part Three focuses on Australia, the subject of Chapter 12. Australia's experience has been shaped by its dual system of legal service delivery: composed of legal aid commissions, the largest sector funded by the state, and community legal centers, grassroots organizations with a more radical ethos. The authors of this study, Fiona McLeay and Lucy Adams, argue that the Australian pro bono movement emerged to "supplement" (not compete with) these organizations, which were to remain the primary sources of legal services for poor and underserved groups. As elsewhere, the movement was built on the liberalization of the law firm sector, transformed between 2000 and 2010, when giant firms from the United States and United Kingdom entered Australia, spurring mergers and growth. Australian firms, many with traditions of public service, took advantage of the expanding network of PILCHs, first launched in New South Wales on the US model and quickly spreading to other states. In what would become a key feature differentiating Australian pro bono from its European counterparts, PILCHs were run by partnerships of community legal centers (in need of private sector resources) and law firm lawyers, forging a close collaboration, even while legal aid lawyers continued to view pro bono as a threat. The pro bono partnership was strengthened in the early 2000s by the creation of the Australian Pro Bono Centre, which has played a crucial role organizing conferences and codifying a definition of pro bono targeting representation to low-income individuals and groups that advocate on their behalf. That definition has been used to measure compliance with the National Pro Bono Target, which has spurred increased pro bono service and channeled that service into the legal representation of poor clients. The authors argue that the primary role of pro bono in Australia is to promote its "best use" as a complement to existing programs – not to displace the role of government. Toward this end, pro bono leaders have backed legal needs surveys and tried to gear pro bono toward gaps in service. The authors also highlight pro bono's secondary effects on social change through volunteer lawyer support of law reform, and its tertiary effects through building careers in pro bono and social justice.

Part Four moves the analysis to Africa. In Chapter 13, Thabang Pooe, Alice Brown, and Jonathan Klaaren place the development of pro bono in the context of South Africa's struggle against the apartheid regime and its legacy. The chapter demonstrates how pro bono builds upon South Africa's long and rich history of providing free legal advice to the Black population, dating back to early community-based service providers and the 1937 establishment of a Legal Aid Bureau in Johannesburg. These organizations counted on critical support from lawyers working pro bono, especially in criminal cases against Black activists. In the 1970s and 1980s, South Africa became the target of legal development initiatives by US foundations, which provided funds for legal clinics, public interest organizations, and Street Law Programs, all of which significantly expanded the infrastructure for pro bono provision. The chapter argues, nonetheless, that the post-apartheid constitutional order was the primary driver of pro bono in the country. The 1996 South African Constitution established a robust Bill of Rights, including provisions for access to justice, leading the government to create the Legal Aid South Africa program, which funded a combination of justice centers and satellite offices to provide legal services to indigent clients and engage in impact litigation. This state-based effort was buttressed by bar initiatives to promote pro bono, resulting in the codification of pro bono rules. In response, the Big Five law firms, as well as smaller firms, have adopted policies in support of pro bono, which vary in format and scope. Pro bono has also been strengthened by the 2006 creation of ProBono.Org, which is an important, though still fledgling, intermediary. Notwithstanding these many accomplishments, pro bono service quality varies, junior lawyers carry a disproportionate load, attorneys are usually not available in the most destitute areas, and clients litigating against corporations have been unable to use pro bono services provided by big firms because of conflicts of interest. A critical challenge to South African pro bono comes from the 2014 Legal Practice Act, which in unifying the profession, mandates pro bono framed as "community service." This has raised concerns that pro bono will be channeled into nonlegal work, draining resources from legal services for those who need it the most.

In Chapter 14, Jayanth Krishnan and Kunle Ajagbe offer an account from Nigeria, a country in which the bulk of the profession historically has consisted of solo practitioners without significant resources to serve clients pro bono. Nonetheless, the authors excavate a pro bono tradition and show how contemporary pro bono builds on a history of volunteer work that has been shaped by the country's experience with authoritarianism and civil society resistance. In 1976, when Nigeria was under military rule, Chimezie Ikeazor, known as the "father of legal aid," led a movement to pass the Legal Aid Act, which provided free legal services to the poor through state-funded lawyers, who relied on pro bono support from the private bar. However, private lawyers were wary of challenging the military government and legal aid was consistently underfunded, which undermined its effectiveness and rendered pro bono work atomistic and ad hoc. After a brief interruption, the return of military rule was a catalyst for greater engagement of private lawyers in pro bono work. In 1987, the Civil Liberties Organization (CLO) was established and, in coordination with private lawyers working pro bono, acted in support of those tormented by the military regime – engaging in heroic (though ultimately unsuccessful) work for the Ogoni nine. Between 1987 and 2000, nearly two dozen groups similar to the CLO were established relying on pro bono lawyers. After Nigeria democratized in 1999, these groups pivoted toward efforts to bring justice to the victims of the military regime by petitioning to commute life sentences of detainees and pursuing claims of human rights abuse through the truth commission. The question now is whether the legacy of CLO-inspired pro bono work can be mobilized to build pro bono culture through the organized bar and in connection with the small but significant corporate law sector. The authors trace important steps forward: in 2009, the Nigerian Bar Association issued a Pro Bono Declaration, while the state requires pro bono service in order for lawyers to be elevated to senior advocate. In the authors' view, these pro bono developments, and others like them, represent Nigeria's own version of pro bono hybridization: refashioning a time-honored principle of professional volunteerism in the context of Nigeria's rapid global integration.

Part Five arrives at Asia. In Chapter 15, Arpita Gupta reports on India, where the state is at the center of the legal services system. Article 39A of the Indian Constitution grants citizens a right to legal aid, dispensed at various geographic levels and within the courts. Yet the government has fallen far short in meeting its promises. While this represents a pro bono opportunity for the private bar, there are significant challenges, not the least of which is the high level of professional stratification: with a small number of large firms and most earnings concentrated in a handful of senior advocates. Nonetheless, the severity of the justice gap has motivated pro bono action, which builds upon the Indian profession's duty to serve those "genuinely in need of a lawyer." Pro bono development has been enabled, in part, by economic liberalization and the growing (but still small) number of large domestic firms, along with the impending entry of foreign firms, bringing to India the trends of CSR and the large-firm pro bono model. Domestic and global actors have also coalesced around the pro bono cause. Inside the country, the Society of Indian Law Firms, representing the most globally connected firms, has launched a pro bono initiative, while academics have spearheaded the creation of ProBono India, a clearinghouse in Gujarat. These efforts have been buttressed by the India-focused work of global intermediaries such as iProbono, TrustLaw Connect, and the Lex Mundi Pro Bono Foundation. Yet the most important push for pro bono comes from the Indian state, seeking to shore up the faltering legal aid system. In 2017, the Ministry of Law and Justice, in partnership with the UNDP, launched a Pro Bono Legal Services Initiative, urging private lawyers to provide a fuller range of pro bono services – including litigation – and stating that such pro bono work would be considered for lawyers to be "appointed to appropriate positions." The Supreme Court followed suit and, borrowing from Nigeria, made pro bono a requirement for achieving the status of senior advocate. These initiatives have influenced the nature and scope of India's evolving pro bono landscape. Whereas solo lawyers tend to work in close collaboration with rights-based organizations to undertake public interest litigation, large-firm lawyers typically engage in transactional pro bono for NGOs and social enterprises, while also doing various kinds of nonlegal work. In a theme echoed throughout the book, Gupta notes that large-firm pro bono in India is increasingly tied to CSR, leading some large Indian law firms to perform "proxy pro bono" – the donation of funds to legal aid and legal rights organizations – in lieu of actual service.

In Chapter 16, Helena Whalen-Bridge and Robert Granfield report on Singapore, a common-law country where the historical development of pro bono has been shaped once again by the evolution of legal aid policy. Although the authors acknowledge the influence of the US model on the discursive rise of "pro bono," they argue that pro bono's actual development in Singapore owes little to direct foreign intervention. Foreign firm participation in areas such as criminal and family law is negligible in the country (due to a high degree of market protectionism), and global NGOs and intermediaries play a limited role in fostering pro bono practice. Instead, the chapter portrays how changing approaches to criminal and civil legal aid have influenced the rise of pro bono. A major impetus was the 1995 amendment to the national Legal Aid and Advice Act, which removed the never-implemented provisions on noncapital criminal representation from the ambit of legal aid, channeling noncapital cases into the pro bono system – organized primarily through the volunteer-run Criminal Legal Aid Scheme (CLAS). Although the government recently announced it would provide support for indigent defendants in noncapital cases – launching an "enhanced" version of CLAS – the legal aid system overall is structured around a public–private division of labor. In the criminal domain, the bulk of noncapital cases are undertaken by CLAS volunteer lawyers, while capital cases continue to be handled by the state-run system. On the civil side, indigent persons who meet the eligibility requirements of the Legal Aid Bureau receive assistance from legal aid staff, while those who do not (but still cannot afford to pay) seek advice from legal clinics, primarily the Law Society–run Community Legal Clinics, before turning to Law Society Pro Bono Services. For many reasons (including concerns about branding), the attitude of firms toward pro bono has become more positive, and a growing number of firms have agreed to take on CLAS cases and staff legal clinics, while a smaller number either require their lawyers to do pro bono or adopt low bono schemes such as fixed fees. In this way, pro bono culture in Singapore continues to deepen.

In Chapter 17, Jin Dong and Qian Cheng examine pro bono in China, a country in which law practice has been transformed by the advent of the state's "rule by law" program in the 1990s. Professional growth has uplifted pro bono work, while also challenging its meaning. At one level, Chinese pro bono appears to follow global scripts: large law firms advertise their pro bono work on websites and produce reports; law schools have adopted a US-based clinical legal education model that promotes service; and foreign intermediaries and NGOs, like PILnet, have provided training and recognition. However, local politics have dramatically shaped Chinese pro bono, which has been officially promoted as a way to shore up the inadequate state-run legal aid system while allowing the Chinese Communist Party to define and control the terms of professional service. Toward this end, the government-controlled All Chinese Lawyer Association has required that local bars encourage "public interest" service, while producing reports on the "social responsibility" of Chinese lawyers. As the authors show, these efforts have stimulated the revival of "private public interest lawyers," who operate through two modes of practice: "safe" and "challenger." The safe mode focuses on state-run legal assistance, training, civic engagement, and community service activities, all of which are constrained by the power of the Chinese state and designed to generate a good image for the professionals involved. The challenger mode focuses on cases relating to important social issues and defies state power by asserting human rights. The challenger mode is thus more in tune with political liberalism and attempts to promote the rule of law. While China's structure may make it an outlier, its experience provides important evidence that pro bono's global development is not bound to produce inevitable convergence of practices and meanings. Rather, domestic political authority leads to unique hybrid forms and adapts the meaning of pro bono to local ends.

NOTES

1. DEBORAH L. RHODE, PRO BONO IN PRINCIPLE AND IN PRACTICE (2005).
2. Scott L. Cummings, *The Politics of Pro Bono*, 52 UCLA L. REV. 1 (2004); *see also* PRIVATE LAWYERS AND THE PUBLIC INTEREST: THE EVOLVING ROLE OF PRO BONO IN THE LEGAL PROFESSION (Robert Granfield & Lynn Mather eds., 2009).
3. *See, e.g.*, YVES DEZALAY & BRYANT GARTH, ASIAN LEGAL REVIVALS: LAWYERS IN THE SHADOW OF EMPIRE (2010).
4. STUART A. SCHEINGOLD & AUSTIN SARAT, SOMETHING TO BELIEVE IN: POLITICS, PROFESSIONALISM, AND CAUSE LAWYERING (2004).
5. Mauro Cappelletti & Bryant G. Garth, *Access to Justice: The Newest Wave in the Worldwide Movement to Make Rights Effective*, 27 BUFFALO L. REV. 181 (1978).
6. *See* Robert Granfield & Lynn Mather, *Pro Bono, the Public Good, and the Legal Profession: An Introduction*, *in* PRIVATE LAWYERS AND THE PUBLIC INTEREST, *supra* note 2, at 1.
7. Cummings, *supra* note 2; Rebecca L. Sandefur, *Lawyers' Pro Bono Service and American-Style Civil Legal Assistance*, 41 LAW & SOC'Y REV. 79 (2007).
8. LATHAM & WATKINS, A SURVEY OF PRO BONO PRACTICES AND OPPORTUNITIES IN 84 JURISDICTIONS (prepared for the Pro Bono Institute, 2016).
9. This project owes a debt to and builds upon important dialogues in other spaces. It grew out of conversations with Robert Granfield, whose volume (with Lynn Mather) on US pro bono is a critical model and whose work on Canada and Singapore was the original impetus for a comparative project. Conversations continued to flourish through the Global Pro Bono Conference held at Harvard Law School on April 18, 2014, supported by the Harvard Law School Center on the Legal Profession. The Center also supported the Globalization, Lawyers, and Emerging Economies (GLEE) Project, spearheaded by David Wilkins and David Trubek, who convened scholars from India, China, and Brazil

to explore the changing role of the corporate legal sector in those countries and who made pro bono one of the central aspects to be examined comparatively. The editors and some of the authors in this volume have been part of these conversations and enormously benefited from them.

10. Robert L. Nelson & David M. Trubek, *Arenas of Professionalism: The Professional Ideologies of Lawyers in Collective and Workplace Contexts*, *in* LAWYERS' IDEALS/LAWYERS' PRACTICES: TRANSFORMATIONS IN THE AMERICAN LEGAL PROFESSION 1 (Robert L. Nelson & David M. Trubek eds., 1992).
11. CARROLL SERON, THE BUSINESS OF PRACTICING LAW: THE WORK LIVES OF SOLO AND SMALL-FIRM ATTORNEYS (1996).
12. In the United States, government lawyers report far fewer hours on average than private practice lawyers. In contrast, legal aid and public interest lawyers report extremely high levels of pro bono, although we suspect that this is seamlessly connected to their regular work. *See* RONIT DINOVITZER ET AL., AFTER THE JD III: THIRD RESULTS FROM A NATIONAL STUDY OF LEGAL CAREERS 39 (2017).
13. Transnational pro bono includes legal work by a domestic lawyer on behalf of an individual, organization, or governmental entity located outside of the lawyer's home jurisdiction on the full range of pro bono issues (such as access to justice, human rights, and economic development). It also includes representation by a lawyer of a domestic client in an international forum, like a regional human rights body. *See* Sara Andrews & Lisa Dewey, *Pro Bono Goes Global*, STAN. SOC. INNOVATION REV. (2016); Maya Steinitz, *Internationalized Pro Bono and a New Global Role for Lawyers in the 21st Century: Lessons from Nation-Building in Southern Sudan*, 12 YALE HUM. RTS. & DEV. L.J. (2009); *see also* Darhiana Mateo, *Pro Bono Goes Global: A Look at Lawyers Without Borders*, BUS. L. TODAY, Jan.-Feb. 2006, at 35.
14. But see, for example, public interest litigation in the European Union, as well as evidence of cross-border work in this book from India and Nigeria.
15. Fabio de Sa e Silva, *Doing Well and Doing Good in an Emerging Economy: The Social Construction of Pro Bono among Corporate Lawyers and Law Firms in São Paulo*, *in* THE BRAZILIAN LEGAL PROFESSION IN THE AGE OF GLOBALIZATION: THE RISE OF THE CORPORATE LEGAL SECTOR AND ITS IMPACT ON LAWYERS AND SOCIETY 210 (Luciana G. Cunha, Daniela M. Gabbay, José G. Ghirardi, David M. Trubek & David B. Wilkins eds., 2017).
16. *See* Cummings, *supra* note 2. On institutionalization, see generally Paul J. DiMaggio & Walter W. Powell, *Introduction*, *in* THE NEW INSTITUTIONALISM IN ORGANIZATIONAL ANALYSIS 1 (Walter W. Powell & Paul J. DiMaggio eds., 1991).
17. YVES DEZALAY & BRYANT G. GARTH, THE INTERNATIONALIZATION OF PALACE WARS: LAWYERS, ECONOMISTS, AND THE CONTEST TO TRANSFORM LATIN AMERICAN STATES (2002).

18. *See* Annette Olesen & Ole Hammerslev, Chapter 11 in this volume.
19. THE BRAZILIAN LEGAL PROFESSION IN THE AGE OF GLOBALIZATION, *supra* note 15; THE INDIAN LEGAL PROFESSION IN THE AGE OF GLOBALIZATION: THE RISE OF THE CORPORATE LEGAL SECTOR AND ITS IMPACT ON LAWYERS AND SOCIETY (David B. Wilkins, Vikramaditya S. Khanna & David M. Trubek eds., 2017).
20. Luciana Gross Cunha et al., *Globalization, Lawyers, and Emerging Economies: The Case of Brazil, in* THE BRAZILIAN LEGAL PROFESSION IN THE AGE OF GLOBALIZATION, *supra* note 15, at 1.
21. The influence of neoliberalism can be seen even in countries without a significant welfare state tradition, like Nigeria, where US agents played a significant role in transplanting features of US law and legal practice that resonated with neoliberal aims and helped build the foundation for contemporary pro bono development. *See* Jayanth K. Krishnan, *Academic SAILERS: The Ford Foundation and the Efforts to Shape Legal Education in Africa, 1957–1977*, 52 AM. J. LEGAL HIST. 261 (2012).
22. Deborah L. Rhode, *Pro Bono in Principle and in Practice*, 53 J. LEGAL EDUC. 413, 436–37 (2003).
23. Sandefur, *supra* note 7.
24. Scott L. Cummings & Deborah L. Rhode, *Managing Pro Bono: Doing Well by Doing Better*, 78 FORDHAM L. REV. 2357 (2010).
25. Yves Dezalay & Bryant G. Garth, *Corporate Law Firms, NGOs, and Issues of Legitimacy for a Global Legal Order*, 60 FORDHAM L. REV. 2309 (2012).
26. Nancy Fraser, *From Progressive Neoliberalism to Trump – and Beyond*, 1 AMERICAN AFFAIRS (2017), https://americanaffairsjournal.org/2017/11/progressive-neoliberalism-trump-beyond/ (last visited July 29, 2020). Fraser conceptualizes progressive neoliberalism as combining a finance-centered political economy and a progressive politics of recognition. For debate about the meaning of progressive neoliberalism, see Johanna Brenner & Nancy Fraser, *What Is Progressive Neoliberalism?: A Debate*, 64 DISSENT 130 (2017).
27. For a critical history of the trickle-down concept and its use in development theory and practice, see H. W. Arndt, *The "Trickle-Down" Myth*, 32 ECON. DEV. & CULTURAL CHANGE 1 (1983).
28. Rebecca L. Sandefur, *Lawyers' Pro Bono Service and Market-Reliant Legal Aid, in* PRIVATE LAWYERS AND THE PUBLIC INTEREST, *supra* note 2, at 95.
29. Scott L. Cummings & Ingrid V. Eagly, *After Public Interest Law*, 100 NW. U. L. REV. 1251 (2006).
30. For a survey of the benefits of privatization, see DAVID OSBORNE & TED GAEBLER, REINVENTING GOVERNMENT: HOW THE ENTREPRENEURIAL SPIRIT IS TRANSFORMING THE PUBLIC SECTOR (1992). For critical assessments of privatization, see Bryan Evans, Ted Richmond & John Shields, *Structuring Neoliberal Governance: The Nonprofit Sector, Emerging New Modes of Control and*

the Marketisation of Service Delivery, 24 POL'Y & SOC'Y 73 (2005); and William Walters, *Some Critical Notes on Governance*, 73 STUD. IN POL. ECON. 27 (2004).

31. *See* Scott L. Cummings, *The Pursuit of Legal Rights – and Beyond*, 59 UCLA L. REV. 506 (2012).
32. The notable exception to the association of pro bono and democratic governance is China, which, very tellingly nonetheless, developed its institutions of "rule by law," including its pro bono industry, as a national response to progressive neoliberalism. *See* Jin Dong & Qian Cheng, Chapter 17 in this volume.
33. *See generally* DEZALAY & GARTH, *supra* note 17; THE NEW LAW AND ECONOMIC DEVELOPMENT: A CRITICAL APPRAISAL (David M. Trubek & Alvaro Santos eds., 2006).
34. *Who We Are & Pro Bono Promotion*, CYRUS R. VANCE CENTER FOR INTERNATIONAL JUSTICE, www.vancecenter.org (last visited Apr. 16, 2020).
35. *Id.*
36. Steven A. Boutcher, *Private Law Firms in the Public Interest: The Organizational and Institutional Determinants of Pro Bono Participation, 1994–2005*, 42 LAW & SOC. INQUIRY 543 (2017).
37. For a discussion of how lawyers emulate corporate client giving, see Richard L. Abel, *The Paradoxes of Pro Bono*, 78 FORDHAM L. REV. 2443, 2446 (2010).
38. Ronen Shamir, *Socially Responsible Private Regulation: World-Culture or World-Capitalism?*, 45 LAW & SOC'Y REV. 313 (2011); *see also* Ronen Shamir, *Between Self-Regulation and the Alien Tort Claims Act: On the Contested Concept of Corporate Social Responsibility*, 38 LAW & SOC'Y REV. 635 (2004).
39. *See* John W. Meyer & Brian Rowan, *Institutionalized Organizations: Formal Structure as Myth and Ceremony*, 83 AM. J. SOC. 340 (1977).
40. Although many clearinghouses follow a similar global template, not all are legal transplants. For example, the South African Society for Labour Law has established a Pro Bono Project that coordinates pro bono services from specialist legal practitioners for low-income clients in labor courts in Johannesburg, Durban, Cape Town, and Port Elizabeth.
41. Atinuke Adediran, *Solving the Pro Bono Mismatch*, 91 U. COLO. L. REV. 1035 (2020).
42. AM. BAR ASS'N, SUPPORTING JUSTICE: A REPORT ON THE PRO BONO WORK OF AMERICA'S LAWYERS 7 (2018).
43. *Id.* at 7, 33. The *American Lawyer* reported that, in 2016, US-based lawyers in *AmLaw* 200 firms averaged nearly 57 hours of pro bono per year. AM. LAW., PRO BONO RANKINGS (2017).
44. AM. BAR ASS'N, *supra* note 42, at 29.
45. *Id.* at 7–9 (noting that nearly one-third of lawyers reported providing pro bono service to "an ethnic minority," and one-quarter to a single parent).
46. *Id.* at 14.

47. *See* SCHEINGOLD & SARAT, *supra* note 4.
48. *See, e.g.*, ALAN WATSON, LEGAL TRANSPLANTS: AN APPROACH TO COMPARATIVE LAW (1974).
49. ANTHONY T. KRONMAN, THE LOST LAWYER: FAILING IDEALS OF THE LEGAL PROFESSION (1993).
50. RICHARD L. ABEL, AMERICAN LAWYERS (1989).
51. *See, e.g.*, LAW AND THE NEW DEVELOPMENTAL STATE: THE BRAZILIAN EXPERIENCE IN LATIN AMERICAN CONTEXT (David M. Trubek et al. eds., 2013).
52. *See* Edwin Rekosh & Lamin Khadar, Chapter 6 in this volume.
53. Scott L. Cummings & Louise G. Trubek, *Globalizing Public Interest Law*, 13 UCLA J. INT'L L. & FOR. AFF. 1 (2008).

PART ONE

THE AMERICAS

CHAPTER TWO

RATIONALIZING PRO BONO: CORPORATE SOCIAL RESPONSIBILITY AND THE REINVENTION OF LEGAL PROFESSIONALISM IN ELITE AMERICAN LAW FIRMS

John Bliss and Steven A. Boutcher

INTRODUCTION

The term "pro bono publico" has a long-standing tradition within the American legal profession, although its definition and organizing principles have dramatically changed over time. In this chapter, we review the historical development of the contemporary US pro bono regime and then discuss the recent emergence among elite American law firms of corporate social responsibility (CSR) as a rationale for pro bono practice. In contrast to the legal professionalism rationale for pro bono, wherein lawyers owe a distinct professional obligation to provide meaningful access to the legal system, the CSR rationale locates pro bono under the umbrella of broader commitments to public service, including diversity, philanthropy, environmental sustainability, and global corporate citizenship.

We draw on interviews with pro bono coordinators and content analysis of pro bono and social responsibility statements from leading law firms to examine how CSR interacts with other pro bono rationales to generate overlapping, contested, and sometimes conflicting understandings of pro bono practice and legal professionalism. We posit sources of the CSR movement, primarily rooted in firms' efforts to market themselves to corporate clients. Yet, CSR is more than mere marketing rhetoric for these firms, but rather appears to substantially influence how firms structure, implement, and understand their pro bono contributions. The chapter concludes by discussing implications for the future of US legal professionalism and the provision of pro bono legal services. By shifting attention away from pro bono as a matter of lawyers' distinctive duties and capacities, the CSR framework alters the traditional legitimating narratives of the profession and, we suggest, may ultimately jeopardize the *AmLaw* sector's robust commitment to pro bono participation.

PRO BONO IN HISTORICAL CONTEXT

Providing legal access to poor individuals has been a long and challenging process across the history of the American legal profession. The tradition of providing access to counsel in criminal cases has its origins in the English system, where defendants were allowed legal representation at the court's discretion.[1] The American colonies, skeptical of the centralized power of the state, provided the right to counsel in the Sixth Amendment to the Constitution. However, this right was not interpreted to mean counsel for everyone who could not afford representation.[2] The interpretation was broadened in *Gideon v. Wainwright*, which mandated that criminal defendants be offered legal representation, regardless of any ability to pay.[3] At the time that *Gideon* was decided in 1963, two-thirds of the states already had provisions to provide counsel in felony cases.[4]

Although *Gideon* established a constitutional guarantee to counsel in criminal matters, this guarantee has never been extended to civil matters. Instead, the provision of civil legal aid has been left to individual lawyers. Early attempts to organize representation for civil disputes emerged with the creation of legal aid societies during the late nineteenth century. The first such society was formed in New York City in 1876 to assist German immigrants. These societies diffused across major metropolitan cities, operating as charities and funded primarily through private resources. In 1919, Reginald Heber Smith published *Justice and the Poor*, a scathing assessment of the inherent inequalities between poor and rich in gaining access to the legal system.[5] Smith's book prompted the organized bar to take a more facilitative role in expanding access to representation.[6] The legal aid movement grew from forty societies when *Justice and the Poor* was published to seventy societies by 1946.[7] Funding for this early legal aid movement came primarily from charitable sources, and its reach was extremely limited. In 1963, for example, it was estimated that only four hundred legal aid lawyers were available to assist 50 million eligible clients.[8]

Legal aid organizations were not the only actors working to provide civil legal access; the organized American bar has long turned to individual lawyers to contribute voluntary pro bono representation services. The origins of pro bono have been traced to earlier legal traditions, including Roman and English common-law systems. Pro bono found expression within the American legal profession as early as 1908, when pro bono was inscribed in the Canons of Professional Ethics. Canon 4 stated that "a lawyer assigned as counsel for an indigent prisoner ought not to ask to be excused for any nontrivial reason," and Canon 12 stated that "the reasonable requests for assistance of brother lawyers, and of their widows and orphans without ample means, should receive special and kindly consideration."[9] Although these early Canons recognized the role that lawyers have in addressing unmet legal needs of the poor, it was expressed purely as a charitable act on the part of the individual lawyer and not as a broad component of professional responsibility.[10]

Pro Bono, Civil Rights, and Professional Responsibility

Pro bono found renewed expression amid the popular social movements of the 1960s and 1970s, including the civil rights, women's rights, environmental, antiwar, and antipoverty movements. These movements energized law students to work in the public interest and were perceived as threatening to law firm recruitment. Indeed, increasing activism and the maturing public interest law field were drawing top students away from jobs at large firms.[11] For example, one firm that was contemplating whether to adopt a public interest program wrote in a 1969 memo: "It has become increasingly evident that there is a tendency among younger lawyers, particularly those with *highest academic qualification*, to seek out public service-oriented careers as an alternative to practice in the larger metropolitan law firm" (emphasis in original).[12] In addition, increasing diversity in the legal profession led more lawyers and students to demand increased opportunities to work in the public interest.[13]

Within the context of expanding social activism in broader American society, the ABA looked to modernize the ethical rules of lawyers and developed the 1969 Model Rules of Professional Responsibility. Although the new ethical considerations reinforced the emerging interest in public service as a basic responsibility of the lawyer, it did not define that responsibility. Ethical Consideration 2–25 stated:

> Historically, the need for legal services of those unable to pay reasonable fees has been met in part by lawyers who donated their services or accepted court appointments on behalf of such individuals. The *basic responsibility* for providing legal services for those unable to pay ultimately rests upon the individual lawyer, and personal involvement in the problems of the disadvantaged can be one of the most rewarding experiences in the life of the lawyer. Every lawyer, regardless of professional prominence or professional workload, should find time to participate in serving the disadvantaged (emphasis added).[14]

As the ABA began to frame pro bono service to the poor as a "basic responsibility" of the lawyer, some law firms began to organize their pro bono practices. The extent of this reorganization is not entirely clear, but in one study Joel Handler and his colleagues identified twenty-four formalized programs in large firms in 1973.[15] Many of these firms incorporated elements of organized pro bono programs that have widely diffused today, including pro bono partners, committees, policies, and in some cases public service departments within the firm.[16] While some firms were initiating an early wave of strong pro bono commitment, the majority of lawyers in private firms remained largely indifferent toward pro bono service.[17]

The Watergate scandal in the early 1970s highlighted the necessity of revisiting the ethical duties of lawyers. A politically motivated burglary and ensuing cover-up led to an impeachment process against President Richard Nixon and the indictment of top aides and officials in his administration. Since Nixon and several of the leading figures in the scandal were lawyers, Watergate brought about a widespread "demolition" of public confidence in the legal system and lawyers in particular.[18] In response, the ABA created the Special Commission on Professional Standards to review the ethical codes and make recommendations for change.[19] The ensuing Kutak Commission proposed dramatic changes to the definition of a lawyer's public responsibilities.

Pro bono service was a salient issue for the Kutak Commission. The Commission proposed that a mandatory, quantitative requirement for pro bono service be included in lawyers' ethical codes.[20] According to Maute, "the very first, 'truly tentative' pro bono draft rule proposed forty hours per year of mandatory service, or its financial dollar equivalent."[21] The proposed requirement stirred a substantial backlash among lawyers, especially among solo and small-firm lawyers who felt that this would burden them more than the large firms that could afford to opt out of the time requirement.[22] After numerous rounds of debates and revisions, the ABA House of Delegates finally adopted the new pro bono rule in 1983 without a specified time commitment and without a mandatory requirement. Model Rule 6.1 thus stated:

> A lawyer should render public interest legal service. A lawyer may discharge this responsibility by providing professional services at no fee or a reduced fee to persons of limited means or to public service or charitable groups or organizations, by service in activities for improving the law, the legal system or the legal profession, and by financial support for organizations that provide legal services to persons of limited means.[23]

The Model Rule was revised a decade later specifying a quantitative aspiration of 50 hours. The revised Model Rule 6.1 now states:

> Every lawyer has a professional responsibility to provide legal services to those unable to pay. A lawyer should aspire to render at least (50) hours of pro bono publico legal services per year. In fulfilling this responsibility, the lawyer should:
>
> (a) provide a substantial majority of the (50) hours of legal services without fee or expectation of fee to:
> (1) persons of limited means or
> (2) charitable, religious, civic, community, governmental and educational organizations in matters which are designed primarily to address the needs of persons of limited means; and
>
> (b) provide any additional services through:
> (1) delivery of legal services at no fee or substantially reduced fee to individuals, groups or organizations seeking to secure or protect civil rights, civil liberties or public rights, or charitable, religious, civic, community, governmental and educational organizations in matters in furtherance of their organizational purposes, where the payment of standard legal fees would significantly deplete the organization's economic resources or would be otherwise inappropriate;
> (2) delivery of legal services at a substantially reduced fee to persons of limited means; or
> (3) participation in activities for improving the law, the legal system or the legal profession
>
> In addition, a lawyer should voluntarily contribute financial support to organizations that provide legal services to persons of limited means.

The revised rule not only quantified the lawyer's pro bono obligation, but it also expanded the types of legitimate clients served under the profession's definition of pro bono.[24] No longer was pro bono solely focused on the poor, but it expanded to include a variety of different causes, including civil rights, civil liberties, the environment, immigrant, LGBT, and other "public rights."[25]

Pro Bono Participation across the Profession

Despite professional efforts to facilitate increased pro bono participation, the lack of a mandatory requirement has meant that large numbers of lawyers end up doing little or no pro bono at all without any consequences. In a 2011 survey of American lawyers conducted by the ABA Standing Committee on Pro Bono and Public Service, only about a third of lawyers actually provided enough pro bono legal services to meet the aspirational fifty-hour goal outlined in the Model Rules. In addition, a significant proportion, one-fifth of American lawyers, provided no pro bono legal services to individuals of limited means.[26] In another recent survey of a cohort of midcareer lawyers (identified as twelve years out of law school), 55 percent engaged in some pro bono work, up from 45 percent when that same cohort was surveyed five years earlier, suggesting that lawyers may be more likely to engage in pro bono work as their careers mature within the profession.[27]

When comparing levels of participation across the profession, it is clear that not all lawyers approach the practice with similar orientations toward pro bono. Attorneys working in private practice tend to report more pro bono hours relative to those working in the public sector. However, even in the private sector, pro bono participation appears to increase with the size of the firm.[28] For instance, according to the first wave of the *After the JD* study, solo lawyers reported working close to 48 hours compared to 52 hours for lawyers working in the largest offices of 251 or more attorneys. By contrast, attorneys working in the public sector reported lower participation rates on average; government lawyers averaged 45.7 hours, while public interest lawyers averaged 44.6 hours.[29]

The difference in participation rates between solo and small-firm attorneys on the one hand, and larger firms on the other, may have to do with the mix of organizational, institutional, and practical realities facing lawyers across the profession. For instance, Cummings and Sandefur categorize pro bono orientations along two distinct institutional poles.[30] One end includes the idiosyncratic behavior of individual attorneys picking up pro bono in an ad hoc manner. These individuals may take on pro bono for a variety of individual reasons, including a sense of commitment or duty, or shifting an initial fee-generating case to a pro bono case due to a client's inability to pay. On the other end, pro bono is more organized and structured within the firm similar to any other practice area. In these firms, pro bono is streamlined and the practice of recruiting and training lawyers is centralized, often under the direction of a pro bono manager who also is responsible for matching lawyers to clients.[31]

INSTITUTIONALIZED PRO BONO IN LARGE LAW FIRMS

In the remaining sections of this chapter, we focus on the pro bono practices of large law firms. Large firms have increasingly institutionalized their pro bono practices over the last few decades. During the 1960s and 1970s, the emergence of the public interest field, competition with the legal services movement, and increased social movement activism drew elite law school graduates away from large firms in search of jobs where they could pursue social change.[32] In response to this competition for talent, some large firms began to formalize pro bono programs in order to recruit these students.[33] However, as the height of social activism began to recede in the late 1970s and 1980s, there was less pressure to use pro bono as a mechanism to recruit students, and commitment to pro bono waned.[34]

It wasn't until the turn of the twenty-first century that a new wave of formal pro bono departments took off.[35] However, the new pro bono wave was markedly different from its predecessor of the 1960s. Today pro bono departments can be found in many of the top firms across the country, centralizing the administration of a firm's pro bono practice.[36] These programs, often staffed by a pro bono manager, implement and structure the firm's pro bono practices as well as provide rotating opportunities that connect associates with a network of nonprofit organizations seeking assistance.[37] Although the institutionalization of pro bono within the private bar provides much-needed legal assistance to the poor, it also provides beneficial outcomes for the firm. Pro bono entrepreneurs, bar leaders, and firm managers are quick to tout the "business case" for pro bono. Increased commitment to pro bono, they argue, leads to successful retention of good associates, provides learning opportunities where associates can diversify their legal training, and provides good publicity for the firm.[38]

Pro Bono Participation

The institutionalization of pro bono across large law firms affects how firms organize their pro bono programs, which has an impact on levels of law firm participation. Surveys of pro bono tend to focus only on individual lawyers and not on law firms. However, since 1998, the *American Lawyer* has been surveying the largest 200 firms about their pro bono participation, including information on the firm's total pro bono hours, the average participation rates per lawyer, and the percent of the firm's lawyers engaging in pro bono work. Between 1998 and 2015, this field of firms gradually increased their overall number of hours from a little over 2 million hours in 1998 to a high of almost 6 million in 2009, representing close to a 175 percent increase in pro bono hours over this time period. However, in subsequent years, pro bono participation decreased to about 4.6 million hours in 2015.[39]

Although these firms have gradually increased their overall participation, not all firms are equally likely to devote as much time to pro bono as their peers. Indeed, large law firms appear segregated based on their ranking.[40] When you compare the top 100 firms to the next 100 firms, it becomes clear that much of the growth in pro bono has been driven by the higher-ranked firms expanding their pro bono participation and not by a uniform shift in pro bono among all large firms.[41] This suggests that although many of the largest law firms have institutionalized their pro bono practices, there remains wide variation in how integrated those practices have become within the firm.

Finally, not all lawyers within firms are equally likely to do pro bono. In this regard, despite pro bono practices being organized, individual attorney orientations may still play an important role in determining who contributes more time toward pro bono. In 1998, about 30 percent of *AmLaw* 200 attorneys reported doing more than 20 hours of pro bono. By 2015, this increased to 45 percent reporting over 20 hours of pro bono on average.[42]

Governance

The institutionalization of pro bono has not only resulted in increasing rates of participation across large firms but also affected how pro bono is organized. Large firms have increasingly formalized their pro bono programs by establishing written pro bono policies, outlining the firm's practical commitment to pro bono, providing billable hour credit to attorneys as an incentive to volunteer for pro bono cases, and even hiring managers to coordinate the firm's pro bono practice. Indeed, in many firms across the field, pro bono has become a formalized practice site, integrated as one of the firm's primary practice areas.

Despite the trend toward formalization, there remains variation in how firms structure their programs. Some elements of pro bono governance are widespread. For example, in an earlier study by the second author,[43] most of the firms surveyed mentioned that they have a formal pro bono policy, possibly indicating that the adoption of a written policy is one of the easiest ways to signal a commitment to pro bono. Adopting a policy requires little cost and effort to implement into existing firm practices. These written policies provide the rationales and parameters of a firm's commitment to individual lawyers within the firm, highlighting how cases are to be undertaken, distributed, and accounted for in terms of attorney time. Other governance features are also common, including a formal committee to review pro bono practices and clients, and providing some form of billable hour credit to incentivize attorneys to take on pro bono cases.

Many firms also have designated an individual (or a team in some cases) to manage the firm's pro bono practice.[44] Some coordinators are responsible for administering the pro bono program in addition to their billable practice, while other firms staff the coordinator as a full-time manager, completely organizing all areas of the firm's pro bono program. There remains variation in whether the pro bono manager position is full-time or part-time. In their survey of pro bono coordinators, Cummings and Rhode found that there has been a dramatic growth in the pro bono coordinator position over time.[45] There were a total of ninety-one pro bono positions in 2008 across seventy-eight firms, demonstrating a remarkable expansion from a decade earlier when only eighteen positions existed in 1998, and only six in 1993. These positions have a direct effect on pro bono participation due, in large part, to the ability to effectively recruit, train, and supervise young lawyers.[46]

Pro Bono Clients

ABA Model Rule 6.1 prioritizes legal services for "persons of limited means." However, a second category of pro bono includes legal services directed more broadly to the public interest, including civil rights and civil liberties groups, the environment, women's rights, and other issues. Existing scholarship shows wide variation in the types of issues that firms assist. For instance, Boutcher found that firms are more likely to assist organizations focused on civil rights and civil liberties, children, and women's rights, and less likely to assist organizations focused on the environment, labor, and animal rights.[47]

There are several reasons why firms may channel their pro bono services toward some organizations and issues over others. Pro bono clients are largely selected based on relationships, which is often the case for both solo and small-firm lawyers as well as large-firm lawyers.[48] Firm partners or associates may serve on a board of an organization, providing a conduit between the two. Firm attorneys may provide pro bono based on their individual interests and tastes. Finally, firms may select issues that avoid damaging relationships with corporate clients, both current and potential. While cases that pose a direct ethical conflict would necessitate avoidance, it is likely that most cases would not pose an ethical conflict as outlined in the Model Rules. Nonetheless, firms may take a broad reading of their perceived conflicts, barring themselves from supporting particular issues.[49] For instance, perceived positional conflicts may shape the likelihood that a firm is willing to take on a labor or environmental issue, even in cases where the Model Rules would not suggest a conflict.[50]

Motivations and Rationales for Pro Bono

Individual lawyers are motivated to do pro bono for a variety of reasons, including personal values and commitments to social justice, the desire to acquire legal skills and training, and as an important mechanism for developing social networks and future clients.[51] Indeed, pro bono has become an important tool for developing individual social capital, especially among elite attorneys.[52] Within the context of the large firm in particular, individual motivations interact with and are shaped by the organizational and economic context of the firm, which can facilitate or inhibit individual participation.

Large firms exist within a competitive field of firms, each concerned about their reputation and status, and their ability to attract top law students and land important corporate clients. Pro bono has emerged as one important way to signal a firm's status to external actors. In hiring, pro bono may allow firms to more effectively recruit and retain junior associates. Student applicants often ask firms about their pro bono programs during interviews. Appearing to lack strong pro bono commitments could turn off some recruits.[53] Large firms are also regularly ranked on their pro bono participation similar to other firm metrics like revenues, profits, and diversity and inclusion. Rankings like the *American Lawyer*'s A-List and pro bono rankings have significantly affected how firms orient their pro bono practices.[54] Finally, clients are also increasingly asking firms about their pro bono numbers (along with diversity numbers) when deciding where to award their business. Although these motivations appear centered on a firm's bottom line, this is not to suggest that some firms are not motivated for more altruistic reasons. Indeed, some firms may have deeply engrained pro bono cultures that have carried over from founding partners or emerged during particular historic moments.[55]

CORPORATE SOCIAL RESPONSIBILITY AND PRO BONO

In this section, we present qualitative findings on the emergence of a CSR rationale for pro bono practice in elite American law firms. In contrast to the profession's official framing of pro bono as a function of lawyers' distinctive duties to the legal system, the emerging CSR rationale frames pro bono in much broader terms within commitments to responsible business and good corporate citizenship.

Among the corporate clients of *AmLaw* firms, CSR has a long and contested history. The roots of the modern CSR discourse are generally traced to the 1940s and 1950s, as corporations enjoyed the benefits of wartime and postwar prosperity.[56] Commentators at the time emphasized corporations' social responsibilities emanating from their economic privileges. Accordingly, CSR came to be defined as a matter of voluntary contributions that go beyond legal requirements and that do not necessarily provide economic benefit to the corporation. These early theorists emphasized that CSR commitments should define a corporation's stakeholders far more broadly than merely its shareholders. In part as a reaction to Friedman's intervention in the 1970s, which sought to narrow CSR to simply the maximizing of shareholder profit,[57] subsequent theories have tended to incorporate profitability within definitions of CSR.[58]

Recently, CSR has emerged as an institutionalized norm among multinational corporations that seek to ensure at least an appearance of social responsibility commitments throughout their supply chains.[59] The diffusion of CSR is bolstered by the pervasive understanding that CSR provides reputational value with implications for profitability.[60] The stakes of CSR are extraordinarily high amid an era of "corporate global rule," where CSR functions as not only a "buffer" by which corporations protect themselves from criticism, but more broadly as a "constitutive force in shaping the relationship between business and society in contemporary global capitalism."[61] Our inquiry in this chapter examines the legal link in corporate supply chains, as corporations' expectations for CSR engagement interact with law firms' existing professional commitments to pro bono practice.

Interviews were conducted with twenty-three pro bono coordinators in elite American law firms in five major markets: New York, Washington DC, Chicago, Los Angeles, and San Francisco. Interviews were also conducted with members of professional bar associations who help to coordinate pro bono practice. The analysis of firms' pro bono and CSR statements began with a thorough review of the primary websites of the *AmLaw* 100 law firms. The pro bono, social responsibility, and "about us" pages of these sites were coded for direct mentions of CSR, CSR rhetoric, and other rationales for doing pro bono. For firms that offered reports, brochures, and videos about their CSR and pro bono programs, we analyzed these materials in the same manner as the web pages. When discussing firms' online materials, we refer to these firms by name. All references to the research interviews exclude the names of respondents' employing law firms.

In our review of these online materials, 20 of the *AmLaw* 100 firms directly mentioned CSR. Another 39 of the 100 firms emphasized nonlegal public service contributions and drew substantially on the language of CSR, using terms such as corporate citizenship, community service, sustainability, diversity, philanthropy, leadership, education, nonprofit support, community partnerships, active board membership, and giving back to local communities and civic and charitable organizations. The remaining forty-one firms did not include separate pages for nonlegal forms of volunteering and, instead, described pro bono primarily in the traditional terms of professional responsibility. Even some of the firms that emphasized traditional pro bono practice included nonlegal charity rhetoric. We begin this section by presenting evidence of these firms' nonlegal public contributions. We then discuss how firms conceived of pro bono in relation to CSR programs.[62]

Nonlegal Public Contributions

In the web pages and reports examined in this study, nonlegal public contributions ranged from local charity to larger social-change efforts, where the firms provide "financial support and leadership" in a wide range of "public policy issues" (Wachtell). Some of these activities had a legal component but did not fall under traditional pro bono representation, such as law-oriented educational programs for high school students. These educational programs were sometimes only tenuously connected to law, as seen in McDermott's description of its Kids First Initiative: "Whether by pursuing education opportunities, family stability, health care or juvenile justice reforms, or by mentoring students in impoverished communities, our lawyers and staff are committed to *ensuring a better future for all children*" (emphasis added). This better future is not framed necessarily as a matter of law reform or providing access to justice.

In some cases, the nonlegal nature of volunteer work was explicitly acknowledged, as Kramer Levin described their lawyers' participation in "a wide range of *non-legal* community service activities" (emphasis added). These nonlegal contributions generally included a wide range of issues. For example, the "philanthropy" page of Kirkland & Ellis's CSR report was broken into sections for legal, community, green, youth, health care, culture and arts, education, and diversity. O'Melveny included a word-tree graphic on the cover of their "Social Responsibility" report, which read: "connection, scholarship, citizenship, volunteer, global, responsibility, support, contribution, give back, commitment 2 community, sustainability, empowerment, leadership, help, collaboration, ethics, change, values, outreach, society, education, charity, people."

This span of abstract social commitments was further reflected in the specific examples firms offered of their charitable and volunteer activities. Locke Lord described a "firm-wide philosophy of inclusion and action, helping raise scholarship money for minority and economically disadvantaged students, hosting holiday parties for lower income children, donating to local food banks and charitable organizations that aid individuals and families in need." Alston & Bird portrayed a particularly nonlegal scope in their social contributions, ranging from "knitting blankets for homeless children and building Habitat for Humanity houses to driving cancer patients to treatment and sending care packages to troops overseas."

This nonlegal service work was often highlighted within firms' "about us" pages, suggesting that these contributions are highly constitutive of law firm identity, at least in terms of publicly expressed identity. The importance of nonlegal charity and volunteering was emphasized at nearly every turn. For example, Hunton & Williams explained that "giving back to the communities in which we live and work" is not only encouraged but is financially rewarded by the firm, as associates can count twenty-five annual billable hours for "disaster relief volunteer time." Counting these volunteer activities as billable hours signals that these contributions are integrated into the firm's core operations.

Nonlegal contributions were also salient in firms' accounts of their international public service. Some of these projects were described with a legal dimension, focusing on human rights or rule of law. Yet, often firms focused more generally on poverty alleviation. See, for example, McDermott Will & Emory's description of "mobilizing broader efforts in response to global crises" in their social responsibility report titled "Protecting the Pursuit of Opportunity":

> Our work has a profound impact, not only at the most personal, individual level, but also at the global level affecting sweeping changes that help a great many people in different places and in different ways.

The nonlegal nature of this international service work was underscored in Mayer Brown's description of seeking to "serve some of the world's most vulnerable populations" by working in multiple continents to "build homes, assist food banks, visit elderly centers, raise funds, and arrange donations of food, furniture and other items for community organizations." Ropes & Gray summarized their "Social Responsibility Initiative" as a means to "ensure we fulfill our responsibilities to the global community with the greatest impact." This focus on global impact extends beyond the traditional notion of lawyers' functional contributions to the American legal system, where the lawyer role is conceived as a "public citizen having special responsibility for the quality of justice" (MRPC preamble [1]). Instead, as Kirkland & Ellis put it, the obligation owed is to "improve the lives and futures of our fellow global citizens." As Greenberg Traurig summarized, "Change has no borders. Neither does Greenberg Traurig's commitment to helping change the world for the better."

Environmental sustainability was consistently emphasized in the web pages and reports. For example, Sullivan & Cromwell prominently claimed that they were "the first major international law firm committed to neutralizing its emissions of greenhouse gases through the purchase and retirement of carbon credits and/or purchase of offsets." The firm conceded in this statement that law practice is not generally a great source of greenhouse gases, but that the firm is "enthusiastic that we will play a pro-active role in mitigating the environmental consequences of our operations." McDermott Will & Emory's "Social Responsibility Report" described a partnership with an organization that is helping to reduce the firm's carbon footprint. This partner organization "weighs containers of the Firm's recyclable materials, records the volume of each container and uses those numbers to track usage trends over time." In Kirkland's CSR statement, environmental efforts were elevated as a central commitment of the firm: "sustainability is a guiding principle of our Firm .... 'Going Green' is more than a catchphrase to us. It is core to responsible business." This nexus between doing good (via environmental practices) and "responsible business" suggests a conception of social responsibility that goes beyond lawyers' distinct public duties as members of a profession.

The emphasis on how public service in legal and nonlegal domains constitutes "good business" was prevalent in these online materials. Norton Rose's corporate responsibility brochure described efforts "to ensure that our behavior conforms at all times with our *business principles*: Quality, Unity and Integrity. Called GPS (Global Practice Standards) they help safeguard our business against a range of risks" (emphasis added). Pepper Hamilton explained that their sustainability efforts speak to the firm's "triple bottom line" as a responsible business:

> We recognize that "Sustainability" entails meeting the "Triple Bottom Line" of economic, social, and environmental responsibility. It is about fostering respect for people and other living things while at the same time wisely using and managing environmental and economic resources. It calls for a careful balancing that takes into account the interests of key stakeholders – partners, associates, employees, and especially our clients – the very parties whose support is critical to the success of Pepper Hamilton .... It is in the best interests of our law firm and society as a whole that Pepper Hamilton move along the path to sustainability.

For firms that emphasized a broad range of social responsibility commitments, pro bono as a central node of professionalism no longer stands out as a core value. Instead, many of these firms portrayed their public responsibilities in terms similar to their corporate clients. Ballard Spahr described their shared interest with clients in contributing to "inner-city" high schools, assisting "sick children and their families," and "being a good neighbor." These contributions were summarized as follows: "Like many of the clients we represent, we consider it a duty and an honor to answer the call to citizenship." Here the lawyer's public role is framed as that of a nonlawyer citizen (likened to clients). In particular, the central commitment is to "being a good corporate citizen" (Mayer Brown) and a "responsible citizen of the global business community" (McGuire Woods).

Pro Bono within Integrated CSR Programs

As these firms increasingly emphasize nonlegal service work, they do not necessarily appear to be shifting away from providing pro bono legal representation. Indeed, as discussed above, elite firms have made abundant pro bono contributions over the past two decades. Furthermore, our interviews and website analysis show a continued emphasis on pro bono legal representation. Yet, we also show that the rationale for pro bono is shifting among many elite firms such that pro bono is included under the umbrella of integrated CSR programs. Accordingly, in the online materials examined, pro bono representation was generally listed as one among several public contributions. For a representative example, the page on Holland & Knight's website titled "Community Commitment" was divided into links for "pro bono legal service," "community service," and "charitable giving." The interviews with pro bono coordinators corroborated this structure, as one respondent explained a firm's social responsibility program: "It's not just pro bono, it's also community service, and it's also charitable giving. So those pieces of it are my responsibility to think about on a global scale as well as on a local scale" (DS 35).

Both the online materials and the interview respondents frequently acknowledged a distinction between pro bono and nonlegal contributions, suggesting that pro bono fits into firms' integrated CSR programs. For example, Sheppard Mullin summarized their public service commitments as follows: "We encourage our attorneys to contribute to their communities *in many ways*, including through the provision of pro bono legal services" (emphasis added).

In some of the social responsibility statements, pro bono was clearly prioritized as the most important of a firm's CSR contributions. A brochure from Pillsbury read: "While pro bono legal counsel is obviously our most valuable public service, the people at Pillsbury serve in other ways as well through volunteer activities and charitable contributions." Pro bono is elevated here, but also framed within a larger commitment to public service. This point was elaborated in a statement from Reed Smith:

> For a law firm, pro bono is at *the heart of any Responsible Business program*. As lawyers, we do pro bono in order to make legal advice and the legal system more accessible to all. Beyond pro bono, lawyers and staff members volunteer their time on a wide variety of community service initiatives in the areas of Pro Bono, Community, Diversity & Inclusion, Environment, Supply Chain and Ethics & Risk Management. [emphasis added]

This statement blends the legal profession's obligation to providing access to justice with a commitment "beyond pro bono" to providing nonlegal contributions as a matter of "Responsible Business." A pro bono coordinator interviewed for this study explained the breakdown of a firm's commitment to these different domains as follows: "Probably say 50% pro bono, 30% charitable giving and 20% community service-type activities" (DS 36). Other firms seemed to place pro bono on equal footing with nonlegal public contributions, as seen in Kilpatrick Townsend's "Corporate Citizenship" page:

> Our lawyers and staff are deeply committed to making positive, lasting change in our communities. We understand that the strategic combination of the various aspects of our IMPACT initiative – community leadership, diversity & inclusion, pro bono, sustainability, and volunteerism – can create a powerful ripple effect in the communities in which we work and live. Functioning together, these elements enable us to more fully engage in the community and produce positive change one life, one project, one commitment at a time.

Kilpatrick Townsend explained their formal integration of pro bono with nonlegal community service commitments not merely as a matter of convenience, but rather as a strategically integrated approach to achieving civic impact and good "corporate citizenship." Their "Impact Highlight Brochure" makes this point explicit:

> While the elements of IMPACT can be considered independently, their *collective impact* reflects our broader commitment to corporate citizenship. Thanks to the integrated nature of our approach, we can multiply the value we deliver, enhance the influence we achieve, and strengthen the effect we can have on our world. (emphasis added)

These holistic and integrated public service efforts were often explicitly labeled as CSR. Pillsbury, cited above as an example of a firm that prioritized pro bono representation, emphasized the "synergy" in an integrated legal/nonlegal CSR program: "With the help of a CSR director, we united our programs – diversity, pro bono and community outreach, and sustainability – under one umbrella to achieve greater synergy and expand our efforts."

Within these synergistic efforts, descriptions of CSR programs included the public service commitments of nonlawyer employees as well as firms' attorneys. For Fenwick & West, this integration was described as a matter of "employee engagement":

> The program integrates key CSR components such as the firm's nationally-recognized and award-winning pro bono work, charitable contributions and volunteerism, with the goal of increasing and focusing employee engagement, and ultimately, making a larger impact within the communities where Fenwick employees live and work.

Pro bono legal representation is subsumed here under the larger, integrated frame of giving back. Katten described this integration (under the initiative titled "Katten Cares") as a means to "promote *a culture of service* by creating opportunities to give back." [emphasis added] The terms of this "culture of service" within CSR programs appear to overlap with the public obligations inherent in lawyers' "culture of legal professionalism," except that the integrated CSR approach deemphasizes lawyers' duties and commitments to the legal system.

Rationalizing Pro Bono as CSR

In their online materials, 39 of the *AmLaw* 100 firms drew on CSR rhetoric when describing their pro bono activities but did not directly use the term "corporate social responsibility" (or variants such as "social responsibility" or "corporate responsibility"). These firms framed pro bono in terms that extend beyond legal duties and law reform. Instead, they rationalized pro bono more broadly as a charitable contribution in response to the financial privileges enjoyed by the firm. One pro bono coordinator respondent explained: "We want to shift the blessings and the bounty that we have in service of those who don't" (DS 36). In particular, giving back was often framed as a commitment to local communities, as another pro bono coordinator explained: "We've been here for ten years. We've really succeeded in this community. We need to give back" (DS 12). Similar rhetoric was prevalent in the online pro bono statements, as evident from Cozen O'Connor: "[Our] growth and success over the past four decades is matched by giving back to those communities where we have placed our roots and built our firm." Pro bono is framed here as a responsibility to community, as described by Hunton & Williams:

> We embrace responsibility for ensuring the firm's actions have a positive impact on the communities where we live and work and on the world we call home. We recruit lawyers and professional staff members who reflect these beliefs and encourage them to take action through community and pro bono service. And, we accept the ongoing challenge of working to improve the world in which we live.

Rather than the specific "professional responsibility" (as it is phrased in Model Rule 6.1) to provide pro bono service, these accounts frame pro bono work as a responsibility to "improve the world" and give back to community. This contrast was explicit in Venable LLP's statement that the firm's pro bono service was motivated by community responsibility rather than professional responsibility:

> Pro bono is *not an ethical obligation* but a way to improve communities:
>
> The firm expects its attorneys to devote their time and diverse talents, on a pro bono basis, to *improving their communities* and the lives of others. [emphasis added]

In their accounts of pro bono, these firms often identified themselves as "responsible neighbors" (McGuire Woods) and "citizens of the communities" where they have offices (Norton Rose Fulbright). Dorsey & Whitney summarized: "We don't just work here. We live here. At Dorsey, community is a core value."

In contrast to the community citizenship framing, some firms strongly emphasized traditional professional responsibility accounts for pro bono rooted in a firm's distinctive culture or in lawyers' general commitment to enhancing the legal system. See, for example, the pro bono statements from Skadden and Latham:

> The firm's long-standing commitment to pro bono work has been based largely on the belief that such work is part of the basic role of lawyers as members of our profession and as officers of the court. (Skadden)
>
> Latham recognizes its duty to help ensure that the doors of justice are open to all, regardless of income, and that the practice of law includes the *unique ability and responsibility* to advocate for equal justice and provide needed representation to persons of limited means. (emphasis added)

These accounts emphasized the distinctly legal nature of lawyers' public responsibilities, echoing the language of the Model Rules. Yet, even accounts focusing on legal professionalism often hinted at broader commitments. For example, White & Case's pro bono statement emphasized the firm's ability to "wield the force of the law," not only to improve the legal order, but to "change *social* order" (emphasis added) and realize their "tremendous power for good." This statement leaves ambiguous whether the "power for good" draws exclusively on legal tools. Other firms emphasized legal professionalism, yet interpreted that professional mandate as a matter of charity and giving back:

> We do believe that as lawyers in particular we have an obligation to give back to our community. We are a privileged organization. We have an amazing skill set that we can offer to people who do not have access to it. (DS 35)

This "amazing skill set" presumably refers to the ability to provide high-quality representation to those lacking access to justice. Yet, this responsibility to use legal skills for charitable purposes is attributed not only to duties of professionalism but also to duties arising from the firm's privileged status. Thus, one respondent described lawyers' dual responsibility as "servants of the law and as part of the community in which we live" (DS 13). Even in accounts emphasizing lawyers' uniquely legal tools, firms consistently emphasized broader commitments to community:

> There are a limited number of people who are fortunate enough to be trained as lawyers and it's our ethical obligation to make sure that not just the wealthy have access to legal assistance but also low-income people and non-profit organizations that can benefit from our services. So I think we're well aware that we have an ethical obligation .... We also feel like, as far as the community goes, we want our lawyers to be involved in the community where they work .... (DS 17)

Even the most traditional accounts of pro bono rooted in legal professionalism were often juxtaposed with firms' nonlegal contributions that satisfy a broader social responsibility mandate, as evident in the example from Troutman Sanders:

> Troutman Sanders' lawyers and staff are dedicated to strengthening the communities where we live and work .... As *officers of the court*, our duties extend beyond the mere representation of our clients. We have a professional and ethical obligation to ensure that justice is accessible

> and fair to all .... Our lawyers and staff also provide leadership and direct service to a variety of local nonprofits, addressing the needs of each of our communities. We generously donate our time by serving on nonprofit boards, organizing fundraising walks and runs, and collecting coats for the homeless and back to school supplies for neighborhood children. We are proud of all our professionals who devote their time and talent to serving our fellow citizens. [emphasis added]

As expressed by Troutman Sanders, lawyers' social responsibilities emanate from their roles as "officers of the court." By echoing the language of the preamble and comments to the Model Rules, this account seems to reflect the legal professionalism rationale for pro bono. Yet, this excerpt also suggests that these emanating responsibilities extend to nonlegal charitable work. Implicit in this framing is a claim that the legal professionalism logic is compatible or even synergistic with broader commitments to community. This integrated public service framework produces contestation over the definition of pro bono by blurring the distinction between legal forms of service and other nonlegal charitable contributions. The resulting ambiguity was evident, for example, in one respondent's characterization of the firm's assistance to an African development project, which the respondent framed as pro bono service although it did not involve legal representation: "It's an extraordinary situation, but I think it clearly ought to be, and we do treat it as pro bono" (DS 14). Given the variety of approaches to pro bono and CSR cited above, we can assume that some *AmLaw* firms might not agree with this respondent's categorization of the development project as pro bono; yet, many firms would publicly celebrate such a project under the CSR umbrella. The transition to a CSR rationale for *AmLaw* firms' pro bono and public service commitments remains contested and incomplete.

Sources of the Emerging CSR Movement

In large corporations, CSR has become institutionalized as a business norm and a perceived precondition of profitability.[63] CSR activities are encouraged by highly publicized social responsibility rankings of major corporations, voluntary external audits of CSR reports, and competition among peer corporations for positive public relations. The United States lacks mandatory reporting requirements, although such requirements are found in many other countries (including all EU Member States pursuant to a 2014 EU directive). Even in countries with reporting requirements, these regulations generally do not stipulate the exact terms and metrics of CSR reporting. Thus, companies are allowed wide discretion to choose the content of their CSR statements, brochures, online materials, and other reports, which may or may not mention pro bono and CSR activities of outside counsel.

Roughly concurrent with the rise of CSR in the corporate sector, corporations have gained greater influence over the inner workings of law firms. This influence is supported by increasing competition among law firms for corporate clients, the dramatic growth of internal legal departments, and the reduction in informational asymmetry between firms and clients.[64] Clients often explicitly request that law firms engage in CSR practice through codes of conduct guidelines issued to law firms. These codes do not generally mention pro bono practice by name, but they include an expectation that firms promote the public interest and the "dignity and integrity of the system of justice" (from Walmart, quoted in Whelan and Ziv 2013).[65] Furthermore, corporations via their inside counsel are cognizant of *AmLaw* rankings and the norms and hierarchies of the legal profession – pro bono is important in these hierarchies, as it is weighted heavily in determining the *AmLaw* A-List and is more generally considered a de facto requirement for membership in the elite *AmLaw* tier.[66]

The pro bono coordinators interviewed in this study explained that clients often raise questions about pro bono work in their inquiries about firms' CSR programs. As one respondent put it, clients "demand pro bono" because of clients' own CSR commitments: "Clients want to see the firms that they are hiring work with their communities to make their communities better because they're doing it and they expect those they hire to do it also" (DS 13).

These client inquiries can extend beyond pro bono representation to include other commitments to social responsibility. In describing a survey from a client, one respondent explained:

> Clients are asking what we're doing on the pro bono front. And they also ask what we're doing on the diversity front. What are you doing on all these other social initiatives? To the extent we have to respond to assorted surveys along the way, that's also been a factor. (DS 19)

This account suggests that client expectations regarding CSR can be influential on law firm behavior. Diversity in particular was a salient theme in respondents' discussions of how clients shape law firms' approaches to social responsibility.

> I think that for many firms they already had an ongoing commitment to pro bono work. And then I think clients started being more community service oriented and started paying attention to diversity and things like that. (DS 38)

In-house lawyers in particular may be an important mechanism for transmitting this influence from clients to law firms. One respondent explained:

> It's when the social conscience, particularly of the law departments – you've got more activist general counsels who said to their management, "We really ought to do more with our suppliers. You're doing it with other kinds of suppliers. We ought to do it with our law firms the same way you're doing it with the people who are selling us paper or doing our janitorial work in the building. We ought to do the same thing with firms. They're just high-priced janitors anyway."(DS33)

Furthermore, one respondent explained that a firm's pro bono participation can be cited by general counsel when explaining their decision to choose a particular firm, even when that decision was made on different grounds:

> [As a general counsel] you're going to have to report who you chose. Well, if you can say, "I chose this firm because I worked there," or "I chose it because I had a case against them and they're good." Are they hugely better? Are there rates incredibly lower? No. But they're a top ten, they're on the A-List, they're on the Am Law A-List. It just gives credibility to a decision that in some ways is completely subjective. (DS 38)

Some respondents acknowledged that law firms' pro bono contributions are not generally the highest priority for corporate clients in deciding whether to award work to a firm, given the high financial stakes of their legal issues. Nevertheless, respondents consistently suggested that pro bono is a significant point of emphasis in law firm marketing:

> In-house counsel will often ask, "What's your firm's commitment to pro bono like? What kinds of cases do you work on?" I'm receiving requests from our marketing people regularly to put a part of a package together for a pitch to a new client .... Pro bono can be a particularly media-friendly component of these pitches. (DS 11)

Marketing is particularly important in the *AmLaw* sector where clients may choose among firms on a narrow basis. Thus, even if pro bono is not a client's highest priority, a robust and "media-friendly" pro bono program could tip the scales in a competitive proposal process. CSR commitments can help a firm distinguish itself from competitors. One respondent explained: "marketing is . . . huge because you need to come up with what's special about you and you need to brand yourself . . . whether it's a particular practice, whether it is corporate social responsibility" (DS 35).

Furthermore, the *AmLaw* sector presents clients with a range of high-quality firms that are generally structured in a highly similar manner, as explained by a pro bono coordinator:

> Everybody [in the top one hundred firms] has a good litigation department. So how do you decide which of these great litigation departments you're going to go to? You look at other factors. Which firms that do the best work also reflect what we are as a company? Whether it be diversity, whether it be pro bono, whether it be the approach of the firm to the practice of law. Are they scorched earth? Are they compromisers? How do they deal with things? So the clients definitely are outcome driven. They want the best representation on any given case. But they have choices because there are so many good law firms and lawyers out there, they can look at other factors to separate out the different firms that do great work. (DS 13)

This marketing imperative was tied explicitly to the CSR trend in *AmLaw* firms by another pro bono coordinator as follows:

> You're seeing this concept of corporate social responsibility kind of develop over time . . . . I think it is tied to the elements of competitiveness in our industry . . . . I think that the legal industry used to be differentiated either because you were a boutique firm and you had a particular legal specialty . . . you also got clients by relationships. And that's changed. That whole environment has become more increasingly competitive. Most law firms, particularly large law firms, we all offer the same services . . . we're all really good lawyers; we're all recruiting from top law schools; we're getting really solid lawyers in the door and we've also expanded what our practices look like. We're not boutiques anymore. There are boutiques that exist, but large law firms are essentially full-service firms. We can do everything possible. So I think it [creates] a need to differentiate. How do you attract clients? How do you get market share? . . . . So I think you're seeing means of differentiating ourselves. (DS 35)

As CSR becomes increasingly institutionalized as a norm in the *AmLaw* field, it may come to function less as a means of differentiation but rather as an expectation associated with elite-firm status. As one respondent put it, "You want to be known as a firm that is giving back to the community .... You don't want to be on the weak side of any clients' lists of considerations of what they're looking for. You want to be in the glowing lights of any list that's of any importance" (DS 13). Another respondent summarized: "A leading law firm by today's definition is one that handles high-visibility pro bono cases ... you look for the biggest, splashiest, loudest client relationship, and then you tell everybody in the world you're doing it" (DS 33).

The importance these firms place on marketing their public service contributions may be further evidenced by the ubiquity of pro bono and CSR pages in the online materials analyzed in this study. The websites of 98 of the *AmLaw* 100 included a pro bono or CSR page. Within the organization of these sites, the pro bono or CSR pages tended to be framed as a centrally important element of a firm's self-presentation. In total, fifty-six (56 percent) of these public service pages were found under a label that denoted law firm identity, such as "about us," "our firm," "our culture," or "who we are." Sixteen percent of these firms included their pro bono and CSR statements under labels that emphasized the firm's values: "principles and values," "culture and core values," "community," "public service," and "citizenship." Another 26 percent included a direct link from the home page to a pro bono or CSR page.

Furthermore, the pro bono and CSR reports that we analyzed tended to reinforce the notion that social responsibility is essential to law firm identity. For example, Alston & Bird explained: "serving those in need occupies a central position in our culture, our business plan and our hearts." Broadly advertising a central commitment to public service appears to be a widely established norm in the field.

In some of the online materials and interviews, we found explicit references to how clients influence law firms' public service activities. For example, Sullivan & Cromwell claimed that their sustainability program was "inspired by our clients who have voluntarily agreed to reduce their carbon footprint in advance of any legal requirement to do so." As one respondent explained, the spread of CSR from corporate clients to *AmLaw* firms is reminiscent of the recent spread of diversity initiatives:

> I think you saw that with the diversity wave ... those corporations that really had a big pull in the market decided diversity was their issue and

> then that made diversity be law firms' issue .... I think the same thing is happening here where there's been a phenomenon of corporate social responsibility .... And I think it started in the corporations to be honest and they were giving back maybe more on the charitable giving sector than they were on the ground doing community service work. But that slowly developed into that as well and so now you're seeing pressure from clients that they're looking at that as whether or not they're going to choose you as your law firm. (DS 35)

This link between the public service work of clients and *AmLaw* firms is further reinforced by the notion that clients seek to work alongside firms in volunteer and charitable projects. A respondent explained:

> There are a lot of companies who are deeply invested in bettering the communities in which they are doing business. The better the community, the stronger the community, the better their business will be. It's a pretty simple calculus, and a lot of companies want to see their lawyers out there in their communities *alongside them* making the communities better and stronger, which creates a better environment for them business-wise and socially and culturally. To a lot of companies it's important that the people that they're doing business with have their same sort of *structural belief in community*. (DS 18a) [emphasis added]

These abstract notions of working in tandem under a "structural belief in community" (note the emphasis on contributing to the community rather than a specific concern about the legal system) were further instantiated in accounts of collaborative public service projects with clients. For example, Baker McKenzie's forty-page report on CSR described the firm's desire to "collaborate with clients who share the same commitment to social justice." They used the example of a collaboration with Hewlett-Packard to "join forces to assist disadvantaged groups and non-profit organizations in their local communities" and to "prove that corporate social responsibility is at its strongest when leaders in their respective fields come together."

A Paul Hastings CSR report described such collaborations across a range of public service projects as "smart business":

> It's smart business to partner with clients on the sustainability issues important to them, as well as the environment at large. And it's smart business to build diverse and inclusive teams rich in talent, experiences, and creativity.

As the following interview excerpt describes, collaborating with clients can lend credence to a firm's claim to genuine public service commitment:

> It's part of the "Do you have a diverse team representing us? Do you have women on the team? Do you have African Americans on the team?" I think the same motivation's going on – "Tell us what pro bono work you're doing. We'd like to see you doing more of it. In fact, can we joint venture with you? Can some of the people in our law department joint venture with you guys at the law firm?" The law firms love that idea. "Yeah, man, we'd love to joint venture with your people. Send them over." (DS 33)

Another respondent explained that collaborative public service projects can promote strong relationships with clients, which furthers the business case (the client retention case) for law firms to engage in charitable and volunteer work:

> There are some clients that ask about [public service] very specifically. There are some requests for proposals that ask for [public service] very specifically. There are some clients with whom we jointly do pro bono programs, or projects. Instead of playing golf with a client, you go to a clinic with a client. It really creates quite a bond. (DS 18a)

In addition to the influence from clients, the CSR trend in *AmLaw* firms may draw on international influences. As *AmLaw* firms expand their practice globally, they come into contact with public service practices and rationales from other national jurisdictions. In discussing their international poverty and human rights projects, these firms often characterized themselves as "global corporate citizens" who "help shape the future in a way that provides economic, ecological and social benefits for all" (Norton Rose Fulbright). These accounts emphasize the global integration of law firms' CSR commitments. A representative example is McGuire Woods: "Each of McGuire Woods' more than 1,000 lawyers in 23 offices around the world, as well as all staff members, takes our social responsibility very seriously."

However, these public service programs are not entirely integrated. These firms' foreign offices generally do not emphasize traditional pro bono client representation, but instead make primarily nonlegal charitable contributions. Abroad, these firms are often restricted from providing pro bono representation by domestic regulation or due to a lack of local bar membership. Furthermore, these foreign offices may be influenced by their neighboring domestic firms, who in most jurisdictions do not carry the same American expectations regarding pro bono legal representation.

It is beyond the scope of our data to make empirical claims about these foreign offices and their impact on firms' overall approaches to public service. Further research is needed to explore the extent of this global influence. It is likely the case that influence between American and foreign offices flows in both directions. For example, one respondent described a firm's efforts to push their foreign offices to engage in pro bono representation in addition to nonlegal charity work:

> My job is to go to the Bangkok office and say, "Here's the kind of program we have .... You don't know that much about [pro bono], but you already support some preschools and you donate money and you help them. That's good. That's good work. In the United States we would call that community service rather than pro bono, but we encourage that. And we do community service work here also." So you try to move them. (DS 34)

This respondent acknowledges the importance of both community service work and a traditional American notion of pro bono legal representation. Assessing how this international exchange may influence *AmLaw* firms in the United States and abroad warrants further research.

DISCUSSION

These findings shed light on contestation over the meaning of pro bono. Where nonlegal contributions are included under the pro bono umbrella or vice versa (where pro bono legal representation is included under CSR), the traditional notion of lawyers' distinct professional responsibilities vis-à-vis the legal system is stretched and perhaps diminished. Yet, the *AmLaw* sector's expansion of nonlegal charitable and voluntary contributions does not necessarily detract from traditional forms of pro bono practice. Indeed, *AmLaw* firms have recently shown a robust commitment to providing pro bono legal representation to those unable to pay.[67] Our contribution in this chapter is to show that these firms' accounts of *why* they do pro bono appear to have substantially shifted toward a more "corporate logic" (rooted in CSR) in contrast to the traditional "professional logic."[68] In addition to and sometimes in place of obligations to the legal system, these firms emphasized broad commitments to their communities and to responsible business practice. We posit that the emergence of this CSR trend owes largely to firms' efforts to market themselves to clients.

Our findings are limited to what we can gather from *AmLaw* firms' online materials and the qualitative responses of pro bono coordinators. These data sources may tend to highlight the images that firms seek to market to the outside world (the online materials likely target clients in particular). In contrast, intrafirm and intraprofessional discourse, where the audience is other lawyers, may tend to emphasize the traditional professionalism account for pro bono, rooted in a strong US legal culture where pro bono is a constitutive element of professional identity. It is beyond the scope of our data to say whether these firms, as they negotiate multiple constituencies, attach greater significance to the CSR account or the professionalism account. However, we can say, based on the interview and online data presented above, that the influence of the marketed imagery (where CSR is emphasized) does not appear to be limited to outward signals but also substantially affects how firms (and lawyers within firms) understand and structure their social responsibility activities.

As pro bono has become increasingly institutionalized over the past three decades, it has developed into a "system of values and practices . . . deeply ingrained as part of the culture of legal professionalism."[69] By framing the profession's public responsibilities in substantially nonlegal terms, the CSR rationale deemphasizes lawyers' roles in the legal system and the role of law as an important tool for doing good. As such, the ascendance of the CSR rationale in the *AmLaw* sector may threaten the strong nexus between legal professionalism and pro bono. Under the CSR view, lawyers are encouraged to align their public service work with the expectations of corporate clients. This view diverges from the bottom-up theory of civic engagement underlying the professionalism account of pro bono, wherein lawyers internalize commitments to the justice system, law reform, and the public good as a matter of professional identity and responsibility.

If elite corporate lawyers become less invested in the notion that lawyers owe a distinct duty to provide legal services to those unable to pay, this trend could jeopardize the stability of the current wave of pro bono participation in the *AmLaw* sector. The American legal system has long been characterized by a peculiar (even "bizarre" and "strange") reliance on volunteer legal services to provide representation to those unable to pay.[70] The *AmLaw* sector in particular has robustly answered this call in recent years. Yet, the rising emphasis on the CSR rationale for pro bono has the potential to shift these firms' attention away from legal representation as their primary form of public contribution. While any charitable work is potentially valuable, the public demand for lawyers' specifically legal skills is particularly critical. Indeed, the American system presents a "shameful irony," pairing distressing deficits in access to justice with one of the highest concentrations of lawyers in the world.[71]

It is possible the CSR trend will remain limited to the *AmLaw* sector, without transformative implications for the rest of the US bar. Yet, diffusion from the *AmLaw* sector to other law firms and other practice settings is plausible given the stature of *AmLaw* firms at the top of the profession's prestige hierarchy.

Concerns about the CSR trend in elite US firms should be contextualized against the backdrop of a profession that lacks strong accountability systems to channel lawyers and firms to work for the public good. Pro bono is framed in the Model Rules of Professional Conduct as a nonobligatory "professional responsibility" (Rule 6.1). The preamble to the Rules describes such aspirational and unenforceable rules as "constitutive and descriptive."

In addition to the organized bar, other regulatory regimes appear to simultaneously promote pro bono practice. The past three decades have seen the rise of professional organizations that monitor, report, and publicly celebrate the pro bono contributions of firms and individual lawyers.[72] Competition from other firms in the *AmLaw* field may further reinforce pro bono commitments, particularly in the elite firm sector where norms and practices tend to diffuse rapidly. Furthermore, the findings in this article emphasize the regulating influence of corporate clients who expect the firms they hire to engage in public service. These overlapping regulatory influences may combine in compatible ways that promote pro bono culture and practice. Yet, for elite American firms residing in an "interstitial space" between the legal profession and the business world, our findings suggest that the influence of corporate clients may be particularly powerful.[73] From a regulatory perspective, relying on client influence to reinforce pro bono participation seems a shaky foundation for a system of voluntary legal aid.

These concerns about sustaining commitments to pro bono participation raise further concerns about how the CSR framing alters the legitimating claims of the legal profession. The traditional justification for the profession's relative autonomy has relied on lawyers' public service contributions, where pro bono figures prominently. Accordingly, the profession is tasked with improving the functioning of the legal system and providing an independent check on the market and state. Commentators suggest that the profession has never fully realized this autonomous and self-regulating vision.[74] The CSR frame seems to further diminish lawyers' claims to these distinctive public contributions. Understanding legal practice primarily as responsible business threatens to collapse the market/profession distinction. This collapse speaks to the long-standing lament about the commercialization of legal practice, particularly in the elite law firm sector. A pro bono coordinator interviewed in this study explained:

> As all the firms grew and became more and more like businesses, the old values that were associated with the profession became more difficult to uphold ... firms have become more and more like corporations .... So one of the reasons that pro bono I think has grown along with [the firms] is so firms can say, "We still have a culture. We still maintain our professional concern." (DS 34)

This excerpt suggests an effort to maintain the legal professionalism ideal while also acknowledging that public service has become a marketing imperative for firms. This dual mandate was described by another respondent as follows:

> Doing pro bono work is a lawyer's highest calling, and I think this firm and many firms recognize that and respond to it because we can do things for disenfranchised and voiceless people that no other profession in the country can do .... But there are also business reasons .... So all of a sudden pro bono becomes an essential element in a firm's national reputation and national standing. So that also creates a huge incentive for firms to have a robust pro bono program. (DS 18a)

As reflected in this excerpt, the notion of doing pro bono as a means to comply with client expectations appears compatible with a sense that pro bono is motivated by professional calling. Yet, if the CSR trend diffuses further in the *AmLaw* sector and beyond to other segments of the bar, this trend could have the capacity to undermine the established bottom-up norms that support a system of voluntary pro bono contributions.

NOTES

1. DEBORAH L. RHODE, ACCESS TO JUSTICE 51 (2004).
2. *Id.*
3. It should be noted that in practice the *Gideon* precedent does not provide the full guarantee of legal representation it appears to promise. Most criminal defendants resolve cases through plea bargaining, while only a small percentage receive legal assistance. *See* GERALD ROSENBERG, THE HOLLOW HOPE: CAN COURTS BRING ABOUT SOCIAL CHANGE? (1991).
4. *See* RHODE, *supra* note 1.
5. REGINALD HEBER SMITH, JUSTICE AND THE POOR (1919).
6. Scott L. Cummings, *The Politics of Pro Bono*, 52 UCLA L. REV. 1 (2004); Robert Granfield & Lynn Mather, *Pro Bono, the Public Good, and the Legal Profession: An Introduction*, *in* PRIVATE LAWYERS AND THE PUBLIC INTEREST: THE EVOLVING ROLE OF PRO BONO IN THE LEGAL PROFESSION 1 (Robert Granfield & Lynn Mather eds., 2009).
7. JOEL F. HANDLER ET AL., LAWYERS AND THE PURSUIT OF LEGAL RIGHTS (1978).
8. DEBORAH L. RHODE, PRO BONO IN PRINCIPLE AND IN PRACTICE: PUBLIC SERVICE AND THE PROFESSIONS 61 (2005).
9. RHODE, *supra* note 1, at 65.
10. F. RAYMOND MARKS ET AL., THE LAWYER, THE PUBLIC, AND PROFESSIONAL RESPONSIBILITY (1972).
11. JEROLD S. AUERBACH, UNEQUAL JUSTICE: LAWYERS AND SOCIAL CHANGE IN MODERN AMERICA (1976); HANDLER ET AL., *supra* note 7; MARKS ET AL., *supra* note 10.
12. MARKS ET AL., *supra* note 10, at 206.
13. RHODE, *supra* note 1.
14. *Id.* at 65–66.
15. HANDLER ET AL., *supra* note 7, at 123.
16. MARKS ET AL., *supra* note 10, at 206.
17. RHODE, *supra* note 8.
18. AUERBACH, *supra* note 11.
19. Judith L. Maute, *Changing Conceptions of Lawyers' Pro Bono Responsibilities: From Chance Noblesse Oblige to Stated Expectations*, 77 TUL. L. REV. 91 (2002).
20. Cynthia Adcock, *Shaped by Educational, Professional, and Social Crises: The History of Law Student Pro Bono Service*, *in* PRIVATE LAWYERS AND THE PUBLIC INTEREST, *supra* note 6, at 25.
21. Maute, *supra* note 19, at 131.
22. Esther F. Lardent, *Mandatory Pro Bono in Civil Cases: The Wrong Answer to the Right Question*, 49 MD. L. REV. 78 (1990); *see also* MICHAEL J. POWELL, FROM PATRICIAN TO PROFESSIONAL ELITE: THE TRANSFORMATION OF THE NEW YORK CITY BAR ASSOCIATION (1988); RHODE, *supra* note 8.
23. Maute, *supra* note 19, at 134.

24. RHODE, *supra* note 8.
25. Steven A. Boutcher, *Lawyering for Social Change: Pro Bono Publico, Cause Lawyering, and the Social Movement Society*, 18 MOBILIZATION: AN INT'L Q. 179 (2013).
26. AM. BAR ASS'N, SUPPORTING JUSTICE: A REPORT ON THE PRO BONO WORK OF AMERICA'S LAWYERS (2018).
27. RONIT DINOVITZER ET AL., AFTER THE JD II: SECOND RESULTS OF A NATIONAL STUDY OF LEGAL CAREERS (2009); RONIT DINOVITZER ET AL., AFTER THE JD III: THIRD RESULTS OF A NATIONAL STUDY OF LEGAL CAREERS (2014).
28. RONIT DINOVITZER ET AL., AFTER THE JD: FIRST RESULTS OF A NATIONAL STUDY OF LEGAL CAREERS (2004).
29. *Id.*
30. Scott L. Cummings & Rebecca L. Sandefur, *Beyond the Numbers: What We Know – and Should Know – About American Pro Bono*, 7 HARV. L. & POL'Y REV. 83 (2013).
31. Steven A. Boutcher, *Private Law Firms in the Public Interest: The Organizational and Institutional Determinants of Pro Bono Participation, 1994–2005*, 42 LAW & SOC. INQUIRY 543 (2017); Scott L. Cummings & Deborah L. Rhode, *Managing Pro Bono: Doing Well by Doing Better*, 78 FORDHAM L. REV. 2357 (2009).
32. AUERBACH, *supra* note 11, at 278–79; POWELL, *supra* note 22, at 161–65; Cummings, *supra* note 6, at 13.
33. HANDLER ET AL., *supra* note 7, at 123.
34. *Id.*
35. Cummings, *supra* note 6.
36. *Id.*
37. Steven A. Boutcher, *From Policy to Practice: Assessing the Effect of Large Law Firm Pro Bono Structure on Pro Bono Commitment*, *in* STUD. IN LAW, POL. & SOC'Y 145 (Austin Sarat ed., 2010); Cummings & Rhode, *supra* note 31.
38. Ronit Dinovitzer & Bryant Garth, *Pro Bono as an Elite Strategy in Early Lawyer Careers*, *in* PRIVATE LAWYERS AND THE PUBLIC INTEREST, *supra* note 6, *at* 115; Cynthia Fuchs Epstein, *Stricture and Structure: The Social and Cultural Context of Pro Bono Work in Wall Street Firms*, 70 FORDHAM L. REV. 1689, 1693 (2001).
39. Steven A. Boutcher, *Growth of Large Law Firm Pro Bono Programs*, *in* BEYOND ELITE LAW: ACCESS TO CIVIL JUSTICE IN AMERICA 270 (Samuel Estreicher & Joy Radice eds., 2016).
40. Steven A. Boutcher, *The Institutionalization of Pro Bono in Large Law Firms: Trends and Variation Across the AmLaw 200*, *in* PRIVATE LAWYERS AND THE PUBLIC INTEREST, *supra* note 6, *at 135*.
41. *Id.*; Boutcher, *supra* note 31, at 556–57.
42. AM. BAR ASS'N, *supra* note 26.
43. Boutcher, *supra* note 37.
44. *Id.*; Cummings & Rhode, *supra* note 31.
45. Cummings & Rhode, *supra* note 31.

46. Boutcher, *supra* note 37.
47. Boutcher, *supra* note 25.
48. Philip R. Lochner Jr., *The No Fee and Low Fee Legal Practice of Private Attorneys*, 9 LAW & SOC'Y REV. 431 (1974).
49. Norman W. Spaulding, *The Prophet and the Bureaucrat: Positional Conflicts in Service Pro Bono Publico*, 50 STAN. L. REV. 1395 (1998).
50. Cummings & Rhode, *supra* note 31.
51. Lochner, *supra* note 48; *see also* Robert Granfield & Philip Veliz, *Good Lawyering and Lawyering for the Good: Lawyers' Reflections on Mandatory Pro Bono in Law School*, *in* PRIVATE LAWYERS AND THE PUBLIC INTEREST, *supra* note 6, *at* 53.
52. Dinovitzer & Garth, *supra* note 38.
53. Boutcher, *supra* note 37.
54. Boutcher, *supra* note 37; Boutcher, *supra* note 31; Cummings, *supra* note 6.
55. Fuchs Epstein, *supra* note 38.
56. MARK S. SCHWARTZ, CORPORATE SOCIAL RESPONSIBILITY (2017).
57. Milton Friedman, *The Social Responsibility of Business Is to Increase Its Profits*, N.Y. TIMES MAG. (1970).
58. Kenneth E. Aupperle et al., *An Empirical Examination of the Relationship Between Corporate Social Responsibility and Profitability*, 28 ACAD. OF MGMT J. 446 (1985).
59. Stephen Brammer et al., *Corporate Social Responsibility and Institutional Theory: New Perspectives on Private Governance*, 10 SOCIO-ECONOMIC REV. 10 (2012).
60. *Id.*
61. Ronen Shamir, *Corporate Social Responsibility: A Case of Hegemony and Counter-Hegemony*, *in* LAW AND GLOBALIZATION FROM BELOW: TOWARDS A COSMOPOLITAN LEGALITY 92, 95 (Boaventura de Sousa Santos & César A. Rodríguez-Garavito eds., 2005).
62. In this chapter, we do not discuss law firms' CSR consulting practices. Such practices appear to be on the rise, and the ABA has established a CSR committee focusing on consulting and compliance. These practices were not emphasized by the pro bono coordinators we interviewed, nor did they overlap with the pro bono and social responsibility materials we examined.
63. Shamir, *supra* note 61.
64. David B. Wilkins, *Team of Rivals – Toward a New Model of the Corporate Attorney-Client Relationship*, 78 FORDHAM L. REV. 2067 (2009).
65. Christopher J. Whelan & Neta Ziv, *Law Firm Ethics in the Shadow of Corporate Social Responsibility*, 26 GEO. J. LEGAL ETHICS 153 (2013).
66. Boutcher, *supra* note 40; Boutcher, *supra* note 31; Cummings, *supra* note 6.
67. Steven A. Boutcher, *Rethinking Culture: Organized Pro Bono and the External Sources of Law Firm Culture*, 8 U. ST. THOMAS L.J. 108 (2010).

68. Boutcher, *supra* note 31.
69. Cummings, *supra* note 6.
70. Richard L. Abel, *The Paradoxes of Pro Bono*, 78 FORDHAM L. REV. 2443 (2009).
71. Deborah L. Rhode, *Access to Justice: A Roadmap for Reform*, 41 FORDHAM URB. L.J. 1227 (2013).
72. Boutcher, *supra* note 67.
73. Boutcher, *supra* note 31.
74. RICHARD L. ABEL, AMERICAN LAWYERS (1989).

CHAPTER THREE

PRO BONO LEGAL WORK IN CANADA

Robert Granfield and Fiona Kay

INTRODUCTION

In this chapter, we examine the historical growth of pro bono legal services in Canada and contemporary patterns of pro bono engagement within the bar. We employ mixed methods, incorporating in-depth interviews with lawyers, legal educators, and leaders in the Canadian bar and a large-scale social survey of attorneys. We begin by tracing the historical development of government-funded legal aid in Canada – through the roles of local bar associations and government-led legislation – and the rise of pro bono service in response to declining resources for legal aid. Next, we outline structural factors connected to the diffusion of pro bono service, especially the spread of nongovernmental organizations (NGOs) in Canada, and we identify several distinguishing characteristics associated with pro bono culture in the country. Our discussion leads us to consider professional-based interests associated with the expansion of pro bono and residual areas of contestation between legal aid and private pro bono legal service providers in the quest to improve access to justice. Finally, we document the distribution of pro bono in Ontario – the province with the largest population of lawyers in Canada. We explore which organizational settings encourage pro bono work and which types of clients are recipients of pro bono service. Our analysis extends beyond a descriptive profile of pro bono work to advance an empirical assessment of the factors (i.e., motivations, organizational context, demographic and educational backgrounds) predicting the incidence of pro bono service and time dedicated to specific types of clients.

HISTORICAL STATE-SUPPORTED LEGAL AID AND THE RISE OF PRO BONO SERVICE

The emergence and institutionalization of pro bono within the Canadian context shares a similar history to other countries, especially the United States. As has been the case elsewhere, volunteer legal services preceded the development of formalized, state-supported legal aid initiatives in Canadian provinces like Ontario. Prior to the development of legal aid in Canada, solo practitioners and lawyers from Bay Street law firms in Toronto provided free legal services to indigent individuals and community-based organizations. Early provisions for legal aid in Ontario date back to the 1920s where legal services were provided on an ad hoc basis. During this time, presiding judges often waived court fees for the poor who were unable to afford these fees. As a result of increasing rates of poverty within Ontario during the 1930s, the Board of Control in Toronto requested that the local bar association provide a lawyer on a voluntary basis to staff an office in the city that would provide free legal aid for recipients of public assistance.[1] Rather than act on the recommendation to create a city office to provide legal assistance to the poor, the local bar association enacted a system of providing lists of lawyers who were willing to give free legal advice within their office to individuals unable to afford legal services.[2] Although the Law Society of Upper Canada expanded this program of voluntary lawyers in later years, it was becoming increasingly apparent that the legal needs of the poor could not adequately be met through the charitable efforts of lawyers.

Responding to the failure of the bar to address the legal needs of the poor, the Ontario government enacted the Law Society Amendment Act in 1951, creating the country's first formally structured legal aid program in partnership with the Law Society of Upper Canada.[3] Under this act, lawyers' services were free to those who met financial eligibility requirements, but the government compensated these lawyers for administrative costs and expenses.[4] In the 1960s, with increasing recognition that volunteerism by the bar was unable to meet the legal needs of the poor, legislation was expanded under the Legal Aid Act to develop a system of government funding for legal services. These services included the creation of certificates (tariffs paid to lawyers by the government), a duty counsel program, and an outline of eligibility requirements and the types of offenses to be covered by the plan.[5] Throughout the 1960s, several other provinces adopted similar programs, and in 1972 the federal government initiated a cost-sharing plan that provided provinces with limited support for legal aid in cases involving the criminal justice system. Throughout the next two decades, demand for services and associated costs for supporting legal aid increased.

Similar to the US decline in state support for legal services during the Reagan administration,[6] legal aid funding across Canada began to decline in the mid-1990s. This was in large part related to the rise of neoliberalism within Canada. When Progressive Conservatives under the leadership of Premier Mike Harris gained power in Ontario in 1995, they implemented reforms that were consistent with a neoliberal ideology. Known as the "common sense revolution," the Harris government (1995–2002) imposed massive spending cuts in health care, postsecondary education, affordable housing, environmental protection, as well as welfare initiatives including legal aid. In Ontario, the province with the largest per capita expenditures on legal aid, funding declined 10 percent in the period 1996–2006.[7] Diminished resources were dedicated to legal aid across Canada as Ottawa's funding for indigent criminal legal matters declined.

This declining state support for legal aid has led to a significant growth of volunteer lawyer services and pro bono activity. Initiated largely through the efforts of the Canadian Bar Association to respond to growing unmet legal needs in Canada due to limitations in legal aid, organized pro bono programs began to develop. Two of the first pro bono initiatives developed in the 1990s in Ontario. First, a collaboration between the United Way of Toronto, the Law Society of Upper Canada, and the Canadian Bar Association (CBA) led to the development of the Volunteer Lawyers Service in 1994 to provide free legal services to charitable and noncharitable organizations. This organization offered free legal advice and services in various areas of the law as well as conducted seminars on such topics as charitable incorporation and board of directors' liability. In establishing volunteer lawyer service centers throughout Canada, the CBA sought to assist nonprofit and charitable agencies that had sprung up to provide services to low-income individuals in the wake of declining federal support for social services. The second and perhaps even more significant initiative, the Pro Bono Students of Canada

(PBSC), was launched two years later at the University of Toronto. Considered Canada's first formalized pro bono organization, the PBSC initiative matched law students with public interest groups, NGOs, legal clinics, agencies, and lawyers who provided pro bono legal services. Having now expanded to twenty-one law schools in Canada, its mandate is to: (1) provide early, practical learning experience for law students; (2) provide high-quality legal services for PBSC's partners and their clients; and (3) promote the value of pro bono among the next generation of lawyers.[8]

Original funding for this initiative was provided by the University of Toronto and the Law Foundation of Ontario, but now has grown substantially to include several large law firms across the country as well as provincial bar associations, Legal Aid Ontario, and other private foundations.

Building on the growing attention to pro bono legal services, several legal academics, judges, and lawyers organized a pro bono summit held at the University of Toronto in 1998.[9] Despite the professional norm among Canadian lawyers to provide occasional pro bono – as expressed in the Canadian Bar Association's 1998 resolution that each member of the legal profession "strive to contribute 50 hours or 3% of billings per year on a pro bono basis" – there were no programs or mechanisms to assist willing lawyers to participate in pro bono activity.[10] The central recommendation that emerged from this summit was a proposal to create a center for the advancement of pro bono service. In 2001, Pro Bono Law Ontario (PBLO), Canada's first pro bono NGO dedicated to identifying and developing pro bono opportunities and linking private lawyers to those initiatives, was incorporated. One of the primary functions of this organization is to work with Ontario-based law firms to facilitate access to pro bono opportunities within the province. In one of PBLO's initial projects, LawHelp Ontario – a court-based legal advice center that provides a continuum of services – served nearly seven thousand clients with the support of over two hundred lawyers who were primarily employed in large law firms in Toronto and Ottawa.[11] Over the years, these pro bono–coordinating NGOs have expanded to several other provinces, including Alberta, Quebec, British Columbia, and Saskatchewan. Currently, there are a number of mostly large law firms that allow firm lawyers to count pro bono hours toward their billable hour requirement. Smaller firms, while often supportive of pro bono, are less likely to support counting pro bono toward billable hours.

STRUCTURAL FACTORS ASSOCIATED WITH THE DIFFUSION OF PRO BONO

Pro bono activity has become increasingly diffused throughout Canada over the past two decades. The landscape of pro bono in Canada occupies a broad base of lawyers across various settings, including solo practitioners, law firm attorneys, government lawyers, and business lawyers, and a diversity of practice areas including corporate law, litigation, and people-oriented law (e.g., family, landlord-tenant, employee benefits). However, unlike pro bono activity in the United States, Canadian lawyers contribute little pro bono activity in the area of criminal law, a point that will be discussed further below. The pro bono landscape in Canada can be best described as a "hybrid" of various other countries, most notably the United States, United Kingdom, and Australia. The "hybridization" of pro bono within Canada is largely due to the history of government support for public institutions such as education and health, as well as its close proximity to the United States, which has fostered a cross-fertilization of ideas and practices. Although Canada has prided itself on differentiating itself from the United States in many regards, the growing internationalization of law and law firms has led to pro bono practices that resemble the US context. Nonetheless, it would be a mistake to attribute the emergence and institutionalization of pro bono in Canada simply to the exportation of US practices across the border. One staff lawyer who worked at the Canadian Bar Association astutely commented that:

> We do always try to keep an eye on the American Bar Association and what they are doing. They have a bigger budget than we do and they have a bigger staff. Their agenda is somewhat different from the way we approach things, but we're always very interested in what they're doing. Do we specifically ask the question what are the Americans doing? Maybe not as much as you'd think. I think there may actually be a fear because there was a sense of an erosion of legal aid in the United States, and that's something we don't want to have happen here. So, it's an awareness mostly bred from concern as opposed to simple emulation. We wouldn't implement a pro bono policy without looking at other countries like the United States. So, we have a fifty-hour recommendation similar to the US model. In the development of our pro bono model, we looked around and adopted different aspects of different models. We would want to know what the American Bar Association is doing with regards to pro bono as well as in various jurisdictions in the UK or Australia. We try to have environmental scans on what's happening. I think there is a concern that is collectively shared that pro bono has to

> complement existing frameworks, including legal aid like in other places in the world.

So, while there are resemblances between the two countries, there are also important and notable differences.

Most of Canada's major population centers are located near the US–Canada border, and this proximity has led to the transmission of some pro bono concepts and practices northward. For instance, many lawyers in the larger Canadian law firms located in Ottawa, Montreal, Toronto, and Vancouver have had direct work experience with US law firms. In some cases, this has simply occurred as a result of cross-border transactions, but in other cases Canadian lawyers have worked for a period of time in US law firms, affording them firsthand insight into US-style pro bono practices and organizational structures. In these cases, Canadian lawyers incorporated these direct experiences into their Canadian law firms. These cross-border lawyers often brought back insights regarding pro bono in large firms, including such concepts as the business case model for pro bono, allowances for billable hours devoted to pro bono cases, and pro bono coordination.

Another source of infusion of US influence on the rise of Canadian pro bono similarly occurred with the relationship that Canadian lawyers, Canadian and Provincial Bar Association staff, and Canadian law faculty had with pro bono advocacy groups in the United States, including the Pro Bono Institute located at Georgetown University. Several Canadian lawyers and bar staff have participated in training workshops held by the Institute over the years. This organization has not only exposed Canadian lawyers and bar staff to US-style pro bono but has also afforded them access to a network of lawyers across the United States who were involved in building pro bono cultures within their own firms. One law firm attorney in Montreal described his experience attending a pro bono workshop in the United States:

> This was an amazing experience. We're not at the same stage as the United States, and the law firms that participated were the biggest law firms who could send five people for a few days to the Institute. I met a lot of interesting people. I met one guy who did a lot of pro bono cases in front of the Supreme Court. I learned a lot from that experience and how to adapt it to Canada.

This lawyer attended the Pro Bono Institute on behalf of the law firm at a time when the firm was beginning to expand its pro bono involvement. Participating in pro bono training opportunities allows lawyers to become ambassadors of pro bono in their firms and to foster a pro bono culture. Many of the leadership staff within the Canadian pro bono coordinating centers, such as PBLO, Pro Bono Law Quebec, and Pro Bono Law Alberta, have not only had direct experience with US pro bono practices in firms but also participated in workshops conducted by US pro bono practitioners and advocates.

However, this is not to suggest that US-style pro bono has been simply mapped onto the Canadian experience. There are several unique features distinguishing Canadian pro bono culture from that of the United States. First, while Canadian law firms, similar to US firms, have policies permitting pro bono and have lawyers seeking out individual pro bono opportunities, the emerging pro bono culture in many provinces in Canada has relied on separate community-based NGOs to coordinate pro bono opportunities for law firm lawyers. Many of these activities involve linking law firm attorneys to larger community projects as opposed to individuals in need. For instance, PBLO has been involved in a number of long-term activities and projects as well as shorter-term initiatives. Working with mostly law firm attorneys across Ontario, PBLO has coordinated pro bono service on a range of initiatives. These include: (1) litigation assistance at walk-in help centers; (2) medical legal partnerships that connect lawyers to health professionals and social workers at Toronto's Hospital for Sick Children to ensure that the legal needs of patients and their families are being met; and (3) an education law initiative that uses pro bono lawyers working with families to help them to better understand their legal rights and to negotiate solutions to conflicts with school administrators and officials. In addition to these initiatives, PBLO brokers relationships between interest groups with legal needs and pro bono lawyers. For instance, PBLO has partnered with the Gowlings Law Firm, with offices in Ottawa, Toronto, Hamilton, and other branch offices, to help coordinate a program to provide legal support to enable Aboriginal artists to generate and sustain their livelihoods.[12] PBLO also works with McCarthy Tétrault in a partnership with the Immigration and Review Board to provide unaccompanied minors arriving at Pearson International Airport in Toronto with pro bono lawyers to help these children complete forms, gather evidence related to their refugee status, and facilitate access to legal aid.[13] Lawyers working in coordination with PBLO provide services to individual clients as well as to charitable and nonprofit organizations. Funding to support PBLO and other pro bono coordinating centers comes from several sources, including provincial bar associations, law firms, and private foundations.

A second distinguishing feature of the pro bono culture that has emerged in Canada is the accommodation made to mostly solo and small-firm practitioners who represent legal aid clients. One lawyer employed in a large Toronto-based law firm who had attended several pro bono workshops in the United States noted this difference by commenting that "pro bono is different here because we have a more robust legal aid system than the US. It's not simply a matter of doing what the US has been doing." Legal aid and pro bono in Canada have historically coexisted with considerable tension. The formal legal aid scheme came into existence primarily as a result of traditional pro bono practices failing to meet growing demands. In turn, the failings of the legal aid scheme have been viewed as a catalyst for the recent rise of pro bono programs.[14] This recent shift has led to concerns that, although the pro bono strategy increases access to justice by serving otherwise unmet legal needs in the short term, it also alleviates political pressure on governments to maintain and/or increase legal aid funding, and hence pro bono arguably weakens the legal service delivery system in the long term.[15]

In addition, because many lawyers are compensated by state-supported legal aid and earn a portion of their annual income through the legal aid tariff, these lawyers felt threatened by the expansion of pro bono, especially its growth in the larger law firms. In the wake of rising pro bono initiatives throughout Canada, solo and small-firm practitioners have raised objections to the expansion of pro bono, contending that it would adversely affect their livelihoods by encouraging potential legal aid–subsidized clients to seek out the services of pro bono lawyers. Several of these solo and small-firm attorneys were also fearful that large-firm lawyers doing pro bono would take away paying clients from them. In addition, there was also the assertion from solo practitioners and small-firm lawyers that big-firm pro bono lawyers, whose clients were typically upper-class individuals or large institutions, were ill-equipped to represent the legal needs of the poor. Subsequently, a decision was made within the emerging pro bono constituency that led to a compromise with solo and small-firm practitioners that provide legal aid services. Advocates for the expansion of pro bono in Canada agreed not to do anything to undermine legal aid any further and to support efforts to expand legal aid where possible.

This compromise resulted in an approach to pro bono that characterized it as "complementing" and not "replacing" legal aid. One lawyer who sits on the board of PBLO recalls how important this phrase was in expanding pro bono efforts in Canada:

> We had to repeat over and over the mantra that pro bono was designed to provide the services to those who are *not* assisted by legal aid. We use the language of "complementary not replacing," and we repeated that over and over. That's one of the reasons why we have Legal Aid of Ontario on the board of PBLO.

Seen through this lens, the expansion of pro bono is considered part of the coordinated effort to increase access to justice within Canada.[16] This approach to pro bono has led to the segmentation of areas into which pro bono lawyers provide services. In most regions in Canada that have seen an expansion of pro bono, there is the recognition that lawyers providing free legal services will avoid areas that have historically been served by legal aid, especially criminal legal matters. One prominent lawyer in the Vancouver pro bono scene described the arrangement in the following way:

> Criminal law was never really much of an issue for us because it's covered by legal aid. Very little pro bono is done for criminal cases. The big attention has been entering the field that was previously covered by legal aid and the view that pro bono attorneys are providing substandard service. We were seen as tourists. Also, when we move into the social movement area, we are sometimes seen as a branch of the government. And we get criticized for that by legal aid lawyers. So, it's a little bit of a difficult dance. We certainly advocate for more legal aid funding, but sometimes we're seen as competitors.

Thus, while there is still recognition that pro bono efforts should, at least in part, be directed at serving underrepresented and low-income groups, pro bono attorneys generally avoid taking on criminal and other matters presently covered by legal aid. Subsequently, the majority of cases handled through pro bono efforts in Canada typically involve meeting the civil legal needs of individuals (i.e., disability and health care benefits, civil rights, housing, labor, etc.) who are unable to afford a lawyer and to public interest groups, charities, and community groups who may (but not necessarily) serve underrepresented and low-income constituencies (i.e., Aboriginal rights groups, arts advocate groups, schools and hospitals, refugee organizations, etc.).

A third distinguishing characteristic of the contemporary pro bono culture in Canada is its connection to the broader concept of corporate social responsibility (CSR). Defined as volunteer efforts undertaken by businesses and companies to operate in a socially, ethically, economically, and environmentally responsible manner, CSR has over the past several years become a significant part of Canada's private sector landscape. The Canadian government proclaimed in 2009, in outlining its strategy for CSR, that Canadian companies are expected to meet the highest standards of CSR in all their domestic and international transactions. While companies are responsible for implementing and practicing CSR activities, the Canadian government supports these efforts through the establishment of offices and centers that work with the private sector to provide assistance in CSR strategies.

Several lawyers interviewed for this project indicated that part of the "business model" argument for supporting pro bono was related to the need to satisfy CSR requirements in an effort to attract large institutional clients. Law firms seeking institutional clients now must respond to formal queries from businesses and corporations, as well as governmental agencies, about the community work the law firm regularly conducts. Typically, these queries take the form of a request for proposal (RFP) for external legal services.[17] For many firms, engagement in pro bono activity is a way to demonstrate in an RFP to potential private and public sector clients their commitment to the betterment of society. As one large law firm attorney noted:

> Those big entities are pushing their law firms into having a pro bono commitment as part of a corporate social responsibility focus. There is a business case for pro bono. Firms can use pro bono on the RFPs that law firms have to fill out to do corporate work. At our firm, we do a lot of government work and a lot of the RFPs that we receive ask us to show them what they're doing in terms of pro bono and telling what we do for the public good.

Many firms demonstrate their own commitment to social responsibility by advertising the pro bono work they perform on their web pages. Very often, this pro bono service is provided to community groups such as Boys and Girls Clubs, museums, social service organizations, disability advocacy groups, and assorted charitable organizations.

A final distinguishing characteristic of pro bono within the Canadian context is its relationship to concerns frequently articulated regarding self-regulation and professional autonomy. Many Canadian legal professionals point to England and Australia, where scandals over lawyer self-discipline, concerns about competitiveness, and a heightened focus on consumer welfare all led to a transformation of self-regulatory models.[18] This anxiety over the potential loss of professional autonomy and the growing concern that the legal profession is not meeting the needs of a large segment of the Canadian population[19] has led many in the profession to view the expansion of pro bono as a necessary strategy toward preserving professional autonomy. As one Canadian lawyer commented:

> Self-regulation of the legal profession is dependent on the public's support of lawyers. In some countries, self-regulation has been seriously eroded – like in England and Australia. So, without public support the same thing could happen in Canada. The Law Society as a self-regulating body of lawyers is a mixture of lawyers and laypeople. Many of the nonlawyers who are part of the Law Society are prominent people. This is true of all self-regulating professions in Canada. My sense is that it's a fairly equal mix. So, one way that self-regulation could be threatened might be that there are more laypeople than lawyers on the Law Society board so that lawyers would be outnumbered by nonlawyers. So, one way to maintain a professional monopoly and control is to make sure that lawyers have a positive reputation and pro bono is part of this. This is not to suggest that this is the only reason why the profession supports pro bono, but it certainly is one of the more important reasons.

Another lawyer drew a connection between the expansion of pro bono and a concern for professional regulation in the following way:

> Pro bono is critically valuable for the image of the profession. I think we constantly have to work on the image of the profession. When you ask someone on the street to rate professions, lawyers always rank lower than others. The legal profession is more regulated in Canada than in the US, and there have been examples in place like England and Australia where the profession has lost the right to self-regulation. Pro bono is probably the best way to work on the image of the profession and help maintain autonomy.

Even bar association and law society leaders contend that concerns with the loss of self-regulation that has taken place in other countries have been an important component in the expansion of pro bono within the Canadian legal profession. As one staff attorney at the Canadian Bar Association commented:

> I think there's a real fear among lawyers of losing the right to self-regulation. It's a well-founded concern because of what happened in the UK. Lawyers in England and Wales are no longer self-regulated. That's a recent memory. It is our opinion that a self-regulated profession is better. The issue for us is the independence of lawyers and of the bar, so we are concerned about that. The CBA is trying to advance the interests of lawyers as an autonomous profession, and pro bono helps build that support for lawyers in the communities.

In summary, there has been substantial growth in pro bono activity within the Canadian legal profession over the past twenty years. While the early history of pro bono in Canada led to a government-based legal aid system, by the 1990s that system was increasingly under stress due to insufficient and reduced funding. Canada's modern pro bono movement emerged during this period and has resulted in a hybrid approach that combines different models of pro bono. In the following section, we provide a portrait of contemporary pro bono legal service in Ontario – Canada's largest legal community.

DISTRIBUTION OF PRO BONO ACROSS ONTARIO'S LEGAL COMMUNITY

How is pro bono service distributed across lawyers in Ontario? Are lawyers working in particular organizational settings (e.g., solo practitioners or large-firm lawyers) more likely to perform pro bono work? What factors encourage lawyers to contribute their time to pro bono service? Is pro bono service most often part of lawyers' jobs (e.g., sponsored by private law firms and counted toward billable hours) or work that is undertaken outside law firm billable hours as "free and voluntary work"? Which clients receive the largest share of lawyers' pro bono legal service?

To answer these questions, we draw on a large-scale survey of lawyers in Ontario. This province is an ideal setting in which to study pro bono service because it is home to the largest proportion of lawyers (35 percent) in the nation.[20] The headquarters of the country's largest corporate law firms are stationed in Toronto, the financial nexus and biggest city in Canada, while the largest concentration of government lawyers work in Ottawa, the nation's capital. There is also considerable diversity of law practice settings scattered in smaller cities and towns across the province. The survey consists of a stratified random sample of lawyers from the membership records of the Law Society of Upper

Canada. We stratified the sample by gender to include equal numbers of men and women called to the Ontario bar between 1990 and 2009. We selected this span of nearly twenty years in order to pay close attention to the formative career years. These are years where one might expect to see considerable pro bono engagement fostered by law school clinic and pro bono service,[21] and by law firms' use of pro bono as a way to provide training and courtroom exposure to junior lawyers.[22]

Law graduates of this era entered practice during a period characterized by women's rising representation in the profession (24 percent in 1991 to 38 percent in 2009) and a growing presence of racial and ethnic minority group members.[23] Many of these lawyers also entered the profession in a period of remarkable change. These changes encompass globalization,[24] two recessionary periods (early 1990s and in 2008), the growth of large law firms,[25] rising billable hours expectations,[26] technological advancement,[27] and the 1990s financial crisis in the government-sponsored legal aid system.[28]

We conducted our survey in September 2009. We mailed questionnaires directly to respondents' places of employment. The survey, with two reminders, received a 47 percent response rate (N=1,270). This is a favorable rate of response, consistent with recent surveys of lawyers in North America.[29] In addition, the demographic characteristics of the sample and distribution across sectors of practice and firm size are consistent with population data.[30]

Table 3.1 provides an overview to the measurement of variables used in our analysis. Our core variables of interest include the incidence and amount of pro bono, whether pro bono is considered part of one's job or not, and the recipients of pro bono legal service. We use several factors to explain the incidence and amount of pro bono. These include: (1) demographics; (2) human capital (e.g., education, areas of law); (3) work context (e.g., solo practice, government, law clinic, business, and law firms of different sizes); (4) power measures (e.g., control over work, decision-making authority, and income); and (5) motivations and collective norms (e.g., self-efficacy, meaningful work, religious faith, political views, and community civic engagement).

In our sample, nearly half the lawyers are women (48 percent), and 13 percent are racial minorities (see Table 3.2). The vast majority of the lawyers are married (78 percent), and just over half have children (56 percent). The average age of lawyers in our sample is 40 years old. Over half the lawyers in our sample work in private law firms (53 percent), and 13 percent work as solo practitioners. Another 15 percent work in

TABLE 3.1 Operationalization and Measurement of Study Variables

Dependent variables

Incidence of pro bono in prior year (yes=1)

Amount of pro bono (hours, range=0–2,450)

Pro bono hours as part of job (hours, range=0–2,300)

Pro bono hours not part of job (hours, range=0–300)

Recipients of pro bono legal work (as a percentage of pro bono time)

Charitable organizations (range 0–100%)

Community service(s) (range 0–100%)

Alumni organizations (range 0–100%)

Poor or low-income individuals (range 0–100%)

Other activities/recipients (range 0–100%)

Independent Variables

Demographics

Gender (women=1)

Racial minority (yes=1)

Marital status (married/cohabitation=1)

Children (has children=1)

Age (self-reported, range=25–67)

Power and income

Control over work: How much control do you have over how you do your work? (1=none, 2=little, 3=some, 4=a great deal)

Decision-making authority: Do you participate in policy-making decisions (for example, having to do with budgets, expenditures, and various other aspects of operation) in your place of work? (1=I do not participate; 2=I do not directly participate, but I provide advice in one or more areas; 3=I directly participate in at least one area; 4=I directly participate in some policy-making decisions; 5=I directly participate in all or most policy-making outcomes).

Income (self-reported, range=$0–td,700,000)

Motivations and collective norms

Self-efficacy: It is important to me to be among the best in all areas of my life (1–5, strongly disagree to strongly agree)

Meaningful work: two-item scale: (1) My work is important to society; (2) By practicing law, I am making a difference to people's lives. Likert-style scale 1–5 (strongly disagree to strongly agree) (alpha=0.91). Standardized item used in regression.

TABLE 3.1 (*cont.*)

Human capital
Elite education (University of Toronto=1)

Areas of law
Business law (corporate and commercial, intellectual property, bankruptcy, insurance=1)
Litigation (civil litigation=1)
People-related law (administrative law, adjudication and/or mediation, estates, wills and trust, family law and divorce, employment and labor relations, real estate=1)
Criminal law (criminal law=1)

Work context
Solo practice (solo practitioner=1)
Government (local, provincial, or federal government, including judiciary=1)
Law clinic (law clinic, legal aid services, public interest organization, educational institution=1)
Business (business, banking/finances, accounting firm, management consulting=1)

Organizational size
Less than 10, 10–49, 50–99, 100–299, 300-plus lawyers (each dummy variable coded: 0,1; organizations of 20–49 lawyers comparison category)

Faith (self-identify with a religion or creed=1)
Political conservative: two-item scale: (1) political leaning on social issues; (2) political leaning on taxation, spending, and social welfare issues (scale 1 to 10, from liberal, moderate, to conservative) (alpha=0.76). Standardized item used in regression.
Community civic engagement: sixteen-item scale: (1) political party, (2) political advocacy group, (3) PTA or other social organization, (4) college alumni associations, (5) law school alumni associations, (6) charities, (7) religious organizations, (8) Canadian Bar Association, (9) Law Society or local bar association, (10) gender-based organizations, (11) community/civic associations, (12) service organizations (e.g., Kiwanis, Rotary), (13) private clubs, (14) organized sports leagues, (15) other. Coded 1–4 (1=not a member, 2=current member, 3=active participant, 4=leader) (alpha=0.69). Standardized item used in regression.

TABLE 3.2 Means and Standard Deviations of Dependent and Independent Variables

	Mean	SD
Demographics and human capital		
Female	0.480	0.500
Racial minority	0.127	0.333
Married	0.783	0.412
Children	0.561	0.496
Age	39.512	7.751
Elite education	0.131	0.338
Areas of law		
Business law	0.254	0.436
Litigation	0.132	0.339
People-related law	0.261	0.439
Criminal law	0.097	0.296
Work context		
Solo practice	0.132	0.339
Private law firm	0.533	0.499
Government	0.154	0.361
Law clinic	0.035	0.185
Business	0.135	0.342
Organizational size		
Fewer than 10 lawyers	0.469	0.499
10–49 lawyers	0.189	0.392
50–99 lawyers	0.054	0.225
100–299 lawyers	0.093	0.290
300+ lawyers	0.195	0.397
Power		
Control over work	3.703	0.568
Decision-making authority	2.206	1.289
Income	162,849.70	153,995.00
Motivation and collective norms		
Self-efficacy	3.367	1.121
Meaningful work	3.438	1.116
Faith	0.454	0.498
Political conservative	4.650	2.072
Community civic engagement	1.372	0.271

Note: N=1,270.

government and 14 percent in business, while a very small amount – just 3.5 percent – work in law clinics. The majority of lawyers work in organizations of fewer than 10 lawyers (47 percent), while nearly 20 percent work in large organizations that employ over 300 lawyers, and 19 percent work in midsize organizations of 10 to 49 lawyers. A much smaller share of lawyers work in midsize organizations: only 5 percent of the lawyers work in places with 50–99 lawyers, and 9 percent in places with 100 to 299 lawyers.[31] The average income of lawyers in our sample is $162,850.

We begin with a description of pro bono activities in our sample of Ontario lawyers (see Table 3.3). Nearly half (49 percent) of the lawyers report doing pro bono work in the last year. Among those doing pro bono, the average number of hours performed is 75 hours. The majority of these hours are considered as part of the lawyer's responsibilities at the firm or "on the clock" (52 hours, on average), and a smaller share consists of pro bono hours contributed beyond what is encouraged or required at the firm (24 hours, on average). After PBLO was founded in 2002, several of the country's largest law firms adopted policies to compensate their lawyers for pro bono work.[32] For example, Blakes was among the first national law firms in Canada to adopt a formal policy that treats time spent on pro bono legal services as equivalent to billable hours.[33] Lawyers working in private practice undertake the majority of pro bono work. Solo practitioners, in particular, are heavily involved in pro bono service: 73 percent reported doing pro bono work. Among private law firm lawyers, 58 percent reported doing pro bono work. A large share of law clinic, legal aid, and public interest lawyers also perform pro bono (40 percent). Among lawyers working in business (e.g., private industry, banking/finances, accounting firms, and management consulting), 27 percent reported doing pro bono work in the last year. Pro bono service is lower yet among government-employed lawyers, where only 17 percent reported doing pro bono work in the last year.

Among lawyers performing pro bono work, the hours vary dramatically with work settings. For instance, not only are solo practitioners more likely to do pro bono, they also spend, on average, more hours in this service than do lawyers in law firms (88 hours compared with 62 hours). Although government lawyers are the least likely of the various types of practitioners to perform pro bono work, those who do dedicate a significant number of hours on average (114 hours annually). And while fewer than half (40 percent) of lawyers working in law clinics, legal aid, and public interest settings do pro bono work, those who do invest considerable time – about 320 hours per year, on average. Yet, there is tremendous variation among

TABLE 3.3 Description of Pro Bono Activities: Incidence, Amount, Recipient, and Type of Practitioners Engaged

Incidence of pro bono work (N=1,270)	%	SD	
Did some pro bono in last year	48.66	50.00	
Total pro bono hours	75.30	159.56	
Pro bono hours as part of job	51.49	155.02	
Pro bono hours not part of job	23.81	39.59	
		Number of hours	
Type of practitioner engaged in pro bono (N=1,270): Pearson Chi-square test difference $p < 0.001$	%	Mean	SD
Solo practitioners	72.62	87.83	104.79
Private law firm lawyers[a]	58.05	61.83	83.42
Government lawyers	16.92	113.61	290.58
Law clinic, legal aid, public interest organization, education	40.00	320.28	669.09
Business	26.74	35.33	29.51
		Number of hours	
Law firm size (N=677): Pearson Chi-square test difference $p < 0.001$	%	Mean	SD
Small firm (fewer than 10 lawyers)	66.82	89.41	191.02
Small-midsize firm 10–49 lawyers	61.73	61.85	98.88
Large-midsize firm 50–99 lawyers	50.00	52.93	66.21
Large firm 100–299 lawyers	52.81	74.19	207.00
Very large firm 300 plus lawyers	47.83	51.45	52.81
Percentage of pro bono hours dedicated to (N=618):	%	SD	
Charitable organizations	31.40	40.79	
Community service(s)	14.98	28.90	
Alumni organizations	1.42	8.20	
Poor or low-income individuals	37.72	43.43	
Other people and organizations[b]	9.99	27.73	

[a] Law firm lawyers comprise 53.3% of the sample (n=677).

[b] This category includes mostly friends and family, but also small businesses, clubs, bar associations, existing clients, child advocacy in education system, trade associations, Commerce Chamber, Arts Council, volunteering with continuing legal education programs, extra services to legal aid, and providing services to clients who could not pay.

these lawyers in just how many hours they commit to pro bono (standard deviation=669.09). The overall pattern suggests that while a minority of government and law clinic lawyers do pro bono work, the hours invested are, on average, considerable – though these hours also vary dramatically among practitioners.

Among law firm lawyers there is marked variation in pro bono service (here we restrict our analysis to private law firms, not simply overall organizational size). Small-firm lawyers (firms of fewer than ten lawyers) are more likely to do pro bono work than are lawyers in bigger firms. Sixty-seven percent of small-firm lawyers reported doing pro bono work, followed by 62 percent of small-midsize-firm lawyers (firms of 10 to 49 lawyers). Among lawyers working in the large-midsize (50 to 99 lawyers) and larger firms (100 to 300 lawyers), about half (50 percent and 53 percent, respectively) reported doing pro bono work. Although much fanfare is made of the growing involvement of big firms in pro bono service in the United States,[34] we find fewer than half (48 percent) of lawyers in Ontario's biggest firms[35] reported doing pro bono work.

Here as well there is considerable variation in pro bono hours across different sizes of law firms. Small-firm lawyers not only are more likely to do pro bono work than lawyers working in midsize and large firms, these lawyers also dedicate more hours to pro bono each year, on average, compared with lawyers in bigger firms. The very large firms of 300 or more lawyers have the lowest percentage of lawyers engaged in pro bono work (48 percent) contributing, on average, the fewest hours per year (52 hours) compared with firms of various other sizes.

It is, of course, useful to know the incidence and amount of pro bono hours, as well as the types of practitioners engaged in pro bono, but perhaps more pressing is the question of who receives pro bono service. We find that lawyers dedicate the largest share of their pro bono hours to low-income individuals (38 percent), followed by charitable organizations (31.4 percent). About 15 percent of pro bono hours go to community service and 1.4 percent to alumni organizations. A further 10 percent, on average, of lawyers' pro bono hours are devoted to other people and organizations. This category includes mostly friends and family, but also small businesses, clubs, bar associations, existing clients, child advocacy in education system, trade associations, Commerce Chamber, Arts Council, volunteering with continuing legal education programs, extra services to legal aid, and providing services to clients who could not pay.

To better understand processes that shape pro bono engagement, we use multivariate analyses to examine the relative effects of demographic and educational background, work context and motivational factors on the incidence of pro bono work, and the share of pro bono time dedicated to various clientele. We begin by assessing factors predicting the incidence of pro bono service (see Table 3.4). The first model considers the impact of demographics as well as educational background and areas of law practiced. Initially, women appear less likely (b = –0.213) than men, and married lawyers (b = 0.292) more likely than singles, to do pro bono work. However, these borderline statistically significant effects ($p < 0.10$) disappear in subsequent models when we take into account practice settings. Thus, the context in which lawyers work (e.g., private practice, government, law clinics, and business) is an important factor mediating the relationships between individual attributes and pro bono service. Areas of law are also relevant. Lawyers working in criminal law (b = 0.790, $p < 0.001$) and people-related law (including family law, employment law, mediation, real estate, and administrative law) are more likely to do pro bono (b = 0.655, $p < 0.001$), but these effects are reduced substantially when we take into account work context in subsequent models. Nonetheless, lawyers working in the area of people-related law remain more likely to engage in pro bono work compared with lawyers in other areas of law, even when considering work context, firm size, job authority, and broader collective norms (b = 0.349; $p < 0.05$; see model 4).

In model 2 we examine the role of work context. Private practitioners, both solo practitioners (b = 1.493, $p < 0.001$) and law firm lawyers (b = 1.365, $p < 0.001$), are more likely to do pro bono service, while government lawyers are less likely to engage in pro bono service (b = –0.649, $p < 0.05$). This is expected given that law firms, especially large firms, typically provide support (financial compensation) for pro bono work,[36] and solo practitioners and small-firm lawyers are known to take on a considerable share of pro bono work for economically disadvantaged clients.[37] Interestingly, lawyers working in the big firms (of over 300 lawyers) are less likely to do pro bono work compared with lawyers in the smaller-sized firms of 20 to 49 lawyers (b = –0.414, $p < 0.05$), but this effect is reduced to nonsignificance when we take into account workplace power, motivations, and collective norms (see models 3 and 4). Power in the workplace also makes a difference: lawyers with positions of greater decision-making authority are more likely to engage in pro bono service (b = 0.347, $p < 0.001$, see model 3).

TABLE 3.4 Logistic Regressions of Demographics, Human Capital, Work Context, Power, and Norms on Incidence of Pro Bono Participation

	Model 1	Model 2	Model 3	Model 4
Demographics and human capital				
Female	−0.213†	−0.050	0.041	−0.067
Racial minority	0.140	0.210	0.236	0.075
Married	0.292†	0.215	0.186	0.199
Children	0.040	0.087	0.015	0.038
Age	0.009	0.011	−0.001	−0.003
Elite education	−0.124	−0.021	0.032	0.070
Areas of law				
Business law	−0.038	−0.290†	−0.314†	−0.238
Litigation	0.655***	0.099	0.110	0.132
People-related law	0.790***	0.304†	0.305†	0.349*
Criminal law	0.169	0.319	0.343	0.360
Work context				
Solo practice	1.493***	1.294***	1.299***	
Private law firm	1.365***	1.403***	1.318***	
Government	−0.649**	−0.512†	−0.613*	
Law clinic	0.427	0.492	0.251	
Organizational size				
Fewer than 10 lawyers	0.052	−0.047	−0.052	
50–99 lawyers	−0.232	−0.182	−0.163	
100–299 lawyers	−0.177	−0.125	−0.101	
300+ lawyers	−0.414*	−0.351†	−0.328	
Power				
Control over work			0.026	0.023
Decision-making authority			0.247***	0.208**
Income			0.000	0.000
Motivations and collective norms				
Self-efficacy				0.060
Meaningful work				0.089
Faith				0.092
Political conservative				−0.168*
Community civic engagement				0.975***
Intercept	−0.871**	−1.550***	−1.772**	−1.765**
Log-likelihood	−851.064	−771.699	−761.779	−737.539
Pseudo R-squared	0.033	0.123	0.134	0.162

Note: N=1,270.
†$p < 0.10$; *$p < 0.05$; **$p < 0.01$; *** $p < 0.001$ (two-tailed test).

When it comes to possible motivations and collective norms that might encourage a willingness to engage in pro bono work, two factors surface (see model 4). First, political conservatives are less inclined to do pro bono work (b = .168, $p < .05$). Second, active participation in community associations (e.g., charities, religious organizations, bar associations, sports leagues, and clubs) increases engagement in pro bono work (b = .975, $p < .001$).

Determining the factors that explain whether lawyers will engage in pro bono work is important, but an essential next step is to explore the extent to which these same factors predict which clients will receive pro bono service. In Table 3.5 we examine three possible recipients of pro bono service: charitable organizations, community services, and low-income individuals. Recall that lawyers dedicate the largest share of their pro bono hours (as a percentage of each lawyer's total pro bono hours) to low-income people (38 percent) and charitable organizations (31 percent), with a smaller share to community services (15 percent).

Our study's results reveal that the processes generating pro bono work (incidence) are not the same as those explaining how much time lawyers contribute to pro bono work and for which clients. For example, the demographic backgrounds of lawyers are not influential determinants of whether lawyers do pro bono, but these background factors shape the percentage of pro bono time lawyers give to different clients. For example, racial minorities dedicate less pro bono time to charitable organizations compared with whites (b = –11.565, $p < 0.01$), but more of their pro bono time to community services than do whites (b = 7.186, $p < 0.05$). Women lawyers, compared with their male counterparts, also give a greater share of their pro bono hours to community services (b = 5.480, $p < 0.05$), but no gender differences surface when we consider the percentage of pro bono hours dedicated to charitable organizations or low-income people. Age was not a significant factor in predicting whether lawyers would do pro bono service (see Table 3.4), and yet we find that older lawyers, compared with younger lawyers, give more of their pro bono time to community services (b = 0.390, $p < 0.05$).

Differences are also noteworthy with reference to education, areas of law, and work context. Graduating from a tier-one law school does not shape whether lawyers do pro bono work, but elite education increases the amount of pro bono time dedicated to charitable organizations (b = 8.847, $p < 0.10$). Lawyers practicing business law (including corporate and commercial, intellectual property, bankruptcy, and insurance)

TABLE 3.5 OLS Regressions of Demographics, Human Capital, Work Context, Power, and Norms on Percentage of Pro Bono Time Dedicated to Various Clients

	Model 1	Model 2	Model 3
	Charitable Organization	Community Services	Low-Income Individuals
Demographics and human capital			
Female	0.093	5.480*	−1.938
Racial minority	−11.656**	7.186*	−0.697
Married	−6.455	3.619	−1.838
Children	1.320	−1.369	2.289
Age	0.147	0.390*	−0.280
Elite education	8.847†	0.105	1.536
Areas of law			
Business law	16.769***	−3.218	−5.394
Litigation	−12.477**	1.076	13.159**
People-related law	2.821	3.259	1.242
Criminal law	−3.499	3.564	9.166
Work context			
Solo practice	−4.358	−6.205	24.593***
Private law firm	6.038	−5.682	9.204
Government	16.836†	8.453	−27.924**
Law clinic	13.271	7.439	−5.555
Organizational size			
Fewer than 10	0.803	−1.102	5.082
50–99	2.672	5.308	−9.382
100–299	8.911	1.797	−9.196
300+ employees	14.284**	0.686	−7.193
Power			
Control over work	−6.438†	−4.216†	7.701*
Decision-making authority	0.966	−0.723	0.288
Income	0.000†	0.000	−0.000†
Motivations and collective norms			
Self-efficacy	2.244†	−1.239	−0.536
Meaningful work	−5.484**	−1.991	6.360***
Faith	2.137	−2.875	2.276
Political conservative	−1.281	4.020**	−3.402†
Community civic engagement	8.242**	10.139***	−9.781**
Intercept	30.149†	19.024	12.915
Adjusted R-squared	0.138	0.061	0.181

Note: N=618 (Analysis includes only those lawyers who engaged in pro bono service during the last year).
†$p < 0.10$; *$p < 0.05$; **$p < 0.01$; *** $p < 0.001$ (two-tailed test).

compared with lawyers in other areas of law give more of their pro bono time to charitable organizations (b = 16.769, $p < 0.001$). Undoubtedly, lawyers working in business law offer expertise of value to charities and nonprofit organizations. For example, Gowlings' intellectual property lawyers offer free copyright and trademark counsel to organizations supporting Aboriginal artists. McCarthy Tétrault lawyers offer ArtScape, a nonprofit organization, free legal help in negotiations for the lease of land, land-use planning and zoning, and easement agreements for artists. Blakes' lawyers provide pro bono legal advice on corporate matters to Boys and Girls Clubs.[38]

Meanwhile, civil litigators give less pro bono time to charitable organizations compared with lawyers in other areas of law (b = –12.477, $p < 0.01$), but litigators also give more of their pro bono time than do lawyers working in other areas of law to low-income persons (b = 13.159, $p < 0.01$). Organizational context also plays a role. Solo practitioners, compared with lawyers in other settings, dedicate a much greater share of their pro bono hours to low-income people (b = 24.593, $p < 0.001$). And while government lawyers give less of their pro bono time to low-income people compared with lawyers in business (private industry), they also give more of their pro bono time to charitable organizations (b = 16.836, $p < 0.10$). Big-firm lawyers, compared with smaller-firm lawyers, give more of their pro bono time to charitable organizations (b = 14.284, $p < 0.01$), but otherwise, firm size does not appear to influence the share of pro bono hours dedicated to different types of clients.

When it comes to power and status in the workplace, control over one's work has an interesting effect on the proportion of pro bono hours dedicated to different clients. Lawyers with greater control over their daily work tend to give more pro bono time to low-income people (b = 7.701, $p < 0.05$). And it appears, at least at a marginal level of statistical significance, that these lawyers also give less pro bono time to charitable organizations (b = –6.438, $p < 0.10$) and community services (b = –4.216, $p < 0.10$) compared with lawyers having less control over their work. Control over one's work, or autonomy, correlates closely with hierarchical position: solo practitioners and law firm partners have greater autonomy than associates in law firms. Hence, we find associates in large law firms engage in pro bono work for charitable organizations, while solo practitioners devote more pro bono service to low-income individuals. It is noteworthy that in our analysis of whether lawyers do pro bono service (incidence) (Table 3.4), decision-making authority was an important factor, but here when we consider percentage of total pro bono time (amount) devoted to different types of clients, it is control over one's work that is the power lever (Table 3.5). Our measure of decision-making authority asks lawyers about their level of participation in policy-making decisions (for example, having to do with budgets, expenditures, and various other aspects of operation) in their place of work, while control over work asks lawyers how much control they have over how they do their work. Perhaps decision-making authority matters for choosing whether to engage in pro bono, but then control over work (i.e., autonomy) shapes how extensive that commitment becomes in terms of hours devoted to specific clients.

Some of these factors may involve cultural norms and motivational influences. For instance, lawyers who describe their work as being deeply meaningful devote a greater share of their pro bono hours to helping low-income people. Of course, it could be that by helping the poor through pro bono service, these lawyers find their work to be more meaningful. Interestingly, the effect is reversed when it comes to charitable organizations: lawyers describing their work as very meaningful give fewer hours to charitable organizations ($b = -5.484$, $p < 0.01$). Organizational context may play a role here. Lawyers in law firms, particularly larger firms, give a greater share of their pro bono time to charities compared with lawyers in smaller firms, while small-firm lawyers dedicate more of their pro bono time to assisting the poor. We find that lawyers in firms with over 100 lawyers give, on average, 25 percent of their pro bono time to charitable organizations compared with 18 percent among lawyers in smaller firms (fewer than 10 lawyers and firms of 10 to 49 lawyers). In contrast, small-firm lawyers give, on average, 32 percent (firms of fewer than 10 lawyers) to 24 percent (firms of 10 to 49 lawyers) of their pro bono time to helping the poor, while big-firm lawyers give only 11 percent (firms over 300 lawyers) to 12 percent (firms of 100 to 299 lawyers) of their pro bono hours to helping the poor.

Lawyers who describe themselves as politically conservative give fewer of their pro bono hours to low-income people ($b = -3.402$, $p < 0.10$) but a larger share of their pro bono time to community services ($b = 4.020$, $p < 0.01$) compared with lawyers who identify as more politically liberal. A significant driver of the distribution of pro bono hours across different clients is the amount of volunteer work lawyers take on outside of pro bono legal service. Lawyers who volunteer heavily (either in several associations or as leaders in associations) direct a larger share of their pro bono hours to community services ($b = 10.139, p < 0.001$) and charitable organizations ($b = 8.242, p < 0.01$), but fewer of their total pro bono hours to assisting low-income individuals with legal matters ($b = -9.781, p < 0.01$). This is suggestive of the role of formal volunteering for building client contacts. Perhaps through community civic engagements, lawyers are encouraged to devote pro bono service to charities and community services; however, the nature of these volunteer engagements less often brings lawyers in contact with economically disadvantaged populations in need of legal services.

SUMMARY

The pro bono landscape in Canada represents a hybrid of forms common to several countries. Although the US model of pro bono legal work has certainly influenced Canadian pro bono, Canada's pro bono culture reveals its own distinct features. These features include: (1) the role of NGOs in coordinating pro bono opportunities for law firm lawyers; (2) coordinated efforts to increase access to justice through segmentation of areas into which pro bono and legal aid lawyers provide services; (3) pro bono as demonstrative of corporate responsibility and therefore attractive to the recruitment of large institutional clients; and (4) the view that pro bono work is important to ensure professional autonomy and self-regulation in Canada.

The contemporary landscape of Canadian pro bono service draws on lawyers across a variety of practice settings. Nearly half (49 percent) of all lawyers report doing pro bono work over the last year. These lawyers consider the majority of their pro bono hours (about 68 percent) to be part of their job, or "on the clock." The largest share of these pro bono hours is dedicated to assisting low-income individuals and charities. Numerous factors drive whether lawyers engage in pro bono work, to what extent and for whom. Organizational context plays a powerful role. Although solo practitioners and lawyers working in private law firms undertake the lion's share of pro bono work, it is noteworthy that a sizable proportion of lawyers working in law clinics, business enterprises, and government also contribute pro bono work. This is an important observation because numerous studies of pro bono work restrict their samples to private practitioners.[39] Within the realm of private practice, we find that the vast majority of small-firm and solo practitioners do pro bono work (over 70 percent), while rates of participation fall closer to half among big-firm lawyers.

Organizational context and areas of law remain key determinants of whether lawyers take on pro bono work even when taking into account lawyers' demographic backgrounds, hierarchical positions, motivations, and collective norms encouraging volunteerism. Private practice lawyers are more likely to do pro bono, while government lawyers are less likely to do pro bono work compared with lawyers in private industry or business. Lawyers working in people-related areas of law (such as family, employment, and mediation) are more likely to do pro bono service, even when considering organizational context and motivations. Although organizational context is important, professional power also matters – lawyers with greater decision-making authority are more likely to take on pro bono work. Motivations and collective norms also influence propensity to do pro bono work: political conservatism dampens inclination to do pro bono work, while active engagement in community civic associations (e.g., volunteering outside work) encourages pro bono legal work.

Interestingly, factors predicting which clients will receive pro bono legal services are often unique from the factors determining whether lawyers will engage in pro bono work in the first instance. For example, demographics do not appear to affect whether lawyers do pro bono work, but they shape which clients receive pro bono legal assistance. Whites dedicate more of their pro bono time to charitable organizations, while racial minorities and women direct a greater share of their pro bono hours to community services. Similarly, age does not influence whether lawyers do pro bono work, but age shapes how lawyers distribute their pro bono time – with older lawyers giving more of their time to community services. Other factors relevant to the incidence of pro bono shape the choice of clients in specific ways. For example, lawyers practicing business law give more of their pro bono time to charities, while civil litigators give more of their pro bono time to low-income persons compared with lawyers practicing in other areas of law. Solo practitioners dedicate more of their pro bono time to assisting the poor, while government lawyers, compared with lawyers in business, give more of their pro bono hours to serving charities. Big-firm lawyers too, compared with smaller-firm lawyers, give more of their pro bono time to charitable organizations. And while decision-making authority influences whether to do pro bono, control over one's work shapes which clients will receive more pro bono time. Control over one's work encourages lawyers to devote more pro bono time to serving the poor. Motivations and cultural incentives are also influential, shaping both the incidence and clients preferred for pro bono service. Lawyers describing their work as deeply meaningful tend to give more pro bono time to assisting the poor. Politically conservative lawyers give less pro bono time to low-income people but more time to community services compared with their liberal counterparts. Finally, community civic engagement encourages pro bono time dedicated to providing legal services to charities and community services, and less pro bono time toward helping low-income people with their legal matters.

In sum, one might characterize pro bono work in Canada as a realm of contrasting tendencies: legal aid for criminal matters and pro bono for civil law claims and disputes; big firms offering pro bono service to charities and solo practitioners and small-firm lawyers aiding the poor. Yet, beneath these simple contrasts, we find powerful forces that drive whether lawyers work pro bono, the amount of time they dedicate to pro bono, and which clients will receive legal assistance. Specifically, professional power, organizational context, gender and cultural background, political leanings, and civic engagement influence whether lawyers do pro bono and how lawyers disperse their pro bono time across different types of clients. When it comes to pro bono service, there is a lack of professional unity. As Heinz and Laumann[40] and others[41] suggest, the profession may be better characterized as having "hemispheres": first, a corporate cluster of fields housed in large law firms that serve primarily corporate clients, and second, an array of fields of law and individual clients serviced by solo practitioners and small-firm lawyers. Our analysis indicates that the nature and extent of pro bono service also fluctuate across these different hemispheres of practice.

NOTES

1. Mary Reilly, *The Origins and Development of Legal Aid in Ontario*, 8 WINDSOR Y.B. OF ACCESS TO JUST. 81 (1988).
2. *Id.* at 81.
3. Frederick Zemans, *Legal Aid and Legal Advice in Canada*, 16 OSGOODE HALL L.J. 663 (1978).
4. Robert Todd, *Legal Aid: A System on Peril*, CANADIAN LAWYER MAG., Oct. 4, 2010, www.canadianlawyermag.com/article/legal-aid-a-system-in-peril-969/ (last visited Aug. 8, 2020).

5. Lorne Sossin, *The Public Interest, Professionalism and Pro Bono Publico*, 46 Osgoode Hall L.J. 131 (2008).
6. Scott L. Cummings, *Community Economic Development as Progressive Politics: Toward a Grassroots Movement for Economic Justice*, 54 Stan. L. Rev. 399 (2002).
7. Melinda Buckley, Moving Forward on Legal Aid: Research on Needs and Innovative Approaches (Canadian Bar Ass'n 2010), www.cba.org/CBAMediaLibrary/cba_na/images/Equal%20Justice%20-%20Microsite/PDFs/Moving-Forward-on-Legal-Aid.pdf (last visited Aug. 8, 2020).
8. *See Pro Bono Students Canada*, Univ. of Toronto Fac. of Law, www.law.utoronto.ca/programs-centres/programs/pbsc-pro-bono-students-canada (last visited Aug. 8, 2020).
9. Law Soc'y of B.C. & Canadian Bar Ass'n (B.C. Branch), Pro Bono Publico – Lawyers Serving the Public Good in British Columbia (2002), www.lawsociety.bc.ca/Website/media/Shared/docs/publications/reports/ProBono_02-06.pdf (last visited Aug. 8, 2020).
10. Lynn Burns, *Pro Bono North of the Border: The Canadian Experience*, 11 Dialogue 1, 1–2, 5–6 (2007).
11. Roy McMurtry, Marion Boyd & John McCamus, Listening to Ontarians: Report of the Ontario Civil Legal Needs Project (2010), http://plelearningexchange.ca/database/listening-to-ontarians-report-of-the-ontario-civil-legal-needs-project-2/ (last visited Aug. 8, 2020).
12. Cathexis Consulting, Evaluation of Pro Bono Law Ontario: Final Report (2010).
13. *Id.*
14. Sossin, *supra* note 5, at 131.
15. Jamie Maclaren, *Pro Bono: Ubiquitous Saviour or Reluctant Crutch?* Just. Issues, Nov. 5, 2011, www.slaw.ca/2011/11/15/pro-bono-ubiquitous-saviour-or-reluctant-crutch/ (last visited Aug. 8, 2020).
16. Richard Abel, *State, Market, Philanthropy, and Self-Help as Legal Services Delivery Mechanisms*, Private Lawyers and the Public Interest: The Evolving Role of Pro Bono in the Legal Profession 295 (Robert Granfield & Lynn Mather eds., 2009); Andrew Boon & Avis Whyte, *Charity and Cheating Begins at Home: The Aetiology of the New Culture of Pro Bono Publico*, 2 Legal Ethics 169 (1999).
17. Vawn Himmelsbach, *Building a Better RFP*, Canadian Law. Mag., Dec. 29, 2015.
18. Paul Paton, *Between a Rock and a Hard Place: The Future of Self-Regulation – Canada Between the United States and the English/Australian Experience*, J. Prof. Law. 87 (2008).
19. *See* Buckley, *supra* note 7.
20. Federation of Law Societies of Canada, Our Members: Canada's Law Societies (2017), http://flsc.ca/about-us/our-members-canadas-law-societies/ (last visited Aug. 8, 2020); Law Society

OF UPPER CANADA, STATISTICAL SNAPSHOT OF LAWYERS IN ONTARIO (2016), www.lsuc.on.ca/uploadedFiles/Equity_and_Diversity/Members2/Lawyer-Snapshot%202015.pdf (last visited Aug. 8, 2020).

21. Benjamin P. Cooper, *Mandatory Pro Bono Redux: Guest Correspondent's Report from the United States*, 15 LEGAL ETHICS 135 (2012); Ann Juergens & Diane Galatovitsch, *A Call to Cultivate the Public Interest: Beyond Pro Bono*, 51 J. LAW & POL'Y 95 (2016); Anne R. Traum, *In Law School, It's Pro Bono from Day One*, NEVADA LAW., Sept. 2014, at 44–45.
22. Michael P. Downey, *Pro Bono*, INTRODUCTION TO LAW FIRM PRACTICE 169 (2010); Cynthia F. Epstein, *Stricture and Structure: The Social and Cultural Context of Pro Bono Work in Wall Street Firms*, 70 FORDHAM L. REV. 1689 (2002); Fiona McLeay, *The Legal Profession's Beautiful Myth: Surveying the Justifications for the Lawyer's Obligation to Perform Pro Bono*, 15 INT'L J. LEGAL PROF. 249 (2008); Stephen Parker, *Why Lawyers Should Do Pro Bono Work*, 19 LAW IN CONTEXT 5 (2001); Deborah L. Rhode, *Survey Indicates Little Emphasis on Public Service*, NAT'L L.J., Sept. 12 (2005).
23. The Law Society reported that 15.7 percent of the candidates in the licensing admission process self-identified as racial minorities in 2007 and by 2014 this percentage had risen to 24 percent. The profession consisted of 18.6 percent racial minority lawyers in 2016. *See* FEDERATION OF LAW SOCIETIES OF CANADA, *supra* note 20; LAW SOCIETY OF UPPER CANADA, *supra* note 20; LAW SOCIETY OF UPPER CANADA, 1990 ANNUAL REP. (1991); LAW SOCIETY OF UPPER CANADA, 2008 ANNUAL REP. (2009), https://lawsocietyontario.azureedge.net/media/lso/media/legacy/pdf/a/ar/arep_full_08.pdf (last visited Aug. 8, 2020); LAW SOCIETY OF UPPER CANADA, 2013 ANNUAL REP. (2014), www.annualreport.lsuc.on.ca/2013/en/index.html (last visited Aug. 8, 2020).
24. Steven A. Boutcher & Carole Silver, *Gender and Global Lawyering: Where Are the Women?* 20 INDIANA J. GLOBAL LEGAL STUDIES 1139 (2013).
25. Marc Galanter & William Henderson, *The Elastic Tournament: A Second Transformation of the Big Law Firm*, 60 STAN. L. REV. 1867 (2008).
26. Andrew Francis & Hilary Sommerlad, *Access to Legal Work Experience and Its Role in the (Re)production of Legal Professional Identity* 16 INT'L J. LEGAL PROF. 63 (2009).
27. Linda Duxbury, Christopher Higgins, Rob Smart & Maggie Stevenson, *Mobile Technology and Boundary Permeability* 25 BRIT. J. MGMT. 570 (2014).
28. Mary Jane Mossman, *From Crisis to Reform: Legal Aid Policy-Making in the 1990s*, 16 WINDSOR Y.B. ACCESS TO JUST. 261 (1998).
29. In a survey of Harvard Law School graduates (classes of 1975, 1985, 1995, and 2000), Wilkins and colleagues reported a response rate of 35 percent. The *After the JD*, a national study of US law graduates who

entered law practice in 2000, received a response rate of 51 percent in wave 2 conducted in 2007. Finally, a national study of Canadian lawyers conducted in 2012 reported a response rate of 46 percent, after adjusting for eligibility. *See* Ronit Dinovitzer, LAW AND BEYOND: A NATIONAL STUDY OF CANADIAN LAW GRADUATES (2015), http://individual.utoronto.ca/dinovitzer/images/LABReport.pdf (last visited Aug. 8, 2020); Ronit Dinovitzer & John Hagan, *Hierarchical Structure and Gender Dissimilarity in American Legal Markets*, 92 SOCIAL FORCES 929 (2014); David B. Wilkins, Bryon Fong & Ronit Dinovitzer, THE WOMEN AND MEN OF HARVARD LAW SCHOOL: THE PRELIMINARY RESULTS FROM THE HLS CAREER STUDY (HLS Center on the Legal Profession Research Paper No. 2015–6, 2015), https://clp.law.harvard.edu/assets/HLS-Career-Study-FINAL-2.pdf (last visited Aug. 8, 2020).

30. LAW SOCIETY OF UPPER CANADA, *supra* note 23.
31. The measure of organizational size captures not only law firms but also other settings where lawyers work (i.e., Department of Justice in the federal government and corporations that employ lawyers as in-house counsel).
32. *See* Jacquie McNish, *Pro Community, Pro Service, Pro Bono*, THE GLOBE & MAIL (2007) [updated 2017], www.theglobeandmail.com/report-on-business/pro-community-pro-service-pro-bono/article686963/ (last visited Aug. 8, 2020).
33. *See Pro Bono*, BLAKES, www.blakes.com/English/WhoWeAre/SocialResponsibility/Pages/ProBono.aspx (last visited Aug. 8, 2020).
34. Scott L. Cummings & Deborah H. Rhode, *Managing Pro Bono: Doing Well by Doing Better*, 78 FORDHAM L. REV. 2357 (2010); Cynthia F. Epstein, *Issues Entrepreneurs: Charisma, Charisma-Producing Events, and the Shaping of Pro Bono Practice in Large Law Firms*, *in* PRIVATE LAWYERS AND THE PUBLIC INTEREST, *supra* note 16, *at* 211; Rowena Maguire, Gail Shearer & Rachael Field, *Reconsidering Pro Bono: A Comparative Analysis of Protocols in Australia and the United States*, 37 UNIV. N.S.W. L.J. 1164 (2014); Deborah L. Rhode, *Rethinking the Public in Lawyers' Public Service: Strategic Philanthropy and the Bottom Line*, *in* PRIVATE LAWYERS AND THE PUBLIC INTEREST, *supra* note 16, at 251; Rebecca L. Sandefur, *Lawyers' Pro Bono Service and Market-Reliant Legal Aid*, *in* PRIVATE LAWYERS AND THE PUBLIC INTEREST, *supra* note 16, at 95.
35. In the Canadian context, we define these as firms with over three hundred lawyers.
36. *See* Sandefur, *supra* note 34; Andrew Boon & Robert Abbey, *Moral Agendas? Pro Bono Publico in Large Law Firms in the United Kingdom*, 60 MODERN L. REV. 630 (1997); Steven A. Boutcher, *The Institutionalization of Pro Bono in Large Law Firms: Trends and Variation Across the AmLaw 200*, *in* PRIVATE LAWYERS AND THE PUBLIC INTEREST, *supra* note 16, at 135; Scott L. Cummings, *The Politics of Pro Bono*, 52 UCLA L. REV. 1 (2004).
37. Jill Anderson & Gordon Renouf, *Legal Services "for the Public Good,"* 28 ALTERNATIVE L.J. 13 (2003).

38. *See* McNish *supra* note 32; *Community*, McCarthy Tétrault, www.mccarthy.ca/en/community/community (last visited Aug. 8, 2020); *Pro Bono*, Blakes, *supra* note 33.
39. *See* Steven A. Boutcher, *From Policy to Practice: Assessing the Effect of Large Law Firm Pro Bono Structure on Pro Bono Commitment*, Stud. Law, Pol. & Soc'y 145 (2010); Boutcher & Silver, *supra* note 24; Robert Granfield, *Institutionalizing Public Service in Law School: Results on the Impact of Mandatory Pro Bono Programs*, 54 Buff. L. Rev. 1355 (2007); Robert Granfield, *The Meaning of Pro Bono: Institutional Variations in Professional Obligations Among Lawyers*, 41 Law & Soc'y Rev. 113 (2007); Robert Granfield & Philip Veliz, *Good Lawyering and Lawyering for the Good: Lawyers' Reflections on Mandatory Pro Bono in Law School*, Private Lawyers and the Public Interest, *supra* note 16, at 53; Sandefur, *supra* note 34.
40. Jack P. Heinz & Edward O. Laumann, Chicago Lawyers: The Social Structure of the Bar (1982).
41. John P. Heinz, Robert L. Nelson, Rebecca L. Sandefur, & Edward O. Laumann, Urban Lawyers: The New Social Structure of the Bar (2005).

CHAPTER FOUR

PRIVATE LAW PRACTICE AND THE PUBLIC GOOD: INDIVIDUAL PRO BONO'S INSTITUTIONALIZATION IN SÃO PAULO LAW FIRMS

Fabio de Sa e Silva

INTRODUCTION

While the diffusion of pro bono – private lawyers offering free services to people in need – has affected and reconfigured corporate law practice in many jurisdictions around the world, the Brazilian case remains particularly intriguing.[1] In São Paulo – the largest market for legal services in Brazil – a pro bono movement emerged in 2001 and led to the creation of Instituto Pro Bono (IPB), a clearinghouse and advocacy center for the cause of voluntary legal work. Although firms were not the drivers of this process, they quickly lent support to IPB and demonstrated interest in pro bono work.

In spite of this promising start, pro bono was met with significant resistance, led by three main groups. First, access-to-justice activists feared that pro bono might result in legal aid being privatized, at a time when they were campaigning for the creation of a state public defender's office. Second, some law firms understood that pro bono was being used by their counterparts as a tactic of unfair competition and client recruitment – which the Brazilian legal ethics code prohibits – and brought the issue to the São Paulo state bar. Third, a large contingent of solo and small-firm lawyers providing legal aid through a judicare system administered jointly by the São Paulo state government and the São Paulo Bar Association – in 2012, this system involved more than 44,000 professionals at a cost of US $142 million – feared that their market niche could be overtaken by large-firm pro bono lawyers.

To mediate between these conflicts and factions, the bar association decided to regulate pro bono. In August 2001, the bar issued a Pro Bono Resolution, which placed considerable limits on the ability of firms to engage in pro bono. According to the Resolution, firms were allowed to provide pro bono only in the form of transactional services to non-profits. Litigation and individual representation were, therefore, excluded and lawyers providing these types of services pro bono could be disciplined for ethical violations. Pro bono activists and some law firms rejected the rationale behind the Pro Bono Resolution and claimed a right to provide pro bono services, including legal representation, to individuals. But the bar association did not back off in its regulatory doctrine.

Change only started to happen in 2013, when – under a credible threat of litigation from federal prosecutors – the Federal Bar Association decided to draft new regulations addressing the provision of pro bono services with a national scope. This came in 2015 and, while it still included some restrictive stipulations – for instance, pro bono services to political parties and candidates were prohibited – lawyers were at last allowed to represent individuals in court on a pro bono basis. Pro bono activists received these changes with high hopes. They expected that firms would naturally expand their pro bono work and begin to serve individual clients. But three years later, these expectations were not met. Only two firms became more organically involved in individual pro bono services, while law firm lawyers overwhelmingly understood pro bono to be restricted to work provided to charity, religious, civil society, or educational entities (Figure 4.1).

What explains the decision of firms regarding whether or not to engage in pro bono? Drawing from a long-term investigation of pro bono's institutionalization in São Paulo, with an especially close look at São Paulo corporate law firms,[2] this chapter points to structural forces and agency dynamics that bring private law practice and the public good together – or drive them apart. More specifically, I argue that while firms may be responsive to their embedding institutional context – the field of corporate law practice – this process is mediated by their cost-benefit calculations as "rational" organizations. But organizational rationality[3] and the constant pursuit, by firms, of an optimal cost-benefit ratio are not all that shape law firm pro bono. Entrepreneurial intermediaries can "lower the costs" and idealist lawyers can sustain, and expand the meaning of, pro bono work within these firms. I posit that these findings have important implications for the sociology of the

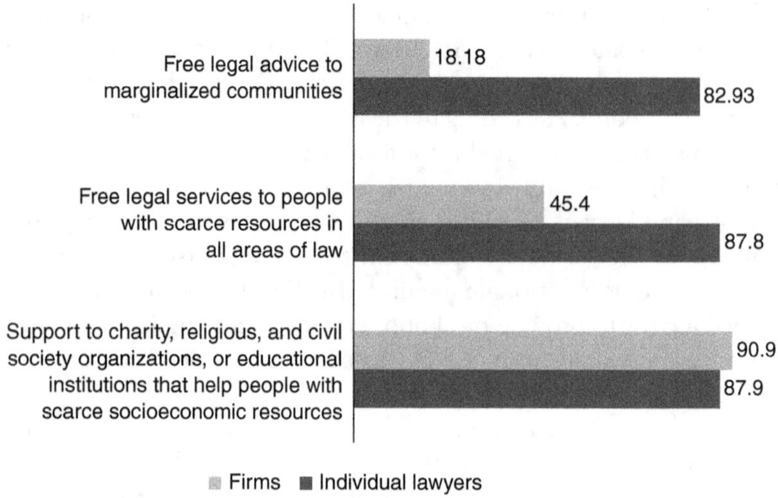

Figure 4.1. Activities qualified as pro bono by survey respondents
Source: Author's elaboration based on Natalia Serrano, Julián Díaz, & Daniel Bonilla Maldonado, El trabajo jurídico pro bono en Brasil: Discurso, prácticas y límites 2005-2017, 10 *Revista Direito e Práxis* 1, at 488.

legal profession and the sociology of law firms, as well as to access-to-justice research and policy.

The chapter proceeds in four sections. First, I review the literature on pro bono's institutionalization, with an emphasis on the explanations for why firms engage/do not engage in pro bono work. I then report on the methods used in the research that informs the chapter. Next, I present my findings. Lastly, I advance concluding thoughts.

LITERATURE REVIEW

The Anglo-American scholarship on pro bono was initially driven by normative concerns. Scholars[4] approached the growth in pro bono work in light of long-standing claims or expectations about the public role of lawyers and their duties, as professionals, to society at large. Implicit in these views may have been a "classical theory" of professionalism, in which the power and privilege society affords to lawyers must be compensated with free services to those unable to pay for legal fees. But the theory was taken as a given, rather than critically and objectively tested.

It did not take long for law and society scholars to subject the Anglo-American pro bono movement to a deeper, empirical scrutiny. Many authors in this vein focused on individual motivations of lawyers to do pro bono. They drew from surveys,[5] and occasionally interviews,[6] to highlight the role of gender, race, class, law school credentials, and personal values as drivers of participation in pro bono programs. These studies offered important contributions to our general understanding of pro bono's institutionalization. More broadly, they demonstrated that the professional "call" for pro bono resonates quite differently across subsets of the legal profession. In addition, they demonstrated how participation in pro bono may factor in, and help reproduce, inequality within and across firms – for instance, elite lawyers may strategically engage in pro bono to expand their social capital[7] – although sometimes pro bono also offers minority lawyers the chance to build alternative career pathways.[8]

While some of these studies did look at the role of workplace settings in shaping pro bono participation,[9] none of them took the firm as the unit of analysis to ask: "Why did these firms come to participate in and eventually institutionalize pro bono?" This gap began to be filled by Scott Cummings' *The Politics of Pro Bono*.[10] Cummings situated the growth of pro bono in law firms amidst larger structural trends, such as the firms' growth in size and their consequent potential to supply pro bono services; the declining role of state-sponsored legal aid through the Legal Services Corporation; efforts by the bar to promote pro bono as a form of professional virtue; and a societal shift toward volunteerism. Yet he recognized that while some of these trends created demands for firms to offer pro bono services, firms were also driven by the tangible benefits they saw in this move. These benefits could be financial/material (the "business case" for pro bono[11]) or organizational (the ability to train young associates or to recruit and retain talents). Hence, Cummings suggested that the decision by firms to engage in, and institutionalize, pro bono was part of an attempt to navigate – and take the most from – a changing structure of opportunities and constraints for the commercial practice of law.[12]

The studies that followed ultimately ran along two tracks. Some drew from market control theories of professionalism and a critique of the commercialization of law practice to claim that pro bono's institutionalization in law firms resulted from a rational calculation.[13] For instance, Rebecca Sandefur indicated that US firms tended to offer more pro bono services if their monopoly over legal services was under threat locally.[14]

A commonly raised critique in this vein was that, as rational agents, law firms would limit their areas of pro bono work and the number of hours they would be willing to donate based on cost-benefit considerations and what they found to be their "bottom line." This included both the economic well-being of firms – firms would offer pro bono services only if they were doing well enough in the market – and their relationship with clients – firms would not take cases that put them in positional conflicts and made them lose their paying corporate clients.

Others drew from organizational sociology and neoinstitutional approaches to highlight the role of internal and environmental factors as drivers of pro bono's institutionalization in law firms. The most comprehensive effort in this direction was put together by Steven Boutcher.[15] Drawing from panel data on a subset of elite US corporate law firms (the *AmLaw* 200) and using quantitative analytical techniques, he argued that money is not all that matters in the decisions of firms to do pro bono, there being reasons why firms may take pro bono work beyond their "bottom line."

For example, he demonstrated that some firms increased lawyers' volume of pro bono work during trying economic times to keep their talents – that is, to nurture their "human capital." He also found that some firms donated more than others based on distinctive organizational and cultural factors. Lastly, he found that firms committed to pro bono in response to the "institutional environment" in which these firms were embedded – or the "field" of elite corporate law practice. For example, he found a positive effect of rankings systems and exposure to a "corporate logic of doing good" on the number of hours donated by firms. The irony here is that commercialization of law practice seemed to be promoting, rather than undermining, the commitment of firms to public good.[16]

While studies along both of these tracks offer valuable insights into the understanding of law firm pro bono, they still leave empirical and theoretical lacunae. To begin with, they typically draw from data on US law firms, at a time when both the big-firm model and pro bono have gone global.[17] In addition, they typically involve analyses of the quantitative outcomes of – how much pro bono is done – and motivations for pro bono's institutionalization in firms, rather than on the decision-making processes behind these developments. Relatedly, even when recognizing that pro bono programs involve collaboration with others outside of firms,[18] they typically overlook the agency and links of individuals and organizations within and beyond the firm structure.[19]

This chapter fills in some of these lacunae. In doing so, the chapter demonstrates both the power and the limits of the scholarship summarized here. My data and analysis both corroborate and modulate accounts from the market control/commercialization critique and the organizational/institutional perspective. In addition, I call for approaches that pay greater heed to entrepreneurial intermediaries and idealist individuals who work to facilitate, sustain, and expand law firm pro bono work.

METHODS

In 2012 and 2013 (in this chapter, this period will be referred to as research stage 1), I conducted systematic research on pro bono's institutionalization among São Paulo corporate lawyers and law firms. Having obtained a list of all the lawyers and law firms providing pro bono services through IPB, I selected a sample of ten corporate law firms (N=33) and two general counsel's offices (N=4) for in-depth interviews. To ensure validity, the law firm sample was stratified[20] to purposely include firms of different sizes and tradition in the São Paulo market for corporate legal services.[21] Some of the selected firms had been in business for decades; others had just been launched. Of the ten firms, six had over one hundred lawyers and four ranged from twenty to one hundred lawyers.

The respondents to these interviews were partners or pro bono managers for the law firms and heads of general counsel's offices. My interview protocols included questions on the history of pro bono's institutionalization in Brazil and the firm or general counsel's office, the procedures used by interviewees and their organizations to select and conduct pro bono cases, and their opinion about the future of pro bono in the country and the São Paulo jurisdiction. The interviews took an average of one hour. The records were anonymized, coded, and analyzed along with other data sources such as fieldwork notes, documents, and literature sources.

In January 2018, I decided to follow up on my previous research (in this chapter this will be referred to as research stage 2). I contacted IPB with questions about the involvement of corporate law firms in individual pro bono services, given the regulatory changes reported in the introduction. What I learned was twofold. First, this process was happening slowly, and only one firm had taken more decisive steps to start offering individual pro bono services on a consistent basis (in this chapter, this will be referred to as firm A). Second, IPB itself was undertaking a project to facilitate the engagement of private lawyers – whether in corporate law firms or in solo and small-firm practice – in individual pro bono services.

This project was meant to provide legal representation to criminal defendants in custody hearings. Such custody hearings were established by the Brazilian judiciary, which, since 2015, has required the police to present detainees before a judge within 24 hours of detention. In these proceedings, judges should: (1) determine whether the detainee must wait for trial in custody or whether he or she could qualify for alternatives to pretrial detention (for example, release with bail); and (2) verify whether there are signs that the detainee has been subjected to torture and, if there are, order the appropriate investigation to start. By the time of my data collection, the project had secured the participation of lawyers from a second law firm (in this chapter, this will be referred to as firm B).

After this review, I set up interviews with pro bono activists and with lawyers from firms A and B. In both firms, I talked to partners and pro bono coordinators, as well as to individual lawyers involved in the custody hearings project. The final component for research stage 2 involved observation. During two days in June 2018, I joined different teams of law firm lawyers who were participating in the custody hearings project. These activities gave me the chance to better know the firm lawyers involved and the pro bono work they do in this project, as well as to engage in lengthy informal conversations about the lived reality of pro bono in their firms and the role of pro bono work in their professional and civic lives.

FINDINGS

The findings from my research corroborate, modulate, and expand the literature on why law firms do pro bono. As I demonstrate in this section, pro bono emerged in São Paulo amid changes in the institutional field of corporate law practice. The field became increasingly populated by calls for corporate social responsibility (CSR), foreign law firms with well-institutionalized pro bono practices, and concerns with promotion of the "rule of law." Pro bono grew in São Paulo firms as a response to these changes. But this response was mediated – and oftentimes moderated – by organizational rationality and the constant pursuit, by firms, of an optimal cost-benefit ratio in their activities and initiatives. With organizational rationality being so central, what creates, maintains, and eventually expands space for pro bono in law firms beyond their technical "bottom line"? My research points to two factors: the social entrepreneurship and organizing role of IPB and the work of idealist-firm lawyers.

Embedding Logics and Organizational Rationality: The Structural Context of Law Firm Engagement in Pro Bono (2001–15)

Pro bono's institutionalization in São Paulo law firms took place amid more radical changes affecting corporate law practice in Brazil. By 2001, Brazil had been influenced by what, at least at that time, was becoming a global consensus on free markets and the rule of law. Lawyers played important roles on all fronts of this script: they would protect rights/democracy, support civil society initiatives, and facilitate business transactions.[22] Global businesses, transnational law firm partnerships, and law school programs to train the next generation of "public interest lawyers" were some of the conduits through which this orthodoxy could be disseminated.[23]

The events that led to the creation of IPB display these influences. One of the architects of IPB was Oscar Vilhena Vieira, the current dean of Fundação Getúlio Vargas law school. Vieira combines training in law and political science with an LL.M. from Columbia Law School and working experience in the New York public interest law industry. He held an "old belief" that Brazilian lawyers should do more to help the poor and disadvantaged.[24] But it was the time he spent in the United States and the contact he then had with pro bono work that helped him translate those intentions into feasible action.[25] In the early 2000s, with support from the Ford Foundation and the Open Society Institute, Vieira organized a series of meetings with "distinguished São Paulo lawyers" to promote pro bono work. These meetings featured Daniel Grunfeld, the then-executive director of the Public Counsel Law Center in Los Angeles, and Ellen Chapnik, a law professor at Columbia Law School.[26] IPB was created as a culmination of these meetings.

The São Paulo business community was also being influenced by – and pulling the corporate bar toward – global calls for CSR. When I asked a law firm lawyer whom I interviewed during research stage 1 about the history of her involvement with pro bono, she said: "It begins with clients who wanted to form nonprofits to support CSR projects."[27] CSR projects undertaken by São Paulo companies included, for example, musical education for children in *favelas* and training programs for juveniles in poor urban areas.

These projects had some intrinsic legal needs, such as with tax planning or incorporation of nonprofit entities. Milu Villela, a social entrepreneur with ties to the financial sector whom Vieira calls IPB's "godmother," realized that pro bono work could help companies meet these needs. In 2001, which the United Nations had designated the International Year of Volunteers, Villela held meetings with Brazilian big businesses to discuss their CSR practices. A large law firm lawyer who was also invited recalls that he heard of pro bono for the first time in one of these meetings. Villela asked him and a few other lawyers attending "what they could do to exercise social responsibility." When they failed to respond, she suggested that free legal work to companies structuring CSR projects might be a valuable contribution.

Firms were able to perceive – and respond to – these changes in their surrounding institutional context. In my interviews with pro bono activists during research stage 1, for example, I learned that positive coverage in the *Latin Lawyer* magazine became an important stimulus for firms to do more pro bono. This activist said, "They (*Latin Lawyer*) keep publishing about it . . . and since law firms are always interested in appearing on their pages, they have become more aware of how pro bono can be important" as an indicator of status in elite corporate law practice. In a more recent study of São Paulo firms, Natalia Serrano, Julián Díaz, and Daniel Bonilla Maldonado came across similar findings. More than half of the firms they surveyed (n=11) reported publicizing their pro bono activities (Figure 4.2). In addition, about a third of the firms they interviewed included a member of their communications team in their "pro bono committees." Lastly, all of the firms they interviewed that contributed financially to IPB and had received recognition as "amicus pro bono" displayed this "symbol of distinction" on their websites.[28]

But, in my research, I found that this response, too, was mediated – and oftentimes moderated – by organizational rationality and the constant pursuit, by firms, of an optimal cost-benefit ratio.[29] For example, the provision of free legal services to people in need was not completely foreign to most of the São Paulo firms. Their lawyers were more than used to representing "friends," "family members," and "firm janitors" for no charge.[30] This was common in cases of "family law," "consumer protection," and "small claims," with work being done "after regular work hours" or "during lunchtime."[31] Firms realized that, by making pro bono an official policy, they could both have a better

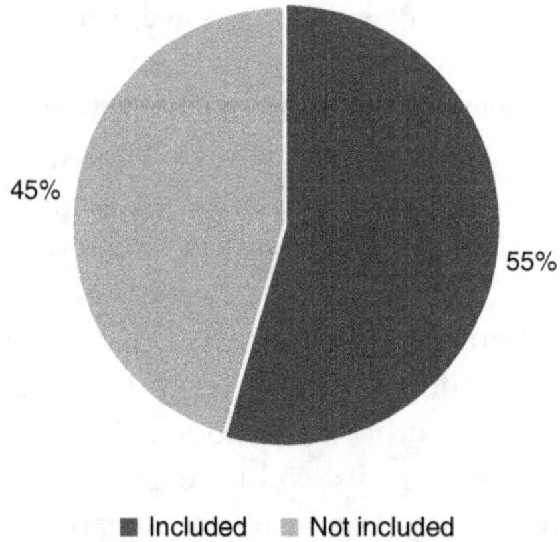

Figure 4.2. Pro bono work in law firm publicity among survey respondents (n=11)
Source: Natalia Serrano, Julián Díaz, & Daniel Bonilla Maldonado, "El trabajo jurídico pro bono en Brasil: Discurso, prácticas y límites 2005–2017," *Revista Direito e Práxis* 10(1), at 507.

management of, and take greater reputational benefits from, these practices.

Firm partners and administrators also realized that many of their staff lawyers found personal and professional satisfaction in their interaction with pro bono clients. Pro bono gave these lawyers the chance to learn new legal subjects and develop new professional skills, having to work with a clientele that had other needs and was not as sophisticated as the one they traditionally dealt with. Pro bono also gave many the sense that they were at last "helping somebody" and giving back to their community.

Economic benefits were, of course, part of these considerations. Since Brazil was becoming more integrated with the global economy, particularly after an era of privatization,[32] legal transactions involving foreign investors were growing tremendously. Firms, nevertheless, knew that they had some homework to do in order to appear as trustworthy agents locally. They set up a think tank called CESA, or Center for Studies on Law Firms, seeking to anticipate the needs of their prospective clientele. In this process, they learned that pro bono had become a defining feature of the modern corporate law sector around the globe and the United States in particular. Embracing pro bono and supporting IPB would resonate well with this target audience.[33]

But the economic benefits of pro bono became even more tangible when firms had to negotiate their service contracts with this changing clientele. For example, a lawyer I interviewed during research stage 1 said that pro bono became "a sort of tiebreaker" in the dealings between companies and firms they were hiring. According to this lawyer, "If companies wanted to work with five firms and had to decide among many with similar conditions, this [dedication of firms to pro bono work] is something they began to consider."[34] Likewise, a lawyer interviewed by Natalia Serrano, Julián Díaz, and Daniel Bonilla Maldonado said, "Other firms of the same size as ours do pro bono and our clients prefer firms that do pro bono."[35] Hence, these authors concluded: "Pro bono work allows firms to enter, or to stay in an exclusive group of transnational law firms .... Not having a pro bono program means that Brazilian firms cannot portray themselves as partners in a market that is becoming ever more competitive and demanding. Not having a pro bono program means that firms cannot appeal to a discourse that has become common in global legal dialogues."[36]

Ironically, this role of organizational rationality helps explain why few firms went the extra mile required to provide pro bono services to needy individuals once the Pro Bono Resolution was overruled by the bar association, in 2015. In my interviews with IPB officials during research stage 2, I learned that firms had "become more conscious about what they want ... and like anything else in a firm, their decisions regarding pro bono ultimately come down to what they understand they can get from it."[37]

As firms sort out "what they can get" from pro bono, individual pro bono services can prove tricky. During research stage 2, Instituto Pro Bono officials said to me that there are "easy cases," such as those in which firms "are asked to support NGOs [nongovernmental organizations] that are already litigating on behalf of individuals, but which need support in high-profile cases that have been sent for review by higher courts." These are cases that bring "high 'gains'" to firms; they "involve strategic work and generate visibility, so firms will hardly hesitate to take."[38] But as a rule, "firms do not want to take responsibility for cases that no one knows how long it is going to take for courts to try."[39] And even when firms want to be more open to individual pro bono representation and take up more "ordinary" cases, rational considerations come into play. Individual cases open doors for issues – especially those related to class and race – that can be delicate for firms to become involved with, given the larger interests they serve. Hence, said my interviewees:

> What we notice is that, in these firms, the beneficiaries of individual pro bono services tend to be women victims of domestic violence, refugees, and LGBT people; racial discrimination sometimes is included, but class-related issues are always avoided. And why is that? First, because class-related issues can lead to conflicts of interest, such as in labor or housing cases. Second, because the emphasis on issues of identity echoes international trends. These are the cases that are "hot" in the United States, so there is a message being sent out by the firms that will resonate with their peers and potential clients around the globe.[40]

Professional Disputes and the Political Economy of Access to Justice Lawyering: Additional Costs to a Rational Endeavor

Since its early days, pro bono in Brazil is caught up in disputes over the prerogative to provide legal services to the poor. Even though regulatory restrictions were lifted and private lawyers were entirely freed to do pro bono, this did not change. Solo judicare lawyers continue to resist pro bono and seek protection for their market niche. During research stage 2, law firm lawyers who participated in the custody hearings project said to me that "since day one in that project, such judicare lawyers give [them] a hard time .... And [the law firm lawyers] understand it, because [the judicare lawyers] make their living out of the cases they get."[41] I was also told – and sometimes even witnessed – that judicare lawyers "look down" on their pro bono counterparts, or that "in the [room that is normally reserved in courtroom buildings for lawyers to gather], they sometimes won't let [the pro bono lawyers] be served with coffee or cookies."[42]

A more intriguing dispute, however, grew involving the Public Defender's Office. As reported above and elsewhere,[43] those fighting for the creation of the Public Defender's Office were initially sceptical of pro bono, which they saw as a threat to "privatize" legal aid to the poor. Once the Public Defender's Office was created, it often stood side by side with pro bono activists, both opposing the bar association's protectionist stances in disputes over access-to-justice policies.[44] Then again, when the restrictions to individual pro bono services were removed, the Public Defender's Office began to act very quickly and carefully to protect its jurisdictional power and its political prestige in the market for legal aid services.

The custody hearings project offers examples of such protectionism. The project began to be conceptualized in 2016, after a Latin American

Pro Bono Forum was held in São Paulo with the purpose to "generate ideas about how the Brazilian pro bono movement could move forward with pro bono under the new regulatory framework, especially when it comes to serving individual clients."[45] But the project could not take off for the next eighteen months. "The Public Defender's Office would not accept the idea that pro bono lawyers would be in charge of individual representation in the custody hearings," and a compromise was only found when the parties agreed that the services should be provided in a state county that was not yet served by the Public Defender's Office.[46]

How may these disputes affect the decision by law firms of whether or not to do pro bono? Firm A, whose story of engagement in individual pro bono services I studied during research phase 2, offers an example. The firm collaborates in the custody hearings project and has partnered with NGOs to recruit individual pro bono clients. But in its first attempt to provide individual pro bono services post-2015, the firm contacted the Public Defender's Office with an offer to represent women victims of domestic violence.

According to informants from this firm, the conversations on this offer lasted for over a year, during which the parties "sorted out what kinds of cases could be taken up by the firm, and how the firm was going to proceed with the cases." When there seemed to be an agreement about the scope of the pro bono work to be performed and the proposal moved up the decision-making chain, said a firm A lawyer, "we heard that the project would only be accepted if we agreed to take up a 'significant number' of cases, which they estimated as twenty per month." The Public Defender's Office also "required that we set up a room at the firm, with a sign stating that here are offered legal aid services" and determined that the firm "couldn't reject any of the cases it would be sent." To this lawyer, "this meant [her firm] would be transformed into a legal aid branch." Given the role of organizational rationality in the development of law firm pro bono, the time and energy involved in these negotiations represented a "cost" that firms were not always willing to bear. Hence, in the end, one of these informants said, "We thought, 'OK, we don't want to deal with these issues now. Let's find another way to move forward.'"[47]

Agency Back In (I): Intermediaries and the Reduction of Transactional Costs

Concerns of firms with costs and benefits are not absolute impediments for their engagement with pro bono work. The role of IPB in the custody hearings project demonstrates ways in which such engagement can happen. For the project to be put into practice, it took more than traditional clearinghouse work from IPB. IPB staff members had to figure out project details, anticipate problems – and possible solutions – and develop partnerships to ensure that the implementation would be successful or at all possible, like in the eighteen months of negotiation with the Public Defender's Office reported above.

One example of this social entrepreneurship involved follow-ups to the custody hearings. Though these had not been thought of when the project was initially being drafted, IPB officials reported that they "reflected further and concluded that there was no way to walk out of a hearing with a decision, by the judge, to illegally keep a defendant imprisoned, and not challenge this decision."[48] They then "decided to expand the scope of the project, to also file appeals or habeas corpus petitions pro bono against decisions that kept clients in pretrial detention or that allowed them to leave on bail but on terms that, in practice, meant that they would remain in pretrial detention."[49] Needless to say, when the number of individuals arrested was too high and the number of releases was too low, the decision to present additional appeals or habeas petitions could put a little too much on the plate of the lawyers attending the hearings. IPB officials then coordinated with a separate network of pro bono lawyers, who were willing to write these petitions from home or their offices, based on photocopies from court case dockets.

Another example involved the preparation of would-be pro bono lawyers. In this case, IPB partnered with civil society organizations to develop training programs for the lawyers joining the project. "We could not put lawyers to work in these hearings and not give them any prior training," said the IPB officials I interviewed during research stage 2. "So, anyone who joins the project, including lawyers from big firms, has to go through this training. And the training has five basic topics – rights of incarcerated women, torture, habeas petitions, effective legal defense strategies, international human rights law – and others that we add later," they concluded.[50] Training activities eventually evolved into strategic planning. IPB officials realized that "many of these lawyers want to go beyond the hearing and the appeals or habeas petitions." So, once a month, they began to gather these lawyers for a "legal strategy workshop, to think how we can change the prison system in the jurisdiction that we serve and how we can even mobilize politically, beyond the legal process. So, it is an entirely new area of work that we discovered."[51]

How does this social entrepreneurship affect the decision by law firms of whether or not to do pro bono? At the very least, it reduces the transactional costs involved in the decision of firms to take up individual pro bono cases, facilitating their engagement in the provision of these services significantly. Further reports from firm A's saga to provide individual pro bono serve to illustrate this point. After unsuccessful attempts to work with the Public Defender's Office in cases of violence against women, firm A has also reached out to São Paulo NGOs, seeking to identify potential cases to be brought on behalf of individuals that these NGOs serve.[52] In at least one case this approach was successful, but even then, numerous difficulties were encountered. According to firm A lawyers, "There was a degree of mistrust on the part of the NGO we never expected. They asked why a corporate law firm would be wanting to offer free legal services to their clients."[53] With time and "several meetings," firm A managed to convince the NGO officials that "they had a genuine interest in helping," but it took six months for them to be able to take up the first few cases from this partnership, and "it mattered that the NGO had a legal department, which helped build a common understanding between the NGO and the firm about what the pro bono work to be offered would involve."[54] In the custody hearings project, none of this was in place. All the details had been sorted out by the organizing work carried out by Instituto Pro Bono.

Agency Back In (II): Idealist Professional Identities

Whereas the decision of whether or not to engage in individual pro bono services is deeply linked to law firm organizational rationality and the constant pursuit, by firms, of an optimal cost-benefit ratio, this is not the only force at play in the firms I researched during research stage 2. Instead, in both firms, a great sense of professional idealism – a vision of what a "good lawyer" is, which encompasses a duty to help others in need and promote equal justice for all – could be noticed, and clearly informed their initiative to take on individual pro bono cases. An early-career lawyer in firm B said, "I cannot deny that [pro bono work] has positive implications for the firm, but the real reason why we do it is, we think of the lawyers we are as tools for justice."[55] A senior lawyer in law firm A said, "Since some partners are more concerned with the benefits that pro bono creates to the firm, it is important that we demonstrate that these benefits exist. But what drives us, the very true reason why we do pro bono, is what the expression 'pro bono' means: for the public good."[56]

This vision has roots in both personal and socioprofessional factors. Lawyers participating or influencing the firms in their move toward individual pro bono services normally share a predisposition to help others, which is due to varied events shaping their life histories. For example, law firm A has a founding partner who played a key role in promoting pro bono within the firm and making it a front-runner in the provision of individual pro bono services. He is known for "always having a knack for service," for coming from a "very humble background," for being "the first in his family to go to college," and for having a "great sense of giving back."[57] Likewise, a senior lawyer in firm A said that by the time she came across the notion of pro bono, she "had someone in her family who was very sick and was desperately wanting to do volunteer work."[58] And a junior lawyer in firm B said that "when I was a kid, before thinking of law school, I wanted to be a fireman. I always wanted to help others."[59]

But this vision really develops as these lawyers come to participate in professional circles or spaces in which their role in society is called into question. Hence, the senior lawyer in firm A previously cited locates the origins of her pro bono work in events that happened thirty years ago, when she was:

> Working with [the above-cited founding partner], and he went to give a talk at PUC [the Pontifical Catholic University of São Paulo Law School]. And when he came back, he was deeply troubled. [The PUC Constitutional law professor] Jose Eduardo Cardozo, [who later served as minister of justice and solicitor general under President Dilma Rousseff], was with him on the panel. Cardozo said, "These big law firms, they just serve the big money, they do not care about justice," and then left. When it was time for [the partner] to speak, he joked, as he introduced himself, that "[he] was an expert in tax law, and a partner in a law firm that does not care about justice and just serves the big money." After that, [the partner] kept saying that "we need to do something."[60]

Similarly, a firm B lawyer said about her motivation to do pro bono and participate in the custody hearings project:

> I think I bring this from law school, which made me think of things I had never thought of. I was also an intern for the Public Defender's Office, and when we start to see how the criminal justice system works, we see so much disregard and dehumanization of the others [that] it becomes impossible for us to alienate ourselves from these issues. I would not be a full-fledged criminal lawyer if I could not give some of my time to these

> issues and to people who have no one else to look at their cases and help.[61]

These often unplanned experiences of professional socialization open the eyes of lawyers to issues of justice and equality, and foster in them a need to "give back," which they carry into, and search for ways to perform during, their law firm careers. Pro bono appears as a legitimate vehicle for them to meet these needs and be fulfilled as both professionals and individuals. Then again, the mere contrast between the two accounts brought up above indicates the different ways in which idealism can appear and operate in firms. In firm A, the idealist vision was nurtured by a founding partner and, from its very early days, influenced by scripts and models of professional responsibility circulating globally. Indeed, as this partner grappled with the need to "do something," the firm A lawyer quoted previously said:

> He had read a "very cool book, about a lawyer in a big law firm," and he made me purchase this book, *The Street Lawyer*, by John Grisham. And I started doing research on pro bono. And we found out that there was an Institute, the Pro Bono Institute, in Washington DC, [and] that the founder of it was an Ashoka fellow, and it looked like something very cool and well-established in the US, and [the partner] said, "We are going to do something of that sort here."[62]

Without a doubt, both of these factors were important for the vision to spread through the firm's culture and become constitutive of the firm's identity. From his privileged position of power, the cited firm A founding partner could "push the firm toward pro bono, influence the other partners, and continue to influence the firm's trajectory in this area until these days."[63] And by demonstrating that his concerns have been not only shared but also institutionalized in modern law firms internationally, this partner and those who followed his lead could persuade others that firm investment in pro bono was consistent with good practices of firm organizing and management globally. Hence, said the senior law firm A lawyer quoted above, "when the prohibition was lifted, service to individuals was a natural progression of what we were doing, and the question was how we were going to adapt our governance models and structure the offer of pro bono services to those individual clients."[64]

In firm B, in turn, the provision of individual pro bono services and the participation in the custody hearings project were driven by the idealism of criminal lawyers, among whom many junior lawyers were included. On one hand, this may make the move toward individual pro bono work more contained within the criminal law sector of the firm. But on the other hand, it places this work within a more specific – and in many ways more radical – set of assumptions about the role of lawyers in society. Hence, when I asked a law firm B lawyer about her motivations to participate in the custody hearings project, she said:

> It makes no sense to become a criminal lawyer and not help those who had no access to what I had. And that includes anybody, but especially those who, given the legal and political context we face, of heightened punitivism and incarceration, need it the most; it is a real mission. When I am in that courtroom, seeing nine out of ten people staying in prison for no good legal reasons, I cannot stay inert.[65]

Similarly, when another law firm B lawyer was explaining the procedures for taking and handling individual pro bono cases, he gave the following and telling example:

> My supervisor took on a pro bono case, and she was also writing a memo for a regular firm case. She was handling both cases at once. She then met the partner for our area and said, "I wanted to talk to you. I am running a little late with the pro bono case." The partner then asked, "Why are you late?" She said, "Because this new paid case came in and I am giving it priority." The partner responded, "But wait, isn't the pro bono client in jail? So that is the one you should be prioritizing. Finish the pro bono assignment first, and then get back to the paid case." And she finished the pro bono job on that same day. And, incredibly, we won, and the client was released two weeks later. But had she focused more on the other case, the client would be sitting in jail for another day.[66]

There is no evidence that this particular form of idealism observed among firm B lawyers translates into a more effective representation of their pro bono clients. But the professional identity it fosters – in which a more direct concern with liberty and justice, instead of a generic, if laudable, aspiration to "give back" – allows for new and promising forms of engagement. Hence, when the same law firm B lawyer quoted above was describing the work he and his peers do in the custody hearings project, he reported that they recently "had the initiative to set up a taskforce in the firm, to study and strategize." He explained:

> We work hard and put a lot of preparation into these hearings, but when we end up releasing one in eight, that is too little. So, once a month, after our work hours, we meet and discuss the outcomes of the cases we

> are handling and the pathways we can follow. Should we try to improve the arguments we are presenting these judges with? Or are we before more systemic illegalities and maybe we should reach out to one of the bar association's panels or other areas in the firm for support?[67]

CONCLUDING CONSIDERATIONS

This chapter has drawn from a long-term investigation of pro bono's institutionalization in São Paulo – the largest market for legal services in Brazil, where pro bono has developed in nonlinear and intriguing ways. The chapter responds to an important question in pro bono scholarship: "Why do law firms do pro bono?" The existing literature, which is by and large derived from studies of firms in the Anglo-American world, follows two explanatory tracks. Some argue that firms do pro bono because of the tangible benefits – financial or organizational – it generates. Others contend that firms do pro bono in response to their embedding environmental/institutional logics and based on distinctive organizational/cultural factors.

The data and analysis in this chapter both corroborate and modulate such arguments. I find that São Paulo firms came to do pro bono to enjoy some of the prestige and status that is afforded by their surrounding environment – one that has been increasingly populated by CSR practices, foreign law firms with well-institutionalized pro bono practices, and a global movement for the "rule of law." But it was also noticeable that, at some point, most firms expect that such prestige and status would be translated into tangible economic benefits as well. In other words, the response to an embedding institutional logic is mediated – and often times moderated – by the organizational rationality of firms.

While organizational rationality remains central in the structure of pro bono work in São Paulo law firms, what creates, maintains, and eventually expands space for pro bono in law firms beyond their technical "bottom line"? My research points to two factors: the social entrepreneurship and organizing role of IPB, and the work of idealist-firm lawyers. IPB – which at this point has become more than a traditional clearinghouse in the São Paulo pro bono industry – helps "lower the costs" of pro bono for firms. Idealist professional identities were crucial for firms to accept the challenge to provide individual pro bono services and commit to the custody hearings project in both firms I studied during research stage 2.

These findings have important implications to research and policy on lawyers, law firms, and access to justice. To begin with, they call for studies that pay greater heed to intermediaries such as IPB in the organization of pro bono work. In these studies, it might be particularly fruitful for scholars to incorporate concepts and tools from network theory – arguably the least explored theoretical strand in pro bono studies.[68] How do intermediaries help establish links between firms, legal aid agencies, and NGOs? In what ways do these links challenge law firm organizational rationality and "bring professional values" back into law firm practice? How does this all affect contestations over the meaning of pro bono within firms and, more generally, in the profession? Unfortunately, these are questions that have been neglected by scholars and rendered invisible by both the market control/commercialization critique and the organizational/institutional perspective.

Similarly, my findings highlight the role of idealist individuals in the processes by which the – once again, contested – meaning of pro bono is shaped within firms. Here – especially at a time when democracy and the "rule of law" in Brazil and many other countries are being undermined – a crucial question is, "How is idealism socially produced?" In one of the first attempts to better understand the causes of pro bono growth in the United States, Robert Granfield asked whether participation in mandatory pro bono programs in law school had an independent effect on the motivation of lawyers to participate in law firm pro bono.[69] He found no such effect. My research finds, indeed, that idealism is due to more complex processes, cutting across socioprofessional experiences and life histories. What are these? How can law schools, legal aid agencies, and other "communities of practice"[70] be more effective in nurturing and transmitting idealism, as we learn that this can have more systemic effects in the profession? These are questions that should continue to deserve the attention of scholars and policymakers.

Last but not least, my findings moderate, and to some extent contradict, Boutcher's argument about the effects of corporate clients and a "corporate logic of doing good" on law firm commitment to pro bono. Boutcher finds that firms do more pro bono due to the reputation and status that this generates in the "field" of elite corporate law practice.[71] My research demonstrates that firms are, indeed, responsive to this external "logic." But this logic constrains as much as it enables firms in their commitment to pro bono. São Paulo law firms may resist traveling the extra mile to offer individual pro bono services precisely because transactional legal work to NGOs meets the "corporate logic" of doing good, while the corporate world offers little incentive for these firms to support needy individuals. Quite the opposite, individual legal representation can raise issues inconvenient to both companies and firms, such as conflicts of interest and increased expenditures due to the complexity of litigation in the Brazilian legal system. The exception is the client domain that represents the agenda of "diversity" and identity politics, as captured in one of my interviews with some pro bono activists and identified (and denounced) by Nancy Fraser as a pillar of "progressive neoliberalism."[72] In other words, São Paulo tells us that not all chips must be put on the "corporate logic of doing good" when it comes to aspirations of equal justice for all.

NOTES

1. Fabio de Sa e Silva, *Doing Well and Doing Good in an Emerging Economy*, *in* THE BRAZILIAN LEGAL PROFESSION IN THE AGE OF GLOBALIZATION: THE RISE OF THE CORPORATE LEGAL SECTOR AND ITS IMPACT ON LAWYERS AND SOCIETY 210 (Luciana Gross Cunha, Daniela Monteiro Gabbay, José Garcez Ghiradi, David M. Trubek & David B. Wilkins eds., 2018) [hereinafter *Doing Well and Doing Good*]; Fabio de Sa e Silva, *"A Little More Complex": Commitment to Pro Bono Among São Paulo Corporate Law Firms*, INT'L J. LEGAL PROF. (forthcoming) [hereinafter *"A Little More Complex"*]; Oscar Vilhena Vieira, *Public Interest Law: A Brazilian Perspective*, 13 UCLA J. INT'L L. & FOREIGN AFF. 219 (2008); *see also* MARCOS FUCHS, EXPANDING ACCESS TO JUSTICE: THE INSTITUTO PRO BONO IN SÃO PAULO: A TACTICAL NOTEBOOK PUBLISHED BY THE NEW TACTICS PROJECT OF THE CENTER FOR VICTIMS OF TORTURE (2004) (*ebook*).
2. *See* de Sa e Silva, *Doing Well and Doing Good*, *supra* note 1; *see also* de Sa e Silva, *"A Little More Complex," supra* note 1.
3. Organizational rationality is herein understood in the Weberian sense of formal rationality, that is, a purposeful calculation of the most efficient means and procedures to realize goals. *See* MAX WEBER, ECONOMY AND SOCIETY: AN OUTLINE OF INTERPRETIVE SOCIOLOGY 85 (1978).
4. DEBORAH L. RHODE, PRO BONO IN PRINCIPLE AND IN PRACTICE: PUBLIC SERVICE AND THE PROFESSIONS (2005); Irma S. Russell, *The Lawyer as Public Citizen: Meeting the Pro Bono Challenge*, 72 UMKC L. REV. 439 (2004); Lucie E. White, *Pro Bono or Partnership? Rethinking Lawyers' Public Service Obligations for a New Millennium*, 50 J. LEGAL EDUC. 134 (2000).
5. Ronit Dinovitzer & Bryant G. Garth, *Pro Bono as an Elite Strategy in Early Lawyer Career*, *in* PRIVATE LAWYERS AND THE PUBLIC INTEREST: THE EVOLVING ROLE OF PRO BONO IN THE LEGAL

PROFESSION 115 (Robert Granfield & Lynn Mather eds., 2009); Robert Granfield, *The Meaning of Pro Bono: Institutional Variations in Professional Obligations Among Lawyers*, 41 LAW & SOC'Y REV. 113 (2007); Rebecca L. Sandefur, *Lawyers' Pro Bono Service and American-Style Civil Legal Assistance*, 41 LAW & SOC'Y REV. 79 (2007).

6. David B. Wilkins, *Doing Well by Doing Good? The Role of Public Service in the Careers of Black Corporate Lawyers*, 41 HOUS. L. REV. 1 (2004).
7. Dinovitzer & Garth, *supra* note 5.
8. Wilkins, *supra* note 6.
9. Granfield, *supra* note 5.
10. Scott L. Cummings, *The Politics of Pro Bono*, 52 UCLA L. REV. 1 (2004).
11. THE PRO BONO INSTITUTE, MAKING THE BUSINESS CASE FOR PRO BONO (2000).
12. *Id.*
13. Richard Abel, *The Paradoxes of Pro Bono*, 78 FORDHAM L. REV. 2443 (2010); Stephen Daniels & Joanne Martin, *Legal Services for the Poor: Access, Self-Interest, and Pro Bono*, *in* ACCESS TO JUSTICE: SOCIOLOGY OF CRIME, LAW AND DEVIANCE 145 (Rebecca L. Sandefur ed., 2009); Bryant Garth, A *Competition to Do Good: Big Firms Are Getting into Pro Bono for Business, Recruiting Reasons*, A.B.A. J., Oct. 1995, at 99; Deborah L. Rhode, *Rethinking the Public in Lawyers' Public Service: Pro Bono, Strategic Philanthropy, and the Bottom Line*, 77 FORDHAM L. REV. 1435 (2009).
14. Sandefur, *supra* note 5.
15. Steven A. Boutcher, *Private Law Firms in the Public Interest: The Organizational and Institutional Determinants of Pro Bono Participation, 1994–2005*, 42 LAW & SOC. INQUIRY 543 (2017).
16. *Id.*
17. de Sa e Silva, *Doing Well and Doing Good*, *supra* note 1; de Sa e Silva, *"A Little More Complex," supra* note 1; Arpita Gupta, *Pro Bono and the Corporate Legal Sector in India*, *in* THE INDIAN LEGAL PROFESSION IN THE AGE OF GLOBALIZATION: THE RISE OF THE CORPORATE LEGAL SECTOR AND ITS IMPACT ON LAWYERS AND SOCIETY 275 (David B. Wilkins, David M. Trubek & Vikramaditya Khanna eds., 2017); Arpita Gupta, Chapter 15 in this volume; Jin Dong & Qian Cheng, Chapter 17 in this volume.
18. Cummings, *supra* note 10.
19. *But see* Steven A. Boutcher, *Lawyering for Social Change: Pro Bono Publico, Cause Lawyering, and the Social Movement Society*, 18 MOBILIZATION: INT'L Q. 179 (2013); Cynthia Fuchs Epstein, *Issues Entrepreneurs: Charisma, Charisma-Producing Events, and the Shaping of Pro Bono Practice in Large Law Firms*, *in* PRIVATE LAWYERS AND THE PUBLIC INTEREST, *supra* note 5, at 211; Cynthia Fuchs Epstein, *Stricture and Structure: The Social and Cultural Context of Pro Bono Work in Wall Street Firms*, 70 FORDHAM L. REV. 1689 (2002).
20. Jan E. Trost, *Statistically Nonrepresentative Stratified Sampling: A Sampling Technique for Qualitative Studies*, 9 QUAL. SOC. 54 (1986).

21. In 2018, I was told by Instituto Pro Bono officials that they were working with a "firmer number" of fifteen corporate law firms and five General Counsel's offices. In methodological terms, this boosts the validity of my findings from 2011 to 2012. Not only did I capture pro bono institutionalization at corporate law firms at its peak, but I also took care to ensure the "representativeness" that is desired in qualitative research.
22. Yves Dezalay & Bryant G. Garth, Asian Legal Revivals: Lawyers in the Shadow of Empire (2010); Yves Dezalay & Bryant G. Garth, Global Prescriptions: The Production, Exportation, and Importation of a New Legal Orthodoxy (2002); Yves Dezalay & Bryant G. Garth, The Internationalization of Palace Wars: Lawyers, Economists, and the Contest to Transform Latin American States (2002).
23. The corporate law sector itself was reconfigured as a result of these changes. Back in the day, this was the province of "grand advocates" who built on family capital, part-time academic appointments, and connections with state politics to nurture clients and deliver services within small offices. Dezalay & Garth, The Internationalization of Palace Wars, *supra* note 22; Jayanth K. Krishnan, Vitor M. Dias & John E. Pence, *Legal Elites and the Shaping of Corporate Law Practice in Brazil: A Historical Study*, 41 Law & Soc. Inquiry 346 (2016). As of the 1990s, it began to feature organizational forms (big law firms and general counsel's offices) and styles of practice analogous to their US counterparts. *See generally* The Brazilian Legal Profession in the Age of Globalization, *supra* note 1.
24. Personal communication with the author during research stage 1.
25. *Id.*
26. *Id.*
27. Interview with a midsize law firm lawyer conducted during research stage 1, São Paulo (Aug. 2013).
28. Natalia Serrano, Julián Díaz & Daniel Bonilla Maldonado, *El Trabajo Jurídico Pro Bono en Brasil: Discurso, Prácticas y Límites 2005–2017*, 10 Revista Direito e Práxis 507 (2019).
29. Organizational rationality also affected the practices by which firms handle pro bono. While these firms initially took pro bono cases on an ad hoc basis – cases were brought by partners or through informal referrals and idiosyncratically distributed to lawyers – they adopted sophisticated policies and procedures for case selection, management, and monitoring. See details in de Sa e Silva, *Doing Well and Doing Good*, *supra* note 1. For similar developments in the United States, see Scott L. Cummings & Deborah L. Rhode, *Managing Pro Bono: Doing Well by Doing Better*, 78 Fordham L. Rev. 2357 (2010).
30. de Sa e Silva, *Doing Well and Doing Good*, *supra* note 1, at 221.
31. *Id.*
32. Luciana Gross Cunha, Daniela Monteiro Gabby, José Garcez Ghirardi, David M. Trubek & David B. Wilkins, *Globalization, Lawyers, and Emerging Economies: The Case of Brazil*, *in* The Brazilian Legal Profession

IN THE AGE OF GLOBALIZATION, *supra* note 1, at 1; Maria da Gloria Bonelli & Pedro Fortes, *The Transformation of the Brazilian Legal Profession: Fragmentary Development, Democratisation, and Globalisation of Lawyers in Brazil*, *in* LAWYERS IN 21ST CENTURY SOCIETIES: NATIONAL REPORTS (Richard L. Abel, Ole Hammerslev, Hilary Sommerlad & Ulrike Schultz eds., 2020); Daniela Monteiro Gabbay, Luciana Ramos & Ligia Pinto Sica, *Corporate Law Firms*, *in* THE BRAZILIAN LEGAL PROFESSION IN THE AGE OF GLOBALIZATION, *supra* note 1, at 33; David B. Wilkins, David M. Trubek & Bryon Fong, *Globalization, Lawyers, and Emerging Economies: The Rise, Transformation, and Significance of the New Corporate Legal Ecosystem in India, Brazil, and China* (HLS Center on the Legal Profession, Research Paper No. 2019-1, and Univ. of Wisconsin Legal Studies, Research Paper No. 1486, 2019), https://ssrn.com/abstract=3453908 (last visited Sept. 5, 2020).

33. de Sa e Silva, *Doing Well and Doing Good*, *supra* note 1.
34. *Id*. at 221
35. Serrano, Díaz & Bonilla Maldonado, *supra* note 28, at 508, originally in Spanish.
36. *Id*.
37. Interviews conducted during research stage 2, various officials, Instituto Pro Bono, São Paulo (Jan. 2018); de Sa e Silva, "A *Little More Complex*," *supra* note 1.
38. Interviews, Instituto Pro Bono, *supra* note 37.
39. *Id*.
40. *Id*. It should be noticed, however, that even the issues of "women victims of violence, refugees, LGBTQ+, and [sometimes] racial discrimination" can be problematic for firms operating in a context of growing intolerance, as is the case of Brazil under Jair Bolsonaro and many other markets for legal services undergoing far-right turns. It does take, therefore, some courage for firms to take this path, as the cost-benefit ration it involves is not – in fact, it is less and less – clearly positive.
41. Interviews conducted during research stage 2, São Paulo (Jan. 2018); de Sa e Silva, "A *Little More Complex*," *supra* note 1.
42. Interviews and observation conducted during research stage 2, São Paulo (Jan. 2018); de Sa e Silva, *Doing Well and Doing Good*, *supra* note 1.
43. de Sa e Silva, *Doing Well and Doing Good*, *supra* note 1, at 234–36.
44. *Id*.
45. Interviews conducted during research stage 2, Instituto Pro Bono (Jan. 2018).
46. *Id*.; *see also* de Sa e Silva, "A *Little More Complex*," *supra* note 1.
47. Interviews with firm A lawyers conducted during research stage 2 (Jan. 2018); *see also* de Sa e Silva, "A *Little More Complex*," *supra* note 1.
48. Interviews conducted during research stage 2; *see also* de Sa e Silva, "A *Little More Complex*," *supra* note 1.
49. *Id*.
50. Interviews conducted during research stage 2; *see also* de Sa e Silva, "A *Little More Complex*," *supra* note 1.

51. Interviews, *supra* note 50.
52. *Id.*
53. *Id.*
54. *Id.*
55. *Id.*
56. *Id.*
57. *Id.*
58. *Id.*
59. *Id.*
60. *Id.*
61. *Id.*
62. *Id.*
63. *Id.*
64. *Id.*
65. *Id.*
66. *Id.*
67. *Id.*
68. For a survey of theoretical perspectives in the study of law firms, see Alan James Kluegel, *The Firm As a Nexus of Organizational Theories: Sociological Perspectives on the Modern Law Firm*, 12 ANN. REV. L. & SOC. SCI. 459 (2016).
69. *Institutionalizing Public Service in Law School: Results on the Impact of Mandatory Pro Bono Programs*, 54 BUFF. L. REV. 1355 (2007); *see also* Deborah L. Rhode, *Cultures of Commitment: Pro Bono for Lawyers and Law Students*, 67 FORDHAM L. REV. 2415 (1999).
70. Lynn Mather, Craig A. McEwen & Richard J. Maiman, DIVORCE LAWYERS AT WORK: VARIETIES OF PROFESSIONALISM IN PRACTICE (2001).
71. Boutcher, *supra* note 15.
72. Nancy Fraser, *From Progressive Neoliberalism to Trump – and Beyond*, AM. AFF., Winter 2017, at 46, https://americanaffairsjournal.org/2017/11/progressive-neoliberalism-trump-beyond/ (last visited Sept. 5, 2020). Fraser conceptualizes progressive neoliberalism as a blend of a finance-centered political economy and a progressive politics of recognition. For debate about the accuracy of concept, see Johanna Brenner & Nancy Fraser, *What Is Progressive Neoliberalism?: A Debate*, 64 DISSENT 130 (2017).

CHAPTER FIVE

THE MANDARINS OF THE LAW: PRO BONO LEGAL WORK IN ARGENTINA, CHILE, AND COLOMBIA

Daniel Bonilla Maldonado

INTRODUCTION

In liberal democracies, lawyers have societal obligations that are directly connected to the right of access to justice. Access to justice provides citizens with the ability to turn to the judicial and administrative bodies of the state to enforce their rights.[1] The right of access to justice is multifaceted. It may include the ability to introduce and challenge evidence presented at trial, to have a translator when necessary to understand the trial proceedings,[2] and to have a lawyer represent one's interests before state judicial and administrative bodies.[3] Modern liberal democracies have developed four institutions to realize the state's and lawyers' obligations to the right of all members of the political community to access a lawyer: public defender's offices, court-appointed counsel, legal clinics, and pro bono work. These institutions aim to eliminate the access-to-justice deficit that exists in all modern liberal democracies to varying degrees. This chapter focuses on only one of these strategies: pro bono legal work. More precisely, this chapter seeks to describe and analyze the pro bono discourse and practices developed in Argentina, Colombia, and Chile. In the chapter, I offer the following five ideas related to this object of study.

* This is a revised and shorter version of a much longer article, published as *The Mandarins of Law: Pro Bono Legal Work from a Comparative Perspective*, 27 IND. J. GLOB. LEGAL STUD. 131 (2020).

First, I argue that the pro bono discourse and practices in Argentina, Chile, and Colombia are the result of a legal transplant between the legal elites of North and South America. The Argentine, Chilean, and Colombian legal elites import this set of practices and theories; the US legal elites export them.[4] Second, I argue that this legal transplant has not taken root in the private spheres of the importing liberal states, and that it has had minor impact on the realization of the right of access to justice.[5] Third, I argue that the importing and exporting legal elites exchange legal knowledge for reasons of principle, as legal elites seek to meet the social obligations that they have assumed, and for strategic reasons, as lawyers in both importing and exporting states seek to improve their reputation and consolidate their position in an increasingly global legal market. Regardless of their motivation, importers and exporters of pro bono knowledge put into place what is commonly known in comparative law as a functionalist methodology.[6] Fourth, I present and analyze why the legal transplantation of pro bono work has achieved what it has, as well as the local interpretations and variations of the transplant that we are beginning to witness. Finally, I argue that six main factors explain the lack of consolidation of a pro bono culture: the low degree of commitment to pro bono work among the legal elites that control the business structures that provide these kinds of legal services; the institutional and political weaknesses of the organizations that promote pro bono work; the assistentialism of pro bono policies; the characteristics of the legal market in the importing countries; the lack of a philanthropic culture in these political communities; and class and epistemological differences between the legal elites and pro bono clients that do not allow for the fluid and stable communication necessary to resolve pro bono cases successfully.

The chapter is divided into five sections in order to support and develop these ideas. In section 1, I examine the subjects that exchange legal knowledge and the legal knowledge that they exchange; in section 2, I examine the causes that explain this legal transplant. In section 3, I examine the connections and tensions between the legal transplant, pro bono clients, and the state. In this section I also explore the marginal local variations that the transplant has experienced. In section 4, I study the strength of the transplant. In the final part, section 5, I offer some very brief conclusions.

The comparative analysis presented in this chapter is informed by fieldwork done in Bogotá by the University of the Andes and Fordham University in 2013, and in Buenos Aires and Santiago by the Public

Interest Law Group (GDIP) of the University of the Andes in 2014. During fieldwork, research teams conducted 183 semistructured interviews with the staff of foundations that work on pro bono issues in Argentina, Chile, and Colombia, as well as with lawyers who work at the firms that created and are affiliated with these organizations. The analysis is also based on three online surveys that were sent to all of the firms affiliated with the pro bono foundations. These surveys aimed to collect quantitative information to complement the qualitative information collected during fieldwork. In the case of Chile, the analysis also uses statistical information published by the Chilean Pro Bono Foundation that covers the period between 2008 and 2013. The semistructured interviews and the online surveys concern the work done by the three organizations and their firms from the moment of their creation until 2013 and 2014, when Uniandes and Fordham did the fieldwork.

There were four reasons for selecting Argentina, Chile, and Colombia as case studies of this research project. On the one hand, although lawyers and social organizations have made efforts to institutionalize pro bono work in Latin America over the past three decades, there are currently no academic articles that describe and analyze this work in a precise and complete manner.[7] The relationships between the right of access to justice and pro bono work in this region have not been thoroughly studied.[8] Nor have the connections between social obligations of lawyers, liberal democracies in process of consolidation, and pro bono work been positioned as a valuable object of study in the local or international literature.

On the other hand, the processes aiming to promote pro bono work in Colombia, Argentina, and Chile were developed in the same time frame. Consequently, this variable remains stable and allows the analysis to focus on pro bono discourse and practices. The projects were started with the creation of the Chilean Pro Bono Foundation, the Argentine Public Interest and Pro Bono Work Commission, and the Colombian Pro Bono Foundation. The first two organizations started their work in 2000, while the third did so in 2006. To date, the three initiatives have developed their work continuously.

Thirdly, the pro bono processes of Argentina, Chile, and Colombia are the oldest in Spanish-speaking Latin America and are comparatively more consolidated.[9] The three pro bono foundations in these countries started with the goal of serving as a clearinghouse for pro bono work for the elite firms in Santiago, Buenos Aires, and Bogotá, as well as promoting pro bono work in their larger legal communities.[10] The three organizations created formal and informal channels of communication to share their positive and negative experiences. These experiences have been communicated with other countries through institutions like the International Pro Bono Network and the Cyrus Vance Center for International Justice in New York.[11] The processes and structures that these first pro bono organizations created to develop pro bono work became examples for initiatives seeking to create a pro bono culture in other countries in the region, such as the Dominican Republic, Perú, and México.

Finally, the legal and political systems of Argentina, Chile, and Colombia are analogous. The three countries are liberal democracies in the process of consolidation and have historically identified as part of the civil law tradition.[12] Chile and Argentina are still grappling with the effects of dictatorships on their democratic institutions, while Colombia confronts the consequences of fifty years of armed conflict. The states of the three countries are profoundly centralized, and they have a weak presence in some of their provinces, particularly in impoverished rural regions far from the political center.[13] The levels of inequality and poverty in these countries are also noteworthy. The Gini coefficient for Chile in 2014 was 0.50, for Argentina 0.41, and for Colombia 0.53.[14] In Chile, in 2011, 22.2 percent of the population was considered to be impoverished, and 0.5 percent in extreme poverty.[15] In Argentina, in 2011, the percentages were 11.6 and 1.4, respectively.[16] In Colombia, they were 32.7 and 5.6.[17] The three legal systems also share a notable lack of realization of the right of access to justice.[18] Indices showing levels of satisfaction of legal needs are low. In Colombia,[19] Argentina, and Chile, the gap between the normative discourse and the realization of the rights to access to justice remains worrisome.[20]

The legal systems of the three countries are based on the Romano-Germanic tradition.[21] Their style, tradition, and ideology, the three criteria traditionally used in comparative law to classify legal systems, support classifying them as part of the civil law family.[22] However, since the second half of the twentieth century, the three legal systems have been noticeably influenced by US legal theory, doctrine, and practices.[23] Many legal transplants have the United States as exporter and Colombia, Chile, and Argentina as importing countries, and they affect key aspects of their legal systems.[24] The transplant of the accusatory criminal system, neoclassical labor law, liberal theory of law, and liberal constitutionalism are four noteworthy examples. A fifth example, fundamental for this article, is pro bono work. Pro bono in Latin America has developed along discursive patterns and practices created by the US legal community, in particular, those of the large New York law firms affiliated with the Vance Center. The similarities in the legal and political context of Chile, Argentina, and Colombia allow for this analysis to focus on the pro bono discourse and practices.

THE TRANSPLANT OF PRO BONO WORK: THE SUBJECTS WHO TRANSPLANT AND THE KNOWLEDGE TRANSPLANTED

Pro bono legal work is a transplant in Argentina, Chile, and Colombia. The subjects who exchange pro bono legal knowledge in this case are clearly identifiable. In Argentina, Chile, and Colombia, the subjects who import are elite lawyers from Buenos Aires, Santiago, and Bogotá, as well as the organizations that these lawyers created to boost pro bono work in their legal communities: the Chilean Pro Bono Foundation, the Colombian Pro Bono Foundation, and the Argentine Public Interest and Pro Bono Work Commission.[25] In each country there are some lawyers who appear repeatedly when the circumstances in which pro bono work emerged and was developed are examined. These lawyers are not the only ones who have contributed to the process, but they are the ones who have come to symbolize it: in Argentina, Martín Zapiola; in Colombia, Paula Samper; and in Chile, Beatriz Corbo, Ciro Colombara, María Paz Garafulic, Pablo Guerrero, Juan Pablo Olmedo, and Francisco Orrego. These lawyers had a noteworthy presence in the creation of the three pro bono organizations and in exchanges with US legal mandarins.[26]

The number of lawyers who contribute to and put imported pro bono legal knowledge into practice has expanded significantly. Today, the Chilean Pro Bono Foundation has fifty affiliated firms,[27] the Colombian Pro Bono Foundation has thirty-one,[28] and the Commission has twenty.[29] These law firms belong to the legal elite of Bogotá, Santiago, and Buenos Aires, and their lawyers are the ones who take the pro bono cases distributed by the organizations. These firms contribute to the management of the foundations and pay an annual fee to support them.[30]

In the three countries, a few legal academics from private universities like University of Palermo, University of the Andes, and University

Adolfo Ibáñez contributed in the transplant process or in its consolidation. But their role is minor compared with the roles that the firms and the pro bono organizations have played in the creation and consolidation of pro bono work in their countries. In Argentina, academics like Martín Bohmer recognized the value of pro bono work, created a space to reflect on its implementation in the country, made the first contacts with the partners of elite US law firms who knew about the issue, and contributed to the management of the Commission.[31] In Chile and Colombia, academics like Verónica Undurraga[32] and Daniel Bonilla,[33] respectively, contributed to establishing or managing pro bono foundations, creating channels of communication between the organizations and legal academia, or championing the formal study of the subject in universities.

In the United States, the exporting subjects are the Cyrus Vance Center for International Justice and the law firms that are a part of it.[34] The Vance Center is a social organization that aims to promote pro bono work both in the United States and internationally.[35] Currently, twenty-one firms in New York are part of the board of directors of this organization.[36] All of these are elite law firms, some of which are the largest and most influential law offices in the world.[37] Firms like Debevoise & Plimpton, Sullivan & Cromwell, and Davis Polk & Wardell are part of the organization.[38] These firms have also been particularly active agents in the exchange of pro bono knowledge with Latin America.[39] Lawyers from these firms, along with Vance Center employees, promoted the drafting of the Pro Bono Declaration of the Americas;[40] organized or participated in seminars on pro bono in Latin America;[41] have managed the shipment, use, and application of its publications; and have maintained continual dialogue with the Latin American pro bono organizations.[42]

The subjects who promote the exchange of pro bono legal knowledge between Argentina, Chile, Colombia, and the United States are partners in elite law firms.[43] All are lawyers who are at the peak of their legal communities. All are lawyers solidly positioned in the legal market. The conceptual apparatus that supports pro bono legal work does not exclude independent lawyers. Nevertheless, this is a discourse that has been developed, disseminated, and implemented by legal elites organized in law firms with high economic and social capital. The state and the potential pro bono clients have also been outside the process that has allowed for the transplantation and implementation of pro bono knowledge. The states of Argentina, Chile, and Colombia have not had any presence in the process. No social organizations representing the interests of the population with few socioeconomic resources in these countries have participated in its development or establishment. The pro bono clients of these three countries receive the benefits of pro bono work. However, they have not been part of the processes that have allowed for its importation and implementation.

The pro bono legal knowledge that has been imported and exported is a set of practices collected in a literature formed by a set of primers and documents of diffusion of what we could call pro bono policies.[44] The knowledge that is exchanged has been acquired by elite US firms, particularly those based in New York, and collected in a series of documents published by the Vance Center.[45] These are not academic publications; these are not texts that profoundly examine pro bono work. Their aim is to describe and promote the standard pro bono practices of the large New York firms.[46] These texts cover the basic concept of pro bono work, the internal structures that the firms require to implement it, the virtuous practices that would have to be learned, and the negative experiences that would have to be avoided.[47]

Pro bono legal knowledge has also arrived in Latin America through formal and informal personal exchanges. The Latin American lawyers who have led the process of transplanting pro bono work have visited both the Vance Center (or its predecessor, the City Bar Justice Center) and the firms that form it numerous times.[48] The lawyers who led the transplant process in Chile did so before creating the pro bono foundation. Before starting the process in Santiago, they wanted to learn from the pro bono experiences of the large US law firms. Participating in a case before the Inter-American System of Human Rights allowed some of the leading Latin American pro bono lawyers to enter into contact with US pro bono work.

The Argentine lawyers interested in the issue invited the director of New York Lawyers for the Public Interest, Joan Vermeulen, to Buenos Aires at the end of the 1990s to meet with the law firms that might be interested in working on pro bono issues.[49] Shortly before this visit, Vermeulen became the founding director and executive director of the Vance Center (she held this last position for ten years). After its creation, the Commission and its directors met with the staff of the Vance Center on multiple occasions to discuss the ways they could promote and establish pro bono work in Argentina.[50] The Colombian lawyers who led the process from the beginning have met in both New York and Bogotá on multiple occasions with the staff of the

Vance Center or its firms.[51] Lawyers from the US firms linked to the Vance Center have participated in seminars and private meetings on pro bono work that have been organized by the Vance Center in association with the three Latin American pro bono organizations.[52] These private or public events have taken place in New York, as well as in Santiago, Bogotá, and Buenos Aires.

The enormous specialized literature that exists in the United States with respect to pro bono work has not circulated among the organizations that promote it in Argentina, Chile, and Colombia and the firms that form them. This literature is not mentioned by the lawyers involved in pro bono, does not appear cited in the publications of the organizations, and is not discussed by its members. Neither is this literature widely known in Latin American legal academia. Courses on professional ethics tend to move between two extremes: a formalist examination of the codes of professional ethics and an analysis of moral theory, for example, deontologism or utilitarism.[53] The theoretical and empirical study of the social responsibilities of lawyers in democracies in consolidation, such as the Latin American democracies, is at the margins of the legal academia of the region.

In Latin America, the literature on this issue in general, and on pro bono work in particular, is scarce.[54] To date, there is not a single book dedicated to examining pro bono work from an academic point of view or entering into dialogue with the literature produced in other countries. The organizations that promote pro bono work in Argentina, Chile, and Colombia have produced some documents promoting it or gathering quantitative information about the work that their firms do.[55] Nevertheless, the organizations do not have standardized patterns to collect, systematize, and analyze this information.[56] In consequence, the data they offer are not always reliable and precise. The organizations and their firms are not certain of the dynamics and characteristics of their pro bono work.[57]

The transplant of pro bono legal knowledge is evidenced in five fundamental aspects of the pro bono discourse and practices in Argentina, Chile, and Colombia. First, the concept of pro bono work internalized by the lawyers linked to the pro bono foundations of Colombia, Chile, and Argentina is the same one promoted by the Vance Center and endorsed by the firms that form it.[58] The empirical work shows an absolute homogenization of the legal consciousness of the Latin American lawyers interviewed on this matter. Documents like the PBDA Implementation Handbook: A Guide to Establishing a Pro Bono Program at Your Law Firm,[59] Statement of Pro Bono Principles[60] by the

Vance Center, the Pro Bono Declaration of the Americas,[61] Ways Offices Can Increase Their Pro Bono Contribution,[62] and the Guide for the Implementation of Pro Bono Programs in the Law Firms of Latin America,[63] published by the three Latin American organizations, state that pro bono work is a set of free legal services that lawyers voluntarily provide to people with few socioeconomic resources or to benefit the public interest.

In none of the 183 interviews conducted was the concept of pro bono work found to be outside of these parameters. Lawyers might refine some of its elements; for example, pro bono lawyers might require clients to pay for the costs of the legal or administrative proceedings, or argue that activities that law firms do, like philanthropy, should also be included in the concept of pro bono work. Nevertheless, these details were the exception and did not change the standard concept of pro bono work promoted by the Vance Center and disseminated by the Latin American pro bono organizations.

Second, the transplant of pro bono legal knowledge is evidenced in the internal structures that allow for its development within the firms.[64] Both the Latin American and New York law firms have a hierarchical pro bono structure that revolves around the following figures: the pro bono committee, the pro bono partner, and the pro bono coordinator. Pro bono committees establish the pro bono policies of the firm. They generally include lawyers that occupy a high position in the firm's hierarchy, such as partners and senior associates. The pro bono partner is in charge of leading the pro bono activities within the firm and managing the execution of pro bono policies. Finally, the pro bono coordinator is in charge of the daily administration of the firm's pro bono program. Usually, junior lawyers who are just starting their careers occupy this position. In Latin American law firms, the coordinator is the first point of contact between the firm and the pro bono organization, and this person is in charge of distributing information about the pro bono cases available and, in some cases, following up on their development. This structure is promoted explicitly by the literature published and disseminated in Latin America by the Vance Center.[65]

The third aspect where the transplant is evinced is the very existence of the pro bono organizations in Chile, Argentina, and Colombia. The three organizations perform functions analogous to those performed by the Vance Center. They are the institutions created by elite law firms to promote pro bono work in their communities.[66] The three Latin

American foundations and the US organization are also in charge of mediating between the supply of and demand for free legal services.[67] The Chilean, Colombian, and Argentine organizations function as clearinghouses.[68] Consequently, they are in charge of receiving potential pro bono cases, evaluating them, and, if applicable, accepting these cases to then distribute among the affiliated firms. The Vance Center promotes the creation of these kinds of institutions nationally and internationally, works with affiliated law firms on pro bono cases for international clients, and puts international clients in contact with law firms so they can take pro bono cases.[69]

Fourth, all the offices that participate in the three Latin American pro bono organizations have signed the Pro Bono Declaration of the Americas.[70] This Declaration was promoted by the Vance Center and drafted by a diverse group of five lawyers from the Americas.[71] The Declaration is a normative document that defines the concept of pro bono work, explains the reasons lawyers should do this kind of work, and articulates a series of principles that should guide it. This international document reproduces the concept, bases, and principles of the pro bono discourse promoted by the Vance Center[72] and accepted and disseminated by the foundations in Colombia, Chile, and Argentina.[73] The only concrete obligation that the signatories of the Declaration assume is 20 hours of pro bono work per lawyer per year.[74] The three Latin American organizations aim to comply with this obligation.[75] The lawyers who are committed to the management of the foundations or to the administration of the pro bono programs at their firms also have this figure as a goal.

THE CAUSES OF THE TRANSPLANT

The exchange of pro bono legal knowledge between the United States and Latin America is explained both by the functionalism implicit in the importing and exporting elites and by the geopolitics of legal knowledge. The transplant of pro bono work in Argentina, Chile, and Colombia puts in motion and illustrates the functionalist theory dominant in contemporary comparative law.[76] Functionalists think that transplants are the primary engine of legal change in the world.[77] This argument is explained by the fact that all political communities face similar problems and because the strategies they develop to solve them are not always analogous.[78] The most efficient way a political community can solve a problem is to learn from the successful experiences that other groups have had with the same challenge.[79] The importation and exportation of legal theories, practices, doctrines, or norms reduces the economic, political, and temporal costs that usually must be paid when seeking to create an original solution.[80]

Some of the most noted functionalists also argue that legal transplants are commonly managed by the political and economic elites of the countries involved.[81] In this sense, the possible tensions between the culture of the issuing country and the culture that the imported legal product intersects with are irrelevant.[82] The elites are not necessarily familiar with, interested in, or willing to prioritize "culture." They emphasize the technical character of the problem and its "universality."[83] Elites import legal knowledge for many other reasons, from their political legitimation[84] to the search for a merely symbolic efficacy of the law that allows them to elude the problem concerned without having to pay a cost to do so. Transplants may or may not take root in the receptor country. However, the cultural differences between the receptor country and the issuing country do not explain the failures in the operation of the transferred legal product.

The leaders of pro bono in Chile, Argentina, and Colombia all report that the initiatives were set in motion in a three-stage process. In the first stage, the leaders recognized the serious problems of access to justice, as well as the difficulties of consolidating rule of law, in their communities. In the three countries, the lawyers interviewed described socioeconomic inequalities, epistemological inequalities, and inequalities in the legal market as explaining the difficulties that people with few financial resources have in accessing a lawyer.[85] They consider these inequalities as completely unjustified. There are no reasons that can support the radical differences that exist between the legal mandarins (and other social elites) and the serfs of law.

In the second stage, pro bono leaders accepted the principle that lawyers have an obligation to contribute to solving these problems. The reasons for this obligation are the same in the three countries: the principle of solidarity and the virtue of charity.[86] Nevertheless, different countries emphasize different aspects of these reasons, which they also perceive as composed of slightly different content. In Chile, the religious argument was the only one commonly offered as creating the obligation to do pro bono work.[87] Lawyers affiliated with the pro bono foundation continually referenced their religious convictions to ground the work that the organization does. They connected their religious beliefs with pro bono legal work, as well as with other types of charitable work that they commonly do, such as participating on the boards of directors of social organizations, donating money to social projects, and performing volunteer work in community activities.

In the Argentine case, the most common argument among lawyers to explain the obligation to do pro bono work was the principle of solidarity.[88] Lawyers interpret this argument in a general manner as the obligation to help those who have less in society. However, this obligation is also based on the educational benefits that lawyers obtained from the political community, particularly if they studied law at a public university. Those interviewed continually mentioned the University of Buenos Aires, their alma mater, as the reason why they had to do pro bono work.[89] In their reasoning, lawyers like them had to "pay society back" through pro bono work for having received a free, high-quality university education.

In Colombia, lawyers offered an unusually diverse array of arguments as to the source of the obligation to do pro bono work.[90] The argument of solidarity was the most common, although the virtue of charity also appeared in the interviews. The principle of solidarity was generically linked to class and epistemological inequalities. Sometimes the lawyers referenced the high levels of poverty in the country, while other times they referred to the private university education they received. They also referred to the privileged socioeconomic position they occupy with their families and the legal knowledge that lawyers control in a monopolistic manner.

In the third stage, pro bono leaders decided to explore the solutions that other legal communities had given to the problem. Everyone involved in the process concentrated their research on the United States.[91] The Colombian and Chilean leaders concluded that the solution given to the problem by US lawyers associated with the Vance Center (or its predecessor or allied centers) was the best available. The Argentine lawyers who came from academia and participated in the creation of the pro bono process in their country thought that New York Lawyers for the Public Interest not only had useful experiences that they could learn from, but that the lawyers from Argentine firms could only be persuaded of the importance of pro bono work by a powerful external agent like this. The social capital of New York Lawyers for the Public Interest, because it was created and supported by large New York law firms, would provide leverage for mobilizing Argentine lawyers around pro bono work. However, the lawyers that belonged to law firms did not have this strategic view of New York Lawyers for the Public Interest or the Vance Center. The current staff of the Commission and the firms that do pro bono work today do not have it either. These pro bono operators interpret the work of the Vance Center and the New York law firms, from a normative point of view, as the best experience available in the market of legal ideas.[92]

The Chilean, Colombian, and Argentine legal mandarins all found a counterpart willing to export the pro bono legal knowledge and to support its consolidation in the receptor countries. One of the Vance Center's objectives is promoting pro bono work internationally.[93] It creates discourse on pro bono work as a product ready for exportation. The Vance Center begins with an assumption that all political communities have greater or lesser deficiencies with respect to the realization of the right of access to justice.[94] The Vance Center also assumes that US pro bono discourse and practices are of high quality and can be exported to solve problems of access to justice that trouble other political communities around the world.

Finally, the Vance Center assumes that lawyers have moral obligations to their political community.[95] The Center met in New York with Chilean and Colombian lawyers who were seeking pro bono legal knowledge to import. The Vance Center also sent its representatives to Argentina so that they could meet with the promoters of the pro bono initiative in the country and with the partners of elite law firms, who could give pro bono the boost it needed to get started. The Center has also maintained close contact with the three Latin American pro bono foundations.[96] This contact has translated into the exchange of literature, the organization of events for the promotion of pro bono work among the firms, support in seeking financing, and seminars aimed at incentivizing the participation of law schools in pro bono work.[97]

Now, it is important to state that legal elites did not solely appeal to reasons of principle to justify the importation and exportation of pro bono knowledge to Argentina, Colombia, and Chile, and from the United States. The partners of elite law firms of both regions of America also appeal to strategic reasons to justify the transplant and to contribute to its local consolidation. Today, pro bono discourse is a prestigious transnational discourse among global legal elites.[98] The firms that are not part of international pro bono networks and do not do pro bono in their countries are affected both in terms of their reputation and in the probability of their entering or expanding their presence in certain legal markets.[99] The law firms that do not adopt the discourse as their own, even formally, will see their commitment to the ideals of the profession questioned and will probably find obstacles in achieving the highest positions in the formal or informal hierarchies of the discipline.

In the United States, publications that rank law firms consider pro bono work as a variable in determining law firms' status.[100] The US legal community recognizes that these classifications have played an important role in the establishment of pro bono work in the country.[101] Occupying a low position or descending in these hierarchies has a negative impact on firms' reputations and, in the long term, can negatively affect their position in the market. In Latin America, there are no rankings of law firms that take this variable into account. In fact, there are no publications that have systematically and continuously ranked Latin American law firms. Nevertheless, journals like *Latin Lawyer*,[102] which is focused on the Latino legal market in the United States as well as the Latin American and European legal markets, continually discuss pro bono and law firms' achievements on the matter.[103] This kind of publication is attractive to the partners of elite law firms of Argentina, Chile, and Colombia. It is a valuable source of professional recognition. Likewise, for the highest legal mandarins of these three countries to remain outside of the pro bono network would imply remaining outside of one of the most select clubs of the profession; it would mean remaining outside of a source of prestige and local professional recognition.

Today's legal market also has global dimensions.[104] The large firms of the world, particularly US firms, have affiliates or work with allies in multiple countries.[105] Latin America is an attractive emerging market for the large firms of the United States.[106] Promoting pro bono in the region allows US firms to have a local presence and to be in touch with the most prestigious firms in countries like Argentina, Chile, and Colombia. For lawyers in these three countries, interacting with lawyers from some of the largest and most prominent law firms in the world is attractive. This is a source of professional recognition and opens a space for finding new legal business. When the New York lawyers visit Buenos Aires, Bogotá, or Santiago, the meetings on pro bono work become a relevant professional event.[107] A lot more lawyers attend these pro bono gatherings; a lot more partners do so as well. In contrast, at the routine meetings of pro bono organizations or national events for the promotion of this kind of work, fewer lawyers and far fewer partners participate.

Finally, importing and exporting pro bono knowledge, as well as putting it into practice in liberal democracies in the process of consolidation, counteracts the negative social image of lawyers.[108] It is widely known that lawyers are perceived negatively in countries such as the United States, Colombia, Argentina, and Chile. They are seen as dishonest, as individuals who do not really help resolve social conflicts but promote and amplify them for their own benefit, and as subjects who serve the interests of the most powerful in the socioeconomic hierarchy.[109] Doing pro bono work, importing it from a prestigious country like the United States, and exporting it toward democracies in the process of consolidation allows firms to project a positive social image in their communities. Thus, pro bono work is a way for law firms to recognize and realize their social obligations. It allows them to spread the idea that they have a commitment to the weakest members of society.

The geopolitics of legal knowledge is the second reason for the transplant of pro bono knowledge from the United States to Latin America.[110] This transplant, like the majority of transplants, travels in only one direction: North-South. Legal products migrate from the Global North, particularly the United States and Western Europe, toward the Global South, Latin America, Africa, and the greater part of Asia.[111] Colombia, Chile, and Argentina, like the rest of Latin America, have historically been classified as poor contexts for the production of legal knowledge.[112] The United States, in contrast, has been classified as a rich context for the creation of original legal products.[113] The Argentine, Chilean, and Colombian partners of elite law firms could have decided to create their own discourse and practices to provide free legal services to people with few resources in their countries. They could have opened spaces for discussion with universities, bar associations, and local social organizations. Instead, they decided to look toward the United States from the beginning of the process and to explore the legal products that US lawyers had created in the area.

Efficiency explains this attitude in part.[114] It is much less costly to import existing products that have proven their value in legal practice than to create new legal material that runs the risk of failing, or that would have to go through a long period of development and adjustment in order to meet its objectives appropriately. The market of legal ideas has a global and, it is assumed, multidirectional dimension.[115] The best legal products can and should be created in any part of the world and travel toward any part of the globe.[116] Nevertheless, the attitude of the importers and exporters of pro bono knowledge is also explained by the premises internalized by both Latin American lawyers and US lawyers regarding the geopolitics of legal knowledge. The prestige that the United States enjoys makes US lawyers and, in this case, Latin American lawyers, assume that US legal products are valuable and exportable. The United States is assumed to be a well of production of original legal knowledge,[117] its products are presumed to be of high quality,[118] and its operators are interpreted as capable of using them efficiently and ethically.[119] In contrast, Latin America is interpreted as a space of diffusion and reproduction of legal knowledge created in other latitudes, its legal products are assumed to be of low quality, and its operators inefficient and ethically naive or questionable.

PRO BONO CLIENTS, THE STATE, AND THE LOCAL VARIATIONS OF THE TRANSPLANT

The transplant of pro bono knowledge, as stated above, occurred between partners of elite law firms. It is important to make explicit that neither the state nor potential or actual pro bono clients have been part of the process of transferring this type of knowledge and putting it into practice. The absence of the state is understandable given the conceptual architecture that supports the pro bono discourse. The space of pro bono is the private sphere, and two groups of citizens that are connected through a moral obligation that is acquired autonomously are thought as its active and passive subjects. From the beginning, the state is not part of this conceptual frame. Involving it would mean questioning the premises of pro bono work. Making the state part of pro bono discourse and practices would also not necessarily help to consolidate it or make it more effective.

The absence of pro bono clients in the importation and realization of pro bono work in Argentina, Chile, and Colombia is also understandable if one appeals to its conceptual architecture. The partners of elite law firms control legal knowledge; they are the active subjects of the system and of pro bono knowledge. The clients, in contrast, are unfamiliar with legal practices, theories, doctrines, and norms; they are passive subjects of both the legal order and lawyers. The epistemological distance between one and the other is so wide that it is understandable, within the discourse, that lawyers do not ask clients what pro bono should be and how it should be put into operation. It is also unimaginable that clients would request a space to present their points of view on pro bono work. In Argentina, Chile, and Colombia, they have not been invited to do so. Nevertheless, there have been no reports that the clients, individually or collectively, have wanted to open a space within pro bono discourse and practices. The conceptual architecture of the institutionalized free legal services makes this undesirable. It is not within the horizon of perspectives that both lawyers and clients are immersed in.

Nevertheless, the absence of pro bono clients in pro bono's discourse and practice is problematic. In the narrative and in the legal consciousness of those who internalize pro bono discourse, the clients are understood as mere passive receptors of a practice that has a sizable impact on their finances, liberty, and individual and collective stability. Pro bono work therefore runs the risk of making the same mistakes made by the free legal services that have historically been provided in the region.[120] Pro bono work is a type of legal service that is not differentiated in its objectives from the services provided by legal clinics, some social organizations, and public defender's offices. These institutions have been questioned because they marginalize clients from the articulation of the problem and from the means of solving it.[121] The lawyer determines the concept and the means for providing the free legal services, and how the problem that the client faces is defined and solved.[122]

Lawyers from the elite Chilean, Colombian, and Argentine law firms may have difficulties establishing a dialogue with the clients or the organizations that represent them about the way pro bono discourse should be developed and implemented. Law firms do not have the time or the knowledge on participative processes to do so. Nevertheless, it is not clear why the pro bono foundations could not advance this dialogue. Their mission is precisely to promote and establish free legal services. It would seem that, to reach these objectives, it would be critical to establish channels of communication with the people their work is directed at. Although it cannot be demanded of lawyers from firms that they create a process to construct pro bono discourse in a participative manner, it could be demanded that they create a more horizontal relationship with their clients, for example, allowing clients to have a more active role in the definition and solution of their cases.

However, to finalize this section, it is useful to indicate that the transplant of pro bono knowledge still has not undergone variations or interpretations that distinguish it from the original US product. The Chilean, Argentine, and Colombian pro bono discourse and practices still reflect the US model precisely. The standard pro bono concept, structure, and practices have not been adjusted to make them suitable for local contexts, make them more effective, or transform them into a new institution. The only practice that departs from the conceptual architecture of pro bono work and the way it is put into practice in the United States is the Chilean Pro Bono Foundation's practice of making ties with a significant number of independent lawyers.[123] In 2014, the organization had 250 individual lawyers among its affiliates.

This practice sensibly adjusts US practice to account for differences in the legal markets: the Chilean legal market in particular and the Latin American legal market in general are still dominated by lawyers who work independently, in association with a small group of colleagues, or as employees of the state.[124] These associations, however, are not constituted as corporate entities like the law firms. Lawyers do not create an independent legal entity, but they agree to share a space and the basic expenses required for their professional activity. This practice of the Chilean foundation demonstrates the way the transplant can be adapted to the local context, and how these adaptations can transform part of the conceptual architecture that supports pro bono work.

The discourse on the matter could then cease to revolve solely around elite firms. This would allow for including a greater number of lawyers and questioning the idea that only the large law firms can provide free legal services in a permanent and formalized manner. Nevertheless, this change is only just beginning. Independent lawyers, as mentioned above, are at the margins of the Pro Bono Foundation of Chile and of the pro bono work that is done in the country. Independent lawyers are not part of the administrative bodies that guide the organization's policies and direct it. The transplant's lack of stability can be explained by the relatively short time it has been in operation, and because it still has not managed to take root and consolidate in the importing legal communities, as will be seen in the next section.

THE SOLIDITY OF THE LEGAL TRANSPLANT

The pro bono organizations of Argentina, Colombia, and Chile have made valuable advancements in the difficult process of creating a pro bono culture in their legal communities. They have created three organizations that aim to promote and institutionalize pro bono work. The sustained existence of the three foundations is an important achievement. The Chilean and Argentine foundations have existed for fifteen years,[125] while the Colombian foundation has existed for six years.[126] The foundations have committed staffs that have invested significant amounts of time and energy in the promotion of pro bono work. The fieldwork shows that the firms' evaluation of the work that these organizations do is very positive. In particular, the firms find that the foundations have been especially effective in their work as mediators of the supply and demand of free legal services. The organizations have managed to create solid standards for the reception, admission, and distribution of pro bono cases.

The three organizations generally receive their cases from two sources: an internet platform that any potential client can access, and agreements with social organizations that work with people with few socioeconomic resources.[127] The three organizations evaluate potential pro bono cases using two criteria: one economic, and the other related to the public interest.[128] In the first factor, the organizations make sure that the potential pro bono clients actually belong to a low socioeconomic stratum and therefore cannot hire a lawyer.[129]

In the second factor, they determine if the claim serves the public interest, even if the person requesting the service has the financial resources to pay for a lawyer.[130] These criteria are basically used to determine if a social organization serves people with few financial resources or the public interest as its mission. Theoretically, the criteria may also be used to evaluate cases that aim to contribute to the solution of a structural social problem through tools like strategic litigation or lobbying. Nevertheless, the firms affiliated with the three pro bono organizations have taken very few public interest cases.[131] Furthermore, those they have taken have not always arrived through the foundations. Once the cases are admitted by the organizations, they are sent to all affiliated firms weekly via email.

The three initiatives have also managed to make pro bono discourse known among the elite firms of Bogotá, Santiago, and Buenos Aires. All the lawyers interviewed knew of the existence of an area of professional practice named with the words "pro bono."[132] Much more importantly, all of the lawyers interviewed had internalized the concept of pro bono work promoted by the foundations.[133] The diffusion advanced by the three organizations has managed to homogenize the legal consciousness of the lawyers who work for the affiliated law firms. All lawyers indicate that pro bono work is the set of free legal services that lawyers voluntarily provide at no charge to people with few financial resources or in defense of the public interest. This is not a minor achievement. Before the creation of the three organizations, the words "pro bono" were not part of the vocabulary of Chilean, Argentine, and Colombian lawyers. This discourse has also started to permeate universities and some sectors of independent lawyers. The organizations have developed activities of dissemination with universities like the University of Rosario and University of the Andes in Colombia; the University of Palermo and University of San Andrés in Argentina; and the University of Chile.[134]

The diffusion of pro bono discourse has also managed to get a significant number of the affiliated firms to agree to create structures for the administration of pro bono work.[135] The majority of offices have incorporated some variant of the tripartite structure recommended by the foundations to administer pro bono programs, creating a pro bono committee, pro bono partner, and pro bono coordinator. The size and commitment of the firms determines which have all three levels of the structure, which have a partner who is also the coordinator, and which have only the position of coordinator. The creation of these structures, without taking their efficiency into account, is a valuable step forward for the future consolidation of pro bono work in Argentina, Chile, and Colombia. The institutional frames that would allow for efficiently advancing pro bono work already exist in many of the firms formally committed to the discourse supporting it.

Finally, the firms affiliated with the pro bono organizations have taken a low number of cases annually.[136] For the clients served, the advice or representation of a competent lawyer like the ones who work at the affiliated firms is important. Without the support of a foundation and its firms, these people would probably not have access to any lawyer. Without the pro bono work of these professionals, they would not be able to defend their interests and rights. The interviews show that the feedback that the organizations and lawyers receive from their clients is positive. Nevertheless, it is important to note that none of the organizations have stable and efficient procedures to follow up on the cases and to evaluate the quality and effectiveness of the service they provide.[137] In this sense, it is not known with certainty what effects the cases have and how the clients evaluate the service received.

However, in spite of these noteworthy advances, the transplant of pro bono legal knowledge still has not managed to take root in the Colombian, Chilean, and Argentine legal communities.[138] The conceptual architecture that supports pro bono discourse and practices links lawyers and clients based on a moral obligation that the mandarins assume autonomously. This obligation aims to contribute to protecting the clients' rights and achieving their full inclusion in the political community. This conceptual architecture also imagines that the social and epistemological inequalities that create the obligation can gradually be corrected in a liberal state. The time of the discourse is linear, and it is imagined with an end. The discourse is committed to the idea of progress of the political community. The state, primordially, has the obligation to correct these inequalities. Nevertheless, according to the discourse, lawyers have the obligation to contribute to their elimination through pro bono legal work. With this objective in mind, the partners of elite law firms of Argentina, Chile, and Colombia imported pro bono legal knowledge from the United States. In consequence, the consolidation of pro bono work must be measured not only in terms of its taking root in the local legal culture; it should also be measured in terms of the actual impact on the realization of the right of access to justice, and therefore the elevation of levels of social justice in the political community.

When evaluating pro bono work in Chile, Argentina, and Colombia in light of these two criteria, we should conclude that it still has not managed to become firmly institutionalized in the law firms that imported it or promote it today, and that the impact that pro bono has had on the right of access to justice is minor.[139] The objectives pursued via its exportation and importation have not managed to materialize to a sufficient degree. The initiatives have not succeeded in creating a pro bono culture within the firms. The pro bono work that is done in Argentina, Chile, and Colombia still has not developed a set of clear, precise, and efficient policies to guide its implementation in law firms. The pro bono structures that firms have are also not efficient enough. In many of the firms, the formal structures do not advance the continuous and systematic tasks necessary to promote and administer law firms' pro bono work. Pro bono work remains on the margins of daily life for the law firms linked to the pro bono foundations. It still has not taken root in the business structures of Chilean, Colombian, and Argentine law firms.

Likewise, the number of pro bono cases taken by Chilean, Argentine, and Colombian firms is notably low, and the impact of the cases on the satisfaction of legal needs is therefore minor. During the fifteen years of existence of the Chilean and Argentine foundations and the six years of existence of the Colombian one, the firms worked on an average of 344 cases annually.[140] The lawyers who work for the law firms have also not managed to meet the objective of 20 hours per year per lawyer recommended by the Pro Bono Declaration of the Americas, the international document signed by the great majority of law firms that work with these three organizations.[141] These numbers are particularly telling if we contrast them with the economic, political, and legal power that these firms gather.[142] Many of the lawyers who direct the firms also have political power or access to those who do. Due to their class status, or for professional reasons, they have channels of communication with the financial and political leaders of their countries. Likewise, the legal knowledge and experience their lawyers bring together are extraordinary. Many of the best lawyers from Argentina, Colombia, and Chile work in these law firms.

The reasons that the process of consolidation of the transplant of pro bono knowledge has not been effective are various and diverse in nature. The first and most important is a lack of commitment to pro bono work from the partners of elite law firms who control the business structures that provide this kind of legal service.[143] This lack of commitment has particularly serious effects for the consolidation of pro bono work given the hierarchical structure that law firms have. Associate and junior lawyers cannot do anything other than what their superiors instruct them to do. The discretion lower-level attorneys enjoy to choose the tasks that they must advance within the office is notably little.

The fieldwork shows that partners, on average, are formally committed to pro bono discourse. Nevertheless, this formal commitment does not materialize in decisions that allow for its effective implementation within law firms. In particular, partners have not made the decision that would have the greatest impact on the quantity and quality of pro bono work that is done in their firms: equating billable hours with pro bono hours. The firms typically establish some goals for billable hours that all lawyers must meet on a monthly basis. The number of hours varies depending on the firm. Nevertheless, it is usually in the range of 140 to 170 hours a month, or between 1,600 and 2,000 hours a year.[144] This is a sizable number for any individual. Complying with it requires a high investment of time and energy.

Meeting these goals has significant economic and professional effects for lawyers. Satisfying these objectives determines promotions, bonuses, and sometimes salaries. As a consequence, if assuming that pro bono is a type of work that should be done after completing the pro lucro hours established by the firms, it becomes improbable that pro bono will be able to take root within law firms' structures. The material conditions that the law firms establish make pro bono work very difficult to realize. In the best of cases, some Chilean, Argentine, and Colombian firms use pro bono work as an auxiliary criterion in the annual evaluations that determine issues like bonuses or promotions.[145]

These working conditions also create an unfair distribution of burdens and benefits. The lawyers are the ones who have the obligation to do pro bono work in their "free time." Nevertheless, the firms are the only ones who receive the global credit for the pro bono work that their lawyers do. The offices increase their levels of social recognition, enter into contact with the international networks of lawyers that promote pro bono work, and have the possibility of getting new clients with the promotion of the pro bono work that their lawyers do. The only strategies that the Argentine, Chilean, and Colombian firms have developed to incentivize pro bono work are soft strategies like diplomas and honors, trips, and dinners.[146] The lawyers who do pro bono, in consequence, get only the possibility of satisfying moral obligations and receiving minor recognition for their work.

The lack of an effective commitment to pro bono work by the highest mandarins is not only manifested in formal issues like official policies and incentives. It is also expressed in informal attitudes and practices. On average, partners take very few pro bono cases and participate little in internal or external activities related to the administration or promotion of pro bono work. The informal practices that the partners assume on issues like pro bono are fundamental for their consolidation. If the low-level and midlevel lawyers see that partners do not take pro bono work seriously, they will not do so either. For example, when it is clear that the partners participate in pro bono meetings or seminars only when lawyers from New York firms linked to the Vance Center attend, the associates and junior lawyers interpret that the value of this type of work within the firm is not big.[147] If partners do not take pro bono cases regularly, the associates and junior lawyers will not feel the need to do so either. If partners indicate or argue that junior lawyers should accept the majority of pro bono cases, the lowest in the hierarchy, they are sending the message to their organizational structures that this type of work is not very relevant in the life of the law firm.

The fact that partners have not articulated formal incentives and, in practice, promote informal disincentives with respect to pro bono work is reflected in the following facts: It is telling that the empirical work shows that those who do more pro bono work within the firms are the junior lawyers and pro bono partners.[148] The fieldwork consistently showed that the former, on average, have a genuine interest in pro bono. There are still some elements in their legal consciousness that link law to social justice. They are also starting their professional career, and their levels of consumption are minor in comparison with the other lawyers from the firms. The latter have a large degree of autonomy within the firms, financial stability, and an old or new interest in social justice.

In contrast, the lawyers that, on average, do less pro bono work in Chile, Argentina, and Colombia are the associate lawyers.[149] They are typically in a particular moment of their personal and professional lives. They have greater financial burdens, usually due to family issues, and they are in a decisive moment for their rise within the hierarchy of the firm. Pro bono work is at the margins of the professional life of the midlevel mandarins inasmuch as it does not play any role in achieving their legitimate objectives of professional ascent and financial stability. The absence of "hard" incentives for doing pro bono work within the firms means that associate lawyers are not interested in this kind of work. It also means that the junior lawyers are the perfect "victims" of pro bono work: they are willing to do it, and they are at the bottom of the hierarchy and thus cannot refuse it when it is assigned to them formally or informally. Similarly, this pattern makes it possible for pro bono partners to be the ones who put pro bono discourse into practice. For them, formal incentives are irrelevant given their professional and financial position, and the informal disincentives created by other partners do not affect them personally.

The partners' lack of commitment to pro bono work is also connected to the gender inequalities that exist within their firms.[150] Gender inequalities in law firms are reproduced in pro bono work. In countries like Chile, Colombia, and Argentina, few women occupy positions of power within law firms.[151] The number of female partners is notably less than the number of male partners. In the case of pro bono work, this hierarchy is reproduced in a very visible manner: while the great majority of pro bono partners, the members of pro bono committees, and the board of directors of the foundations are men, the pro bono coordinators and the staffs of the foundations are women.[152]

In Argentina and Chile, for example, 90 percent and 66.66 percent, respectively, of the coordinators are women.[153] The staffs of the

Colombian Pro Bono Foundation and the Argentine Pro Bono Work Commission are formed only by women; in the case of Colombia, two female lawyers;[154] and in the case of Argentina, a female lawyer and a female communications associate.[155] In Chile, seven of the eight members of the staff are women.[156] This "feminization" of pro bono work is explained by the idea, structural in a patriarchal society, that women should ideally occupy the private sphere, are naturally inclined to do social work, and when it is inevitable that they work, they should occupy themselves with "soft" tasks like those related to solidarity or charity.[157] The problem, of course, is not in the women who do pro bono work within and outside law firms in a committed and serious manner. Without the work that these women have done in the pro bono foundations, it is not likely that the things mentioned above would have been achieved. The problem is in a structure that hierarchizes pro lucro work as "serious" and pro bono work as "weak," and that links the former with men and the latter with women.

The second reason for the fragility of the legal transplant are the institutional and political weaknesses of the foundations that promote pro bono work in Argentina, Colombia, and Chile.[158] The creation of the organizations, as mentioned above, was an important step in furthering the process of consolidation of pro bono work. The organizations' staffs are also serious and committed. However, two of them, the Colombian Pro Bono Foundation and the Argentine Pro Bono Work Commission, do not have the financial and human resources necessary to effectively advance their work. The annual budget of the former is approximately $100,000, and that of the latter is approximately $32,000.

In Colombia, the money available covers the salaries of two young lawyers and a secretary. The lawyers have to do all kinds of tasks: from answering the phones, maintaining and administering the internet platform, coordinating interns, and organizing fundraising events, to organizing meetings with social organizations, universities, and firms, and writing and processing proposals to get international funding. The salary that they earn is also low, and there are no alternatives within the organization for them to grow professionally. Nevertheless, the organization has a (leased) headquarters, and the law firms pay the annual fees they have committed to the foundation with regularity.

In Argentina, the lawyer and the communications associate work part-time for the Commission, earn a low salary, have an almost nonexistent budget, and do not have their own office; the headquarters of the organization is in the Bar Association of the City of Buenos Aires, a private organization. However, the law firms pay their pro bono fees to the foundation regularly. The case of the Chilean Pro Bono Foundation, in contrast, is different. In 2013, its annual budget was a little more than $340,000; it has a staff of eight people; it has its own headquarters on lease; and it has a reasonable expense budget.[159]

Nevertheless, the three organizations have a profoundly vertical relationship with the firms that form and finance them. Their autonomy is very low, and the political capital they have with respect to the firms is minimal. The staffs of the pro bono organizations, while appreciated, are typically perceived and treated as low-level employees at the service of the firms. In this sense, the capacity they have to decide autonomously on the paths to take within the policies articulated by the firms through the boards of directors is quite reduced, and their capacity for negotiation with law firms is minimal. The staffs of the foundations are immersed in a situation they cannot easily escape: the firms consider these foundations to be their organizations, but also require results from them that would depend in part on their autonomy. Law firms demand significant results and that their levels of efficacy be increased, but they do not contribute with the financial resources necessary for this to happen, or they do not assume the number of pro bono cases that would be necessary to have the impact they would like to have in the political community.

The third reason for the fragility of the legal transplant is the assistentialist character of the legal services they provide to people with few financial resources.[160] The strategy assumed to confront the problems of access to justice by the pro bono foundations of Chile, Argentina, and Colombia is not notably different from the strategies developed and implemented at the end of the 1960s and beginning of the 1970s by governments, universities, and social organizations.[161] This model, which had a notable impact in Chile and Colombia, was also a transplant imported from the United States.[162] The US government, through its international development agency and with the support of organizations like the Ford Foundation, exported institutions like legal clinics and promoted the creation or strengthening of institutions like public defender's offices and legal social organizations to protect the right of access to justice.[163]

The Latin American countries that imported these legal products were persuaded by the arguments offered by the law and development movement to justify them.[164] The key premise of this intellectual movement's line of argumentation was that there was a directly proportional relationship between economic development and social justice, on the one hand, and liberal law, on the other.[165] Economic development in Latin America had stagnated, and its levels of social justice were not desirable, it was argued, because its legal systems were formalist and exclusive.[166] Consequently, the dominant legal consciousness in the region had to be transformed, along with the practices it created. For example, law schools needed to change their pedagogical methods in favor of the study of case law and the Socratic method common in US legal academia.[167] Likewise, their legal systems needed to be much more inclusive and thus create institutions like legal clinics to allow people with few financial resources to be able to access justice.

The justification for the legal services that were developed and implemented during the 1970s in Latin America is different from that of the pro bono legal services of the twentieth century. Pro bono work does not appeal to developmentalist arguments as justification. Nevertheless, the strategies that both use to attack the same problem, the lack of access to justice among people with few economic resources, are the same. The two models revolve around free legal services that focus on individual cases and do not offer any participation to the clients in the conceptualization or development of these services or in the articulation or implementation of the cases they are involved in. It is true that the model of the 1970s emphasized litigation,[168] while the model of the new century emphasizes advising.[169] Nevertheless, the difference is not one of principle; practical issues motivate it. Lawyers from elite firms do not generally accept cases that involve litigation. They would have to invest too much time and energy, and the justice system is very slow. In a country like Chile, these are the kinds of cases that the independent lawyers affiliated with the pro bono foundation would take.

However, the kinds of cases that the two models usually accept are the same. The empirical work shows that the pro bono cases are the same as those that the specialized literature indicates as the typical cases of the legal services based on the law and development movement.[170] In the two models, the cases address minor criminal, civil, family, and labor issues that an individual or a small group of individuals is involved in. This form of conceiving and materializing free legal services was severely and repeatedly criticized in the 1980s.[171] Some of the most well-known leaders of the law and development movement argued, repentantly, that it was unlikely that the lives of people with few financial resources would be positively and effectively affected through these legal actions.[172] If the source of the problem is not attacked, they argued, individual problems will keep emerging and will do so indefinitely; if the clients' opinions of the services provided are not kept in mind, one runs the risk of developing paternalistic legal services that do not take the true interests of the people and communities involved into account.

The pro bono initiatives of Chile, Argentina, and Colombia have asserted the need to take public interest cases, those in which a structural social problem can be confronted through law. Nevertheless, the empirical work shows that the number of public interest projects that have actually been taken is very low. Lawyers from the three countries repeatedly mention the same cases to illustrate the collective interest work that their firms or organizations do: in Argentina, the elimination of all barriers in public and private schools in Buenos Aires that obstruct children with disabilities to move freely, and the right that all citizens have to access the federal senate's employee census as well as the budget used to pay the salaries of these employees; in Colombia, the Islote Case, where the rights to health and a healthy environment of an Afrocolombian community in the Caribbean coast of Colombia were protected; and in Chile, *The Last Temptation of Christ* Case, where freedom of speech, freedom of religion, and freedom of conscience were protected against the Chilean state attempts to censor this movie.[173] Even so, the interviews show that lawyers from the three countries want to take more projects of this type. In fact, they repeatedly question their foundations for not finding and distributing more public interest cases. However, this ambition enters into conflict with the common characteristics of these types of projects: given their complexity, lawyers must invest more time and energy than what they must employ in an individual pro bono case; given their polemic and high-profile character, they may create conflicts of interest with their pro lucro clients or with the state.

Public interest cases usually have multiple legal and political dimensions, can only be resolved in the medium or long term, and are technically and administratively challenging for those who work on them. If the pro bono lawyers of Argentina, Chile, and Colombia have difficulties finding the time that would allow them to take a simple pro bono case, they would have much more difficulty finding the time necessary to work on a structural case. These projects are also usually morally and politically polarizing, and can therefore create a social debate that the firms do not want to be involved in. Likewise, these cases may easily come up against the economic interests of the firms' regular clients, or they may lead to questioning the relations that many of the elite law firms have with the governments of their countries.[174]

In Argentina, a significant part of the pro bono work that is done is presented as for the public interest.[175] However, the cases that are catalogued in this way both by the Commission and by its firms are those in which corporate-type advising is done for social organizations, such as being incorporated, changing organizational rules and principles, or registering a brand or patent. The argument used to qualify this type of pro bono work as public interest is the supposed multiplier effect of the work that social organizations do. Nevertheless, neither the Commission nor the firms have criteria to determine which organizations actually create these broader virtuous cycles. In practice, this type of work is done because the needs of the social organizations can be satisfied with the corporate knowledge and practices common in law firms. Also, some of this work is done for the foundations created by pro lucro clients. These are the organizations through which the firms' regular clients materialize their corporate social responsibility. This type of work is undoubtedly valuable for social organizations. However, it could hardly be said that the law firms are contributing to solving a structural social problem with this work.

The fourth reason has to do with the characteristics of the legal market in the importing countries. In Argentina, Chile, and Colombia, there are no external incentives for the firms to commit to pro bono work.[176] The empirical research shows that this kind of work is still not relevant as it is in the United States, for example, for recruiting new talent, keeping the talent that firms have already hired, or getting new clients.[177] As long as pro bono work is marginal in their legal communities, recent graduates will not use it to determine where they want to work, and associate or junior lawyers will not use it as a criterion to decide if they want to remain at a firm or switch to another. Potential national or foreign clients only rarely ask about the pro bono work of the firms to determine which firm they want to hire. Finally, there are no mass media monitoring and evaluating the pro bono work that the firms do, and there are no rankings of Latin American firms that take pro bono work into account as one of their criteria.

These characteristics of the Latin American legal market have determined that the firms do not use pro bono work as a marketing strategy.[178] Most law firms include information about their pro bono work on their websites or institutional brochures. However, it is not a tool that they continuously and systematically use to open new markets. It is still not considered to be an effective instrument for the materialization of their business mission. However, this is not the only reason why they do not steadily advertise their pro bono work. The firms also argue that they do not do so because lawyers should not benefit from fulfilling their moral obligations.[179] In this manner, an ethical moral argument, possibly of direct or indirect religious origin, limits the use of pro bono work as a tool of promotion of the law firms in Chile, Argentina, and Colombia.

The fifth reason is the lack of a philanthropic culture in these three political communities.[180] In Latin America, it is not common for individuals to donate their time or financial resources to charitable institutions or activities. Pro bono work therefore does not have a cultural context that can be adhered to or that can serve as support for entering into lawyers' consciousness. Most Colombian, Chilean, and Argentine jurists, like most of the citizens of these countries, do not have volunteer activities on their moral radar.

The sixth and last reason are the class and epistemological differences between the legal mandarins and serfs of law that do not allow for the fluid and stable communication that is necessary to bring pro bono cases to a good end.[181] The empirical work shows clearly and precisely that it is difficult for lawyers from elite firms to initiate fruitful dialogues with their pro bono clients, and vice versa. Class markers are an obstacle to the creation of these channels of communication. Pro bono clients feel uncomfortable in the neighborhoods where the firms are located, as well as in their offices. The kinds of language used by one and the other are also different. The criteria to determine what is relevant or the best paths to follow to resolve the conflict are not similar. As a consequence, it is difficult to plan the cases, implement these plans, and create the levels of confidence necessary for the cases to be successfully advanced.

CONCLUSIONS

Pro bono work is a legal transplant in Argentina, Chile, and Colombia. In spite of some valuable achievements, this legal product has still not taken root in the importing legal communities. In Argentina, Chile, and Colombia, there is still not a culture of pro bono work; there are no solid structures and policies within the law firms that promote this kind of work, and the impact it has had on the right of access to justice is minor. Time will tell if this transplant manages to take root in the local legal cultures. Hopefully it will: pro bono work is one of the instruments through which lawyers realize their social obligations. It is a tool that may be useful in democracies in the process of consolidation both to realize the rights of people with few financial resources and to achieve their full political inclusion.

NOTES

1. *See* MAURO CAPPELLETTI & BRYANT G. GARTH, EL ACCESO A LA JUSTICIA: LA TENDENCIA EN EL MOVIMIENTO MUNDIAL PARA HACER EFECTIVOS LOS DERECHOS 12–13 (1996).
2. *See, e.g.*, Corte Constitucional [C.C.] [Constitutional Court], Septiembre 9, 1998, M.P: Fabio Morón Diaz, Sentencia T-476/98 (Colom.) and Corte Constitucional [C.C.] [Constitutional Court], Noviembre 17, 2005, M.P: Jaime Cordoba Triviño, Sentencia C-1177/05 (Colom.).
3. *See, e.g.*, G.A. Res. 217 (III) A (Dec. 10, 1948) and the International Covenant on Civil and Political Rights art. 14, Dec. 19, 1966, 999 U.N.T.S. 14668.
4. *See El Trabajo Pro Bono en Argentina 2000–2015*, *in* LOS MANDARINES DEL DERECHO (Daniel Bonilla ed., 2017), at Sections III.C, III.C.2, and IV.A [hereinafter *Informe-Argentina*]; *El Trabajo Pro Bono en Chile 2000–2014*, *in* LOS MANDARINES DEL DERECHO, *supra*, at Sections III.A, III.D, and IV.A [hereinafter *Informe-Chile*]; *El Trabajo Pro Bono en Colombia 2009–2012*, *in* LOS MANDARINES DEL DERECHO, *supra*, at Section III.B [hereinafter *Informe-Colombia*].
5. *Informe-Argentina*, *supra* note 4, at Section III.C.2; *Informe-Chile*, *supra* note 4, at Sections III.D.2, III.D.6, and IV.A; *Informe-Colombia*, *supra* note 4, at Sections III.A.1, III.B.5, and III.D.4.
6. *See* ALAN WATSON, SOCIETY AND LEGAL CHANGE (2001).
7. One of the few Latin American law professors who has explored the topic is Martín Böhmer. Martin Böhmer, *Igualadores Retóricos: las Profesiones del Derecho y la Reforma de Justicia en la Argentina*, 15 CUADERNOS DE ANÁLISIS JURÍDICO 187 (2003); Martin Böhmer, *Trabajando Como Si No Pasara Nada. Las Obligaciones del Derecho en Sociedades Desiguales*, SELECCIÓN DE JURISPRUDENCIA ARGENTINA, Feb. 24, 2010.
8. *Id.*
9. The pro bono work done in Brazil is old, valuable, and notably well consolidated. *See, e.g.*, BRAZILIAN PRO BONO FOUNDATION, www.probono.org.br/ (last visited Oct. 1, 2020). Nevertheless, the budgetary limits of the research project that this article is based on

meant that fieldwork in Brazil would be conceived as part of the project's second stage.

10. *See Informe-Argentina*, *supra* note 4, at Section III.B; *Informe-Chile*, *supra* note 4, at Section III.C.3; *Informe-Colombia*, *supra* note 4, at Section III.C.
11. *See Informe-Argentina*, *supra* note 4, at Section III.B; *Informe-Chile*, *supra* note 4, at Section III.C.3; *Informe-Colombia*, *supra* note 4, at Section III.C.
12. David Clark, *The Idea of the Civil Law Tradition*, *in* COMPARATIVE AND PRIVATE INTERNATIONAL LAW 11 (David Clark ed., 1990).
13. Egon Montecinos, *Los Estudios de la Descentralización en América Latina: una Revisión sobre el Estado Actual de la Temática*, 31 EURE (SANTIAGO) 73 (2005).
14. *Índice de Gini*, EL BANCO MUNDIAL, http://datos.bancomundial.org/indicador/SI.POV.GINI (last visited Oct. 1, 2020).
15. *Id.*
16. *Poverty & Equity Data Portal: Argentina*, THE WORLD BANK, http://povertydata.worldbank.org/poverty/country/ARG (last visited Oct. 1, 2020).
17. *Poverty & Equity Data Portal: Colombia*, THE WORLD BANK, http://povertydata.worldbank.org/poverty/country/COL (last visited Oct. 1, 2020).
18. The three systems recognize the right of access to justice as a fundamental right. *See* CONSTITUCIÓN POLÍTICA DE COLOMBIA [C.P.] art. 13 (equality before the law), art. 29 (due process and right to defense), and art. 213 (access to justice); CONSTITUCIÓN POLÍTICA DE LA REPÚBLICA DE CHILE [C.P.] art. 19, number 3.
19. CORPORACIÓN EXCELENCIA PARA LA JUSTICIA, LINEAMIENTOS DE POLÍTICA PÚBLICA EN MATERIA DE ACCESO A LA JUSTICIA A PARTIR DE UN ESTUDIO DE NECESIDADES JURÍDICAS INSATISFECHAS 9–12, http://www.cej.org.co/files/DOCS_POLITICA_PUBLICA_Y_ACCESO_A_LA_JUSTICIA_1.pdf (last visited Oct. 1, 2020).
20. Fundación John Merck & Facultad de Derecho Universidad Diego Portales, *Acceso a La Justicia*, *in* INFORME ANUAL SOBRE DERECHOS HUMANOS EN CHILE 177 (2008).
21. JOHN HENRY MERRYMAN & ROGELIO PÉREZ PERDOMO, THE CIVIL LAW TRADITION: AN INTRODUCTION TO THE LEGAL SYSTEMS OF WESTERN EUROPE AND LATIN AMERICA 1–4 (2007).
22. The classification of the three legal systems within the Romano-Germanic family is widely accepted. Elaborating on the characteristics of each system and comparing them with the systems that give rise to the family is a task that lies beyond the bounds of this article. *Id.*
23. *Id.* at 57, 60.
24. R. Daniel Kelemen & Eric C. Sibbitt, *The Globalization of American Law*, 58 INT'L ORG. 103 (2004).
25. The firms that are affiliated with the organizations that promote pro bono work in Chile, Colombia, and Argentina are some of the largest and most recognized law firms in each of these three countries. *See*

Miembros, COMISIÓN PRO BONO (Argentina), www.probono.org.ar/miembros.php (last visited Oct. 1, 2020); *Miembros*, FUNDACIÓN PRO BONO (Chile), www.probono.cl/miembros/ (last visited Oct. 1, 2020); *Miembros*, FUNDACIÓN PROBONO COLOMBIA, http://probono.org.co/quienes-somos/miembros/ (last visited Oct. 1, 2020).

26. *See* FUNDACIÓN PRO BONO, www.probono.cl/paula-samper-directora-de-pro-bono-colombia-%E2%80%9Cel-desafio-sera-motivar-a-los-abogados-a-que-no-vean-el-voluntariado-como-una-carga-adicional%E2%80%9D/ (last visited Oct. 1, 2020); *Informe-Chile*, Section III.A; *Martín Zapiola Guerrico Recibió el Premio al Abogado Pro Bono del Año*, COMISIÓN PRO BONO (Apr. 2, 2015), http://comisionprobono.blogspot.com.co/2015/04/martin-zapiola-guerrico-recibio-el.html (last visited Oct. 1, 2020); *Nuestros Profesionales*, GÓMEZ-PINZÓN, www.gpzlegal.com/nuestros-profesionales-es/socios-es/r-t-es/profesional-1-es (last visited Oct. 1, 2020); *Pro Bono*, GÓMEZ-PINZÓN, www.gpzlegal.com/pro-bono-es/ (last visited Oct. 1, 2020).
27. *Historia*, FUNDACIÓN PRO BONO, www.probono.cl/fundacion/historia/ (last visited Nov. 20, 2019).
28. *Firmas de Abogados que Creen y Trabajan con la Fundación ProBono*, FUNDACIÓN PROBONO COLOMBIA, https://probono.org.co/actores-probono/ (last visited Oct. 1, 2020).
29. COMISIÓN PRO BONO, *supra* note 25.
30. *See Informe-Argentina*, Section III.B; *Informe-Chile*, Section III.A; *Informe-Colombia*, Section III.C.5.
31. Informe Pro Bono Argentina, Interview No. 27, Partner, Co-founder of the Commission (July 2, 2014).
32. She is part of the Board of Directors of Fundacion Pro Bono Chile. *See Directorio*, FUNDACIÓN PRO BONO, www.probono.cl/fundacion/directorio/ (last visited Oct. 1, 2020).
33. He is an honorary member of the Board of Directors of Fundación Pro Bono Colombia and designed and promoted the research project that is analyzed in this article. *See* FUNDACIÓN PROBONO COLOMBIA, INFORME DE GESTIÓN (2014), http://probono.org.co/wp-content/uploads/2015/03/Informe-de-Gesti%C3%B3n-2014-PDF.pdf (last visited Nov. 13, 2019).
34. *Pro Bono Network of the Americas*, CYRUS R. VANCE CENTER FOR INTERNATIONAL JUSTICE, www.vancecenter.org/vancecenter/index.php/our-partners/pro-bono-partnerships (last visited Oct. 1, 2020).
35. NGO *Legal Support*, CYRUS R. VANCE CENTER FOR INTERNATIONAL JUSTICE, www2.nycbar.org/vancecenter/index.php/what-we-do/ngo-legal-support (last visited Oct. 1, 2020).
36. *Law Firms*, CYRUS R. VANCE CENTER FOR INTERNATIONAL JUSTICE, www.vancecenter.org/vancecenter/index.php/our-partners/law-firms (last visited Oct. 1, 2020).
37. *Vance Center Committee*, CYRUS R. VANCE CENTER FOR INTERNATIONAL JUSTICE, www.vancecenter.org/vancecenter/index.php/who-we-are/vance-center-committee (last visited Oct. 1, 2020).

38. *Id.*
39. William Dean, *Pro Bono: A Professional and Ethical Obligation*, N.Y.L.J., Jan. 2, 2004.
40. *Declaración Pro Bono para las Américas*, RED PRO BONO DE LAS AMÉRICAS, http://redprobono.org/declaracion-pro-bono-para-las-americas/ (last visited Nov. 6, 2019); *see also* BASHAM, www.fundacionbasham.org.mx/index.php?ate=historia-de-pactos-latinoamerica&hl=es_MX (last visited Aug. 28, 2020); CYRUS R. VANCE CENTER FOR INTERNATIONAL JUSTICE, GUÍA PARA LA IMPLEMENTACIÓN DE PROGRAMAS PRO BONO EN LAS FIRMAS DE ABOGADOS DE LATINOAMÉRICA, www.probono.cl/wp-content/uploads/2013/08/guia-pro-bono-para-estudios-juridicos-de-latinoamerica.pdf (last visited Oct. 1, 2020).
41. Four of the most important events that the Vance Center organized and that are connected to the drafting of the Pro Bono Declaration of the Americas are the Conferences on Pro Bono in Buenos Aires (2001), Santiago (2002), and São Paulo (2003), and the Strategic Summit of the Americas in New York (2005). *See* CYRUS R. VANCE CENTER FOR INTERNATIONAL JUSTICE, *supra* note 40. For some of the most recent events, see *Events*, CYRUS R. VANCE CENTER FOR INTERNATIONAL JUSTICE, www.vancecenter.org/events/ (last visited Oct. 1, 2020).
42. *Bringing Access to Justice*, LATIN LAW. (Mar. 13, 2012), https://latinlawyer.com/benchmarking/january-february-2012/1092232/bringing-access-to-justice (last visited Nov. 13, 2019). In the following link find the ample number of partners that the Vance Center has for pro promoting pro bono in Latin America: *Clearinghouses*, CYRUS R. VANCE CENTER FOR INTERNATIONAL JUSTICE, www.vancecenter.org/vancecenter/index.php/our-partners/clearinghouses (last visited Oct. 1, 2020).
43. *See supra* notes 25 and 26.
44. The documents produced by the Vance Center on pro bono work have been very influential in Latin America. Perhaps the most important has been the Guide for the Implementation of Pro Bono Programs in the Law Firms of Latin America (The Guide). *See* CYRUS R. VANCE CENTER FOR INTERNATIONAL JUSTICE, *supra* note 40. Also see the manual that complements the Guide. CYRUS R. VANCE CENTER FOR INTERNATIONAL JUSTICE, FREQUENTLY ASKED QUESTIONS: A SUPPLEMENT TO THE PBDA IMPLEMENTATION HANDBOOK, www.vancecenter.org/vancecenter/images/stories/vancecenter/pro%20bono%20guide_2011%20supplement.pdf (last visited Oct. 2, 2020).
45. *See, e.g.*, CYRUS R. VANCE CENTER FOR INTERNATIONAL JUSTICE, *supra* note 40, at 2.
46. *Id.* at 2.
47. *Id.* at 3.

48. *See generally Informe-Argentina, Informe-Chile, Informe-Colombia, supra* note 4.
49. *Informe-Argentina, supra* note 4, at Section III.A.1.
50. *See id.*; *see also* CYRUS R. VANCE CENTER FOR INTERNATIONAL JUSTICE, LA DECLARACIÓN DE TRABAJO PRO BONO PARA EL CONTINENTE AMERICANO, www.vancecenter.org/vancecenter/images/stories/vancecenter/111811spanishversion.pdf (last visited Oct. 2, 2020).
51. *See, e.g.*, *Informe-Colombia, supra* note 4, at Sections III.A.1, III.B.5, and III.D.4; *Round Table Invitation*, NEW YORK CITY BAR, http://www.citybarjusticecenter.org/wp-content/uploads/images/stories/pdfs/roundtableinvitation.pdf (last visited Nov. 13, 2019).
52. Evelyn Quezada, *Fundación Pro Bono Conversa Sobre el Pro Bono en América Durante el Foro Pro Bono Europeo 2014*, FUNDACIÓN PRO BONO, www.probono.cl/fundacion-pro-bono-conversa-sobre-el-pro-bono-en-america-durante-el-foro-pro-bono-europeo-2014/ (last visited Oct. 2, 2020); Evelyn Quezada, *Fundación Pro Bono Participó en el Primer Congreso Internacional sobre el Pro Bono y Acceso a la Justicia en República Dominicana*, FUNDACIÓN PRO BONO, www.probono.cl/fundacion-pro-bono-participo-en-el-primer-congreso-internacional-sobre-el-pro-bono-y-acceso-a-la-justicia-en-republica-dominicana/ (last visited Oct. 2, 2020); Evelyn Quezada, *Integrantes de la Red Pro Bono Internacional se Reunieron en Chile en el Marco de Conmemoración de 14 Años de Trabajo*, FUNDACIÓN PRO BONO, www.probono.cl/integrantes-de-la-red-pro-bono-internacional-se-reunieron-en-chile-en-el-marco-de-conmemoracion-de-14-anos-de-trabajo/ (last visited Oct. 2, 2020); Evelyn Quezada, *Red Pro Bono de las Américas Realizó Mesa de Trabajo en Panamá sobre Trabajo Pro Bono*, FUNDACIÓN PRO BONO, www.probono.cl/red-pro-bono-de-las-americas-realizo-mesa-de-trabajo-en-panama-sobre-trabajo-pro-bono/ (last visited Oct. 2, 2020); *see also Etiqueta: Cyrus Vance Center*, FUNDACIÓN PRO BONO, www.probono.cl/tag/cyrus-vance-center/ (last visited Oct. 2, 2020); *Future of Pro Bono Discussed in Chile*, LATIN LAWYER, Apr. 8 2011, www.probono.cl/wp-content/uploads/2011/05/future-of-pro-bono.pdf (last visited Oct. 2, 2020).
53. *See generally* RODOLFO VIGO, ÉTICA DEL ABOGADO: CONDUCTA PROCESAL INDEBIDA (1997).
54. *See* Martín Böhmer, *Igualadores Retóricos, supra* note 7.
55. *See, e.g.*, FUNDACIÓN PROBONO COLOMBIA, SISTEMA DE MANEJO DE CASOS PROBONO GUÍA PARA FIRMAS Y ABOGADOS INDEPENDIENTES, https://docplayer.es/amp/1783356-Sistema-de-manejo-de-casos-probono-guia-para-firmas-y-abogados-independientes.html (last visited Oct. 2, 2020); *Compromiso de Buenas Prácticas Pro Bono*, COMISIÓN PRO BONO, www.probono.org.ar/compromiso-de-buenas-practicas-pro-bono.php (last visited Oct. 2, 2020); *Memorias*, FUNDACIÓN PRO BONO, www.probono.cl/publicaciones/memorias/ (last visited Oct. 2, 2020); *Presentación Buenas Prácticas*, FUNDACIÓN

ProBono Colombia, http://probono.org.co/wp-content/uploads/2012/03/Presentaci%C3%B3n-Buenas-pr%C3%A1cticas-Vance-Center.pdf (last visited Aug. 28, 2020).

56. *See Informe-Argentina, supra* note 4, at Section III.B.1; *Informe-Chile, supra* note 4, at Section I; *Informe-Colombia, supra* note 4, at Section III.C.4 and V.B.
57. *See Informe-Argentina, supra* note 4, at Section III.B.1; *Informe-Chile, supra* note 4, at Section I; *Informe-Colombia, supra* note 4, at Section III.C.4 and V.B.
58. *See Informe-Argentina, supra* note 4, at Section III.A.2; *Informe-Chile, supra* note 4, at Section III.B; *Informe-Colombia, supra* note 4, at Sections III.A y III.A.1.
59. Cyrus R. Vance Center for International Justice, PBDA Implementation Handbook: A Guide to Establishing a Pro Bono Program at your Law Firm, www.vancecenter.org/vancecenter/images/stories/vancecenter/pro_bono_guide_ar.pdf (last visited Oct. 2, 2020).
60. New York City Bar, Statement of Pro Bono Principles, www.nycbar.org/images/stories/pdfs/pbpstatement.pdf (last visited Oct. 2, 2020).
61. *Pro Bono Declaration for the Americas*, Cyrus R. Vance Center for International Justice, www.vancecenter.org/wp-content/uploads/2018/03/English.pdf (last visited Nov. 6, 2019); *see also* Declaración Pro Bono para las Américas, *supra* note 40.
62. Ronald J. Tabak, Formas en que los Estudios Jurídicos Pueden Actuar para Incrementar su Representación del Trabajo Pro Bono, www.probono.cl/documentos/documentos/Formas%20en%20que%20los%20estudios%20jur%C3%ADdicos%20puedesn%20incrementar%20su%20trabajo%20pro%20bono%20%28Ronald%20Tabak%29.pdf (last visited Oct. 2, 2020).
63. *See* Cyrus R. Vance Center for International Justice, *supra* note 44.
64. *See Informe-Argentina, supra* note 4, at Section III.C; *Informe-Chile, supra* note 4, at Section III.C; *Informe-Colombia, supra* note 4, at Section III.A.1.
65. Cyrus R. Vance Center for International Justice, *supra* note 40, at 4–7.
66. *See La Comisión Pro Bono*, Comisión Pro Bono, www.probono.org.ar/la- comision.php (last visited Nov. 20, 2019); *Misión*, Fundación Pro Bono, www.probono.cl/fundacion/mision/ (last visited Nov. 20, 2019); *Our Mission*, Cyrus R. Vance Center for International Justice, www.vancecenter.org/vancecenterlindex.php/what-we-do (last visited Nov. 20, 2019); *Visión*, Fundación Pro Bono Colombia, http://probono.org.co/quienes-somos/nuestra-organizacion/vision/ (last visited Nov. 20, 2019).

67. *See Informe-Argentina*, *supra* note 4, at Section III.B; *Informe-Chile*, *supra* note 4, at Section III.C.3; *Informe-Colombia*, *supra* note 4, at Section III.C.
68. *See Informe-Argentina*, *supra* note 4, at Section III.B; *Informe-Chile*, *supra* note 4, at Section III.C.3; *Informe-Colombia*, *supra* note 4, at Section III.C.
69. *See Our Approach*, CYRUS R. VANCE CENTER FOR INTERNATIONAL JUSTICE, www.vancecenter.org/our-approach/ (last visited Oct. 2, 2020); *Our Mission*, VANCE CENTER, *supra* note 66.
70. *See Declaración Pro Bono para las Américas*, *supra* note 40.
71. *Id.*
72. *Pro Bono Network of the Americas*, *supra* note 34.
73. *See Declaración del Trabajo Pro Bono Para el Continente Americano*, FUNDACIÓN PROBONO COLOMBIA, http://probono.org.co/quienes-somos/declaracion-del-trabajo-pro-bono-para-el-continente-americano/ (last visited Oct. 2, 2020).
74. *See* NEW YORK CITY BAR, www2.nycbar.org/citybarjusticecenter/pdf/PBDA_Text_Castellano.pdf (last visited Oct. 7, 2018).
75. *See Informe-Argentina*, *supra* note 4, at Section III.C.2; *Informe-Chile*, *supra* note 4, at Section III.D.2; *Informe-Colombia*, *supra* note 4, at Section III.A.1.
76. Mark Tushnet, *The Possibilities of Comparative Constitutional Law*, 108 YALE L.J. 1225, 1225–39 (1999).
77. Alan Watson, *Legal Transplants and European Private Law*, Electronic J. Comp. L., Dec. 2000, www.ejcl.org/44/art44-2.html (last visited Oct. 2, 2020).
78. Pier Giuseppe Monateri, *"Everybody's Talking": The Future of Comparative Law*, 21 HASTINGS INT'L COMP. L.J. 825 (1998).
79. *Id.* at 844.
80. *Id.*
81. Watson, *supra* note 77, at 3.
82. Daniel Bonilla, *Introducción – Teoría del Derecho y Transplantes Jurídicos: la Estructura del Debate*, *in* TEORÍA DEL DERECHO Y TRANSPLANTES JURÍDICOS 23-28 (Daniel Bonilla ed., 2009).
83. *Id.*
84. *See* Monateri, *supra* note 78, at 840.
85. *See Informe-Argentina*, *supra* note 4, at Sections II.A.1 and III.A.3; *Informe-Chile*, *supra* note 4, at Section III.A and III.B; *Informe-Colombia*, *supra* note 4, at Section III.A.
86. *See Informe-Argentina*, *supra* note 4, at Sections II.A.1 and III.A.3; *Informe-Chile*, *supra* note 4, at Section III.A and III.B; *Informe-Colombia*, *supra* note 4, at Section III.A.
87. *Informe-Chile*, *supra* note 4, at Section III.A.
88. *Informe-Argentina*, *supra* note 4, at Section III.A.3.
89. *Id.*
90. *Informe-Colombia*, *supra* note 4, at Section III.A.

91. *See generally Informe-Argentina, Informe-Chile, Informe-Colombia, supra* note 4.
92. *Id.*
93. *Our Mission*, VANCE CENTER, *supra* note 66.
94. In the United States, the unmet legal needs of citizens are also high. *See* Deborah L. Rhode, *Access to Justice: Again, Still*, 73 FORDHAM L. REV. 1013, 1015 (2004); Deborah Rhode, *Access to Justice: An Agenda for Legal Education and Research*, 62 J. LEGAL EDUC. 531, 534 (2013).
95. *See NYC Bar Association*, CYRUS R. VANCE CENTER FOR INTERNATIONAL JUSTICE, www.vancecenter.org/vancecenter/index.php/who-we-are/nyc-bar-association (last visited Oct. 2, 2020).
96. *See generally* sources cited *supra* notes 50, 51, and 52.
97. *Id.*
98. Maya Steinitz, *Internationalized Pro Bono and a New Global Role for Lawyers in the 21st Century: Lessons from Nation Building in Southern Sudan*, 12 YALE HUM. RTS. DEV. L.J. 205 (2009).
99. Ronit Dinovitzer & Bryant G. Garth, *Pro Bono as an Elite Strategy in Early Lawyer Careers*, *in* PRIVATE LAWYERS IN THE PUBLIC INTEREST (Robert Granfield & Lynn Mather eds., 2009).
100. Scott L. Cummings, *Access to Justice in the New Millennium: Achieving the Promise of Pro Bono*, 32 HUM. RTS. 6, 6 (2005).
101. The most influential ranking is in *The American Lawyer*. Cummings, *supra* note 100, at 7.
102. LATIN LAW., http://latinlawyer.com/ (last visited Oct. 2, 2020).
103. Latin Lawyer and the Vance Center do an annual survey on pro bono work in Latin America: *Latin Lawyer-Vance Center Pro Bono Survey Extended*, LATIN LAW. (Aug. 25, 2015), http://latinlawyer.com/news/article/48583/latin-lawyer-vance-center-pro-bono-survey-extended/ (last visited Oct. 2, 2020). Also see examples of the information regularly published by *Latin Lawyer* about pro bono work: Vincent Manancourt, *Latin Lawyer Announces Pro Bono Lawyer of the Year Award*, LATIN LAW. (Mar. 6, 2015), http://latinlawyer.com/news/article/47932/latin-lawyer-announces-pro-bono-lawyer-year-award/ (last visited Oct. 2, 2020); Lulu Rumsey, *Pro Bono Profile: Instituto Pro Bono*, LATIN LAW. (Mar. 6, 2015), http://latinlawyer.com/news/article/47929/pro-bono-profile-instituto-pro-bono/ (last visited Oct. 2, 2020).
104. Nuno Garoupa, *Globalization and Deregulation of Legal Services*, 38 INT'L REV. L. ECON. 77 (2014).
105. Carole Silver, Nicole De Bruin Phelan & Mikaela Rabinowitz, *Between Diffusion and Distinctiveness in Globalization: US Law Firms Go Glocal*, 22 GEO. J. LEGAL ETHICS 1431 (2009).
106. Linda Chiem, *Law Firms Eye Outposts in Africa, Latin America in 2014*, LAW360 (Jan. 1, 2014), www.law360.com/articles/489572/law-firms-eye-outposts-in-africa-latin-america-in-2014 (last visited Oct. 2, 2020); María Inés Bergoglio, *Cambios en la Profesión Jurídica en*

América, 5 ACADEMIA: REVISTA SOBRE ENSEÑANZA DEL DERECHO 9, 18 (2007).

107. *See, e.g.*, *Informe-Colombia*, *supra* note 4, at Section III.B.
108. Cynthia Fuchs Epstein, *Stricture and Structure: The Social and Cultural Context of Pro Bono Work in Wall Street Firms*, 70 FORDHAM L. REV. 1689, 1693 (2002).
109. Mauricio Rojas, *No el Abogado, "Mejor el Doctor": La Imagen Social del Profesional en Derecho*, 11 REVISTA ESTUDIOS SOCIO-JURÍDICOS 281 (2009).
110. Daniel Bonilla, *La Economía Política del Conocimiento Jurídico*, 2 BRAZ. J. EMPIRICAL LEGAL STUD. 26 (2015).
111. *See* Lee Epstein & Jack Knight, *Constitutional Borrowing and Nonborrowing*, 1 INT'L J. CONST. L. 196 (2003).
112. Daniel Bonilla, *Towards a Constitutionalism of the Global South*, *in* CONSTITUTIONALISM OF THE GLOBAL SOUTH (Daniel Bonilla ed., 2013).
113. Bonilla, *supra* note 110.
114. *See* Monateri, *supra* note 78.
115. Bonilla, *supra* note 110.
116. *Id.*
117. Daniel Bonilla, *Legal Clinics in the Global North and South: Between Equality and Subordination*, 16 YALE HUM. RTS. DEV. L.J. 176 (2013).
118. *Id.*
119. *Id.*
120. Burton Fretz & Gridley Hall, *Legal Services in the Third World*, 24 CLEARINGHOUSE REV. 782 (1990–1991).
121. Joseph R. Thome, *New Models for Legal Services in Latin America*, 6 HUM. RTS. Q. 521, 525–26 (1984).
122. Marc Galanter & David Trubek, *Scholars in Self-Estrangement: Some Reflections on the Crisis in Law and Development Studies in the United States*, 4 WIS. L. REV. 1062 (1974).
123. *Historia*, *supra* note 27.
124. Bergoglio, *supra* note 106, at 14, 19.
125. *La Comisión Pro Bono*, *supra* note 66; *Historia*, *supra* note 27.
126. *Nuestros Logros*, FUNDACIÓN PROBONO COLOMBIA, http://probono.org.co/quienes-somos/nuestra-organizacion/nuestros-logros/ (last visited Nov. 20, 2019).
127. *See Informe-Argentina*, *supra* note 4, at Section III.B.2; *Informe-Chile*, *supra* note 4, at Section III.C.3; *Informe-Colombia*, *supra* note 4, at Sections III.C.2 and III.C.3.
128. *See Informe-Argentina*, *supra* note 4, at Section III.B.2; *Informe-Chile*, *supra* note 4, at Section III.C.3; *Informe-Colombia*, *supra* note 4, at Sections III.C.2 and III.C.3.
129. *See Informe-Argentina*, *supra* note 4, at Section III.B.2; *Informe-Chile*, *supra* note 4, at Section III.C.3; *Informe-Colombia*, *supra* note 4, at Sections III.C.2 and III.C.3.

130. *See Informe-Argentina*, *supra* note 4, at Section III.B.2; *Informe-Chile*, *supra* note 4, at Section III.C.3; *Informe-Colombia*, *supra* note 4, at Sections III.C.2 and III.C.3.
131. *See Informe-Argentina*, *supra* note 4, at Section III.C.1; *Informe-Chile*, *supra* note 4, at Section III.C.2; *Informe-Colombia*, *supra* note 4, at Section III.D.1.
132. *See* Thome, *supra* note 121, at 527; *see also Informe-Argentina*, *supra* note 4, at Section III.A.2; *Informe-Chile*, *supra* note 4, at Section III.B; *Informe-Colombia*, *supra* note 4, at Sections III.A y III.A.1.
133. *See Informe-Argentina*, *supra* note 4, at Section III.C.1; *Informe-Chile*, *supra* note 4, at Section III.C.2; *Informe-Colombia*, *supra* note 4, at Section III.D.1.
134. For a description of the programs for promoting pro bono work and interns that the Colombian Pro Bono Foundation has with the universities of Rosario, Sabana, Javeriana, and Andes, see *Alianzas*, FUNDACIÓN PROBONO COLOMBIA, http://probono.org.co/quienes-somos/alianzas/ (last visited Nov. 20, 2019). For a description of the Pro Bono Challenge Contest that the Chilean Pro Bono Foundation organizes annually, see *Etiqueta: Desafío Pro Bono Chile*, FUNDACIÓN PRO BONO, www.probono.cl/tag/desafio-pro-bono-chile/ (last visited Nov. 20, 2019).
135. *See Informe-Argentina*, *supra* note 4, at Section III.C; *Informe-Chile*, *supra* note 4, at Section III.C; *Informe-Colombia*, *supra* note 4, at Section III.A.1.
136. This is the average number for 2012, a year for which there is available information for the three organizations. In 2012, in Colombia 212 cases were taken, in Argentina 190 (although a very low percentage came from the Commission), and in Chile 756. *See Informe-Argentina*, *supra* note 4, at Section III.B.1; *Informe-Chile*, *supra* note 4, at Section III.C.1; *Informe-Colombia*, *supra* note 4, at Section III.C.1.
137. *See Informe-Argentina*, *supra* note 4, at Section III.B.2; *Informe-Chile*, *supra* note 4, at Sections III.C.3, III.D.1, and III.D.3; *Informe-Colombia*, *supra* note 4, at Section III.B.2; *see also* Rhode, *Access to Justice*, *supra* note 94, at 537.
138. *See* Víctor Abramovich, *Acceso a la Justicia y Nuevas Formas de Participación en la Esfera Política*, 9 REVISTA ESTUDIOS SOCIO-JURÍDICOS 9, 10 (2007); *Informe-Argentina*, *supra* note 4, at Section III.C; *Informe-Chile*, *supra* note 4, at Section III.C; *Informe-Colombia*, *supra* note 4, at Section III.A.1.
139. Abramovich, *supra* note 138; *Informe-Argentina*, *supra* note 4, at Section III.C; *Informe-Chile*, *supra* note 4, at Section III.C; *Informe-Colombia*, *supra* note 4, at Section III.A.1.
140. This is the only period for which there is information about the number of cases taken in the three countries. Between 2009 and 2012 the firms affiliated with the Pro Bono Foundation of Chile took 558, 821, 570, and 573 cases, respectively. The Argentine firms affiliated with the Commission, 160, 200, 200, and 190, respectively. Between 2009 and

2012 the Colombian firms affiliated with the Pro Bono Foundation of Colombia took 128, 209, and 211 cases, respectively. For additional information, see *Informe-Argentina, supra* note 4, at Section III.B.1; *Informe-Chile, supra* note 4, at Section III.C.1; *Informe-Colombia, supra* note 4, at Section III.C.1.

141. *See Informe-Argentina, supra* note 4, at Section III.B.1; *Informe-Chile, supra* note 4, at Section III.C.1; *Informe-Colombia, supra* note 4, at Section III.C.1. In 2013, the Chilean Pro Bono Foundation reported that the affiliated firms had reached this goal for the first time. However, this is probably an imprecise figure. The fieldwork showed that firms in Chile, as in Colombia and Argentina, do not have rigorous standards for tracking and systematizing the pro bono work that law firms do.

142. The Colombian market is smaller than the Argentine and Chilean ones. Nevertheless, "In 2014, for example, Colombian law firms billed 648,970 millions of pesos (324 million dollars); they also control assets worth 516,830 millions of pesos (258 million dollars) and they have a patrimony of 257,692 millions of pesos (129 million dollars)." *Análisis Comparativo de las Firmas de Abogados en Colombia 2012–2015*, Los Datos, www.losdatos.com (last visited Oct. 2, 2020).

143. *See Informe-Argentina, supra* note 4, at Sections III.C.2, III.C.6, and V. B; *Informe-Chile, supra* note 4, at Section III.D.2; *Informe-Colombia, supra* note 4, at Sections III.D.5, III.D.6, and V.B.

144. Interview, partner and founder, Fundación Pro Bono Colombia (Aug. 26, 2015).

145. *See Informe-Argentina, supra* note 4, at Section III.C.4; *Informe-Chile, supra* note 4, at Section III.D.4; *Informe-Colombia, supra* note 4, at Section III.D.8.

146. *See Informe-Argentina, supra* note 4, at Section III.C.4; *Informe-Chile, supra* note 4, at Section III.D.4; *Informe-Colombia, supra* note 4, at Section III.D.8.

147. *See, e.g., Informe-Colombia, supra* note 4, at Section III.B.

148. *See Informe-Argentina, supra* note 4, at Sections III.C.2, III.C.6, and V. B; *Informe-Chile, supra* note 4, at Section III.D.2; *Informe-Colombia, supra* note 4, at Sections III.D.5, III.D.6, and V.B.

149. *See Informe-Argentina, supra* note 4, at Sections III.C.2, III.C.6, and V. B; *Informe-Chile, supra* note 4, at Section III.D.2; *Informe-Colombia, supra* note 4, at Sections III.D.5, III.D.6, and V.B.

150. Mariana N. Sánchez, *Género y Profesión Jurídica*, *in* 8 Anuario VIII (2004– 2005) del Centro de Investigaciones Juridica y Sociales, 451, 453 (2005).

151. "When looking at partners in terms of gender, the participation of women in the law firms in Colombia is 25%, with which it is observed that the presence of female partners in the large firms is quite low." *Análisis Comparativo de las Firmas de Abogados, supra* note 142.

152. *See Informe-Argentina, supra* note 4, at Section III.B; *Informe-Chile, supra* note 4, at Section III.C; *Informe-Colombia, supra* note 4, at Section III.A.1.

153. *See Informe-Argentina, supra* note 4, at Section III.B; *Informe-Chile, supra* note 4, at Section III.C; *Informe-Colombia, supra* note 4, at Section III.A.1.
154. *Informe-Argentina, supra* note 4, at Section III.B.
155. *Nuestro Equipo de Trabajo*, FUNDACIÓN PROBONO COLOMBIA, http://probono.org.co/quienes-somos/nuestra-organizacion/nuestro-equipo-de-trabajo/ (last visited Nov. 20, 2019).
156. *Equipo*, FUNDACIÓN PRO BONO, www.probono.cl/fundacion/equipo/ (last visited Nov. 20, 2019).
157. Sánchez, *supra* note 150.
158. *Informe-Argentina, supra* note 4, at Sections III.B.3, III.B.4 V.A., and V.C; *Informe-Chile, supra* note 4, at Sections III.C.5, III.C.6, and V.B; *Informe-Colombia, supra* note 4, at Sections III.C.4, III.C.5 V.A, and V.C.
159. In 2103, the last year for which there is available data, the Foundation received almost CLP 200'000.000, equivalent to $341,751.82. *Financiamiento*, FUNDACIÓN PRO BONO, www.probono.cl/fundacion/financiamiento/ (last visited Nov. 20, 2019).
160. Thome, *supra* note 121, at 525–26.
161. Peggy Maisel, *The Role of US Law Faculty in Developing Countries: Striving for Effective Cross-Cultural Collaboration*, 14 CLINICAL L. REV. 465 (2008).
162. Fretz & Hall, *supra* note 120.
163. Galanter & Trubek, *supra* note 122.
164. JAMES A. GARDNER , LEGAL IMPERIALISM: AMERICAN LAWYERS AND FOREIGN AID IN LATIN AMERICA 43 (1980).
165. *See* Galanter & Trubek, *supra* note 122.
166. Daniel Bonilla, *El Formalismo Jurídico, la Educación Jurídica y la Práctica Profesional del Derecho en Latinoamérica*, *in* DERECHO Y PUEBLO MAPUCHE 274 (Helena Olea ed., 2013).
167. Thome, *supra* note 121, at 525–26.
168. *Id.*
169. The pro bono clients of Argentine, Chilean, and Colombian law firms are persons that have few social and economic resources. *See Informe-Argentina, supra* note 4, at Section III.B.2; *Informe-Chile, supra* note 4, at Section III.C.3; *Informe-Colombia, supra* note 4, at Sections III.C.3 and III.D.1. The typical pro bono cases are the ones that affect low social and economic strata. *See Informe-Argentina, supra* note 4, at Section III.C.1; *Informe-Chile, supra* note 4, at Sections III.C.2 and III.D.1; *Informe-Colombia, supra* note 4, at Section III.D.1.
170. *Id.*
171. Fretz & Hall, *supra* note 120.
172. Thome, *supra* note 121, at 525–26.
173. *See* La Última Tentación de Cristo (Olmedo Bustos y otros) v. Chile, Inter-Am. Ct. H.R. (ser. C) No. 73, 263, www.corteidh.or.cr/cf/jurisprudencia/ficha.cfm?nId_Ficha=263&lang=es (last visited Oct. 2, 2020).

174. *See* Cummings, *supra* note 100, at 10.
175. *See Informe-Argentina, supra* note 4, at Section III.A.2.
176. *Informe-Argentina, supra* note 4, at Section III.C.5; *Informe-Chile, supra* note 4, at Section III.D.7; *Informe-Colombia, supra* note 4, at Section III.D.7.
177. Rhode, *supra* note 94, at 1446.
178. *Id.*
179. *Id.*
180. Andrés Thompson & Olga Lucia Toro, *El Voluntariado Social en América Latina. Tendencias, Influencias, Espacios y Lecciones Aprendidas*, 3 REVISTA SOCIEDAD CIVIL 27 (1999).
181. *Informe-Chile, supra* note 4, at Section III.D.6; *Informe-Colombia, supra* note 4, at Section III.D.8.

PART TWO

EUROPE

CHAPTER SIX

LE PRO BONO: THE DEVELOPMENT OF LEGAL VOLUNTEERISM IN EUROPE

Edwin Rekosh and Lamin Khadar

INTRODUCTION

At an international conference on access to justice hosted by the Association of the Bar of the City of New York in 2000, Jean-Luc Bedos, a partner in the Paris office of Dentons and a founder of the nongovernmental organization (NGO) Droits D'Urgence, stated point blank: "Pro bono does not exist in France."[1] In the same presentation, Bedos mentioned that four hundred volunteer lawyers were working with his NGO to provide legal assistance to "*sans-papiers*" immigrants, obviously seeing no contradiction between the two statements. About a dozen years later, PILnet: The Global Network for Public Interest Law[2] would honor Bedos and two other French lawyers for their pioneering work in building pro bono culture in Europe, and Bedos now serves on the board of directors of PILnet, which has become the leading promoter of pro bono practice in Europe.

Behind this story lie questions of semantics but also many centuries of European legal history, public policy, and normative development that have shaped European perceptions of the legal profession and its role in society. At the same time, legal globalization has had its influence, with formalized pro bono practices accompanying other cultural influences as "Big Law" has spread throughout Europe.

While the story of the institutionalization of pro bono practice within large law firms is an American one,[3] parallel developments decades later in Europe have been driven, in part, by a variety of endogenous factors, including the history of the European legal profession, the nature of European legal systems and political culture, and some of the specific features of European legal markets. Key historical influences include deeply rooted European values and policy preferences regarding access to formal justice systems. More contemporary influences include the increasing role for European civil society organizations in facilitating public participation.

At the same time, there have been exogenous factors, such as the globalization of the legal profession, marked in part by mergers across Europe that played an important role in creating a new class of "megafirms" with global footprints: Global Big Law. The pro bono culture of the largest US firms has had its impact, via both megafirms of US origin as well as the megafirms of UK origin, which had already adopted some of the trappings of US-style pro bono practice before their global expansion. Institutionalized pro bono developed in large European law firms, first in London and then elsewhere in Europe, for some of the same reasons as in the United States, including the opportunity provided by the administrative capacity and largesse of Big Law as well as the need of large law firms for social legitimacy and the inevitable competition for attention among brand-name law firms.[4]

Despite the dominant role played by Global Big Law in developing institutionalized pro bono in Europe, there are some important differences with the US experience. Unlike the United States, codification of ethical norms by the organized bar, competition over recruiting legal talent, and a preference for a shrinking welfare state do not explain the growth of pro bono. In Europe, the pressure of complying with firmwide policies of global law firm networks has had more influence than the organized bar.

Competitive dynamics among law firms has also played a role in pushing pro bono forward in Europe, but the dynamics are driven by competition over clients rather than for associates. Corporate social responsibility (CSR) norms – which have been codified into EU law to a far greater extent than in the United States[5] – create an incentive for European Big Law to engage in pro bono activity in part to meet the expectations of corporate clients pushing out CSR policies to their supply chains.

After providing an overview of the history of the legal profession and the ethic of legal volunteerism, both of which originate in Europe, this chapter will trace the pathways of diffusion that have led pro bono practice to develop among the large law firms of Europe, in countries as diverse as the United Kingdom, France, Germany, Hungary, and

Poland. After examining a wide variety of influences – both endogenous and exogenous, historical and contemporary – it will describe how pro bono practice has been adapted to fit the European context, followed by some reflections on the limitations and potential value of the European approach to pro bono practice.

EVOLUTION OF THE ACCESS-TO-JUSTICE NORM IN EUROPE

The term for pro bono in the French language is *le pro bono*. Observers in France have noted with irony that pro bono is a Latin term used to describe an Anglo-Saxon concept in the French language. Adding irony on top of irony, a French magazine catering to the legal profession published a cover story on the rise of pro bono in France early on, adding a second borrowed word from English: "*Pro bono des avocats: Nouveau* marketing *ethique?*"[6]

Pro bono in France, as elsewhere in Europe, is used to describe one particular institutionalized form of legal volunteerism, according to which commercial lawyers volunteer their services through programs organized in the private sector, primarily through the offices of large law firms (*les grands cabinets*, or as they are collectively known in the United States, Big Law). While lawyers working in smaller firms or solo practice have an important role to play in securing access to justice through informal volunteer efforts and state-funded legal aid mechanisms, the development of institutionalized pro bono – organized at the law firm level and labeled as pro bono per se – has taken place almost exclusively within European Big Law.

The significance of pro bono developments in Europe cannot be understood properly without considering the broader context of how European legal systems have evolved over time, particularly with respect to legal principles and policies connected to access to justice. Access to justice encompasses a variety of dimensions, including the provision of legal information, reduction of barriers to fair and efficient adjudication, and the like. One critical aspect of access to justice, in recognition of epistemological, socioeconomic, and legal market inequalities,[7] is the opportunity to be represented by legal counsel regardless of the ability to pay for those services. Consequently, assistance by counsel in both civil and criminal contexts is strongly recognized in Europe as a social benefit as well as an inalienable right guaranteed by law.

For the purposes of understanding the particularities and significance of pro bono in Europe, we will focus primarily on the free legal services component of access to justice. In doing so, it is important to consider the normative development of the right to legal counsel as well as the ethic of volunteerism among legal professionals. These two features of the access-to-justice norm have had an intertwining evolutionary path in Europe, and the roots of contemporary European systems designed to institutionalize the norm of access to justice can be traced back to key stages that map onto the evolution of European governance principles and legal systems in general.

The Origins of Access to Justice through Legal Volunteerism

An ethic of legal volunteerism – the provision of legal services without financial compensation to those in need – has deep roots in Europe, going back to the very formation of the legal profession itself. That ethic has taken different forms over the centuries, but it has been consistently reflected in European legal institutions for as long as there have been legal institutions in Europe. Across the centuries, rationales for the ethic have shifted: from kinship ties, communal solidarity, civic duty, patronage and aristocratic duty to Christian charity to professional duty. Nevertheless, elements of each rationale persist to this day, and they can be seen in contemporary justifications for privately organized pro bono practice and governmental policies alike.

The need for professional lawyers first arose in ancient Athens after 600 BC with the emergence of the heliastic courts.[8] In these courts, litigants were required to face large popular juries, and success depended on "carefully prepared and expertly delivered argument."[9] As a result, a practice of retaining professional assistance in the presentation of cases developed, replacing the prior practice of self-representation.[10] The system of legal representation brought with it, in time, the commodification of such services (the practice of paying these professionals for services rendered).

Commodification of legal services met some resistance based on Athenian democratic ideals. As Plato complained, "justice was at the service of whomsoever was able and willing to pay for the services of a professional lawyer."[11] One well-known jurist, Hyperides, wrote: "What is more democratic than that those who are able to plead a cause should come to the aid of those who are themselves unable to do so, particularly if the latter are in dire peril?"[12] As a reflection of those ideals, an ethic of legal volunteerism emerged, as lawyers (the *synegoros* or *hyperapologoumenos*) began to provide representation for free to their relatives, friends, and associates, likely out of the shared sense of communal solidarity or civic duty articulated by Hyperides. The practice took organized form in some Athenian townships and clubs (e.g., fraternities), which would provide legal assistance to inhabitants and members experiencing legal difficulties.[13] This system enabled weaker, less affluent parties to obtain assistance, typically from elected officials acting on their behalf in court as *synegoros*.[14]

Unlike Athens, where the nascent legal profession seemed to challenge democratic ideals, the Roman Republic revered lawyers. The profession emerged from the body of "state priests," *sacerdotes publici*, men of noble origin, patricians, occupying important social or political positions responsible for the interpretation of sacral and secular law. Even in later periods, as the Roman profession transcended its priestly roots and the practice of law became a secular endeavor, the profession was nevertheless stocked with aristocratic men (*patronus*).[15] Owing to their social position, the early aristocratic Roman lawyers did not typically take payment for services rendered. According to cultural norms of the time, it would have been considered beneath them; taking payment was seen to degrade the practice of law, reducing it to a "mercenary business."[16] As a result, legal services were provided out of a sense of public duty, chivalry, honor, and *noblesse oblige*: a duty of the strong to the weak, from the patron to his family, vassals, and neighbors, and even to strangers in need of help.[17]

Nevertheless, as legal practice became more complex, fostered in part by the growing sociopolitical and economic complexity of Roman life, the work of lawyers required more time, training, and specialization and became embraced by men who were not of noble birth and who could not afford to work without remuneration. In turn, this led first of all to the expectation that lawyers would receive some form of remuneration from clients, not as a fee but as a sign of gratitude, and ultimately to the charging of fees.[18] Yet, under the so-called clientele system, men of noble birth – "patricians" – would continue to take it upon themselves to provide protection (including legal services in court) to those within their household as well as others occupying a position of dependency.[19]

The ascendance of Christianity during the Roman Empire had a significant impact on morality within the Roman world. As a result, European attitudes about legal services likewise took a definitive turn from more Republican justifications to a focus on Christian charity and the needs of the poor, which remains a dominant theme within access-to-justice discourse in contemporary Europe. Indeed, the charitable ethic within the legal profession emanates directly from scripture, which mandates that the poor, needy, and weak should be spared from oppression and judged impartially in legal disputes.[20] Flowing from that norm, the church began to produce a range of doctrine and practice concerned with the legal needs of those persons coming under its protection.[21]

During the Middle Ages, legal volunteerism continued, but with a new rationale. As the Christian Church became increasingly influential, it played an important role, too, in shaping the organized legal profession. At first, Christian lawyers provided free legal services, often referred to as *pro deo* (for God),[22] as pious work in spontaneous acts of charity. Saint Yves of Brittany provides an iconic example, eventually becoming canonized for his work for the impoverished.[23] In time, the church produced more sophisticated and institutionalized forms of legal charity. For example, one practice initiated by the church, later spreading to secular courts, was to instruct magistrates to waive the court fees of the poor and sometimes to appoint a private lawyer or a member of the clergy to represent them free of charge (acting for God) or for a small fee.[24] This practice was documented in France, England, Italy, and Germany.[25]

In time, the influence of the Christian ideology of charity, and the practices it spawned, spread to the secular courts and slowly became embraced by the legal systems and emerging legal professions of Europe. From the thirteenth century, the sense of free legal assistance as a Christian duty began to transform into notions of professional duty.[26] In Modena, for example, the role of the clergy in providing free representation to indigent clients shifted to the city's legal guild as the legal profession took shape.[27] Municipal statutes of Modena stipulated that lawyers must provide for the legal needs of the poor, widows, and orphans without taking any fees or other compensation.[28] Although it is unclear how effectively the standard was implemented, it was entirely reliant on legal volunteerism.

Codification of the Access-to-Justice Norm

Thanks to philosophers such as Hobbes, Locke, and Rousseau, the idea emerged in the seventeenth and eighteenth centuries that the state should protect its citizens against encroachment of their rights by either fellow citizens or the state itself, as part of a social contract.[29] The rise of nationalism and the formation of modern European nation-states created new constitutional orders premised on this philosophical foundation. The constitutional orders include the notion of equal protection of the law, implying equal access to the machinery of justice (i.e., the courts and the legal process) on the basis of citizenship.[30] The constitutional guarantees were abstract, however, until laws were enacted to codify a duty of the legal profession to provide free legal services.

Accordingly, the first national-level "proto-legal aid systems" emerged in Belgium (1810 as a prenational law, amended 1889), France (1851), Italy (1865), and Germany (1877), all of them Catholic countries undoubtedly influenced by the *pro deo* practices of the church. Although systematized on a national level, the systems were more akin to an administrative and procedural framework for organized legal volunteerism than a comprehensive state-funded legal aid system.[31] In Belgium, for example, the bar was required to establish legal consultation bureaus tasked with providing legal advice to the poor, staffed with private lawyers working voluntarily on a rota system.[32] Meanwhile, in France, financial barriers to litigation for the poor were removed, unpaid lawyers were appointed to serve at no cost, and court fees were waived.[33] A similar system prevailed in Italy.[34] In Germany, the 1877 Code of Civil Procedure empowered judges to appoint lawyers and waive costs for litigants who could demonstrate their poverty.[35] Similar provisions were in place right across Western Europe, from Spain (1881) and San Marino (1884) to Luxembourg (1893) and Iceland (1907).[36]

In Germany, the welfare state was emerging, with the introduction of social insurance programs, enacted to protect against risks inherent in industrial economies, namely the potential loss of income from contingencies such as old age, sickness, or unemployment.[37] Germany introduced an industrial accident insurance program in 1871, representing the first social insurance program in Europe, followed by the first health insurance and pension programs in the 1880s, and the social innovation quickly spread.[38] The policy preference had emerged under Bismarck, in the context of the formative German nation-state centered around the booming, industrial metropolis of Berlin, replete with increasing social tensions the state sought to mitigate. For similar reasons, German legal academics theorized about the need for free legal assistance to help relieve social pressures around the same time, resulting in a "peace of law" movement that led to the rapid growth of legal aid programs of diverse sorts.[39]

The end result was a proliferation of models for how to put into effect the duties to provide legal assistance delineated in national legislation. One model, supported in large part by the already existing legislative frameworks, was the municipally organized legal aid bureau. This institution – documented in Germany, Poland, Switzerland, the Netherlands, Finland, Estonia, Norway, and Sweden – involved municipalities working with the profession, acting largely on a voluntary basis, to maintain legal aid offices that provided free legal advice to the poor.[40] In Romania, undoubtedly following the French model established in Paris and the provinces,[41] the national bar association organized a legal aid system premised in large part on volunteerism.[42] Under the regulating statute of the Romanian Order of Advocates, each local branch ("Council") of the Romanian bar was required to organize the provision of free legal assistance in its area by setting up a "legal assistance bureau."[43] "Counselors" tasked with setting up each bureau relied on both voluntary assistance provided by private lawyers and the services of salaried lawyers (paid by the Council specifically for this purpose). When the bureau requested a private lawyer to act on an uncompensated basis for a client, compliance was compulsory (including assisting with litigation). Similar arrangements were also in place in Poland, Latvia, and Hungary.

In Germany, trade unions also set up legal aid bureaus for workers to provide advice on accident insurance and social welfare law,[44] adopting a role similar to the one played by churches for centuries. Most of the unions retained lawyers to provide advice and representation to their members, and several also established legal aid offices for that purpose. Similar practices were documented in Czechoslovakia, Danzig, greater Poland, Hungary (both trade unions and church-related organizations), and Latvia (a tenants' association providing free legal advice to its members).[45]

In some European countries, legal aid bureaus relied on law students to supplement the work of volunteer lawyers. In 1885, for example, the Danish Bar Association established the institution of the *Retshjaelp*, a Copenhagen-based organization tasked with coordinating the provision of legal services to the poor by private lawyers and student clerks, both acting voluntarily.[46] The lawyer–student teams would see poor clients and provide advice on a variety of civil legal matters, including financial benefits for foster children, debt matters, divorce, landlord–tenant disputes, and so on. The Society of Students, based at the University of Copenhagen, eventually took over administrative responsibility for the *Retshjaelp*, and by 1927 similar organizations had been established in several provincial towns across Denmark.[47] The Danish model spread to Norway in 1893,[48] and parallel institutions have been documented elsewhere, such as the "Legal Dispensary" at the law school of Edinburgh University in 1900[49] and a similar organization at the University of Glasgow.[50] The influence of the Danish innovation even spread across the Atlantic.[51]

A German statistical report in 1912 provides an overview of private initiatives to provide legal aid; it recorded some 916 legal advice bureaus, of which around half were maintained by trade unions, 145 by church organizations, 119 by local municipalities, and 93 by women's legal aid organizations.[52] Collectively they provided advice to 1.8 million citizens.[53] In a similar vein, a report produced by the Austrian Department of Justice for the League of Nations revealed that, by 1926, there were nearly ninety unions providing free legal advice to their members across Austria, of which around twenty were Christian unions.[54]

No doubt such institutions were pervasive across much of Europe, and they portended the development of full-fledged, state-organized legal aid systems in the next century. For the time being, however, these initiatives still relied largely on volunteerism, whether grounded in notions of charity, communal solidarity, or legal duty.

The Expansion of the Welfare State and the Financing of Legal Aid

The expansion of the welfare state during the twentieth century had a critical influence on contemporary legal aid systems. As welfare states developed in the context of two world wars, procedural frameworks initially dependent on volunteerism and local organizational initiative eventually transformed into administratively centralized state-run institutions providing legal services subsidized by the government, as well as the eventual emergence of a "Social Bar," a subgroup of lawyers who specialize in legal aid cases.

The British welfare state is typically traced back to the liberal government that took office in 1908, in the years prior to World War I. Liberal reforms in England and Wales at the time included the replacement of the seldom used "*in forma pauperis*" procedure with a new Poor Persons' Procedure in 1914, importantly staffing a new "Poor Persons' Department" at the high court with civil servants who would facilitate the assignment of volunteer lawyers to individuals in need.[55] Although the Lord Chancellor's budget funded the administrative functioning of the department, the legal services themselves continued to be the responsibility of volunteer lawyers.[56] In the face of difficulties recruiting the volunteers, the Law Society – the national professional body for solicitors – took on responsibility for administering the Poor Persons' Procedure in 1925, along with inheriting the infrastructure of the Poor Persons' Department and funding to defray the Law Society's administrative expenses.[57]

Similarly, following World War I, the Swedish government adopted the view that the state was obliged to inform poor persons of their rights and facilitate their access to the courts.[58] As a consequence, the Swedish government took the step in 1919 of "nationalizing" several municipal "Poor Man's Advocate offices" that had been set up independently by private lawyers and municipal authorities in various Swedish towns since 1872.[59] Two separate laws enacted that year provided for state financing of poor persons' litigation fees and the subsidy of a national network of legal aid bureaus.[60] The bureaus would qualify for state funding provided that they submitted to regulation of their governance and operations as well as monitoring of their activities through the collection of statistical information by the national government.[61] Costs of the bureaus were shared between the state and the local municipality (approximately a 25/75 percent split), with staff costs constituting the largest portion of expenditure. A similar system of national/municipal funding for legal aid bureaus was adopted in Finland.[62] Meanwhile, in Germany, the basic system established by the 1877 Code of Civil Procedure (i.e., empowering judges to appoint lawyers and waive costs for litigants who could demonstrate their poverty) was revised in 1923 when a law was introduced providing for state funding (i.e., reimbursement of private lawyers) of legal aid work carried out under the 1877 Code.[63] However, such legal aid extended only to counseling and not litigation.[64]

The outbreak of World War II and the resulting mobilization effort produced a new host of needs on the home front in Britain. A principal innovation in addressing legal needs was the creation of the Services Divorce Department to provide legal assistance on matrimonial cases under the Poor Persons' Procedure when one of the parties was a member of the armed services.[65] For the first time, legal services were provided by salaried lawyers through the new department because of a sharply rising backlog of cases and the wartime shortage of solicitors. The precedent, spurred by concerns over the morale of the armed forces during wartime, would become the catalyst for a new approach to how the state would implement its responsibility to provide access to justice following the war, opening the door for arguments in favor of compensating lawyers propounded by the Law Society.[66]

In the meantime, civilians with wartime legal needs turned to Poor Man's Lawyer Centres, part of the Settlement House Movement, a progressive effort in the late nineteenth century to establish pioneering community centers where university student volunteers lived and worked to serve the growing urban poor.[67] The Centres were overwhelmed by demand, a crisis heightened by the increasing shortage of volunteer solicitors available to serve in the Poor Man's Lawyer centres.[68] In response to the unmet civilian needs, the Ministry of Health set up and funded Citizens Advice Bureaus (CABs) to help citizens tracing missing relatives in bombed areas or learning about the new wartime rules and regulations,[69] and they gradually spread throughout the country.[70] Although CAB services did not initially include legal advice or representation, lawyers began volunteering their services, enabling CABs to provide legal advice on housing, employment, family matters, and sometimes even litigation.[71]

After the war, the welfare state took a sharp uptick throughout Europe, driven by a sense that citizens who had endured such hard times required a guarantee of some minimum justice or fairness.[72] Nowhere did the welfare state grow as generously, quickly and comprehensively as in Britain, which introduced a universal approach two or three decades before Continental countries such as France and Italy.[73] In that context, it should be no surprise that the Legal Aid and Advice Act enacted in 1949 represented a watershed in how access to legal counsel was provided in Britain. From that point forward, the government would now compensate lawyers who provided free legal assistance, a system sometimes described as "judicare," with the Law Society continuing to manage it.[74] In the meantime, CABs continued to develop as well, providing a network of community-based advice offices. In 1950, the resulting system provided legal aid to 80 percent of the population, reaching as far as the lower middle class.[75] The coverage has been dramatically reduced since then, declining to a third or less of the population before shrinking again as a result of budget cuts that took effect in 2013, discussed later in this chapter.[76]

After a debate kicked off in the early 1950s, the Netherlands followed a similar path toward judicare in 1957, when the Act on Legal Aid for People of No or of Poor Means was passed. This legislation established a state subsidy for legal aid services provided to persons of low income.[77] Similar to the Swedish system, the legislation also provided for the establishment of several legal aid bureaus staffed by local lawyers. However, unlike the original network of bureaus, lawyers in the new state-sponsored bureaus would not actually provide advice themselves; rather, they would review the legal queries of citizens and issue certificates to those persons who qualified (based on both a merit and a means test). The certificates could then be taken to private lawyers who would receive state-provided compensation on the basis of the certificate. Today, despite some modest reforms in 1994, the Dutch legal aid system remains largely unchanged, although the budget has ballooned in recent decades.[78] It continues to operate through a network of frontline "Legal Services Counters," which perform an assessment, provide limited initial advice, and refer clients on to private lawyers, as necessary, who may be reimbursed by the state (through the Dutch Legal Aid Board). Approximately 36 percent of the Dutch population are eligible for legal aid according to their financial means.[79]

In parallel, the Nordic countries, as part of a common social democratic approach to providing universal coverage of social needs through the welfare state, adopted similarly comprehensive legal aid schemes, led by Finland with the adoption of a legal aid act in 1953 that provided for state-funded services by private attorneys during court proceedings.[80] In the 1960s, Sweden made its already well-established legal aid system more universal in response to pressure from the labor movement by requiring household insurance policies to include legal expense insurance. Today, 96 percent of the Swedish population over the age of sixteen is covered by such insurance.[81] The remainder of the population qualifies for public legal aid if they earn under EUR 28,000 per year. Sweden eventually emulated Finland in adopting a more statutorily unified legal aid system in 1972,[82] followed by Denmark (1974) and eventually Norway (1980).[83]

In the 1970s, during what is often called the "law reform movement," many other European countries revisited their legal aid legislation and embraced the example initially set by the Nordic countries, the United Kingdom, and the Netherlands. As a result, by the end of the 1970s, state-funded legal aid was institutionalized across the western part of the continent.[84]

In France, for example, a law introduced in 1972 replaced the volunteer-based system that had been in place since 1851.[85] The new law introduced a legal aid scheme that was largely modeled after the

British 1949 law, extending state subsidies to private practice lawyers.[86] Taking a far more modest approach, however, the French law subsidized lawyers only for their expenses, leaving fees uncovered.[87] Like the Dutch model, the system also relied on a network of legal aid bureaus, consisting mainly of government officials and lawyers – typically attached to municipal or local courts – to vet applicants and clear them for legal aid.[88] Once an applicant was deemed eligible, the local bar association would appoint a lawyer to represent the client, with the state subsidizing any expenses during litigation. No reimbursement was provided for advisory work.

The French system was significantly updated in 1991 and expanded to include compensation of legal aid lawyers, following the example set in the United Kingdom, Nordic countries, and the Netherlands. Although advice was still to be provided on a voluntary basis by lawyers under the *accès au droit* program coordinated by the French bar,[89] indigent persons could now receive legal representation (*aide juridictionnelle*) from qualified lawyers subsidized by the state and remunerated on a point-based system.[90] *Aide juridictionnelle* lawyers receive a fixed amount depending on the complexity of the matter and the estimated number of hours of legal work required, according to a point system.[91] Between 20 and 40 percent of the French population is estimated to be eligible for legal aid today.[92] Meanwhile, the German system, which had first been established under the 1877 Code of Civil Procedure, was revised in 1923 as discussed above and was revised again in 1980 to extend coverage of state-subsidized legal aid to include litigation as well as counseling.[93]

In short, the United Kingdom, the Nordic countries, and the Netherlands all adopted increasingly unified and comprehensive legal aid systems during the formation and expansion of the welfare state, from World War I through the 1970s. Over time, those systems came to rely on state-subsidized services rather than legal volunteerism. Despite legal aid cuts in each of them in the decades that followed, and partial reliance on insurance schemes in Sweden and the Netherlands, the top four European countries in terms of legal aid spending per inhabitant as of 2012 were (in order) Norway, the United Kingdom, the Netherlands, and Sweden.[94]

By the early twenty-first century, providing legal services to Europeans in need was no longer a *duty of the profession as a whole*; rather, it was a *professional practice area* for certain specialized lawyers who fully expected to be remunerated for their work.

Legal Aid as a Right, Not a Benefit

Along with dramatically expanding the welfare state, postwar Europe began a process of developing regional legal norms, including a human rights treaty backed up by a court. In the area of access to justice, European human rights norms complemented the new welfare state policies.

The European Convention on Human Rights (adopted in 1950) is interpreted by the European Court of Human Rights, whose decisions are binding in international law on countries that have ratified the Convention, including all the members of the European Union. Further, the constitutions of many European countries incorporate international treaty law into domestic law and give priority to human rights treaties to the extent they conflict with national law. In short, the jurisprudence of the European Court of Human Rights carries constitutional-level weight across much of Europe.

In comparison with US constitutional norms and jurisprudence, access to justice has acquired a much stronger constitutional-level protection in Europe through the Convention. With respect to criminal cases, the Convention has always provided an explicit guarantee of the right to legal representation, including free legal assistance "when the interests of justice so require," codifying many years of developing national law and practice in individual European states.[95] In 1950, US law stood in marked contrast. While the US Supreme Court definitively interpreted the US Constitution to provide a right to free legal assistance in the relatively small number of criminal proceedings brought in federal courts,[96] the matter remained unsettled with respect to state courts, which have jurisdiction over the vast majority of criminal proceedings in the United States. As an exception, the US Supreme Court had reversed a state court death penalty conviction because of a failure by the state to provide legal representation (*Powell* v. *Alabama* 1932), but it had decided the other way in a case involving a robbery (*Betts* v. *Brady* 1942).

In 1963, the US Supreme Court overturned *Betts* v. *Brady* in the case of *Gideon* v. *Wainright*, finding that the US Constitution required free legal assistance to the indigent, through interpretation of the Sixth Amendment right of the accused in criminal prosecutions "to have the assistance of counsel for his defense" and the Fifth Amendment right to "due process." The US jurisprudence has never been extended to civil matters, although there has been a mounting effort by progressive lawyers to call for "a civil Gideon."

In contrast, the European Court of Human Rights "discovered" a right to free legal assistance in civil matters in the European Convention, despite the absence of any explicit reference in the text. The Court first held that the right to fair trial guaranteed in Article 6 of the Convention implies a right to access to a court on civil matters (*Golder* v. *United Kingdom* 1975). It then expanded on the *Golder* ruling to find that access to court could not be meaningful without the implied right to free legal assistance even in civil cases, depending on the complexity of the procedure or the type of case (*Airey* v. *United Kingdom* 1979). The Court made that ruling despite the fact that Article 6 of the treaty specifies the right to free legal assistance in criminal matters but says nothing about free legal assistance in civil matters.

As a result of the *Airey* decision, and cases that followed it, European human rights guarantees include an inalienable right to free legal assistance in civil cases, at least for complex matters of significance. Although welfare state policy reforms were expanding legal aid systems in many European countries in parallel, the existence of an internationally guaranteed right, and a well-developed jurisprudence to illuminate it, has been an important driver of further reforms, particularly in the eastern part of Europe, which lagged behind Western Europe. As a consequence, state-funded legal aid programs were expanding in Eastern Europe during the fifteen years following the fall of the Berlin Wall, years before pro bono programs began to develop in the region.[97]

Access to Justice in the Eastern Part of Europe

Postwar Central and Eastern Europe followed a path diverging from Western Europe, adopting the socialist legal system until the fall of the Berlin Wall. In the socialist legal system, commercial law was unnecessary, and the civil code was simplified and reduced in scope. Criminal law remained well developed, but there was little need for the traditional liberal legal profession; the modest civil law needs of citizens were met by lawyers attached to the courts who could provide simple services at modest rates.[98] As a result, Eastern European countries did not follow the Western European trend of incorporating state-subsidized legal aid systems into the burgeoning welfare state. As one authoritative source puts it: one can accurately say, at one and the same time, that "there [was] no comprehensive Soviet program of legal aid" and, on the other hand, "the entire Soviet legal system constitute[ed] a system of legal aid."[99]

This would all change following the fall of the Berlin wall. As the legal systems of Central and Eastern Europe underwent a rapid transformation to adjust to market economies, legal aid – which quickly became necessary again – was provided by a bar- or court-appointed (*ex officio*) system, which had been the pre-Communist default, similar to most of prewar Western Europe. According to that system, legal aid was once again a professional obligation of the members of the bar, acting voluntarily. A combination of pressure from civil society groups, government reformers, and the legal profession, along with the drive to modernize laws to meet the technical conditions for membership in the European Union and the norms provided by the European Convention on Human Rights and related jurisprudence, resulted in significant legal aid reforms across the region.[100]

Between 2005 and 2012, new legal aid legislation was introduced across much of Central and Eastern Europe. The Dutch legal aid system offered an especially influential model, primarily because it represented a practical hybrid of the UK common-law approach and the less comprehensive French and German civil law models that had so influenced the prewar legal systems restored across Eastern Europe in the 1990s.[101] In Hungary, for example, a new civil legal aid law was adopted in 2003, which established a national legal aid system largely fashioned after the Dutch and English models. The law removed the mandatory requirement for all lawyers to provide legal aid on a voluntary basis and created a nationwide legal aid service with national and regional offices.[102] In 2006, Bulgaria passed a legal aid law establishing a system similar to the one adopted in Hungary.[103]

Similar legislative developments unfolded in Slovakia (2005), Latvia (2006), Georgia (2007), Moldova (2007), and Ukraine (2011).[104] Consequently, by the beginning of the 2010s, state-subsidized and sometimes even state-organized legal aid systems had been established across much of Central and Eastern Europe, mirroring the systems in place across Western Europe.

Legal Volunteers and the Social Bar

Despite the trend toward formalizing legal aid and granting compensation to an increasingly specialized subset of lawyers that provide it, voluntary efforts among mainstream lawyers have coexisted, continuing to fill gaps of unmet need. During the 1960s and 1970s, tracking trends in the United States, Europe also experienced the development of "neighborhood law centers," which were established in England, the

Netherlands, Belgium, and Norway.[105] In England, for example, the Law Centre Movement of the 1970s saw an estimated 3,300 lawyers collaborating with community workers to provide heavily discounted legal assistance to persons who were not otherwise being serviced by the profession (in the model of a family/community doctor).[106] In the Netherlands and Belgium, during the same time period, there emerged a student-led "law shop" (*recthswinkel/wetswinkel/boutique de droit*) movement, while in Norway there was the "law bus" (*juss bus*) movement.[107] The central idea behind all of these movements was to involve law students and volunteer lawyers in the provision of free legal services to individuals in poor communities and rural communities who fell beyond the reach of the mainstream legal community.

Such volunteerism within portions of the European legal professions has continued into the present day as evidenced, for example, by the European clinical legal education movement, which has spread across much of Europe, engaging law students working alongside qualified lawyers to provide free legal services to the poor and marginalized.[108] Although the advent of clinical legal education in Europe derives from influences outside the region, especially the US experience, it is also the product of intrinsic European values and historical antecedents.[109] Indeed, in Belgium, for example, the legal aid system still relies largely on voluntary efforts from within the Belgian bar.[110]

Nevertheless, by the turn of the twenty-first century, most European governments were improving access to justice in large part by compensating the lawyers who provided legal aid.

The result, across Europe, was the emergence of what might be referred to as a "Social Bar"[111] – lawyers working in private practice who specialize in areas of law typically relevant to the problems of the poor and whose work is subsidized by the state. Such lawyers develop practices that concentrate around family law, immigration law, criminal law, employment, and housing.

Of course, the size of the Social Bar varies dramatically among European countries. In some countries, there is a discernible segment of the private profession that has clearly specialized in legal aid work, whereas in others there remains broader engagement in legal aid work across the profession (see Table 6.1 below). In any case, it is clear that specialization has been underway across Europe for some time. In the Netherlands, for example, the percentage of lawyers engaged in the provision of legal aid as a proportion of the total legal profession

TABLE 6.1 Percentage of lawyers engaged in legal aid work (as a percentage of the total legal profession)

France[112]	48%
Netherlands[113]	44%
Spain[114]	28%
England & Wales[115] (civil only)	24%
Belgium[116]	24%
Latvia[117] (civil only)	10%
Hungary[118] (civil only)	4%

dropped from around 85 percent in the mid-1980s to 44 percent in 2012.[119] Meanwhile, in Britain, the figure for solicitors acting in civil legal aid matters has dropped from around 60 percent in the mid-1960s to 24 percent in 2016.[120] In France, legal aid services are concentrated in law firms of two or three lawyers, predominantly women, for which legal aid comprises 80 percent of the workload.[121] Perhaps specialization is necessary in that the only way for lawyers to handle legal aid work in a profitable manner is "through mass production."[122] On the other hand, concentration of legal aid services within a subgroup of the overall profession may be a factor in the marginalization of legal aid providers and disillusionment of the public about legal aid policies – evident to some degree even in the Nordic countries that have arguably gone farthest in adopting a universal approach to legal aid.[123]

THE SPREAD OF BIG LAW PRO BONO TO EUROPE

So why did pro bono develop in Europe, and is the provision of legal services *pro bono publico* anything more than a secular rebranding of *pro deo* policy and practice, with its roots in ancient Greece and Rome and the Middle Ages?

To further sort out these questions, it is first necessary to specify what the term "pro bono" actually refers to in the European context, particularly since the term was not widely used to describe any practices in Europe until about a decade ago. As mentioned earlier, pro bono has come to be associated in Europe with privately organized efforts to encourage lawyers, especially within the largest law firms, to volunteer their time to address unmet legal needs.

European pro bono practice, understood in that sense, has been influenced strongly by the development of pro bono in the United States. In particular, it has been modeled after the organized form of pro bono practiced in Big Law, at the largest US law firms, and the spread of the practice to Europe has tracked the internationalization of those firms.[124] Even that story, however, is more complex, as the diffusion of the underlying ethics, policies, and practices that undergird even Big Law pro bono has been multidirectional for more than a century.[125] The preceding section described the European experience with those underlying ethics, policies, and practices, and there were parallel and related antecedents in the United States that influenced the development of Big Law pro bono there as well.[126]

Looking beyond origins, however, the trajectory of Big Law pro bono in Europe can perhaps be best understood as the search by this new resource, or rather by those wishing to deploy it, for the most effective ways in which it could serve societal needs. In that sense, the development of pro bono in Europe differs from prior European efforts to serve the same needs, which were strongly driven by centralized authorities, such as the ruling classes in ancient Greece and Rome, the Catholic Church in the Middle Ages, and the governments of modern nation-states, in the context of the normative development of the legal system itself. The key distinguishing features with respect to pro bono, as compared with prior European efforts to assure access to justice, are the nature of the legal resource and the primary actors who are driving the institutionalization of that resource.

The Emergence of Global Big Law

Changes in the structure of the legal profession globally that began in the 1970s and accelerated in the 1990s were key to bringing about the new model of organized pro bono practice in Europe.[127] The emergence of megafirms in both the United States and London and the accompanying rapid internationalization of those firms created the conditions out of which the new, increasingly institutionalized and increasingly globalized model of legal volunteerism emerged.

Between the 1950s and the 1990s, the average size of commercial law firms expanded rapidly. In America, the fifty largest firms in 1950 employed an average of only forty-nine lawyers. That number more than quadrupled in the following three decades and nearly tripled from there in the subsequent two decades.[128] As of 2015, there were twenty-three US law firms with more than one thousand lawyers (several multiples in some cases), and the top one hundred firms employed an average of nine hundred lawyers.[129] Meanwhile, in England, a legal restriction in place until 1967 limited law firms to no more than twenty partners, although there were already thirty-eight firms with more than fifty lawyers each by 1950.[130] Once the restriction on the number of partners was removed, English law firms also expanded quickly. By 1997, the top twenty British firms employed an average of just under two hundred lawyers, and by 2015, the top one hundred firms averaged over five hundred lawyers each. By the late 1990s, the top five or so English firms (often referred to as the "Magic Circle") rivaled the top one hundred US firms.

In Continental Europe, law firms were initially less subject to the market-driven imperative to expand. In Germany, unlike the United Kingdom, the federal nature of the legal system created major legal markets in a number of German cities. Until 1989, German law firms were prohibited from practicing in more than one city, undoubtedly prompted by the protectionist impulses of the bar, which is organized independently in each German state. The prohibition effectively prevented the emergence of large law firms;[131] when the restriction was lifted, German firms began to merge and consolidate, connecting offices in multiple major economic centers (Dusseldorf, Frankfurt, Hamburg, Munich, and Berlin). Similarly, French law firms were also prohibited from having more than one office until 1989.[132] The Netherlands was exceptional in that it did not have such restrictions. As a result, by the mid-1980s, it boasted larger law firms than any other Continental European country.[133] Across the rest of Continental Europe, with the exception of a handful of large French firms, European firms remained relatively small until a wave of globalization of legal practice kicked off in the 1990s.[134]

The relaxation of prohibitions on consolidation of large law firms also led to an easing of restrictions on the entry of foreign law firms into Continental European markets. The late 1980s into the 2000s saw extensive international expansion among large American and English law firms.[135] Table 6.2 below illustrates the incredibly rapid rate of internationalization among six leading global law firms. Across the six firms, there was an average increase of nearly 350 percent in the number of foreign offices between 1987 and 2016.

TABLE 6.2 Expansion of selected global law firms[136]

	Number of staff				Number of foreign offices			
Firm	1987	2002	2016	% Increase 1987 to 2016	1987	2002	2016	% Increase 1987 tc 2016
Baker & MacKenzie (US)	1,070	3,762	4,200	+292%	30	68	69	+130%
Clifford Chance (UK)	803	3,180	3,400	+323%	12	33	34	+183%
Jones Day (US)	933	1,735	2,500	+167%	5	29	24	+380%
Freshfields (UK)	351	1,604	2,460	+600%	4	28	26	+550%
Sidley & Austin (US)	689	1,278	1,779	+158%	3	8	10	+233%
Skadden & Arps (US)	852	1,680	1,700	+99%	2	22	14	+600%

TABLE 6.3 Top locations for Global Big Law[137]

Rank	City
1.	London
2.	New York
3.	Frankfurt
4.	Hong Kong
5.	Washington
6.	Brussels
7.	Paris
8.	Singapore
9.	Tokyo
10.	Moscow
11.	Amsterdam
12.	Berlin
13.	Budapest
14.	Prague
15.	Chicago
16.	Los Angeles
17.	Munich
18.	Dusseldorf
19.	Bangkok
20.	Milan

In particular, there has been a dramatic increase in the number of European offices maintained by American and English firms. A 2000 study revealed that of the top twenty cities where large law firms maintained offices, twelve were in Europe.

The expansion of Anglo-American firms into Europe, which began with the expansion of transnational legal practice in the 1980s,[138] was met with varying degrees of caution, protectionism, or outright hostility by the local legal professions. For example, in 1984, the Brussels bar allowed members to enter into partnerships with foreign lawyers but imposed a quota on non–European Community lawyers.[139] In France, a 1992 law prohibited any foreign law firm established after 1971 from practicing French law and prevented any established prior to 1971 from using their foreign firm name.[140] In Spain, foreign law firms were prohibited from employing Spanish lawyers, and Swedish law prohibited cross-border mergers.[141] This pattern was common to much of Continental Europe, and US and UK law firms managed to operate in

Europe only through ad hoc arrangements with local regulators or by finding other ways to circumvent the restrictions.[142]

Large foreign law firms nonetheless persisted in their efforts to expand their European footprints, driven by economic globalization and the increasing demand for cross-border legal work that resulted.[143] Ultimately, local regulators, undoubtedly unable to withstand the increasing pressures of economic globalization, acquiesced through a series of reforms over a period of time, with the adoption of the EU "Establishment Directive"[144] in 1998, which represented a watershed. The Directive required EU countries to adopt legislation allowing European law firms to establish branch offices in other EU member states and to employ lawyers from multiple EU countries within the same firm. Throughout the 1990s and 2000s, Continental European firms, both in response to US firms and as a result of the Establishment Directive, pursued their own internationalization strategies. Dutch firms were the first to engage in transnational mergers in the early 1990s, pursuing tie-ups with firms in Belgium, France, and Luxembourg.[145] In Germany, there was a series of mergers with large British and US firms in the year 2000.[146] The German mergers in particular led to wider expansion into Europe more generally, as the German firms had already established strong presences in Central and Eastern as well as Southern Europe, resulting in extensive pan-European office networks for a number of British firms.[147]

Institutional Drivers across Global Megafirms

There were a variety of factors that led to the gradual internalization of pro bono culture within Big Law in the United States, including: efforts by large commercial law firms to attract top law students who might otherwise pursue public service careers; the introduction of an aspirational pro bono hours target (of 50 hours per lawyer per year) within the American Bar Association's model legal ethics rule on pro bono; the introduction of pro bono as a criterion for ranking commercial law firms in the *American Lawyer* magazine; and of course the cuts in US federal legal aid funding during the 1980s that led to a big push by the American Bar Association to promote pro bono practice.[148]

Further, the growing size of leading US law firms led to the development of pro bono infrastructure that would be crucial for the development of organized large-firm pro bono practice. One key feature of the American law firm business model, and a driver for the growth of US law firms, has been the employment of large teams of lawyers available to serve labor-intensive needs of large corporate clients at a moment's notice, as a business deal or litigation need develops without warning. As a result, law firms hired more lawyers than they needed at a given moment, with a business practice of pooling profits, enabling the firm to spread the risk of excess capacity. At the same time, that excess capacity created the opportunity to provide pro bono services without having as much of an impact on profitability as would be the case for a smaller firm.

As law firms grew, they also needed infrastructure to manage the business side of the firm,[149] creating an opportunity for firms to build in some infrastructure to manage pro bono practice in ways similar to any other area of practice and harness the full marketing value of the work. The result was a gradual institutionalization of pro bono, which spread along with the geographic footprint of the largest law firms.[150]

Although pro bono first became incorporated into US law firm practice on an institutional level in the 1970s, pro bono programs expanded dramatically beginning in the 1990s. Between 1993 and 2015, the total number of pro bono hours provided by the top 200 firms increased by over 200 percent.[151] Common features of the formal pro bono programs that developed to organize the work included: a pro bono committee, composed of firm lawyers tasked with identifying and reviewing potential pro bono cases; a system for assigning individual lawyers to pro bono cases; and a formal commitment from the firm to release lawyers for pro bono work.

One study suggested that, by 1973, at least twenty-four large US law firms had formalized pro bono programs. The most well-established pro bono programs were found in the largest firms and the largest cities, where those firms maintained offices. Typically, much of the pro bono work supported public interest legal advocacy NGOs and other non-profits; however, a significant portion (perhaps up to a third) was carried out directly for individual clients.[152] As those programs grew, firms began to hire or assign lawyers to work exclusively on managing them, and as of today the Association of Pro Bono Counsel, a membership organization for full-time pro bono managers, claims to include "over 200 attorneys and practice group managers who run pro bono practices in over 100 of the world's largest law firms."[153]

Meanwhile, in London, a 1992 effort by leading lawyers dubbed the Pro Bono Working Party failed to overcome resistance in the Law Society, but eventually led to the creation of the successful Solicitors

Pro Bono Group (SPBG) in 1996.[154] SPBG was established, without any formal support from the Law Society, with the purpose of uniting and centralizing the pro bono efforts of lawyers across England and Wales.[155] Its membership grew rapidly, and by 2000 it comprised 130 firms, including 40 percent of the top fifty firms.[156] Initially funded by a group of large law firms, it grew into a well-established charity, known as LawWorks, which is now funded by a mixture of charitable and public money.

A process of institutionalizing pro bono practice commenced at the very top English law firms as they began to appoint full-time pro bono managers and directors and implement pro bono policies. The first was Hogan Lovells (perhaps unsurprisingly an Anglo-American firm) in 1997, followed by Clifford Chance a few months later, and Linklaters and Allen & Overy followed shortly behind. By 1999, there were six firms that maintained full-time pro bono personnel.[157]

Two key drivers for this development were derived from the corporate culture of the clients of Global Big Law,[158] naturally propelled by law firms incentivized by competition over corporate clients. One driver was the emergence of an ethos of community-based volunteerism connected to the concept of CSR, as reflected in the work of the UK charity Business in the Community (BITC). BITC was influential in the initial abortive 1992 effort to promote pro bono in the United Kingdom, and it was responsible for incorporating into the earliest discussions of pro bono an understanding much broader than the US one, encompassing volunteer efforts of nonlawyer staff and charitable financial contributions.[159]

A second and related development was that corporate clients of large law firms began to promote CSR norms throughout their supply chains, inevitably reaching suppliers of legal services. British Aerospace, for example, adopted a policy in 1999 requiring law firms to undertake pro bono work or face being dropped from their panel of legal advisers. Increasingly, law firms report that they are asked about their CSR practices when they are being evaluated by prospective corporate clients; being in a position to describe a robust set of pro bono activities can give them a competitive advantage over their peers.[160]

Undoubtedly, however, another important driver for the development of pro bono in the United Kingdom was the increasing presence in London of law offices connected to large US firms, with their well-developed pro bono programs and firmwide efforts to promote them across offices. As both US and UK law firms expanded globally – to meet the demands of their multinational corporate clients – they sought to take their newly international pro bono practices with them. To some extent, law firms had an inherent interest in creating cohesive institutional cultures as they expanded geographically. In the words of Suzanne Turner (partner and chair of Dechert's firmwide pro bono practice), speaking to *American Lawyer* in 2003, "our commitment to pro bono is global in nature ... one firm, one commitment, one policy."[161] Likewise, the ethical dimension of pro bono knew no borders. Speaking in 2015, Turner justified a firmwide approach to pro bono another way: "There is legal need in *all* jurisdictions so to require pro bono in the US but not in Kazakhstan does not hold water."[162] Both management priorities and values were often transmitted by individual US lawyers, given the model of internationalization pursued by many US firms, at least initially, which was to send US-trained and qualified lawyers to open foreign offices.[163] Turner, for example, was based for many years in Dechert's London office.

In addition to the imperative of firm management priorities and the universal aspects of pro bono values, internal pressures may have also contributed to the drive by the megafirms to spread pro bono responsibilities across offices throughout the world. US megafirms needed to report pro bono hours only for lawyers in their US offices in order to be ranked among their peers in the annual pro bono survey conducted by *American Lawyer*, ultimately influencing whether they landed a coveted spot among the magazine's "A-List" of top twenty firms. Within a global law firm, the disproportionate pressure on billing hours felt by US partners was a potential source of tension within the global partnership, and that may have been one of the factors prompting the spread of law firm pro bono responsibilities more broadly. When *American Lawyer* documented pro bono hours per lawyer outside the United States for the first time, in 2014, the divergence between the US and non-US offices of the same firm was stark, with few exceptions, despite the overall spread of pro bono culture.[164]

In any case, the developments in the late 1990s and early 2000s led to the gradual institutionalization of pro bono practice in large commercial law firms in England. In 2002, just 15 percent of lawyers at large English firms (with over eighty-one partners) were engaging in pro bono practice. By 2012, that figure had soared to 45 percent.[165] Even in 2009, in the midst of the financial crisis, the largest city firms were reporting growing rates of pro bono.[166] Linklaters reported a 23 percent increase of pro bono activity in their London office between 2007–08 and 2008–09.[167] Clifford Chance reported an 8 percent increase in the same period and indicated that over half of its lawyers were now involved in pro bono work of some kind. Tom Dunn, the pro bono director at Clifford Chance, said at the time: "I put the increase in pro bono activity at Clifford Chance down to its steady on-going institutionalization."[168] Of course, by this time, several of the largest British firms had merged with major German practices, which had also yielded them practices in Central and Eastern Europe amongst other places.

In sum, by the end of the first decade of the 2000s, pro bono practice had been significantly institutionalized in the top one hundred American firms as well as the top ten or so British firms. While institutionalized pro bono was still unheard of within the largest Continental European firms, many of these firms had already merged with UK or US firms by the late 2000s, thus paving the way for pro bono in Continental Europe along with the widespread adoption of the Anglo-American law firm business model.

The Role of Pro Bono Entrepreneurs and Intrapreneurs

There were a number of efforts to explore the potential for actively developing pro bono practice in Continental Europe. One of the first was undertaken by the Cyrus R. Vance Center for International Justice, at the Association of the Bar of the City of New York. Joan Vermuelen, the founding executive director of the Vance Center, was the key organizer behind the International Conference on Access to Justice in 2000, referred to in the introduction. Along with the conference, Vermuelen was keen to find ways to deploy pro bono resources to contribute to civil society development efforts in Central and Eastern Europe, though concrete results never materialized.

Later in the 2000s, three London-based lawyers, one American and two British, began an initiative to extend the growing interest in pro bono practice among London law firms to counterparts on the Continent. Working within global megafirms and driven by a sense of "intrapreneurial" altruism, Dechert pro bono partner Suzie Turner, White & Case pro bono counsel Felicity Kirk, and Debevoise & Plimpton pro bono manager Florence Brocklesby (notably all representing US firms) joined together to establish informal pro bono roundtables for law firm lawyers in Paris and Frankfurt to discuss the possibilities for developing pro bono practice within French and

German commercial law firms.[169] The challenge that these early pro bono intrapreneurs faced was that they were trying to promote pro bono practice across multiple locations with diverse legal systems, and they had very limited networks within local civil society or the legal professions (beyond Global Big Law).

Ultimately, PILnet: The Global Network for Public Interest Law, an NGO then known as the Public Interest Law Institute (PILI) and founded by one of the authors, became the most important pro bono promoter in Continental Europe by bringing together a critical mass of actors motivated to help build pro bono culture. PILnet, in contrast with the law firm professionals referred to above, was well-connected in Continental civil society, and it was in a good position to build relationships with local bar organizations across much of Europe. Building such networks had been a primary focus for PILnet (established in 1997 with seed funding from the Ford Foundation). PILI had the original objective of promoting public interest law culture across Central and Eastern Europe and had done so successfully between 1997 and 2004, playing a role in establishing almost one hundred university law clinics across the region, collaborating with advocacy groups and expert bodies to promote legal aid reform and organizing scores of conferences bringing together relevant stakeholders (such as human rights NGOs, local lawyers, law schools, bar organizations, and government ministries).[170] PILnet would go on to embrace the roundtable format, first pioneered by the pro bono professionals in Paris and Frankfurt, and deploy it across the continent to great effect.

For PILnet, there had been an earlier false start or two with pro bono – most notably a failed conference at the University of Warsaw in 2003.[171] The conference had been coorganized with the Legal Clinics Foundation of Poland, a longtime partner of PILnet that successfully promoted and developed clinical legal education in Poland. The conference was so poorly attended that the couple of law firm lawyers who had decided to show up wondered why they had come.

Initially daunted, PILnet tried again two years later in 2005 after an informal study by a British summer associate seconded to the Budapest office of Allen & Overy revealed that attitudes of the Hungarian managing partners of large law firms might be shifting in favor of exploring the possibilities for developing pro bono in Hungary.[172] After developing a pilot clearinghouse initiative in Budapest to match local law offices with NGOs needing legal assistance, and having successfully initiated a small number of pro bono projects, PILnet undertook a more ambitious effort to institutionalize pro bono culture in Hungary and disseminate it throughout Europe.

PILnet's first move in its regional strategy was the tentative step of holding an international convening in Budapest in 2007, in large part intended to call positive attention to the nascent developments in Hungary, deploying a tactic widely used in the region to reinforce innovations in one country by "showing off" to peers in other European countries. PILnet dubbed the conference the European Pro Bono Forum – a title that may have seemed at the time a bit grandiose for what could have been a one-off event. The title reflected the intention of PILnet and several American law firm pro bono professionals who developed an early stake in the strategy that, if successful, the conference would become an annual convening, fueling development of pro bono culture in Europe. The initiators were inspired by the success of the Pro Bono Institute's annual convening in Washington, DC, which helped accelerate and deepen the development of pro bono in the United States, as well as a more nascent effort by LawWorks to hold convenings in London with a similar intention.

With those experiences in mind, PILnet held its inaugural European Pro Bono Forum. Organizers were pleasantly surprised at the substantial turnout, with 122 participants from 20 countries, including 62 lawyers and 60 NGO representatives attending to find out more about the possibilities for developing pro bono in a European country. The high turnout was due to a combination of PILnet's strong relationships with NGOs in the region and the pent-up curiosity generated within Global Big Law from exposure to pro bono via firmwide communications networks and generated more intentionally by the initial group of stakeholders from US megafirms.

With the significant numbers of participants, and the unusual opportunity for European NGOs and commercial lawyers to interact with each other, the Forum succeeded in creating an atmosphere that made participants feel like they were witnessing the beginning of something important and inevitable. By the end of the event, it was clear that a follow-up conference would be held the next year. With the second European Pro Bono Forum, PILnet was already dubbing it an annual event, and participation grew dramatically. The first three forums (2007, 2008, and 2009) all took place in Budapest, drawing participants from increasing numbers of countries; the 2009 forum attracted 150 participants from thirty-two countries.[173]

In 2010, PILnet decided to hold the Forum in Paris, building on the preexisting series of self-organized roundtable discussions among French law firms with international connections.[174] As a result, that year's Forum became the first major international gathering on pro bono to take place in Continental Europe outside of Budapest. It marked a turning point for the spread of pro bono culture in Europe, but it also represented a watershed in the perceptions of the Parisian legal community – at least within the higher echelons of the Paris bar as represented by the bar leadership and the French equivalent of Big Law.[175]

PILnet staff set the stage during the year leading up to the 2010 Forum with key partners who were already convinced of the desirability of promoting pro bono through participation in the local roundtables and by attending the Forum in Budapest. They worked together to facilitate behind-the-scenes discussions and persuasion efforts to promote the concept of pro bono among French law firms and within the organized bar. As a result, resistance within the French bar to the "Anglo-Saxon" institution of pro bono had broken down significantly by the time of the event. Jean Castelain, then *Bâtonnier* of the Paris bar, used the occasion to state in his official welcome note:

> The 2010 European Pro Bono Forum marks a turning point holding great promise.
>
> Little by little, many law offices within the Paris bar, in keeping with the practices of Anglo-Saxon firms, are making pro bono services a distinct segment of their overall activities.
>
> Mentalities have evolved and so has our culture: individual initiative is taking precedence in a domain in which serving the public interest used to be the business of the State alone.
>
> The Public Interest Law Institute (PILI) pursues the goal of "Mobilizing private sector resources for the public good."
>
> The Paris Bar also subscribes to this goal, without reservation. To achieve it, the Bar is working to create an institution focused on bringing together, encouraging and supporting personal initiatives through legal, logistical and financial assistance.
>
> This institution, undoubtedly organized as a foundation, will be able to receive donations and will include a Pro Bono Council composed of lawyers and leading figures, known and acknowledged for their social commitment.
>
> Our society has no alternative but for civil society to participate in pursuing the public interest.

> The voluntary provision of expertise constitutes a new means for expressing solidarity. This needs to be encouraged with all our energy.[176]

During his keynote address at the Forum, Castelain reiterated the Paris bar's commitment to contributing to the institutionalization of pro bono practice – including through the disbursement of private funds as part of a new *fond de dotation* set up for that purpose. As a consequence, Castelain provided official imprimatur both to the vocabulary and to the spirit behind pro bono legal practice as a component of French legal culture.

A cover story appeared the following spring in *Culture Droit: Le Magazine Interprofessional* (*Legal Culture: The Interprofessional Magazine*) under the title "*La Mode Pro Bono*" ("Pro Bono Fashion"). The cover story and accompanying articles documented the arrival of pro bono among *les grands cabinets*, most of them now affiliated with US or UK law firms. While it was clear that the concept had arrived within the upper echelons of the French legal profession, the coverage offered a healthy dose of skepticism about how much substance there was to the trendy adoption of an inherently Anglo-Saxon idea.

Nevertheless, pro bono practice has continued to develop in France. Coming around full circle from where the story started in New York, PILnet honored Jean-Luc Bedos during the 2013 Forum in Poland – together with the cofounder of his NGO and a member of the Paris bar council who had championed the 2010 Paris Bar Initiative – with an award for their pioneering work.[177] French law firms continue to undertake pro bono work, and pro bono programs have proliferated in Paris (Alliance of Lawyers for Human Rights, Pro Bono Lab, the Good Lobby). As the Paris Forum demonstrated, and later forums repeated, the hosting of the Forum had a strong validating effect for local pro bono champions because of the large numbers of engaged mainstream lawyers descending on the local legal community – prominent European officials and corporate leaders among them – along with the evident endorsement by Global Big Law and corporate brand names sponsoring the event.

There were a total of ten annual European Forums held as of 2017, when PILnet changed its strategy to hold one global forum a year, rather than convene regional gatherings. The European Forum typically welcomed several hundred participants, including representatives from a broad array of commercial law firms and NGOs that collaborate with them from all parts of Europe. In addition, PILnet successfully leveraged the conferences to launch so-called "sister clearinghouses": intermediaries mandated to connect law firms, nationally, with local NGOs that need legal assistance.[178] Clearinghouses have been established, for example, in Poland, the Czech Republic, Romania, France, Italy, and the Netherlands.[179] Each of these organizations (which typically charge firms annual membership fees or solicit charitable donations in order to sustain themselves) created opportunities for commercial lawyers to do pro bono work, further institutionalizing pro bono culture domestically and within large law firms across the continent. As a consequence of PILnet's collaborative efforts to link civil society and the legal community around legal volunteerism, the term "pro bono" has entered the vocabulary of lawyers whose mother tongues encompass the full variety of European languages.

In short, there are a number of factors that have resulted in a growing resource for free legal services in Europe: the globalization of Big Law practice and the spread of the Anglo-American law firm business model; the institutional infrastructure to support pro bono practice throughout new global law firm networks, though centered in the headquarters of such firms in locations such as New York, Washington, DC, and London; and the development and spread of a network of intermediary NGOs, such as PILnet, capable of connecting that resource to specific legal needs.

CONSTRAINTS ON ADAPTATION TO THE EUROPEAN CONTEXT

The Role of the Organized Bar

As discussed at the outset, the legal profession as such has its origins in Europe, and an ethic of legal volunteerism developed along with it as a means to ensure equal access to justice. With the advent of the welfare state, however, the dominant European model for securing access to justice gradually shifted to state subsidy for legal services provided by an expanding Social Bar. As a consequence, when Global Big Law began to undertake pro bono work in Europe, the organized bar initially resisted it, seeing the promotion of pro bono practice as a threat to the tradition of state support for legal aid.[180]

In the United States, the American Bar Association formally incorporated an expectation of pro bono service into standards of legal ethics,[181] a trend given renewed force following dramatic funding cuts to federal legal aid by President Ronald Reagan, beginning in 1980.[182] Accordingly, the organized bar was one of the main driving forces for the expansion of US pro bono practice. There were parallel efforts, as described above, within the Law Society of England and Wales in the 1990s, and then at the Bar Council, eventually resulting in a more tacit form of support from the organized profession. In Continental Europe, however, the organized bar was not initially supportive at all. Reactions to the first exploratory steps to developing pro bono practice in Continental Europe mirrored the same chilly reception given to the initial expansion of global law firms across the region. A large majority of the members of national bars on the Continent consisted of lawyers working within small local law firms or solo practices, many of whom actively participated in the Social Bar, and relatively few of whom worked in Global Big Law. As a result, the priorities of Global Big Law and the organized bar in Europe were not naturally aligned. Pro bono was often perceived by the bar leadership as just another competitive advantage for the global law firms. According to that perception, pro bono would provide just one more means for those market disrupters to use their superior communications and management infrastructure to call attention to themselves in a bid to outcompete local service providers for the most lucrative corporate clients.[183]

In order to navigate concerns from the organized bar about unfair competition or the potential to undermine ongoing debates with the government about levels of state subsidy for legal aid, many of the European clearinghouses (discussed earlier) that were set up to promote pro bono defined the term carefully to avoid rankling the leadership of the organized bar. When these national clearinghouses were established, they typically required their founding members, local offices of Global Big Law, to sign on to a "pro bono declaration" committing the firms to participate and support the development of pro bono. In concessions to the national bar associations, several of the declarations explicitly excluded the provision of legal services to individuals, defining pro bono as the provision of free legal services to nonprofit organizations.[184]

United Kingdom: Struggling over the Purse Strings

As described earlier, the design of the legal aid system in the United Kingdom dates back to liberal reforms in the period leading up to World War I, in particular the replacement of the antiquated *in forma pauperis* procedure with the Poor Persons' Procedure, a more organized, charitable system originally intended to include a fund to compensate litigants for out-of-pocket expenses and witness fees.[185] The Law Society of England and Wales was a key stakeholder from the beginning, with an explicit interest in ensuring that the burden of providing access to justice was spread evenly among the profession, at the same time guarding against the possibility that some lawyers would take advantage by touting their practices and thus gaining undue commercial advantage from charitable acts.[186]

Mounting pressure on the system in the wake of World War I, particularly the high demand generated by a strong surge in divorce, prompted transfer of administrative responsibility to the Law Society, along with a grant to cover administrative costs.[187] From that point forward, the groundwork was laid for a system premised on professional independence, but funded by the state.[188] As it evolved, the UK legal aid system perhaps inevitably grew to benefit – for a significant period – from the highest state funding per capita of anywhere in the world.[189]

The upward trajectory in state-funded legal aid in the United Kingdom hit a significant bump in the road in 2013, when the UK Legal Aid, Sentencing and Punishment of Offenders (LASPO) Act took effect, drastically cutting the national budget allocated to civil legal aid in the name of austerity. The budget cuts have continued, reaching a cumulative total of 40 percent over a five-year period, triggering outrage in the legal community, including a strike by barristers.[190] For years, pro bono proponents in the United Kingdom repeated, like a mantra, the phrase "pro bono is an adjunct to, not a substitute for, publicly funded legal services" in order to avoid handing a political justification to the UK government to reduce legal aid funding.[191] Yet, legal aid funding was cut significantly nonetheless, over the strong objections of the Legal Aid Society and the Bar Council.[192] Moreover, the worst fears of pro bono advocates have been borne out by decisions to refuse legal aid and other state-supported services in cases in which voluntary services were deemed to be available to the applicant.[193]

The budget cuts put pressure on pro bono resources that had developed to fill gaps in what had been a generally robust and generously funded civil legal aid system. The law firms that take on the most pro bono responsibility in the United Kingdom have also been quickest to point out that their services are most effective when leveraged by a strong legal aid system, including – in the United Kingdom – networks of charitable organizations that help to structure the inputs of law firm pro bono programs.[194] Moreover, they argue, the skillset of commercial pro bono lawyers at large law firms do not match up well with the individual-oriented legal needs that the formal legal aid system is designed to meet.

Germany: Regulating Fees

When Big Law pro bono first gained some traction in Germany around 2006, through the Frankfurt and Munich pro bono roundtables, there was significant doubt as to the very legality of pro bono work under German professional rules. Compensation of lawyers was regulated by a federal law (the German Act on Legal Counseling, "*Rechtberatungsgesetz*" or "*RBerG*"), which expressly prohibited the provision of free legal advice.[195] In December 2006, the RBerG was replaced with the Lawyers Compensation Act ("*Rechtsanwaltsvergütungsgesetz*" or "*RVG*"), which was hardly more supportive. The new regulatory framework was slightly more liberal, permitting lawyers to negotiate fees with clients with respect to advisory work, but fees in a litigation context were strictly regulated and determined in accordance with the "value of the claim" (e.g., calculated based on the value of the underlying transaction or damages claimed).[196] Despite the removal of the outright prohibition, the permissibility of Big Law pro bono under German law remained unclear at best (and appeared to be explicitly precluded with respect to litigation). The regulatory ambiguity created an understandable reluctance among German law offices to engage in pro bono, reinforced by the hostility of the German state and federal-level bars, which took the position that pro bono was prohibited under German law.[197]

The Global Big Law firms present in Germany tentatively engaged in pro bono work nonetheless – often restricting themselves to supporting cross-border projects outside Germany to avoid the regulatory question. In the meantime, they sought a more benign interpretation of the law regulating fees, as reflected in the publication of an article "*Rechtsberatung pro bono publico in Deutschland-eine Bestandsaufnahme*,"[198] authored by several lawyers advocating for pro bono practice from their Global Big Law perches. The article engaged in a detailed analysis of the provisions of the new legislation, working from the premise that pro bono advice was, by its very nature, provided to clients (singling out nonprofits in particular) who could not (and *would* not) pay for legal services in the regular marketplace. Moreover, unlike needy individuals, nonprofits could not qualify for legal aid and so would therefore go without legal services altogether if not for the availability of pro bono. The authors argued that the historical prohibition on free legal services (and the regulation of lawyers' fees under the new regime) was intended primarily to tackle anticompetitive price dumping practices, a purpose irrelevant to underresourced nonprofits, which would not be in a position to purchase legal services regardless of price.[199] The authors also noted that the new legislation explicitly permitted nonlawyers to provide free advisory legal services (provided they were supervised by a professional) and reasoned that professional lawyers should be permitted to provide pro bono advisory services by implication, even if they were excluded from litigating on a pro bono basis.[200]

In an opening keynote address at the 2011 PILnet Forum in Berlin, the head of the German Federal Bar confirmed that analysis, adding a further interpretation to support the provision of pro bono legal services even in a litigation context.[201] In a video address to the conference, the EU's European commissioner for justice, Viviane Reding, embraced pro bono practice, providing authoritative Europe-wide legitimacy for the concept.[202]

WHAT DOES EUROPEAN PRO BONO LOOK LIKE?

The Nature of the Resource

Who are the beneficiaries of European Big Law pro bono? There are a wide range of pro bono clients including individuals, nonprofit entities, corporate foundations, social investment funds, small and medium-sized social enterprises, academic institutions and groups, public benefit institutions (e.g., UN agencies and international organizations), and even countries and government departments (typically developing and transitional countries).

The overwhelming majority of recipients of Big Law pro bono services in Europe, however, are nonprofit NGOs. Asked to estimate the approximate distribution of pro bono work between nonprofit clients and individual clients, surveyed pro bono counsel revealed an average ratio of approximately 85 percent of pro bono work carried out for nonprofits, social enterprises, or public benefit institutions and 15 percent for individuals.[203] Considering that DLA Piper, which arguably has the most developed individual client pro bono practice in Europe, carried out only 3 percent of its pro bono work for individual clients in Continental Europe in 2017 (and 15 percent in the United Kingdom), it is likely that the true balance may be even more skewed toward organizational clients.[204]

But heavy emphasis on organizational clients stands in sharp contrast with US practice, where institutionalized pro bono practice originated. A 2016 survey revealed that 85 percent of US pro bono lawyers had provided services directly to individuals as compared with 35.5 percent who had provided assistance to organizations.[205] A 2012 survey focusing exclusively on large firms (with more than 100 lawyers) showed that 70 percent of those lawyers provided free legal services to persons of limited means in the last year (including advice, representation, and mediation) compared with 42 percent who provided advice to organizations in the same period.[206] Thirty-two percent indicated that they "typically" served organizations as pro bono clients.[207]

It is against such data that we can make sense of Scott Cummings' claim that in the United States, "pro bono has thus emerged as the dominant means of dispensing free representation to poor and underserved clients, eclipsing state-sponsored legal services and other nongovernmental mechanisms in importance."[208] Compared with the distribution in Europe, this is a marked divergence.

There are a number of reasons why pro bono in Europe is targeted more at nonprofit organizations than in the United States. First, the well-developed, and relatively well-funded, state-sponsored legal aid systems in place across most of Europe have meant that individuals' legal needs have been addressed to a large extent by state-subsidized lawyers comprising a relatively well-developed Social Bar. There are nonetheless some significant gaps of course, especially due to a spate of drastic budget cuts in the United Kingdom as well as dislocations caused by economic and political transformation in the newer member states of the European Union.

Second, the organized bar throughout Europe resisted Global Big Law pro bono, at least initially, partly because the promotion of pro bono was perceived as a marketing tool that could advantage the large globally connected law offices over smaller national firms, and partly to protect a Social Bar that comprises a substantial segment of the overall profession and is dependent on state-subsidized fees. For that reason, European Big Law has emphasized the provision of pro bono service to organizational clients as a priority, with the important exception of the United Kingdom, where there has been an imperative to fill the dramatic gap caused by legal aid cuts.

Third, the NGO sector in Europe has developed rapidly in the past several decades, continuing to be pushed along by trends in public–private partnership and pressures on traditional welfare state policies.

Of particular relevance, European NGOs pursuing social change through legal strategies have developed in recent decades, driven by diffusion of public interest law models in the eastern part of Europe following the fall of the Berlin Wall.[209] Such NGOs continue to be fueled by the law-centric global human rights movement, the influence of the European Court of Human Rights, and the advocacy opportunities presented by the supranational EU legal system and the increasingly technocratic and legalistic nature of EU policy.

Fourth, the work of key diffusers of law-based social change strategies, such as PILnet, the Open Society Foundations, and the Ford Foundation (among others), has had a significant effect on shaping the expectations of the legal community itself with respect to the demand for pro bono assistance. NGOs in Europe are historically less legally oriented than their counterparts in the United States, but from a law firm perspective, that looks like opportunity and need.[210] The growing number of legal advocacy NGOs in particular offers an appealing example to law firms, providing a wide range of strategically significant projects that appeal to pro bono lawyers seeking to achieve social impact and recognition from peers in their own firms and the broader legal community. In addition to creating opportunity at legal advocacy NGOs, that model drives lawyers to seek ways to offer similar assistance to NGOs that lack legal advocacy capacity altogether.

Fifth, NGOs are attractive pro bono clients for European Big Law because they are similar in some respects to the corporate clients that European Big Law generally serves. Client relationship protocols for NGOs are similar, it is easier to limit the scope of representation to a specific input, and the legal research, governance, and other transactional needs of NGOs often require a skill set similar to the needs of corporate clients.

Sixth, European Big Law is populated by large numbers of lawyers working outside their home jurisdictions, often working on cross-border regulatory or transactional legal issues for their corporate clients.[211] Such lawyers are often unqualified to provide pro bono services on matters of local law to individual clients. Moreover, Global Big Law's full-time pro bono managers, who are disproportionately based in New York, Washington, DC, and London for historical reasons, can most readily develop relationships through transnational NGO networks. Internationally connected pro bono clients are especially welcome because they serve overall law firm management goals when they spur multioffice teams that work on pro bono projects involving multiple jurisdictions, languages, and legal cultures.

Putting the Resource to Best Effect

The emphasis by European Big Law on organizational clients has been of great benefit to the formal civil society organizations that have blossomed, especially in the eastern part of Europe, during the last thirty years. Furthermore, the resources of European Big Law are providing much-needed capacity to NGOs to engage on law and governance issues on behalf of their respective constituencies, both within their own countries, and importantly, across the European legal order. The gradual construction of the institutions and legal order of the European Union has resulted in a policy context characterized by a plurality of judicial sources and authorities. In the process, the EU has created new, increasingly legalized and technocratic modes of governance and democratic participation that have profoundly shaped the nature and practice of law and policy.[212]

Today, the EU institutional and legal order radiates outwards, acting on an ever-increasing range of issues both within Europe and beyond. The supranational EU governance structure and its major institutions have become immensely powerful, substantially shaping the everyday lives of Europeans. In Europe, the EU legal and institutional order is made all the more complex by its coexistence with other international institutions emerging from agreements both among EU member states and other governments, and between the EU and third countries as well as international organizations. The World Trade Organization and the Council of Europe, for example, have their own dispute resolution mechanisms, which generate overlapping legal norms.

Ultimately, then, we are left with a legislative, judicial, and policy landscape in Europe characterized by vertical and horizontal pluralism as well as other forms of complexity.[213] There is vertical pluralism in the overlap and interaction among local, national, European, and international legal norms and norm-generating bodies. There is horizontal pluralism in the growing relevance of legal norms generated in one part of Europe for the rest of Europe; for example, norms generated in Hungary or Sweden can be significant in Latvia or Italy. In addition, there is also intense procedural and substantive complexity. To pursue policy change, private sector and civil society actors alike must proceed along multiple avenues in the legislative, judicial, and policy processes (litigation, administrative actions, consultations, petitions, etc.) as well as acquire significant specialized knowledge of various fields (environmental law, asylum law, discrimination, labor and social law, free movement law, etc.). As a result, both commercial and noncommercial actors aiming to influence the regulation of their respective industries/ policy areas must engage at multiple levels.[214]

The resultingly complex array of institutions and legal norms are an important target for civil society organizations aiming to achieve positive social impact. First, EU institutions have powerful effects on society, for better or worse. Second, reforms and policy changes in one part of the system can have an impact across the whole system. Meanwhile, Brussels begins to develop the lobbying culture of Washington, DC. From tobacco companies and food manufacturers to airlines and banks, big business is keen to have the ear of EU institutions and willing to invest vast sums of money to secure favorable policy outcomes.[215] Modestly resourced civil society groups pursuing their own goals cannot easily compete for influence because of the need for significantly detailed knowledge about comparative law and policy as well as expertise in navigating sophisticated avenues for participation.

At the same time, the growth of European Big Law has been driven in large part by the global business need to engage with the increasingly complex legal and governance structure of Europe. European Big Law formed as the result of mergers across European jurisdictions, which created large multioffice law firm networks well-suited to providing comparative analysis of specific laws and legal and administrative practices across European jurisdictions for their commercial clients. As a result, pro bono lawyers practicing in European Big Law are particularly well-suited to help NGOs engage effectively in the complex legislative, judicial, and policy processes of Europe.[216] European governance/policy requires comparison and analysis of specific laws and legal and administrative practices across multiple jurisdictions. It should be no surprise, then, that comparative legal research forms a very large part of the pro bono work that goes on across Europe. Comparative legal research forms a very large part of the pro bono work that goes on across Europe. A survey carried out by one of the authors among 100 NGOs listed in the European Transparency Register revealed that just under 80 percent of them had received or were interested in receiving pro bono "legal research" assistance. This made legal research the most popular form of pro bono legal assistance by a margin of over 15 percent (followed by "governance/corporate" advice).[217]

A typical example would be the work of Clifford Chance on behalf of Fair Trials International in 2014. Clifford Chance undertook multijurisdictional research on breaches of Articles 5 and 6 of the ECHR through the efforts of twenty-eight lawyers across eighteen European offices. The work contributed to the development of three EU directives on the right to translation and interpretation and the right to information during criminal proceedings, as well as the right to access to a lawyer and communication with a consular official or nominated person.[218] It would be difficult for an NGO to be able to secure the financial resources needed to conduct research on that scale on its own.

Similarly, the Romanian LGBTi advocacy group Accept teamed up with White & Case to achieve a sophisticated legal judgment at the European Court of Justice in 2017. In *Coman* v. *Romania*, a team composed of experienced corporate commercial litigators and Romanian human rights lawyers persuaded the Grand Chamber of the Court of Justice to hold that the term "spouse" includes same-sex spouses of EU citizens for the purpose of freedom of movement and residency rights in the EU. While there had been a series of cases at the European Court of Human Rights protecting the rights of LGBTi persons, the case was remarkable in that it represents one of the first times that a commercial law firm and an NGO have successfully teamed up before the European Court of Justice (a court that is traditionally far less relevant and accessible for NGO advocacy than the European Court of Human Rights).

CONCLUSION

While the development of Big Law pro bono practice in Europe may have been inevitable given the strong global trends that have driven its growth around the world, pro bono in Europe has developed unique features, shaped by history and traditions, European human rights norms, a strong preference in favor of welfare state polices, and the deeply rooted role of an extensive Social Bar subsidized by the state.

A tradition of legal volunteerism runs deep in Europe; indeed, it is the foundation for modern legal aid systems across the Continent. But the most distinctive feature of European pro bono, compared with the American variant, is the heavy emphasis on providing services to nonprofit organizational clients. There are many reasons for that divergence, but the most significant root cause is the relatively extensive availability of legal aid services in Europe, even in civil matters, which is not only assured by policy preferences and tradition but is also backed up to a significant degree by the case law of the European Court of Human Rights.

While European Big Law pro bono does not play as essential a role in providing access to justice for individuals as it does in the United States, the dramatic increase in pro bono support for civil society organizations over the past decade is significant in a number of ways. In particular, the Big Law pro bono community in Europe constitutes an important new group of stakeholders for access to justice and human rights. In the United Kingdom, for instance, where a once generous legal aid system has been cut back dramatically, the well-established law firm pro bono community has risen to the defense of legal aid lawyers and the charitable organizations that work hand in hand with them.

Moreover, law firms across Europe now provide critical assistance to NGOs promoting citizen engagement on important social issues like LGBTi and Roma rights as well as immigration, climate change, human trafficking, and many other issues. As a result, European pro bono is helping make EU democracy work, and it is supporting the realization of human rights, reinforcing liberal democratic European values in the process. At the same time, European Big Law pro bono offers important resources and assistance to burgeoning NGO sectors that are playing a growing role in filling gaps created by shrinking welfare states.

Ultimately, the European experience with pro bono represents something of a conundrum. When law firms step up to contribute pro bono services, do they mitigate, or do they contribute to the eroding support for a robust state responsibility to provide access to justice? Is law firm support for EU democracy and citizen engagement sufficient to compensate for any weakening in state support for access to justice? Will the role of NGOs continue to grow in Europe, and will pro bono legal services – facilitated through collaboration between European Big Law and civil society – continue to grow along with it?

NOTES

1. *Roundtable: Pro Bono and Volunteer Practices April 8, 2000*, 24 FORDHAM INT'L L.J. S 341, 353 (2000).
2. One of the authors, Edwin Rekosh, is the founder of PILnet.
3. *See generally* Scott L. Cummings, *The Politics of Pro Bono*, 52 UCLA L. REV. 1 (2004).
4. *Id.* at 33–41.

5. *See* Jette Steen Knudsen, Jeremy Moon, & Rieneke Slager, *Government Policies for Corporate Social Responsibility in Europe: A Comparative Analysis of Institutionalisation*, 43 POL'Y & POL. 81 (2015); Ayselin Yıldız & Gokay Ozerim, *Corporate Social Responsibility in European Context*, *in* CONTEMPORARY ISSUES IN CORPORATE SOCIAL RESPONSIBILITY 43 (Duygu Türker, Huriye Toker & Ceren Altuntas eds., 2014).
6. CULTURE DROIT, May 2011.
7. Daniel Bonilla, Access to Justice and Public Interest Law (2017).
8. Anton-Hermann Chroust, *Legal Profession in Ancient Athens*, 29 NOTRE DAME L. REV. 339, 342–44 (1954).
9. *Id.* at 344.
10. *Id.* at 353.
11. *Id.* at 355.
12. *Id.* at 372.
13. *Id.* at 352; *see also* LENE RUBINSTEIN, LITIGATION AND COOPERATION: SUPPORTING SPEAKERS IN THE COURTS OF CLASSICAL ATHENS 230–31 (2000).
14. *Id.* at 230–31.
15. Anton-Hermann Chroust, *Legal Profession in Ancient Republican Rome*, 30 NOTRE DAME L. REV. 97, 105–08 (1954).
16. *Id.* at 136; ROSCOE POUND, JURISPRUDENCE 697 (1959).
17. Mauro Cappelletti & James Gordley, *Legal Aid: Modern Themes and Variations Part One: The Emergence of a Modern Theme*, 24 STAN. L. REV. 347, 349 (1972); Chroust, *supra* note 15, at 136.
18. Chroust, *supra* note 15, at 136, 137.
19. Pound, *supra* note 16, at 696, 697; Chroust, *supra* note 15, at 105–06; Cappelletti & Gordley, *supra* note 17, at 349.
20. DEUTEROTOMY 24:14; PROVERBS 14:20. For a discussion of the religious roots of professional charity, see James A. Brundage, *Legal Aid for the Poor and the Professionalization of Law in the Middle Ages*, 9 J. LEGAL HIST. 169, 170 (1988); Donald B. Robertson, John Lynch & Mary Anne Noone, *Pro Bono as a Professional Legacy*, 19 LAW IN CONTEXT 97, 103 (2001).
21. Brundage, *supra* note 20, at 170, 171; Cappelletti & Gordley, *supra* note 17, at 351.
22. Nick Huls, *From Pro Deo Practice to a Subsidized Welfare State Provision: Twenty-Five Years of Providing Legal Services to the Poor in the Netherlands*, 5 MD. J. CONTEMP. LEGAL ISSUES 333, 333 (1994).
23. Cappelletti & Gordley, *supra* note 17, at 351.
24. Brundage, *supra* note 20, at 173; Cappelletti & Gordley, *supra* note 17, at 351.
25. Cappelletti & Gordley, *supra* note 17, at 352.
26. *Id.*
27. Brundage, *supra* note 20, at 174, 175.
28. *Id.* at 174.

29. Michael Lessnoff, Social Contract: Issues in Political Theory 42, 71 (1986).
30. *Id.*; Brundage, *supra* note 20, at 174. See Sidney B. Jacoby, *Legal Aid to the Poor*, 53 Harv. L. Rev. 940, 940–41 (1940), for an interesting discussion in this context of the Equal Protection Clause of the US Constitution in the 1940s.
31. Ernst Joseph Cohn, *Legal Aid for the Poor: A Study in Comparative Law and Legal Reform*, 59 L.Q. Rev. 250, 254 (1943); Cappelletti & Gordley, *supra* note 17, at 356.
32. Cohn, *supra* note 31, at 254, 255.
33. Cappelletti & Gordley, *supra* note 17, at 356.
34. *Id.*
35. *Id.*
36. Iceland: Law of November 16, 1907; Luxembourg: Law on Legal Aid, March 23, 1893; San Marino: Law on Legal Aid for Poor Persons, December 20, 1884; Spain: Civil Procedure Law of February 3, 1881. *See generally* League of Nations, Legal Aid for the Poor, V. Legal (1927).
37. Christopher Pierson, Beyond the Welfare State? The New Political Economy of Welfare 103 (1998).
38. *Id.*
39. Erhard Blankenburg, *The Lawyers' Lobby and the Welfare State: The Political Economy of Legal Aid*, *in* Transformation of Legal Aid: Comparative and Historical Studies 113, 115–18 (Don Fleming, Francis Regan, Tamara Goriely & Alan Paterson eds., 1999). It was around this time that the first legal aid program was set up in the United States by the German Legal Aid Society, which later became the Legal Aid Society of New York. *See* Edwin Rekosh, *Constructing Public Interest Law: Transnational Collaboration and Exchange in Central and Eastern Europe*, 13 UCLA J. Int'l L. & Foreign Aff. 55, 93 (2008).
40. Cohn, *supra* note 31, at 257; Erhard Blankenburg & Jeremy Cooper, *A Survey of Literature on Legal Aid in Europe*, 2 Windsor Y.B. Access Just. 263, 276 (1982). *See generally* League of Nations, *supra* note 36.
41. League of Nations, *supra* note 36, at 430.
42. *Id.* at 209, 452.
43. Law concerning the Organisation and Unification of the Order of Advocates, August 29, 1925. *See* League of Nations, Legal Aid for the Poor, V. Legal 1927, 209–11.
44. Blankenburg & Cooper, *supra* note 40, at 281.
45. League of Nations, *supra* note 36, at 423, 424, 439, 443, 451.
46. Albert H. Jessel, *A Poor Man's Lawyer in Denmark*, 7 L.Q. Rev. 176, 177 (1891).
47. League of Nations, *supra* note 36, at 423, 425.
48. Olaf Halvorsen Rønning, *Legal Aid in Norway*, *in* Outsourcing Legal Aid in the Nordic Welfare States 15, 18 (Ole Hammerslev & Olaf Halvorsen Rønning eds., 2018).

49. Hector Lewis MacQueen, *Lawyers' Edinburgh 1908–2008*, 8 BOOK OF THE OLD EDINBURGH CLUB – NEW SERIES 27, 38 (2010).
50. *Id.*; ROBERT EGERTON, LEGAL AID 38 (ILS ed., Routledge 1998) (1945).
51. Prominent US law reformers observed the innovative involvement of Danish law students in expanding the resources available to provide access to justice, and that provided an early inspiration for what eventually became the robust field of clinical legal education in the United States. *See* Rekosh, *supra* note 39, at 84.
52. Blankenburg & Cooper, *supra* note 40, at 281.
53. Incidentally, all of these organizations were subsequently dissolved in 1933/34 by the Nazi regime, and their functions were ostensibly absorbed by the *Rechtsfürsorge*. *See* Blankenburg & Cooper, *supra* note 40, at 281.
54. League of Nations, *supra* note 36, at 413, 414.
55. Richard I. Morgan, *The Introduction of Civil Legal Aid in England and Wales, 1914–1949*, 5 TWENTIETH CENTURY BRIT. HIST. 38, 41–42 (1994).
56. *Id.* at 43.
57. *Id.* at 47–50.
58. Egerton, *supra* note 50, at 45.
59. Cohn, *supra* note 31, at 258, 259; Egerton, *supra* note 50, at 45.
60. The two laws were the Law Concerning Free Legal Proceedings and the Royal Decree Concerning the Grant of Government Subsidies to Public Legal Aid Institutions, both enacted in 1919. Jon T. Johnsen, *Nordic Legal Aid*, 5 MD. J OF CONT. LEGAL ISSUES 301, 304 (1994).
61. Cohn, *supra* note 31, at 258, 259; Egerton, *supra* note 50, at 45, 46.
62. Johnsen, *supra* note 60, at 305.
63. Karl August Klauser & Robert A. Riegert, *Legal Assistance in the Federal Republic of Germany*, 20 BUFF. L. REV. 583, 585 (1971).
64. James Maxeiner, *A Right to Legal Aid: The ABA Model Access Act in International Perspective*, 13 LOY. J. PUB. INT. L. 61, 83–84 (2012).
65. Morgan, *supra* note 55, at 57.
66. *Id.* at 58.
67. The movement was a precursor to the profession of social work. *See* Stefan Köngeter, *Transnational Roots of the Settlement Movement: The Example of St. Christopher House in Toronto, Canada*, 2 TRANSNAT'L SOC. REV. M-43 (2012). The two most prominent examples were Cambridge House and the Mary Ward Centre in London, both of which continue to provide community-based legal services to this day. Morgan, *supra* note 55, at 61.
68. Morgan, *supra* note 55, at 61.
69. *Id.*
70. Ernst Joseph Cohn, *Legal Aid to Soldiers in the British Army*, 92 U. PA. L. REV. 166, 167 (1943).
71. *Id.* at 167; Cohn, *supra* note 31, at 258.
72. TONY JUDT, POST WAR: A HISTORY OF EUROPE SINCE 1945, at 76 (2005).

73. *Id.* at 75, 372.
74. Morgan, *supra* note 55, at 66–70.
75. *Id.* at 73.
76. Yohanna Sallberg & Benjamin Politowski, *Civil Legal Aid: England and Wales, Scotland and N Ireland Compared* 6 (June 9, 2016) (House of Commons Library, Briefing Paper No. 7603, 2016).
77. Blankenburg & Cooper, *supra* note 40, at 276.
78. RAAD VOOR RECHBIJSTAND, LEGAL AID IN THE NETHERLANDS: A BROAD OUTLINE (2015).
79. *Id.* at 5.
80. Ole Hammerslev & Olaf Halvorsen Rønning, *Outsourcing Legal Aid in the Nordic Welfare States, in* OUTSOURCING LEGAL AID IN THE NORDIC WELFARE STATES, *supra* note 48, at 311, 312; Antti Rissanen, *Legal Aid in Finland, in* OUTSOURCING LEGAL AID IN THE NORDIC WELFARE STATES, *supra* note 48, at 77.
81. Isabel Schoultz, *Legal Aid in Sweden, in* OUTSOURCING LEGAL AID IN THE NORDIC WELFARE STATES, *supra* note 48, at 43, 44–46.
82. *Id.* at 45
83. Hammerslev & Halvorsen Rønning, *supra* note 80, at 312.
84. Starting in the early 1970s, a series of legal aid statues were introduced across Europe. In addition to those countries already mentioned, examples include France (1972), Germany (1972), and Italy (1973). *See* Mauro Cappelletti, *Legal Aid in Europe: A Turmoil*, 60 AM. BAR ASS'N J. 206, 206 (1974). Denmark introduced a general obligation on authorities to provide free legal advice to help citizens overcome social obstacles as part of general social welfare legislation enacted in 1974, and it created a full-fledged lawyer-based free legal aid scheme in 1978. Bettina Lemann Kristiansen, *Legal Aid in Denmark, in* OUTSOURCING LEGAL AID IN THE NORDIC WELFARE STATES, *supra* note 48, at 99, 101–02.
85. Loi du 3 Janvier 1972, No. 72, 11, JO para. 15.
86. Blankenburg & Cooper, *supra* note 40, at 286.
87. *Id.* at 286; Mel Cousins, *Legal Aid Reform in France and the Republic of Ireland in the 1990s, in* ACCESS TO JUSTICE IN CENTRAL AND EASTERN EUROPE: SOURCE BOOK 135, 137–38 (Public Interest Law Initiative ed., 2003).
88. Blankenburg & Cooper, *supra* note 40, at 287.
89. LATHAM & WATKINS LLP, A SURVEY OF PRO BONO PRACTICES AND OPPORTUNITIES IN 84 JURISDICTIONS 202 (2016), https://www.lw.com/admin/Upload/Documents/Global%20Pro%20Bono%20Survey/A-Survey-of-Pro-Bono-Practices-and-Opportunities.pdf (last visited Aug. 8, 2020).
90. *Id.* at 203.
91. *Id.* at 204.
92. Maurits Barendrecht, Laura Kistemaker, Henk Jan Scholten, Ruby Schrader & Marzena Wrzesinska, *Legal Aid in Europe: Nine Different Ways to Guarantee Access to Justice? Executive Summary*, HIIL 37

(2014), www.hiil.org/wp-content/uploads/2018/09/Legal-Aid-in-Europe-Executive-Summary.pdf (last visited Aug. 8, 2020).

93. Maxeiner, *supra* note 64, 83–84.
94. *See* Johnsen, *supra* note 60, at 252. According to data from the Council of Europe's European Commission for the Efficiency of Justice, legal aid cuts have resulted in the United Kingdom slipping further down the list, situating it between Sweden and the Netherlands. *See* https://public.tableau.com/profile/cepej#!/vizhome/CEPEJ-Explorerv4_0/Tables (last visited Feb. 26, 2019).
95. "Everyone charged with a criminal offence has the following minimum rights: . . . (c) to defend himself in person or through legal assistance of his own choosing or, if he has not sufficient means to pay for legal assistance, to be given it free when the interests of justice so require." EUR. CONV. ON H.R. AND FUNDAMENTAL FREEDOMS, Art. 6(3).
96. Johnson v. Zerbst, 304 US 458 (1938).
97. *See* Rekosh, *supra* note 39.
98. Imre Szabo, *The Socialist Conception of Law, in* INTERNATIONAL ENCYCLOPEDIA OF COMPARATIVE LAW VOL. II, THE LEGAL SYSTEMS OF THE WORLD: THEIR COMPARISON AND UNIFICATION 17 (1975).
99. Cappelletti & Gordley, *supra* note 17, at 389, 390.
100. Rekosh, *supra* note 39, at 94–95; Roger Smith, *Human Rights and Access to Justice*, 14 INTL. J. LEGAL PROF. 261 (2008).
101. *See generally* ACCESS TO JUSTICE IN CENTRAL AND EASTERN EUROPE: SOURCE BOOK, *supra* note 87.
102. Report, Access to Justice in Central and Eastern Europe, 2nd European Forum on Access to Justice 13–14 (Organized by the Public Interest Law Initiative in collaboration with the Open Society Justice Initiative, Budapest, Hungary, Feb. 24–26, 2005).
103. *Id.* at 12.
104. Georgia: Law of Georgia on Legal Aid No. 4955, July 2, 2007; Latvia: Act on State Legal Aid, Cabinet Regulation No. 920 of November 6, 2006 on forms of legal aid; Moldova: Law No. 198-XVI of July 26, 2007 on State Guaranteed Legal Aid; Slovakia: Act No. 327/2005 on the provision of legal aid to persons in material need (the Legal Aid Act); and Ukraine: Law No. 3460-VI of June 2, 2011 on Free Civil Legal Aid.
105. BRYANT G. GARTH, NEIGHBORHOOD LAW FIRMS FOR THE POOR: A COMPARATIVE STUDY OF RECENT DEVELOPMENTS IN LEGAL AID AND THE LEGAL PROFESSION 52–63 (1980); Steven Gibens, *Legal Aid in Belgium: The Absence of a Tradition?*, 13 INT'L J. LEGAL PROF. 3, 3–18 (2006).
106. Andrew Boon & Avis Whyte, *"Charity and Beating Begins at Home": The Aetiology of the New Culture of Pro Bono Publico*, 2 LEGAL ETHICS 172, 176, n.44 (1999).
107. Garth, *supra note* 105, at 118–29; *see also* Jon T. Johnsen, On the Origins of the Juss-Buss (2011) (unpublished manuscript on file with authors).

108. *See generally* REINVENTING LEGAL EDUCATION: HOW CLINICAL EDUCATION IS REFORMING THE TEACHING AND PRACTICE OF LAW IN EUROPE (Alberto Alemanno & Lamin Khadar eds., 2018).
109. Rekosh, *supra* note 39, at 83–92.
110. Steven Gibens & Bernard Hubeau, *Socially Responsible Legal Aid in Belgian Society*, 1 INT'L J. LEGAL PROF. 20, 67–86 (2013); Steven Gibens & Jean Van Houtte, *Towards a More Effective Legal Aid: The Belgian Case in Comparative Perspective*, 2 SOCIOLOGIA DEL DIRITTO 83 (2011).
111. The "Social Bars" of Europe have become organized to some extent, forming associations for legal aid lawyers, family lawyers, children's rights lawyers, immigration lawyers, etc. Members of this professional subgroup tend to receive lower levels of remuneration than the mainstream of the profession, and they are often situated geographically in poorer neighborhoods or outside of capital cities. The concept of a "Social Bar" seems to have been coined by German sociologist Erhard Blankenburg in 1982 when referring to the experience of legal aid in the United Kingdom and the Netherlands. *See* Erhard Blankenburg, *European Experience in Innovating Legal Services*, 2 WINDSOR YB ACCESS JUST. 247, 248 (1982).
112. Figures for 2012–13. *See* Steven Gibens & Bernard Hubeau, *National Report – Belgium*, ILAG, DEN HAAG 5.2.2 (2013).
113. Figures for 2014–15. *See* Raad voor Rechtbijstand, *Legal Aid in the Netherlands – A Broad Outline – 2016*, DEN HAAG 29 (2013).
114. Figures for 2014–15. *See* LATHAM & WATKINS, *supra* note 89, at 616.
115. Figures for July 2016. Based on the number of solicitors firms engaged in civil representation work. *See* Solicitors Regulation Authority, Legal Aid Statistics England and Wales (July 2016); Solicitors Regulation Authority, Regulated Population Statistics (Solicitors) (July 2016).
116. Figures for 2012–13. *See* Gibens & Hubeau, *supra* note 117, at 5.2.2.
117. Figures for 2012–13. *See* Agris Batalauskis, "National Report – Latvia," International Legal Aid Group (ILAG) Conference (June 2013) at 7.
118. Figures for 2007–08. *See* Márta Pardavi, *The Legal Profession in Hungary*, ORGANIZATION FOR SECURITY AND CO-OPERATION IN EUROPE 16 (2008), www.osce.org/odihr/36305.
119. For 1983 figure, see Richard L. Abel, *Law Without Politics: Legal Aid Under Advanced Capitalism*, 32 UCLA L. REV. 474, 507 (1984).
120. For 1966 figure, see *id.* at 508.
121. Audrey Guinchard & Simon Wesley, *The French Approach to Access to Justice*, *in* ACCESS TO JUSTICE: BEYOND THE POLICIES AND POLITICS OF AUSTERITY 259 (Ellie Palmer, Tom Chordford, Audrey Guinchard & Yseult Marique eds., 2016).
122. Abel, *supra* note 112, at 561.
123. Hammerslev & Halvorsen Rønning, *supra* note 80, at 319.
124. LAMIN KHADAR, THE GROWTH OF PRO BONO IN EUROPE: USING THE POWER OF LAW FOR THE PUBLIC INTEREST 17 (2016), https://

probonoconnect.nl/wp-content/uploads/2017/03/PILnet-pro-bono-report.pdf (last visited July 16, 2020).

125. Rekosh, *supra* note 39, at 78.
126. *See generally*, Cummings, *supra* note 3.
127. KHADAR, *supra* note 124, at 17; *see also* Cummings, *supra* note 3, at 97.
128. The fifty largest firms in the United States averaged 231 lawyers in 1979, rising to 621 lawyers in 2001. Cummings, *supra* note 3, at 35; Marc Galanter, *Mega-Law and Mega-Lawyering in the Contemporary United States*, *in* THE SOCIOLOGY OF THE PROFESSIONS: LAWYERS, DOCTORS, AND OTHERS 152 (Robert Dingwal & Philip Lewis eds., 1983).
129. *The Am Law 100*, AMERICAN LAWYER (May 2015).
130. Robert G. Lee, *From Profession to Business: The Rise and Rise of the City Law Firm*, 19 J. L. & SOC'Y 31, 33 (1992).
131. Christoph Luschin, *Large Law Firms in Germany*, 14 TOURO INT'L L. REV. 26, 30 (2010).
132. Richard L. Abel, *Transnational Law Practice*, 44 CASE WESTERN RESERVE L. REV. 737, 783 (1993).
133. *Id.* at 795.
134. *Id.* at 782–818.
135. *See* JON BAUMAN, PIONEERING A GLOBAL VISION: THE STORY OF BAKER & MCKENZIE (1999); Jonathan V. Beverstock, Peter J. Taylor & R.G. Smith, *The Long Arm of the Law: London's Law Firms in a Globalising World Economy*, ENV'T & PLANNING: ECONOMY & SPACE 31 (1999); James R. Faulconbridge, Jonathan V. Beaverstock, Daniel Muzio & Peter J. Taylor, *Global Law Firms: Globalization and Organizational Spaces of Cross-Border Legal Work*, 28 NW. J. IN'TL L. & BUS. 455 (2008).
136. Figures for 2016 retrieved from firm websites as visited in 2016: www.bakermckenzie.com/en, www.cliffordchance.com/people_and_places.html?_charset_=UTF-8&fname=&lname=&tags=all&tags=all&office=all&query=&x=0&y=0#partners, www.jonesday.com/en/locations, www.jonesday.com/en/lawyers, https://www.freshfields.com/en-gb/, www.sidley.com/en/locations/offices, www.sidley.com/en/global/people/, www.skadden.com/locations, www.skadden.com/professionals. Figures to 2002 collected from: Faulconbridge et al., *supra* note 135, at 459; *see also* Beverstock et al., *supra* note 135; Bauman, *supra* note 135.
137. Faulconbridge et al., *supra* note 135, at 460.
138. *See generally* Abel, *supra* note 132. Abel suggests several possible explanations for the emergence of transnational legal practice, including increased international trade and finance, the emergence of the global corporation, the emergence of supranational governance centers, and competition within the domestic marker. *Id.* at 739–40.
139. *Id.* at 797.
140. *Id.* at 785.
141. *Id.* at 787, 806.

142. *Id.*
143. *Id.*
144. Directive 98/5/EC of the European Parliament and of the Council of 16 February 1998 to facilitate practice of the profession of lawyer on a permanent basis in a member state other than that in which the qualification was obtained, OJ L 77, 14.3.1998.
145. Patrick Stewart, *Have Dutch Lawyers Found the Key to European Expansion?*, 11 IN'TL FINANCIAL L. REV. 12 (1992).
146. Clifford Chance merged with Pünder, Volhard, Weber & Axster; Freshfields united with both Deringer Tessin Herrmann & Sedemund and Bruckhaus Westrick Heller Löber; Lovells with Boesebeck Droste; and Linklaters with Oppenhoff & Rädler. *See* Richard Parnham, To What Extent Has Research Conducted by the GaWC Research Network Aided Our Understanding of Large EU Law Firm Geography? 207 (Ph.D. Dissertation, University of Westminster, Department of Philosophy 2016). Large US firms such as Latham & Watkins, Weil Gotshal, and Orrick also merged with German counterparts around the same time.
147. *Id.* at 141.
148. *See generally* Cummings, *supra* note 3.
149. The widespread adoption of standard business practices by large law firms during the 1980s and 1990s has been described as a paradigm shift. Russell Pearce, *The Professionalism Paradigm Shift: Why Discarding Professional Ideology Will Improve the Conduct and Reputation of the Bar*, 70 N.Y.U. L. REV. 1229, 1250–56 (195).
150. JOEL F. HANDLER, ELLEN JANE HOLLINGSWORTH & HOWARD S. ERLANGER, LAWYERS AND THE PURSUIT OF LEGAL RIGHTS 123 (1978); Cummings, *supra* note 3; Steve Boutcher, The Institutionalization of Pro Bono Publico in Large Law Firms: An Analysis of the Causes and Consequences of Large Firm Pro Bono Programs (Ph.D. Dissertation, University of California, Irvine, Department of Sociology, 2010).
151. *Pro Bono Report 2015: Treading Water*, AM. LAW., July 20, 2015.
152. HANDLER, HOLLINGSWORTH & ERLANGER, *supra* note 150, at 123.
153. *Membership*, THE ASSOCIATION OF PRO BONO COUNSEL, https://apbco.org/about/membership/ (last visited Dec. 21, 2018).
154. Boon & Whyte, *supra* note 106, at 177–85.
155. *Id.*
156. *Id.*
157. *Who Is Behind Pro Bono? As the Director of the Solicitor's Pro Bono Group Resigns, Matheu Swallow Asks Where the Group Goes from Here*, LAWYER, Sept. 27, 1999, 14.
158. Boon & Whyte, *supra* note 106, at 187.
159. *Id.*
160. Dentons Europe LLP (for which one of the authors works as a pro bono manager) receives at least two CSR-related inquiries from clients per week and has seen a large increase in such inquiries from both US and

European corporations in recent years as corporations increasingly engage with CSR (including diversity and inclusion, sustainability, human rights, and community engagement). The EU announced its intention to develop policies on CSR with the 2001 publication of a Green Paper, "Promoting a European Framework for Corporate Social Responsibility." The momentum for information gathering and disclosure about nonfinancial social impact as part of CSR has accelerated in recent years, as reflected in a growing number of regulatory and voluntary standard-setting efforts, including the EU directive on the disclosure of nonfinancial and diversity information by large corporations (Directive 2014/95/EU), the OECD Guidelines for Multinational Enterprises, the UN Global Compact, the ISO 26000 Guidance Standards on Social Responsibility, the ILO Tri-partite Declaration of Principles Concerning Multinational Enterprises and Social Policy, the UN Guiding Principles on Business and Human Rights, the Sustainable Development Goals (Goal 17 in particular on public–private partnerships), and independent benchmarking systems such as the Global Reporting Initiative and Ecovadis.

161. Michael D. Goldhaber, *A World of Good*, AM. LAW., June 27, 2012.
162. KHADAR, *supra* note 124, at 17.
163. Sigrid Quack, *Recombining National Variety: Internationalisation Strategies of American and European Law Firms*, 5 J. STRATEGY & MGMT. 154, 162, 163 (2012).
164. Michael Goldhaber, *Pro Bono Empire*, AM. LAW., Oct. 2014, at 82.
165. The Law Society, Strategic Research Unit, "The Pro Bono Work of Solicitors: Findings from Omnibus Survey Nine" (2002), at 5; The Law Society, "The Pro Bono Work of Solicitors: PC Holder Survey" (2014), at 5.
166. For parallels with the United States, see Scott L. Cummings & Deborah L. Rhode, *Managing Pro Bono: Doing Well by Doing Better*, FORDHAM L. REV. 2357, 2378–80, 2394–405 (2009).
167. *Pro Bono Work Flourishes in Spite of Economic Downturn*, LAWYER, Nov. 9, 2009, at 56.
168. *Id.*
169. KHADAR, *supra* note 124, at 21.
170. *Id.* at 17.
171. *Id.* at 54, n.117.
172. *Id.* at 18.
173. *Id.* at 23.
174. *Id.*
175. *Culture Droit n°27* – Mai 2011; Herve Delannoy, *PILnet: The Global Network for Public Interest Law*, JURISTE D'ENTERPRISE MAG., July 2013, at 36.
176. Jean Castelain, Welcome, Program Brochure for European Pro Bono Forum 3 (PILnet 2010).
177. *2013 European Pro Bono Awards: PILnet Honors Exemplary Pro Bono Achievements*, PILNET: THE GLOBAL NETWORK FOR PUBLIC

INTEREST LAW, www.pilnet.org/events/195–2013-european-pro-bono-awards-.html (last visited Feb. 26, 2019).

178. KHADAR, *supra* note 124, at 22, 23.
179. *Id.*
180. Goldhaber, *supra* note 161, at 69.
181. Cummings, *supra* note 3, at 29–33.
182. *Id.* at 19–25.
183. Concerns by local regulators about the marketing muscle of large law firms have been inspired by even more attenuated causes than potential publicity around a law firm's pro bono work. As one of the authors recalls, the Budapest bar brought a disciplinary action against one global law firm in the early 2000s based on rules governing lawyer advertising because the firm had sent out a change-of-address mailing with high production values showing the prestigious and beautiful view of the firm's new office location overlooking the Danube.
184. KHADAR, *supra* note 124, at 30, 44. For example, the Czech Pro Bono Declaration explicitly states: "The Pro Bono Centre services are provided exclusively to non-profit organizations that engage in socially responsible activities. PBC does not provide legal services to individuals." *See Program Pro Bono Centre*, PRO BONO CENTRUM, https://www.probonocentrum.cz/english/pro-bono-declaration (last visited July 17, 2020). Meanwhile the Dutch Clearinghouse states on its website: "Pro Bono Connect lends its services to organizations representing the public interest in the field of human rights, vulnerable groups, conservation of the environment and animal welfare." *See What Do We Do?*, PRO BONO CONNECT, https://probonoconnect.nl/en/ (last visited July 17, 2020).
185. Morgan, *supra* note 55, at 42.
186. *Id.* at 43.
187. *Id.* at 49.
188. *Id.* at 50.
189. Earl Johnson, Jr., *Equal Access to Justice: Comparating Access to Justice in the United States and Other Industrial Democracies*, 24 FORDHAM INT'L L.J. S83 (2000). Johnson's study did not take into account legal aid spending through the kind of mandated insurance schemes adopted in Nordic countries, and as pointed out by a former head of the Law Society, the UK common-law system inherently involves services by private lawyers to be a significant cost factor in the legal aid system. Andrew Caplen, *Access to Justice: The View from the Law Society*, *in* ACCESS TO JUSTICE: BEYOND THE POLICIES AND POLITICS OF AUSTERITY, *supra* note 114, at 3. In any case, as described earlier, the United Kingdom fell significantly from its top spot in per capita legal aid spending, surpassed by both Norway and Sweden in more recent years.
190. *The Guardian View on Legal Aid: Cuts Have Caused Chaos and Must Be Reversed*, GUARDIAN, Aug. 12, 2018.
191. Paul Yates, *CourtNav and Pro Bono in Times of Austerity*, *in* ACCESS TO JUSTICE: BEYOND THE POLICIES AND POLITICS OF AUSTERITY, *supra* note 114, at 207.

192. *See, e.g.*, The General Council of the Bar of England and Wales, LASPO Five Years On: Submission to the Ministry of Justice LASPO Post-Implementation Review, Sept. 27, 2018.
193. *Id.* at 208–09.
194. *See* Steven Hynes, *Pro Bono Cannot Plug the Gap Left by Legal Aid Cuts*, GUARDIAN, Dec. 7, 2011.
195. LATHAM & WATKINS, *supra* note 89, at 85.
196. *Id.* at 82.
197. Kilian Bälz, Henning Moelle & Finn Zeidler, *Rechtsberatung Pro Bono in Deutschland-eine Bestandsaufnahme*, 61 NEUE JURISTISCHE WOCHENSCHRIFT 3383 (2018).
198. *Id.*
199. *Id.*
200. *Id.*
201. Axel C. Filges, Keynote Speech, The Role Pro Bono (Can) Play in German Society, European Pro Bono Forum 2011, Berlin, Germany, Nov. 17–18, 2011, www.pilnet.org/dmdocuments/Axel%20Filges%20on%20pro%20bono%20in%20Germany.pdf (last visited Feb. 26, 2019).
202. Edwin Rekosh, Fighting for a Common Cause at the Pro Bono Forum, www.pilnet.org/public-interest-law-news/blogs/30000-feet/132–2011-forum-blog.html (last visited Feb. 26, 2019).
203. Lamin Khadar, *PILnet Anonymous European Pro Bono Survey* (2016). This ratio was further supported by law firm interviewees, most of whom confirmed that the overwhelming majority of their pro bono work was carried out for nonprofits. KHADAR, *supra* note 124.
204. Internal DLA Piper 2017 Pro Bono Report for Mainland Europe (on file with authors).
205. APRIL FAITH-SLAKER, SUPPORTING JUSTICE: A REPORT ON THE PRO BONO WORK OF AMERICA'S LAWYERS 8 (Am. Bar Ass'n 2018).
206. JANET BUCZEK, KAREN STUTH & APRIL FAITH-SLAKER, SUPPORTING ACCESS TO JUSTICE III: A REPORT ON THE PRO BONO WORK OF AMERICA'S LAWYERS A-8 (Am. Bar Ass'n 2013).
207. *Id.* at 11.
208. Cummings, *supra* note 3, at 1.
209. Rekosh, *supra* note 39, at 62–64, 79–82.
210. A survey carried out by one of the authors among 100 EU policy NGOs revealed that just 32 percent of them had lawyers on staff. Only 16 percent had more than one lawyer on staff, and some of the lawyers were responsible exclusively for compliance and operational matters rather than contributing to advocacy campaigns and programmatic work. Lamin Khadar et al., *The Good Lobby Legal Needs Survey: 2016 Final Report* (2016). Meanwhile, a 2004 survey among more than 300 public interest NGOs in the United States revealed that over 50 percent of them had more than five lawyers on staff, and 40 percent had ten or more lawyers on staff. Laura Beth Nielsen & Catherine R.

Albiston, *The Organization of Public Interest Practice: 1975–2004*, 84 N. C. L. REV. 1591 (2006).

211. The bulk of lawyers populating the European offices of large international law firms are transactional lawyers who have specialized in transactional law from an early stage in their career. As Richard Abel noted in 1993, "any law firm that aspires to become transnational . . . must emphasize transactional lawyering rather than advocacy." Abel, *supra* note 132, at 73.

212. Joanne Scott & David M. Trubek, *Mind the Gap: Law and New Approaches to Governance in the European Union*, 8 EUROPEAN L.J. 1 (2002).

213. Several factors have led to this normative plurality, including legal doctrines originating in both the European Union and the Council of Europe (via the jurisprudence of the European Court of Human Rights) designed to retain a flexible degree of national sovereignty within Europe, such as "consistent interpretation," "consensus," "margin of appreciation," and "subsidiarity." In addition, there is interplay between European-level and national norms through a general process of harmonization of law within the EU, the incorporation of European human rights law and other international law jurisprudence into EU jurisprudence and vice versa, and the EU policy process, which is informed by constant surveying of national legal systems in various policy areas. As a result, European lawyers (judges, academics, policy makers, legislators, public interest lawyers, etc.) need to have strong grounding in comparative law (for both horizontal and vertical comparisons).

214. For example, tobacco companies have been vigorously resisting the introduction by the EU of tobacco advertising regulation through a complex multipronged strategy. They have litigated in multiple national jurisdictions, at the European Court of Human Rights and the European Union Court of Justice, and they have engaged in lobbying both EU institutions and member state governments. Engaging in such a multipronged strategy requires significant financial resources, but it can be crucial to success within the European governance, legislative, and judicial framework. Eva Nanopoulos & Rumiana Yotova, *"Repackaging" Plain Packaging in Europe: Strategic Litigation and Public Interest Considerations*, 19 J. INT'L ECON. L. 175 (2016).

215. David Coen, *Business Lobbying in the European Union*, *in* LOBBYING THE EUROPEAN UNION: INSTITUTIONS, ACTORS, AND ISSUES 145 (David Coen & Jeremy Richardson eds., 2009).

216. KHADAR, *supra* note 124, at 34, 35.

217. Khadar et al., *supra* note 210.

218. KHADAR, *supra* note 124, at 34.

CHAPTER SEVEN

AN EXPLOSION OF LEGAL PHILANTHROPY? THE TRANSFORMATION OF PRO BONO LEGAL SERVICES IN ENGLAND AND WALES

Andrew Boon and Avis Whyte

INTRODUCTION

A tradition of pro bono publico legal work (hereafter "pro bono") existed in England and Wales for centuries and was adopted, along with many other traditions, in the legal systems of British colonies. The questions we address here are how pro bono legal services in the jurisdiction have changed and why. In considering these questions, we are concerned with the infrastructure of provision (the architecture of pro bono), the volumes and nature of work performed (the typology of pro bono), and the causative factors underlying current patterns (the genealogy of pro bono). The answers to our research questions are relevant to understanding the significance of pro bono services. This will assist with practical issues, such as the reliability of pro bono provision in supporting access to justice, and theoretical issues, such as the significance of pro bono to legal professionalism.

A theoretical framework for considering the motivations underpinning pro bono legal services is provided by substantial literature on legal professions. The perspective in such work has shifted over time. The early literature on the professions assumed that they were characterized by high ethical standards and by the way they conducted work in a spirit of public service.[1] Consistent with these public interest theories is the assumption that pro bono is motivated by a desire to provide access to justice, and hence support for the rule of law. On this view, pro bono is part of the ethical commitment of lawyers to fulfil the needs of clients.[2]

A competing theory of motive sees professionalism simply as a form of market control.[3] From this perspective, pro bono services are potentially part of an elaborate ideological smokescreen[4] or a bargaining chip in an ongoing "negotiation" between legal professions and the state over the recognition of monopolies or other privileges.[5] Within this framework, pro bono is more likely to be seen as part of a *noblesse oblige* tradition[6] in which lawyers voluntarily correct distortions in access to justice in return for a monopoly of litigation and advocacy. Their underlying motive is likely to be seen as manipulative, for example, to forestall state regulation of legal services or to improve their public image.[7]

The groundwork for our analysis was work we did in the late 1990s.[8] Fortuitously, this period was a watershed moment in the development of pro bono in the jurisdiction. In updating that work we now draw on data published by professional bodies and others and previously unpublished quantitative and qualitative material of our own, including interviews with leading figures in the pro bono movement. We begin with a brief introduction to the jurisdiction focusing on the two most significant legal professions in England and Wales, the barristers and the solicitors and their professional bodies.[9] We then identify key institutional actors (government, professions, organizations), the types and volume of pro bono work, and the causative factors shaping current manifestations of pro bono culture. We also consider the implications of recent quantitative data.

THE PROVISION OF "FREE" LEGAL SERVICES

Public Philanthropy for the Good of the State

Legal historians suggest that lawyers' charitable responsibility for the poor and the dispossessed were established in the medieval period. The right to sue *in forma pauperis*[10] was linked to the right of the court to assign lawyers to act for litigants without a fee.[11] Ad hoc legal aid was sometimes available for special types of cases,[12] and free representation was not limited to the poor. The provision of free services continued to be characterized by exceptionalism. For example, by the 1700s it was conventional for those appearing on treason charges to be represented pro bono.[13] Since pro bono obligations typically attached to courtroom representation and barristers had a monopoly of advocacy, such obligations probably applied only to them. The narrowness of the obligation suggests that the primary motivation was to assist the judge in managing cases, although concern for the rights of litigants may have been a factor.

Legal Welfarism

The character of pro bono probably changed at the end of the nineteenth century with establishment of a Poor Man's Lawyers movement by charities based at Mansfield House and Toynbee Hall in East London.[14] These drew on the expertise of solicitors and barristers providing pro bono advice but stopped short of representation in court. The provision of broad-based advice and representation occurred when Poor Persons' Committees were established.[15] This followed the outbreak of World War I, which resulted in a substantial increase in poor persons petitioning for divorce.[16] Taxing masters adopted the practice of allowing the payment of solicitors' out-of-pocket expenses in these cases (including clerk's time and office overheads).[17]

The voluntary nature of the divorce scheme and the difficulties encountered by people in meeting even limited costs was problematic. A Committee of Inquiry, chaired by Justice Lawrence, was appointed to enquire into the administration of the Poor Persons Rules.[18] Following the Committee's report in October 1919, new rules were introduced that confined recoverable costs to actual out-of-pocket expenses only.[19] The legal services provided reflected the distinct monopolies and symbiotic relationship of the professions at this time. Solicitors, although they could appear in minor courts, tended to prepare litigation and brief barristers to conduct advocacy.

The Poor Man's Law movement was assisted by many philanthropically minded lawyers, but there are also suggestions that it was sometimes abused by lawyers or unqualified parties touting for work.[20] There were apparently differences in the attitudes of barristers and solicitors to the work produced by the Poor Persons' Committees. Many barristers were happy with the pro bono arrangement because, for them, an appearance in court was free advertising. Solicitors, particularly in some regions, resented the volume of free work and advocated the introduction of state assistance for divorce clients.[21]

When the legal aid scheme was introduced in 1949, following World War II, it responded to demand for "private plight" work, such as divorce. Legal aid rates were set at slightly below standard legal charges but provided a solid and regular income to smaller local solicitors' firms and to barristers specializing in these areas. The wide availability of legal aid encouraged the development of social welfare as a distinct field of law. It may also have contributed to the inculcation of a "social service" ethos for the large sectors of the barristers' and solicitors' professions engaged in legal aid work.[22]

The advent of legal aid coincided with a significant growth of citizens' advice services during the 1950s. Funded by local authorities and charities, they provided commonsense advice to ordinary people. During the 1960s and 1970s, their services became more specifically legal, sometimes supported by local lawyers giving free "legal advice sessions."[23] This was perhaps the clearest example of solicitors working pro bono at that time.[24] The motives of different lawyers offering these free sessions were probably mixed. For lawyers building practices they provided opportunities to identify strong cases eligible for legal aid.[25] From the 1970s, some local authorities funded local law centers staffed with lawyers, offering free legal services, including, in some cases, court and tribunal advocacy.

The attitude of the legal professional bodies to pro bono during the second half of the twentieth century was cautious if not a little hostile. Neither the Bar Council, nor the solicitors' professional body, the Law Society, provided any infrastructure or support for pro bono. Indeed, the Law Society treated voluntary sessions at advice agencies as unfair attraction of business until 1977,[26] when waivers from practice rules began to be granted. The Law Society's reluctance was largely because the solicitors' profession had grown considerably as a result of legal aid funding. The profession was very aware of a real risk that advice agencies could be a long-term competitor to this sector of private practice.

An area in which the pro bono participation of lawyers was encouraged was in handling appeals against the imposition of the death penalty from former British colonies in the Caribbean. Many of these countries retained appeals to the Judicial Committee of the Privy Council on independence.[27] In the case of death penalty appeals, English solicitors were needed to prepare the paperwork and barristers were needed to argue the cases before the Judicial Committee. The tradition was that this rather exotic area of work was performed pro bono. London firms that were willing to do it joined a panel and were allocated cases in turn.

When a breakthrough in providing infrastructural support for pro bono came in 1972, it was the initiative of a group of bar students attending the Inns of Court School of Law in Gray's Inn, London.[28] Dissatisfied with what was a sterile substantive vocational course, they formed Bar Students for Legal Advice, operating out of a pub in central London. The students provided legal representation in those tribunals that had been created after World War II to deal with social security, welfare benefits, and employment cases. These had been designed to discourage lawyer involvement, and legal costs were not recoverable. This had the result that employers, local authorities, and government agencies often appeared using in-house lawyers, while applicants were unrepresented. The bar students leveled the playing field.

In the 1980s, the provision of free legal services became a little more ambitious, certainly in and around London and some other centers. Bar Students for Legal Advice had been renamed the Free Representation Unit (FRU) and operated out of an office in the Temple, one of the Inns of Court, opposite the Royal Courts of Justice.[29] Solicitors working in law centers, or pro bono in Citizens' Advice Bureaux (CABx), provided initial contact and advice and referred suitable cases to organizations such as FRU to allocate advocates to cases. South Bank University ran two advice sessions at CABx, at Streatham and North Lambeth, staffed by practitioner academics and students, and there was also a student law clinic operated by Warwick University Law School.[30] The rationale of these sessions was, however, the educational experience of the students more than the provision of free services.[31]

The political environment in which the legal professions operated began to change in the 1980s. The Conservative Party under Margaret Thatcher adopted a neoliberal political perspective that involved rolling back the boundaries of the welfare state. In the 1990s, various measures were introduced to curb expenditure. Administration of legal aid was taken away from the Law Society and given to the Legal Aid Board, a state agency.[32] Ending case-by-case remuneration and pegging eligibility rates worked temporarily. The next step was to end individual applications and to impose fixed budgets on those solicitors' practices and advice agencies selected to offer legally aided services.

The bureaucratic and auditing requirements of the franchising and contracting regimes caused many solicitors' firms to stop legal aid work. At the same time as restricting legal aid, successive governments sought to increase competition in consumer-based markets for legal services, reducing market control by the legal professions.[33] By the 1990s, the demand for legal assistance caused legal aid budgets to spiral out of control. In 1994, a newly invigorated Labour Party under Tony Blair was gearing up for its first period of government since 1979. Blair had confronted the hard left of the party and adopted a neoliberal world view. This included dealing with rising levels of legal aid expenditure and falling levels of legal aid eligibility.

In May 1994, the Law Society published a report by a working party established to consider the issue of solicitors' pro bono work.[34] At a Law Society conference in October 1995, Tony Blair praised CABx and called for law firms to do more pro bono work.[35] Paul Boateng, the Shadow Justice Secretary, continued this campaign, arguing that small-firm solicitors should provide advice and large firms should provide money to support access to justice.[36] When it was elected in May 1997, the Labour Party's determination to control public spending confronted a significant problem that Blair had undoubtedly anticipated: declining access to justice.

The Labour Party's solution to public spending constraints was to seek a "third way" in collaboration with social democrats in the United States and the EU. Echoing American presidential campaigns, Blair called for civil society and "volunteering" to play key roles in an era of productive cooperation.[37] In April 1999, a round table discussion took place in Washington, DC, with US president Bill Clinton (Democrat); Tony Blair; the German chancellor, Gerhard Schröder; the Dutch prime minister, Wim Kok; and the Italian prime minister, Massimo D'Alema (as Europe's social democrats) included among the discussants.[38] The following June, Blair and Schröder launched a joint document, Third Way – Die Neue Mitte. With a Republican, George W. Bush, entering the White House and Schröder taking a more left-wing stance,[39] the Third Way became a historical footnote.[40]

The Law Society Working Party report had reflected antagonism between government and sections of the legal profession, particularly on the issue of legal aid. The report argued that providing access to legal services was a government responsibility and lawyers did their share by accepting the 10 percent discount intrinsic in legal aid rates. Further, it suggested that the efforts of successive governments to promote competition in the market for legal services weakened any obligation lawyers had. This no doubt explained the generally negative attitude to the idea of a pro bono tradition. Indeed, the report suggested renaming pro bono "voluntary legal services," which it argued solicitors already did plenty of. It offered the example of solicitors unpaid by recalcitrant clients, a contribution that stretched the meaning of "voluntary."[41]

None of the six recommendations made by the Law Society's Pro Bono Working Party report were ever implemented,[42] but developments at the Bar in the same period were more propitious. The Bar had a close relationship with FRU, which received contributions from the Bar Council and Inns of Court to support its operating costs and a number of other pro bono schemes.[43] The Bar Council's chairman-elect, Peter Goldsmith QC, had attended the Law Society conference at which Tony Blair spoke in 1995. He had immediately pledged to form a bar pro bono unit and to personally contribute three days a year.[44] In 1996, Goldsmith began his year in office by founding the Bar Pro Bono Unit (BPBU), an independent charity supported by Bar funding, which referred pro bono applicants to volunteer barristers.[45] The Law Society proposed establishing a Solicitor Representation Unit, on similar lines to FRU,[46] but nothing came of the idea.

Corporate Social Responsibility

In October 1996, shortly after the report of the Law Society's Pro Bono Working Party was published, a solicitor and founder of a leading charities firm and a moving force behind the Law Society Working Party, Andrew Phillips, called a public meeting to discuss solicitor pro bono.[47] Held at the Law Society, the fact that the meeting was opened by its deputy vice president, Michael Matthews, suggested that the Working Party report had split opinion at the professional body. Another potentially significant fact was that a large part of the audience represented large City of London law firms.[48] As corporate/commercial firms they had never been involved in legal aid, or even in work for private clients. They had, however, become notably successful and immensely wealthy. It would be pure speculation to suggest that, in the *noblesse oblige* tradition, this increased a sense of obligation to pro bono.

The large firms had grown exponentially since the lifting of a cap on the numbers of partners in the 1960s.[49] Many had benefited from doing legal work for the privatization of state assets by conservative governments. By the 1990s, the top ten large firms by gross income were competing with the US behemoths in international legal services markets. After a morning lamenting the failure of the report to offer a firmer lead, it was decided to elicit interest at a further meeting at the offices of one of the Magic Circle firms in London. This meeting led to a commitment of funding from a number of large firms to support the formation of the Solicitors' Pro Bono Group (SPBG) with a full-time coordinator.[50]

It is arguable that one of the biggest influences on the development of solicitor pro bono was the concept of corporate social responsibility (CSR), which emerged in the 1960s as a more or less distinctive model of corporate self-regulation.[51] While the meaning, scope, and significance of CSR had always been contested,[52] it was promoted as a more effective means of controlling corporations and promoting the public good than state law.[53] CSR was introduced to the United Kingdom following a meeting of leaders of large Anglo-American corporations in 1980. The meeting, jointly hosted by the British minister for local government and the US ambassador,[54] was attended by the senior executives of major firms in the United States and the United Kingdom, together with those from the United States with direct experience at the most senior level of private sector initiatives within the community. The aim was:

> to explore the concept of corporate social responsibility and to provide the opportunity for an exchange of experience between the two countries, particularly for individuals working outside government with an interest in greater community involvement by large firms.[55]

The conference concluded that interventions needed to be more active and that there was a need for "discussion and action to achieve a more innovative approach for business in contributing resources to urban renewal."[56]

The Anglo-American conference led to formation of a charitable nongovernmental organization (NGO), Business in the Community (BITC), in 1982. Some notion of the importance attached to BITC is evident from the appointment of the Prince of Wales as president from 1985. As described by professor David Grayson, former joint managing director of BITC, it had three phases of development: in the 1980s, corporate community involvement; in the 1990s, corporate community investment; and, from 2000, corporate responsibility. The first phase aimed to help business regenerate local economies depressed by corporate closures; the second encouraged business to organize its involvement; and the third phase focused on responsible business practices and sustainability.[57]

In the 1990s, in the second phase of development, its initial concerns, the economic and ethical dimensions of corporate governance, expanded to embrace a corporate philanthropic dimension.[58] During that period large corporations in the United Kingdom were under political pressure to adopt a CSR agenda.[59] In the course of our earlier research we were told that BITC's strategy at that time was to approach directly the head of any organization it sought to recruit. Their pitch was to emphasize the business advantages to businesses participating in community programmes as much as a reaction to the preceding "decade of greed."[60] It was in the second development phase that BITC formed a Professional Firms Group (PFG) specifically to outline the "business case" for "corporate action" in professional firms and to target employee volunteering. Of the two hundred members of the PFG at that time, forty were law firms.[61]

It seems likely that the work the PFG had done with large law firms led to formation of the SPBG. Caroline Knighton, the director of business of the PFG, was the contact point given in the press release announcing the Law Society event;[62] she accompanied Andrew Phillips and spoke at the meeting.[63] The positive response of large firms to the initiative may also have reflected a number of other factors. These included a huge increase in trainee solicitor numbers, which had accompanied the expansion of corporate firm personnel, and the appointment of in-house training coordinators. The sessions at local advice service offices provided neophyte lawyers with client interaction, an opportunity to develop legal skills, and a much needed sense of purpose. Therefore, pro bono fitted into a suite of training opportunities for trainees that the large firms had geared up to provide.

Large firms adapted conceptions of pro bono to their cultures. It became more common for senior lawyers to do free work for charitable organizations. This might have been conveyancing of property or other assistance with the commercial dimensions of charitable work. There were also attempts by some firms to wrap up pro bono in a philanthropic package, whereby legal work was lumped with nonlegal charitable work or financial donations. This had several advantages. It allowed the firms to make nonspecific claims of philanthropic activity without losing the billable hours from legal work, and it allowed nonlegal staff, who were employed in increasing numbers by large firms, to participate. There is no doubt that many firms took CSR very seriously, to the extent that they gave senior partners overall responsibility for it and allowed pro bono contributions to count as billable hours. Many also appointed lawyers as pro bono coordinators to manage the pro bono workload and ensure that it was done properly.

An Assessment of Pro Bono Work by 2000

In this section we base a number of conclusions regarding infrastructure, volumes, culture, and motivation on our work on pro bono set out in the introduction. This work provided the baseline data considered in the rest of this section.

Infrastructure

The BPBU immediately attracted volunteer panel members, including the leading practitioners, Queen's Counsel.[64] In its first year it had 350 volunteer barristers on its panel, 1 part-time staff member, and matched 110 cases.[65] By the end of that year it had 720 barristers, including 120 QCs. These numbers crept up gradually in the early days,[66] and by 2000 the BPBU had 1,000 barrister volunteers.[67] It deployed a senior review panel assessing all cases for merit, suitability, and financial eligibility. This enabled selection of important cases and, because they invariably involved advocacy, ensured that preparation time could be invested in them.[68] The BPBU then referred to a suitable barrister but played no further role in the matter; any subsequent relationship was directly between counsel and the client.[69]

After its creation in 1996, the SPBG established itself in a campaigning role, attracting new members and helping to raise the profile of pro bono. Most importantly, it managed to enlist large firms beyond the original corpus of enthusiasts. By 2000, over 40 percent of the top fifty law firms were members and many claimed to be performing thousands of hours of free work.[70] Perhaps more significantly, by 2001, thirteen of the top twenty firms had appointed full-time pro bono coordinators, claims about pro bono work began to appear in client brochures, and the promise of opportunities to conduct it in trainee recruitment literature. Because of its noninvolvement in service delivery, the SPBG failed to demonstrate a clear impact on the delivery of pro bono legal services.

Volumes

In 1996, the BPBU received 250 applications for help (increasing to over 2,000 in 2019.[71] When a barrister was assigned to a case, the expectation generally was that it would involve a court appearance. It is arguable, therefore, that the BPBU was more concerned about the quality than the volume of interventions.

In contrast, the claims made for solicitor pro bono were always about quantity. In this regard, it appeared that the claims of the Pro Bono

Working Party for the high volume of solicitor pro bono work were not well evidenced. A survey of 123 local Law Societies that the working party conducted in November 1993 produced only 32 responses. These apparently referred to the "many" practitioners on CABx rotas but confirmed that there were no formal records.[72] Nor did the Working Party's claim chime with other existing data. A Law Society survey of 978 private practitioners conducted in 1989 had found 41 percent claiming to carry out "public service work for which [they did] not charge fees," but only 3 percent doing more than 5 hours a week.

One concrete source of information on the volumes of activity was pro bono work done by lawyers in advice agencies. Only four years before the Working Party report, a survey of all 559 members of the Law Centres Federation had found 369 wholly or partly qualified lawyer volunteers, far fewer than 1 percent of the solicitors then holding practicing certificates.[73] In 1997, the Law Society included questions on pro bono in its annual survey of solicitors. This found that solicitors performed 37 hours of free or substantially undercharged work a year. Based on this rather dubious definition, the Law Society claimed that solicitors performed £124 million worth of pro bono per annum.[74]

Our survey of the one hundred largest firms[75] had few swift and positive responses. After two waves of follow-up calls we had sixty-one responses and found fifty-three firms performing pro bono work. Less than 50 percent of these (n.20) kept any records of it. Of these, nine claimed to have done work worth more than £100,000 in the previous year. Only six published a pro bono policy. This apparent indifference to pro bono in large London firms was also found by Galanter and Palay, who conducted qualitative interviews in city firms between 1990 and 1994.[76]

Culture

Our assessment of the types of pro bono performed in the period approaching the millennium was that it consisted of four strands. First, local solicitors and barristers assisted local CABx and advice agencies by providing advice sessions and, occasionally, help in pursuing cases. Second, a number of pupil and junior barristers provided advocacy through FRU. Third, a significant number of large firms were beginning pro bono programs, typically based in local advice agencies. Fourth, the Law Society claimed that many solicitors provided pro bono on an ad hoc basis, although their definition led us to doubt the significance of this.

There were tenuous links between these various kinds of pro bono. For example, lawyers attending external advice sessions might well work on cases pro bono from their office. Second, large firms often followed the student model for sessions at advice centers staffed by teams of qualified and unqualified personnel. Third, lawyers working at advice centers might seek the services of FRU to secure advocates for pro bono clients. Despite these connections, the culture of pro bono was fragmentary and unformed. Even the definition of what constituted pro bono was uncertain.

Despite the rather patchy large-firm commitment to pro bono we found in 1996, we saw signs of the emergence of a distinctive pro bono culture in a minority of large firms. Under the umbrella of CSR, large law firm pro bono changed character. It was no longer a manifestation of an individual commitment to access to justice but a manifestation of a firm's social responsibility and, often, a responsibility to a particular community. This was manifest in the assignment of work to trainees, the presence of large numbers of trainees from single firms in different advice agencies, and the organized contribution of partners' legal work, such as conveyancing, to charitable organizations.

In the CSR model, which many large firms signed on to, pro bono was only part of the offering. In fact, in the determination to ensure that a philanthropic contribution was mainstream and inclusive, they tended to elide the distinction between legal pro bono and other forms of employee philanthropic contribution, such as working on reading schemes in local schools. One of the recommendations of our Nuffield report was that this tendency should be resisted. Rather, we argued that the distinctiveness of pro bono should be preserved as a "way of inculcating an ethos of public service, improving the public image of lawyers and establishing collegial relations between different sections of the profession."[77]

Motivation

It is clear that, for much of the 1990s, the growing culture of rights and the low political priority afforded legal aid presented an irresolvable political dilemma to government. For a period, pro bono seemed to be part of a potential solution. The bar's positive response was a personal initiative of its chairman Peter Goldsmith QC in direct response to a speech by Tony Blair. It may be coincidental Goldsmith became a Labour politician only a little later.[78] At the time, we were told that the bar had been subject to a parliamentary campaign of lawyer denigration intended to create an environment receptive to legal services reform.[79] Andrew Phillips admitted that part of his motivation for his pro bono initiative was that, as a member of the House of Lords, he was subjected to a "drip, drip of denigration of lawyers by government spokesmen."[80]

Large firms may also have responded directly to Labour's campaign. The probability that they were its real target is suggested by the fact that they were threatened, variously, with a levy to support access to justice or some other compulsion.[81] At the time, we suggested that the phenomenon of large-firm pro bono reflected a response to a number of interacting pressures: idealism (of young trainees in particular), professionalism (an obligation for lawyers to respond to legal need), and commercialism (growing pressure from corporate clients). To these we speculatively added the force of globalization, represented by CSR.

CSR entered the frame at the right time. Although it came about through an interaction with US business leaders and politicians,[82] it was also a very neoliberal response to a problem created by neoliberal economics. It emphasised the win-win possibilities of worker involvement in feel-good activity for social benefit. Not only would pro bono work polish the firms' public image, it would make employees feel better and help to build more successful organizations. By embracing pro bono, large firms were potentially killing these several birds with a single stone, seizing the initiative and possibly heading off government intervention.

Whatever the pressures on professions and firms, there were no new demands to bridge the widening access gap in the aftermath of Labour's electoral success in 1997. It is not clear whether the formation of the BPBU and the SPBG was deemed a sufficient response. Officially, ministers pinned hopes on increasing the efficiency and profile of existing advice services under the umbrella of a new Community Legal Service,[83] which included bringing together the various advice agencies into a mutually supportive network. If so, the policy shift may have reflected a decision that access to justice could not depend on lawyers providing free work.

Evolution of the New Pro Bono Culture Since 2000

Since 2000, a number of actors have directly or indirectly shaped the provision of free services: government, NGOs, large law firms, academia, legal practitioners, and the legal professions. In this section we consider the impact of these various "players" in the evolution of the new culture of pro bono, particularly in terms of the growth of pro bono institutions and infrastructure.

Government

After 2000, government continued to reduce the level of legal aid and reliance on legal aid as the principal means of providing access to justice. The plan to provide the Community Legal Service, reducing reliance on private practice lawyers, was largely unsuccessful and was formally abandoned in 2005.[84] The Legal Services Act 2007 aimed to create legal services "supermarkets" using nonlegal capital and management. The relative failure of this experiment has led government agencies to advocate encouraging competition from unregulated legal service providers.[85]

More successful efforts to reduce reliance on legal aid were the introduction of alternative ways of funding litigation from the late 1990s, so-called conditional fee agreements, a species of previously forbidden contingency fee agreements for damages claims.[86] At the same time, court procedures were adjusted to reduce dependence on lawyers; introducing "litigant friendly" civil procedure rules, increasing judicial control of the process and placing greater emphasis on alternative dispute resolution.[87] The latest phase of this strategy includes proposals for online courts dealing with claims up to £25,000. These will exclude lawyers, either formally or through costs mechanisms.[88]

In 2012, the Legal Aid Sentencing and Punishment of Offenders Act 2012 (LASPO) at s.44 legalized damages-based agreements, essentially a conventional contingency fee arrangement, but removed substantial parts of some areas of law – family, immigration, welfare benefits, employment, and clinical negligence – from the scope of legal aid.[89] In the financial year following LASPO, net expenditure on legal aid fell from £1,916.7[90] million to £1,709.5[91] million; funded individual acts of assistance dropped from 2.3 million[92] to 1.8 million.[93] Further reductions were expected to significantly reduce legally aided acts of assistance.[94] By 2017, the decline of legal aid, and the reduced profitability of conveying real property, meant that many small firms no longer achieved 30 percent profit, the traditional benchmark for solicitors' practices.[95]

In the period after 2000, government did not ignore the pro bono issue. In fact, it became directly involved. The impetus was provided by Peter Goldsmith QC, founder of the BPBU, who was called into Blair's cabinet as attorney general in June 2001. In 2002, Goldsmith formed the Attorney General's Pro Bono Co-ordinating Committee (A-GPBC),[96] which adopted the mission of promoting, developing, and coordinating pro bono. Goldsmith appointed a leading solicitor, Michael Napier, "pro bono envoy"[97] to carry the message to professions and practitioners.

One of the A-GPBC's first acts was to issue a pro bono protocol[98] (see Appendix) defining pro bono legal work as "legal advice or representation provided by lawyers to individuals and community groups who cannot afford to pay for that advice or representation and where public funding is not available."[99] It also legislated to ensure that costs could be recovered when litigants were assisted. The creation of pro bono costs orders[100] mitigated the impact of the recovery principle in relation to costs; the rule that a claimant could only recover costs actually expended. The Act also created a charitable foundation to receive costs awarded and fund pro bono initiatives.[101] The protocol[102] was endorsed by the Law Society, which uses this definition throughout its pro bono manual,[103] the Bar Council, and the Chartered Institute of Legal Executives.[104] Lawyers and firms may voluntarily sign up to the protocol.[105]

Another initiative brokered by the A-GPBC had an enduring impact: National Pro Bono Week (NPBW).[106] Held since 2002, the week comprises a series of events celebrating the legal professions' efforts and awarding prizes for outstanding individual performances. When Goldsmith left government office,[107] the A-GPBC continued under successive office holders. The climax event of NPBW is generally attended by one or more of the government law officers. This gives pro bono the stamp of political approval now bestowed rarely on the legal professions.

The Pro Bono Organizations

After 2000, the BPBU continued in much the same way it had since establishment. Its panel of barristers grew incrementally a little each year, as did the number of cases it handled. In 2002, it was reported that the BPBU had set up a solicitors' panel of eleven firms, including most of the Magic Circle firms, for cases that needed the support of solicitors for case preparation.[108] In 2000, it established Bar in the Community (BIC) to provide barrister trustees to voluntary organizations.[109]

After 2000, the SPBG tried to present itself as the face of solicitor pro bono across the board and made a strategic change of direction. It adopted the title LawWorks in 2006, and with this change of operating title, it adopted a more proactive role in service delivery. This was achieved by establishing a referral system to match lawyers with advice centers in the Law Centres Federation.[110] By 2006, fifty-five of these free clinics had been established for work not supported by legal aid.[111] By 2013, it also had a number of delivery modes, offering case brokerage and email advice.

In 2010, a National Pro Bono Centre was established.[112] The Centre brought together the charities dedicated to the provision of pro bono legal services and access to justice in a building in Chancery Lane, the London avenue that links the Law Society and the Inns of Court.[113] At various times it has housed organizations including the BPBU, LawWorks, CILEx Pro Bono Trust (established for legal executives), the Access to Justice Foundation, the London Legal Support Trust, the Environmental Law Foundation, and i-ProBono.[114]

Following the evisceration of legal aid provision by the LASPO Act 2012, in 2013, LawWorks received 2,883 enquiries, an increase of 56 percent from the previous year.[115] It quickly became apparent that drastic action was required to preserve the expertise of legal aid practitioners in many areas of law. In response, LawWorks launched Secondary Specialisation, a program employing specialists in a range of social welfare law disciplines. The aim was to train and supervise lawyers from member organizations to advise and represent vulnerable clients in cases concerning welfare benefits, housing, community care, and family cases (including domestic violence) – areas of expertise in real danger of extinction.[116] The firms with resources to commit to developing secondary specialization were, typically, top 100 firms.[117]

Large Law Firms

Published data rarely distinguishes contributions by size or type of private practice firm. It is therefore difficult to assess how widespread contributions are. It seems likely that large law firms make a very significant contribution to the total of solicitor pro bono hours. Many claim to provide thousands of hours each year, and many of the top fifty aspire to contribute at least 25 hours per fee earner.[118] After 2000, considerable effort was invested in trying to ensure that pro bono was seen as an initiative of the whole profession. In the LawWorks pro bono awards there are distinctions made in the categories covering, for example, size of firm, status of individual practitioners, and size of team.[119]

Large firms continue to be influenced, directly or indirectly, by CSR. This is generally confirmed by stories in the trade press about corporate clients calling for their lawyers to demonstrate community commitment or requiring CSR to be addressed in pitches for work.[120] Recent analysis of the websites of large law firms in England and Wales by Vaughan et al. suggests that pro bono continues to sit within a broader CSR framework.[121] CSR disclosures by the one hundred largest law firms found that activity tended to be grouped in three areas: (i) pro bono and community giving; (ii) diversity and inclusion; and (iii) environmental matters.[122] It noted that many of the top 100 firms made no distinction between pro bono and other categories of CSR, and that the majority disclosed no data regarding their pro bono work.[123] Therefore, there was no way of distinguishing legal advice from wider "community giving."

The business rationale for working pro bono persists in large law firms. Tender documents and law firm panel appointment procedures continue to emphasize the role of CSR in attracting employees and increasing work satisfaction[124] rather than, for example, the professional obligation of lawyers to provide free legal services. Vaughan et al. suggest that firms' literature addresses both internal and external audiences and that pro bono is a potential source of good news stories. They view "the widespread references to awards and external recognition for CSR on many law firm websites" as "part of the "media-isation" of legal practice, and one concrete aspect of the wider pan-promotionalism of contemporary culture."[125]

The Academy

The academy potentially served a role in shaping the character of the new culture of pro bono. It is plausible that our report for the Nuffield Foundation, *Something for Nothing*, had some impact, particularly on the Attorney General's Pro Bono Committee. The report was actively promoted by Michael Napier in promotional speeches given in his envoy role. He supported our strict definition of pro bono activity and invariably mentioned our conclusion that pro bono might be a mechanism for "reinvigorating professionalism." Napier also ensured that copies of *Something for Nothing* were distributed at the committee's first meeting. Although we interviewed Lord Goldsmith and specifically asked whether the report had influenced him on the need for pro bono costs orders and the Access to Justice Foundation, he was unable to recall any impact on his thinking.[126]

The other role of the academy was as a place for student voluntary legal service. As described above, this long predated the designation of such work as "pro bono." Nevertheless, the pro bono label may have helped to ensure that the three active law school "clinics" in England and Wales were joined by more in the succeeding decades. Most of the new clinics followed the Law Centre model, with a clinic located in the law school or in a nearby agency. A notable exception was the Centre for Capital Punishment Studies program at Westminster University, which sent students and recent graduates to assist with death penalty appeals in the Caribbean and United States.[127]

The growth of law school pro bono clinics was influenced by LawWorks, which launched an initiative to develop pro bono in universities.[128] By 2014, although the rate of growth was beginning to slow, 70 percent of all law schools had pro bono projects.[129] Although the main focus of most of these clinics remained student education and training, their rebranding or labeling as pro bono activities had advantages, such as making them eligible for national pro bono awards.[130] By 2010, more than 64 percent of law schools had some such activity, by this time often referred to as pro bono clinics.[131] Many of these clinics are increasingly central to law schools' core business. In 2017, for example, Nottingham Law School was granted a license to operate a teaching law clinic as part of an alternative business structure providing initial advice to small businesses. Although any profits would support an existing law clinic, it is a legal business rather than pro bono.[132] It could be argued, however, that law students will acquire a habit of providing pro bono services which might be carried into practice.

Legal Practitioners

Although all sections of both professions are engaged in pro bono, there are reasons why engagement is particularly strong among trainees at large solicitors' firms and among junior barristers.[133] Many law graduates might be tempted to join large solicitors' firms because they offer a disproportionate number of training contracts and provide generous financial packages. These firms typically employ their trainees in the routine aspects of corporate or commercial transactions and rarely provide client contact. Pro bono provides an opportunity for trainees in large firms to experience, and to gain experience of, "real" legal work.[134] Barristers, on the other hand, are self-employed. At the start of their careers, they rely on the chambers clerk to allocate them work, and it may be thin on the ground. Pro bono allows them to obtain experience so that they can "hit the ground running" when the chance arrives. This is not to suggest that many young practitioners are not idealistic in the pursuit of pro bono, but their motives may be mixed.

Many practitioners followed existing routes in developing their pro bono work, but several examples in the LawWorks national awards demonstrate that pro bono is often important in keeping advice services alive during difficult times.[135] This includes the women-only service at Toynbee Hall.[136] The awards also highlighted some who had pursued interesting new avenues, often with a view to assisting pet causes. A notable area of development was in pro bono work overseas. The awards literature highlights examples of such work conducted by teams from specific law firms, but data suggests that international work is a particular area of barrister activity.

The winner of the Bar Pro Bono Award in 2017 established a program assisting individuals convicted of capital offenses in Uganda.[137] Initially working through the Centre for Capital Punishment Studies, Tanya Murshed wrote submissions for around sixty individuals facing the death penalty and made applications for resentencing.[138] Around 243 prisoners were either resentenced or released as a result of this work. Many of the pro bono practitioners recognized through awards also set up organizations to continue the work that they had been doing.[139]

Legal Professions

The campaign to promote pro bono had an impact on the professions. The General Council of the Bar, the barristers' professional body, had a close hold on pro bono from 1996, no doubt partly because the BPBU was the initiative of its sitting president. From 1999, it received core funding from the Bar Council and the four Inns of Court.[140] The Bar Council provided 50 percent of operating costs, around £60,000 in 2012. It was also broadly supported by barristers. From 2013, an Authorisation to Practice Appeal invited them to contribute £30 each to the BPBU while renewing their practicing certificates.[141] By 2016, 8,297 barristers, including 85 percent of QCs, each volunteered to contribute £30 to the BPBU when renewing their practice certificates,[142] bringing in a total to the unit of £248,910. This enabled the BPBU to support a relatively high level of staffing; thirteen in 2016.[143] For financial year 2015–16, the Bar Council and Inns of Court also donated £64,800 and £5,000 respectively to FRU.[144] In the period 2015–16, FRU employed administrators and a solicitor to prepare more complex cases.[145]

The Law Society's approach to pro bono reflected ambivalence. This may have been due to attitudes partly fostered by the reliance of many small firms on legal aid. Locked in a philosophical battle with successive governments about legal aid, the Law Society was in defensive mode on pro bono. Although it emphasized its formal support for the principle of pro bono and for the SPBG,[146] it kept both at some distance. It has made various grants to the SPBG over the years, becoming a major funder in 2011. It currently provides around a quarter of LawWorks income[147] (the remainder being provided by charitable trusts and, notably, the Big Lottery fund).[148] Perhaps the underlying problem for the Law Society was that pro bono reinforced a schism, latent in the solicitors' profession, between firms representing different interests. Legal aid firms represented something approaching a "social service" ethic for legal practice,[149] whereas corporate/commercial firms had hitherto focused almost purely on business. By crossing the divide, large firms were not only taking small firms' business, they were taking their raison d'être.

In 2017, the Law Society launched a Pro Bono Charter.[150] It included forty-six "founding signatories," including many large firm members of the SPBG.[151] Given the existence of the SPBG, it is unclear what the Law Society hoped to achieve by this initiative. Two possible reasons were that it was not content in its relationship to the SPBG, or that it wanted a vehicle that emphasized a more overt commitment to pro bono. The package of benefits offered to firms adopting the charter included three month's free membership of the SPBG,[152] which suggests it was the latter.

A number of factors may have led to the Law Society's change of direction on pro bono. First, the creation of the National Pro Bono Centre in 2010 began a process of developing a national and integrated pro bono culture, providing an opportunity for the professional body to occupy local space in relation to solicitors. Second, the decades-long battle over legal aid was largely lost; it had never developed electoral traction and, despite the devastation wreaked by LASPO 2012, access to law, unlike access to health or education (apart from university fees), was not a policy of any of the parties in the general election of 2017.

Legal aid was not the only battle with government the Law Society had lost. The third factor probably influencing the Law Society's decision to launch the Pro Bono Charter was that, under the Legal Services

Act 2007, it had been stripped of all regulatory power, leaving only "representative" functions. The professional body was in search of both a role and activity that reflected credit on the organization; pro bono contributed to both objectives. At its launch, the Law Society president, Robert Bourns, stated that "the Pro Bono Charter offers a framework to unite the solicitor profession's pro bono strategies, policies and learning and further enhance the impact of the pro bono work carried out by our members."[153] This involved subscribing to a joint pro bono protocol and contributing data, including best practice information, which would help the Law Society demonstrate that its initiative had impact.[154]

The webpage setting out details of the Pro Bono Charter includes a familiar disclaimer about pro bono not replacing legal aid, though also incorporating other campaign messages. It read:

> Pro bono must never be viewed as a substitute for a properly funded legal aid system but rather should be seen as part of a coordinated strategy promoting access to justice, alongside public legal education and tackling barriers to access such as court fees.[155]

This emphasizes that the Law Society still, as it always had, saw pro bono as a bargaining chip in an oblique negotiation between professions and government about the terms of access to law.

THE GROWTH AND CHARACTER OF PRO BONO LEGAL SERVICES

In this section we present available data on the delivery of pro bono legal services in England and Wales since our earlier research, first by considering the contribution of solicitors and then that of barristers.

Solicitors

Demographic

Between 2000 and 2019, the population of practicing solicitors rose from nearly 101,000[156] to just over 146,000.[157] Of these, around 20 percent were typically employed in government or industry. In 2019, firms with more than twenty-six partners offered nearly 50 percent of all trainee placements.[158] The City of London, where most of the 100 largest firms are located, accounted for one-third of all traineeships registered.[159]

Data Collection

As there is no regulatory requirement to provide pro bono services, the Law Society's Annual Statistical Review did not collect relevant information. The Law Society's Pro Bono Work of Solicitors Annual Omnibus Survey of individual PC holders was started in the early 1990s. Telephone interviews were conducted with a representative sample of practitioners from private practice, central and local government, and other in-house (primarily commerce and industry, but also including charities, health, educational establishments). Total sample size was not less than 1,200. Since 2012, the Individuals Omnibus Survey is referred to as the Practising Certificate Holder Survey and the sample has increased to 1,500 individuals. Pro bono data has been collected as part of a wider survey.[160] From 2012, the Law Society adopted the Pro Bono Protocol definition of pro bono, so the figures prior to that are not directly comparable.

Proportion of Different Practice Types Performing Pro Bono

Figure 7.1 sets out the proportion of practicing solicitors providing pro bono work in three significant sectors: government, in house, and private. The first year in which comparable data was collected was 2002. It showed that the proportion of solicitors in private practice performing pro bono work was over three times that in commerce and industry, the next largest proportion. It also showed an overall pro bono participation rate of around 33 percent of practitioners. The same kinds of data were not collected again until 2012. At that time, levels of engagement had slightly increased for private practitioners and in-house solicitors (the equivalent of commerce and industry), but fallen for those in government positions.[161] Over the four-year period since, overall levels of participation hovered around the 40 percent mark.

Grade of Private Practice Solicitor Performing Pro Bono

Figure 7.2 shows the proportion of solicitors of different grades performing pro bono work between 2009 and 2015. While the proportion of associate solicitors doing such work remained fairly constant between these two points, the proportion of sole practitioners nearly doubled and the proportion of partners more than doubled. During the period between 2009, the first year the data distinguished between equity and salaried partners, and 2015, the proportion of equity partners participating rose from 32 to 51 percent while the proportion of salaried partners rose from 13 to 58 percent. At the beginning of the period (2009), salaried partners and sole

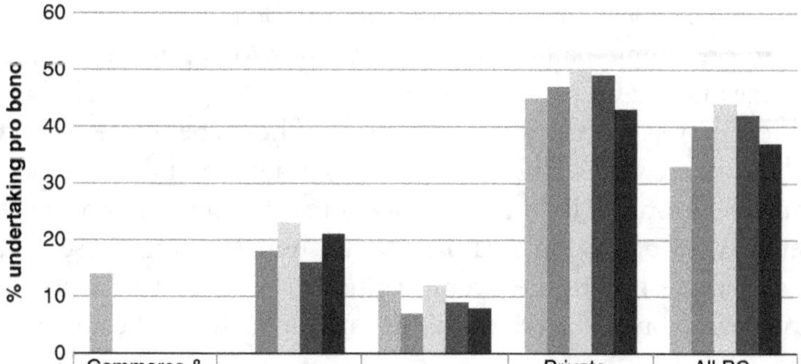

	Commerce & Industry	In-house	Govt	Private Practice	All PC Holders
2002 (n=1,127)	14		11	45	33
2012 (n=1,503)		18	7	47	40
2013 (n=1,506)		23	12	50	44
2014 (n=1,517)		16	9	49	42
2015 (n=1,502)		21	8	43	37

Figure 7.1. Proportion (%) of solicitors providing pro bono work by sector (2002, 2012–2015)

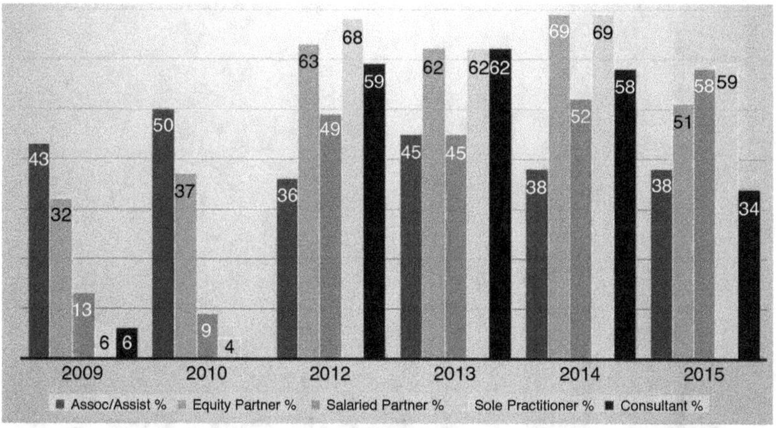

Figure 7.2. Proportion (%) of private practice solicitors at different grades providing pro bono work

practitioners were among those contributing the least as a proportion of practitioners in these grades. By the end of the period (2015), they were contributing the most. This, we hypothesize, might be because pro bono had been defined to include providing free legal work to charities. It might also have been a response to campaigns by the pro bono organizations and others anticipating the impact of LASPO, which was not implemented until 2013.

The Financial Value of Private Practice Pro Bono Work

Based on sample data, some solicitors provide up to 600 hours of pro bono work in a year.[162] These outliers are not represented in Figure 7.3, which shows that the average number of hours performed by pro bono solicitors between 2012 and 2014 was around 50 hours a year. Across the profession, including solicitors not working pro bono, the average per private practitioner is around 23 hours. Using these data, it is possible to estimate the overall value of solicitors' pro bono contributions based on the average charge rate for each year between 2011–12 and 2014–15.

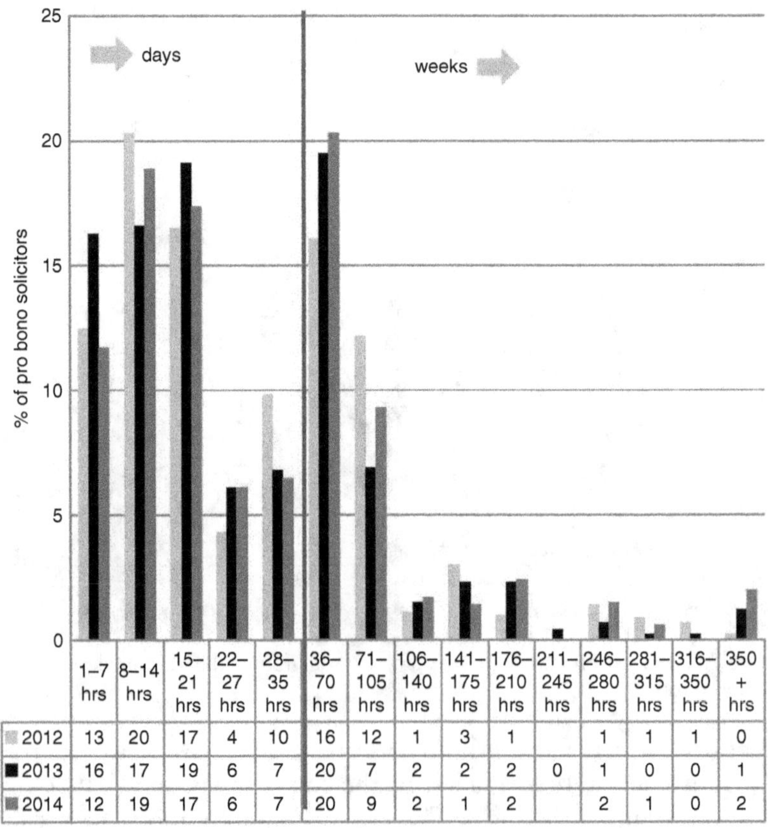

	1–7 hrs	8–14 hrs	15–21 hrs	22–27 hrs	28–35 hrs	36–70 hrs	71–105 hrs	106–140 hrs	141–175 hrs	176–210 hrs	211–245 hrs	246–280 hrs	281–315 hrs	316–350 hrs	350+ hrs
2012	13	20	17	4	10	16	12	1	3	1		1	1	1	0
2013	16	17	19	6	7	20	7	2	2	2	0	1	0	0	1
2014	12	19	17	6	7	20	9	2	1	2		2	1	0	2

Figure 7.3. Pro bono hours worked, by pro bono solicitors in the previous 12 months (2012–2014)

Based on the data in Table 7.1, the total value of solicitors' pro bono work rose from £513 million to £592 million between the beginning and end of the four-year cycle. This represented 2.7 percent of the total turnover of solicitors' firms at the start of the period and 2.4 percent at the end. Unfortunately, because of definitional and methodological problems, it is not possible to accurately compare this with the value of pro bono work at the beginning of the period under discussion. In our earlier article we referred to a Law Society claim that "solicitors give at least £124 million of free legal help a year" and an average of 37 hours from each private practitioner.[163] Even if this claim was wildly inflated, as seemed probable based on the data we had collected from large firms, the fivefold increase in the twenty years since is dramatic, and it is not explained by the admittedly large increase in the number of solicitors since 2000 referred to under the heading "Demographic" at the start of the section. Moreover, following LASPO, it is roughly equivalent to a third of the civil legal aid budget, meaning that solicitors are now making a significant contribution to legal services.

Barristers

Demographic

The bar is a much smaller profession than the solicitors, and it has expanded at a slower rate.[164] Between 2010 and 2017 the number of practicing barristers, including QCs, rose from around 15,000 to around 16,500. During the same time frame, the number of employed barristers also rose from around 2,700 to 2,900. There were around 1,800 self-employed QCs between 2009 and 2011, but numbers began to gradually decline, to around 1,600 in 2017.

Data Collection

The Bar Standards Board (BSB) ran its Biennial Survey in 2013, which included statistics on pro bono work.[165] However, in 2014, prompted by several issues with the survey as it stood,[166] a decision was taken not to continue with it. And though much of the information on the makeup of the bar is now covered in other publications, the BSB does not currently publish or collect any data on pro bono work. In 2016, the Bar Council ran a survey about pro bono work, but the response rate was too low to provide any meaningful data. The Bar Pro Bono Unit (now named Advocate) collects some information, but this is not comprehensive. Indeed, it was only in February 2017 that the BPBU

TABLE 7.1 The financial value of solicitors' pro bono between 2011–12 and 2014–15

Value calculation (financial figures have been rounded)	2011–12 (n=308)	2012–13 (n=345)	2013–14 (n=312)	2014–15 (n=268)
Average charge out rate	£254 (£215 median)	£259 (£220 median)	£256 (£213 median)	£283 (£240 median)
Average number of pro bono hours by pro bono solicitors	49 hours (25 hours median)	47 hours (20 hours median)	53 hours (25 hours median)	53 hours (30 hours median)
Average number of hour across all private practitioners	23 hours	23 hours	26 hours	23 hours
Average value of pro bono work (for those providing pro bono services)	£12,446 (£5,375 median)	£12,173 (£4,400 median)	£13,568 (£5,325 median)	£14,999 (£7,200 median)
Average value of pro bono work across all private practitioners	£5,850	£6,087	£6,648	£6,509
Total number of solicitors in private practice	87,768	86,840	90,306	91,029
Percent of private practice doing pro bono work	47%	50%	49%	43%
Estimated number of solicitors offering pro bono	41,251	43,420	44,250	39,142

TABLE 7.1 (*cont.*)

Value calculation (financial figures have been rounded)	2011–12 (n=308)	2012–13 (n=345)	2013–14 (n=312)	2014–15 (n=263)
Estimated financial value based on figures averaged across the profession	£513m	£529m	£601m	£592m
Total turnover	£19bn[5]	£21bn[5]	£23bn[7]	£23bn[8]
Estimated percent of total turnover	2.7% (1.1% median)	2.5% (1.9% median)	2.6% (2.2% median)	2.4% (2.8% median)
Total number of pro bono hours by private practitioners	2.0m hours	2.0m hours	2.3m hours	2.1m hours

Source: The Pro Bono Work of Solicitors PC Holder Survey 2015, p. 11, www.lawsociety.org.uk/support-services/research-trends/solicitors-pro-bono-work-2015/.

announced its intention to send an individualized overview to every chamber that supports it in order to report on ways those chambers contribute to the Unit.[167] As a result, the bar has no comparable data for more recent years or data that compares with the Law Society's Annual PC Holders Survey.

The BSB are keen to fill the data gap in the future and are currently reviewing what information on the profession needs to be collected and published. This may lead to changes to the information it aims to collect from barristers and how this information is collected. For example, the Board fulfilled its 2017 plan to add a question to the Authorisation to Practice process on the amount of pro bono work barristers undertake annually.[168] The results have not been made available, so the statistical information contained in this section is more limited than that on solicitors' involvement in pro bono.

Involvement in Pro Bono Activity

Membership of the BPBU jumped significantly in the years following LASPO 2012. In 2011, the BPBU reported over 2,000 barrister members, including more than 250 QCs. In 2013, this rose to 3,300 members, including one-third of all QCs. In 2016, the BPBU had 3,749 volunteer barristers on its panel. Membership does not necessarily involve working on cases, since this depends on referrals. The barristers' working lives survey did find that 39 percent of those interviewed had undertaken some legal pro bono work in 2013.

The BPBU is keen to refresh its pro bono offering and reengage the bar at all levels, so it recently launched its FABFeb (Find a Barrister February) campaign, which saw it contacting all heads of chambers, senior clerks, and chambers directors at barrister sets with over twenty members, asking them to appoint a pro bono champion.[169] There are about four hundred sets of chambers[170] and, by April 2018, fourteen sets had stepped up to nominate their champions.[171] Since the scheme officially launched at a special event in June 2018, 102 of 175 signatory chambers have appointed a champion.[172]

Volume of Activity

Some idea of the volume of activity can be gained from the annual reports of the different barrister pro bono organizations. In 2016, the BPBU had 2,169 requests for help, and matched 848 cases.[173] In the year ending March 2015, 1,200 cases were referred to FRU.[174] Its representation in employment cases declined to March 2015, from 434 to 210, a drop of approximately 50 percent.[175] This is almost certainly due to the introduction of employment tribunal fees in July 2013.[176] In 2016, 1,500 cases were referred to FRU. It provided representation in 407 Social Security cases (37 percent of such cases referred).[177]

Although the BPBU and FRU are obvious ways for barristers to provide pro bono services, they are not the only ways. As demonstrated in Table 7.2, only 21 percent of barristers claiming to provide free legal work do so through participation in the BPBU. It is doubtful, however, that an accurate idea of barrister pro bono could be obtained by multiplying the BPBU caseload by a factor of five. More would need to be known about the details of arrangements before they could be counted as genuine pro bono work, for example, pro bono work accepted informally from a solicitor, the largest percentage category.[178]

TABLE 7.2 Means by which barristers provide pro bono support[179]

Through what route do barristers provide pro bono support?	Percent taking route	Range in hours volunteered
Bar Pro Bono Unit	21%	1–100 hours pa
Other schemes, e.g. CLIPS, etc.	8%	2–30 hours pa
Legal Advice Centres	6%	1–240 hours pa
Informally through a solicitor	37.5%	1–800 hours pa
Direct access	18%	1–400 hours pa
Other	14%	2–300 hours pa

Categories of Work

The Barristers' Working Lives survey data set out in Table 7.3 produced unexpected results. For example, significant categories are criminal work for which legal aid is available and personal injury for which new funding arrangements are available. Another surprise is a relatively large engagement by barristers in international pro bono work. It is not known how much of the work revealed overlaps with either BPBU or FRU caseloads.

Profile of Barristers Doing Pro Bono Work

The barristers' working lives survey found that, within the 39 percent doing pro bono work, barristers with certain characteristics were more likely to be involved (see Table 7.4); they were self-employed rather

TABLE 7.3 Number of hours of pro bono work in 2012–13 by practice area (percent)[180]

	Criminal (n=746)	Civil (n=746)	Personal negligence/ personal injury (n=215)	Commercial & chancery (n=352)	Family (n=387)	International/ other (n=61)
Zero	67	53	59	66	66	57
< 50 hrs	19	31	34	29	30	30
≥ 50 hrs	14	16	7	5	7	13
Total %	33	47	41	34	37	43

than employed, of Black and minority ethnic origin rather than white, and relatively young rather than older.[181] The biggest difference was between barristers who were self-employed and those who were employed,[182] despite the fact that the BSB Handbook does not prevent employed barristers doing pro bono work.[183] This discrepancy may be because of insurance issues. All self-employed barristers must be members of the Bar Mutual Indemnity Fund whereas, generally speaking, employed barristers need not be insured if only providing services to their employers. They do, however, require insurance cover if they are providing legal services to others, including pro bono work.[184] The Bar Council's recent call for professional indemnity insurance to cover employed barristers was approved in November 2017.[185] So, in time this gap may be reduced.

TABLE 7.4 Characteristics of barristers undertaking pro bono work (2012–13)[186]

Characteristic	Percentage	Percentage Difference
Self-employed	44	
Employed	15	29+
Self-employed disabled	63	
Self-employed without disability	43	20+
BME	48	
White	38	10+
Dependent children	43	
Without dependent children	35	8+
Young Bar < 8 years since call	59	12+
1–3		
4–7	47	
Self-employed barristers qualifying aged 30 plus	50	
Self-employed barristers qualifying under 30	43	7+
Self-employed civil barristers	56	
Self-employed barristers in the international/EU/other practice area	67	
QCs	45	

CONCLUSION

Evaluation of the position in England and Wales throws new light on the architecture, typology, and genealogy of the prevailing culture of pro bono. In our analysis it would not be true to say that the development of pro bono in England and Wales is the consequence of an unbroken historical tradition. Indeed, we argue that there are distinct phases in the development of the pro bono culture of the legal profession and that the current phase is not like those preceding it. This current phase is characterized by a marked increase in levels of activity, particularly in solicitors' pro bono contributions, which apparently increased from £124 million in 1997 to £600 million in 2014. Bearing in mind that the 1997 figure was probably inflated by the wide definition of pro bono used, and that the 2014 figure is based on the more restricted definition in the pro bono protocol, this growth is striking. We suggest that it is partly due to the growth of pro bono infrastructure and a more positive culture of pro bono that this has engendered.

At the end of our research into pro bono in the 1990s we observed that the legal profession had potentially embarked on a new direction in the conception and delivery of pro bono. This was marked by the formation of the BPBU, very much an initiative of the professional body, and the SPBG, very much an initiative of large firms. The period since the millennium has seen several developments that might be viewed as attempts to engage the whole solicitors' profession. The A-GPBU sought to involve both professional bodies more directly in pro bono. As part of this initiative it brokered an Annual Pro Bono Week. The success of this strategy may be measured by the belated launch of a Law Society pro bono initiative.

The issue of a protocol by the A-GPBC helped to clearly define pro bono work as essentially legal and distinctively voluntary. It also helped to rescue the term from the risk of redefinition as proposed by the Law Society Working Party and from the risk of being subsumed within the general concept of corporate philanthropy used by CSR. Clarity has also been provided by the SPBG, which, as LawWorks, has sought to emphasize the pure definition of pro bono and to be inclusive in terms of its membership. It has stressed the importance of large firms delivering legal services as part of their CSR programs and built on its connections with the advice network to become more active in the delivery of services. Its annual awards seek to recognize the efforts of different parts of the profession. In its secondary specialization scheme, it tries to blend the resources of large practices with the expertise of former legal aid practitioners to preserve expertise in the social welfare field in the face of legal aid cuts.

Our analysis points to there being a new culture of pro bono in England and Wales. This builds on preexisting models but has a wholly new infrastructure and is based on broader engagement from all the major players. Regarding the aetiology of this new movement, there is some evidence that this phase may have originally resulted from pressure, particularly from Labour Party politicians, to demonstrate that the legal professions could contribute to Tony Blair's "third way." One of the risks of the large firms' response was that pro bono would be subsumed within a broader philanthropic concept: CSR. Although there is some recent evidence of this happening, confusion of pro bono with other philanthropic activity was largely avoided by widespread acceptance of the pro bono protocol proposed by the A-GPBC and by the SPBG's efforts.

Our earlier work noted that the diverse pressures (from politicians, clients, NGOs, and others) and motives (altruism, rights building, and skills acquisition) led inevitably to the conclusion that pro bono publico could only be described as "mixed motive altruism."[187] With hindsight we think that this explanation is only valid if pro bono is viewed from a distance. The closer the focus on the actual situation, the clearer the different motives of different actors appear. Politicians more or less demanded a contribution by lawyers to replacing legal aid. The bar and large law firms responded fairly quickly, and the Law Society has done so over time. Many more lawyers than were previously engaged in pro bono have responded positively to the call.

The professions have worked with elements of government to provide infrastructure to support pro bono. This provides motivation, guidance, and recognition of practitioners engaged in pro bono work, many of whom would probably be positively motivated without the infrastructure of support and recognition. We conclude that developments in England and Wales over the past twenty years have enabled the professional community of lawyers to move toward a common conception of what constitutes pro bono, to maintain an institutional commitment to its continuance, and, hence, to ground a credible claim to support the rule of law.

APPENDIX: THE PRO BONO PROTOCOL

The Pro Bono Protocol was developed to promote and support consistently high standards of pro bono work. The protocol in no way replaces but rather seeks to build upon the Professional Codes of Conduct that set out the standards and requirements that all lawyers must achieve and observe.

The Protocol was developed under the auspices of the Attorney General's Pro Bono Coordinating Committee and has been endorsed by the Law Society of England and Wales, Bar Council of England and Wales, and Chartered Institute of Legal Executives.

At all stages throughout their career many lawyers regard pro bono legal work as an integral part of being a member of the legal profession, in providing access to justice and meeting unmet legal need.

This Protocol has been agreed to set out the core values of such work and to assist both those who undertake it and their clients.

Many lawyers undertake charitable work of many different kinds. However, the purpose of this protocol is to concentrate specifically on the provision by lawyers of their legal knowledge and skills in the form of pro bono legal work.

1. What is Pro Bono Legal Work?

1.1. When we refer to Pro Bono Legal Work we mean legal advice or representation provided by lawyers in the public interest including to individuals, charities and community groups who cannot afford to pay for that advice or representation and where public and alternative means of funding are not available.

1.2. Legal work is Pro Bono Legal Work only if it is free to the client, without payment to the lawyer or law firm (regardless of the outcome) and provided voluntarily either by the lawyer or his or her firm.

1.3. Pro Bono Legal Work is always only an adjunct to, and not a substitute for, a proper system of publicly funded legal services.

2. How should Pro Bono Legal Work be done?

2.1. Pro Bono Legal Work should always be done to a high standard. That means in particular that:

2.2. The availability of appropriate publicly funded legal advice or representation and opportunities for alternative funding should always be considered before a lawyer undertakes Pro Bono Legal Work.

2.3. When a lawyer is requested to agree to undertake a piece of Pro Bono Legal Work the lawyer should give his/her decision within a reasonable time.
2.4. The terms on which the Pro Bono Legal Work is undertaken including the circumstances in which the relationship may be terminated should be made clear at the outset.
2.5. The Pro Bono Legal Work should only be undertaken by a lawyer who is adequately trained, has appropriate knowledge, skills and experience and, where necessary, is adequately supervised for the work in question.
2.6. The lawyer undertaking a piece of Pro Bono Legal Work (and where appropriate his or her supervisor) should have no less than the minimum level of legal expertise and experience as would be required if the particular work in question was paid work.
2.7. In no case should the client be misled as to the lawyer's skill or ability to undertake the Pro Bono Legal Work.
2.8. Once a lawyer has agreed to undertake a piece of Pro Bono Legal Work the lawyer (and if appropriate his or her firm) must give that work the same priority, attention and care as would apply to paid work.
2.9. Pro Bono Legal Work must not be undertaken without appropriate insurance.
2.10. A lawyer in doubt or difficulty in relation to a piece of Pro Bono Legal Work should seek advice from a Pro Bono organisation or from the Bar Council, the Law Society or the Chartered Institute of Legal Executives.
2.11. Lawyers undertaking Pro Bono Legal Work should advise their client of the risk of an adverse costs order if the client is unsuccessful. Equally they should consider whether a 'pro bono costs order' under section 194 of the Legal Services Act 2007 in favour of The Access to Justice Foundation is available if the client is successful.

3. What about other ways in which lawyers use their legal knowledge or their legal skills?
3.1. The profession also supports further ways in which lawyers use their legal knowledge or their legal skills, without charge, for public benefit. Examples of using their legal knowledge include providing the community with access to legal information and education through legal literacy projects, citizenship work and

other forms of public legal education. Examples of roles in which professional skills might usefully be deployed include acting on the board of trustees for a charity or as a school governor.

3.2. A professional approach is important here as elsewhere. The lawyer's contribution should be made to a high standard and with proper commitment. Suitable training should be undertaken where appropriate.

ANCILLARY PROVISIONS

1. RELATIONSHIPS BETWEEN PRO BONO ORGANISATIONS AND LAWYERS
   1.1. Where practical, lawyers able to undertake pro bono work are encouraged to do so through a pro bono organisation, through the not-for-profit sector, or through both.
   1.2. Pro Bono Legal Work will be more effectively delivered through co-ordinating the relationships between lawyers, pro bono organisations, and not-for-profit agencies such as Law Centres and CABx.
   1.3. When a lawyer is asked by a pro bono organisation or not-for-profit agency to undertake a particular piece of Pro Bono Legal Work, the lawyer is expected to have proper regard to any prior confirmation given to the pro bono organisation or not-for-profit agency that the lawyer was prepared to undertake Pro Bono Legal Work.
   1.4. Sets of chambers, law firms and legal departments should, wherever possible, seek to encourage and support the undertaking of appropriate Pro Bono Legal Work by their lawyers, including the undertaking of that work 'in-house'.
2. THE CONTRIBUTION OF PERSONS WHO ARE NOT QUALIFIED, OR ARE UNABLE TO DO PRO BONO LEGAL WORK
   2.1. Non-lawyer staff within a set of chambers or a firm should be enabled to make the same contribution to the undertaking of a piece of Pro Bono Legal Work as they would for a piece of paid work.
   2.2. Law students, pupil barristers and trainee solicitors have an important contribution to make to Pro Bono Legal Work. However that contribution must be properly supervised and must be preceded by proper training.
   2.3. Where suitably qualified and experienced, academic lawyers and employed lawyers are particularly encouraged to consider providing training to others to enable them to undertake Pro Bono Legal Work if they are not able themselves to provide legal advice or representation. The provision of pro bono legal training without charge is an important contribution to Pro Bono Legal Work.
3. PARTICIPATION IN PRO BONO LEGAL WORK AS A CHARACTERISTIC OF BEING A MEMBER OF THE LEGAL PROFESSION

3.1. A commitment to the delivery of Pro Bono Legal Work is encouraged throughout a lawyer's professional life, as a student and in practice, through to and including retirement.

NOTES

1. See, for example, Roscoe Pound, *The Lawyer from Antiquity to Modern Times: With Particular Reference to the Development of Bar Association in the United States* and the discussion in ANDREW BOON & JENNIFER LEVIN, THE ETHICS AND CONDUCT OF LAWYERS IN ENGLAND AND WALES (1999).
2. Lorne Sossin, *The Public Interest, Professionalism and Pro Bono*, 46 OSGOODE HALL L.J. 131 (2008).
3. *See* MAGALI S. LARSON, THE RISE OF PROFESSIONALISM: A SOCIOLOGICAL ANALYSIS (1977); Andrew Abbott, *Jurisdictional Conflicts: A New Approach to the Development of Legal Professions*, 11 AM. B. FOUND. RES. J. 187 (1986); Richard L. Abel, *Between Market and State: The Legal Profession in Turmoil*, 52 MOD. L. REV. 285 (1989); Richard L. Abel, The Decline of Professionalism?, 49 MOD. L. REV. 1 (1986).
4. Richard. L. Abel, Why Does the ABA Promulgate Ethical Rules?, 59 TEX. L. REV. 639 (1981).
5. RICHARD L. ABEL, ENGLISH LAWYERS BETWEEN MARKET AND STATE: THE POLITICS OF PROFESSIONALISM (2003); Alan A. Paterson, *Professionalism and the Legal Services Market*, 3 INT'L J. LEGAL PROF. 137 (1996); Terry Johnson, *Expertise and the State*, *in* FOUCAULT'S NEW DOMAINS 139 (Mike Gane & Terry Johnson eds., 1993).
6. DONALD NICOLSON & JULIAN WEBB, PROFESSIONAL LEGAL ETHICS: CRITICAL INTERROGATIONS (2000).
7. BOON & LEVIN, *supra* note 1, at 541.
8. *See* ANDREW BOON & AVIS WHYTE, SOMETHING FOR NOTHING?: THE PROVISION OF LEGAL SERVICES PRO BONO PUBLICO (2001); Robert Abbey & Andrew Boon, *Moral Agendas?: Pro Bono Publico in Large Law Firms in the United Kingdom*, 60 MOD. L. REV. 630 (1997); Robert Abbey & Andrew Boon, *The Provision of Free Legal Services by Solicitors: A Review of the Report of the Law Society's Pro Bono Working Party*, 2 INT'L J. LEGAL PROF. 26 (1995); Andrew Boon & Avis Whyte, *Charity and Beating Begins at Home: The Aetiology of the New Culture of Pro Bono Publico*, 2 LEGAL ETHICS 169 (1999); Andrew Boon & Avis Whyte, Pro Bono Publico: Problems and Possibilities: Full Report (1999) (unpublished report submitted to the Nuffield Foundation).
9. Although many aspects of traditional demarcation between the professions have broken down, it is still true to say that solicitors can operate in partnerships or as sole practices and are the larger profession. Barristers,

meanwhile, are usually self-employed advocacy specialists whose preferred practice mode is to be briefed by solicitors to advise or appear in court. The Law Society is the independent professional body for solicitors, and the Bar Council represents barristers in England and Wales. *See* www.lawsociety.org.uk and www.barcouncil.org.uk.

10. J. A. Brundage, *Legal Aid for the Poor and the Professionalisation of Law in the Middle Ages*, 9 J. LEG. HIST. 169 (1988).
11. A right to sue *in forma pauperis* was established by statute in 1495 but probably has earlier origins. *See* John M. Maguire, *Poverty and Civil Litigation*, 36 HARV. L. REV. 361 (1923). A similar example of court-assigned advocates is the dock brief in criminal trials, whereby the judge asks an advocate to appear for an unrepresented defendant. *See* WILFRID R. PREST, THE RISE OF THE BARRISTERS: A SOCIAL HISTORY OF THE BAR 1590–1640 22 (1986).
12. Sir Henry Brooke, *Appendix 6: The History of Legal Aid 1945–2010*, *in* LORD WILLY BACH, THE RIGHT TO JUSTICE: THE FINAL REPORT OF THE BACH COMMISSION (2017).
13. Thomas Erskine famously represented Tom Paine pro bono when he was charged with seditious libel in connection with publication of *The Rights of Man*. JOHN HOSTETTLER, THOMAS ERSKINE AND TRIAL BY JURY 89 (2010).
14. BACH, *supra* note 12.
15. Tamara Goriely, *Gratuitous Assistance to the "Ill-Dressed": Debating Civil Legal Aid in England and Wales from 1924 to 1939*, 13 INT'L J. LEGAL PROF. 41 (2006). This earlier history is covered in detail elsewhere. *See* BOON & LEVIN, *supra* note 1.
16. *Lord Chancellor's Office: Committee to Enquire into Poor Persons Rules 1919*, NAT'L ARCHIVES, http://discovery.nationalarchives.gov.uk/details/r/C10270 (last visited July 4, 2018).
17. *Id.*
18. *Id.*
19. *Id.*
20. Some poor man's lawyers claimed a share of damages. R. F. Scott, *The Poor Man's Lawyer*, SPECTATOR, July 15, 1938, at 13. This was illegal under rules against maintenance and champerty (supporting or profiting from another's litigation).
21. Goriely, *supra* note 15.
22. GERARD HANLON, LAWYERS, THE STATE AND THE MARKET: PROFESSIONALISM REVISITED (1999).
23. Tamara Goriely, *Law for the Poor: The Relationship Between Advice Agencies and Solicitors in the Development of Poverty Law*, 3 INT'L J. LEGAL PROF. 215 (1996).
24. Lynda Hiscock & Godfrey Cole, *The Motivation, Use and Future of Volunteer Lawyers in Law Centres*, 6 J. SOC. WELFARE & L. 404 (1990).
25. Barristers might have hoped that they would later be briefed to appear in cases referred to local solicitors.

26. MICHAEL ZANDER, *Restrictions on Lawyers Working for the Poor*, *in* LAWYERS AND THE PUBLIC INTEREST: A STUDY OF RESTRICTIVE PRACTICES 238 (1968).
27. Robert Verkaik, *Law: Last Appeal to a Lost Empire*, INDEPENDENT, May 25, 1999, www.independent.co.uk/arts-entertainment/law-last-appeal-to-a-lost-empire-1095796.html (last visited July 5, 2018).
28. For this and further information in this paragraph, see BOON & LEVIN, *supra* note 1.
29. FRU is authorized by the Bar Council in relation to each of the tribunals in which its representatives appear.
30. There was also a student-run clinic offering advice to students at Kent University, which now also provides advice to local people. Kent Law Clinic, UNIVERSITY OF KENT, www.kent.ac.uk/law/clinic (last visited July 3, 2018).
31. Andrew Boon, Michael Jeeves & Julie Macfarlane, *A Working Model for Clinical Legal Education: Testing the Definition Against a Range of Examples*, 21 LAW TCHR. 172 (1987).
32. Brooke, *supra* note 12. The Legal Aid Board was replaced by the Legal Aid Commission in 2000, which was in turn replaced by the current Legal Aid Agency in 2013. *Id.*
33. As regards monopolies, for example, by the introduction of a conveyancing profession in the 1980s and by allowing solicitors to compete with barristers for higher court advocacy in the 1990s. As regard powers, by the requirement that legal professions separate representative and regulatory functions. *See* Andrew Boon, *England and Wales: Cocktails of Logics: Reform of Legal Services Regulation in England and Wales*, *in* INTERNATIONAL PERSPECTIVES ON THE REGULATION OF LAWYERS AND LEGAL SERVICES 209 (Andrew Boon ed., 2017).
34. LAW SOCIETY, REPORT OF THE PRO BONO WORKING PARTY (1994).
35. *For Love – Not Money – an Assessment of Free Work Already Conducted by Solicitors*, LAW SOC'Y GAZETTE, Oct. 25, 1995.
36. *Labour Creates Future Vision*, LAW SOC'Y GAZETTE, Feb. 22, 1995, at 68; *Pro Bono Wrangle*, LAW SOC'Y GAZETTE, Dec. 13, 1996, at 6.
37. Volunteerism was the core of H. W. Bush's presidential nomination acceptance speech in 1988, *Address Accepting the Presidential Nomination*, AMER. PRESIDENCY PROJECT, www.presidency.ucsb.edu/documents/address-accepting-the-presidential-nomination-the-republican-national-convention-new (last visited Sept. 6, 2020), and, in the United Kingdom, of Tony Blair's "Third Way," launched at a meeting of Blair and Bill Clinton in New York in September 1998, Anne Mellbye, *A Brief History of the Third Way*, GUARDIAN, Feb. 10, 2003, www.theguardian.com/politics/2003/feb/10/labour.uk1 (last visited Sept. 6, 2020), and Prime Minister David Cameron, *Big Society Speech*, GOV.UK (July 20, 2010), www.gov.uk/government/speeches/big-society-speech (last visited Sept. 6, 2020).
38. Mellbye, *supra* note 37.

39. *Id.*
40. Iain Hollingshead, *Whatever Happened to the Third Way?*, GUARDIAN, Oct. 29, 2005, www.theguardian.com/politics/2005/oct/29/labour.uk (last visited Sept. 14, 2020).
41. Abbey & Boon, *The Provision of Free Legal Services by Solicitors*, *supra* note 8.
42. *Id.*
43. Especially the regional schemes run on the Northern Circuit, Western Circuit and Wales, and Chester Circuit, and the schemes run by subject area bar associations, for example, the Employment Law Bar Association Scheme, the Planning Bar Association's Free Advocacy Scheme, and Environmental Legal and Mediation Service. Vanessa Sims, *Legal Education and Practice Pro Bono at the Bar*, 4 AMICUS CURIAE 21 (1998).
44. *Id.*
45. In October 2018, the Bar Pro Bono Unit changed its name to Advocate but remains a national charity finding free legal help from barristers in any area of law and in any court or tribunal across England and Wales. *See We Are Advocate*, ADVOCATE, https://weareadvocate.org.uk/we-are-advocate.html (last visited Sept. 14, 2020).
46. *Id.*
47. Letter from Andrew Phillips (Oct. 1999), *see also* Boon & Whyte, *Charity and Beating*, *supra* note 8, at 176.
48. Matheu Swallow, *Who Is Behind Pro Bono?*, LAW., Sept. 27, 1999.
49. In the Companies Act 1965; *see* John Flood, *Mega-Law in the UK, Professionalism or Corporatism?: A Preliminary Report*, 64 IND. L.J. 569 (1989).
50. *Solicitors Vote for Boost to Pro Bono*, LAW., Nov. 12, 1996, at 1.
51. Archie B. Carroll, *A History of Corporate Social Responsibility: Concepts and Practices*, *in* THE OXFORD HANDBOOK OF CORPORATE SOCIAL RESPONSIBILITY 19 (Andrew Crane ed., 2009).
52. Ronen Shamir, *Socially Responsible Private Regulation: World-Culture or World-Capitalism?*, 45 LAW & SOC'Y REV. 313 (2011).
53. Joel Bakan, *The Invisible Hand of Law: Private Regulation and the Rule of Law*, 48 CORNELL INT'L L.J. 279 (2015).
54. *Our History*, *About Us*, BITC, www.bitc.org.uk/about-us/what-we-do/our-history (last visited July 5, 2018).
55. *Id.*
56. *Id.*
57. *Id.*
58. Archie B. Carroll, *The Pyramid of Corporate Social Responsibility: Toward Moral Management of Organizational Stakeholders*, 34 BUS. HORIZONS 39 (1991).
59. *See also* Constantina Bichta, Corporate Social Responsibility: A Role in Government Policy and Regulation 9–11 (Research Report 16, 2003).

60. Sally Wheeler & Gary Wilson, *Corporate Law Firms and the Spirit of Community*, 49 N. IR. LEGAL Q. 241 (1998).
61. Though we were not told, we surmised that the remaining members of the PFG were accountants, engineers, architects, and estate agents.
62. *Pro Bono – Where Next?*, LAW., Oct. 15, 1996, www.thelawyer.com/pro-bono-where-next (last visited July 6, 2018).
63. *Solicitors Vote for Boost to Pro Bono*, *supra* note 50.
64. *See About Barristers*, THE BAR COUNCIL, www.barcouncil.org.uk/about-the-bar/about-barristers (last visited Sept. 14, 2020).
65. THE BAR PRO BONO UNIT, THE EVOLUTION OF THE BAR PRO BONO UNIT: ANNUAL REVIEW 2016, at 3 (2016), www.barprobono.org.uk/public/downloads/XyJXX/FINAL_BarProBono_AnnualReview_2016_DIGITALSPREADS.pdf (last visited Sept. 14, 2020).
66. By 1998, the number had crept up to 800, including 130 QCs. Sims, *supra* note 43. In 2002, 1,220 barristers were registered. Sally Weale & Clare Dyer, *Heard the One About the Lawyer Who Works for Nothing …*, GUARDIAN, June 11, 2002.
67. *Overview*, THE BAR PRO BONO UNIT, www.barprobono.org.uk/overview.html.
68. S. Solley & R. D'Cruz, *Deliverance from Death Row?*, COUNSEL, Oct. 1998, at 22.
69. The Unit itself does not provide any legal advice or assistance or "instruct" counsel. THE BAR PRO BONO UNIT, *supra* note 67.
70. In 2001, Allen & Overy claimed 12,232 hours and Clifford Chance 18,000 hours per annum. Lucy Hickman, *Pro Plus*, LAW SOC'Y GAZETTE, July 13, 2001, www.lawgazette.co.uk/news/pro-plus/34465.article (last visited July 6, 2018).
71. *Our History*, ADVOCATE, https://weareadvocate.org.uk/our-history.html (last visited Sept. 14, 2020).
72. LAW SOCIETY, REPORT OF THE LAW SOCIETY'S PRO BONO WORKING PARTY Annex C para. 1 (1994).
73. Hiscock & Cole, *supra* note 24. This was significantly fewer than the three thousand solicitors that the Benson report estimated were supporting advice agencies in 1979. SIR HENRY BENSON, ROYAL COMMISSION ON LEGAL SERVICES FINAL REPORT (1979).
74. BOON & LEVIN, *supra* note 1, at 233 (citing Law Society Press release).
75. At that time, they had a mean number of 48 partners, 172 associates, and 42 trainees.
76. Marc Galanter & Thomas Palay, *Large Law Firms and Professional Responsibility*, *in* LEGAL ETHICS AND PROFESSIONAL RESPONSIBILITY 189–202 (Ross Cranston ed., 1995).
77. BOON & WHYTE, SOMETHING FOR NOTHING?, *supra* note 8, at 1.
78. Goldsmith became a Labour life peer in 1999 and attorney general to Blair's government in 2001.
79. Boon & Whyte, *Charity and Beating*, *supra* note 8, at 182.

80. Andrew Phillips, A *Want of Experience*, LAW SOC'Y GAZETTE, Apr. 28, 1999, cited in Boon & Whyte, *Charity and Beating*, *supra* note 8, at 182.
81. *Labour Suggests Levy to Support Legal Assistance*, LAW., Sept. 27, 1994, at 3; *Labour Eyes US Pro Bono Model*, LAW., Nov. 8, 1994, at 2.
82. DAVID GRAYSON, BUSINESS-LED CORPORATE RESPONSIBILITY COALITIONS: LEARNING FROM THE EXAMPLE OF BUSINESS IN THE COMMUNITY IN THE UK 17 (2007), https://sites.hks.harvard.edu/m-rcbg/CSRI/publications/report_26_GraysonBus-LedCRCoalitions.pdf (last visited Sept. 14, 2020).
83. *See, e.g.*, LORD CHANCELLOR'S DEPARTMENT, MODERNISING JUSTICE: THE GOVERNMENT'S PLANS FOR REFORMING LEGAL SERVICES AND COURTS (1998); Karen Mackay, *Evaluating the Community Legal Service*, *in* SOURCEBOOK ON THE ENGLISH LEGAL SYSTEM 446 (2001); Gary Slapper, *Modernising Justice*, *in* SOURCEBOOK ON THE ENGLISH LEGAL SYSTEM 439 (David Kelly & Gary Slapper eds., 2001).
84. Brooke, *supra* note 12, at 14–20.
85. *See* Boon, *supra* note 33.
86. Legal Aid, Sentencing and Punishment of Offenders Act 2012, § 45 (UK).
87. Civil Procedure Rules 1998 (UK).
88. LORD JUSTICE BRIGGS, CIVIL COURTS STRUCTURE REVIEW: FINAL REPORT 36 (2016), www.judiciary.uk/wp-content/uploads/2016/07/civil-courts-structure-review-final-report-jul-16-final-1.pdf (last visited July 6, 2018). The online pilot civil claims has now gone live and spread across England and Wales. *See Quicker Way to Resolve Claim Disputes Launched Online*, HM COURTS & TRIBUNAL SERVICE (Apr. 6, 2018), www.gov.uk/government/news/quicker-way-to-resolve-claim-disputes-launched-online (last visited July 6, 2018); and *Online Civil Claims Pilot Now Public Across England and Wales*, EVERSHEDS SUTHERLAND (Apr. 24, 2018), www.eversheds-sutherland.com/global/en/what/articles/index.page?ArticleID=en/Litigation_Support/online-civil-claims (last visited July 6, 2018).
89. Catherine Baksi, *Civil Legal Aid: Access Denied*, LAW SOC'Y GAZETTE, Apr. 7, 2014, www.lawgazette.co.uk/law/civil-legal-aid-access-denied/5040722.article (last visited July 6, 2018).
90. LEGAL SERVICES COMMISSION, ANNUAL REPORT AND ACCOUNTS 2012–2013 23 (2013).
91. LEGAL AID AGENCY, ANNUAL REPORT AND ACCOUNTS 2013–2014 19 (2014).
92. LEGAL SERVICES COMMISSION, *supra* note 90.
93. LEGAL AID AGENCY, *supra* note 91.
94. The government acknowledged that in April 2013 the LASPO Act had resulted in large reductions in legal help workload and that the overall trend had subsequently leveled out at around one-third of pre-LASPO levels. *Legal Aid Statistics in England and Wales April to June*

2016, MINISTRY OF JUSTICE, www.gov.uk/government/statistics/legal-aid-statistics-april-to-june-2016.

95. *Market Financials: Turnover and Profitability*, LEGAL SERVICES BOARD, https://research.legalservicesboard.org.uk/analysis/supply/market-financials/turnover-and-profitability (last visited July 6, 2018).
96. Press release from the Attorney General's Chambers, 23 April 2002; Victoria MacCallum, *Lord Goldsmith Unveils Pro Bono Drive to Co-ordinate Work Across the Country*, LAW SOC'Y GAZETTE, Apr. 25, 2002.
97. President of the Law Society (2001).
98. The term "pro bono" caused persistent definitional issues. *See The Pro Bono Protocol*, LAWWORKS, www.lawworks.org.uk/why-pro-bono/what-pro-bono/pro-bono-protocol (last visited July 6, 2018); *Joint Protocol for Pro Bono Legal Work*, THE BAR PRO BONO UNIT, www.barprobono.org.uk/pro_bono_protocol.html (last visited July 6, 2018); Victoria MacCallum, *Attorney-General Unveils Protocol That Sets Out Key Elements of Pro Bono Work*, LAW SOC'Y GAZETTE, Apr. 3, 2003, at 4; Michael Napier, *Delivering Hope on Pro Bono*, LAW SOC'Y GAZETTE, Apr. 3, 2003, at 13.
99. *The Pro Bono Protocol*, *supra* note 98.
100. Under the indemnity principle, the losing party in litigation is only liable for costs actually incurred by the winner. Under the Legal Services Act 2007 s.194, a pro bono costs order could be made against a losing party where a case has been won with pro bono help, and the losing party would otherwise have escaped liability for costs. *See also* Civil Procedure Rule 46.7 & Practice Direction 46 – Costs Special Cases: Personal liability of legal representative for costs – wasted costs orders: rule 46.8, 4.1 (a party who has pro bono representation prepares, files, and serves a written statement of the sum equivalent to the costs that party would have claimed for that legal representation had it not been provided free of charge).
101. The charity prescribed by the Lord Chancellor to receive sums raised by pro bono costs orders is the Access to Justice Foundation (AJF). The Legal Services Act 2007 (Prescribed Charity) Order 2008 (UK). *See further* Legal Services Act 2007, §194(3) and (8) (UK); *Pro Bono Costs*, ACCESS TO JUSTICE FOUNDATION, www.atjf.org.uk/pro-bono-costs-orders.html (last visited July 6, 2018).
102. *See The Joint Protocol for Legal Work*, LAW SOCIETY OF ENGLAND AND WALES, www.lawsociety.org.uk/Support-services/Practice-management/Pro-bono/The-pro-bono-protocol (last visited July 6, 2018), which also carries the protocol as an appendix.
103. LAW SOCIETY OF ENGLAND AND WALES, PRO BONO MANUAL: A PRACTICAL GUIDE AND RESOURCE KIT FOR SOLICITORS (2016), https://events.lawsociety.org.uk/uploads/files/c9556625-e3e7-416c-bdc3-52b3c1107ca8.pdf (last visited Sept. 14, 2020).

104. The "third branch" of the legal profession in England and Wales. *See* CHARTERED INSTITUTE OF LEGAL EXECUTIVES, www.cilex.org.uk (last visited Sept. 14, 2020).
105. For protocol signatories, *see Protocol Signatories*, LAWWORKS, www.lawworks.org.uk/why-pro-bono/pro-bono-protocol/protocol-signatories (last visited Sept. 14, 2020).
106. *Power of Pro Bono*, LAW SOC'Y GAZETTE, Apr. 25, 2002.
107. He became the leader of European litigation in the City office of Debevoise & Plimpton LLP, an American corporate firm, in 2007. Clare Dyer, *So Lord Goldsmith, what first attracted you to the £1m-a-year job at a US law firm?*, GUARDIAN, Sept. 27, 2007, www.theguardian.com/politics/2007/sep/27/uk.topstories31 (last visited July 6, 2018).
108. *BPBU Creates Solicitor Panel*, LAW., Jan. 28, 2002.
109. BAR IN THE COMMUNITY, www.barinthecommunity.org.uk (last visited Sept. 14, 2020).
110. The Solicitors Pro Bono Group brochure (undated) as cited in Boon & Whyte, *Charity and Beating*, *supra* note 8, at n.9.
111. Clare Dyer, *Win or Lose, No Fee: Pro Bono Week Promotes Free Legal Services*, GUARDIAN, June 5, 2006, at 14.
112. *About Us*, THE NATIONAL PRO BONO CENTRE, www.nationalprobonocentre.org.uk/about-us (last visited July 6, 2018).
113. *Id.*
114. *Id.*
115. THE PRO BONO YEARBOOK OF ENGLAND AND WALES (J. Robins ed., 2013).
116. *LawWorks Secondary Specialisation Programme*, LAWWORKS, www.lawworks.org.uk/system/files/Membership%20Pack%20Insert%20-%20LawWorks%20Secondary%20Specialisation%20Programme.pdf (last visited Sept. 14, 2020).
117. The welfare benefits first-tier support and advocacy scheme partners include Islington Law Centre, Child Poverty Action Group (CPAG), volunteer solicitors from Norton Rose Fulbright LLP, Kirkland & Ellis LLP and Berwin Leighton Paisner (BLP) LLP, Clyde & Co., and Sidley Austin LLP, to provide specialist assistance and advocacy at First-Tier Social Security Tribunals on Employment and Support Allowance (ESA) and Personal Independence Payments (PIP) appeals. More than one hundred volunteer lawyers from affiliated firms have been trained by the CPAG (a leading training provider in social welfare law). *Id.* The housing and community care services scheme involves work with the charity Together for Short Lives to support clients challenging local authority decisions in relation to housing allocations and community care services. *Id.*
118. Steven Vaughan, Linden Thomas & Alastair Young, *Symbolism Over Substance? Large Law Firms and Corporate Social Responsibility*, 18 LEGAL ETHICS 138 (2015).

119. *LawWorks Annual Pro Bono Awards*, LAWWORKS, www.lawworks.org.uk/solicitors-and-volunteers/get-involved/lawworks-pro-bono-awards/lawworks-annual-pro-bono-awards-20-0 (last visited Sept. 14, 2020).
120. *See* Boon & Whyte, *Charity and Beating*, *supra* note 8, at 108; Joanna Goodman, *Corporate Social Responsibility – Community Spirit*, LAW SOC'Y GAZETTE, Oct. 4, 2016, https://ww.lawgazette.co.uk/features/corporate-social-responsibility–community-spirit/5058438.article (last visited July 3, 2018).
121. Vaughan et al., *supra* note 118.
122. *Id.*
123. *Id.* at 154 (table 8).
124. Vaughan et al., *supra* note 118 (citing Edward Weeks, *Why Firms Should Embrace CSR*, LAW., Dec. 4, 2006).
125. *Id.*
126. Interview by Andrew Boon in 2012.
127. Andrew Boon & Peter Hodgkinson, *Life and Death in the Lawyer's Office: The Internship in Capital Punishment Studies*, 30 LAW TCHR. 253 (1996).
128. DAMIAN CARNEY, FRANK DIGNAN, RICHARD GRIMES, GRACE KELLY & REBECCA PARKER , THE LAWWORKS LAW SCHOOL PRO BONO AND CLINIC REPORT 2014 10 (2014), www.lawworks.org.uk/sites/default/files/LawWorks-student-pro-bono-report%202014.pdf (last visited Sept. 14, 2020).
129. Frank Dignan, Richard Grimes & Rebecca Parker, *Pro Bono and Clinical Work in Law Schools: Summary and Analysis*, 14 ASIAN J. LEGAL EDUC. 1, 4 (2017).
130. *See LawWorks and Attorney General's Student Pro Bono Awards 2018*, LAWWORKS, www.lawworks.org.uk/solicitors-and-volunteers/get-involved/student-pro-bono-awards/lawworks-and-attorney-generals (last visited Sept. 14, 2020).
131. CARNEY ET AL., *supra* note 128, at 10.
132. Nottingham Trent University, *Business Law Advice Service Launched at Nottingham Law School*, www.ntu.ac.uk/about-us/news/news-articles/2017/05/business-law-advice-service-launched-at-nottingham-law-school (last visited Sept. 14, 2020).
133. BOON & LEVIN, *supra* note 1, at 567–68.
134. Andrew Boon, *From Public Service to Service Industry: The Impact of Socialisation and Work on the Motivation and Values of Lawyers*, 12 INT'L J. LEGAL PROF. 193 (2005); *see also* Scott L. Cummings & Deborah L. Rhode, *Managing Pro Bono: Doing Well by Doing Better*, 78 FORDHAM L. REV. 2359 (2010).
135. *Pro Bono Awards 2017: The LawWorks Annual Pro Bono Awards & Lecture*, LAWWORKS, www.lawworks.org.uk/sites/default/files/LawWorks-AwardsBrochure2017-Final-Web-ready.pdf (last visited June 18, 2018).

136. *See further* TOYNBEE HALL, WOMEN ONLY GENERAL ADVICE, www.toynbeehall.org.uk/women-only-general-advice (last visited Sept. 14, 2020).
137. *Bar Pro Bono Award 2017: Winner Announced!*, THE BAR PRO BONO UNIT, www.barprobono.org.uk/tanya-murshed-winner-bar-pro-bono-award-2017.html (last visited June 18, 2018).
138. These followed from the landmark Uganda Supreme Court decision, *Attorney General v Susan Kigula and 417 Ors* ((CONSTITUTIONAL APPEAL NO. 03 OF 2006)) [2009] UGSC 6 (21 January 2009), https://ulii.org/node/15313, which held that automatic death sentences were unconstitutional.
139. Murshed, for example, launched an organization called Evolve and trained Ugandan law students to collect evidence and mitigation for resentencing appeals. *See further Tanya Murshed*, EVOLVE, https://evolvefila.org/founder/ (last visited July 6, 2018).
140. Two other core funders are sets of chambers. THE BAR PRO BONO UNIT, *supra* note 65, at 17.
141. In 2016, over 50 percent of the bar made this contribution during the Authorisation to Practise (ATP) process, including over 85 percent of QCs, with the majority of donations coming from the publicly funded bar, *Authorisation to Practice Appeal*, THE BAR PRO BONO UNIT, Mar. 15, 2017, www.barprobono.org.uk/atp-appeal.html (last visited July 6, 2018).
142. THE BAR PRO BONO UNIT, *supra* note 65, at 17.
143. *Id.* at 3.
144. FREE REPRESENTATION UNIT, ANNUAL REPORT AND FINANCIAL STATEMENTS 31 MARCH 2016 3 (2016), www.thefru.org.uk/sites/default/files/FRU%20Signed%20Accounts%202015-16.pdf (last visited Sept. 14, 2020).
145. Help was provided by the Bar Council (33 percent), the Inns of Court (26 percent), covenants from individual barristers (20 percent), subscriptions from referral agencies, and income from training days. *FRU – The Bars Contribution*, COUNSEL, Apr. 1994, at 23.
146. Law Society Council Minutes, Sept. 24, 1998.
147. *Funders*, LAWWORKS, www.lawworks.org.uk/about-us/funders (last visited July 6, 2018).
148. *See also* Mark Smulian, *How the LawWorks Project Obtained Its Big Funding*, LAW SOC'Y GAZETTE, Mar. 3, 2006, www.lawgazette.co.uk/analysis/how-the-lawworks-project-obtained-its-big-funding/2776.article (last visited July 6, 2018).
149. HANLON, *supra* note 22.
150. *Pro Bono Charter*, THE LAW SOCIETY, www.lawsociety.org.uk/my-law-society/pro-bono-charter (last visited July 6, 2018).
151. *Founding Signatories of the Law Society Pro Bono Charter*, THE LAW SOCIETY (Feb. 20, 2017), www.lawsociety.org.uk/news/press-releases/founding-signatories-law-society-pro-bono-charter (last visited July 6, 2018).

152. *Pro Bono Charter*, *supra* note 150, at 2.
153. *Founding Signatories of the Law Society Pro Bono Charter*, *supra* note 151, at 2.
154. *Pro Bono Charter*, *supra* note 150.
155. *Founding Signatories of the Law Society Pro Bono Charter*, *supra* note 151.
156. LAW SOCIETY, TRENDS IN THE SOLICITORS' PROFESSION: ANNUAL STATISTICAL REPORT 1999 (2000); SOLICITORS REGULATION AUTHORITY, REGULATED POPULATION STATISTICS, www.sra.org.uk/sra/how-we-work/reports/data/population_solicitors.page (last visited Feb. 13, 2018).
157. SOLICITORS REGULATION AUTHORITY, *supra* note 156.
158. LAW SOCIETY, TRENDS IN THE SOLICITORS' PROFESSION: ANNUAL STATISTICAL REPORT 2018, at 37 (2019).
159. *Id.* at 36.
160. The PC Holder Survey has been primarily a vehicle for the Law Society's Corporate Responsibility, Equality and Diversity and Inclusion (CREDI) team to collect data on the protected characteristics of the profession, working hours, and earnings.
161. Private practice solicitors were more likely to report having adequate opportunity to do PB work (63 percent) than those in the employed sector (44 percent) or government (26 percent). THE LAW SOCIETY, THE PRO BONO WORK OF SOLICITORS – PC HOLDER SURVEY 4 (2015).
162. Some such outliers are mentioned in the Annual Pro Bono Awards. For example, Tanya Murshed, *supra* note 139, apparently spends a quarter of her working time on her pro bono project.
163. Boon & Whyte, *Charity and Beating*, *supra* note 8, at 179 n.68 (citing a news release by THE LAW SOCIETY, Oct. 14, 1997).
164. The statistics in this paragraph are taken from the data spreadsheet 2000 to 2017 found on the BSB. *Practising Barrister Statistics*, BAR STANDARDS BOARD, www.barstandardsboard.org.uk/media-centre/research-and-statistics/statistics/practising-barrister-statistics (last visited July 4, 2018).
165. THE BAR COUNCIL & BAR STANDARDS BOARD, BARRISTERS' WORKING LIVES, A SECOND BIENNIAL SURVEY OF THE BAR 2013, www.barstandardsboard.org.uk/uploads/assets/3eda875f-c7bb-4f95-aa70c7ebbf1fc516/biennialsurveyreport2013.pdf (last visited Sept. 14, 2020).
166. First, the survey was commissioned jointly by both the Bar Standards Board (BSB) and the Bar Council. It was felt that this led to issues with the design and publication of the survey as the information requirements of the regulatory and representative arms were different. In addition, it was felt that the areas of the survey that covered the main areas of interest to the BSB were – to a large extent – duplicating information the Council collected and published elsewhere (see, for example, statistical information published on its website, www.barstandardsboard.org.uk/media-centre/research-and-statistics/statistics), and

it was a more sensible use of resources to concentrate on improving the Council's own data collection. By improving the data the Council collected from barristers, this would enable it to publish statistics on the whole profession, rather than relying on a survey sample that it could not be certain was representative. The information contained in this footnote was provided to us by the BSB Research Team (May 2017).

167. *Guest Blog: Bar Pro Bono Unit Reports to Each Chambers for the First Time*, BAR COUNCIL (Feb. 22, 2017), www.barcouncil.org.uk/media-centre/bar-blog/contributing-writers/2017/february/guest-blog-bar-pro-bono-unit-reports-to-each-chambers-for-the-first-time (last visited July 6, 2018).

168. *Id.* The AtP process represents a more structured approach to barristers' registration, bringing it into compliance with the Legal Services Act 2007. *Authorisation to Practice*, BAR STANDARDS BOARD, https://www.barstandardsboard.org.uk/authorisation-to-practise (last accessed July 6, 2018).

169. Richard Simmons, *Landmark, Littleton and 7KBW Among Chambers Appointing Pro Bono Champions*, LAW., Apr. 30, 2018, www.thelawyer.com/bar-pro-bono-champions/?nocache=true&adfesuccess=1 (last visited July 6, 2018).

170. *Chambers Statistics*, BAR STANDARDS BOARD, www.barstandardsboard.org.uk/media-centre/research-and-statistics/statistics/chambers (last visited July 6, 2018).

171. *Simmons*, *supra* note 169.

172. *Id.*; *see also Pro Bono Champions*, ADVOCATE, https://weareadvocate.org.uk probonochampions.html (last visited February 16, 2021).

173. THE BAR PRO BONO UNIT, *supra* note 65, at 3.

174. FREE REPRESENTATION UNIT, *supra* note 144, at 3. FRU works with over two hundred referral agencies. *List of Agencies*, FREE REPRESENTATION UNIT, www.thefru.org.uk/get-advice/list-of-agencies (last visited July 6, 2018).

175. *Id.*

176. Indeed, this compares to the 60 percent decline in the tribunal's quarterly receipts over the same time span. *Id.*

177. FREE REPRESENTATION UNIT, *supra* note 144, at 3.

178. The way in which such arrangements operate is unclear. For example, are the solicitors themselves acting pro bono and, if so, do they brief barristers in a conventional way (i.e., through the barrister's chambers (and clerking system))?

179. *How Do Barristers Provide Pro Bono Support?*, THE BAR COUNCIL: BAR PRO BONO HUB, www.barcouncil.org.uk/media-centre/campaigns/bar-pro-bono-hub (last visited July 6, 2018).

180. IES/ERL 2013 as cited by THE BAR COUNCIL, *supra* note 165, at 61, Table 5.7. Note the first biennial survey contains no reference to pro bono work.

181. *Id.* at 62.

182. *Id.*
183. *BSB Handbook Explained – Barristers Working Pro Bono*, BAR STANDARDS BOARD, www.barstandardsboard.org.uk/regulatory-requirements/regulatory-update-2016/bsb-regulatory-update-january-2016/bsb-handbook-explained-%E2%80%93-barristers-working-pro-bono (last visited July 6, 2018). Note that employed barristers in "recognized bodies" are already able to volunteer through the Bar Pro Bono Unit. *Bar Council Insurance Call for Employed Barristers Gets Go-Ahead*, BAR COUNCIL (Nov. 13, 2017), www.barcouncil.org.uk/media-centre/news-and-press-releases/2017/november/bar-council-insurance-call-for-employed-barristers-gets-go-ahead%E2%80%8E (last visited July 6, 2018).
184. PROFESSIONAL ETHICS 37 (Robert McPeake ed., 16th ed., 2015).
185. THE BAR COUNCIL, *supra* note 165.
186. *Id.*
187. Carrie Menkel-Meadow, *The Causes of Cause Lawyering: Toward an Understanding of the Motivation and Commitment of Social Justice Lawyers*, *in* CAUSE LAWYERING: POLITICAL COMMITMENTS AND PROFESSIONAL RESPONSIBILITIES 31 (Austin Sarat & Stuart Scheingold eds., 1998).

CHAPTER EIGHT

NO LAWYERS WITHOUT GENEROSITY: LESSONS ON PRO BONO FROM FRANCE

Louis Assier-Andrieu and Jeremy Perelman

INTRODUCTION

This chapter develops a *vision d'ensemble*, or intertwined vision, of what is known conventionally as lawyers' pro bono practice, an increasingly major field of research at a time largely seen as one in which the legal profession undergoes – and will undergo – its greatest transformations. It offers some insights and snapshots on pro bono as a phenomenon operating and spreading in legal practice, including in and through corporate law firms. At the same time, it approaches pro bono through an anthropological lens, as a concept related to the assumption that a structured legal institution exists in society. As such, while this chapter sheds some light on the origins and features of pro bono in France,[1] it aims to provide a narrative and rationale for pro bono beyond its borders.

The French pro bono "story" echoes, to a certain extent, those examined elsewhere in this volume. There is indeed a similar set of actors and drivers, both local and global, which have led to the current development and "momentum" of pro bono in the French context. Those actors, drivers, and factors may be examined through the lens of two dominant, and partly overlapping, approaches to pro bono. The first is a primarily sociological approach, which essentially sees pro bono as a stratagem organized by the legal profession to gain prestige and to conquer new clients. The other, developed by scholars of the legal profession, interprets pro bono as the transposition of corporate social responsibility (CSR) in the legal world.

On the one hand, sociologists (such as Brian Garth and Yves Dezalay[2]) construe pro bono practices as a strategy by law firms of maximizing their commercial positions through charity events and actions. Engaging in the so-called charity business is, pursuant to this view, part and parcel of a domination strategy orchestrated by the legal profession in order to increase its power. Sociologists thus analyze the pro bono movement as a short-term phenomenon, enabling law firms to pursue short-term objectives (i.e., turnover increase, conquest of new market shares made possible thanks to reputational gains, etc.). European and American sociologists thus tend to find a relatively recent origin to pro bono and to locate the emergence of this phenomenon in the United States, which subsequently spread to the world following the American model.

On the other hand, specialists of the legal profession tend to consider pro bono primarily from the perspective of the recently theorized CSR. The CSR approach to pro bono practices – perceived as one facet of responsible capitalism – has a rather subtle, structural origin: it rests on the assumption that capitalism affects the legal profession to such an extent that the latter becomes exclusively capitalistic. Because of the capital-intensive nature of the large or "big" law firm model (generalized through global networks), the entire legal profession is now entitled to remedy imbalances structurally induced by capitalism, like other profitable corporations. Accordingly, legal practitioners should fully assume this social responsibility (i.e., the corollary of the profits realized thanks to capitalism) by offering free legal "services" to people or causes that cannot afford them.

In this chapter, we suggest that both of these perspectives, while capturing part of the story, are limited. The recent momentum of pro bono in France, examined through the lens of these two perspectives, appears as the result, in large part, of the diffusion of the US "big law" model and of the emergence of CSR within the legal profession. The picture is one of an encounter with local institutions and actors, of resistances, reappropriations, and realignment of interests and hierarchies, in which hybridization emerges, as it does in many parts of the world and in this volume, as a central dynamic of the story. This chapter suggests, however, that the story of diffusion, resistance, and hybridization and the analytical framework it relies on are somewhat limited and have to be recontextualized within a broader conceptual lens and a longer historical time frame. It situates the current pro bono momentum within social, cultural, and economic relationships, related to broader dynamics at play in the evolution of legal professions across the world and in the structural features of contemporary capitalist processes. And, going further, it relates it to the fundamental function of lawyers in a structured legal institution. As such, it resists the suggestion that a radical, historical change is at work in the evolution of the legal professions. It does so by drawing on an understanding of pro bono related to the concept of lawyers' generosity and linking it to lawyers' functional obligation of securing the matrix of their own existence within a structured legal institution. Historically, the practice of counseling, defense, and pleading used to be entirely free and thereby became an institutional element of the rule of law, along with judging and doctrine. Serving the people – and, through the people, the rule of law – is therefore crucial and related to the development of generosity and pro bono as a condition of any lawyer's practice. The manner in which lawyers are often analyzed as paradoxically giving free services in order to strategically make more profit therefore ought to be understood as related to the fact that lawyers belong to the structure of legally grounded societies. And as such, they must prove, consciously or not, that they belong to the people, just like doctors or judges, before being allowed to practice asymmetrical powers over the people. Lawyers practicing lawyering as if it were free and as if lawyers were still and always friends of the people, at least in part, means lawyers accepting their function in a secular legal institution. While the term "generosity" refers to caring for humankind, lawyers and attorneys, while caring for democracy and the rule of law, have never ceased to care for their own structural functions.

PRO BONO IN FRANCE AND THE POLITICAL ECONOMY OF HYBRIDIZATION

There is a current momentum for pro bono practice in France. In significant ways, this momentum echoes what Ed Rekosh and Lamin Khadar have described in this volume as the (Western) European story. This story highlights the centrality of the encounter between the globalizing Big Law model of professional practice and its US-inspired pro bono framework, on the one hand, and the French local context, institutions, actors, and interests, on the other. In this story, the pro bono momentum that has been taking place in France over the last decade – and/or the resistances to it – is centered primarily on the influence of global Anglo-American law firms. These firms have indeed diffused and arguably transplanted a US-inspired pro bono model, and, after some reticence, inspired initiatives by the French and particularly the Paris bar. These practices and dynamics take place within the broader context of the French access-to-justice system, which includes a relatively familiar set of actors and institutions.[3]

The Actors

The first is a system of socialized legal aid, funded by the French state. It is the result of the (relatively, in historical terms) recent socialization of a long-standing pro bono tradition, which we will explore further in the chapter, and carries a notion of access to justice as an individual right in both civil and criminal cases. As a result, qualified lawyers, paid by the state through local bar associations, provide means-tested, free or partially free legal aid called *aide juridictionnelle*. The program has more than doubled its size since the early 1990s, with 971,181 cases announced by the Ministry of Justice in 2016 as having been referred to the *aides juridictionnelles* and involving around 25,000 lawyers in at least one case each year (mostly small daily matters, as well as criminal cases through *commission d'office* organized by the bar). As a result, an important constituency of lawyers, many of them small practitioners, relies financially on cases referred through this program, which at the same time has regularly come under budgetary pressure linked to the comparatively slow but seemingly inevitable "rationalization of the welfare state" over the last three (and especially the last) decades.

In parallel to the *aide juridictionnelle* program, France has a mixed *accès au droit* (access to justice) system, which includes county-based "access to justice councils," local bar associations, city halls, and non-governmental organizations (NGOs). The system provides "access to legal knowledge and information" through pro bono lawyer consultations held in courthouses and city halls, covering a wide range of issues, as well as free consultations by lawyers and other legal professionals in 137 local government (county level)-run *maisons de la justice et du droit* ("justice and law houses") and *points d'accès au droit* ("access points to law"). The *défenseur des droits* ("defender of rights," public ombudsman), which draws on teams of professional in-house jurists, focuses on discrimination issues and children's rights protection, as well as information rights for users of public services and investigations related to police and security services. Both citizens and noncitizens can solicit the *défenseur*, and its investigative powers have made it an increasingly important and visible actor in the access-to-justice landscape. After a period of resistance, which subsequent sections will examine, the Paris bar, which represents more than 40 percent of French attorneys (the number of which has increased by almost twofold over the last decade), has adopted a pro–pro bono discourse and taken a variety of initiatives to develop its practice. Those include the lawyer solidarity leave initiative, as well as partnerships with NGOs through its *Barreau de Paris solidarité* started in 2003 with the NGO *Droits d'urgence*, and which since 2011 has received the financial support of an endowment. As a result, Parisian lawyers engage in an increasing range of activities and initiatives, including the well-publicized "Solidarity Bus," the "lawyer in the city" week, and the *Trophées du pro bono* ("Pro Bono Awards") awarded since 2012 to both large firms and individual practitioners.

Parallel law firm initiatives have emerged, mostly in global or internationally networked Anglo-American firms belonging to the increasingly powerful Parisian *barreau d'affaires* ("corporate bar"). While some are driven by local partners, many appear as the French chapter of a more global, firmwide pro bono policy, monitored by a dedicated pro bono officer, off council, partner, or team based either in Paris or elsewhere in Europe (often in London), which organizes and publicizes the participation of lawyers in pro bono activities. A few domestic firms, increasingly large ones competing with global Anglo-American firms, have developed pro bono initiatives and programs, albeit less systematically and systemically. Firms that provide pro bono typically offer their support through the free individualized legal consultations *accès au droit* ("access to justice") network. Many provide support to and through other actors, such as selected NGOs (both locally and internationally), foreign governments in arbitration procedures (subject, however, to numerous conflict of interest obstacles), social entrepreneurs, start-ups, as well as law clinics, which themselves offer pro bono support to individual clients or NGOs.

At the medium-sized level, arguably because of a loss of pro bono culture examined below, initiatives are largely left to individual attorneys in relation to their personal interest, and pro bono is more tolerated than programmatically promoted. Some organize themselves in more or less formalized pro bono networks related to a specific cause (e.g., defending victims of the Khmer Rouge genocide in Cambodia). Smaller firms or solo practitioners, working on immigrant rights, labor, women's rights, environmental, or family law, are also part of the picture, albeit on a much more limited (and less publicized) scale.

Most of those practitioners consider themselves cause lawyers; they include older or semiretired practitioners, established practitioners practicing pro bono in parallel to their regular activities, as well as younger, often female lawyers. Many of these practitioners form the limited pool upon which emerging French law clinics rely for pro bono supervision of students and clinical projects operating in these areas of law.

Three other type of actors complete the picture. First, and partly in response to the increasing demands of medium-sized, primarily French law firms, as well as the influence of pan-European initiatives such as PILNet and the European Pro Bono Forum, dedicated pro bono clearinghouses or platforms have begun to emerge recently, even if still modestly. Those include the Paris Bar Endowment Fund, the *Alliance des avocats pour les droits de l'homme*,[4] and *Pro bono lab*, the launch of which was promoted by the Paris bar in 2014 in a very public endorsement of pro bono after years of resistance. Second, a number of specialized NGOs play an increasingly important role as both a vehicle for and a recipient of pro bono. Some act partly as pro bono platforms, such as *Droits d'urgence* within the access-to-justice network or *Avocats sans frontières* ("Lawyers Without Borders"), which provides opportunities for lawyers to work on a pro bono basis on human rights cases, primarily in francophone Africa, and arguably along "transnational" dynamics of global pro bono that reflect North/South power dynamics.[5] Exclusively public interest law firms are relatively inexistent in France, although a couple of historic NGOs, such as the *Groupe d'Information et de Soutien des Travailleurs Immigrés* (GISTI, focusing on immigrant labor rights), have played and continue to play an important role in providing pro bono legal assistance to specific individuals or groups, in particular through strategic litigation. Furthermore, a number of smaller and recently created NGOs or initiatives, often created and/or run by former lawyers, former in-house lawyers of large international human rights NGOs, or young law clinic graduates, are emerging. Many of those aim to develop the relatively underdeveloped practice of strategic litigation, in part with the pro bono help of individual cause lawyers and law clinics. Those operate in new areas (in France) such as class action in the field of antidiscrimination law (one example is *la Fondation des femmes*) or environmental law (*Notre Affaire à tous*).

Third, and finally, law clinics have emerged as providers of pro bono in a variety of areas and, in many cases, as a recipient of pro bono work and thereby as de facto clearinghouses.[6] A case in hand, which directly informs the viewpoint developed in this chapter, is that of the Sciences Po Law School. An elite institution created in 1872 in the aftermath of the Franco-Prussian War with the aim of training high-caliber civil servants, Sciences Po opened a graduate-level (master's) law school in 2009, which grants its graduates access to the bar examination. In 2011, it created a clinical program, which currently engages in legal assistance, advocacy, and policy-oriented applied research through partnerships with a number of actors. Those include access-to-justice institutions, local and international human rights and immigrant rights NGOs, international organizations, professional and public institutions, local government actors, social enterprises, as well as CSR and human rights departments within companies.

This clinical program offers an interesting vantage point on pro bono practice in that it is both a provider and a recipient of pro bono legal assistance. It is, classically, a pro bono provider through the public interest projects and services carried out by its students and their supervisors, some directly serving individual clients, others in support of NGOs or other public or private organizations. It is also a pro bono recipient, since its economic model, mainly because of a lack of resources typical of the US law school, does not rely on full-time clinical instructors to supervise students but rather on part-time lecturers, doctoral students, as well as lawyers acting pro bono. The story of its creation features many dimensions, including intellectual and epistemological ones.[7] It also relates to the broader story of the law school's creation and the role of the corporate bar. At the heart of that specific strand of the story is a set of multiple and at times overlapping, conflicting dynamics, which in part reflects what this chapter identifies as the broader dimensions that underlie, beyond a story of diffusion and hybridization, the current pro bono "moment."

At first sight, the Paris corporate bar's support for and involvement in the creation of a clinical program at Sciences Po echoes the role played by law firms in the United States in the exponential rise in experiential training within US law schools over the last decade. In the wake of the 2008 global financial crisis and the partly related crisis of the big law model, US law firms to a large extent amended the preexisting consensus in American legal education. This consensus implied that professional, practical training would happen post–law school graduation and "in house," through the billable hours of first-year associates. Over the last decade, pressed by their clients following the global financial crisis and by the impact of technological innovation on legal services, law firms have pressed law schools to provide this professional training through experiential training. As a result, such training has become a staple of US law schools. It includes both new forms of low-cost pedagogical models such as externships or simulations, as well as increasingly professionalizing law clinics, many of which have departed from "traditional" clinical legal education understood as exclusively public interest or social justice-oriented and organized in small intensive coursework around live clients. Beyond these factors, some of which are similar in France and in the specific context of Sciences Po,[8] pressure for and support by law firms of clinical programs within law schools can also be understood, in France and elsewhere, as reflecting the two partly overlapping analytical lenses identified above as accounting for the rise of pro bono.

In one interpretation, the support by large and primarily Anglo-American global law firms implanted in France for the creation of law clinics can be characterized as one original example of the diffusion of the American model analyzed by sociolegal scholars and involves primarily strategic dimensions. In this sense, and in a context in which the primacy of publicly funded *aide juridictionnelle* involved until recently a lack of well-identified pro bono recipients and clearinghouses, clinics, and in particular the Sciences Po clinic, provide an avenue for law firm associates or partners to provide pro bono assistance to clients and NGOs, through student supervision. Participation in pro bono clinical legal assistance may open up new marketplaces for legal services directly, for instance, through senior lawyers acting as pro bono clinical supervisors in the development of CSR and human rights tools for public or private actors, which, once conflict-of-interest requirements expire, could become future clients. Or indirectly, mostly through reputational gains, including among elite law students who, along the way, get trained in areas that will allow them to capture new markets for CSR-related legal services for their employers in the future. In this logic, and while engagement with and support of clinics may relate to firms' or senior partners' social/ideological preferences, it is often framed and selected in terms of primary areas of expertise and contingent on conflict-of-interest and market-based considerations.[9] In another parallel and overlapping interpretation, supporting the emergence of clinics gives firms a particularly convenient vehicle and outlet for the development of "law firm CSR" (LCSR),[10] which has been internalized by actors within firms not only as a strategic means but as inherent to the very notion of "modern" professional legal practice and "responsible" capitalism.[11]

While consciously developing projects that either examined or developed the LCSR approach, the clinic's underlying objective has been to both question and expand this notion, beyond responsible capitalism, within the training of future elite lawyers. It has done so by systematically selecting projects that would fit the double purpose of pedagogical innovation and training, on the one hand, and public interest/access to justice/social justice, on the other, without consideration for economic (conflict of interest) or ideological compatibility with pro bono support to clinical projects – thereby expressly resisting a logic of privatization of public interest practice. This has taken the shape, in particular, of a transparent and selective call for projects for its human rights clinical program, which has attracted an increasing range of both national and international NGOs. And it has led the law school to consciously reject the creation of a professionalizing business/start-up incubator-type law clinic. The clinic has also aimed to deliberately expose students, both through clinical seminars and by incorporating nonclinical academics (doctoral candidates and faculty members) in student supervision teams, to key elements at stake in clinical, public interest, and pro bono practice. This includes exploring and engaging with the deep-seated historical roots of pro bono practice, and in particular of the long-standing social role and ethos of lawyers in France, beyond economistic approaches to the profession. It also involves critically examining the dilemmas and trade-offs between primarily professionalizing clinical legal education, including in its LCSR version, on the one hand, and social justice–oriented clinical initiatives, on the other. And it implies using the classroom as a reflective space to highlight the hierarchies and imbalances of power or the disciplinary effects that can be created, overtly or not, by students and supervising lawyers drawing on legal norms and professional practices while acting in pro bono mode on their projects and with their clients. The objective, in the long run, is to not only raise awareness about but also deepen, expand, and reframe the understanding of the social role of lawyers in society and generate a renewed set of professional practices and aspirations beyond LSCR.

The Political Economy of Hybridization

The way the various actors of the French pro bono momentum interact echoes in part some of the analyses presented in this volume. To some extent, it echoes the American, British, and Australian analyses pointing to the influence, and multiple interpretations that can be made, of CSR as a framework to capture pro bono dynamics. To another, it reflects some of the similar hierarchies and power struggles at play in the legal culture through which pro bono is hybridizing in Latin America.[12] And in particular, it points to the broader Western European story and to the Spanish and Portuguese stories of both momentum and limits to the diffusion and hybridization of the US pro bono model.[13]

In France, the existence of a socialized legal aid model has been a constraint on the development of pro bono. Its promoters, just like those of law clinics, had to convince the initially resisting bar that it would complement rather than threaten the *aide juridictionnelle*. As will be examined below, this initial resistance in defense of the *aide juridictionnelle* was not only linked to the existence of a key constituency of solo or small-size practitioners who financially rely on it. Resistance was also related to a transformed legal profession over the last half century, which adhered to the merchandization of its services and was happy to devolve legal aid to the welfare state, thereby ignoring its historical social mission. As stated by a prominent former president of a provincial bar association:

> I come from the "old" Bar, in which we had strict rules. Those rules included confraternity, equality among all of us, the absence of advertising – all of that fell apart. Not just today, but over the last thirty, forty years, all of this fell apart, the spirit of the Bar, in Paris or here in Montpellier, it all changed. We now have way too many lawyers, like in America: there are lawyers at every corner of the street, lawyers are authorized to do anything, they are real estate agents, they do business of all kind, they advertise as being the best in all domains . . . this is far from the ethics we practiced during centuries.[14]

Diffusion thus happens, in part, through the influence of the increasingly powerful Parisian *barreau d'affaires*, affected by the globalization of legal services and the legal profession. Pro bono promoters within this corporate bar, mostly Anglo-American firms, have indeed played an important role in eroding the resistance to and encouraging the diffusion of pro bono. They have done so, for instance, by framing US- and UK-style pro bono models as a natural complement of publicly funded *aide juridictionnelle* and other existing access-to-justice mechanisms,[15] if not as a necessary replacement of the inevitably shrinking welfare state. Most of these firms present themselves as progressive examples of "responsible" legal practice, understood as operating through organizations increasingly run and managed as corporations geared toward the delivery of legal advice and strategic counseling, and adhering to an "LCSR" ethos. They typically present obstacles to the development of pro bono in France in terms of restriction on merchandization (e.g., restrictions on advertising, until 2014, lack of a specific tax regime for pro bono hours and of professional insurance for lawyers covering their pro bono activities).[16] In this understanding, the pro bono momentum is related to the diffusion of a model that is highly contingent on market-based factors and calculations.[17]

A study of LCSR within the Paris bar, conducted by the Sciences Po Law Clinic in partnership with an LCSR-promoting global law firm, reveals the acceptance of this understanding of pro bono.[18] The sample of Parisian corporate bar practitioners involved in the study thus understood LCSR primarily in terms of competitive advantage. This includes LCSR as a response to CSR requests by current or potential clients, as an avenue to develop new domains of expertise (including in the increasingly legal domains of CSR),[19] and, in particular, as a means to enhance "human capital loyalty" and attract new talents.[20] They identified obstacles to its development that can and ought to be "overcome" in both technical (e.g., size of firms; lack of integration of pro bono in working hours and career advancement of lawyers; or difficulty for firms to identify public interest projects that can use their legal expertise)[21] and cultural (e.g., reliance on French socialized legal aid; reluctance by French firms of similar size to develop the type of systematic LCSR policies of large Anglo-America large firms) terms. In this self-perception, the deeply rooted social role of lawyers seems to be captured and reframed through the "modern" prism and lens of LCSR, in which social responsibility is understood as that of the firm as a higher-impact, collective structure of professional practice, transcending and arguably discharging the individual social responsibility of lawyers to the firm. In this context, the ability for a firm to engage in pro bono is often linked by its corporate bar promoters to "innovation" in professional practice and has become a strong argument in debates agitating the bar among those seeking to challenge professional regulatory restrictions against fully commercial partnership structures, akin to those existing in the United Kingdom or the United States.

At the same time, however, and pointing to more subtle and complex dynamics and modes of consciousness at play, the same sample of actors also understood LCSR as allowing lawyers to perpetuate or even renew their traditional function in French society, and as relating to the history and consciousness of professional ethics and lawyers' roles as servants of the rule of law.[22] And unlike in the United States, where the tendency is to stretch LCSR beyond it, pro bono appears as the most significant element of what LCSR is understood to mean, and of how it actually should translate into in practice, despite the existence and attachment to socialized legal aid.[23] Arguably, similar dual dynamics occur at the level of the bar. The various initiatives adopted over the last decade, in terms of pro bono and more broadly LCSR,[24] appear primarily as a reflection of the evolution of interests and power within the bar, including the increasingly powerful players within the Paris *barreau d'affaires* adopting and diffusing the pro bono and LCSR model. The bar's moves can be interpreted as responding to this shift in power, and as attempting to both capture and harness this movement in order to include and manage it within its active role in the French access-to-justice system, as a complement to socialized legal aid. At the same time, bar initiatives can be seen as reflecting and tapping into the idea of a return to lawyers' long-standing tradition and consciousness, either as a direct manifestation of this consciousness or as a strategic move in light of long-term challenges faced by a transforming profession – or as a mix of both. The French story of hybridization, it seems, thus involves a complex set of dynamics, which includes but goes beyond a relatively short-term sequence, in historical and fundamental, social and institutional terms, of diffusion/resistance/adaptation of an outside model.

BEYOND HYBRIDIZATION: PRO BONO AND THE HISTORY, CULTURE, AND IDENTITY OF THE FRENCH AVOCAT

The two approaches at play in contemporary analyses of the globalization of pro bono practice, which this chapter has identified respectively as the sociological approach and the legal professions approach, both highlight primarily conjunctural factors – the diffusion of a charity business linked to the American models of professional practice, and the transposition of CSR in the legal profession – as the main drivers at play. Accounts of local hybridization, reappropriations, and resistances, while acknowledging and highlighting deep local historical and cultural factors, often frame contemporary practice primarily as reactions to/in terms of the US and CSR-centered movement of contemporary diffusion. While partly reflecting the story, including in France, such approaches seem insufficient and at times erroneous in contemplation of the long-term historical roots and ethical principles of the legal profession.

Pro Bono and the Foundations of the Rule of Law

As opposed to the financial sector, which almost never engaged in charitable activities, or to the recent CSR movement in the corporate world, pro bono practices have been at the heart of legal ethics since the invention of the law itself in Rome some 2,500 years ago.[25] Pro bono is obviously not a recent phenomenon, chronologically speaking, and was not born in the United States at the turn of the last century. Law was invented in the fifth century BC in Rome by rebellious intellectuals who did not want to obey pontiffs and consuls anymore, that is, religious and political authorities. They invented a normative category that has the particularity of being self-referential: in other words, one must obey the law because it is the law, without any reasons, simply because it is written or engraved in marble. One may trace the origin of law to the drafting of the Law of the Twelve Tables[26] between 451 and 449 BC. This first legal document stems from an analysis of three years of trials held in the Lazio region conducted by a group of ten men. This wind of change unfolded in the aftermath of a conflict resembling Shakespeare's *Romeo and Juliet* tragedy: a plebeian wanted to marry an aristocrat but was barred by the pontiffs' and consuls' rules. The plebs revolted in order to end this caste system, and the aristocrats finally yielded so as to agree on a common and independent rule governing human relations in society. Furthermore, pro bono appeared even before the formalization and theorization of the law. By the fourth century BC, Athenian litigants could request the assistance of an orator in public hearings. The culture of selflessness hence appeared at that time, since it was prohibited to be paid for this occasional representation activity.[27]

Since then, the role and structural function of lawyers is correlated to a foundational notion: defending the rule of law. And pro bono is part of the lawyer's DNA.

To function, the law is inseparable from the existence of the jury. Legal normativity differs from religion to the extent that a nonecclesiastical religion can exist without clerks and rely solely on a belief system. On the contrary, law is ecclesiastical in essence: it cannot exist in the absence of dedicated professionals. There must be agents invested with the mission of recalling the primacy of the rule of law, especially when a political community is under the threat of religious absolutism or when its leaders are tempted by absolute power. These agents – the lawyers – are the necessary guardians of the secular state and liberal democracies in that they fight against all manifestations of arbitrariness and reaffirm that the legal norm must prevail at the end of the day. In France, one may identify a "foundational trio," including the judge (acting as the guarantor of justice), the prosecutor (guarantor of the institutions, representative of the state's interests), and the lawyer (representative of the people in general).

Structurally speaking, lawyers are thus not law merchants in their raison d'être. Accordingly, in terms of social prestige, considering lawyers as "bourgeois" (equivalent to doctors or pharmacists) is a quite recent invention, dating back to the 1950s. The "law merchants" conception is even more recent in France, corresponding to the massive implantation of Anglo-American law firms in the 1990s. For centuries, lawyers were closer to the aristocracy than to the business world, forming an independent *militia legum.* There is indeed a fundamental distinction between lawyers and the public in general, which is accentuated in English with the "lawyers" and "laypeople" linguistic antagonism. This differentiation refers to the distinction between the sacred and the profane: while the *militia celestis* has the sacred mission to save the people's souls, the *militia legum* is correspondingly invested with the sacred mission of preserving the rule of law for the people. Unlike other honorable professions, the entire destiny and modalities of existence of the social body rests on the lawyer's shoulders. This superior status (the sacred attributions entailing higher social prestige) was not only true for France but could be observed in virtually all Western societies. As an example, Tocqueville wrote that if one sought to situate aristocrats in the American society, it would be among lawyers and judges, not among captains of industry or the richest few.[28] The aristocracy described by Tocqueville refers to an elite that is responsible for the totality of society. The aristocratic affiliation of lawyers is historically linked to their status of advocates of the rule of law.

Defending the rule of law means to ensure that the secular legal order finally prevails over political command or religious prescriptions, whichever they are. As in Rome, consuls and pontiffs ultimately have to bow before the legal authority. The functioning of this principle has been fluctuating in history, adopted by democracies but also by other forms of government such as monarchies or empires.[29] Law's success throughout history is enigmatic: invented in Latium 2,500 years ago, it has transcended ages, survived different modes of production, and covered ever larger geographical areas, so as to appear today as a universal category.

The rule of law is hence inseparable from lawyers – a profession with the sacerdotal mission of constantly reminding the value of this fragile system. It is no coincidence that totalitarian regimes first target lawyers as their public enemies, along with journalists: they are both sentinels of the rule of law, and in the most extreme cases, the last bulwark against arbitrariness. This is precisely the origin of pro bono: prior to the defense of private interests, lawyers are first and foremost the benevolent "knight-servants" of the rule of law. In his 1992 "Who Should Regulate Lawyers?"[30] article, David Wilkins highlights a distinctive character of lawyers who "zealously defend individual rights against state power,"[31] and who "must be able to defend vigorously the rights of accused citizens without fear of retribution by state authorities."[32]

As champions against all forms of arbitrariness, lawyers defend the public interest without being paid for it: doing so is the bedrock of their activity since the origins of the legal profession in the West.[33] French lawyers were inspired by prominent intellectuals fighting injustice, such as Voltaire or Victor Hugo. In defending Calas, Sirven, or the Chevalier de la Barre in the eighteenth century, Voltaire not only invented the figure of the intellectual engaged in the protection of liberties and in the struggle against injustice but also offered to lawyers a cultural representation that they have used since then for the greater benefit. Voltaire succeeded in transforming individual cases into public affairs, attracting the interest of the whole nation if not the whole of Europe. On the other hand, Hugo stood as a passionate advocate for the abolition of the death penalty in the nineteenth century,[34] which inspired subsequent generations of lawyers including Robert Badinter, who actually succeeded in 1981 as minister of justice of the socialist government led by François Mitterrand. As the French sociologist Lucien Karpik suggests, while judges are the voice of the sovereign, lawyers are the voice of the nation.[35]

Following these illustrious examples, lawyers have been an atom of society[36] upholding civil liberties for free, far from today's fee-based exercise and market dimension of the legal profession. One question remains, however: If lawyers used to work for free, how did they make a living? This is where the notion of "decency" comes into play. In societies where decency stands as a fundamental value, it would be unbecoming for the beneficiary of a lawyer's benevolence not to offer something in return. This attitude of decency is reflected in the Latin etymology of the French word "*honoraire*" (i.e., legal fees), which means "honoring the lawyer." In 1911, the Dalloz Repertory held that "the *honoraire* is the recognition of a blessing rather than the payment of the lawyer's work."[37] This commitment to honor the lawyer may take various forms, such as offering farm animals or compensating with money.

However, this glorious conception and representation of a generous and selfless lawyer, who defends the humble and fights injustice (by publicly opposing powers of all kinds), is now competing with the image of a lucrative profession in tune with the emergence of a new society governed by economics and economic thought.[38]

The Value of Trust: A Historical Construct

The relationship between the lawyer and client is essentially based on one irrational element: trust.[39] In France, trust is the product of a historical osmosis between the public and its lawyers, from the defense of the Jansenists against the church and the monarchy in the early eighteenth century to the legal purge after World War II (i.e., the *épuration légale*) to the Algerian war trials.[40] Indeed, and as demonstrated by Karpik, the professionalization of lawyers has been structured over three centuries through the cultivation of a strong bond with the public.[41] This public trust toward lawyers is the result of the political history of France since the nineteenth century, in which the democratization of French politics led to the emergence of what is often referred to as the "republic of lawyers." During the short-lived Second Republic (1848–51), lawyers entered the spheres of government. Under the longer-lasting Third Republic (1870–1940), lawyers formed a ruling majority in parliament and were nominated or elected at both the Presidency of the Council and of the Republic. The legal profession was entitled to occupy the highest offices insofar as the dignity of lawyers allowed them to make the most impactful decisions for the people. This period was marked by a sense of convergence between the public interest defended in politics and the public interest advocated by lawyers, symbolized in the defense of the rule of law. Pierre-Antoine Berryer, the finest orator of his time, put an emphasis on this "completely common interest" that unites lawyers and the people.[42] Defending civil liberties while embodying the values of the French republican democracy (at least during the Third Republic) made the legal profession legitimate and respected, and allowed it to benefit from a positive social representation. Throughout history, and in particular during the Third Republic, the legal profession in France thus appears to have sealed an alliance with the public, so as to become the "spokespersons" for the public.[43] Thanks to their central privilege, namely their independence, lawyers achieved this status and gained trust, which became the cement of the profession and the foundation of its relationship with society.

The quintessence of the lawyer's prerogative consists in representing laypeople, whether rich or poor. It is the only configuration in society where someone entrusts freedom, family, fortune, fate, and sometimes even life, to another person: the representation of someone else is the most specific and unique function devolved to the lawyer (with perhaps psychoanalytic transfer).[44] Throughout generations, lawyers have thus enjoyed what can be called a presumption of trustworthiness, because giving is altogether the consequence of trust and produces it. The lawyer, however, will act on behalf of the client's interests, but not only: in defending the client's private interests, the lawyer at the same time has to serve the law and defend the interests of the multitude. As soon as private interests are protected by law, these interests somehow become public. Wilkins illustrates this double allegiance: "By vigorously defending the rights of their clients, criminal defense lawyers stand as a bulwark against state power, not just for the accused, but for all who might be accused in the future."[45] As a consequence, a lawyer is not and cannot be the client's employee: the lawyer always remains under the strain of stringent ethics, as a servant of the law. This sovereign independence enjoyed by the lawyer as a servant of the law (necessary to perform the duty of representation) inspires respect and entails trust: from the moment of accepting a case, a lawyer can no longer betray the client. Trust thus refers to a mutual tribute, an idea expressed in many languages since the origins of writing, from the Latin tradition (*fides*) to ancient Indian and Iranian idioms. This reciprocal commitment is hence distinct from profit or interest considerations: it is rather a relationship in which decency is paramount.

Economic analyses of law envisage this particular attorney–client relationship under the prism of "legal privilege," which stems from the interpersonal trust between the lawyer and client. Even in large firms, one may identify a point of contact between the client and the lawyer at a certain level: generally, the client (or its officials for corporations) and a senior partner lawyer. This interpersonal contact will structure the entire collaboration between the firm and the client (even on a corporate deal), and this trust must be protected. The rationale behind legal privilege is that trust relationships ought to be insulated and safeguarded from outside interference, including that of the state.

Pro Bono in France: Historical Perspectives

The Legal Profession in the Age of Modern History (Fifteenth Century Onwards)

To understand pro bono in France, it appears essential to revisit the peculiar history of its legal profession. Indeed, the evolution of the historical pact sealed by lawyers with French society determines the contemporary role of lawyers and is crucial to make predictions about the future of the profession.

In France, lawyers never formed a "corporation" in the sense of a "group of merchants or traders united in trade guild."[46] One may better define lawyers as a particular grouping, which started to unite in the twelfth century in order to teach law, at the time the first European universities opened. These pioneers rediscovered Roman law and invented academic degrees: it is the birth of the doctorate in law. Doctors in law were assimilated to *domini* ("lords") and inherited the qualification of *militia legum* ("militia of the law"). It is therefore more of a nobiliary order than of a mercantile corporation, such as that of stonecutters. Lawyers become genuine pillars of society and sometimes servants of the state, representing the state's interests in specific circumstances.

In the European tradition (including Great Britain), the lawyer is in principle free. This gratuity aims to alleviate the consequences of the dismantling of feudalism. The former serfs – who became free – no longer enjoy their masters' protection and often fall into poverty. The legal profession spearheaded a widespread tactic in Europe, in which the *militia legum* mobilizes to take care of the poor, who represented a large portion of the population.[47] The "attorneys of the poor" gradually appeared in the bars of many European cities, from the depths of Italy to Portugal, Spain, France, and the Netherlands. These advocates willing to defend the poor for free were the most eminent and respected practitioners: at the end of the fifteenth century, being an attorney of the poor was considered almost a title of nobility. In France, Louis Raoul founded an *avocaterie des pauvres* in 1459 in Nîmes, an institution that spread in southern France between the fifteenth and the sixteenth centuries.[48] This tradition of an *avocature des pauvres* persevered throughout time: in Nîmes, lawyers still elect their *bâtonnier* (i.e., president of the bar) as well as an official "attorney of the poor." This kind of institution allowed lawyers to become savvy observers of the human condition and contributed to building the professional identity of lawyers on fundamentally humanistic principles.[49] This is reflected in today's oath for lawyers entering the profession: "I, as a lawyer, swear to perform my duties with dignity, trust, independence, probity and humanity."

Besides the institution of attorney of the poor, pro bono is incorporated in the lawyer's day-to-day practice: in choosing clients, a lawyer already knows, without asking for it, the reward that might or might not be received. By accepting to represent poor clients, lawyers already know that they may receive little or no monetary compensation. Deontological considerations encourage French lawyers to accept clients regardless of their financial capacities insofar as pecuniary interest must never be the motive of the lawyers' actions. In this historical deontological sense and representation of professional practice, wealth can be a consequence of a lawyer's career, but their prime motivation must never be the pursuit thereof: whoever becomes a lawyer for greed or vanity is a "mercenary," who deviates from the nobility of the profession.[50] This characteristic state of mind can be illustrated by the former president of the French *Cour de Cassation* ("civil and criminal law Supreme Court") Raymond-Theodore Troplong (1795–1869):

> A man does not work only for money, he also works for glory, for his country, for humanity. This explains why there are necessary inequalities between professions . . . . Some are subaltern, which are in general those that speculate on the men's physical needs; profit is their purpose, and money their retribution. The others, which are greater, address the men's moral needs.

Naturally, lawyers belong to the latter.[51]

While historically situated, this vision of lawyers' role and deontology is visible in a variety of contemporary features of the legal profession. One of them, quite symbolic, is the recovery of legal fees. Classically, a lawyer and client enter into an agreement setting the amount of legal fees. In many situations, clients do not pay their lawyers, which results in a contractual breach. For a long time in France, lawyers were prohibited from suing their former clients to recover their fees. The recovery of one's owed legal fees became legally possible only in the 1950s, although it remained considered as highly inappropriate by the overwhelming majority of the profession. In 1956, a lawyer admitted to the Paris bar tried to recover his fees, generating heated reactions from prominent figures of the bar. Maurice Garçon, a towering figure of the profession at the time, wrote a widely publicized pamphlet to discredit such a lawsuit and recall some foundational deontological principles. More than a pamphlet, Garçon's argumentation was rather a manifesto rehabilitating the honour of lawyers and marginalizing such attempts to sue bad payers.

The Historical Involvement of the French State in Pro Bono and Its Consequences

As mentioned in the opening sections of this chapter, France is home to a specific access-to-justice landscape, the structure of which partly explains the political economy of momentum/resistance and hybridization of pro bono practice as understood in the US and CSR approaches. This structure is built around what essentially amounts to a "state pro bono" system of socialized legal aid.

While lawyers were for a long period the only social actors in charge of organizing and providing free legal counsel and thereby of ensuring access to justice for the poor ("attorney of the poor" model), this situation changed in the mid-nineteenth century. Influenced by social Catholicism, the French Second Empire developed a bold solidarity policy that culminated with the 1851 law on "judicial assistance,"[52] which aimed to guarantee equitable access to justice and to courts for the needy. In other words, the state chose to subsidize lawyers to defend the poorest litigants. This state-organized judicial assistance mechanism gained a momentum until the 1890s: between 1851 and 1855, 38 requests for judicial assistance before civil courts out of 1,000 were recorded, while between 1886 and 1890, 270 requests for judicial assistance out of 1,000 were recorded, showing a clear increase.[53] This 1851 statute was replaced by the Law No. 72–11 as of 3 January 1972, which recognized a means-tested right to jurisdictional assistance based on personal earnings.[54] While pro bono activities used to be fully organized and carried out by the legal profession, the emerging French welfare state's intervention from the mid-nineteenth century onwards resulted in the demobilization of many lawyers.

Indeed, over the last 150 years, French lawyers have not felt obligated to perform pro bono activities insofar as the state took the responsibility to pay lawyers who provided legal aid: pro bono gradually became a duty of the state, and a public service. In other words, because pro bono has been socialized by the state through the *aide juridictionnelle* mechanism, lawyers have felt exempted from their historic obligation. In this new cultural configuration, public generosity appeared as the exclusive privilege of the state.[55] Despite its laudable purposes, jurisdictional assistance *à la française* has thus had the perverse effect of demobilizing lawyers who would otherwise engage in pro bono individually, and assume the costs thereof (i.e., the opportunity cost of the time not spent on lucrative cases).

Such a demobilization can be problematic to the extent that one understands the social role of lawyers as being intimately related to all segments of society, as defenders of both the poor and the rich, but also of business interests, and above all, of the rule of law. For these reasons, and while making sure that this isn't used as an argument to brutally downsize the financing of legal aid as any other public service in a neoliberal "structural reform" mode, there is a case to be made for lawyers to resume their historical role of organizing legal aid. Solidarity as a guiding principle not only strengthens the ability of lawyers to exercise their profession (notably through trust), it also testifies to the rooting of this particular professional community in society, in the nation, and in civilization.[56]

Postwar Economic and Sociological Analyses of the Legal Profession

During the second half of the twentieth century, economic analysis of law as well as sociological approaches to the legal profession put forward new paradigms. Sociologists contemplate the legal profession as one among many trades, that is, a profession that sells specific knowledge to third parties (i.e., the clients). This body of knowledge has previously been encrypted as expertise so that lawyers can legitimize their intervention and maximize their benefits in giving legal advice or litigating. Information asymmetry is thus used as a means to perpetuate the power of the legal profession over laypeople. Sociological analyses, however, do not sufficiently take into account the specific nature of the legal profession, in particular lawyers' traditional social role and their engagement in the defense of the rule of law and civil liberties. Economic analyses of law, on the other hand, reason in terms of interests: all that does not generate pecuniary interest is deemed irrational.[57]

In the wake of the triumph of neoliberalism in the 1980s, elevating the market economy as a universal model, the legal profession indeed experienced a series of notable changes. In Ronald Reagan's America and Margaret Thatcher's Britain, followed by many Western countries including France, the legal profession witnessed the inflation of its profits as well as a "merchandization" of its performances, leading to the adoption of the commercial terminology "legal services." In the 2010s, the globalization of the "law firm model" gave birth to the so-called legal industry. Thus, for economists, lawyers essentially provide paid-for services. The European Court of Justice and the European Commission share this vision, as illustrated by the 2006 European Union Directive on Services in the Internal Market,[58] which treats lawyers as service providers and therefore trivializes the profession.[59] In this prospect, pro bono – the free supply of legal services from an economic vantage point – appears as a nonsense at the microeconomic level. It is only from a macroeconomic standpoint that pro bono becomes more rational, along with CSR strategies, aiming to repair damages induced by deregulated capitalism.

Indeed, where does this social responsibility come from? To understand the CSR trend, it appears necessary to shed light on one major paradox in the functioning of capitalism. The capitalist mode of production is entirely directed toward the accumulation of profit. Capitalism is therefore geared toward the production of social goods that are critical to the perpetuation of society. The only social relations deemed necessary in the realm of capitalism are those between economic agents, competing in the conquest of profit through the use of commercial acts. As a result, capitalism does not need such things as family or other social units.[60] Further, capitalism deems solidarity as an irrational behavior: all initiatives falling within the ambit of social action are characterized as "negative externalities." This explains why the system aims at the disappearance of government intervention by privatizing the state's traditional prerogatives and turning them into marketable merchandise. Therefore, capitalism – as the ordering principle of social relations – is itself devoid of the means to perpetuate society, the latter being supposed to produce the consumers needed by capitalism to exist and thrive. Human beings are perceived through the exclusive lens of the consumer pays principle. The aforementioned paradox arises: capitalism needs the reproduction of society, but it rejects the perpetuation of society by the state (by collectivizing and allocating resources for this purpose). Instead, capitalism proposes to create private offers of services (health, education, or pensions) to individuals against money. While certain social strata can afford these private services, a substantive fraction of society remains unable to access them.

Some actors belonging to the capitalist system have become aware of the substantial part of society left behind (being the necessary consequence of neoliberalism) and decided to take action by reinjecting marginal portions of their benefits into CSR, so as to repair social damages that capitalism has itself produced. From this standpoint, social responsibility is not even the fruit of moral guilt: it becomes a rational, pragmatic tool to perpetuate society and ensure the regeneration of future consumers on which capitalism relies to thrive.[61] In a nutshell, the system fosters social responsibility as one way to strengthen its basis of (poor) consumers and safeguard the system from its own collapse.[62] The origins of this contemporary call for pro bono are hence more systemic than altruistic. One may notice that among pro bono advocates in the United States or the United Kingdom, no mention is made of the aforementioned core reason justifying the existence of pro bono practices in the realm of neoliberalism. There is no satisfying definition of the reasons underlying the CSR call for pro bono, save the alleged pretence of generosity.

How Sustainable Is this Macroeconomistic, Neoliberal Perspective?

In a survey conducted during the second semester of 2016, a sample of young lawyers were asked whether or not new technology could pose a threat to their profession. An overwhelming majority (87 percent) answered in the affirmative, stating that automation, standardization of many tasks (e.g., due diligences in M&A transactions), or the democratization of legal knowledge thanks to the internet could hurt the whole profession. In this context, the doctrines – or "narratives" – developed by both economists and sociologists collapse with the advent of new technologies. These technologies indeed abolish (at least in part) information asymmetry for "law consumers" who are – more than ever – able to access legal information without a lawyer. Barriers to information are falling down, and legal knowledge becomes less encrypted. Sociological theories according to which the legal profession organizes its domination over society by cultivating hermetic, expertise-based knowledge are less relevant. On the other hand, from an economic standpoint (which assesses the value of a service based on its scarcity and on the information asymmetry existing between providers and consumers), new technologies highly threaten the sustainability of the legal profession given the ever-increasing access to legal information by the public.

On a related note, three-quarters of services provided by law firms (if they are considered as selling "services") could be performed by individuals with a minimum legal education, that is, without necessarily being admitted to a bar. The "commercial lawyer" hence has no raison d'être insofar as a person educated in law – although not admitted to a bar – could perform the vast majority of activities simply by using information resources and legal databases available. This is why a growing number of firms, in particular medium and large firms, are now outsourcing their services to emerging countries, where labor costs are lower,[63] while billing the overall amount of hours in New York or London. As suggested by Wilkins, emerging countries in which such services are outsourced have begun to rationalize strategies in order to address a growing demand and in the medium to long term plan to support local providers that can enter into direct competition with Western law firms by circumventing outsourcing and offering their services directly to Western clients.[64] Furthermore, the advances of artificial intelligence (AI) also pose a threat to lawyers who usually carry out higher-value, strategic work: AI is about to design M&A strategies, corporate strategies, or financial schemes without human intervention. Therefore, new technologies do not only threaten lawyers performing "grass roots" and "day-to-day" commercial work, but also senior lawyers handling more subtle tasks.

Over the past fifty years or so, a substantial part of the legal profession has converted their activity to capitalism. This shift has had consequences in sociological terms: lawyers fell off their aristocratic pedestal to embrace the materialistic bourgeoisie means and ways of living. In doing so, lawyers made a short-term choice: having made some profits by embracing capitalism for nearly half a century, the legal profession made itself vulnerable to the realities and dangers of market competition. After having subscribed to the economic doctrine – because it would serve its immediate interest – the legal profession now faces its downsides. Lawyers have been increasingly perceived as "cogs" of the market economy, performing a support function to business (as opposed to "core business"). However, cogs can be replaced by more efficient cogs, following Schumpeter's creative destruction theory. Technological advances now suggest, economically speaking, that some tasks that were previously performed by lawyers will be performed by AI, entailing two major consequences: the old status that lawyers used to enjoy no longer justifies their current remunerations as their input is decreasing in the short run, while in the long run, technology threatens the very existence of the corporate lawyer.

It is ironic to note that corporate lawyers have locked themselves into this support function during the last decades instead of overlooking the market by virtue of their historical authority and of the self-referential nature of legal normativity to which they owe their status. Servants of the law are supposed to escape from the rules of trade because, in Western culture, law is the "matrix reference" permitting the inscription of humans in society. In other words, law is the founding code of the social order. As a consequence, no competing normativity should encompass or subject the law, at the risk of "breaking up" future generations.[65]

The adherence to the ephemeral opulence of capitalism not only entails economic consequences but questions the role of lawyers in society more generally. The pursuit of profit has often taken over the pursuit of justice, resulting in intellectual vacuity at least in the way the people perceive lawyers. In France, this threatens the very pact between lawyers and society. The relations between lawyers and clients become those of merchants to buyers, undermining the sacred trust relationship that is essential to the art of representing the interests of someone else. Negotiating the fee agreement beforehand is one symptom of this impairment of trust: if one negotiates the price of trust, then trust is not worth much. The increase of material wealth for legal professionals (some would equate it to the climbing of the social ladder) has entailed an obvious decline: that of the lawyers' symbolic status.

STATE OF PLAY AND PROSPECTIVE THOUGHTS

France and North America: A Diverging Perception of Pro Bono

There has always been a need for affordable justice. Over the last decades, we have witnessed an increase of legal aid structures in North America (this movement started in Ontario and spread throughout the continent). These structures may include law graduates who nonetheless are not admitted to a bar and who may be referred to as "paralegals." In France, the *Conseil National des Barreaux* (CNB)[66] was reluctant and first prohibited this practice (i.e., pro bono by nonattorneys), despite a growing demand. And as mentioned above, the bar associations were originally resisting the emergence of law clinics and students not admitted to the bar doing pro bono work.

Beyond reasons related to the political economy of the legal aid system (and notably the existence of an important constituency of lawyers "living" on low-paid state-funded legal aid), there is a parallel, and perhaps more structural reason explaining such reticence to pro bono by nonattorneys. Lawyers – in the sense of attorneys admitted to a bar – have historically been the exclusive guarantors of the people's access to justice, to the extent that lawyers *are* the law. From an anthropological viewpoint, the primary image that individuals conceive when they think about the law or when they seek advice or representation is the image of "the lawyer." Further, it can be argued that in litigating or in advising a client, a lawyer who applies the law uses and renews the legal rule so as to adjust human relations according to previously accepted or transformable principles.[67] This ability to maintain an established order or to promote change through the law illustrates the structural role of the legal profession in the overall organization of society.

A further explanation of the French bars' reticence with respect to contemporary forms or discourses of pro bono may reside in cultural considerations. Morals and ethics underlying pro bono indeed differ in North America, and especially the United States, and Europe. In North America, the Protestant tradition of public benevolence prevails and encourages benefactors to communicate about their good deeds, show their accomplishments, and lead by example. This is consistent with the old puritanical culture of extensive social control over individuals, where the acts of each and every one are scrutinized by all members of the community. As Roscoe Pound showed in *The Spirit of the Common Law* (1921), "puritanism of itself and possibly because of the deeper-seated causes of which it was a manifestation, has been a significant factor in moulding the spirit of our common law."[68] Culturally speaking, it is hence not surprising that pro bono – nurtured by Puritan ethics of public benevolence – gained a momentum in a jurisdiction like the United States. This conception contrasts with Catholic or Jewish traditions of charity, which value all the more an act of charity when done discretely. One is accountable to God and God only, not to the community. Moreover, Catholic and Jewish charities do not impose the heavy burden of gratitude upon the beneficiary: charitable acts must be intrinsically free.

As a consequence, pro bono gained a momentum in the United States without contradicting the genuine business orientation of American Bar Association. One can witness in the United States a constant quest for "virtue" through the multiplication and display of pro bono practices, as well as the involvement of major law firms in charitable, educational, or humanitarian causes. However, French bars have long been reluctant to use the term "pro bono," perceiving it as an American import. This perception is erroneous: pro bono is the short for "pro bono publico," a Roman term. After this time of relative reluctance, the term "pro bono" has finally been revitalized and is now actively promoted and used in official bar associations' discourse. It appears that the development of pro bono was critical to the flourishing of the legal profession in the first place and, arguably, will be critical to its survival.

The Return to the Legal Profession's Traditional Values

Although a portion of lawyers have gradually abandoned the access-to-justice tradition, one may still find themes such as civil liberties or human rights advocacy in modern-day bar associations' discourse. However, in the twenty-first century, this question must no longer be asked in terms of access to justice but in terms of access to legal knowledge. The legal profession is likely to suffer from a strong popular disavowal, insofar as lawyers can be blamed for trading something that now belongs and is accessible to virtually everyone thanks to new technologies: the law. Lawyers were so far responsible for disseminating this legal knowledge, but they may become obsolete on the market as technology empowers individuals. While the legal profession used to enjoy immense prestige, notably in virtue of the aforementioned pact with the citizenry, lawyers now face the risk of falling into disgrace and, arguably, becoming redundant.

As a result, one may discern a recent move in California or in the United Kingdom, in which lawyers, perhaps conscious of this challenge, are gradually abandoning the exclusively economic model corresponding to the capital-intensive, profit-seeking paradigm. Instead, some seem to be coming back to or (re)discovering "traditional" values, emphasizing the defense of civil liberties – including liberties that ought to be defended in light of the evolution of society and technology, such as privacy in the realm of Big Data. On the contrary, French lawyers, late perhaps by a couple of decades, largely continue to rush into the capitalist economic model described above, despite the array of future negative prospects for the legal profession.

Indeed, a recent report on the future of the legal profession in France submitted to the minister of justice pleaded in favor of the introduction of nonlawyers in the equity of law firms. In 2007, the Australian law firm Slater & Gordon launched an initial public offering and became listed on the national stock exchange for the first time. That same year, the United Kingdom passed legislation that allowed nonlawyer investors to acquire shares in law firms.[69] Transforming law firms into public companies (whose shares are traded on a stock exchange) or into mundane corporations in the case of Britain leads to the banalization of the legal profession. Worse, it can force lawyers to meet higher profitability requirements, and in certain cases it can make the legal profession an object of financial speculation, which dangerously threatens its independence and deals a fatal blow to the self-referential character of the law. Having noticed the side effects of such evolutions, lawyers in the United Kingdom have reacted by advocating a return to traditional values. In France, several associations of young lawyers (e.g., *Fédération Nationale des Unions de Jeunes Avocats*, or *Union des Jeunes Avocats*) still call for "innovation" and the "modernization" of the legal profession in France, although "modernity" is understood as it was twenty or thirty years ago in the Anglo-American world. It appears that young lawyers fully adhere to this market logic without measuring its pitfalls: the return to traditional values among lawyers across the Channel should be interpreted as a serious caveat to the neoliberal, competitive, market-based model of legal professional practice.

The aforementioned renewal through a return to the so-called traditional values, mostly in some parts of the United States and in the United Kingdom, and in burgeoning segments of the French bar, can be related to three overlapping elements. The first can be found in the new storytelling strategies adopted by bar associations and individual lawyers, willing to change the image of lawyers. Perceived as greedy since the 1980s, the transactional lawyer advises, negotiates, but does not plead. This image is replaced by the more traditional image of the eloquent lawyer wearing a gown while representing clients in court, in particular for lawyers pleading before judges or arbitration panels. In this renewed aesthetics, which draws on traditional values, the lawyer is restored as a speech artist who wields the words of the sword better than anybody else and appears as the designated spokesperson for the voiceless. Lawyers must endow their image with the ability to console, to demonstrate empathy, to think broadly, and to tell a story that generates meaning for their fellow citizens.

A second element resides in the replenishment of the bonds of trust. A substantial part of the legal profession is expected to leave corporate structures (i.e., large Anglo-American law firms) to follow less profitable but more loyal clients based on a renewed mutual trust. Lawyers in the twenty-first century will be more likely to relocate their activity and follow families in need of "ordinary" legal advice, for example. A lawyer will be in charge of advising and representing members of one family at every step of life and business, from fiscal considerations to criminal charges, and therefore needs to develop a "generalist" approach to the law (as opposed to today's extreme specialization of lawyers). In the same way as there are family general practitioners, lawyers will join family circles. This is already the case in several states in the United States, especially for well-off families who can afford "their" lawyer, who devotes almost all of her time to the client–family.

A third element can contribute to the renewal of the legal profession: high-quality and tailored interventions, as opposed to standardized services. These requirements of quality and flexibility are essential to restore the degraded bond of trust that used to unite the French people and its lawyers in virtue of the "pact with the nation." As the judge adapts the law to the case (in common-law systems, the judge infers the applicable rule of law from the nature of the facts and their possible resemblance with judicial precedents, while in civil law systems the judge legally qualifies the facts and through deductive reasoning applies the law and makes a decision), the lawyer needs to adapt advice to the client's peculiarities. This justifies the return to human-scale, generalist law firms, adapting to specific, individual situations.

The Disengagement of the State and the Future of Pro Bono in France

History is more of a cyclical phenomenon than a linear one. The historical period identified as the "mercantile cycle" is now reaching its limits, even though economic theory still widely presents capitalism – the system's driving ideology – as the only valid system. In France, as in other Western nations, the welfare state era seems to have reached an end, despite recurrent political upheavals and social movements appearing, at times in contradiction to concurrent claims, to be holding on to it. The foundations of the French welfare state have been repeatedly and increasingly weakened since the end of the "Glorious Thirty," notably through the waves of liberalization that unfolded since the early 1980s. The current dominant ideology, of which the present French government is a particularly symbolic example, calls for the disengagement of the state, which necessarily implies that non-state bodies assume certain welfare prerogatives.

When a crucial element disappears, or when a crisis upsets a system, one may witness a return to the configuration that existed before the start of the crisis. In the 1990s, the effects of the first liberal policies implemented by the socialist government of François Mitterrand (i.e., privatizations, deregulation, disintermediation, cuts in public spending) translated into the closing of mines in northern France, the closing of many factories prefiguring France's deindustrialization, the emergence of the so-called new poverty, and the aggravation of social exclusion. A variety of initiatives appeared in France at that time to palliate the absence of the state in some areas, like comedian Coluche's *Restos du Coeur* that aimed to provide free food for people in need. This latter initiative recalls Saint Ignatius in sixteenth-century Barcelona, illustrating the aforementioned cyclical dimension of time.

This reasoning may be conclusive with regard to the history of pro bono. While one can regret and strongly resist it, including by making sure the emergence of pro bono and law clinics doesn't become a justifying argument to amplify it, the movement of state disengagement will inevitably impact the budget of the Ministry of Justice, including funds allocated to judicial assistance. If state-sponsored legal aid is eroded or removed, and given the erosion of community solidarity, a substantive number of people will be deprived of access to justice, and one may legitimately expect the decline of the rule of law in the face of economic normativity.

Within this context, the legal profession should not be viewed as a technical tool (a cog in the legal machinery) but as a prominent resource for a community that intends to renew its social ties despite dwindling state support. How to play again this fundamental role that lawyers used to play in society? One strategy for the legal profession consists of going back to its traditional values – including trust, eloquence, confraternity, and selflessness. These values are essential to the extent that no one else but a lawyer can perform the rhetorical art of pleading in a courtroom. More and more law students are taking theater or eloquence lessons, confirming the aforementioned trend among new generations of lawyers. The popular success in France of the documentary *A Voix Haute* ("Aloud"), featuring attorney at law Bertrand Périer giving weekly eloquence lessons to young underprivileged students, is another example.[70] Reconnecting progressively with pro bono beyond LCSR-motivated strategies, and with the traditional values that built the lawyers' prestige and legitimacy, will be likely to allow the return of the public trust toward lawyers.

As suggested by a former provincial president of the bar:

> When justice is not rendered as it should be, there still is a spirit of assistance, a spirit of serving justice. There are some things left, to revive .... I say there is still some fire under the ashes. And one day when we will realize we are heading toward nonsense – can you imagine, in France there are more than 50,000 lawyers! – when we will realize all that nonsense that is being done, then maybe we will get back to the origins.[71]

Pro bono is thus an occasion for lawyers to renew their old alliance with the public – an alliance that has been eroded in recent years with capitalistic perceptions of lawyers, including the widespread idea that lawyers are too expensive. Thanks to values-grounded pro bono practice, lawyers can stay "in touch" with their own society and participate again in the production of law. Moreover, in an increasingly socially and ethnically diversified French society, pro bono can serve as a way to resolve potential conflicts between the French "national culture" and imported "foreign culture," and thus stands as a factor of social integration and inclusion (offered by the legal profession, with no state intervention).[72]

On another note, the introduction of the Priority Preliminary Ruling on the Issue of Constitutionality[73] by the constitutional reform of 2008 gives room to new claims subject to constitutional judicial review, whether they involve civil liberties or individual rights. Lawyers articulating these claims can play a fundamental role in French democracy by representing claimants regardless of their ability to pay and strengthening the rule of law. Pro bono therefore stands as a tremendous opportunity for lawyers to show their solidarity with the broader society.

Finally, another "survival strategy" employed by the legal profession is to develop clinics. A law clinic is a place to rethink the fundamental contradictions shaping the ever-changing defence of the rule of law. In the United States, there is one professional legal culture so to speak, namely that of "lawyers." By contrast, in France and in civil law jurisdictions, there are three professional legal cultures: the culture of the *avocats* ("attorneys"), the culture of the magistrates (judges and prosecutors), and finally the culture of the doctors and professors (the academia, or the intellectuals of the law). Clinics in France can provide a bridge between the academic culture and the two other cultures of legal practitioners, whether they are judges or attorneys. The majority of clinical projects undertaken by students are submitted by professionals and allow for the mixing of theoretical and practical thinking. Crucially, they introduce law students – future lawyers – to selflessness, social justice, the defense of human rights, and fundamental freedoms as key foundational dimensions of the legal profession.

CONCLUSION

This chapter has provided a *vision d'ensemble* – at times empirical, conceptual, historical, and prospective – of pro bono. It has explored it as a phenomenon and a story of contemporary momentum, based on both French and global factors. It has attempted to provide a narrative and rationale for understanding pro bono beyond the momentum story, from a French perspective but beyond the French case. This rationale draws on the assumption that a structured legal institution exists in society. The legal institution can disappear. Or it could never have existed. Although different, life would be possible without it. But as and since it has existed in society, it has been related to the notion of structure, which does not necessarily relate to reactionary tradition. Structure means the sine qua non components of the legal institution. Advocacy, adjudication, and doctrine embody – besides case law, statutes, and codes – the less abstract, more human figure of the structure. Attorneys, judges, and jurists, to this day, are first and foremost humans, granted with flaws and abilities. While the two latter, judges and professors, must be functionally prominent within the structure to decide cases and teach accurate knowledge, attorneys, functionally, are people's daughters and sons, friends and saviors, so much so that originally, there was no need to be a lawyer to be an advocate: simple friendship is necessary, sufficient, and free. Throughout French medieval, modern, and contemporary history and cultures, and while attorneys have been feudal lords, kings' officials, major opponents to the church and monarch, fathers of the revolution, and children of the Republic, they still remain *avocats* – from the Latin *ad-vocatus*, that is, whoever is called for talking ("attorney" coming from the French word *à-tourner*). As this chapter has shown, attorneys, up to the contemporary practice of pro bono in large business forms, have never ceased to care for their own structural functions. As long as the legal institution shall bear people's trust and confidence, judges will be respected and obeyed, law schools' students will mostly learn law from their learned professors, and, consciously or not, attorneys will accept through pro bono to do their share of secular legal institution resilience.

NOTES

1. Part of this chapter draws on a limited body of qualitative and quantitative empirical data consisting in questionnaires, surveys, and interviews, as well as participant–observer insights, drawn from a project on the corporate social responsibility of Paris-based law firms (or Law Firm CSR ("LCSR") in this chapter). This project (LCSR Project) was carried out in 2012–14 by one of the clinical programs at the Sciences Po Law School, under the cosupervision of Jeremy Perelman, director of the clinic. This chapter also draws on interviews and conversations with lawyers practicing beyond Paris-based law firms, as well as with former heads of provincial bar associations. The chapter finally draws on Louis Assier-Andrieu's involvement in and interactions with members of the *Commission de perspective* of the French National Bar Council, which helped him develop an intersubjective vision on the condition and social role of lawyers (rather than "the legal profession") in France today. This vision builds on legal realist (in Karl Llewellyn's sense), anthropology of modernity (in Louis Dumont's sense), sociology of lawyers (primarily Lucien Karpik's), and historical perspectives. For a particularly notable example, see LUCIEN KARPIK, FRENCH LAWYERS, A STUDY IN COLLECTIVE ACTION, 1274–1994 (1999); POLITICAL LAWYERING, JUDICIARIES, AND POLITICAL LIBERALISM (Lucien Karpik, Terence C. Halliday & Malcom Feeley eds., 2006). Assoer-Andrieu further draws on a book that resulted from his research with the *Commission de prospective*, LOUIS ASSIER-ANDRIEU, LES AVOCATS: IDENTITÉ, CULTURE ET DEVENIR (2011), as well as on L'INDÉPENDANCE DES AVOCATS: LE LONG CHEMIN D'UNE LIBERTÉ (Louis Assier-Andrieu ed., 2015).
2. YVES DEZALAY & BRIAN GARTH, GLOBAL PRESCRIPTIONS: THE PRODUCTION, EXPORTATION, AND IMPORTATION OF A NEW LEGAL ORTHODOXY (2002); *see also* Ronit Dinovitzer & Brian Garth, *Pro Bono As an Elite Strategy in Early Lawyer Careers*, *in* PRIVATE LAWYERS AND THE PUBLIC INTEREST: THE EVOLVING ROLE OF PRO BONO IN THE LEGAL PROFESSION 115 (Robert Granfield & Lynn Mather eds., 2009) (distinguishing legitimacy and market-driven, demand creation-related rationales for pro bono, and assimilating both within a Bourdieusian perspective). French sociolegal studies on the legal profession include authors such as Anne Boigeol, Pierre Bourdieu's student Jacques Comaille, or more recently, on cause lawyering, Liora Israël. *See, e.g.*, Liora Israël, *Mobilisations du Droit et Engagements des Juristes, XXe Siècle*, ANNUAIRE DE L'EHESS 428 (2013); *see also* Charles Bosvieux-Onyekwelu, *Law Firms and Lawyers' Pro Bono Practice: A Comparative Approach to US and French Legal Fields*, 12 REVISTA DEBATES 33 (2018).
3. For a descriptive overview by a global law firm actively promoting pro bono practice in France as a "complement" to an increasingly under-resourced socialized legal aid system, see LATHAM & WATKINS, PRO BONO PRACTICES AND OPPORTUNITIES IN FRANCE (2016).

4. Founded in 2009, it claims that more than twenty-six thousand lawyers voluntarily provide written pro bono assistance to NGOs and institutions dealing with issues of human and children's rights, social and solidarity economy, comparative law, and professional training.
5. For an analysis, see Daniel Bonilla, Chapter 5 in this volume, and Sarah Dezalay, *Lawyers in Africa: Brokers of the State, Intermediaries of Globalization: A Case Study of the "Africa" Bar in Paris*, 25 INDIANA J. GLOBAL LEGAL STUD. 639 (2018).
6. For a comprehensive identification of the key drivers of and challenges faced by the French clinical movement, see LES CLINIQUES JURIDIQUES (Xavier Aurey & Marie-Joëlle Redor-Fichot eds., 2016). Specifically on the emergence of the French clinical legal movement in this volume, see Jeremy Perelman, *L'Enseignement du Droit en Action: l'Émergence des Cliniques Juridiques en France*, LES CLINIQUES JURIDIQUES, *supra*, at 61–105, pointing to both internal and external factors such as debates within French academia about the limits of formalist, black letter legal education in France, and the reemergence in academic literature of early twentieth-century European and French ideas that originally inspired American legal realism; debates within national and local bar associations about the quality of professional training provided by postgraduate bar schools; and the influence of the emerging global clinical movement.
7. Jeremy Perelman, *Penser la Pratique, Théoriser le Droit en Action: Des Cliniques Juridiques et des Nouvelles Frontières Épistémologiques du Droit*, 73 REVUE INTERDISCIPLINAIRE D'ÉTUDES JURIDIQUES 133 (2014).
8. The French context is different, with the traditional "French compromise" consisting of public universities (*facultés*) teaching black letter law at the undergraduate level, on the one hand, and professional training through "bar schools" run by bar associations, in which students attend classes while training in law firms as "student–lawyer" interns, on the other. The Paris corporate bar's dissatisfaction about this compromise explains in part their support for the creation of a graduate-level law degree at Sciences Po and of a clinical program within the school. For further analysis, see CHRISTOPHE JAMIN, LA CUISINE DU DROIT: L'ÉCOLE DE DROIT DE SCIENCES PO: UNE EXPÉRIMENTATION FRANÇAISE (2012) and Perelman, *supra* note 6.
9. As an example, partners at a large American law firm office repeatedly had to give up on expressed intentions to collaborate with the Sciences Po Clinic on an amicus brief on behalf of communities affected by extractive projects in the Global South, because of conflicts of interests with global clients of the firms. On the privatization of public interest law in the United States, for context see Scott L. Cummings, *Privatizing Public Interest Law*, 24 GEO. J. LEGAL ETHICS 1 (2011); see also Edwin Rekosh & Lamin Khadar, Chapter 6 in this volume.
10. As the director of Sciences Po's clinical program, I was involved in the LCSR Project carried out by one of the clinic's four programs on *Responsabilité et Innovations Sociale des Entreprises* (RISE, or corporate

social responsibility and innovation). The project sought to survey and report on the emerging notion and practice of LCSR and to examine the challenges it faces in its development. This project led to a 2014 report copublished with the Paris Bar Association, which was the result of an inquiry led by students, under the dual supervision of clinical instructors and a team at Linklaters LLP Paris, acting pro bono. This report relied on both quantitative and qualitative data gathered from fifty law firms in Paris, as well as surveys of student–lawyers in the Paris *Ecole du Barreau* (professional bar training school, which students integrate into after passing the entry-level bar exam and which trains each year about two thousand new lawyers, i.e., about half of the national total, in parallel to their mandatory internships as student–lawyers). The questionnaire included thirty questions, focusing on (1) the general engagement of the firm in terms of CSR (definition, origins, level of engagement, support); (2) client relations; (3) the internal functioning and governance of the firm; (4) pro bono practice; and (5) actions focused on the environment. It was sent to about fifty Paris law firms of different sizes. A new series of questions, drawing on the analysis of the data obtained in the first round of answers, was sent to the same firms in the fall of 2013. These questionnaires were completed by follow-up interviews with managing partners, as well as general counsels, CSR coordinators, communications managers, and associates in the spring of 2013. Further interviews were carried out in the fall of 2013, notably with the candidates and winners of the *Trophées du Pro Bono* (Pro Bono Prize) organized for the first time by the Paris Bar Association in 2012. Furthermore, web-based surveys were sent in the spring of 2013 to associates within the same Paris law firms, and in the fall of 2013 to student–lawyers at the Paris Bar School. Finally, the report relied on secondary sources such as academic literature, reports on the legal profession by bar associations, the National Bar Council, as well as reports on CSR by law firms.

11. The clinic's RISE program received direct support by Paris-based partners of large global corporate firms, through both seed funding and pro bono student supervision. As per interviews done in the context of the LCSR Project, these partners conceived this support as a way to channel their vision of CSR. This vision included the firm's CSR, through pro bono supervision of clinical students by senior and managing partners (as an example, a large international law firm recently entered a partnership with the Sciences Po Law School Clinic, in which associates and partners of the law firm, where pro bono is mandatory as per the law firm's CSR policies, are given access to engage with selected projects and cases on the clinic's docket as cosupervisors or technical resources for students, subject to prior approval by the clinic's scientific board, as well as by the firm in terms of conflicts of interests). It also included the firms' corporate clients' CSR, which demanded that firms they contracted with adopt their own CSR practices and which the clinic, in turn, would assist in further developing their CSR and, increasingly, human rights strategies and tools. Students participating in such programs

would thus become familiarized with both company and law firm CSR practices and ethos, with the hope that they would in turn reproduce and develop it further in their professional trajectories (Interviews with law firm partners, LCSR Project, Sciences Po Law Clinic, 2013).

12. Daniel Bonilla, Chapter 5 in this volume.
13. *See* Leire Larracoechea San Sebastián, Michelle Ha & S. Todd Crider, Chapter 9 in this volume; Edwin Rekosh & Lamin Khadar, Chapter 7 in this volume; and Susana Santos, Chapter 10 in this volume.
14. Interview by Louis Assier Andrieu with François Bedel de Buzarengues, former president, French Council of the Presidents of the Bar (June 2018).
15. *E.g.*, LATHAM & WATKINS, *supra* note 3, at 8.
16. *Id.*
17. *E.g.*, Interview with managing partner of the Paris office of a large British law firm (June 2013) (suggesting that the pro bono momentum, as a supplement to socialized legal aid, was halted by the financial crisis and its impact on the big law model and its diffusion in France, and that the LCSR framework is a way to regain momentum. One can also point to the idea, expressed by various authors in this volume, that pro bono and its publicity (e.g., by gaining awards or prizes, or media coverage) by a firm often constitutes a competitive strategy to attract talent and to control the activities of younger associates within a firm.
18. LSCSR Project (2014). LCSR is understood by respondents as consisting of four dimensions: client relations, through which firms ensure the respect of good practices by their clients (including anti-money laundering, trackability of payments, conflict of interest, data protection, as well as the promotion of socially responsible practices within the firms' sphere of influence) but which essentially derive from compliance with legal or professional ethics obligations; the internal operating mode of the law firm, which includes the quality of the working environment, actions in favor of professional training, and human resources initiatives benefiting associates and salaried employees, as well as the promotion of gender equality and diversity (relatively new and rare within the French bar, which counts about twice as many female associates than male, but twice as many male partners); environmental initiatives; and, finally, pro bono, defined and understood by respondents not as servicing indigent clients but more broadly as "lawyers putting their legal expertise in support of public interest projects by working with stakeholders outside the law firm" and identified as the domain in which their firm deploys the most efforts (e.g., taking pro bono practice into account for career advancement or working hours by some, mostly Anglo-American firms).
19. For example, development of CSR tools and risk management strategies, related, for instance, to the new requirements for large multinational corporations from the French Law No. 2017–399 of March 27, 2017, on the corporate duty of vigilance for parent and instructing companies, or to criminal complaints lodged by NGOs against corporations (such as Samsung and its French subsidiary in 2013 [dismissed] and 2018

[ongoing] for deceptive commercial practice in relation to its publicized ethical commitments [2013, dismissed] and human rights violations [2018, ongoing] related to the manufacturing of its products in China).

20. LCSR Project (2014), including a survey of the 2013 graduating class of the Paris Bar School, suggesting that 60 percent of the 100 student–lawyers (out of 1,717 in total) who responded to a survey suggested that law firms' socially responsible practices will play a key role in their choice of employment, and 90 percent that the development of LCSR is a key issue for the evolution of the legal profession.
21. *See* LSCR Project (2014) (examining views of the actors on the rationales behind the interest of Parisian Anglo-American corporate firms for the development of law clinics).
22. *Id.* A significant number of interviewees considered that LCSR offered law firms and lawyers working within those firms an opportunity to perpetuate their historical social role and engagement, and the collective identity of a profession grounded in values of "conscience, independence, probity and humanity."
23. For further analysis on this historically ambiguous "attachment," see *infra*, "The Historical Involvement of the French State in Pro Bono and Its Consequences."
24. Other initiatives, related to the broader concept of LCSR, include the French National Bar Council's general assembly resolution of 2011 on the adoption of a Charter of the Responsible Citizen Lawyer; the Paris Bar Association in the 2012 report "A Sustainable, Responsible and Partner Bar Association," which suggests the evolution of the legal ethics code toward a full inclusion of all aspects of social responsibility; the Paris bar's promotion of the adoption of ISO 26000 norms by law firms, through financial assistance offered to those wishing to do so, and by becoming in 2013 the first French Bar Association granted with the label; and finally the Paris bar's elaboration of a *Charte des bonnes pratiques de la collaboration* (Best Practices Charter, which includes issues such as the status of the salaried associate, the promotion of gender equality, diversity, well-being at work, notably in light of family situations, and conflict prevention mechanisms) and carbon footprints reports since 2013.
25. SHUGAAR ANTONY, CARDEN JEREMY & ALDO SCHIAVONE, THE INVENTION OF LAW IN THE WEST (2012).
26. Latin: *Leges Duodecim Tabularum* or *Duodecim Tabulae*.
27. ASSIER-ANDRIEU, *supra* note 1, at 81.
28. ALEXIS DE TOCQUEVILLE, DE LA DÉMOCRATIE EN AMÉRIQUE (Flammarion 2010) (1835–40).
29. Although not a democrat, Emperor Napoleon I is the instigator of the French Civil Code of 1804.
30. David B. Wilkins, *Who Should Regulate Lawyers?*, 105 HARV. L. REV. 799 (1992).
31. *Id.* at 813.
32. *Id.* at 859.

33. According to Christophe Jamin and Thierry Wickers, lawyers are "the best servants of the public interest." Christophe Jamin & Thierry Wickers, *L'avenir de la profession d'avocat*, 2010 COMMENTAIRE 996 (2010), *cited in* ASSIER-ANDRIEU, *supra* note 1, at 46.
34. VICTOR HUGO, CLAUDE GUEUX (Paul Savey-Casard ed., Presses Universitaires de France 1956) (1834); VICTOR HUGO, LE DERNIER JOUR D'UN CONDAMNÉ (Editions Hatier 2005) (1829).
35. Lucien Karpik (1992), at 3293, *cited in* ASSIER-ANDRIEU, *supra* note 1, at 125.
36. ASSIER-ANDRIEU, *supra* note 1, at 98.
37. *Id.* at 132.
38. *Id.* at 28–29.
39. Trust is in many ways a precapitalist notion and became later on a prerequisite to capitalism: without trust, there can be no market economy. Prior to the emergence of capitalism, relations between lawyers and their clients were already built on trust.
40. ASSIER-ANDRIEU, *supra* note 1, at 29.
41. *Id.* at 29–30.
42. *Id.* at 126.
43. *Id.* at 32.
44. *Id.* at 30.
45. Wilkins, *supra* note 30, at 865.
46. *Corporation*, MERRIAM-WEBSTER DICTIONARY ONLINE, www.merriam-webster.com/dictionary/corporation (last visited Sept. 22, 2020).
47. One may notice that this mobilization is also true for doctors and hospitals, which were equally engaged in assisting the poor for free.
48. ASSIER-ANDRIEU, *supra* note 1, at 104.
49. *Id.* at 10.
50. *Id.* at 87.
51. *Id.* at 91.
52. Loi du 22 janvier 1851 sur l'Assistance Judiciaire [Law of January 22, 1851 on Judicial Assistance], Journal Officiel de la République Française [J.O.] [Official Gazette of France], Aug. 20, 1944.
53. Emile Yvernès, *L'assistance judiciaire (1851–1891)*, 36 JOURNAL DE LA SOCIÉTÉ STATISTIQUE DE PARIS 221 (1895).
54. *Loi 72–11 du 3 janvier 1972 instituant l'aide judiciaire* [Law 72-11 of January 3, 1972 Instituting Legal Aid], Journal Officiel de la République Française [J.O.] [Official Gazette of France], Aug. 5, 1972, p. 164.
55. ASSIER-ANDRIEU, *supra* note 1, at 115.
56. *Id.* at 144.
57. SOPHIE HARNAIS & CAMILLE CHAZERON, MINISTRE DE LA JUSTICE, L'ANALYSE ÉCONOMIQUE DES AVOCATS (2013).
58. Directive 2006/123/EC of the European Parliament and of the Council of 12 December 2006 on services in the internal market, 2006 O.J. (L 376) 36.

59. Lawyers cannot, in the eyes of the author, be considered as simple service providers. Lawyers perpetuate a form of humanistic solidarity that covers virtually all aspects of life, just as doctors and priests do. Lawyers are committed to relieving social ills to the full extent of the ethically possible. CATHERINE FILLON, HISTOIRE DU BARREAU DE LYON SOUS LA TROISIÈME REPUBLIQUE (1995), *cited in* ASSIER-ANDRIEU, *supra* note 1, at 80.
60. Margaret Thatcher: "There is no such thing as society."
61. A bold (and excessive) parallel could be made with ALDOUS HUXLEY, BRAVE NEW WORLD (1932), where a "predestination service" cynically produces the exact number of people for each function in society, corresponding to the needs of the labor market.
62. It can be argued that the universal income also serves capitalism: universal income means the collectivization of an annuity through taxation. Then the use of this annuity is privatized insofar as all goods and services are exclusively provided by the private sector. Public aid goes to private hands, which serves the initial purpose of capitalism.
63. Personal communication of David Wilkins (Aug. 2010) (on file with the American Bar Association), *cited in* ASSIER-ANDRIEU, *supra* note 1, at 41.
64. *Id.*
65. Pierre Legendre, *cited in* ASSIER-ANDRIEU, *supra* note 1, at 42.
66. National Council of the Bars. "The *Conseil national des barreaux*, a public interest body as well as a legal entity, is the national institution that represents all practicing lawyers in France, with all lawyers also being registered in one of 161 local bars. The law assigned it some very specific mandates, and its functioning is governed by legal provisions and decrees, backed by internal rules." *Mandates of the Conseil national des barreaux*, CNB LES AVOCATS, www.cnb.avocat.fr/en/mandates-conseil-national-des-barreaux (last visited Sept. 22, 2020).
67. ASSIER-ANDRIEU, *supra* note 1, at 27.
68. ROSCOE POUND, THE SPIRIT OF THE COMMON LAW (1921).
69. The UK legislation, adopted as of October 2007, applies to England and Wales. Milton C. Regan Jr., *Lawyers, Symbols, and Money: Outside Investment in Law Firms*, 27 PENN ST. INT'L L. REV. 407 (2008).
70. A VOIX HAUTE – LA FORCE DE LA PAROLE (My Box Productions, 2017).
71. Interview, *supra* note 14.
72. One may look at the example given by Alison Dundes Renteln, although in the United States, where lawyers and lawsuits were used to delineate the law between a family's cultural rights and the national culture (i.e., the child's rights), with respect to a Hmong newborn in need of surgery. *Cf.* Alison Dundes Renteln, *The Significance of Cultural Differences for Human Rights*, *in* HUMAN RIGHTS: THE HARD QUESTIONS 79 (Cindy Holder & David Reidy eds., 2013).
73. Question prioritaire de constitutionnalité (QPC), 1958 CONST. 61-1, in force since March 1, 2010.

CHAPTER NINE

NARROWING THE JUSTICE GAP: CLEARINGHOUSES FOR SPAIN

Leire Larracoechea San Sebastián, Michelle Ha, and S. Todd Crider

INTRODUCTION

The Spanish constitutional and legal system grants the right to free legal assistance for Spanish citizens as well as foreign nationals in Spain who lack the financial means to litigate or are part of certain vulnerable groups. However, many poor individuals do not meet the means test to qualify for free legal aid, as the economic threshold is very low and many nonprofit organizations are also not eligible. The decade-long (2008–2018) economic downturn, from which Spain only recently emerged, led to drastic funding cutbacks in government support, which have not been fully restored. In addition, other administrative obstacles may effectively prevent access to legal aid. For example, even those who qualify for free legal aid may not be able to effectively access the help of a legal aid lawyer in practice, as is typically the case for asylum seekers in Spain.

Despite its potential to help address access-to-justice needs, pro bono legal services are not widespread and are not a component of a concerted response by the Spanish legal profession. Pro bono initiatives and platforms have started to emerge, but the lack of broad-based, collaborative clearinghouse mechanisms has limited the growth of pro bono in Spain. There are few open communication channels among the key stakeholders, mechanisms for effective and sustainable coordination of the work among pro bono providers, and discussions regarding strategic ways to identify and select those nonprofit entities and cases that fit the lawyers' interests and expertise and better harness the power of law for the public good. Ultimately, many foundations, associations, and other nonprofit organizations that would like to access pro bono services do not know where to start. Vulnerable groups have even less ability to access resources.

This chapter discusses the role pro bono clearinghouses could play in promoting access to justice by facilitating the creation of an efficient pro bono "ecosystem" in Spain. It examines publicly subsidized legal aid, as well as the reasons behind the lack of pro bono institutionalization in Spain, and investigates how pro bono can supplement and strengthen the state legal aid system, looking at the situation of asylum applicants as a relevant case study of the need and promise of pro bono in Spain. The chapter also explores examples of clearinghouses from Latin America and Europe, assesses the role they have played in the institutionalization of pro bono, and discusses how, considering the different cultural and societal contexts, lessons learned in other geographies could be applied in Spain. Finally, it discusses the newly created *Fundación Pro Bono España*, a collaborative pro bono clearinghouse platform.

BACKGROUND

In Spain, justice is expensive and legal proceedings are complex, lengthy, and unaffordable for many individuals and nongovernmental organizations (NGOs) that need access to free legal services.[1] The latest figures indicate that 16.7 percent of the Spanish population is unemployed,[2] and 12.8 million people are at risk of poverty or social exclusion.[3] There have also been significant cuts in state and local funds for NGOs, 60 percent of which depend on public funding.[4] During the 2008–2018 economic crisis, between 20 and 30 percent of NGOs in Spain dissolved or ceased activities due to lack of funds.[5]

While the number of those who cannot afford legal services has increased, the accessibility of free legal aid has been jeopardized by drastic reductions in government funding. Even though Spain guarantees the right to legal aid within its Constitution[6] and has a well-established legal aid system, the cutbacks in national and regional funding to the legal aid system since 2011 have ranged from 20 percent in some Spanish regions to 40 percent in others.[7] In Madrid, for instance, public funding for the bar association's free legal guidance services (*servicios de orientación jurídica*) was entirely removed in 2012 and has thereafter been subsidized by members' annual contributions.[8]

That same year, the fees paid to lawyers according to the schedule set by the state in compensation for services provided by the legal aid bar (*turno de oficio*) were reduced by 20 percent.[9] Publicly funded legal services are slowly recovering as Spain emerges from its decade-long economic downturn, but effective access to justice is still far from being fully realized.

This situation, however, is not unique to Spain. The justice crisis seems to be a reality everywhere.[10] In Europe, even though the European Convention on Human Rights requires European Union Member States to provide its citizens without sufficient financial means with free legal assistance,[11] many European legal aid systems do not meet this need.[12] In the United States, studies have consistently estimated that over four-fifths of the individual needs of the poor and a majority of the needs of middle-income Americans remain unmet.[13] Countries and lawyers around the globe are facing this grim reality, and in a growing number of jurisdictions, pro bono work has played a significant role in narrowing the justice gap.[14]

The idea that providing pro bono services to those in need is an ethical duty inherent to the legal profession has been a strong driver of its promotion and development globally.[15] As the practice of law became more specialized, lawyers who possessed the requisite knowledge of law and, over time, an exclusive right to act before courts became critical to effective access to justice.[16] The balance of the scales of justice often depend upon access to lawyers and the quality of lawyers placing their thumbs on either side of the scale, and conversely, lack of access to a lawyer – or a skilled lawyer – tends to be indicative of, perpetuate, and result in exclusion and marginalization. In this context, lawyers provided uncompensated legal services to individuals in need, based on relationships, charity, or court designation.

However, over the last thirty-five years, and due to factors such as growth patterns in large firms, inadequacies in state-funded legal aid, bar initiatives to promote pro bono activity, and law firm rankings based on pro bono participation, private bar efforts for the "public good" have undergone a transformation,[17] evolving from mostly ad hoc individual efforts into sophisticated pro bono programs and organizations that involve a wide variety of stakeholders: from transnational law firms to midtier firms and solo practitioners, NGOs, universities, bar associations, the government, and companies.[18]

In many countries, pro bono clearinghouses[19] have been essential to structure and articulate this complex and fundamental justice service in an efficient and collaborative manner.[20] These intermediary entities connect vulnerable individuals and communities with attorneys in a position to provide legal advisory services or representation.[21] In addition to playing this role as a broker between the supply and demand sides of pro bono, pro bono clearinghouses have proved useful in addressing the problem of lack of access to justice across borders by deepening pro bono culture within the legal profession and building a strong collaborative infrastructure. In Latin America, clearinghouses have played a significant role in pro bono's institutionalization and growth,[22] with fourteen operating across the region today. In continental Europe, these coordinating centers have also developed in the last decade and have been key to expanding pro bono within law firms and internationally.[23] At present, over a dozen are helping bridge the justice gap in Europe.[24] Further, some clearinghouses are going beyond matchmaking to embrace a specialist role by developing pro bono teams with deep expertise in the various matters they broker, as well as a "thought leadership" role in innovating pro bono in support of positive social change.[25]

In Spain, however, while some bar associations, law firms, universities, and nonprofit organizations are doing exemplary pro bono work, the lack of a collaborative pro bono clearinghouse has limited the growth of pro bono legal work. Pro bono remains a relatively foreign concept in Spanish legal culture, especially outside Madrid and Barcelona, and – until now – no collaborative and inclusive platform has emerged that organizes the pro bono work of the different stakeholders, including bar associations, law firms, law firm foundations, law schools, and solo practitioners. NGOs and individuals may not know that many law firms and independent lawyers are able and willing to provide pro bono assistance. The lack of clear organization, development, and specialization among the key pro bono players also means that lawyers do not know how to become involved and are not well prepared to meet the needs of pro bono clients. The result, all too often, is a "market" failure in which pro bono demand in the form of unmet legal needs is not matched with supply in the form of underutilized pro bono legal resources.

Specialized and broad-based matchmaking services between pro bono lawyers and not-for-profit entities working with those seeking advice have an important role to play in strengthening access to justice in Spain. This chapter illustrates the current state of pro bono in Spain and the interaction between the state-funded legal aid system and pro bono development, examining access to legal assistance in the asylum context as an example of how pro bono clearinghouses in Spain could promote efficient, effective, and sustainable pro bono service gestation and delivery. It covers the objectives of these intermediary entities, assesses the role that they have played in the institutionalization of pro bono in the Americas and Europe, and discusses how to apply these experiences to Spain, considering the different cultural and societal contexts.

The chapter starts from the premise that pro bono in Spain must play a complementary role to the publicly funded legal aid system, as it is most effective when it supports the work of the public legal aid system and fills in the coverage gaps. More study regarding the efficiency and quality of pro bono services is necessary, as the field currently lacks detailed descriptions and metrics that substantiate the role pro bono plays as a stand-alone measure in providing access to justice.[26] Consequently, much of this chapter relies on reports that analyze the trends in pro bono activities on a country-by-country basis and pays special attention to interviews with experts on the pro bono movement: leading members of bar associations, law firms, law schools, clearinghouses, and NGOs. It does so with the understanding that pro bono is part of a larger, broader movement to improve access to justice, in which the state-sponsored legal aid system is front and center.

The ultimate potential of pro bono legal services, however, extends beyond the "gaps" in any state-sponsored legal services system. By involving large numbers of lawyers in private practice in the challenges of access to justice, pro bono engages private sector lawyers and law firms in the issues of poor people and disadvantaged communities. This engagement can serve as a bulwark against governmental abuse or neglect and mobilize top legal talent and law firms in public service work. Pro bono, at its best, has a dynamic effect on the legal profession and the administration of justice.

THE CURRENT STATE OF PRO BONO SERVICES IN SPAIN

Diagnosis of the Situation of Pro Bono Legal Services in Spain

According to the 2016 TrustLaw Index on pro bono trends around the globe, the number of hours lawyers in Spain devote to pro bono legal services is among the lowest in Europe: an average of 11.4 hours of pro bono per lawyer in 2016.[27] By contrast, in the rest of Europe (excluding England and Wales, where pro bono is more developed), though still very low, lawyers worked an average of 15.2 hours of pro bono service each in 2016.[28]

The first study on pro bono in Spain conducted on a national level was published in 2014 and, to date, no other national survey has been conducted.[29] According to the study, only 57.5 percent of respondents were aware of pro bono opportunities in Spain. Most of these lawyers worked for the largest law firms, which represent a small fraction of overall lawyers in Spain. Three out of four respondents were familiar with the concept of pro bono, while only 41.8 percent of the respondents actually reported providing pro bono services. It is important to note that solo practitioners also reported providing pro bono legal services.[30] Among the lawyers who were not familiar with pro bono previously, 88.1 percent (most working at midtier or small firms) indicated a willingness to participate, which points to the lack of pro bono visibility as a strong explanatory factor for the low numbers of pro bono lawyers and the potential for major growth in the supply of pro bono lawyers. The fact that the Spanish legal market is atomized,[31] fragmented, and complex,[32] with a few large and economically successful firms but dominated numerically by small firms and solo practitioners, many of which struggle to eke out a living, also makes it challenging for those other than the largest or more successful firms to allocate significant resources to pro bono. Nonetheless, because pro bono legal service involves a lawyer's time and does not necessarily require other resources, there is substantial opportunity for growth in pro bono among smaller law firms and solo practitioners.

Meanwhile, demand for pro bono services, especially among NGOs,[33] is high. A 2017 survey by The Good Lobby (TGL) and the Madrid Bar's Center for the Legal Profession's Social Responsibility (*Centro de Responsabilidad Social de la Abogacía Madrileña*, CRSA)[34] showed that nearly 65.9 percent of NGOs require legal assistance at least once a year and, out of that, nearly one-third require legal services at least once a month.[35] The Spanish Association for Foundations (*Asociación Española de Fundaciones*, AEF), an umbrella organization for foundations in Spain, reveals that one in two members asks for legal advice on a regular basis.[36] Yet, few NGOs have in-house lawyers, and two-thirds pay external lawyers for the legal assistance that they need, with fees being allocated out of the budget that could otherwise be directed toward mission-driven activities and services.

The reasons behind the insufficient pro bono development in Spain are complex. While the Spanish Constitution does recognize the right to free legal assistance, it does not refer to pro bono work. The term "pro bono" is not used in the Spanish jurisprudential lexicon,[37] and there are no specific professional or ethical rules governing the delivery of pro bono services in Spain.[38] The Spanish legal system lacks instruments for promoting pro bono, and pro bono was viewed as potentially presenting tax costs. Specifically, law firms were concerned that value-added tax would be payable as to services provided on a pro bono basis and that related expenses might not be deductible from income for tax purposes.[39] The fact that discussions on pro bono have been isolated and limited to academic circles[40] poses another obstacle to institutionalizing and developing pro bono in Spain.

Broader cultural, political, and historical dynamics also play a role. Culturally, even though familial and social solidarity are characteristic of the Spanish culture, due in part to a centralized statist tradition and highly hierarchical church structure, civic associations and private philanthropy are less developed in Spanish culture. Indeed, as noted above, many community-based organizations remain dependent upon government support for funding. There is little tradition of community-based initiatives aimed at collaboratively promoting and ensuring social justice.

Historically, the Catholic Church and the state have sustained charity and volunteer activities. Drawing upon theological understandings of justice, in the High Middle Ages, the Catholic Church emphasized the role of the clergy in providing free legal assistance to those who could not afford it themselves at a time in which the legal profession as a whole was becoming more and more relevant.[41] Given the overlap between the various responsibilities of the church and the state in Spain until the twentieth century, the duty of providing legal assistance to economically disadvantaged people eventually shifted from the church to local municipalities who would pay for legal representation for the disadvantaged.[42] Eventually, these local efforts toward free legal aid would become institutionalized within the social welfare state in Spain in the twentieth century. Nonetheless, it would take a series of stages and legal movements throughout much of the century, particularly a movement that arose in the 1970s called the Movement for Access to Justice (*Movimiento para el Acceso a la*

Justicia),[43] for the government to recognize access to justice as a fundamental right and incorporate it in the Spanish Constitution of 1978,[44] together with the right to free legal assistance for those who have insufficient means to litigate.[45] The French influence on the development of the idea of rights in Spain dating back to the eighteenth century has also been a recurring ideological underpinning for the long-standing consensus in Spain about the role of government as the protector of rights.[46]

In the early 2000s, nonetheless, things began to change: pro bono stakeholders started to institutionalize the pro bono work that they had been doing for years.[47] Prompted in part by the vocation and demands of lawyers, who were aware of the potential to do something meaningful and sought to express the values of social volunteerism through their profession, law firms in Spain began looking to international models for inspiration on how to properly formalize their ad hoc pro bono activities. Cuatrecasas, for example, launched its pro bono program in 2007, after a trip to New York organized in coordination with the Cyrus R. Vance Center for International Justice of the New York City Bar Association (the Vance Center), where it visited various law firms, the bar association, and various legal services NGOs and clearinghouses to learn about the institutionalization of pro bono practice.[48] The program focuses on offering legal advice and representation to those in need.[49] Even before, in 2005, *Fundación Profesor Uría* was founded to promote voluntary social work within Uría Menéndez.[50] Gómez-Acebo & Pombo's Fernando Pombo Foundation was created in 2010, inspired by the idea of the legal profession's ethical responsibility and duty to help others.[51] Gradually, as these and other law firms developed their pro bono programs, various firms realized the opportunity to develop a collaborative platform to structure and articulate pro bono practice in an efficient and collaborative manner, which led them to establish a working group to analyze the possibility of establishing a clearinghouse – the so-called Group of Seven.[52]

Simultaneously, some universities started developing the first Spanish legal clinics, with the aim of providing students with the opportunity to be involved in social work and engage in practical training.[53] Interest in exposing students to social work with the third sector and the need for a more practical system, promoted with the enactment of Law 34/2006 on Access to the Professions of Lawyer and Attorney of the Courts,[54] greatly influenced the appearance of legal clinics and the practice of law in Spain.[55]

Various bar associations launched the first pro bono programs around the same time. In Madrid, for instance, the bar association created CRSA in 2008, to promote social responsibility among lawyers, including through engagement of lawyers with communities and NGOs, providing training to citizens as to legal rights, civic and social engagement, and other initiatives.[56] In 2011, CRSA organized the first Meeting on Social Responsibility of the Legal Profession, which is viewed as a major catalyst to the growth of pro bono practice in the country.[57] Know Your Laws, a pioneer program of the Community of Madrid aimed at providing immigrant populations with primers on the Spanish legal and institutional system, became the first public-private pro bono partnership in Spain, with many law firms, lawyers, and the CRSA participating.[58]

The PILnet European Pro Bono Forum, an annual event that shifts among leading European cities, held in Madrid in 2012, with the collaboration and support of the Madrid Bar Association and several Spanish law firms, was also an important catalyst for pro bono development in Spain.[59] Amidst a rising sense of urgency caused by the economic crisis, various stakeholders from the legal community convened to discuss the need for pro bono as well as novel strategies and structures that could strengthen pro bono work.[60] This convening of stakeholders provided a foundation from which pro bono efforts in Spain began to arise.[61]

Thereafter, new pro bono players emerged in Spain: *Fundación Hazloposible*, a Spanish NGO with a broad purpose of engaging civil society with NGOs, and *Fundación Aranzadi Lex Nova* (afterward renamed *Fundación Más Que Derecho*, although it no longer exists), a Spanish foundation focused on issues of legal education and access to justice. At the time, these two organizations jointly launched Probonos.net,[62] an online clearinghouse platform that connects professionals in legal services, technology, communications, marketing, and fundraising with NGOs who are otherwise unable to afford providers,[63] and a web page,[64] which were received favorably by the legal community in Spain but not focused exclusively on legal pro bono.[65] Prompted and encouraged by these and other developments, several firms implemented new pro bono practices. By way of example, Garrigues launched its pro bono program in 2012 to formalize the pro bono activities that they had been doing for years and provide tools to professionals willing to become involved.[66] Bar associations also developed new and preexisting pro bono initiatives after the forum.[67]

University legal clinics also proliferated from 2010 to 2015. These legal clinics are typically structured to offer practical learning by having students provide supervised legal services on a pro bono basis. Most clinics also seek to use this platform to expose Spanish law students to pro bono legal work and expand pro bono practice at large in Spain.[68] Currently, there are approximately twenty-five legal clinics in Spain. Some are general legal clinics that serve any particular case, while others are specialized and focus on certain vulnerable groups and types of cases.[69] In addition to providing experiential learning opportunities for students, legal clinics have added benefits for the legal and academic community writ large, cultivating a broader sense of community responsibility and fostering a commitment to social service.[70]

A contributing factor to the recent growth of pro bono in Spain is a recognition by law firms, companies, and universities that social responsibility is exceedingly important among millennials.[71] A recent survey by Deloitte found that almost 76 percent of millennials believe that the business they work for should have a positive social impact,[72] and some Spanish companies have begun to publicize and promote public interest work, including legal pro bono, that they do.[73] In fact, companies in Spain are also starting to take pro bono into consideration in choosing external legal counsel,[74] and even launching their own pro bono programs.

Addressing the justice gap is only one of the motivations driving lawyers and law firms to do pro bono. Although the emphasis is on the moral and altruistic meaning of pro bono,[75] the business case for implementing a solid pro bono program in a law firm is also driven by the increasingly global and competitive environment in which law firms operate.[76] Law firms are conscious that pro bono can help recruit and retain the best lawyers, increase job satisfaction, accelerate professional development, improve firm image, and even attract more clients.[77]

The advancement of pro bono in Spain is demonstrated by recent data, which shows pro bono activity to be modest but growing. According to a study done by TGL and CRSA in 2017, in 2014, only 27 percent of NGOs were familiar with the pro bono system, and out of those who knew about it, fewer than half had used pro bono legal services,[78] but in 2017, 80 percent of the NGOs surveyed reported some experience with pro bono legal services in Spain.[79] *Fundación Hazloposible*'s online pro bono program has also reported some of their results: in 2015, they published over 100 petitions for pro bono work, largely related to tax, labor, administrative, and civil law, which resulted in 600 hours of pro bono legal work completed.[80] In 2016, Probonos.net reported 135 completed pro bono cases.[81] The average number of pro bono hours per lawyer in Spain among survey respondents almost doubled between 2015 and 2016,[82] and the number of partners at law firms who dedicated time to pro bono in 2016 increased by 86 percent compared with 2015. Although survey respondents self-select to those firms and lawyers more likely to be informed and engaged with pro bono, it attests to the growth and potential for further growth.

While the progress of pro bono activity in Spain is encouraging, reservations remain regarding the quality of pro bono work being done. While many NGOs surveyed by TGL and CRSA were satisfied with the pro bono assistance they received, approximately two-thirds reported having a negative experience during their engagement with pro bono lawyers related to factors such as delays in the delivery of the service, the limited involvement and engagement of the pro bono lawyers, and their lack of expertise.[83] In addition, 55.6 percent of the legal needs of NGOs stem from the specific field in which a particular NGO works.[84] This is particularly true across a range of areas of practice: 55.6 percent of NGOs require legal assistance related to human rights issues, 41.3 percent on labor law, and 32.6 percent in regards to immigration and asylum issues.[85] A pro bono lawyer's lack of experience or substantive knowledge limits his or her ability to meaningfully contribute in matters in which either or both are required.[86]

When asked about how this service can be improved, the majority of the respondents referred to the need to optimize services, such as managing deadlines, establishing more frequent and fluid communication with the lawyers, implementing pro bono policies within the legal profession, and reducing the amount of bureaucratic tasks.[87] Some NGOs and pro bono clients in Spain noted their experience with what seems to be a lack of attention from the pro bono attorneys, especially when billable matters take priority.[88] It is clear that concerns with quality control and project management must be addressed in order for pro bono to be useful and meaningful as a social resource, as well as to guide its proper development.

In light of the opportunity for pro bono enhancement in Spain, and conscious of the need to better gauge the pro bono stakeholders' interest in developing pro bono, representatives of the Vance Center, which has had a leading role in the growth of pro bono in Latin America and sub-Saharan Africa,[89] traveled to Madrid in June 2016. The Vance Center team arranged meetings with leading law firms, the leadership of the Madrid Bar Association, and leaders of the existing initiatives and ventures in the legal social responsibility and pro bono space. The Vance Center representatives identified a strong interest[90] in a shared, privately supported platform that would permit lawyers to work collaboratively toward the advancement of pro bono practice. In order to further that objective, as well as to exchange best practices with representatives of different pro bono providers, in October 2016, the Vance Center hosted a delegation of several Spanish law firms and the Madrid Bar Association in New York City.[91] The visit concluded with a consensus among participants that pro bono work in Spain could benefit significantly from the collaboration through a broad-based clearinghouse.[92] Consequently, a new working group (Working Group), in some regards a successor to the efforts of the Group of Seven, was established to develop a business plan for a clearinghouse.[93]

Shortly after, the General Council of Spanish Lawyers (*Consejo General de la Abogacía Española*, Council),[94] "aware of the importance that social responsibility can play today in a world where both public and private operators must work together to effectively protect and promote rights and freedoms," formalized its commitment to promote pro bono in the country for the first time in history, incorporating its development as one of the 163 measures and 23 objectives that are part of their 2017–2020 Strategic Action Plan.[95] Spurred by this objective, in February 2018, the Council organized the first Informative Day on Pro Bono Advocacy. During its opening remarks, Luis Nieto, Council elective committee member, discussed the need for a systematized and coordinated approach to the many individual and dispersed pro bono initiatives, which was one of the main reasons why pro bono was incorporated into the 2017–2020 Strategic Action Plan.[96] He also emphasized the supplementary nature of pro bono work with respect to free legal assistance.

In order to understand pro bono in Spain, one must understand its system of government-funded free legal aid. The next section will consider the relationship between the state-sponsored legal aid system and pro bono, and how pro bono can serve as a complement to legal aid to enhance access to justice in Spain.

Pro Bono Assistance as a Complement to State-Funded Legal Services

The existence of an expansive and strong state-funded legal aid guarantee in Spain explains, to some extent, the low levels of pro bono visibility in the profession and to the general public. For certain segments of the Spanish legal market, as will be discussed in more detail later in this section, pro bono is perceived as unnecessary due to the existence of the state-funded legal services system, or worse, as presenting a threat to the legal services system itself. However, understanding the scope of coverage of state-supported legal aid and how it is disbursed through local bar associations demonstrates the gaps in access to state-supported legal aid that pro bono may be able to fill and, rather than being duplicative of or in competition with the existing legal aid system, how pro bono might support and coexist with legal aid to improve access to justice in Spain.

The Spanish constitutional system grants both citizens and noncitizens the right to free legal assistance (*asistencia jurídica gratuita*),[97] which is financed by the state and organized and managed by the bar association of each Spanish region through the legal aid bar. Generally speaking, these public services cover the fees of legal defense and representation for those who are economically excluded from the legal services market, as well as for members of certain vulnerable groups, including victims of gender-based violence, children, and foreigners.[98] Through this judicare system,[99] these clients receive legal representation in court by attorneys whose fees are paid by the state. The right to legal aid also includes reduced fees for access to public registries and documents. In addition to the right to legal aid contained in the Law on Free Legal Assistance, certain bar associations and regional and local administrations have created and disbursed several services that complement the above services, including legal guidance services. Certain vulnerable groups, such as victims of gender-based violence, immigrants, and people with disabilities, have special legal guidance services focused on their areas of need.[100] However, not every area of law is covered by legal aid, and few of the individuals who are in need of free legal assistance meet the economic threshold set out by law in order to qualify for legal aid from the state; many individuals, NGOs, and communities without sufficient resources to retain experienced representation also do not qualify to access this service.[101] In order to be eligible for free legal aid, an individual must prove that their family income does not exceed 532.51 euros per month.[102] This threshold was established in reference to the Public Index of Income and has been frozen since 2010. Individuals must send applications to local legal aid committees (*Comisiones de Asistencia Jurídica Gratuita*) organized by municipal bar associations that evaluate applications on a case-by-case basis.

Legal aid assistance, for the most part, is directed at individuals. Spanish law provides that NGOs are also included as entities with the right to legal aid, provided that they are public interest associations or foundations registered with the appropriate Public Registry and lack sufficient means to litigate.[103] However, other than the smallest, it is likely very difficult for NGOs to pass the means test due to this restrictive financial requirement, and furthermore, many NGOs do not know that they are eligible and fail to apply for legal aid in the first place.

In addition, during the 2008–2018 financial crisis, there were drastic cutbacks to publicly funded legal aid.[104] In regions such as Madrid, legal aid–related expenditures gradually declined from 2011 to 2016. Compensation for legal aid lawyers, which is determined by a fees schedule from 2003, was reduced by 20 percent,[105] whereas the number of these lawyers has increased every year.[106] The government also halted funding to legal guidance services, which are now maintained by bar associations themselves if they can afford to do so, as is the case in Madrid.[107]

One of the main reasons for the immaturity of pro bono in Spain is the debate regarding its compatibility with the state-funded legal aid system, which has deterred its adoption. Whereas the United States has a developed pro bono culture that aims to be universal, as the right to state-funded legal assistance is limited to criminal cases (excluding appeals) and there are consequently many legal needs that are not covered by public resources,[108] in mainland Europe, including Spain, pro bono services are – and perhaps should be – more limited, due to the existence of a more expansive legal aid guarantee, both in substance and in terms of its beneficiaries.[109] Unlike government-funded legal aid and public defenders in the United States, who tend to embrace the engagement and resources of pro bono lawyers to supplement scarce resources and overwhelming case dockets and demand, lawyers in Spain who provide government-funded legal services are critical about the "unfair competition" that allegedly could arise from lawyers delivering free pro bono legal services when the legal aid bar lawyers (*turno de oficio*) are already providing legal services for a fee as part of the state-funded legal aid system.

Unlike some countries in which government-funded legal aid is provided through specialized legal services organizations, these services are generally provided through the bar associations in Spain. Any lawyer who has habitual residence or an open firm within the area of the bar, with three-year requisite experience, and who has passed the courses or tests of access to the *turno de oficio*, can sign up with the bar association to provide legal services.[110] These individual lawyers provide legal services to indigent clients and receive payment from the bar association of amounts per the government's approved fees schedule. The large number of Spanish lawyers who derive a portion of their earnings through this *turno de oficio* system creates a large constituency prone to view pro bono legal services with concern as potentially "unfair" or "disloyal" competition. One of the main concerns is that pro bono representations could reduce the cases available through the *turno de oficio*. Although not supported by the facts, the state-funded legal services bar's perception of pro bono as dominated by lawyers from large and prosperous firms who do not charge for the same services they provide for which they are paid – albeit poorly and late – generates concern and suspicion.

Some lawyers think that pro bono is unnecessary and that lawyers who wish to engage in pro bono work should also join the legal aid bar instead. However, there are several considerations that complicate this approach from the perspective of both law firm and individual lawyers, including a law firm's imperative to review substantive conflicts as well as direct client conflicts; the interest of firms to identify areas of interest or expertise to design a law firm's pro bono portfolio, which is difficult to do within the legal aid bar where neither the client nor the lawyer is at liberty to choose the other; the necessity of a pro bono client to be signed on by the law firm as a client in order for a lawyer to be able to represent the client in a pro bono capacity, which cannot be done within the legal aid bar; the prior practice requirement, which is five years for the immigration section of the legal aid bar and by default excludes new lawyers from participating; and the limitation of working on direct client representation rather than a large-scale project on a longer time horizon, such as strategic litigation.

A key distinction between the state-sponsored legal services system in Spain and pro bono legal work is generally a question of qualifiers: only the economically disadvantaged and certain vulnerable groups and NGOs are eligible for publicly funded legal services, due to the restrictive means test, but in principle there are no such limitations on pro bono legal work, which enables access by populations in need who do not qualify for state-sponsored legal aid. Consequently, pro bono advocates in Spain, including the authors of this paper, insist on the complementarity and compatibility of pro bono legal services and the state-sponsored legal services system. There is an opportunity for pro bono providers and bar associations to work collaboratively to identify areas and beneficiaries of their respective services and to address their needs. The focus should be on filling gaps in the current system without competing with the existing state-funded system.[111]

Indeed, the impetus for developing pro bono systems is consistent, rather than in tension, with the public interest in ensuring access to justice. The complementarities between the two are illustrated by the three axes by which pro bono legal work promotes the public interest: (i) helping address the need for the realization of the fundamental right to access to justice,[112] (ii) standing against discrimination and protecting the most vulnerable in society, and (iii) promoting values necessary for democracy and the rule of law.[113] Pro bono may best be characterized as an "externalization of services" that can be made to fit the mold of the needs of the existing state-funded legal services system.[114]

Case Study A: Access to Legal Assistance for Asylum Seekers in Spain

The unmet needs of particular groups of asylum seekers in Spain illustrate that legal guarantees and an apparatus to deliver free legal aid alone may be insufficient to ensure meaningful access to justice, and how pro bono could play an important role even in contexts where legal aid is established by law.

Asylum seekers are individuals who have fled their home countries and are requesting international protection in another, exercising their right to seek asylum under international refugee law.[115] States parties to international refugee law instruments, such as the Convention and Protocol relating to the Status of Refugees (Refugee Convention), are required to evaluate asylum claims submitted by these individuals and determine whether they qualify for refugee status according to the criteria established within the Refugee Convention or other types of protection as each state may specify within its domestic laws.[116] Asylum seekers tend to lack formal status within the countries in which they seek international protection and may also be fleeing persecution or grave harms within their countries of origin. Only upon being recognized as a refugee according to the Refugee Convention definition or eligible for another form of international protection are they granted access to various benefits and social services that are due to them according to their status; therefore, they constitute a particularly vulnerable group.

Asylum seekers in Spain are entitled to a state-funded lawyer. Article 16 of Law 12/2009, the law in force regulating asylum in Spain, states that asylum seekers have a right to free legal assistance,[117] which is also listed in Article 18 of the same law as a right to which asylum seekers are entitled.[118] The immigration section of the legal aid bar within the Madrid Bar Association is tasked with providing free legal assistance to asylum seekers in Madrid. In practice, all asylum seekers are covered by the legal aid system: no asylum seeker has been denied state-funded legal representation by failing the means test determined by the income ceiling.[119] The legal need requirement for asylum seekers is satisfied by way of an affidavit attesting that the asylum seeker lacks sufficient funds to pay for a lawyer.[120] In effect, the burden of proving financial need is waived for asylum seekers, recognizing that many asylum seekers lack the documents necessary to prove their identity, let alone their financial status.

While all asylum seekers have a right to free legal aid, only those who apply for asylum at the border, airports, and from within migrant detention centers (*Centros de Internamiento de Extranjeros*, CIE) are required to be assisted by a lawyer. Asylum seekers who are applying within the territory – that is, those asylum seekers who are already located in Spain and not in detention or deportation proceedings – may choose to decline legal assistance. However, it is puzzling that the immigration section of the Madrid Bar Association received zero legal aid requests from asylum seekers applying within the territory between 2013–2016.[121] In contrast, they assisted 268 asylum seekers who applied at the border and within CIE in 2016 alone.[122] Even the coordinator for the immigration section of the state-funded legal services at the Madrid Bar Association himself questioned why every asylum seeker applying for protection within the territory in Madrid would decline the free help of a qualified lawyer in preparing an application.[123] In addition, according to Ministry of Interior statistics, less than 10 percent of asylum seekers in Madrid were accompanied by a lawyer during their asylum interviews during the first half of 2016.[124] Lawyers are permitted a large breadth of advocacy activity on behalf of their clients during asylum interviews in Spain,[125] including the ability to intervene during the asylum interview by asking or suggesting additional questions to clarify or further substantiate the asylum claim.[126]

Given the important role lawyers can play in ensuring that an asylum application is thoroughly and effectively presented, it is troubling that more asylum seekers are not benefiting from the presence and support of legal counsel during their asylum interviews.

Some hypotheses for the reasons behind the dearth of requests for legal assistance by asylum seekers include the state's failure to provide information to asylum seekers regarding the availability of free legal aid and their right to be assigned an attorney at no cost; the lack of translation services or information provided in languages other than Spanish, if relevant information is provided at all; and asylum seekers themselves deciding to forgo legal assistance because the delays in appointment times would not allow them to meet a legal aid lawyer before their scheduled asylum interview. One of the most compelling explanations indicates that the point in time in which an asylum seeker is given information regarding their right to a free legal aid lawyer is problematic: asylum seekers may receive this information only once they arrive at their asylum interview, not when they are prompted to make an interview appointment by calling the hotline number.[127] When given this information at the interview, even if the asylum seeker would like to meet with a state-funded lawyer, it would not be possible to meet the lawyer prior to the scheduled interview, and asylum seekers are also not likely to know that the asylum interview could be postponed to a later date in order to allow for a meeting with the state-funded lawyer – and that this delay in the interview would not prejudice the case. Therefore, asylum seekers fail to avail themselves of assistance from a state-funded lawyer. In effect, the right to a publicly funded lawyer, which is guaranteed to asylum seekers according to Spanish law, is hollowed out due to deficiencies in the system, and legal needs remain unmet.

Case Study B: Project Jones Day – Strategic Litigation on Behalf of Migrant Youth

Project Jones Day is a collaborative effort among the Madrid office of Jones Day, a global law firm, the Raíces Foundation, an NGO that works with children and vulnerable youth, and the legal clinic at *ICADE–Universidad Pontificia Comillas* (ICADE legal clinic),[128] bringing together the distinct skills and resources of each party toward a shared goal and allowing them individually to also achieve their own missions: the law firm's need for meaningful pro bono opportunities, the NGO's need for free legal services, and the legal clinic's need for significant and immersive practice experiences for their students. The development of this strategic litigation project aiming to protect the rights of unaccompanied minors illustrates the critical need and potential for collaborative pro bono networks and specialized local pro bono coordinators in Spain in order to facilitate the proper growth and development of pro bono.

The Raíces Foundation had been assisting two unaccompanied minors[129] with social services and throughout the course of administrative procedures related to age determination and residency.[130] Both clients were found, according to questionable age determination procedures, to be above the age of majority, when in fact both were minors at the time, which meant they had the right to be sheltered in support centers for minors (*centro de menores*) and access other protections and social services.[131] At the same time, the ICADE legal clinic was designing a course on strategic litigation for the upcoming 2016–17 school year, and had been in contact with the Madrid office of Jones Day, which had previously developed a legal assistance project at the United States–Mexico border and, based on the success of that project and its desire to continue expanding its immigration pro bono portfolio among its global offices, was looking to start a similar project helping migrants in Spain.[132] Based on the strong foundation of pro bono contacts developed by Gail Harvey, the Europe–Middle East business development and communication manager at Jones Day Madrid, Jesús Gimeno and Jesús Merino, respectively of counsel and associate in the office at the time, had been conducting individual outreach to various NGOs working with child migrants to scout partnership opportunities.[133] Ultimately, Jones Day, together with ICADE and the director of the ICADE legal clinics at the time, María Concepción Molina, organized a seminar at ICADE where NGOs working with refugees and interested in collaborating with Jones Day in a pro bono capacity were invited to participate. It was here that Jones Day made contact with the Raíces Foundation, who they believed would be the ideal partner, and together along with ICADE created the ICADE legal clinic's first strategic litigation project: Project Jones Day, which aims to challenge the age determination policies for unaccompanied minors in Spain and bring justice to those who were erroneously found to be above the age of majority, both before Spanish domestic organs such as the Prosecutor's Office (*Fiscalía*) and Spanish courts, as well as in the international arena.[134]

As a model pro bono initiative, Project Jones Day shows the collaborative potential of different stakeholders in the legal sector, including NGOs, private law firms, and law school clinics.[135] The development of the project also underscores the laborious process that brought the parties together, including organizing the seminar and active outreach by Gail Harvey laying the foundation, as well as ICADE legal clinic's key role as a broker in the absence of a central coordinating mechanism. Many NGOs do not have capacity to engage in such coordination activity due to a lack of resources and focus on mission-driven activities; ICADE legal clinic's focus is – as is the case for any other law school clinic in Spain – teaching and training new generations of lawyers, not identifying parties in need of pro bono services and others who are able to provide pro bono assistance. Further, given their ultimate goal, as Molina explains, legal clinics within a law school faculty tend to be limited in their capacity by natural student turnover and the academic year,[136] which poses some challenges to the possibilities for long-term engagement, such as the second phase of Project Jones Day and other large-scale litigation matters.[137]

These collaborations to enhance access to justice and effect positive social change are difficult to achieve and could be more effectively designed by professional and specialized entities that focus on matching pro bono needs to law firms with resources and expertise. Examples of this already exist and are active in other contexts around the globe. The next section covers these pro bono clearinghouses: describing their form and function illustrated through examples in Latin America and Europe, and proposing a model tailored to the Spanish context.

PRO BONO CLEARINGHOUSES AND PRO BONO DEVELOPMENT

The previous account of the need for free legal services in Spain, combined with the nascent scaffolding of pro bono in Spain and the challenges faced by its players, shows the important role Spanish clearinghouses could play in orchestrating pro bono to maximize its efficiency and effectiveness, promoting pro bono culture and measuring its impact and, ideally, developing models tailored to Spain's access-to-justice needs.

Global pro bono has both induced and required the development of clearinghouses. As pro bono programs at global law firms have become increasingly formalized, diversified, and sophisticated over the past decades, pro bono clearinghouses have also spread and evolved to conform to this emerging landscape.[138] During the first Global Pro Bono Conference held at Harvard Law School in 2014, Edwin Rekosh explained that global trends have driven the growth of locally based NGOs because the clearinghouse network helps them frame their needs as legal matters that law firms can address and understand.[139] "Above all," Rekosh affirmed, "global pro bono is about connecting local lawyers to local needs around the globe."[140] A4ID, PILnet, the Pro Bono Institute, and the Vance Center are some of the global pro bono clearinghouses that have been instrumental in promoting pro bono expansion and institutionalization against this backdrop.[141]

The following analysis of pro bono clearinghouses is drawn from a worldwide movement aiming to institutionalize pro bono legal services[142] and draws from the experiences of specific clearinghouses in Latin America and continental Europe. Spain's geographic presence in the European continent, the parallel sociopolitical circumstances between Spain and other EU member states, as well as the shared legal and regulatory traditions that shape their domestic legal architectures[143] point to the potential benefits of comparative analysis between Spain and its European neighbors. In fact, Spain's exceptionalism within Europe may be one of the most interesting comparisons: whereas over a dozen European jurisdictions have developed clearinghouses, until recently Spain was one of the only countries that had still not managed to unite the main pro bono stakeholders to support a common clearinghouse. Latin America provides inspiration for Spain due to their deep historical and cultural ties. The Spanish legacy and long-standing legal culture and tradition undoubtedly left a significant mark during Spain's three centuries of colonial presence in this region. Furthermore, the presence and growth of the top-tier Spanish law firms in Latin America as well as the investments of Spain's leading companies in the region invites consideration of the local pro bono movement in order to import into Europe some of the key takeaways from the promising story of pro bono implementation in Latin America.[144] The fact that Spain functions as the European point of entry for Latin America makes this ongoing cross-pollination potentially more meaningful.[145] In building from these experiences, Spain's legal structure, culture, and demands will be considered in order to customize pro bono clearinghouses to the national context.[146]

Clearinghouses: Form and Function

The term "clearinghouse" refers to organizations that coordinate and generate pro bono matters as well as work to develop pro bono culture and a broader pro bono ecosystem.[147] Clearinghouses facilitate access to justice by providing free legal advice to vulnerable communities, disseminating legal knowledge, promoting the practice of pro bono work, and raising awareness within the legal profession about the importance of pro bono. However, their main areas of activity, personnel, governance, and administration structure and means of financing differ depending on their areas of focus and priorities, geographic area, and stakeholders. Clearinghouses are created in relation to the needs of each country, or smaller geography (i.e., state or city), and the ideas that emerge around pro bono work; there are clearinghouses of all shapes and sizes, even within the same jurisdiction. Clearinghouses can be general and broad in approach, by covering all types of referrals, or narrow, by focusing on specific areas of need (e.g., rights of children or advocacy for minority rights).

Clearinghouses provide the coordination mechanism necessary for the proper development and execution of pro bono projects. In many countries, class divisions and stratification generate insurmountable chasms between law firms and NGOs, so neutral referral organizations are key to developing a relationship of trust between them.[148] By understanding the kind of work done by not-for-profit entities, the communities they serve, and the specific needs they have, clearinghouses can find the most suitable law firm or solo practitioner that matches an NGO's ethical and professional requests. On the other side, clearinghouses can also facilitate private sector fulfilment of its professional and ethical responsibilities toward civil society and the public good.

Clearinghouses help filter and define the legal needs of individuals, NGOs, and governments and connect them with pro bono lawyers who have the relevant skills to help.[149] They shoulder for law firms the time, opportunity, and monetary costs of matching pro bono lawyers with clients in need of pro bono services and provide structure, metrics, and efficiency so that resources are efficiently deployed. Through repeated experience, clearinghouses accumulate "tacit relational knowledge" over time, which allows them to gain expertise in client, case, and partner selection as well as relationship management and development.[150] Their brokering services thus become even more valuable over time.

As noted above, clearinghouses can prioritize different types of representations and clients. In the United States, pro bono has historically related primarily to the representation of poor individuals in litigation, criminal appeals, housing disputes, and other matters affecting the poor. In Latin America, however, because most large firms are substantially composed of business lawyers, some clearinghouses have focused on the needs of NGOs rather than individual clients. In addition, in Brazil, the rules of the bar association historically limited pro bono efforts to NGOs to avoid competition with state-funded legal services offered through the bar association in a structure similar to that in effect in Spain. Most clearinghouses in Latin America, however, do provide pro bono assistance to individuals in need, and there is growing expertise within the clearinghouses and law firms related to individual representation.

Clearinghouses not only connect pro bono needs with resources but also act as the necessary supporting infrastructure for coordination as well as "co-opetition,"[151] promoting efficiency through organizing competition and cooperation between the various actors. Participating stakeholders – whether NGOs, law firms, governments, or individuals – often lack the resources to tackle coordination. With a separate and dedicated staff, clearinghouses plan, manage, support, and improve the initial matchmaking service, taking on "responsibility for intake, screening, packaging, referral, follow up, promotion and communication"[152] for pro bono matters, allowing parties to focus on their own missions.

A growing body of evidence demonstrates that in countries with pro bono clearinghouses, firms have higher pro bono output due to clearinghouse support.[153] Antonia Stolper, a member of the Vance Center's executive committee and partner at Shearman & Sterling, explains: clearinghouses "allow the firms to act collectively, which clearly has a positive impact for technical assistance and sourcing matters."[154] Furthermore, the pro bono framework that is created through the coordination managed by clearinghouses adds to the creation of an efficient system by "bring[ing] heterogeneity to the network, which leads to competition for cases among the law firms," as well as facilitating the transfer of know-how among the actors, allowing for "the network as a whole [to benefit] directly."[155] Clearinghouses, as both "network developer[s]" and "network articulator[s],"[156] are thus essential to pro bono "ecosystems," in both generating these environments and developing them.

Clearinghouses perform several core functions including outreach, vetting, matchmaking, and follow-up.[157] During the outreach and vetting processes, clearinghouses screen potential clients based on eligibility and the availability and expertise of law firms while at the same time educating potential clients on the benefits of free legal assistance and what they can expect from it. They do so proactively, while law firms normally undertake pro bono projects and conduct due diligence reactively. Clearinghouses meet with nonprofit organizations to understand what they need and search, select, filter, and develop the best pro bono projects, guiding the process from start to finish. They also liaise with law firm pro bono programs and other members of the legal profession to understand their interests and the expertise and resources available for pro bono work in order to match them with appropriate matters.

Once the client is prescreened, clearinghouses identify the type of expertise required in the pro bono project. They play a key role in preparing the legal proposal, as NGO clients seeking pro bono support may not be familiar with legal procedures and concepts, or how to articulate the issue at hand as a legal question.[158] Whatever the case may be, correctly addressing and articulating the legal need in a project description is essential in order to find the right pro bono attorney. In placing matters through its normal procedure, PILnet's Global Pro Bono Clearinghouse, for instance, prioritizes the best interests of the NGO client, taking into account the lawyers' level of experience and expertise and the need for equitable distribution among member law firms. However, time-sensitive pro bono requests that fall under its urgent procedure may be placed on a first-come, first-served basis, depending on the circumstances.[159] In all cases, the matter description must be clear so that all stakeholders know what to expect from the engagement.[160] In Latin America, clearinghouses such as *Fundación Pro Bono Colombia* have developed all types of pro bono models and formats, including pro bono service proposals, pro bono advice request forms, pro bono implementation manuals, and support guides and videos on legal issues relating to vulnerable groups, in order to more efficiently and effectively match pro bono matters. The *Fundación Barra Mexicana*, one of the Mexican clearinghouses, for its part, has developed Quolaw, a pioneering system for digitizing and managing pro bono cases,[161] which has been instrumental in the generation and efficient organization and distribution of pro bono projects among its members and clients.

While a clearinghouse may limit its activity to matchmaking and hand off the matter to the partners once they are matched, it is advisable for clearinghouses to maintain some degree of involvement with the project in order to ensure smooth project execution.[162] Indeed, experts agree that the best clearinghouses are those that stay involved; provide substantive expertise, training, or at least backup; and have expert resources.[163] This allows them to ensure that the matter is solved in the most professional way possible, there is a good relationship between the parties, the case is handled within a reasonable time frame, and the client is satisfied with the result. It also enables them to verify whether the matter is in compliance with application regulations regarding pro bono activity and that all stakeholders involved are clear about their capacity in terms of both resources and time.[164] Although some US clearinghouses will sometimes act as counsel to the pro bono client with the indirect support of a law firm acting on a pro bono basis or as co-counsel with the law firm, this would be atypical in Latin America. The supporting and monitoring activity by a clearinghouse generally does not involve acting as co-counsel.

Clearinghouses in Latin America and Europe: Lessons for Spain

In both the United States and Latin America, clearinghouses have been protagonists in the institutionalization and development of pro bono. According to Wendy Atrokhov, Latham & Watkins director of global pro bono, "Clearinghouses have been complete game-changers" in the US pro bono landscape.[165] In the US context, where pro bono was already widely understood, clearinghouses taught people how to get involved;[166] they connected supply and demand, created partnerships between the different legal market actors, and shared know-how.[167] Whereas in the United States they appeared at a moment in which pro bono had already walked its first steps, in Latin America these intermediaries appeared to consolidate a phenomenon that was still in its early stages, with the support of US lawyers and institutions like the Vance Center.

In concert with a variety of pro bono stakeholders,[168] Latin American clearinghouses have played an important role in the establishment of a pro bono culture and practice in the region.[169] As Todd Crider, coauthor of this chapter, partner at Simpson Thacher & Bartlett LLP, and member of the Vance Center executive committee, says, "Thanks largely to the leadership of the clearinghouses in the region, pro bono has evolved over the last decade from being a new word and concept in need of definition, to being enshrined as a necessary component of legal practice at most significant firms."[170] In 2011, in response to the successful development of pro bono in the region, various Latin American clearinghouses came together to develop the Pro Bono Network of the Americas,[171] an umbrella organization built to exchange best practices and promote increased institutionalization of pro bono in the region.[172] In Europe, PILnet's activity in hosting pro bono forums, as well as roundtables and different types of convening in various countries, has also markedly contributed to the development of pro bono culture, as was the case in Spain. For example, the PILnet European Pro Bono Forum in 2015, held in Rome, was helpful in bringing more NGOs into the Pro Bono Roundtables that PILnet was already hosting in the country, enabling the members to enlarge their scope of activity, including liaising with local bar councils and forensic associations to include them in the discussion.[173] Through the Roundtable discussions, stakeholders in Italy's pro bono movement developed a definition of pro bono to clarify the concept and tailor it to Italy's specific legal context,[174] providing a base for its successful development. More than four years since the first roundtable held in Milan, Pro Bono Italia was established in May 2017 as the first not-for-profit, independent association of lawyers, law firms, and forensic associations devoted to fostering a culture of pro bono throughout Italy. Its members offer free legal advice to NGOs and private individuals in need, and promote open dialogue and cooperation with NGOs, clearinghouses, and legal clinics operating nationally and abroad, as well as with the international public interest law community. Training seminars and larger events on relevant legal, social, and cultural matters are organized on a regular basis, aimed at facilitating the performance of pro bono services as a means of upholding human rights and improving the Italian judicial system.[175]

At the local level, clearinghouses have also been key to pro bono development. They allocate important resources to educate the public on pro bono work and encourage its development: to eliminate existing confusion about the meaning of pro bono and how it differs from legal aid; to portray a socially conscious image of the legal profession; and to create synergies with the media, with whom collaboration is essential to increase visibility and propagate a pro bono culture. In some jurisdictions, pro bono growth has been impaired by an overassociation of pro bono projects with specific law firms or firms who were early adopters, and by the perception of pro bono as solely a marketing tool for law firms. Shared clearinghouse platforms serve to redirect, to mutual benefit, the competitive energy of law firms toward a common project.

The Chilean *Fundación Pro Bono* (FPB),[176] which serves as the leading pro bono clearinghouse in Chile and coleads, with the Vance Center, the Pro Bono Network of the Americas, prioritizes pro bono promotion such as seminars, workshops, and talks targeting lawyers and encourages them to participate in public debate around access to justice.[177] FPB also helps law firms disseminate and highlight their pro bono work through keeping track of the number of pro bono hours completed and a personalized annual report on pro bono to each firm; it also contributes to creating best practice manuals for pro bono.[178] FPB arranges meetings and agreements with local and international NGOs to give pro bono a higher profile.[179] Disseminating the pro bono work done by attorneys among other legal professionals and the public –through internal and external media – is one of FPB's main missions. The ultimate goal is to encourage volunteer work by attorneys in order to consolidate pro bono assistance and extend its coverage.

Many clearinghouses on a global scale attach particular importance to training pro bono lawyers and clients. They develop and provide training courses, materials, and guides for lawyers from social organizations and other legal practitioners on common legal issues and pro bono matters, and also organize initiatives and events for new lawyers and law students. Students in particular benefit from the opportunity to acquire practical experience in socially responsible advocacy by being involved in the cases coordinated by the clearinghouse together with the law firms and universities, and attending – and even teaching – seminars, courses, and lectures aimed at nonprofit entities.[180] Through educational workshops, trainings for nonprofit leaders, individual counseling, and a series of publications, clearinghouses can also help NGOs maximize their performance and their impact.

The range of opportunities for clearinghouses to promote pro bono is broad: clearinghouses may also help law firms recruit and mentor lawyers who may be interested in pro bono activities; provide advice to law firms looking to implement pro bono systems internally; and organize conferences or grant awards to lawyers for their pro bono commitment as a motivational tool.[181] In Europe, clearinghouses such as *Centrum Pro Bono* in Poland have always prioritized this function. Through initiatives such as its annual pro bono award, which is organized in collaboration with one of the main national newspapers, the Polish clearinghouse has engaged various stakeholders from the Ministry of Justice, the Supreme Court, and the bar association, among others, in the development of pro bono. The working groups composed of members of the clearinghouses in Germany (*Proboneo*), Italy (*Pro Bono Italia*), and other European countries have also been essential in this regard.

In South America, clearinghouses have played a crucial role as promoters of pro bono. The Argentinian clearinghouse of the Buenos Aires Bar Association (*Comisión Pro Bono*), for example, created a pro bono coordinators roundtable, a monthly meeting of the pro bono coordinators of the clearinghouse member law firms to share best practices and discuss the challenges each faces. These roundtables have allowed *Comisión Pro Bono* to better understand pro bono supply and demand, thus substantially improving the services it provides to NGOs, which has been essential in the development of pro bono both inside and outside firms.

The Pro Bono Peru Alliance (the Alliance) serves as a clearinghouse with seventeen firms currently providing financial support. A distinctive project of the Alliance is its Pro Bono Challenge, an annual contest aimed at law students in Peru where students identify a legal problem facing a vulnerable community and develop a pro bono project to address it. The winning project is then implemented in collaboration with one of the Alliance law firm members. The Challenge encourages law students to become involved in pro bono advocacy while promoting and improving the pro bono programs of the Alliance's firms and providing an opportunity for law students to work directly with a top law firm on the project. Its success has been such that it has been replicated in several Latin American countries.

Brazil's *Instituto Pro Bono* (IPB), a nonprofit organization founded in 2001 dedicated to access to justice for vulnerable populations through volunteerism, was also vital in the promotion of pro bono in the country.[182] Despite the obstacles imposed on pro bono work by the Brazilian Bar Association, IPB continued to work toward its mission of building a pro bono culture in Brazil and acting as a clearinghouse for the pro bono representation of NGOs. The Brazilian Bar Association treated pro bono work as ethically dubious behavior due to potentially "disloyal competition" and concerns related to the state-funded legal aid that, like Spain's system, is generally administered through the relevant bar association and benefits private sector lawyers who provide their services for a fee. In fact, the Brazilian Bar Association's decision in 2015 to allow free legal services for individuals and nonprofit organizations that cannot afford the costs of a lawyer[183] was due, in large part, to IPB's efforts.[184]

In each country, an essential component of creating a pro bono ecosystem is to organize a shared pro bono platform, funded by law firms and in-house legal departments, that functions as a clearinghouse and otherwise provides permanent support to a pro bono legal culture. These efforts benefit from sharing best practices, ideas, and experiences with lawyers in other jurisdictions.

Specialized Clearinghouses and Pro Bono Practice Development

As the pro bono landscape develops and evolves, clearinghouses also adapt and innovate. While clearinghouses in Europe and Latin America begin with a broad pro bono mandate, in the more developed cultures of the United States, United Kingdom, and Australia, more specialized clearinghouses have emerged. One model of specialization drawing increased attention is the "co-counseling model," in which the clearinghouse serves as co-counsel on a matter alongside pro bono counsel. Clearinghouses employing the co-counseling model develop expertise in particular areas. They then employ this expertise to provide tailored consultation to both NGO clients and to the pro bono lawyers and law firms partnering on the matter at hand throughout the lifetime of the project, ensuring that client needs are served in a thorough manner from beginning to end.[185]

For example, for many of its matters, the Vance Center uses a co-counseling model that employs specialized lawyers on the Vance Center staff who serve clients alongside pro bono law firms in the areas of human rights, the environment, and good governance.[186] Its level of involvement in projects depends on NGO client needs, pro bono partner experience and expertise, and the nature of the matter; it can range from facilitating communication with the client, to directing pro bono counsel to relevant resources and reviewing the work product, to playing the lead role in project execution. The Vance Center's work in support of the peace process in Colombia illustrates the potential of the co-counseling model. Staff attorneys at the Vance Center worked alongside law firm partners researching the legality of amnesty for members of the Revolutionary Armed Forces of Colombia (FARC) rebels in peace agreements. As part of this effort, the Vance Center supported groups in Colombia working on implementing the peace accords, including a project with Afro-Colombian women.[187] Marie-

Claude Jean-Baptiste, programs director at the Vance Center, was able to identify the exclusion of Afro-Colombian women as a pressing issue due to her familiarity with the peace process and experience working with Afro-Colombian victims.[188] Based on this insight, the Vance Center organized a seminar alongside the National Conference of Afro-Colombian Organizations in April 2017, where over forty Afro-Colombian women leaders as well as Colombian and international civil society organizations came together to discuss how Afro-Colombian women could participate in the implementation of the peace agreement, particularly in the Special Peace Tribunal and the Truth Commission created for the postconflict transition.[189]

Specialized clearinghouses also engage in advocacy, law reform, and in-depth initiatives on particular areas of practice.[190] While a clearinghouse focusing on matchmaking alone may lack the resources and capacity to pursue advocacy projects, specialized clearinghouses may have in-house lawyers and external volunteers who are experts in a specific area of practice. TrustLaw is an example of a specialized clearinghouse that is developing an issue-focused approach, paying particular attention to issues facing women, such as gender-based violence and child marriages,[191] and generating investigative reporting as well as novel legal research.[192] Specialized clearinghouses or specialists within clearinghouses also frequently provide training to pro bono lawyers as well as ongoing support by consulting with pro bono lawyers during the representation. Issue-focused specialized clearinghouses provide an answer to some of the most serious criticisms of pro bono, namely, the lack of substantive expertise among pro bono volunteers and the limited time that law firms dedicate to pro bono work.[193]

Some specialized clearinghouses have also sought to play a "thought leadership" role in the pro bono field. Under the leadership of its president, Garth Meintjes, PILnet has been exploring the possibility of innovating public interest lawyering, shifting away from reactive models of advocacy that focus on rights violations and redress mechanisms and toward employing transactional lawyering skills that aim to manage and mitigate risks for civil society, much as private lawyers use contracts and negotiations to serve the business interests of paying clients.[194] PILnet has also worked to change the narrative of pro bono practice from focusing on access to justice as a distributive question of primarily economic concern to questioning the role of law itself as a social process and institution that creates unequal outcomes – a process that will bias the scales in favor of the wealthy and powerful in society even if every indigent individual were provided free legal aid or a pro bono lawyer.[195] The success of such "think tank" specialized clearinghouses in influencing the way pro bono is imagined will depend on the clearinghouse's ability to design and carry out successful case studies that can serve as proof of concept and be duplicated and scaled for wider impact. Nonetheless, clearinghouses are best positioned to engage in such thought leadership, due to their expertise in the field of pro bono practice and unique role as mediator and facilitator, brokering partnerships between civil society actors and the private sector in pursuit of the public good.[196]

Recently, the Vance Center, with the support of the Ford Foundation, has created the Lawyers Council for Civil and Economic Rights for the Americas, which brings together top private sector lawyers from across the region to design and implement a proactive, cross-jurisdictional strategy to utilize pro bono resources to bring about greater economic and social rights. Like PILnet, this initiative seeks to take the pro bono model from reactive to proactive and drive a reform agenda in areas that cut horizontally across the Americas. Early areas of focus include corruption, selection of judiciary, and protecting and cultivating the NGO sector in civil society.

To maximize impact, clearinghouses should also collect, systematize, and update information on the pro bono work of their clients and their members through generating research and analysis such as statistics, follow-up briefs, and annual reports on pro bono. As Jennifer Daniels, former NCR corporate general counsel, underscored at Harvard's Global Pro Bono Conference, "Ranking surveys and other statistical measures of pro bono enable us to understand to what extent we are making a difference, if we are developing programs that are efficient, and what the NGOs think of the help we are offering."[197] As a cultivator and provider of vital statistics and information regarding pro bono, clearinghouses should contribute to the development and professionalization of pro bono culture in ways that more effectively improve access to justice and the rule of law. Yet, it is clear that pro bono services consistently face the challenge of lack of reliable benchmarks, accurate reporting, and transparency.[198] Social enterprises, individuals, and lawyers do not have good data on pro bono providers, structures, or benefits, which prevents stakeholders from accessing the service. Clearinghouses can also help address this issue.

BRINGING IT ALL TOGETHER: NEW DEVELOPMENTS AND PROPOSALS FOR PRO BONO IN SPAIN

Fundación Pro Bono España: A New Spanish Pro Bono Clearinghouse

In June 2018, *Fundación Pro Bono España* (*Fundación*), a pro bono clearinghouse, was founded in Spain with the support of twenty-eight Spanish and global law firms.[199] The foundation aspires to "driv[ing] the development of pro bono legal services by promoting, organizing, raising awareness of and extending pro bono practice, while acting as an intermediary between lawyers and the nonprofit sector, academic circles and key pro bono stakeholders at an international level."[200]

The decision to launch this clearinghouse came after extensive study of its need by the Working Group organized by the Vance Center.[201] According to the Working Group's business plan, among the reasons underpinning the establishment of *Fundación* are the need to "join a global (pro bono) movement via an effective platform with proven results," promote a pro bono culture in Spain to raise awareness of an unfamiliar yet sought-after service, "meet and coordinate the growing demand to collaborate in social development," "provide the right tools to maximize the development of pro bono work," and "reinforce free legal aid by providing complementary services."[202]

To help address those needs, *Fundación* determined three main areas of focus: "(i) facilitating access to specialised legal assistance for non-profit organizations; (ii) providing law firms, in-house counsel, university clinics, bar associations and other pro bono actors with the tools required to expand their scope of work; and (iii) offering legal professionals opportunities to get involved in promoting justice and equality before the law."[203] Conscious of the need to develop pro bono hand in hand with the existing state-supported legal aid system, *Fundación* explicitly committed in its bylaws not to interfere with the state-supported legal services provided through the bar associations and to act collaboratively with the bar associations to develop pro bono practice.[204]

The launch of *Fundación* marks an inflection point in the history of pro bono in Spain. Previously, efforts to create collaborative spaces for Spanish law firms have encountered limited success, given the branded nature of certain law firms' pro bono initiatives and foundations that limited their potential as collaborative spaces.

The project has been received positively by the legal community, regarded as a milestone in Spain's pro bono development, while also being met with skepticism by others.[205] Going forward, it will be important for *Fundación* to build bridges and common spaces with the existing system of legal aid that is sponsored by the state through the bar associations. Because this work represents a significant source of livelihood for a large number of lawyers in Spain, any potentially "competitive activity" is viewed with mistrust. As previously noted, *Fundación* intends to focus on representing NGOs instead of individuals to the extent that they do not qualify for assistance by state-sponsored legal services. At the same time, *Fundación* also intends to explore opportunities for pro bono lawyers to collaborate with the lawyers providing state-funded legal services. Indeed, for special cases, state-funded lawyers could be encouraged to request assistance from *Fundación* in the form of pro bono resources, much as legal services organizations in the United States seek to leverage pro bono resources. Finally, pro bono counsel, by seeking to identify obstacles to persons asserting legal rights, would seek to add to demand for state-sponsored legal services as barriers are overcome.

The principal challenge for *Fundación* will be to build a network of relationships with NGOs to identify and operationalize pro bono projects that enable pro bono lawyers to engage effectively and productively. The true value of pro bono rests upon its ability to deliver needed legal services that make a difference in the lives of those who are in need. Time and effort are required to build relationships with community-based organizations and train their teams to identify potential pro bono projects and bring those to the attention of *Fundación*. *Fundación*'s staff will also need to sustain the attention and loyalty of the law firms and lawyers that are supporting *Fundación* by delivering attractive pro bono projects and otherwise creating opportunities for those lawyers to participate.

At the time of submission of this chapter, *Fundación* was newly created. Operations commenced in September 2018. Leire Larracoechea, coauthor of this chapter, left the Vance Center to serve as the executive director of *Fundación*. As she explained,

> The establishment of *Fundación* is only a first step in proving the thesis in this chapter that a pro bono clearinghouse can find fertile ground in Iberia and act as the primary catalyst to cultivating a pro bono culture. The team will work hard to realize the promise of pro bono in Spain,

trying to expand its remit beyond Madrid to the rest of the country. Whether and to what extent *Fundación* will be successful in servicing as a key pro bono promoter in Spain, replicating the success of other international clearinghouses, remains to be seen.

A Specialized Clearinghouse in Spain with Expertise in Asylum and Refugee Law

The main indicator of *Fundación*'s success would be its ability to instill a pro bono culture in the whole country, albeit in different ways and at varying speeds depending on the region and institution, and to serve as an effective middleperson between unmet needs for legal services and legal professionals willing to provide pro bono legal representation. Success will come client by client (NGO by NGO), in obtaining access to justice and in proving to the law firms and lawyers assisting with the work the value of a clearinghouse as an intermediary for pro bono legal services. Above all, *Fundación* should have a pedagogical role by contributing to a healthy and growing pro bono culture, with a genuinely altruistic aim, within both the legal market and society.

Looking ahead, while *Fundación* intends to act broadly to develop the Spanish pro bono space, it is likely that, over time, space for specialized clearinghouses, such as those that have emerged in more developed pro bono jurisdictions, will grow. For example, what if, in the future, there were a specialized clearinghouse in Spain that focused on asylum and refugee matters? Certain challenges, due to their complexity, require specialized knowledge and sustained and dedicated resources to address.

The strategic litigation in Project Jones Day (see "Case Study B: Project Jones Day – Strategic Litigation on Behalf of Migrant Youth") targets an important and pressing problem that pro bono collaboration could address in the field of asylum: the gap in protection for unaccompanied minors. While a system exists within each autonomous region in Spain for unaccompanied minors to receive state protection and support within designated centers (*Centros de Protección de Menores*), these minors often lack documents to prove their age, and age determination procedures, such as forensic examination of the wrist, have a high margin of error that lead to erroneous determinations that a minor is actually of the age of majority. The result is that these vulnerable youth fall outside of the system of protection that they have a right to access, as is the case for the plaintiffs in Project Jones Day. A specialized clearinghouse in Spain with in-house experts on asylum and refugee law and a broad network of NGO and law firm partners could play the role of coordinator, facilitator, and strategist in developing a strategic litigation pro bono project like Project Jones Day more efficiently. It could have the expertise to understand the thematic issues at hand and think strategically about how pro bono could best be utilized. All parties involved in the project – the pro bono lawyers, the legal clinic, and the NGO and its clients – could approach this centralized hub and consultancy service to be matched with each other and design together in a collaborative forum a pro bono project that best utilizes the resources and skills of each party in pursuit of genuine impact on the social good. Indeed, the refugee crisis requires coordination from different actors, both locally and transnationally.[206] This specialized local clearinghouse could connect Spanish actors to this global effort, coordinating the work of firms and NGOs in Spain that also have offices or counterparts abroad and get involved in cross-border collaboration on projects with Spanish and international actors.[207]

Asylum and refugee issues are areas particularly ripe for pro bono collaboration. NGOs and pro bono and legal aid lawyers in Spain already collaborate in different ways within the field of asylum and immigration, mostly on providing Know Your Rights workshops and trainings: the Fernando Pombo Foundation has partnered with NGOs to create training guides for lawyers assisting migrants in detention within the CIEs through its Project EXEQUO;[208] the ICADE legal clinic regularly partners with organizations and lawyers to provide its students with opportunities to support the development and execution of "Street Law" chats and legal orientation sessions with migrant communities;[209] and the Madrid bar's CRSA also collaborates on projects in service to immigrants, such as preparing multilingual Know Your Rights and Know Your Laws guides and supplementary manuals in preparation for the Spanish citizenship exam.[210] Around 33 percent of the volunteer lawyers active within the CRSA are also members of the state-supported legal services bar.[211]

It is important to note again that, even though there is no regulation that prevents pro bono lawyers from doing so, pro bono in this area should not attempt to substitute or duplicate the role that state-supported legal services play in assisting those in need. In the area of direct assistance to immigrants and asylum seekers, for example, the immigration section of the state-supported legal services bar is well equipped to fulfill this function. There are standards in place to ensure adequate training and ability: lawyers wishing to enroll are required to have at least five years of experience as a practicing lawyer and to successfully complete a training course in asylum law and pass the qualifying exam.[212] In addition, several expert bodies collaborate with and contribute to the training curriculum and programs for legal aid lawyers, including ACNUR and the Spanish Lawyers' Foundation (*Fundación Abogacía Española*).[213] As of May 2017, there were around 670 lawyers admitted to assist asylum seekers within the legal aid bar,[214] so supply of trained lawyers is also not an issue.

However, due to its mandate to provide direct client services, the state-supported legal services bar is unlikely to be able to tackle the problem of barriers to delivery of legal services that prevent asylum seekers from requesting or obtaining its help in the first place, as explained in "Case Study A: Access to Legal Assistance for Asylum Seekers in Spain." This could be an entry point for pro bono lawyers to engage by acting in support of the work of the immigration section of the state-supported legal services bar. For example, pro bono lawyers could work together on a research project to determine the causes underlying the dearth of legal aid requests from asylum seekers applying within the territory, engaging with stakeholders, including state organs such as the Asylum and Refugee Office (*Oficina de Asilo y Refugio*) and the Ministry of Interior and independent bodies such as the Office of the Ombudsman (*Defensor del Pueblo*), and monitoring access points through which asylum seekers ought to receive information regarding their right to legal aid. Furthermore, pro bono lawyers could assist in determining why such a substantial percentage of asylum seekers are unrepresented in their hearings, despite the availability of state-supported legal services.

In cooperation with the state-supported legal aid services, pro bono lawyers could also become involved in designing and implementing a solution to problems identified by the research project, thus facilitating asylum seekers' access to their rights as well as the proper functioning of the legal aid bar and potentially increasing the demand for its services. This kind of targeted collaboration also fulfills pro bono's mission and foundational impetus to fill in the gaps of legal aid coverage to ensure a more complete realization of equality before and equal access to law and, by extension, justice.

CONCLUSION

During Spain's recently concluded decade-long economic downturn, the gap between the advantaged and the disadvantaged continued to grow, as it has in many parts of the developed and underdeveloped worlds. Social and economic inequality both exacerbates and is exacerbated by legal inequality. Spain continues to lag behind certain other countries in addressing the justice gap and developing pro bono, which go hand in hand. Improving access to justice in Spain can aid in breaking down legal inequality that, in turn, is an important step toward tackling social inequality.

Even though pro bono is far from a panacea, experience in other jurisdictions has shown that it may help address this gap in access to justice, and that clearinghouses could play a pivotal role in institutionalizing and maximizing the impact of pro bono. Pro bono clearinghouses have been crucial to developing the architecture of pro bono in Latin America, and the proliferation of clearinghouses and pro bono activity has occurred in parallel across much of Europe. Drawing from the experiences of Latin American and other European countries and adapting a structure and strategy of pro bono clearinghouses that suits Spain's particular social, legal, and cultural circumstances could provide the needed impetus to develop pro bono culture in Spain. Time will tell whether the newly created *Fundación Pro Bono España* can serve as a successful clearinghouse model in Spain, and whether pro bono will further develop as a positive force that contributes to the movement to bring access to justice closer to reality.

NOTES

1. Throughout this paper, NGOs will be referred to as nonprofit organizations or nonprofits, foundations, or third-sector entities interchangeably. In Spain, "third sector" is the term used to refer to the nonprofit sector.
2. *See Economically Active Population Survey*, SPANISH NATIONAL STATISTICAL INSTITUTE 1 (Apr. 26, 2018), www.ine.es/en/daco/daco42/daco4211/epa0118_en.pdf (last visited Sept. 20, 2020).
3. *Radiografía del Tercer Sector Social en España: Retos y Oportunidades en un Entorno Cambiante*, FUNDACIÓN PWC 6 (2018), www.pwc.es/es/publicaciones/tercer-sector/fundacion-pwc-tercer-sector-social-2018.pdf (last visited Sept. 20, 2020).
4. FUNDACIÓN PWC, INSTITUTO DE INNOVACIÓN SOCIAL DE ESADE & FUNDACIÓN LA CAIXA, LA REACCIÓN DEL TERCER SECTOR SOCIAL AL ENTORNO DE CRISIS [REPORT ON THE REACTION OF THE THIRD SECTOR IN AN ENVIRONMENT OF ECONOMIC CRISIS] 7 (2014).
5. *Id.* at 7.

6. C.E. ART. 119, B.O.E. n. 311, Dec. 29, 1978, *expanded by* Law of Free Legal Assistance (B.O.E. 1996, 11), *further modified by* Law of 18 July 2005 to Amend the Law of 10 January 1996 (B.O.E. 2005, 171), *and further modified by* Law of 21 June 2017 to Amend the Law of 10 January 1996 (B.O.E. 2017, 148).
7. ABOGACÍA ESPAÑOLA & WOLTERS KLUWER ESPAÑA, S.A., JUSTICIA GRATUITA XI INFORME DEL OBSERVATORIO DE JUSTICIA GRATUITA [FREE JUSTICE, XI REPORT ON FREE LEGAL SERVICES IN SPAIN] 9 (2012–2016).
8. Email interview with María Sol Cuevas Gama, Director, Legal Aid Bar and Legal Guidance Services, Madrid Bar Association (Aug. 3, 2017).
9. As of August 2017, the average remuneration for legal aid lawyers was less than 135 euros per case, while purchasing power remained the same as in 2011, as summarized in the press release on the publication of the XI Report on Free Legal Services in Spain. *See* Luis Javier Sánchez, *Los Abogados del Turno de Oficio Manejan un Poder Adquisitivo del Año 2011*, CONFILEGAL.COM (July 4, 2017), https://confilegal.com/20170704-los-abogados-del-turno-oficio-manejan-poder-adquisitivo-del-ano-2011/ (last visited Sept. 20, 2020). By contrast, the average salary of a lawyer working in a major law firm in Spain with around five years of practice is usually between 3,750 and 6,600 (net) euros per month, reaching a minimum salary of 10,000 euros per month after ten years of experience. *See* Vanesa Matesanz, *¿Cuánto Gana un Abogado en España?*, FORBES.ES (May 1, 2015), http://forbes.es/business/6780/cuanto-gana-un-abogado-en-espana/ (last visited Sept. 20, 2020). Nonetheless, the Madrid Bar Association and the Madrid Government have reached an agreement whereby the 20 percent reduction in the legal aid lawyers' salary should be fully recovered by the end of 2018. Email interview with María Sol Cuevas Gama, Director of the Madrid Bar Association's Legal Aid Bar and Legal Guidance Services (Aug. 3, 2017).
10. COMMISSION ON LEGAL EMPOWERMENT OF THE POOR, UNITED NATIONS, MAKING THE LAW WORK FOR EVERYONE: VOLUME 1 61 (2008), www.un.org/ruleoflaw/files/Making_the_Law_Work_for_Everyone.pdf (last visited Sept. 20, 2020).
11. Article 6(3), European Convention for the Protection of Human Rights and Fundamental Freedoms art. 6(3), Nov. 4, 1950, 213 U.N.T.S. 2889, *as amended by* Protocol No. 11, May 11, 1994, 2061 U.N.T.S. 2889, *and* Protocol No. 14, May 13, 2004, 2677 U.N.T.S. 2899 [hereinafter European Convention on Human Rights].
12. THOMSON REUTERS FOUNDATION, TRUSTLAW INDEX OF PRO BONO 2016, K1-2 (2016), www.trust.org/contentAsset/raw-data/d31d8b72-0f82-4241-88e1-71abc90e3d72/file (last visited Sept. 20, 2020) [hereinafter TrustLaw Index].
13. Deborah L. Rhode, *Access to Justice: An Agenda for Legal Education and Research*, 62 J. LEGAL EDUC. 531, 531 (2013).

14. LEGAL SERVICES CORPORATION, REPORT OF THE PRO BONO TASK FORCE 2 (Oct. 2012), www.lsc.gov/sites/default/files/attach/2015/09/Report-ProBonoTaskForce-2012.pdf (last visited Sept. 20, 2020).
15. That is not to say the concept of pro bono has been a stagnant one; in fact, the "American pro bono phenomenon" has evolved significantly in its definition and scope since the adoption of the ABA Model Rules of Professional Conduct in 1983. *See ABA Model Rules of Professional Conduct (pre-2002)*, LEGAL INFORMATION INSTITUTE, www.law.cornell.edu/ethics/aba/2001/ABA_CODE.HTM (last visited Sept. 1, 2017).
16. Steven B. Rosenfeld, *Mandatory Pro Bono: Historical and Constitutional Perspectives*, 2 CARDOZO L. REV. 273 (1981).
17. *See* Scott L. Cummings, *The Politics of Pro Bono*, 52 UCLA L. REV. 1, 6 (2004) [hereinafter *The Politics of Pro Bono*]; Scott L. Cummings & Deborah L. Rhode, *Managing Pro Bono: Doing Well by Doing Better*, 78 FORDHAM L. REV. 2370 (2010).
18. THE ABA STANDING COMMITTEE ON PRO BONO AND PUBLIC SERVICE, SUPPORTING JUSTICE: A REPORT ON THE PRO BONO WORK OF AMERICA'S LAWYERS 6 (2005).
19. We also include within the term "pro bono clearinghouses" those organizations that focus mainly on pro bono matchmaking between NGOs and individuals in need and lawyers and law firms willing and able to provide free legal services. These entities also look to the development and growth of pro bono as an end goal in itself and may sometimes be referred to as referral organizations, coordinating centers, pro bono organizations, or intermediaries. For the purposes of this chapter, we distinguish pro bono clearinghouses from advocacy organizations with clearinghouse-like functions. *See infra* note 147.
20. Cummings, *The Politics of Pro Bono*, *supra* note 17, at 42.
21. PILNET AND ADVOCATES FOR INTERNATIONAL DEVELOPMENT, PRO BONO CLEARINGHOUSE MANUAL: RESOURCES FOR DEVELOPING PRO BONO LEGAL SERVICES 19 (2011) [hereinafter PRO BONO CLEARINGHOUSE MANUAL].
22. DANIEL BONILLA, THE MANDARINS OF THE LAW: PRO BONO LEGAL WORK FROM A COMPARATIVE PERSPECTIVE 55 (2015).
23. LAMIN KHADAR, THE GROWTH OF PRO BONO IN EUROPE, USING THE POWER OF LAW FOR THE PUBLIC INTEREST 27 (2016).
24. *Where We Work, Other Locations*, PILNET (Jan. 19, 2011), www.pilnet.org/public-interest-lawyers/other-locations.html (last visited Sept. 22, 2020).
25. KHADAR, *supra* note 23, at 47–48.
26. Scott L. Cummings & Rebecca L. Sandefur, *Beyond the Numbers: What We Know – and Should Know – About American Pro Bono*, 7 HARV. L. & POL'Y REV. 85 (2013).
27. TRUSTLAW INDEX, *supra* note 12, at K20. It should also be noted that only nine law firms in Spain provided data for the Index, and all of

them were international firms. Therefore, this can only serve as an estimate of pro bono resources in Spain in past years and, due to its concentration on larger firms who chose to participate, likely overstates the actual time dedicated to pro bono activity. In contrast, thirty-nine law firms with offices in Europe submitted data for the Index.

28. *Id.* at K1.
29. FUNDACIÓN ARANZADI LEX NOVA, INFORME SOBRE CONOCIMIENTO Y PARTICIPACIÓN EN ACTIVIDADES PRO BONO POR PARTE DE ABOGADOS ESPAÑOLES 2014 [REPORT ON KNOWLEDGE AND INVOLVEMENT IN PRO BONO ACTIVITIES BY SPANISH LAWYERS 2014] 48 (2015).
30. According to Jeanne Charn, cofounder of what is now known as the WilmerHale Legal Services Center at Harvard Law School, although big law firms have become the face of pro bono, solo and small firms generally account for more pro bono services and tend to have more relevant expertise. Interview with Jeanne Charn, Senior Lecturer on Law, Harvard Law School (Feb. 9, 2015).
31. According to the General Council of Spanish Advocacy (*Consejo General de la Abogacía Española*, Council), in December 2017, there were 256,644 registered attorneys in Spain. *See Censo Numérico de Colegiados*, CONSEJO GENERAL DE LA ABOGACÍA ESPAÑOLA, www.abogacia.es/2017/02/28/censo-numerico-de-abogados/ (last visited Sept. 9, 2018).
32. In Spain, there are approximately 90,000 firms and, among those, 89 percent are headed by a maximum of three partners. *See En España hay 90.000 Despachos de Abogados*, LEGALTODAY (Mar. 7, 2012), www.legaltoday.com/actualidad/noticias/en-espana-hay-90000-despachos-de-abogados (last visited Sept. 20, 2020).
33. In Spain, as in other European countries, pro bono lawyers mainly cater to NGO clients, whereas legal aid mainly serves individuals. KHADAR, *supra* note 23, at 29.
34. "The study has concentrated on the nonprofit entities that engage in advocacy, understood as defense of the general interests. As they are not registered as such, we contacted around 16 coordinators and distinct social action platforms from the entire Spanish territory in order to obtain the referenced information. We contacted 310 nonprofit organizations, including both the coordinators that also engage in advocacy as well as the nonprofit organizations of an ample range, from the most powerful such as Save, Greenpeace, UNICEF, etc. to the smallest (e.g., ACCP.com). Of the total, approximately, 14% are dedicated exclusively to advocacy, 3% 'almost exclusively,' while the remaining 83%, in addition to advocacy occupy their mission in other various responsibilities, from humanitarian assistance and social intervention to the environment." Email interview with Ruth de Miguel, Director, Center for the Legal Profession's Social Responsibility, Madrid Bar Association (Aug. 24, 2017). "We have used the term 'ENL' (nonprofit) as it is the most inclusive and least restrictive term

to refer to all those entities that work in advocacy (briefly translated as 'defense of the general (public) interest,' a very expansive term in effect, but we have decided to concretize it as 'promotion and defense of the general interests (public interest) such as the protection of public health, the environment, education, employment, etc., at the national and/or international level' so as not to use the anglicism and to further differentiate it from the 'defense of human rights'). I believe I remember that the majority of the responses came from Madrid, and despite including distinct organizations throughout all of Spain, many are headquartered in Madrid." Email interview with Ruth de Miguel, Director, Center for the Legal Profession's Social Responsibility, Madrid Bar Association (Aug. 25, 2017). "I hereby inform you that, of the 50 entities that completed the survey, 34 are based in Madrid." Email correspondence with Elettra Colombi (Aug. 30, 2017).

35. Ilustre Colegio de Abogados de Madrid Centro de Responsabilidad Social de la Abogacia Madrileña & The Good Lobby, Estudio de Necesidades Jurídicas de las ONGs en España 2017 [Study on the Legal Needs of NGOs in Spain 2017] 4 (2017) [hereinafter Study on the Legal Needs of NGOs in Spain].

36. Isabel Peñalosa of the Asociación Española de Fundaciones summarizes the varied nature of their members' legal requests as: obligations *vis-à-vis* the Spanish Protectorate of Foundations; legal regime of acts of property disposal; transparency, accountability, and good governance; prevention of money laundering; new criminal responsibility of legal entities; processes of modification, merger, and extinction of not-for-profits; and tax regime of NGOs. Email interview with Isabel Peñalosa, Director, Institutional Relations and Legal Advice, Asociación Española de Fundaciones (July 8, 2016); *see also* Isanchez, *La Gestión de Litigios Estratégicos, el Gran Reto del Pro Bono de la Abogacía en Nuestro País*, Confilegal (Oct. 26, 2012), www.diariojuridico.com/la-gestion-de-litigios-estrategicos-el-gran-reto-del-pro-bono-de-la-abogacia-en-nuestro-pais/ (last visited Sept. 20, 2020).

37. Latham & Watkins LLP & PBI, A Survey of Pro Bono Practices and Opportunities in 71 Jurisdictions, Prepared by Latham & Watkins LLP for the Pro Bono Institute 300 (2012) [hereinafter Latham & Watkins Survey 2012].

38. Thomson Reuters Foundation & Latham & Watkins LLP, Global Corporate Pro Bono Map, Survey of Pro Bono Practices and Regulations for Legal Departments 113 (2017).

39. Nonetheless, value-added tax (VAT) is not applicable to the delivery of pro bono services by law firms. See the binding decisions from the General Directorate of Taxes (DGT) V236909, of October 26, 2009, and V0185-04, of October 23, 2004. The 2009 decision was obtained as a result of a consultation led by an ad hoc working group of Spanish law

firms (the Group of Seven) organized at the behest of the Cyrus R. Vance Center for International Justice and initially convened by Andres Gil of Davis Polk & Wardwell and S. Todd Crider of Simpson Thacher & Bartlett.

40. TrustLaw Index, *supra* note 12, at K20.

41. María Del Carmen Barranco Avilés , Rafael De Asís Roig & Alberto Iglesias Garzón , Madrid City Bar, Estudio Sobre el Pro Bono en la Comunidad de Madrid [Pro Bono Study on the Madrid Region] 41 (2014) [hereinafter Madrid Pro Bono Study].

42. *Id.* at 43.

43. The "Movement for Access to Justice" was pivotal to the inclusion of access to justice as a right guaranteed in the Spanish Constitution of 1978 because it was part of a broader ideological and political movement to expand the role of the state to include free legal assistance. The establishment of free legal assistance in other European countries helped domestic Spanish groups seeking to improve access to justice in Spain and also allowed them to draw from a variety of structures and models. As such, due to mounting influence from a global movement focused on improving access to justice, foundational ideas about the state as the sole guarantor of legal assistance took hold in Spain. *See* Madrid Pro Bono Study, *supra* note 41, at 49–52.

44. *Id.* at 47–49, 51.

45. C.E. art. 24 & art. 119, B.O.E. n. 311, Dec. 29, 1978, *expanded by* Law of Free Legal Assistance (B.O.E. 1996, 11), *further modified by* Law of 18 July 2005 to Amend the Law of 10 January 1996 (B.O.E. 2005, 171), *and further modified by* Law of 21 June 2017 to Amend the Law of 10 January 1996 (B.O.E. 2017, 148).

46. For more information on the French human rights model, which combines individualism with the protection of the state, see generally Maurizio Fioravanti, Los Derechos Fundamentales: Apuntes de la Historia de las Constituciones [Fundamental Rights: Notes on the History of the Constitutions] (Manuel Martínez Neira trans., Trotta, 2003) (1996).

47. "The civil society in Spain is tremendously supportive and caring. People in Spain have always been involved in voluntary activities and, as lawyers started joining the labor market, they looked for ways to incorporate their vocation into their profession. Solidarity moved us to explore international experiences in formalizing pro bono practice." Email interview with Javier Carvajal, Partner, Pérez-Llorca (then working at Cuatrecasas) (Sept. 9, 2018).

48. Telephone interview with Javier Carvajal, Partner, Pérez-Llorca (then working at Cuatrecasas) (Sept. 7, 2018). The Cuatrecasas team included corporate partners Javier Villasante and Javier Carvajal (then at Cuatrecasas).

49. *La Firma, Pro Bono*, CUATRECASAS, http://cuatrecasas.com/es/firma/ (last visited Sept. 6, 2018).
50. *La Fundación, Qué Hacemos, Origen*, FUNDACIÓN PROFESOR URÍA, www.fundacionprofesoruria.org/la-fundacion/que-hacemos.html (last visited Sept. 11. 2018). Uria partner Rafael Vargas visited New York and the Vance Center in 2005 as part of the design of *Fundación Profesor Uria's* pro bono component.
51. *La Fundación, Quiénes Somos, Fundadores*, FUNDACIÓN FERNANDO POMBO, www.fundacionpombo.org/fundadores/ (last visited Sept. 6, 2018).
52. This working group, convened by the Vance Center, included CMS Albiñana & Suárez de Lezo, Cuatrecasas, Garrigues, Gómez-Acebo & Pombo, Pérez-Llorca, Ramón y Cajal and Uría Menéndez, as well as Andrés Gil, then partner at Davis Polk & Wardwell, and Todd Crider, partner at Simpson Thacher & Bartlett LLP and member of the Vance Center executive committee. Telephone interview with Javier Carvajal, Partner, Pérez-Llorca (then working at Cuatrecasas) (Sept. 7, 2018).
53. In 2006, three universities established legal clinics for the first time in Spanish history: the University of Barcelona (*Clínica jurídica universitaria Dret al Dret de la Universidad de Barcelona*), the University of Valencia, and the University Rovira i Virgili (*Centro de Estudios de Derecho Ambiental de Tarragona de la Universitat Rovira i Virgili*).
54. Law on Access to the Professions of Lawyer and Attorney of the Courts (B.O.E. 2006, 260), *modified by* Royal Decree Law of Mediation in Civil and Commercial Matters (B.O.E. 2012, 56).
55. LATHAM & WATKINS LLP & PBI, A SURVEY OF PRO BONO PRACTICES AND OPPORTUNITIES IN 84 JURISDICTIONS, PREPARED BY LATHAM & WATKINS LLP FOR THE PRO BONO INSTITUTE 615 (2016) [hereinafter LATHAM & WATKINS SURVEY 2016].
56. Information about the CRSA is available on its website: *CRSA*, CENTRO DE RESPONSIBILIDAD SOCIAL DE LA ABOGACÍA, http://crsa.icam.es/web3/cache/CRSA_crsa.html (last visited Sept. 20, 2020).
57. As Carmen Pombo, director of the Fernando Pombo Foundation, explained in the first Informative Day on Pro Bono Advocacy. *Jornada Divulgativa de la Abogacía "Pro Bono"* [*Informative Day on Pro Bono Advocacy*], CONSEJO GENERAL DE LA ABOGACÍA ESPAÑOLA, www.formacionabogacia.es/course/view.php?id=134 (last visited Apr. 29, 2019).
58. Email interview with Javier Carvajal, Partner, Pérez-Llorca (at the time working at Cuatrecasas) (Sept. 9, 2018).
59. Information about past forums is available on the PILnet website: *Past Forums*, PILNET, www.pilnet.org/our-events/past-forums/ (last visited Sept. 20, 2020).
60. MADRID PRO BONO STUDY, *supra* note 41, at 17.

61. LATHAM & WATKINS SURVEY 2012, *supra* note 37, at 613.
62. Probonos.net was created thanks to the financial assistance of *Fundación Aranzadi Lex Nova. See Únete al Pro Bono y Ayuda a ONG con Tus Conocimientos Profesionales*, PROBONOS.NET, https://legal.probonos.net/post/2006/ac%C3%A9rcate-al-mundo-del-pro-bono-con-fundaci%C3%B3n-aranzadi-lex-nova (last visited Sept. 6, 2018). Subsequently, the funding of Probonos.net has come, in large part, through collaboration with Wolters Kluwer. *See Wolters Kluwer y Fundación Hazloposible Firman un Convenio para Impulsar el Pro Bono Legal en España*, PROBONOS.NET, https://legal.probonos.net/post/4035/wolters-kluwer-y-fundaci%C3%B3n-hazloposible-firman-un-convenio-para-impulsar-el-pro-bono-legal-en-espa%C3%B1a (last visited Sept. 6, 2018).
63. PROBONOS.NET, https://legal.probonos.net/ (last visited Apr. 16, 2015).
64. *Conexión ProBono*, FUNDACIÓN ARANZADI LEX NOVA, www.fundacionlexnova.org/probonolegal/probonolegal1.asp (last visited Apr. 16, 2015).
65. As noted in the press release for the event where these platforms were inaugurated on Dec. 18, 2014: www.legaltoday.com/actualidad/probono/fundacion-aranzadi-lex-nova-apoya-el-nacimiento-de-la-primera-plataforma-online-de-coordinacion-de-pro-bono-legal-en-espana (last visited Apr. 29, 2019).
66. *Inicio, Compromiso, Garrigues y la Sociedad, Trabajo Pro Bono*, GARRIGUES, www.garrigues.com/es_ES/commitment/garrigues-y-la-sociedad/trabajo-pro-bono (last visited Sept. 11, 2018).
67. Now, regions like Baleares, Barcelona, Madrid, Málaga, and Valencia have bar associations with well-developed pro bono programs, and their pro bono volunteers are sometimes shared with their legal aid systems. The Madrid Bar's CRSA, for instance, runs a registry of lawyers that have expressed interest in doing pro bono work and connecting them with NGOs that need help. This is not necessarily the case in other Spanish regions.
68. These university legal clinics focus on six types of legal services and activities: legal aid (*asistencia jurídica*), community legal services (*servicios jurídicos comunitarios*), legal representation services (*servicios jurídicos de representación*), street law, alternative dispute resolution, and public interest litigation (*litigación o abogacía de interés público*). DIEGO BLÁZQUEZ MARTÍN, PATRICIA CUENCA GÓMEZ & ALBERTO IGLESIAS GARZÓN, MADRID CITY BAR, GUÍA SOBRE COMO CREAR, ORGANIZAR, GESTIONAR Y CONDUCIR UNA CLÍNICA JURÍDICA EN UNA FACULTAD DE DERECHO [GUIDE ON HOW TO CREATE, ORGANIZE, MANAGE, AND CONDUCT A LEGAL CLINIC AT A LAW SCHOOL] 16 (2014).
69. The legal clinic at European University of Madrid is an example of a general legal clinic, whereas the legal clinic at University of Valladolid is specialized in disabilities, immigration, foreign affairs, and human

rights matters. More information about this university's clinic is available on its website. *Clínicas Jurídicas*, CLÍNICA JURÍDICA DE LA UNIVERSIDAD DE VALLADOLID, http://clinicajuridica.sitios.uva.es/?q=node/1 (last visited Sept. 20, 2020).

70. Marian Martínez, *La Clínica Jurídica Defiende el Modelo Pro Bono para que los Abogados Cojan Experiencia*, LANUEVAESPAÑA.COM, Dec. 12, 2016, www.lne.es/asturias/2016/12/02/clinica-juridica-defiende-modelo-pro/2022164.html (last visited Sept. 20, 2020).
71. While not all universities have pro bono programs, some universities have successfully partnered with NGOs to create pro bono programs. For example, the Fernando Pombo Foundation has partnered with the University Carlos III of Madrid to create a free legal clinic aimed at providing assistance to people who suffer from chronic fatigue syndrome and multiple chemical sensitivities. LATHAM & WATKINS SURVEY 2012, *supra* note 37, at 620.
72. DELOITTE, THE 2017 DELOITTE MILLENNIAL SURVEY 7 (Jan. 2017), www2.deloitte.com/global/en/pages/about-deloitte/articles/millennialsurvey.html(last visited Sept. 20, 2020).
73. MCI Spain, *El 76% de los Millenials Cree que su Negocio Ha de Tener un Impacto Social*, HOSTELTUR.COM (July 19, 2017), www.hosteltur.com/comunidad/nota/019582_el-76-de-los-millenials-cree-que-su-negocio-ha-de-tener-un-impacto-social.html (last visited Sept. 20, 2020).
74. TRUSTLAW INDEX, *supra* note 12, at K20.
75. Deborah L. Rhode, *Profits and Professionalism*, 33 FORDHAM URBAN L.J. 49, 61 (2005).
76. Esther F. Lardent, *Pro Bono Work Is Good for Business*, NAT'L L.J., Feb. 19, 2001, at B20.
77. *Bringing Access to Justice*, LATIN LAW. (Mar. 13, 2012), http://latinlawyer.com/features/article/43161/bringing-access-justice/ (last visited Sept. 20, 2020). Another factor in promoting pro bono with companies and affecting the interest of clients in the pro bono efforts of law firms are CSR programs. More study is required to evaluate the relationship between pro bono and CSR, but these are likely mutually reinforcing.
78. FUNDACIÓN ARANZADI LEX NOVA, INFORME SOBRE CONOCIMIENTO Y PARTICIPACIÓN EN ACTIVIDADES PRO BONO POR PARTE DE ONGS ESPAÑOLAS 2014 [REPORT ON KNOWLEDGE AND INVOLVEMENT IN PRO BONO ACTIVITIES BY SPANISH NGOS 2014] 36 (2015).
79. STUDY ON THE LEGAL NEEDS OF NGOS IN SPAIN, *supra* note 35, at 3.
80. FUNDACIÓN HAZLOPOSIBLE, MEMORIA 2015: CANALIZANDO EL TALENTO HACIA CAUSAS SOCIALES CON IMPACTO [2015 ANNUAL REPORT: CHANNELING THE TALENT TOWARDS SOCIAL CAUSES WITH IMPACT] 12 (2015), www.hazloposible.org/wp-content/uploads/2016/11/MEMORIA-HAZLOPOSIBLE-2015.pdf (last visited Sept. 20, 2020).

81. FUNDACIÓN HAZLOPOSIBLE, MEMORIA 2016: ACOMPAÑÁNDOTE EN EL CAMINO PARA MEJORAR EL MUNDO [ANNUAL REPORT 2016, SUPPORTING YOU TO IMPROVE THE WORLD] 17 (2016), https://www.hazloposible.org/wp-content/uploads/2017/07/hlpmemoriaWEB2016.pdf (last visited Sept. 20, 2020). As noted above, the services provided through this online resource are focused on NGO "clients" and are not limited to legal services.
82. TRUSTLAW INDEX, *supra* note 12, at K20.
83. STUDY ON THE LEGAL NEEDS OF NGOS IN SPAIN, *supra* note 35, at 8.
84. *Id.* at 9.
85. *Id.* at 10.
86. Telephone interview with Lucía de los Reyes Losada, Volunteer, Pueblos Unidos (Aug. 1, 2017).
87. STUDY ON THE LEGAL NEEDS OF NGOS IN SPAIN, *supra* note 35, at 9.
88. Telephone interview with Cristina Manzanedo, Migration Program Coordinator, Entreculturas (July 27, 2017).
89. Email interview with Fabio de Sá e Silva, coeditor of this book (Feb. 15, 2017). We note that the representatives were two of the coauthors, S. Todd Crider, member of the executive committee of the Vance Center (and founding chair), and Leire Larracoechea San Sebastián, at the time employed by the Vance Center. The Vance Center is an international pro bono legal services and human rights organization imbedded in the New York City Bar Association.
90. We refer to "pro bono actors" in general terms. However, during the trip to Madrid, the Vance Center met with only a selection of representatives of Spanish and international law firms, universities, NGOs, and the Madrid Bar Association.
91. Latin Lawyer & Vance Center, *The Latin Lawyer-Vance Center Pro Bono Survey 2016*, 15 LATIN LAW., Nov. 2016, at 6 [hereinafter *Latin Lawyer & Vance Center Survey 2016*].
92. During the visit, the delegation met with the president of the New York City Bar Association, the City Bar Justice Center, pro bono partners, and coordinators of international law firms, NGOs, local and international clearinghouses, and the Vance Center committee and staff.
93. The working group was initially formed by Clifford Chance, Cuatrecasas, Pérez-Llorca and Ramón y Cajal, and was coordinated by the Vance Center by Leire Larracoechea. As the work progressed, and as *Fundación Pro Bono España* began taking shape, various law firms joined the working group, as described in this chapter.
94. The Council represents the lawyers' profession at a national level. It supervises the Spanish bar, which, in turn, organizes and manages the Spanish legal aid system. *See* LATHAM & WATKINS SURVEY 2016, *supra* note 55, at 616.

95. Consejo General de la Abogacía Española, Abogacía 2020 Soluciones 50 (2017–2020) [hereinafter Legal Profession 2020 Solutions (2017–2020)].
96. *Jornada Divulgativa de la Abogacía "Pro Bono"* [*Informative Day on Pro Bono Advocacy*], Consejo General De La Abogacía Española (Feb. 2018), www.formacionabogacia.es/course/view.php?id=134 (last visited Apr. 29, 2019).
97. C.E. art. 119, B.O.E. n. 311, Dec. 29, 1978, *expanded by* Law of Free Legal Assistance (B.O.E. 1996, 11), *further modified by* Law of 18 July 2005 to Amend the Law of 10 January 1996 (B.O.E. 2005, 171), *and further modified by* Law of 21 June 2017 to Amend the Law of 10 January 1996 (B.O.E. 2017, 148).
98. *See* Law of Free Legal Assistance art. 3 (B.O.E. 1996, 11), *further modified by* Law of 18 July 2005 to Amend the Law of 10 January 1996 (B.O.E. 2005, 171), *and further modified by* Law of 21 June 2017 to Amend the Law of 10 January 1996 (B.O.E. 2017, 148).
99. Judicare is a term that refers to a legal aid system in which the government pays private lawyers per case to provide legal assistance to indigent individuals.
100. For an overview of services provided, see *Solicitar Justicia Gratuita*, Abogacía Española Consejo General, www.abogacia.es/2012/07/04/servicios-de-orientacion-juridica-gratuita/ (last visited Sept. 20, 2020).
101. *See* Law of Free Legal Assistance art. 3 (B.O.E. 1996, 11), *further modified by* Law of 18 July 2005 to Amend the Law of 10 January 1996 (B.O.E. 2005, 171), *and further modified by* Law of 21 June 2017 to Amend the Law of 10 January 1996 (B.O.E. 2017, 148).
102. Latham & Watkins Survey 2012, *supra* note 37, at 616.
103. *See* Law of Free Legal Assistance art. 2 (B.O.E. 1996, 11), *further modified by* Law of 18 July 2005 to Amend the Law of 10 January 1996 (B.O.E. 2005, 171), *and further modified by* Law of 21 June 2017 to Amend the Law of 10 January 1996 (B.O.E. 2017, 148).
104. As noted, *supra* note 9, reductions in the public funding to the legal aid system ranged from 20 percent to 40 percent, depending on the Spanish region.
105. The Madrid Bar Association reached an agreement with the Madrid Government in which, by 2019, the reduction of 20 percent in the salary of the legal aid lawyers should be completely recovered. Email interview with María Sol Cuevas Gama, Director, Legal Aid Bar and Legal Guidance Services, Madrid Bar Association (Aug. 3, 2017).
106. Latham & Watkins Survey 2016, *supra* note 55, at 617.
107. Interview with María Concepción Molina, Director of Legal Clinics, ICADE-Universidad Pontificia Comillas (May 4, 2017).
108. The right to counsel in the Sixth Amendment of the US Constitution has been interpreted to require the state to provide legal representation to indigent criminal defendants. However, some legal service providers do receive funding from the Legal Services Corporation (LSC), an

independent nonprofit organization that was established by the US Congress in 1974, to provide civil legal aid. The funds the LSC receives are subject to the congressional budget and thus vary. Moreover, despite LSC funding, roughly half of needy individuals who approach LSC-funded legal services providers for help are turned away because the providers lack sufficient resources to meet demand. *See* LEGAL SERVICES CORP., DOCUMENTING THE JUSTICE GAP IN AMERICA: THE CURRENT UNMET CIVIL LEGAL NEEDS OF LOW-INCOME AMERICANS 8 (2007), www.lsc.gov/sites/default/files/LSC/images/justicegap.pdf (last visited Aug. 16, 2017). As a result of these factors and limitations, LSC has long developed and promoted programs to engage pro bono counsel as a complement to its work.

109. "Although the tradition of pro bono practice has deep roots in Europe, beginning in ancient and medieval Europe, by the 20th century, the prevalence of state-sponsored legal aid systems became the norm in Europe. Although the introduction of state-sponsored legal aid across Europe was a great achievement in most respects and did much to increase access to justice, it unfortunately also had the effect of obliterating the tradition of pro bono among large parts of the European legal professions." Email interview with Lamin Khadar, Pro Bono Associate, DLA Piper, and Cofounder, The Good Lobby (Feb. 13, 2017); *see also* MADRID PRO BONO STUDY, *supra* note 41, at 15.

110. *See* Order of 3 June 1997 art. 1 (B.O.E. 1997, 144) (establishing the minimum general training and specialization requirements necessary to provide free legal assistance), *modified by* Law on Access to the Professions of Lawyer and Attorney of the Courts (B.O.E. 2006, 260), *further modified by* Royal Decree Law of 5 March 2012 (B.O.E. 2012, 56).

111. Although not currently contemplated, it may be possible, for example, to develop in collaboration with the state-funded legal services a program by which, for special cases that may require greater resources than are available to the legal aid private practitioner, pro bono counsel will be provided in a complementary role as co-counsel. This model would need to assure that the fee-earning opportunities for the private lawyer performing state-funded legal services remained, while providing greater resources for potentially significant cases. Any such program should be developed with the support of the local bar and state-supported legal services system.

112. C.E. ART. 24, B.O.E. n. 311, Dec. 29, 1978.

113. MADRID PRO BONO STUDY, *supra* note 41, at 60.

114. Telephone interview with Alberto Iglesias Garzón, then-Program Director, Bartolomé de las Casas Human Rights Institute, Charles III University of Madrid (Feb. 20, 2015).

115. *See* Convention Relating to the Status of Refugees, July 28, 1951, 189 U.N.T.S. 150; Protocol Relating to the Status of Refugees, Jan. 31, 1967, 19 U.S.T. 6223, 606 U.N.T.S. 267.

116. Spain, for example, provides for subsidiary protection for those who may not qualify as Convention refugees but are still deserving of international protection. *See* Law Regulating the Right to Asylum and International Protection art. 4 (B.O.E. 2009, 263).
117. Law Regulating the Right to Asylum and International Protection art. 16 (B.O.E. 2009, 263).
118. *Id.* at art. 18.
119. Interview with Marcelo Belgrano and Mariano Calleja, Coordinating Attorneys, Immigration Section, Bar Association of Madrid (Mar. 15, 2017).
120. *Id.*
121. *Id.*
122. Ilustre Colegio de Abogados de Madrid, Turno de Extranjería: Memoria Año 2016 [Madrid Bar Association, Immigration Section of the Legal Aid Bar: 2016 Memorandum] (on file with author).
123. Panel on Fundamental Rights Violations of Asylum Seekers in Light of the "Refugee Crisis" and Ways to Reestablish These Rights, II Congreso de la Abogacía Madrileña [Second Conference on the Madrid Legal Profession], held by Ilustre Colegio de Abogados de Madrid [Madrid Bar Association] (Apr. 25, 2017).
124. Defensor del Pueblo, Estudio sobre el Asilo en España: La Protección Internacional y Los Recursos del Sistema de Acogida [Office of the Ombudsman, Study on Asylum in Spain: International Protection and Resources of the Reception System] 59 (2016), www.defensordelpueblo.es/wp-content/uploads/2016/07/Asilo_en_España_2016.pdf (last visited Sept. 20, 2020).
125. In fact, in the practice guide it published in partnership with the Madrid Bar Association, the United Nations High Commissioner for Refugees in Spain (La Agencia de la ONU para los Refugiados, or ACNUR) recommends lawyers not to be passive throughout the asylum application process but to actively participate during the interview; the asylum practice guide published by ACNUR and the Spanish Lawyers Foundation (Fundación Abogacía Española) also recommends lawyers to have an active presence and presents best practices and strategies for proper representation, including how to submit supplementary written materials. *See* ACNUR & Fundación Abogacía Española, La Protección Internacional de los Solicitantes de Asilo: Guía Práctica para la abogacía [Practice Guide for the Legal Profession on the Subject of International Protection for Asylum Seekers] (2017), www.abogacia.es/wp-content/uploads/2017/07/VERSION-FINAL-GUIA-PROTECCION-INTERNACIONAL-SOLICITANTES-DE-ASILO.pdf (last visited Sept. 20, 2020); ACNUR & ICAM; Guía de Actuación en la Asistencia Jurídica a Solicitantes de Protección Internacional [The Legal Assistance

PRACTICE GUIDE FOR ASYLUM SEEKERS: IN THE CONTEXT OF LAW 12/2009 OF OCTOBER 30, REGULATING THE RIGHT TO ASYLUM AND SUBSIDIARY PROTECTION] 9 (2011), www.acnur.org/t3/fileadmin/Documentos/Publicaciones/2011/8257.pdf (last visited Sept. 20, 2020).

126. EUROPEAN COUNCIL ON REFUGEES AND EXILES,ECRE/ELENA SURVEY ON LEGAL AID FOR ASYLUM SEEKERS IN EUROPE 37 (2010), www.refworld.org/docid/4d243cb42.html (last visited Sept. 20, 2020).

127. Interview with Marta García, Head of International Protection, ACNUR (July 19, 2017).

128. While this collaborative pro bono project was referred to as Project Raíces by the pro bono lawyers at Jones Day and Project Jones Day by the ICADE legal clinic, we refer to it as Project Jones Day, as this was the name used to introduce the pro bono collaboration to the authors of this chapter during their interview with the ICADE legal clinic to learn more about clinical education and pro bono in Spain.

129. While Project Jones Day started with two unaccompanied minor clients, one more client has since been added to the strategic litigation project. Email from Jesús Gimeno (Jan. 10, 2018).

130. Isabel Diez Velasco, *Clínica Jurídica y Litigación Estratégica: Nuevas Formas de Enseñar y Ejercer el Derecho – Un Caso de la Clínica Jurídica ICADE* [Legal Clinics and Strategic Litigation: New Forms of Teaching and Practicing Law – the Case of ICADE Legal Clinic] 45 (2017) (unpublished manuscript) (on file at ICADE and with the author).

131. *Id.*

132. *Id.*

133. Interview with Jesús Gimeno, Of Counsel, Jones Day Madrid; Jesús Merino, Associate; Jones Day Madrid; and María Concepción Molina, Director of Legal Clinics, ICADE–Universidad Pontificia Comillas (May 12, 2017).

134. Velasco, *supra* note 130, at 45–46.

135. The last update the authors received regarding this project was that Jesús Gimeno, who is now affiliated with a new law firm, will be continuing to collaborate with the Raíces Foundation with the original clients, and that Jones Day will be taking on new clients in collaboration with the ICADE legal clinic. Email from Gail Harvey (June 26, 2018).

136. Project Jones Day will continue for another year with another group of students, and the hope is to continue the following year as well. Email from Jesús Gimeno (Jan. 10, 2018).

137. Interview with María Concepción Molina, Director of Legal Clinics, ICADE–Universidad Pontificia Comillas (June 28, 2017).

138. Michael D. Goldhaber, *A World of Good*, 34 AM. LAW. 67 (2012).

139. Harvard Law School Center on the Legal Profession, *Global Pro Bono Conference: Building Pro Bono Around the World*, YOUTUBE (June 9, 2014),

www.youtube.com/watch?v=eqF9U9QIsuE (last visited Sept. 20, 2020) (panel at Harvard Law School's Globalization and Lawyering in Emerging Economies project, held on Apr. 18, 2014).

140. *Id.*

141. Luis Felipe Gamboa Lozada, Co-Opetition as a Challenge for Network Development: The Case of a Pro Bono Clearinghouse in the Legal Industry in Peru 10 (Aug. 2016) (on file with author) [hereinafter Co-Opetition].

142. Joel F. Handler, *Public Interest Law Firms in the United States*, *in* ACCESS TO JUSTICE: EMERGING ISSUES AND PERSPECTIVES 423 (Mauro Cappelletti & Bryant Garth eds., 1978).

143. *See* European Convention on Human Rights, *supra* note 11; Airey v. Ireland, 32 Eur. Ct. HR (1979); UNDP AND UNDOC GLOBAL STUDY ON LEGAL AID: GLOBAL REPORT 26 (2016), www.unodc.org/documents/justice-and-prison-reform/LegalAid/Global-Study-on-Legal-Aid_Report01.pdf (last visited Sept. 20, 2020).

144. Carlos García-León, *La Pugna de los Grandes Bufetes Españoles por Latinoamérica*, EXPANSIÓN (Sept. 17, 2014), www.expansion.com/2014/09/16/juridico/1410885373.html (last visited Sept. 20, 2020).

145. *Latin Lawyer & Vance Center Survey 2016*, *supra* note 91, at 3.

146. PRO BONO INSTITUTE, GLOBAL DUE DILIGENCE MANUAL: NAVIGATING THE WORLD OF PRO BONO 7 (2016) [hereinafter DUE DILIGENCE MANUAL].

147. Some advocacy organizations also incorporate clearinghouse functions such as matchmaking and training as part of their strategy to advance their missions. The main difference between these organizations and the pro bono clearinghouses that are the focus of this section is that pro bono development is itself a goal for pro bono clearinghouses – more than a tool to achieve advocacy goals, as is the case for advocacy organizations. However, as both pro bono clearinghouses and advocacy organizations with clearinghouse-like functions innovate and evolve, the two forms are increasingly converging. This chapter focuses on development of the clearinghouse side of this dynamic; for an examination of the role of advocacy organizations with clearinghouse-like functions in pro bono development in the United States, see Cummings, *The Politics of Pro Bono*, *supra* note 17, at 45–55; *see also supra* note 19.

148. *Bringing Access to Justice*, *supra* note 77.

149. PRO BONO CLEARINGHOUSE MANUAL, *supra* note 21, at 19.

150. Raymond L. Paquin & Jennifer Howard-Grenville, *Blind Dates and Arranged Marriages: Longitudinal Processes of Network Orchestration*, 34 ORG. STUD. 1623, 1647 (2013).

151. Co-Opetition, *supra* note 141, at 16.

152. *Bringing Access to Justice*, *supra* note 77.

153. Latin Lawyer & Vance Center, *The Latin Lawyer–Vance Center Pro Bono Survey 2014*, 13 LATIN LAW., Nov. 2014, at 15, www.vancecenter.org/vancecenter/images/stories/vancecenter/pro%20bono%20sur

vey%202014.pdf (last visited Sept. 20, 2020) [hereinafter *Latin Lawyer & Vance Center Survey 2014*].

154. *Id.* at 14.
155. Co-Opetition, *supra* note 141, at 16.
156. *Id.*
157. DUE DILIGENCE MANUAL, *supra* note 146, at 4.
158. FUNDACIÓN ARANZADI LEX NOVA, CONEXIÓN PRO BONO: GUÍA PARA LA PRÁCTICA DEL VOLUNTARIADO JURÍDICO [PRO BONO CONNECTION: GUIDE FOR LEGAL VOLUNTEERISM] (2014).
159. Email interview with Marieanne McKeown, Director of Global Pro Bono, PILnet (Aug. 18, 2017).
160. PRO BONO CLEARINGHOUSE MANUAL, *supra* note 21, at 41.
161. This database was developed hand in hand with the Spanish company VLex.
162. DUE DILIGENCE MANUAL, *supra* note 146, at 4.
163. Karen A. Lash, *Pitching Pro Bono: Getting to First Base with the "Big Firm,"* 2 DEPAUL J. SOC. JUST. 141, 166 (2008).
164. DUE DILIGENCE MANUAL, *supra* note 146, at 5.
165. Michael D. Goldhaber, *A New Yardstick for International Pro Bono*, AMERICAN LAW. (June 30, 2014), www.law.com/americanlawyer/almID/1202660208407/a-new-yardstick-for-international-pro-bono/ (last visited Sept. 18, 2020).
166. Telephone interview with Jessica Lauredan, Assistant Director of Pro Bono Programs, New York Lawyers for the Public Interest (NYLPI) (Mar. 27, 2015).
167. *Bringing Access to Justice*, *supra* note 77.
168. Aware of the success that the clearinghouse model was having in the United States, in the early 2000s the Vance Center partnered with its Latin American counterparts to lead the institutionalization of pro bono in the Americas. At that time, this region was already engaged in some pro bono, but it was normally done on an ad hoc basis, without any coordination or infrastructure. *See Bringing Access to Justice*, *supra* note 77. With a view to reinforcing a nascent pro bono culture, the Vance Center, led by one of its founders and first executive director Joan Vermeulen (previously a founder and executive director of New York Lawyers for the Public Interest), organized three consecutive conferences that took place in Buenos Aires (2001), Santiago de Chile (2002), and São Paolo (2003). From these, the so-called Pro Bono Movement emerged in Latin America. Coorganized by each host country's clearinghouse with the Vance Center, at each conference several law firms, bar associations, universities, and NGOs hailing from across the Americas met to exchange best practices and discuss how to advance pro bono. These conferences had a great impact on the institutionalization of pro bono work and helped create professional relationships between the private sector and civil society, promoting pro bono assistance as a way to help address the problem of access to justice in Latin America. The Pro Bono Chain would no longer be a

vague concept; its underlying idea that "pro bono work is about working together" from different sectors of the legal community was reinforced. *See* Emily Russell, *Care for the Community*, LATIN LAW., Dec./Jan. 2003, at 32. The 2005 Conference "Strategy Summit for the Americas: The Crisis in Access to Justice" proved to be a catalyst in this collaborative and multijurisdictional movement. *See Bringing Access to Justice*, *supra* note 77. Five years after the start of the Pro Bono Movement, in December 2015, more than sixty representatives from more than eight countries met in New York at the New York City Bar Association and examined the movement's contribution to improving access to justice and developed an action plan to promote pro bono throughout the Americas. A committee was appointed to draft the eagerly awaited Pro Bono Declaration for the Americas (PBDA). *See* PRO BONO DECLARATION FOR THE AMERICAS, CYRUS R. VANCE CENTER FOR INTERNATIONAL JUSTICE, www.vancecenter.org/vancecenter/images/stories/vancecenter/english.pdf (last visited Aug. 13, 2017). Coming into effect from January 2008, the PBDA, of which the Vance Center is the repository, is considered the cornerstone in the institutionalization of legal pro bono in the region. Its signatories commit to providing an average of 20 hours of pro bono services per lawyer per year. Currently, more than 540 law firms, bar associations, law schools, and other organizations have made this commitment.

169. *Bringing Access to Justice*, *supra* note 77.
170. *Latin Lawyer & Vance Center Survey 2014*, *supra* note 153, at 14.
171. The Pro Bono Network of the Americas, which is headed by the Fundación Pro Bono Chile and the Vance Center, is an informal collaborative mechanism; it has no legal entity.
172. RED PRO BONO INTERNACIONAL, www.redprobono.org (last visited Apr. 16, 2015).
173. In 2017, *Pro Bono Italia*'s membership was around 300 individuals, with around 60 percent from law firms, and the remaining 40 percent from NGOs, civil society organizations, and legal clinics. Telephone interview with Giovanni Carotenuto, Chair, *Pro Bono Italia* (July 31, 2017).
174. *See Italian Pro Bono Definition*, PILNET AND PRO BONO ITALIA, www.pilnet.org/images/Pro_Bono_Publico.pdf (last visited Aug. 31, 2017).
175. Email interview with Giovanni Carotenuto, Chair, *Pro Bono Italia* (July 6, 2018).
176. FPB has been widely seen as an example of a successful pro bono clearinghouse. Marieke Breijer, *Grants to Share*, LATIN LAW. (Nov. 3, 2011), https://latinlawyer.com/article/1091708/grants-to-share (last visited Sept. 18, 2020).
177. *Misión y Objetivos*, FUNDACIÓN PRO BONO CHILE, www.probono.cl/fundacion/mision/ (last visited Apr. 16, 2014).

178. Email interview with Tamara Gutiérrez, Former Director, Transparency and International Area, *Fundación Pro Bono* (Mar. 12, 2015).
179. Telephone interview with Carolina Contreras, Executive Director, *Fundación Pro Bono Chile* (Aug. 3, 2017).
180. An example of this is the Pro Bono Aliance, the clearinghouse of the Czech Republic. PRO BONO ALIANCE, www.probonoaliance.cz/en/ (last visited Sept. 20, 2020).
181. *Latin Lawyer & Vance Center Survey 2014*, *supra* note 153, at 15.
182. Interview with Fabio de Sá e Silva, Coeditor of this book and Research Fellow, Center on the Legal Profession, Harvard Law School (Feb. 23, 2015).
183. Latin Lawyer & Vance Center, *The Latin Lawyer-Vance Center Pro Bono Survey 2015*, 14 LATIN LAW., Nov. 2015, at 13.
184. Marcos Fuchs, IPB's executive director since its beginning, had been lobbying to allow attorneys to provide free legal services and working for the liberalization of the pro bono practice in Brazil. In recognition of such work, he has received several international awards, including the International Bar Association's Pro Bono Award and Latin Lawyer's Pro Bono Lawyer of the Year. *Marcos Fuchs Wins Pro Bono Award from IBA*, LATIN LAW. (OCT. 6, 2015), http://latinlawyer.com/article/1097565/marcos-fuchs-wins-pro-bono-award-from-iba (last visited Sept. 20, 2020).
185. This co-counseling model raises issues of malpractice insurance and ethics that should be carefully considered under the law and regulations of the relevant jurisdiction.
186. Telephone interview with Lara Talsma, Project Coordinator, Pro Bono Connect (July 25, 2017).
187. Lindsay Fortado, *Legal Teams Rally to Defend the Rule of Law*, FIN. TIMES (June 20, 2017), www.ft.com/content/dbea4f34-455f-11e7-8d27-59b4dd6296b8?mhq5j=e1 (last visited Sept. 20, 2020).
188. Interview with Marie-Claude Jean-Baptiste, Programs Director, Vance Center (Aug. 10, 2017).
189. In this case, the Vance Center acted as a necessary expert in a matter because it had the in-house expertise necessary to do so. In fact, for the workshop, no Vance Center Committee firm was involved. It is also important to note that no other law firm or organization had gone beyond the role of Afro-Colombian women as victims of the conflict to look at the active part they can play in the implementation of the peace agreement.
190. As noted in *supra* note 147, these issue-focused clearinghouses may, in some ways, look like advocacy organizations that employ clearing-house-like functions in support of their missions.
191. For more information on TrustLaw's Women's Rights Programme, see *Women's Rights*, THOMSON REUTERS FOUNDATION, www.trust.org/trustlaw/womens-rights/ (last visited Sept. 20, 2020).
192. KHADAR, *supra* note 23, at 48.

193. Cummings, *The Politics of Pro Bono*, *supra* note 17, at 148.
194. Garth Meintjes, *Public Interest Lawyers Need New Tools to Protect the Vulnerable*, OPENGLOBALRIGHTS (July 25, 2017), www.openglobalrights.org/public-interest-lawyers-need-new-tools-to-protect-the-vulnerable/?lang=English (last visited Aug. 30, 2017).
195. *Id.*
196. Interview with Garth Meintjes, President, PILnet (Aug. 17, 2017).
197. Harvard Law School Center on the Legal Profession, *Global Pro Bono: Private Lawyers for the Public Good*, YOUTUBE (June 9, 2014), www.youtube.com/watch?v=f5s4m_ouvWE (last visited Sept. 20, 2020) (panel at Harvard Law School's Globalization and Lawyering in Emerging Economies Project, held on Apr. 18, 2014).
198. PRO BONO INSTITUTE, REPORT ON THE LAW FIRM PRO BONO CHALLENGE 2013, at 11 (2014), www.probonoinst.org/wpps/wp-content/uploads/2013-Challenge-Report.pdf (last visited Sept. 20, 2020).
199. The founding law firms were: Allen & Overy, Andersen Tax & Legal, Arinsa, Ashurst, BLP Abogados, Bufete Barrilero y Asociados, Clifford Chance, Cuatrecasas, De Castro, Dentons, DLA Piper, Elzaburu, Ejaso ETL Global, Eversheds Sutherland Nicea, Garrigues, Huerta & Solana, King & Wood Mallesons, Latham & Watkins, Lean Abogados, MA Abogados, Pérez-Llorca, Ramón y Cajal Abogados, Roca Junyent, Rousaud Costas Durán, Sagardoy, Toda & Nel-lo, Watson, Farley & Williams, and White & Case. We note that, at the time of publication, one of our coauthors, Leire Larracoechea San Sebastián, is executive director and cofounder of *Fundación*.
200. Fundación Pro Bono España, Together We Make Integrated Pro Bono Possible for All 4 (May 2018)(unpublished executive summary) (on file with author) [hereinafter, Fundación Pro bono España Executive Summary].
201. *See supra* note 93.
202. Fundación Pro Bono España Executive Summary, *supra* note 200, at 2–4.
203. *Id.* at 4.
204. FUNDACIÓN PRO BONO ESPAÑA, BYLAWS art. 5 (2018), www.probonoespana.org/quienes-somos/somos-transparentes/ (last visited Sept. 20, 2020).
205. For critical commentary on *Fundación*, see, for example, Mariano Calleja, *De Oficio, Abogado*, CONFILEGAL.COM (July 21, 2018), https://confilegal.com/20180721-de-oficio-abogado/ (last visited Sept. 22, 2020).
206. TRUSTLAW INDEX, *supra* note 12, at K1.
207. The Raíces Foundation, for instance, was part of a broader project with the International Commission of Jurists (*Comisión Internacional de Juristas*). For more information, see *FAIR Project*, FUNDACIÓN RAÍCES, www.fundacionraices.org/?page_id=2578 (last visited Sept. 20, 2020).

208. *See Quienes Somos*, FERNANDO POMBO FOUNDATION, www.fundacionpombo.org/quienes-somos/ (last visited Sept. 20, 2020).
209. Interview with María Concepción Molina, Director of Legal Clinics, ICADE–Universidad Pontificia Comillas (May 4, 2017).
210. *See, e.g.*, CONSEJERÍA DE POLÍTICAS SOCIALES Y FAMILIA & FUNDACIÓN WOLTERS KLUWER, GUÍA PARA LA PRUEBA DE CONOCIMIENTOS CONSTITUCIONALES Y SOCIOCULTURALES DE ESPAÑA [GUIDE TO THE SPANISH CONSTITUTIONAL AND SOCIOCULTURAL KNOWLEDGE EXAM], http://web.icam.es/bucket/GUIA%20PARA%20LA%20PRUEBA%20DE%20CONOCIMIENTOS%20CONSTITUCIONALES.pdf (last visited Sept. 20, 2020).
211. Interview with Ruth de Miguel, Director, Center for the Legal Profession's Social Responsibility, Madrid Bar Association (May 23, 2017).
212. Interview with Marcelo Belgrano and Mariano Calleja, Coordinating Attorneys, Immigration Section, Bar Association of Madrid (Mar. 15, 2017).
213. *See, e.g.*, ACNUR & FUNDACIÓN ABOGACÍA ESPAÑOLA, *supra* note 125, at 9; ACNUR & ICAM, *supra* note 125.
214. Interview with Marcelo Belgrano and Mariano Calleja, Coordinating Attorneys, Immigration Section, Bar Association of Madrid (Mar. 15, 2017).

CHAPTER TEN

PRO BONO IN PORTUGAL

Susana Santos

INTRODUCTION

The aim of this chapter is to present the state of the art of the practice of pro bono in Portugal. To accomplish this, it is necessary to start with a definition. We use pro bono to define the offer of legal services promoted by lawyers for free to individuals or organizations that cannot afford to pay for the services and do not receive state legal aid. We exclude from the definition low bono practice, that is, paying a lower fee for legal services, since it is a more complex activity with multiple causes that distinguish it from the first.

The chapter is divided into three major topics. First, we describe the system of justice in Portugal, focusing on access to and promotion of legal assistance by the state, as well as the role of the Portuguese bar in establishing a network of lawyers, citizens, and the state. We will highlight the tensions arising as a consequence of, on one hand, the continuous demand for lawyers caused by traditional and new social problems and, on the other hand, the rapid expansion of the number of lawyers in the past decades, which compromised access to work for every lawyer.

Second, this chapter examines the first and only clearinghouse in Portugal, showing the difficulties of implementing a project in a country with a long tradition of dealing with pro bono in an individual way, as a matter of good conscience of the lawyer, along with a strong role for the state and bar in regulating access to justice.

We then move to the recent trend of institutionalizing pro bono in law firms, analyzing eight dimensions of the phenomenon in order to establish a comprehensive landscape of the Portuguese legal system.

Lastly, the conclusion highlights how Portuguese law firms, in particular large firms, are establishing special pro bono committees and nominating pro bono coordinators. This trend accompanies the implementation of corporate social responsibility (CSR) norms, more associated with the development of managerial practices and the importance of measuring and publicizing best practices, in which pro bono is an aspect of major concern. Large law firms appear a good choice to present the reality of pro bono in Portugal since they represent (as in other countries)[1] the major driver of pro bono implementation and make the largest contribution to its development.

RESEARCH DESIGN

Our research on the practice of pro bono in Portugal starts with a number of questions not answered in a previous study dedicated to professional socialization of young lawyers.[2] In that study, we focused on the pathways of integration of lawyers in large law firms, and one of the findings emphasized was the importance of doing pro bono as a mechanism developed by firms to provide young trainees with direct contact with clients while at the same time improving their capacities to deal with legal problems during their internships. In this phase, we collected nineteen biographical interviews with female and male lawyers aged between twenty-four and thirty-two years old. The analysis of the interviews allowed us to collect information about the practice of pro bono in large law firms and, simultaneously, to understand that to some extent the practice is understudied in the Portuguese context. Having this starting point, we decided to extend the range of questions in order to be able to present the state of the art of pro bono activities in Portugal, and to map pro bono's actors and institutions. We defined a set of questions: How is pro bono being developed in Portugal? Who are the main drivers? Which types of cases and clients are being selected? And finally, how are these activities crisscrossed by global networks of pro bono?

To accomplish this, we designed a mixed-methods strategy consisting of document analysis, both quantitative and qualitative, and interviews with all types of participants in the Portuguese legal system. Regarding institutions, we focused on documents produced by the

Ministry of Employment and Social Security, the Ministry of Justice, and the Portuguese Bar Association and its regional councils. These are the institutions responsible for the implementation and functioning of the legal aid system. Different types of documentation were analyzed, in particular, reports on legal aid, legislation, and statistics. We also interviewed the legal aid commissioner of the Lisbon regional council of the Portuguese bar, which is the most important council covering one-fourth of the lawyers providing legal aid in the country.[3] In the interview, we were provided information on the organization and structure of the bar as well as a comprehensive description of recent changes in the legal aid system, including the creation of new platforms of contact between individual lawyers and the state operated by the bar.

To advance our interview strategy, we also contacted law firms. Biographical interviews with young lawyers indicated the existence of different activities that combined legal pro bono with fundraising or community support, further described as CSR actions. To better understand the widespread nature of these practices, we collected information on 117 law firms in the country and created a database. From combining the data collected in the database with lawyers' interviews, we selected a subset of six firms to contact. We did interviews with four lawyers, two of them partners, all dedicated to promoting pro bono inside the firms. Along with the interviews, we collected and analyzed firm reports on CSR activities, covering the period from 2013 to 2018.

Pro bono activities bring together different actors, from lawyers to clients, nongovernmental organizations (NGOs), and clearinghouses. In the process of writing this chapter, we followed the creation of the first Portuguese clearinghouse, the Pro Bono Association (PBA), and had three follow-up interviews with the main founder and four volunteers. The NGOs that work closely with PBA are also important for understanding the broader scenario, but it was impossible to reach them. Nevertheless, the information gathered allowed us to categorize the types of NGOs working closely with PBA and law firms in the development of pro bono legal service for their beneficiaries.

Finally, we attempted to gather information, albeit not exhaustive, on what is happening with lawyers in solo practice. Two lines of research were conducted. The first was dedicated to exploring the importance of state legal aid in the professional practice of individual lawyers, combining statistical analysis with an interview with the legal aid commissioner of the bar. The second line tried to understand the reasons why solo practitioners are involved with pro bono, and if they combine it (or not) with state legal aid. To that end, we conducted five interviews with lawyers from different generations.

ACCESS TO AND PROMOTION OF LEGAL ASSISTANCE BY THE STATE

The origins of legal aid in Portugal, as in many European countries, has a long tradition. Legal historians discuss the importance of Roman law and its influence on the concepts of justice, rule of law, and the use of *ius commune* (general law or common law) as the way each community establishes for itself what the law is.[4] The practice of lawyers helping the poor in their contact with legal arenas comes from that period, and its importance in the formation of a European legal culture[5] can still be verified by reviewing law schools' curriculum and the education and training offered by the bar.[6]

During medieval times, kings felt the necessity to organize and to express power through the administration of justice. This movement to centralize power created the concept of a nation distinct from others, governed not only by royal power but by customs codified as law. In different European countries, books of law defining the customs of each kingdom were developed. In Spain, *Ordenanzas Reales de Castela* was published in 1484 by Isabella I. In 1446, *Ordenações Afonsinas*, the first and most complete book of Portuguese law was published, divided into five volumes dedicated to the administration of justice, the relation between the state and the church, civil procedure, civil law, and criminal law.[7] In the third book, dedicated to civil procedure, the fourth part is dedicated to those who could not afford access to a court.[8] Other books followed it, such as *Ordenações Manuelinas* (1512–14)[9] and *Ordenações Filipinas* (1603).[10]

In the modern period, José Maria de Alpoim, minister of justice and member of the Progressive (later Republican) Party published on July 21, 1899, the first modern law dedicated to promoting access to justice and the courts for all citizens. Citizens had to present their case to a commission constituted by a judge, a public prosecutor, and a lawyer. The commission had the power to decide if legal aid should be granted in the case, and only civil and commercial disputes were encompassed.

The Portuguese bar was established by decree in 1926,[11] after several failed attempts to be recognized by the state as an independent and self-regulated profession. Since its foundation, the bar has had its main center in Lisbon, with seven regional councils spread through the mainland and islands. Each regional council has a formal group dedicated to organizing and managing all issues related to access to justice and legal aid.

During the dictatorship period (1928–74), the rules concerning access to justice and the courts remained,[12] even if feelings of injustice grew and courts were used for political judgments.[13] Some lawyers and the bar played an important role in defending political dissidents, most of them for free.[14] The public involvement of the bar in the fight for legal justice and more humane treatment for people incarcerated for political motives[15] helps to explain the good reputation of this professional group. The construction of a professional discourse based on the fight for civil liberties is important to understand pro bono practices and their penetration into Portuguese contemporary legal culture. We can define pro bono activities developed by lawyers as a constitutive part of the ethical and moral code, understood as a core function of the professional habitus.[16] This habitus is important in creating a common professional ideology for its members, and in projecting an ideal of the profession to society.

The new democratic period started in 1974 and combines a set of transformations in the political, legal, economic, and social arenas. As a result, legal aid becomes more effective with the creation of new mechanisms to promote access to justice and the courts for all citizens.

The Portuguese Constitution[17] grants the right of access to justice and to be represented by a lawyer in a court of law to all national citizens, European Union citizens, and asylum seekers. In this sense, like in all Western European states,[18] legal aid services are provided and funded by the state to those who cannot afford legal counseling. The definition of economic hardship is established by law and is applicable to individuals and organizations.[19]

Legal aid is a responsibility of the court and of the judge in a specific case who is to evaluate the economic conditions of the citizen and determine eligibility for legal aid, after the citizen has made a formal request for that aid. These procedural forms have been criticized by judges for taking time from juridical tasks, thereby contributing to an overload of bureaucratic work inside the judicial system, already clogged with the rise of legal proceedings and the general tendency of legal cases to become more complex.

In 2000, new public policies were developed[20] by the government attending to the requests of judges with a double objective: (1) promoting easier access by citizens through the creation of a new service inside local Social Security offices to request all types of legal aid, from legal counseling to representation in court, creating more user-friendly and widespread access across the country; and (2) meeting the demands of judges and public servants to concentrate their activities on juridical tasks. In this new format, after Social Security services determine client eligibility, the request for legal aid is sent to the regional council of the Portuguese Bar Association.

The bar is responsible for the process of selecting and assigning lawyers for each request. For that purpose, a public list of lawyers is organized by subject: public and tax law, civil action, commercial, consumer law, family and minors, criminal, labour, juvenile justice, and general cases (no specification). Crimes against women and domestic violence[21] are a new specialization resulting from a protocol between the bar and the Commission for Citizenship and Gender Equality (CIG),[22] a state agency responsible for implementation and monitoring of gender policies. Every year the general counsel of the bar association defines a period to collect new applications, and every lawyer can become a public legal aid lawyer (*advogado oficioso*). The system does not require that the lawyer should be a specialist or have prior experience in a certain area to accept a case. In practice, a lawyer can apply to work on all types of cases, improving the chance to be contacted in the future but diminishing the possibility for the case to be assigned to a specialist.[23]

In sum, the citizen contacts Social Security services to request legal aid; if the request is accepted, the citizen is contacted by the closest regional council of the bar with a list of lawyers in the vicinity; the chosen lawyer becomes the legal counselor for the process/case and at the end of the case submits a bill to the state and receives reimbursement. Lawyers working for the legal aid system can have other clients during the same period of time, maintaining all the privileges of being a lawyer.[24]

In 2018, the period for applications was in November, and a new list was published in December.[25] Since 2007,[26] the list has been maintained by SINOA (Information System of the Bar Association), an information platform that facilitates direct contact between lawyers, courts, and the bar, serving as an open account where each lawyer can write off all the legal services and generate a payment bill to the minister of justice. The introduction of SINOA[27] was part of a public policy to improve the relation between the bar and the minister of justice in order to solve the problem of constant delays with payments to lawyers,[28] and to have better control over the costs of legal aid services. Delays in payment were responsible for a negative attitude among lawyers regarding their practice in the legal aid system.

Nowadays, lawyers wait an average of fifty days to receive their fees for legal aid services.[29] The legal aid system in recent years has been responsible for many cases, an average of 150,000 per year,[30] with a notable decrease in the years 2012 and 2013 related to the effects of the economic crisis. The system is also expensive; from 2016 to 2018, the minister of justice spent an average of 50 million euros per year on legal aid (estimated numbers).

Another important feature of the legal aid system is its major impact on lawyers' professional activities, especially for lawyers working in small towns and villages. The decrease of economic activity over the years had a negative impact on the activities of courts in the countryside, resulting in some cases in the closing of courts and other judicial or administrative services,[31] aggravating the difficulty of finding clients in certain regions. A greater number of lawyers in those conditions depend on legal aid programs compared with those living in cities or metropolitan areas.[32] The difficulties in finding clients and the dependence on legal aid cases have had an impact on the development of pro bono in the country.[33]

The system combines the right of citizens to legal aid and the right of lawyers to have clients and to continue their professional activities. The system was designed to guarantee equal access to every citizen, by offering legal services and the right of citizens to select a lawyer who best represents their interests in all phases of legal proceedings. However, a great number of citizens have not had prior contact with a lawyer, and they accept the bar's appointment. The lack of knowledge is noted by lawyers interviewed as a fragile part of the system, compromising in some cases the best interest of the citizen, who, without information, can only expect that the system will designate a lawyer who truly understands the problem and has a level of specialization and skill that can be translated into the best legal solution.

PRO BONO ASSOCIATION: THE FIRST PORTUGUESE CLEARINGHOUSE

The creation of the first Portuguese clearinghouse, named the Pro Bono Association (PBA) in 2014, constitutes a transformation in the development of pro bono legal services in the country. The clearinghouse was started by the efforts of two female lawyers working in Lisbon law firms, and the first goal was to implement a platform to help lawyers who wanted to be involved in pro bono but did not have the contacts or the time to reach potential clients.[34] One of the founders had twenty years of experience as an associate and partner in one of the largest and most prestigious firms in the country,[35] and had worked with corporate clients in the areas of cross-border transactions, M&A, capital markets, commercial arbitrations, and joint ventures. The other was a trainee at the time and later become an intern at Public Counsel in Los Angeles.[36]

The idea started as an opportunity to bring to Portugal an international model of pro bono such as the one promoted by organizations like PILnet. The first task was to adapt the model to the Portuguese context using the networks established during the founders' own professional experience. This involved building strong ties between large law firms, corporate clients, and law faculties, where some of the lawyers teach and law firms invest by funding postgraduate and master's programs. The project started with a protocol between the PBA and two law schools in Lisbon (*Faculdade de Direito da Universidade de Lisboa* and *Faculdade de Direito da Universidade Católica de Lisboa*), in which the faculties supported the association by providing a place to conduct meetings and helped with promoting pro bono activities among students. In 2015, the PBA was recognized by the state as a social solidarity organization of public utility.

The first critical factor in the implementation of the clearinghouse was individual agency. The social capital of one of the founders enabled the project to reach a large network, with the help of two important NGOs in the country – *Entreajuda* and *Banco Alimentar contra a Fome*[37] – which proved decisive at the beginning by providing the know-how and technical skills necessary to implement a project based solely on volunteer work. Observing the network of corporations and NGOs revolving around *Entreajuda* and *Banco Alimentar*, we see a solid group of individuals participating as board members. These members are extremely important in organizing voluntary work and supporting the network.

The second critical factor was the state's recognition of PBA as a social solidarity organization. To better understand its importance, we should move to the relation between PBA and the bar. The bar rules, in accordance with the lawyer's legal status, obligate the lawyer to have an office recognized by the bar and dedicated exclusively to conducting professional activities; the bar prohibits lawyers from practicing outside their official offices,[38] except for cases already approved by the bar and its ethics committee, and publicized in the form of a protocol.[39] An important exception is that lawyers may practice in the offices of social solidarity organizations, which may present a request to the bar ethics committee to have lawyers in their spaces offering legal counseling. In those cases, pro bono counseling is permitted, but the lawyer involved cannot become the official lawyer of the case in order to avoid the illegal recruiting of clients.[40] PBA has requested a legal opinion on its activities from the bar and is still waiting for a formal decision. During the interviews, the responsible PBA volunteers mentioned that a decision was on the way, but it was not official.

The PBA is located in Lisbon and works almost exclusively in the Lisbon metropolitan area.[41] The PBA's founders started by organizing a small team of volunteers responsible for presenting the organization to both law students and lawyers. The founders started to spread the idea of what a clearinghouse can do for NGOs and other social solidarity institutions by promoting meetings and sharing cases from other countries. The PBA has a special network with *Fundación Arazandi Lex Nova*, responsible for the publication in 2015 of the guide *Conéxion Pro Bono* with the sponsorship of Thompson Reuters Foundation, dedicated to the promotion and implementation of pro bono best practices in law firms. The guide functions as a marketing tool.

In this guide, ten reasons are advanced in support of pro bono activities: (1) helping society; (2) engaging in rewarding activity; (3) improving the social image of the profession; (4) providing an opportunity to develop new competencies (in particular soft skills); (5) offering the chance to recruit new talents; (6) bringing new cases to courts; (7) improving firms' chances of receiving new clients who value the firms' social commitment; (8) providing benefits for new potential clients; (9) providing an inspiring challenge; and (10) improving society's level of trust in law firms, lawyers, and in the judicial system.[42]

The guide advises law firms to institutionalize pro bono at the highest level of the firms' hierarchy through the constitution of a committee directed by a partner, in order to spread an internal and external message of commitment. The purpose is to reach more lawyers at an internal level and to promote the firm on the external level. The reasons combine individual, organizational, and social benefits and are aligned with the developments underscored by several studies in different countries.[43]

The PBA is organized around three partnerships: (1) with NGOs, working with different segments of the public; (2) with law student volunteers; and (3) with individual lawyers and law firms.

All the work done in the PBA is voluntary, unpaid, and exclusively conducted by law students, who have the chance to make contact with law firms during their first years of undergraduate studies. Students also join the PBA to experience the responsibility of dealing with a real client, even if a nonpaying one, and to manage all the processes going on behind the scenes: filling out forms and mediating the relationship between lawyer, client, and NGO. Students must review a weekly list of pro bono work, organize it, and distribute it to lawyers and law firms. A student is involved in each case in all stages of the process. In its first two years, the PBA provided support in two hundred cases (both to individuals and organizations). Most of the cases were related to family law (divorces and parental regulations) and problems with personal bankruptcy.[44]

The activity report for 2016–17 presents a more detailed register of the different metrics.[45] Based on the data, from 2014 to 2017 the PBA reached 149 NGOs with 5,000 potential beneficiaries, established protocols with 10 law firms and almost 215 lawyers, engaged 839 law students, resolved 155 cases, and maintained 219 pending cases.

The dependence on students, typically from the second, third, and fourth year of undergraduate courses, demands continuing support from law schools. In 2017, the PBA started a new protocol in Porto, the country's second biggest city, with the two most prestigious faculties – the Law School of the Catholic University of Portugal and the Law Faculty of the University of Porto – along with seven NGOs,[46] and four law firms (VdA, PLMJ, Telles, and Delgado & Associates).

The PBA has the goal of becoming international via two different platforms. The first is to enter global pro bono networks. International support can be relevant to enhance the legitimacy of the organization. Presently, the PBA is a member of the European Pro Bono Alliance and PILnet. On November 28, 2018, a PBA delegation joined the Italy Pro Bono Day in Rome to discuss the role of clearinghouses.[47] In the near future, PBA expects to organize the PILnet forum.

Nevertheless, in the interviews, some potential risks of recognition and internationalization were identified. Another organization, the Social Entrepreneurs Agency (SEA),[48] was mentioned as a potential competitor for international recognition, which is an important aspect in applying for funding. In the follow-up interview at the PBA, another volunteer spoke about this, saying that the SEA had contacted them in the past to gather information about their activities, and then the contact stopped. In 2017, the SEA organized the 5th Global Pro Bono Summit in Lisbon, supported by the BMW Foundation and Taproot Foundation, promoters of corporate pro bono worldwide.[49] In a report titled "Pro Bono Portugal Study Final Report 2015,"[50] the SEA explored the potential for corporate pro bono in Portugal, but did not mention other types of pro bono, such as individual services. As it seems, the competition for recognition is focused on creating international networks connecting NGOs and corporations around corporate pro bono. We might expect that the PBA, having difficulties implementing pro bono among lawyers, would seek to develop a model of corporate pro bono, in which broader charitable services, not just legal services, are offered to NGOs.

A second strategy of internationalization can be seen in the joint efforts of law firms and the PBA to provide legal support to individuals and groups in Portuguese-speaking countries in Africa – taking advantage of the business generated in those countries. The PBA's contact with Africa began with a protocol between the Girl Move Foundation,[51] the PBA, and the VdA law firm, which brought two female trainee lawyers from Mozambique to study and work in Lisbon. The PBA received them in their team of volunteers. At the end of the program, the link continued with the idea of establishing a protocol with universities and the bar in Mozambique to create a clearinghouse in the country. The project is still in its embryonic stage.

One of the novelties of the PBA's structure in relation to the access-to-justice system in Portugal is that the PBA does not have a formal rule to define economic need. In order to determine the eligibility of a citizen to receive legal counseling, the PBA uses the rule defined by each NGO, and it is the responsibility of the NGO to select the cases. Because of this system, it is sometimes difficult to understand why NGO partners decline individual representation.

The PBA claims that its work is mostly complementary to state legal aid, and it acts when a citizen who has had prior contact with one of the

NGO partners has a problem and cannot find a solution via traditional channels. Comparing the cases handled by the legal aid system (an average of 150,000 per year) with the cases conducted by the PBA (200 in three years of activity) makes it difficult to support the idea of complementarity. The PBA is, in its current phase, more of an incipient clearinghouse than a full clearinghouse.

THE INSTITUTIONALIZATION OF PRO BONO IN LAW FIRMS

The institutionalization of pro bono in Portugal combines an array of features that make it in some ways similar to and in others distinct from pro bono in other countries. We will thus argue that Portugal is a hybrid case, where we observe the impacts of global movements and trends on pro bono brought by the Anglo-American corporate legal world combined with long-term practices of unstructured and occasional free legal counseling. We also observe a difficult relationship between pro bono and the legal aid system, and attempts by law firms to expand pro bono activities to other jurisdictions, like Portuguese-speaking countries in Africa. To deepen understanding of this hybrid system, the following analysis examines eight central characteristics of pro bono in Portugal.

Legal Aid System and Pro Bono: A Difficult Relationship

The first characteristic identified is the tension between the legal aid system, in particular the bar and the lawyers directly involved, and the PBA. As mentioned earlier, lawyers working in part or almost exclusively for the legal aid system for years had a monopoly on representing low-income clients, filing a significant number of cases in court.[52] The establishment of the PBA – a partnership with the corporate world dedicated to promoting pro bono as an ethical and moral duty for all lawyers, but especially those in large firms – was received with suspicion and dissent by the bar. The controversy and debate over pro bono reflected deeper divisions due to the segmentation and specialization of the profession. These divisions separate lawyers based on the type of clients, areas of practice, revenues, access to power, and internationalization. On the one hand are lawyers who depend on the legal aid system to have clients or whose clients have difficulty making all their payments; have low levels of specialization and work in different areas of practice, but work mostly in criminal and civil law; have low income; do not have access to power; work on a national basis spread throughout the country; and are solo practitioners or share office expenses with other colleagues.

On the other hand are lawyers with corporate clients, some of them international clients; specializing in one area of practice; working in law firms with a clear division of labor and organized in different departments; with higher income (partners earning annual profits); with access to power in its different forms (political, economic, cultural, and symbolic);[53] working in a global environment with international clients and in direct contact with other jurisdictions; and having a cosmopolitan lifestyle of regular travel to business centers around the world.

One of the partners responsible for the development of pro bono in her firm preferred not to discuss the problems between large law firms and the bar, but said that she knows that the PBA's directors have had conflict with the bar over the appropriate role of pro bono in the access-to-justice system. Another pro bono manager recognized that the bar has a hostile position regarding law firms doing pro bono: "The Portuguese bar is not in favor of large law firms offering pro bono services because they consider it's like having sharks stealing the work from the hands of the *descamisados*[54] (lawyers working with legal aid)."[55]

Persistence of Old Practices of Individual and Unstructured Pro Bono

The second characteristic of pro bono in Portugal is the continuity of old practices of doing occasional and unstructured pro bono. Working for free on a special occasion or helping someone with legal advice without expecting payment is a common experience for a lawyer, even if it is not a regular practice. From our interviews with lawyers from different backgrounds, ages, and practice areas, individual pro bono was identified as a matter of personal conscience and an opportunity to help someone in need of legal expertise. All lawyers have done pro bono in the past, but in different circumstances. Solo practitioners have experienced how the legal aid system works and sometimes preferred to offer their legal services without expecting any kind of payment from the state. The main reason identified was bureaucracy: the system involves a lot of paperwork, which causes delays, and sometimes lawyers decided to continue with cases without requesting financial compensation. Occasionally, lawyers would receive new cases or new requests for helping someone from other lawyers and decide to get involved, regardless of the expectation of getting paid. As one lawyer put it, "Sometimes it is a humanitarian issue: you receive in your office a person who is going to be evicted from their home or is a victim of domestic violence, and you don't have the time to work on the case, and you ask among your lawyer friends if someone can help this person for free."[56]

Finally, occasional pro bono can start as an immediate necessity to help someone and then evolve into a lawyer–client relation. In those situations, lawyers instruct the client to contact the legal aid system and formalize the request.

Lawyers working in firms have different approaches. Some have also experienced working with the legal aid system for a period of time. In general, according to what is reported in the interviews, this period corresponds to their first years in the profession or to the period of internship:

> I have registered in the legal aid system in the past because of the professional internship in the bar. We had to have a number of interventions in court, mostly criminal law, before passing the final exam and becoming lawyers. We called it *oficiosas*; basically, we had to go to a court once a month, or sometimes we received a letter from the court to appear, and that day we stayed the whole day in a room waiting to be called to accompany a person who didn't have a lawyer to be presented to a judge in the court. I did it for a year and a half, combining work at the firm with work as a legal aid lawyer in courts.[57]

Other lawyers have the experience of helping a relative, a friend, or an acquaintance, particularly with less complex civil disputes like traffic tickets. Portuguese lawyers view this work as a central part of their cultural and professional ethos. As one interviewed lawyer put it, "Yes, I help my friends, [though in the case of] traffic tickets, only if their driving license is at stake. I've had four large dossiers of road tickets only from my friends. I said one day, 'I'll start working for you, I do not work for the office anymore [laughs],' but, as a general rule, I help people."[58]

Sometimes, lawyers working in firms also handle pro bono cases discretely to preserve the anonymity of the client: "I have represented three clients in court, but not with the intention to promote the law firm; just the opposite, all these procedures were confidential. We helped, but without reporting to the pro bono committee."[59] This kind of individual pro bono service is distinct from what we call organized pro bono activities, which are provided through formal structures in the law firm and vary in the level of institutionalization.

Pro Bono Committees inside Law Firms

The third characteristic of Portuguese pro bono is the presence of pro bono committees inside law firms coordinated by lawyers who are in a power position to handle different types of requests and have the responsibility of transforming individual demands into an institutional response. The institutionalization of pro bono – that is, the transformation of individual lawyer charity into collective action – involves the law firm in a complex web of decisions around the performance of pro bono work, conflicts of interest, publicity, and social recognition.

As with any other client, pro bono is viewed by firm lawyers as work that should be done with professionalism. But it remains important to ensure that accepting nonpaying clients will not affect lawyer performance for paying clients. The creation of pro bono committees facilitates better organization, concentrating all requests in one person who publicizes the work by email or receives declarations by lawyers of their intention to take this kind of work. In all firms contacted, the pro bono work was voluntary, except for trainees. In two law firms, there were discussions about promoting this type of work through equivalence with billable hours in order to attract all lawyers. In periods with a lower volume of work, pro bono can be used to keep lawyers occupied and to maintain their working hours.

The potential for conflicts of interest is one of the main reasons to concentrate pro bono demands in a committee, which has the responsibility to check for potential conflicts before accepting a client or a case: "Before accepting pro bono, we always have to ask the firm first because of potential conflicts of interest. We could receive someone who is having an eviction problem and we as a firm can be representing the bank in other cases, so there is high scrutiny before accepting any case or client, pro bono or not."[60] Pro bono coordinators are also in charge of the production of CSR and pro bono reports working with marketing and communications departments.

The Special Role of Trainees and Women Lawyers

The fourth characteristic of pro bono in Portugal is the special role of trainees and women lawyers. Young lawyers, in particular trainees, are more likely to do pro bono work than other lawyers, especially because they are the only ones who cannot refuse to do it. Of the nineteen lawyers contacted, all did pro bono in their internships.

Young lawyers agreed that doing pro bono has had a positive impact on their professional socialization. They highlighted: (1) more chances to directly contact clients and develop an informal relation; (2) the possibility to use this kind of work to acquire new competencies, mostly soft skills; (3) less pressure; and (4) improved chances to stand out to partners or other senior associates. For the law firm, distributing pro bono work among trainees can have several benefits: (1) professional socialization among peers; (2) including them in teamwork; (3) evaluation; and (4) preparation for "real" clients. During interviews, pro bono coordinators expressed their view that the earlier trainees are socialized to do pro bono, the more positive their opinions will be, and the more likely it is that they will engage in it in the future.

One of the findings of the fieldwork is that women are overrepresented in pro bono committees and are more likely to be engaged in pro bono management. One of the possible explanations advanced is related to the difficulties for women of gaining access to power positions inside the law firm. Following Witz's arguments on different models of leadership,[61] by dedicating their time to pro bono activities, women expect to receive recognition from their fellow partners and to improve possibilities to advance their careers and access power positions. One of the coordinators described her path toward pro bono:

> I started doing pro bono because I have always felt the need to help, to have an ethical position, and because I was working with a partner who does a lot of pro bono. I never thought of doing it for public recognition, but in fact I have received a lot of acknowledgment in the firm since I became the coordinator.[62]

Of course, this approach has risks and cannot be extensively employed by all women, in part, because billable hours receive the most weight in performance evaluations. In addition, we observed that women who are leading pro bono in Portuguese law firms come from an elite social background, which offers them the chance to embrace voluntary activities as a means to distinguish themselves from others with less economic risk. Until recent times, women from the ruling class were not expected to work or to have a professional career, so they engaged in different forms of charity work, usually related to organizations associated with the Catholic Church. This often involved working with poor communities as a way of maintaining their privilege and reputation. The recent growth in the number of women entering law firms (and the fact that women constitute a majority in law schools and other parts of the Portuguese legal profession) suggests that this charitable ethos could become more prominent in law firm pro bono programs.

Match of Expertise as a Precondition to Do Pro Bono

The fifth characteristic of pro bono in Portugal is the match of expertise and specialization between the accepted case and the lawyer or team of lawyers involved. Law firms prefer to dedicate pro bono hours to dealing with legal problems that their lawyers have the skills and competence to handle. As a direct result, law firms prefer to work with organizations rather than individual clients. The main reason presented is related to knowledge and professional expertise. Large law firms work mostly with corporate clients, paying little or no attention to individual problems. So, in order to match the expertise of the firm with the necessities of pro bono clients, the choice to offer pro bono to organizational clients becomes natural. A lot of pro bono is done in order to help create, organize, or restructure NGOs and social enterprises using corporate, tax, and labor law.

This focus on pro bono cases that match law firm expertise can also be understood as a way of avoiding problems with the bar and lawyers working predominantly with legal aid. One of the pro bono counsels we interviewed discussed the firm's reluctance to represent low-income individual clients, even those ineligible to receive legal aid: "Sometimes we accept individual cases, but we don't assist individuals with economic capacity; if we did, it could be understood as unfair competition with solo practitioners, who present reduced and affordable bills to clients. People don't need to go to a big law firm to have a good lawyer."[63]

Focus on NGOs and Social Enterprises

The sixth characteristic of pro bono that we observe in Portugal is the law firm focus on a special kind of client. As the discussion above underscores, law firms prefer not to have individual cases but rather to concentrate their time and skills on NGOs, charities, and social enterprises. Law firms have different strategies for building relationships with these types of clients. Some have a proactive attitude, directly contacting organizations and offering them pro bono services. After an evaluation by the pro bono manager, the firm makes the first contact and establishes a protocol of cooperation offering a number of hours per year. Other firms have a reactive attitude, responding only to requests made by NGOs. The PBA plays an important role in collecting cases from NGOs and presenting them to law firms.

Law firm pro bono involvement with social organizations has other potential benefits, such as introducing the firm to new entrepreneurs. As one lawyer we interviewed reported:

> Last year I did a lot of pro bono, since I'm a member of Team Genesis (a group of lawyers dedicated to start-ups). We help a lot of start-ups in the beginning of the business, both through teaching and legal counseling. In this phase we help a lot without billing. It's a way of doing pro bono by helping entrepreneurs, most of them young people working with very interesting new technologies but without the legal knowledge to make decisions on how to start with the company. This is also a form of doing pro bono.[64]

As this suggests, focusing pro bono activities on organizations can be a strategy to recruit future clients. As one respondent acknowledged, some NGOs represented in a pro bono capacity have now become clients charged what she referred to as a social fee, which is less than the fee charged to corporate clients.

Promoting Pro Bono in Other Portuguese-Speaking Countries

The seventh characteristic of Portuguese pro bono is its spread to other jurisdictions, in particular to Portuguese-speaking countries in Africa. The global promotion of pro bono goes hand in hand with lawyers' and firms' professional activities. Portuguese lawyers act as mediators mainly in international finance projects[65] involving foreign investors, investment banks, local government agencies, and local law firms:

> Here in Portugal, we have a growing number of transactions that are written according to English law. Most of them come from projects that are being developed in Portuguese-speaking countries where the investors are often development banks. I am speaking of the European Investment Bank or the African Development Bank. I have done pro bono in Africa, projects on agricultural development, but it is not substantial; to be honest, I don't think it's substantial. But it is not clear to me where I can find the opportunities to do more. Sometimes we need to go searching for these opportunities.[66]

Portuguese lawyers participating in pro bono projects in Portuguese-speaking countries work as mediators or "shadow advisers," using an expression from Sara Dezalay.[67] The role of mediator is used for two main reasons. First, lawyers do not have a license to operate in a foreign country, which means they cannot practice law, but rather only provide advice. Second, lawyers act as intermediaries of foreign investment, adapting and translating international law to the specific context. Undertaking pro bono is a way to demonstrate commitment to local political, economic, and legal elites. The pro bono initiatives reported in the interviews can vary in format: individual pro bono, cooperation with NGOs, and training of local law students. Regarding individual pro bono, the same pattern found in the Portuguese environment applies. A lawyer is contacted directly or via a third party in order to provide help in solving a legal problem, and the lawyer decides individually, without contacting a pro bono manager:

> We had situations of lawyers doing pro bono in foreign countries without any previous contact with me [the firm's pro bono manager]. In the firm, we have a partner who has been working for years in Mozambique, and he is well known there, and often he is contacted by someone asking for help, and when he can, he does pro bono but only reports it afterward.[68]

Pro bono appears here as another mode of doing business, reinforcing contacts with local NGOs, universities, and governments, while promoting the image of the good Portuguese lawyer. In performing pro bono in these African countries, Portuguese lawyers have advantages over European or American lawyers because they share a common language, understand the culture, and have a shared identity – even though it is mediated by colonial relations.[69]

Pro bono helps to strengthen ties between corporate Portuguese law firms and local governments and political and economic elites in Africa through two different strategies: supporting development initiatives through universities and NGOs, and providing education and training to young law students. Both strategies are being developed in partnerships between law firms and the PBA. The PBA invites African law students to its office and involves them as volunteers, while at the same time law firms accept the students as trainees. In one illustrative case involving the PBA,[70] a Portuguese firm (PLMJ) was contacted to help an NGO in Mozambique, not by providing pro bono but by sponsoring students to work with the NGO. After the law students received training through the PBA and returned to Mozambique, the contact was maintained, and the students became promoters of the PBA, establishing contacts at the university and in the bar to support the development of a clearinghouse and a legal clinic in the country.

Adoption of Corporate Social Responsibility

Finally, the movement toward the institutionalization of pro bono activities in Portugal has developed in parallel with the adoption of CSR practices. This relation is not unique to the Portuguese business landscape, where law firms (in particular large law firms) play an important role; rather, the influence of CSR is widespread around the corporate world. It is difficult to establish the precise direction of the relation, or in other words, who exerts the primary influence: large corporations or large law firms. As Vaughan, Thomas, and Young emphasize,[71] business lawyers are sensitive to changes in the corporate model, particularly the trend of publicizing a group of performance indicators related to CSR. As Boon and Whyte explain, CSR is "a complex interaction between idealism, professionalism and commercialism, to which must be added the force of globalisation."[72]

In Portugal, the adoption of CSR practices is not the only factor responsible for the institutionalization of pro bono but has powerfully influenced its dissemination and growing importance by connecting legal pro bono with other voluntary activities performed by corporations.

The interaction of different social forces shapes legal culture. This culture is exhibited in patterns of behavior and conduct around the rule of law in a specific context,[73] in which lawyers and law firms are influenced by interaction with other lawyers, as well as judges and other agents inside the legal system. And of course, we must consider the important influence of multinational corporations, the best and most influential clients,[74] which impact legal culture from outside the legal system through communications on how to perform, behave, and think, resulting in a structural coupling that produces codependence.[75] This notion of codependence can help to explain how corporate culture permeates the values and culture of law firms and promotes the introduction of CSR as a practice. In other words, the language and discourse used by multinational corporations to describe their activities and their relation with competitors and society are becoming part of the language and discourse utilized by law firms. This interplay has impacted how law firms communicate with the external environment: adopting CSR practices as a way to publicly express their work and their commitment to society.

In addition, it is important to look at external forces shaping legal culture, like popular culture,[76] and to measure the influence of music, television shows, and films, or more recently social media, on the opinions and attitudes of lawyers and law firms regarding social responsibility and their public roles in local and international communities.

The relation between localism and globalism is actually one of the most challenging to understand in the implementation of CSR policies inside law firms. Nowadays, law firms, even smaller and more specialized boutique firms, develop their activities on an internationalized platform of legal services competing and cooperating with others in a globalized environment.[77] We argue that the competition for clients in a global environment strengthens and deepens the circulation of ideas and values between law firms and corporations, and has supported social responsibility as a new form of professionalism. Some of this discussion is present in the work of Hanlon dedicated to exposing transformations inside the profession in a movement he calls commercial professionalism.[78]

> [Lawyers] had to embrace commercialization, put the paying client before all other obligations and restructure their firms in order to add increasing value to client services. For individual professionals, career progression is ever more closely tied to entrepreneurial success and the exhibiting of commercial awareness. This meant a redefining of professionalism so that it came to mean adhering to the goals of the paying client and being commercially aware.[79]

In this sense, it is important for firms to promote an external image that combines local and global aspects. In the Portuguese case, the special bond between NGOs, charities, and social enterprises related to the Catholic Church and the corporate world has created new forms of promoting CSR. GRACE (Group of Reflexion and Support of Corporate Citizenship) is the best-known group,[80] involving 160 members – corporations from different economic sectors, including 8 law firms.[81] GRACE is a nonprofit organization established in 2000, responsible for the promotion and development of the concepts of corporate citizenship and social responsibility in the corporate sphere through diverse member-based activities. It operates through partnerships among corporations, charities, local governments, and NGOs with common goals. Funding comes exclusively from its members through annual membership dues and occasional individual or corporate donations. In addition to the publication of books, articles, and other communications about CSR, GRACE promotes voluntary activities like planting trees, cleaning forests, and painting walls. Operating under the acronym GIRO (GRACE, Intervene, Restore, Organize), these activities involve volunteers from member organizations. Looking at GRACE's 2015, 2016, and 2017 reports, we found participants from law firms in all the activities. These types of activities can be defined as community giving, and they do not have a direct connection with pro bono. Instead, anyone affiliated with a firm can participate since there is no need for technical competence in law. Nevertheless, the involvement of firms is common, and law firms detail such activities in their CSR reports.

In Portugal, CSR is regulated by a set of norms and rules, and certified by Social Accountability International (SAI),[82] a global NGO dedicated to advancing human rights at work.[83] The International Norm ISO26000 defines CSR as "voluntary actions developed by organizations with the purpose of creating or maximizing positive impacts, as well as reducing or eliminating negative impacts."[84] This broad definition can be used to promote all types of activities, but in fact law firms use the concept to promote activities involving pro bono, community giving, networks with universities and NGOs, environmental issues, philanthropy, and staff well-being:

> Even if CSR is a very broad concept and you can find some initiatives like the Green Firm project (environmental sustainability), or the start-up project (dedicated to helping business clients at the beginning of their projects), most of our CSR report is dedicated to presenting our pro bono activities.[85]

Compliance with international CSR norms is voluntary and there is no obligation for law firms to produce a CSR report, but even so, our research reveals an increase of law firm reports, and in some cases they are produced in both Portuguese and English. The bilingual publications can be understood as a product of firms' internationalization – that is, the presence of firms in international markets – and serve as a promotional tool to reach new clients.

We examined a set of reports from medium (between 50 and 100 lawyers) and large firms (over 100 lawyers) based on the Portuguese annual publication, *Anuário das Sociedades de Advogados*,[86] which compiles information about each firm. From that, we developed a database

TABLE 10.1 Existence of reports on pro bono and CSR in law firms by size (%)

	Pro Bono (%)		CSR (%)	
Size of the firm	Yes	No	Yes	No
4 to 10	11.1	88.9	11.1	88.9
11 to 20	12.5	87.5	12.5	87.5
21 to 50	46.7	53.3	46.7	53.3
51 to 100	62.5	37.5	50	50
More than 100	85.7	14.3	85.7	14.3

Number of valid cases = 106

of 117 cases (one large firm does not appear in the publication and was included afterward).

Looking through the data, we see that both pro bono activities and CSR reports are published by a great number of law firms. However, the level of dissemination is unequal among firms. We found that the larger the firm, the greater the chance it will publish a CSR report in which pro bono activities are mentioned.[87]

As seen in Table 10.1, the size of the firm is positively correlated with production of CSR and pro bono reports. Small firms are the least likely to produce such reports. When we look at medium-size firms (51 to 100 lawyers) and large firms (more than 100 lawyers), we see increasing proportions publishing CSR and pro bono reports. One difference can be found in medium and large firms where the existence of reports varies between 62.5 percent and 85.7 percent in the case of pro bono and between 50 and 85.7 percent in the case of CSR reports.

Community Giving

Law firm community giving combines the elite Portuguese tradition of promoting charity through Catholic organizations with new international trends in the corporate sphere, specifically, promoting the image of corporate Good Samaritan while taking care of the firm's human resources by promoting well-being among employees. This type of community giving as a strand of CSR was found during fieldwork. Using different expressions, three coordinators of pro bono committees we interviewed established a connection between Catholic culture and their firm's approach to helping local communities, promoting lawyer volunteer work in the "spirit of the Catholic mission." Community work varies in form and scope, from fundraising, to donations, to painting walls or planting trees, but such activities all have two common features. First, they are promoted through networks of people and organizations within the sphere of influence of the Catholic Church. Most of the time these networks have been developed previously to mobilize voluntary work in connection with scouts, student associations, and other groups, and are reactivated in the professional sphere.

Second, all community giving activities are used for self-promotion by firms on websites and in CSR and other reports, producing an image of firms with ethical values involved with poor communities. It is difficult to measure the impact on the beneficiaries but is easier to evaluate benefits for the firm. Community giving is a sophisticated form of creating and maintaining a good reputation while navigating publicity restrictions on lawyers. Community giving also breaks down service boundaries between lawyers and nonlawyers, and helps develop social capital among firm members. In sum, we conclude that community giving has more impact inside the law firm than on the potential beneficiaries of the actions.

Rock'n'Law[88] is a good example of a form of community giving with an impact that transcends the main goal of fundraising. Rock'n'Law started ten years ago in Lisbon as an initiative of a group of business lawyers who had the idea to organize a charity rock concert to help a social cause. In ten years, they raised more than 500,000 euro and helped sixteen different NGOs working with cancer patients, the homeless, persons with disabilities or mental illness, and on human rights.

In 2010, the project was implemented in Madrid and Barcelona, Spain.[89] In 2018, Rock'n'Law celebrated is tenth annual concert with nine bands, all composed of lawyers, and for the first time with a band of judges, *Audiência Prévia*.[90] The bands gather lawyers from all levels, from trainees to partners, and have names that directly relate to their professional activity. Uría Menéndez is represented by *Herois del despacho*,[91] Morais Leitão with Tier One Band, PLMJ with *Fora da Lei*,[92] SRS with *Lawcura*,[93] and there is also a band with members from two firms, CMS and Linklaters, called Out of Office.

The Rock'n'Law project promotes social responsibility through leisure and the collective participation of lawyers, while also involving friends and family, and other workers of the firms. One of the positive impacts noted is the construction of better relations at work through music rehearsals, usually late in the evening after a day at the office, which are viewed as important for developing a firm's culture. One example is the case of the firm SRS, whose pro bono coordinator is also responsible for the band rehearsals, is lead singer, and serves as the main point of contact for the project.[94] Overall, Rock'n'Law is a charity event with a lot of propaganda involved and a professional communication staff working on spreading the message through different channels, from social media like YouTube[95] and Facebook,[96] to the national economic press,[97] and by giving a concert on a national radio station.[98]

CONCLUSION

Our study had as its first objective to present the current state of pro bono in Portugal. To accomplish it, we began by examining the long tradition of legal aid in the country – responsible for ensuring that all citizens can have access to justice and to courts – showing that the system has problems for both citizens and lawyers. For citizens, the system can be bureaucratic and lack of knowledge can compromise the chance to have the best lawyer for each case. For lawyers, bureaucracy has a different consequence, namely delays in payments.

The legal aid system is an obstacle to the development of pro bono in its institutionalized form. Throughout the chapter, we have described the professional culture of Portuguese lawyers and showed that occasional pro bono is present in their practices. The novelty is the institutionalization of pro bono inside law firms with the creation of pro bono committees, responsible for incorporating pro bono in the division of work; promoting pro bono activities among lawyers, in particular young trainees; dealing with conflicts of interest; matching the expertise of lawyers to cases; and choosing clients.

The main drivers of institutionalization are law firms and the PBA, the first clearinghouse in the country. The PBA was born from the initiative of two lawyers with long experience in large law firms, dealing with corporate clients in a global environment, and with the social, cultural, and economic resources to understand how the international clearinghouse model could be transposed to Portuguese society. The launch of the clearinghouse was made possible by the support of two important NGOs in Portugal, *Entreajuda* and *Banco Alimentar*, which offered existing knowledge of the third sector in Portugal and models of pro bono organization and implementation in the country. Since its formation, the PBA has had modest results, which include building a network of law students, lawyers, and NGOs, first in the capital and recently in another city.

Overall, the development of pro bono in Portugal is shaped by two major processes: segmentation and globalization. The institutionalization of pro bono highlights segmentation in the legal profession in Portugal. Pro bono divides the profession among lawyers from large law firms who can find the space and the opportunity to develop such practice, legal aid lawyers who depend on the state to continue in the profession, and lawyers in small firms or individual practices who cannot afford the altruism of accepting pro bono cases if they do not come via legal aid.

Law firms, in particular large law firms, are working in a globalized environment where adaptation to international clients, competition with national and international firms, and a search for new business in foreign jurisdictions have all come together. Pro bono is an opportunity to respond to this new world by offering a mix of services to traditional paying clients and pro bono clients, in which the former can be attracted by the firm's social responsibility activities, and the latter can become a paying client in the future.

NOTES

1. Scott L. Cummings & Deborah L. Rhode, *Managing Pro Bono: Doing Well by Doing Better*, 78 FORDHAM L. REV. 2360 (2010).
2. Susana Santos, *Becoming a Lawyer in a Large Law Firm: The Idea of the Unstoppable Worker*, 8 PROF. & PROFESSIONALISM 2285 (2018).
3. Data from December 2017: 3,495 lawyers enrolled in legal aid in the Lisbon regional council from a total of 13,480 lawyers in the country. Information available in Portuguese via *Acesso ao Direito | Resultado da 11ª Candidatura ao SADT*, ORDEM DOS ADVOGADOS, https://portal.oa.pt/comunicacao/noticias/2017/12/resultado-da-11%C2%AA-candidatura-ao-sadt/ (last visited Sept. 15, 2020).
4. *See* ANTÓNIO MANUEL HESPANHA, CULTURA JURÍDICA EUROPEIA: SÍNTESE DE UM MILÉNIO 122–23 (2003).

5. *Id.* We use the expression "European legal culture" from António Manuel Hespanha to emphasize the common patterns among national legal cultures in Europe.
6. Roman law is still taught in some European law schools. In Portugal, Roman law is offered to law students as an option, with the exception of the law faculty of the University of Lisbon, where the course is mandatory. This is a direct result of the reduction in the number of years of undergraduate courses (from five to four) as a consequence of the implementation of the Bologna Declaration.
7. ORDENAÇÕES AFONSINAS, LISBOA: FUNDAÇÃO CALOUSTE GULBENKIAN (Serviço de Educação 1999).
8. ORDENAÇÕES AFONSINAS, LISBOA LIVRO III 16 (1446) Facsimile edition available at: www1.ci.uc.pt/ihti/proj/afonsinas/l3p16.htm (last visited Sept. 15, 2020).
9. HISTÓRIA DO DIREITO PORTUGUÊS, FUNDAÇÃO CALOUSTE GULBENKIAN (1992).
10. ORDENAÇÕES AFONSINAS, LISBOA, *supra* note 7.
11. Decreto n° 11:715, Diário do Governo n° 124/1926 de 12 de junho [Decree no. 11:715, Government Diary no. 124/1926 of 12 June], https://dre.pt/application/conteudo/153731 (last visited Sept. 23, 2020), establishes the Portuguese Bar Association and defines access, control, and sanctions inside the profession and the structure of the organization.
12. In 1944, a new law decree on judicial assistance and legal aid was published, but followed the same structure with a commission and was only applicable to civil and commercial disputes. Decreto-Lei n° 33:548, Diário do Governo n° 37/1944 de 23 de fevereiro [Decree-Law no. 33:548, Government Diary no. 37/1944 of 23 February], https://dre.pt/application/conteudo/399594 (last visited Sept. 23, 2020).
13. FERNANDO ROSAS, IRENE FLUNSER PIMENTEL, JOÃO MADEIRA, LUIS FARINHA & MARIA INÁCIA REZOLA, TRIBUNAIS POLÍTICOS: TRIBUNAIS MILITARES ESPECIAIS E TRIBUNAIS PLENÁRIOS DURANTE A DITADURA E O ESTADO NOVO (2009).
14. *See* FRANCISCO SALGADO ZENHA, QUATRO CAUSAS: PEÇAS FORENSES (Four Causes: Forensic Cases) 53-119 (1969). In this book, the lawyer exposes four cases in different courts that had in common the imprisonment of citizens for political reasons. One of the cases is dedicated to Humberto Lopes, a prestigious lawyer, incarcerated for three years for suspicion of being a member of the illegal Portuguese Communist Party. In the trial, more than twenty lawyers, including the president of the bar, offered favorable testimonies.
15. *See* ORDENAÇÕES AFONSINAS, *supra* note 10, at 157–58. The First Congress of Lawyers held in 1972 discussed the necessity of better representation in court, improvement in the communication between lawyers and clients in custody, access to clients in prisons, and the end of political courts, the infamous *tribunal plenário*.
16. Pierre Bourdieu, *The Force of Law: Toward a Sociology of the Juridical Field*, 38 HASTINGS L.J. 814 (1987).

17. *See Constituição da República Portuguesa* art. 20°, Decreto de aprovação da Constituição n° 86/1976 de 10 de abril, https://dre.pt/web/guest/legislacao-consolidada/-/lc/34520775/view (last visited Sept. 23, 2020) (stating that "all citizens have the right to information and law protection"); *see also* Decreto-Lei n° 387-B/87 de 29 de dezembro [Decree-Law no. 387-B/87 of 29 December], https://dre.pt/application/conteudo/670072 (last visited Sept. 23, 2020) (integrating the novelties of comparative law into the Portuguese rule of law).
18. *See* CEPEJ, COUNCIL OF EUROPE, EUROPEAN JUDICIAL SYSTEMS: EFFICIENCY AND QUALITY OF JUSTICE 26, 71–91 (2018 ed. 2016).
19. *See* Lei n° 34/2004 de 29 de julho [Law no. 34/2004 of 29 July], https://dre.pt/application/conteudo/502394 (last visited Sept. 23, 2020) (determining a common set of rules for transnational legal proceedings inside the European Union in matters of access to justice and courts). The law has been updated and republished in 2007: Lei n° 47/2007 of de 28 de Agosto [Law no. 47/2007 of 28 August], https://dre.pt/application/conteudo/641076 (last visited Sept. 23, 2020). Articles 8°, 8°A, and 8°B establish the definition of economic need (indexed to the scale of social benefits), the type of documentation and forms for the beneficiary to complete, and Article 9° defines that in these cases all justice taxes are free of payment.
20. *See* Lei n° 30-E/2000 de 20 de dezembro [Law no. 30-E/2000 of 20 December], https://dre.pt/application/conteudo/315338 (last visited Sept. 23, 2020).
21. *Ordem Vai Criar Lista de Advogados Especialistas em Violência Doméstica*, PUBLICO, www.publico.pt/2018/07/06/sociedade/noticia/ordem-vai-criar-lista-de-advogados-especialistas-em-violencia-domestica-1837108 (last visited Sept. 23, 2020) (last visited Sept. 23, 2020).
22. More information about the work of the commission can be found at COMISSÃO PARA A CIDADANIA E LA IGUALDADE DE GÉNERO, www.cig.gov.pt.
23. Interview with Manuela Frias, Legal Aid Commissioner, Lisbon Regional Council (May 7, 2018).
24. Lawyers' status was published in the form of legislation. Lei n° 145/2015 de 9 de setembro [Law no. 145/2015 of 9 September], https://dre.pt/application/conteudo/70236273, establishes the new status of the Portuguese bar; in particular, Article 69 on "freedom of practice" regulates the right of all lawyers, enrolled members of the bar, to practice all types of acts regarding the profession in total independence from any private or public authority.
25. *Processo de Inscrição dos Advogados no Sistema de Acesso ao Direito e aos Tribunais*, ORDEM DOS ADVOGADOS, https://portal.oa.pt/comunicacao/noticias/2018/10/processo-de-inscricao-dos-advogados-no-sistema-de-acesso-ao-direito-e-aos-tribunais/ (last visited Sept. 23, 2020).
26. *See* Lei n° 47/2007 de 28 de agosto [Law no. 47/2007 of 28 August], https://dre.pt/application/conteudo/641076 (last visited Sept. 23, 2020)

(promoting the simplification of the legal aid system by the use of an ITC platform).

27. Interview with Manuela Frias, *supra* note 23.
28. Interview with two lawyers working in individual practice (May 20 and 25, 2018). Both confirmed the delays of the minister of justice in payment for legal aid services in the 1990s and 2000s.
29. *See Estado Pagou no Ano Passado 59 Milhões de Euros a Advogados em Apoio Judiciário*, PUBLICO, www.publico.pt/2016/07/04/sociedade/noticia/estado-pagou-no-ano-passado-59-milhoes-a-advogados-em-apoio-judiciario-1737170#&gid=1&pid=2 (last visited Sept. 23, 2020).
30. Data from the minister of justice.
31. Susana Santos, *Novas Reformas, Velhos Debates: Análise das Políticas de Justiça e dos Seus Impactos no Sistema Judicial* [*New Reforms, Old Debates: Analysis of Legal Policies and Their Impact in the Judicial System*], 13 CONFIGURAÇÕES 11 (2014).
32. Interview with Manuela Frias, *supra* note 23.
33. The discussion on this topic is developed further in this chapter, *infra* "The Institutionalization of Pro Bono in Law Firms."
34. Interview with Teresa Morais Leitão and Marta Vasconcelos Leite (Oct. 24, 2017).
35. *Teresa Morais Leitão*, LINKEDIN, www.linkedin.com/in/tleitao/ (last visited Sept. 23, 2020).
36. *Inês Graça*, LINKEDIN, www.linkedin.com/in/inescfgraca/ (last visited Sept. 23, 2020).
37. *Entreajuda* is a platform for NGOs responsible for gathering organizations with common goals by promoting contact and sharing of resources. *Banco Alimentar* is a member of the European Federation of Food Banks. In Portugal, the activities are spread throughout the country, and it is the best-known NGO with thousands of volunteers, organizing massive collections of food in supermarkets with the help of young volunteers, mostly Catholic scouts.
38. Lei n° 49/2004 de 24 de agosto [Law no. 49/2004 of 24 August], https://dre.pt/application/conteudo/479604 (last visited Sept. 23, 2020) (defining and regulating all professional activities allowed to lawyers and solicitors), known as LAPAS – *Lei dos Actos Próprios dos Advogados e dos Socilitadores*.
39. Lei n° 49/2004 de 24 de agosto [Law no. 49/2004 of 24 August], https://dre.pt/application/conteudo/479604 (last visited Sept. 23, 2020). Articles 5 and 15 establish the necessity of a protocol between an external entity (NGO, trade union, municipality) and the bar to open a space where citizens can have direct contact with a lawyer for a special fee.
40. Lei n° 34/2004 de 29 de julho (Law no. 34/2004 of 29 July), https://dre.pt/application/conteudo/502394 (last visited Sept. 23, 2020), *as amended by* Decreto-Lei n° 71/2015 de 6 de maio [Decree-Law no. 71/2015 of 6 May], https://dre.pt/application/conteudo/67144143 (last visited Sept. 23, 2020), *and* Lei n° 49/2004 de 24 de agosto [Law no.

49/2004 of 24 August], https://dre.pt/application/conteudo/479604 (last visited Sept. 23, 2020). Law no. 47/2007 regulates the system of access to courts and legal aid. Regional council ethics commissions have publicized several decisions on these matters reinforcing the idea of illegal recruitment of clients whenever protocols are not signed, and the bar is not contacted in advance. Decision n° 38/PP/2012–P and n° 10/PP/2011–P, Ethics Commission, Porto Regional Council; Decision n° 24/PP/2018–C, Coimbra Ethics Commission.

41. The Lisbon Metropolitan area concentrates the political, economic, and social powers in the country.
42. Fundación Aranzadi Lex Nova, Conexión Pro Bono: Guía Para la Práctica de Voluntariado Jurídico (2015).
43. Robert Abbey & Andrew Boon, *Moral Agendas? Pro Bono Publico in Large Law Firms in the United Kingdom*, 60 Mod. L. Rev. 630 (1997); Martha F. Davis, *Access and Justice: The Transformative Potential of Pro Bono Work*, 73 Fordham L. Rev. 903 (2004); Rebecca L. Sandefur, *Lawyers' Pro Bono Service and American-Style Civil Legal Assistance*, 41 Law & Soc'y Rev. 1 (2007).
44. Follow-up interview with António Morais Leitão, Francisco Maia Cerqueira, and Marta Vasconcelos Leite, volunteers, PBA (May 11, 2018).
45. Pro Bono Ajuda Legal, Relatório de Atividades 2017–2018, https://docs.wixstatic.com/ugd/7068a1_67e05890fa6d42b48d4e84ccc101abcd.pdf (last visited Sept. 23, 2020).
46. *Centro Social do Barredo, Vida Norte, Norte Vida, SAOM, Qualificar Para Incluir, Movimento de Defesa da Vida, Movimento 1 Euro.*
47. *Italy Pro Bono Day*, Pro Bono Italia, http://probonoitalia.org/en/event/236-italy-pro-bono-day (last visited Sept. 23, 2020).
48. Agência Empreendedores Sociais, www.seagency.org (last visited Sept. 23, 2020) (last visited Sept. 23, 2020).
49. *Global Pro Bono Summit*, Global Pro Bono Network, https://globalprobono.org/events/summit/ (last visited Sept. 23, 2020).
50. SEA, Pro Bono Portugal Study Final Report (2015), https://app.box.com/s/3oa2kclht1kbkqg8bykfsyei34jlymq6 (last visited Sept. 23, 2020).
51. Girl Move is an NGO with offices in Lisbon and Nampula, Mozambique. The main goal of the organization is to empower girls through education. Girl Move, www.girlmove.org (last visited Sept. 23, 2020).
52. In 2015, the legal aid system supported 153,914 cases in court. Data is available only for the total number of cases; it is not possible to obtain the numbers for each type of court.
53. Yves Dezalay, Marchands du Droit: La Restructuration de l'Ordre Juridique International par les Multinationales du Droit (1992); Bourdieu, *supra* note 16.
54. In English, "shirtless." The term is used to refer to the poor and low-income classes, comparable with the expression *sans culottes* used by the elite during the French Revolution to refer to the groups that

supported the revolutionary cause. In the twentieth century the expression *descamisados* became popular in Argentina during the presidency of Perón.

55. Interview with a pro bono coordinator (Nov. 2017).
56. Interview with a solo practitioner (Jan. 2018).
57. Interview with a lawyer from a large law firm (Nov. 2016).
58. Interview with a lawyer working in a large law firm in Lisbon (Sept. 8, 2017).
59. Interview with a lawyer from a large law firm (Aug. 2016).
60. Interview with a lawyer working in a large law firm (Sept. 2016).
61. ANNE WITZ , PROFESSIONS AND PATRIARCHY (1992).
62. Interview with a pro bono coordinator (Feb. 2017).
63. Interview with a pro bono manager (Oct. 2017).
64. Interview with a lawyer from Morais Leitão.
65. *E.g.*, *Linklaters Wins Two Africa Deal of the Year Awards at the PFI Awards 2017*, LINKLATERS, www.linklaters.com/en/about-us/news-and-deals/news/2017/linklaters-wins-two-africa-deal-of-the-year-pfi-awards-2017 (last visited Sept. 23, 2020). Linklaters law firm won the Africa Deal of the Year 2017 in the category of project finance with the Nacala Corridor Rail and Port Project in Mozambique and Malawi and the Coral South Floating Liquefied Natural Gas, also in Mozambique. The London and Lisbon offices worked together.
66. Interview with a lawyer from a multinational law firm (July 2016).
67. Sarah Dezalay, *Lawyers in Africa: Brokers of the State, Intermediaries of Globalization: A Case Study of the "Africa" Bar in Paris*, 25 IND. J. GLOBAL LEG. STUD. 649 (2018).
68. Interview with a pro bono manager, PLMJ (Oct. 20, 2017).
69. *See generally* Dezalay, *supra* note 67.
70. When the fieldwork started, these young lawyers had already finished their internship in both VdA and the PBA and had returned to Mozambique.
71. Steven Vaughan, Linden Thomas & Alastair Young, *Symbolism over Substance? Large Law Firms and Corporate Social Responsibility*, 18 LEG. ETHICS 138 (2015).
72. Andrew Boon & Avis Whyte, "*Charity and Beating Begins at Home*": *The Aetiology of the New Culture of Pro Bono Publico*, 2 LEG. ETHICS 169 (1999).
73. David Nelken, *Using the Concept of Legal Culture*, 29 AUSTL. J. LEG. PHIL. 1 (2004).
74. DEZALAY, *supra* note 53.
75. NIKLAS LUHMANN , LAW AS SOCIAL SYSTEM (2004).
76. Lawrence M. Friedman, *Law, Lawyers, and Popular Culture*, 98 YALE L.J. 1579 (1989).
77. John Flood, *The Re-landscaping of the Legal Profession: Large Law Firms and Professional Re-Regulation*, 59 CURRENT SOC. 507 (2011).
78. *See* Gerard Hanlon, *Professionalism as Enterprise: Service Class Politics and the Redefinition of Professionalism*, 32 SOC. 43 (1998).

79. Gerard Hanlon, *Sacking the New Jerusalem? – The New Right, Social Democracy and Professional Identities*, SOCIOLOGICAL RESEARCH ONLINE (May 31, 2000), www.socresonline.org.uk/5/1/hanlon.html (last visited Sept. 23, 2020).
80. More information can be found at *A Nossa História*, GRACE, www.grace.pt/sobre_o_grace/historia (last visited Sept. 23, 2020).
81. The president of the NGO is Margarida Couto, partner and pro bono director of VdA law firm (2018–20).
82. *NP 4469 - Sistemas de Gestão da Responsabilidade Social*, SGS, https://www.sgs.pt/pt-pt/sustainability/social-sustainability/social-responsibility-sr/social-responsibility-management-systems (last visited Sept. 23, 2020).
83. Social Accountability International, www.sa-intl.org/index.cfm?fuseaction=Page.ViewPage&pageId=472 (last visited Feb. 28, 2019).
84. Definition found in SRS ADVOGADOS, RELATÓRIO DE RESPONSABILIDADE SOCIAL 2016 3 (2017).
85. Interview with a pro bono manager (Oct. 10, 2017).
86. NEGÓCIOS [BUSINESS], ANUÁRIO DAS SOCIEDADES DE ADVOGADOS 2015 (2016). The publication is offered to readers of the economic newspaper *Negócios* once a year. Even if this is a paid publication, and in that sense a form of advertising prohibited by the Portuguese Bar Association, the publication is presented as a national directory.
87. The relation between pro bono reports and the size of the firm is confirmed by two statistical units of measure, a chi-square test (χ^2 (4) =27.599; p=0.000 and V of Cramer=0.510). The same tests were conducted to analyze the relation between CSR and the size of the firm, chi-square test (χ^2 (4)=27.989; π=0.000 and V of Cramer=0.533). Both tests confirm that an association of medium intensity exists.
88. *Rock'n'Law 2019*, ROCK'N'LAW, www.rocknlaw.pt/evento-rock-n-law/ (last visited Sept. 23, 2020).
89. ROCK'N'LAW, www.rockandlaw.org/index.html#que (last visited Sept. 23, 2020).
90. The Portuguese term for the first hearing by a judge in a judicial process.
91. Heroes of the office.
92. Outlaw.
93. A pun with the words "law" and "*cura*" (healing), in Portuguese a phonetical resemblance with "*loucura*" (madness).
94. Interview with a pro bono coordinator, SRS (Oct. 16, 2017).
95. Rock'n'Law Lisboa, *ROCK'n'LAW 2018 - Uma Década a Apoiar Causas*, YOUTUBE, www.youtube.com/watch?v=f6VeatogMko (last visited Sept. 23, 2020).
96. *Rock'n'Law*, FACEBOOK, www.facebook.com/Pagina.Rock.n.Law/ (last visited Sept. 23, 2020).

97. Filipa Ambrósio de Sousa, *10 Anos de Rock 'n' Law: Veja Aqui o Vídeo*, ECO, https://eco.pt/2018/10/19/10-anos-de-rock-n-law-veja-aqui-o-video/ (last visited Sept. 23, 2020).
98. Carolina Rico, *Silêncio no Tribunal, que se Vai Cantar. Bandas de Advogados Defendem Causa Solidária*, TSF, www.tsf.pt/cultura/interior/silencio-no-tribunal-que-se-vai-cantar-bandas-de-advogados-defendem-causa-solidaria-10073742.html (last visited Sept. 23, 2020).

CHAPTER ELEVEN

LAWYERS' PRO BONO WORK IN DENMARK

Annette Olesen and Ole Hammerslev

INTRODUCTION

Voluntary work has always been a part of Danish lawyers' DNA and is an integrated part of their self-understanding.[1] However, to understand the extent and development of legal pro bono work in Denmark, which is the aim of this chapter, it is important to emphasize the duality between the restructuring of the modern universal welfare state and the marketization of legal practice. Denmark has a population of nearly 5.8 million and approximately 15,700 legal professionals. Anyone with a master's degree in law is called a "jurist" and considered a member of the legal profession. The title qualifies for many career paths and, with further training, also grants access to monopolized positions as lawyers (or advocates), judges (magistrates, high court, and supreme court judges), and public prosecutors. Approximately one-third of all jurists work in public administration (government departments, counties, and municipalities) and one-third as lawyers or attorneys-at-law.[2]

The development of the Danish welfare state escalated after World War II, propelled by the trade union movement and the Social Democratic Party. The development was founded on the principles of solidarity, equality, and individual autonomy. This welfare state model placed (and still places) great responsibility on the tax-financed public sector to perform as the main protector of all citizens' rights and as promoter of universal welfare benefits and services within education, health, disability, eldercare, and childcare.[3] The strong welfare state aimed to remedy many ills facing Danish society, including its own failures. A public sector complaints-handling system helped citizens resolve their problems with public administration through complaints commissions, appeal committees, and ombudsmen, and even helped to adjust the private market through, for example, consumer councils and housing complaints commissions dealing with landlord–tenant issues.[4] Even though the Danish welfare state is still based on the "universalist" welfare paradigm, its founding principles have been challenged since the economic crises ended the "golden welfare years" in the 1980s.[5] To improve financial viability and create resources for welfare during the austerity policy of the 1980s, the market gained influence on the distribution of wealth, which resulted in the partial contracting out of welfare services.[6] Ever since, the Danish welfare system has undergone fundamental and substantial changes that have enhanced the more libertarian and individualistic nature of the state.[7] In continuation of the reconfiguration of the welfare state, free legal advice has gone from being a welfare state responsibility to a "service" mainly provided by legal expenses insurance (LEI) and different third-sector suppliers.[8]

Simultaneously with the changing welfare structure, pervasive marketization and globalization changed the structure of law firms on both an organizational and a behavioral level. Since the 1980s, the legal market has been liberalized through an unsteady process, which transformed the legal field toward a new capitalistic spirit[9] and rising marketization. The industry differentiated internally and developed into – to use Heinz and Laumann's telling metaphor – "two hemispheres"[10] with a small number of large law firms (creating a legal elite) and a majority of small law offices. On the one hand, large law firms developed through waves of mergers in the early 1980s, which were heavily inspired by the global Anglo-American law firms' organizational structures and legal practices. The US sources of inspiration contributed to the large Danish law firms' focus on corporations and organizations, while they downgraded their businesses concerning legal counseling to individuals. The lawyers employed at the large firms became more specialized and the firms developed new strategic business structures to attract and maintain the best clients, which were increasingly price-conscious and not loyal to one firm. In strategic ways, the law firms furthermore sought to recruit the best graduates directly from law schools. On the other hand, an increasing number of lawyers developed solo practices or small offices, focusing on individual counseling and hence maintaining a more generalist expertise profile.[11]

Considering the reconfiguration of the Danish welfare state and the changing character of the Danish law firms, the purpose of this article is to outline the evolution of legal voluntary work in Denmark in the period 1976–2018. Analytically, we operate with two different definitions of lawyers' commitment to volunteering, which mirror the development of the legal industry toward a more global and market-oriented format. "Legal voluntary work" is the umbrella term we use to characterize the often tacit, unsystematic, and locally based work performed by lawyers who offer legal expertise for low or no payment to (mainly) citizens in need or small businesses. Contrary to the official Danish judicare legal aid scheme, this kind of legal voluntary work is by default neither state-supported nor subjected to any state restrictions. Another way for lawyers to deliver free legal services is by performing pro bono work. "Pro bono" as a term and concept slowly entered the Danish vocabulary and the largest law firms around the early 2000s, which meant that a part of lawyers' voluntary activities were now defined in a wider sense and significantly more systematized by, for example, pro bono budgets, programs, and policies.[12]

In order to draw a comprehensive picture of the changing attitude toward the voluntary endeavor of lawyers and law firms, we will contextualize the present situation of legal aid activity and access to justice by examining recent amendments, changing priorities for, and cutbacks on legal aid provided by lawyers in relation to reconfigurations of the Danish welfare state. Next, we present the methodology of the empirical study. We then empirically analyse the structures and rationales that have dominated and defined the trajectory of Danish lawyers' voluntary work for the last forty-two years. The analysis is divided into three subsections. First, it identifies how voluntary work is understood and carried out in many different ways, depending on the size and profile of the law firms. Second, it examines how voluntary work underwent a systematization process inspired partly by US firms and lately by linking to global organizations. Third, it discusses how law firms' competitive environment and focus on branding has influenced law student culture and self-branding. Finally, we conclude on our analytical findings.

CONTEXTUALIZING DANISH LEGAL AID

The Danish welfare model of legal aid is based on a judicare scheme, which is regulated in the Danish Administration of Justice Act §§

323–324 and includes three types of legal aid institutions, namely legal aid offices, private lawyers, and "Lawyers on Call." The 1960s prevalence of legal aid offices was initially considered an alternative to public legal aid provided by private lawyers, but over the years, the three traditional legal aid providers have supplemented one another. It is the Department of Civil Affairs that decides whether a legal aid office or Lawyers on Call can be licensed as subsidy eligible in legal aid cases. Eligible recipients can annually request government subvention from the Department of Civil Affairs to cover equitable operating costs, such as rent, office supplies, informative work, fees to managers, and on special occasions to counselors (e.g., if in a certain area it is particularly difficult to recruit unpaid, voluntary counselors). Government subventions are grants allocated from the national budget to a specific legal aid fund.[13] Government subventions are thus limited, and Lawyers on Call as well as legal aid offices heavily rely on unpaid voluntary work.

The current legal aid scheme is founded on a unified set of rules based on three stages: stage 1 consists of basic oral legal advice. It is free of charge to all citizens and performed voluntarily by lawyers without any state allowance; stage 2 consists of extended legal advice (beyond oral advice), which includes drawing up simple complaints or applications in writing, such as a summon; stage 3 also consists of extended legal advice, including, for example, settlement negotiations. Contrary to stage 1, clients applying for legal aid on stages 2 and 3 must meet the financial eligibility criteria. While Lawyers on Call, staffed by voluntary, unpaid lawyers and assistant attorneys-at-law, offer free basic oral legal advice (stage 1), private lawyers and legal aid offices, staffed by primarily unpaid, volunteer law students, offer legal aid at all three stages. Private lawyers undertaking legal aid work on stages 2 and 3 require a fixed time rate paid partly by the client and partly by the state.[14] To receive subvention, lawyers nevertheless face a highly bureaucratized reimbursement process, which includes having to request that the client's insurance company or the district court cover that aspect. The regulation of legal aid and of litigation aid refers to civil matters only. Criminal cases, on the contrary, are regulated by the rules concerning appointed attorneys.[15]

The Position of the Danish Bar and Law Society

The Danish Bar and Law Society has always argued "for a prudent legal aid scheme supported by lawyers and to some extent supporting lawyers."[16] Their proposal for a delivery model for legal aid was and is still today centered on lawyers being paid a reasonable fee for legal aid cases. In 1976, lawyers' fixed fee for legal aid cases was considered so low that it was characterized as a "poverty rate," which "caused giggles and pleasantries" among members of the bar.[17] Today, the fixed fee for legal aid cases is still considered unreasonably low and reimbursement unnecessarily bureaucratic.[18] The Danish Bar and Law Society, which refers to itself as "an independent, self-governing and self-funding public law institution comprising all lawyers [in Denmark],"[19] has repeatedly engaged in discussions on government abdication regarding public legal aid and lawyers' legal aid work. The head of council of the Danish Bar and Law Society has emphasized:

> It was never the intension that legal aid provided by [private] lawyers should have an element of charity. And it is obviously unfair when the state and insurance companies force lawyers to work far below the market price and claim it is for the sake of clients' rule of law. This gives rise to frustrations that in a rash moment may cause a lawyer to question whether they should at all perform pro bono work.[20]

The Danish Bar and Law Society thus continues to stir up the debate and fight for taxpayer-subsidized legal aid that mirrors market prices and is provided by private lawyers.

Previous Legal Aid Changes

Since 2007, comprehensive amendments have been launched that have changed the priority list for legal aid suppliers, the infrastructure of the legal aid field, and the role of lawyers. Public expenditure on legal aid provided by lawyers has been cut more than 75 percent since 2006.[21] Litigation aid provided by private lawyers has also recently faced a tightening of the financial eligibility criteria and user charges.[22] Simultaneously with the financial downgrading of private lawyers, expenses to legal aid offices staffed by mainly volunteer law students have increased by more than 50 percent. In line with this development, LEI was approved to overrule the Danish legal aid scheme in 2007. This means that citizens who have an LEI by default are excluded from litigation aid. Instead, they must fill out an application to their insurance company to get (part of) their lawyer or court expenses covered. LEI mainly covers assistance in court cases and arbitration cases. It was introduced to the Danish market in 1970, but unlike many other countries, it is not possible to take out a Danish subscription for an independent LEI. Instead, household insurance and all-risk insurance are prescribed to include LEI, which is why LEI presently is the primary source of legal assistance, as it is included in more than 90 percent of Danes' household insurance policies. The minority without an LEI have the opportunity to apply for litigation aid. However, many concerns regarding LEI have been raised, such as that this kind of legal assistance almost never covers pretrial processes,[23] entire areas of law are without or insufficiently covered by the LEI scheme, and copayments can be so comprehensive that underprivileged policyholders lack the financial means to claim their rights.[24] Moreover, poor payment and burdensome administration are tantamount to few law firms conducting LEI complaints, and even fewer perform their obligations under the LEI scheme.[25]

Changes in the legal aid field are not only mirrored in new supplier priorities and a changing money flow; they are also reflected by areas of law being removed from the scope of the legal aid scheme and a tightening of the eligibility criteria for legal aid clients.[26] To mention an important area of law excluded from the scheme, legal aid assistance in administrative matters regarding claims against or processed by public authorities and cases processed by boards of appeal was ruled out in 2007 as part of a larger reform aiming to modernize and simplify legal aid. Based on a general assessment of the administration of justice, the Committee on the Administration of Justice argued that regarding public administrative cases it was neither necessary nor desirable for citizens to team up with private lawyers offering public legal aid to address public authorities, when public authorities were (already) obligated to assist citizens with justiciable welfare rights.[27] Thus, a citizen cannot seek legal aid until the public authorities have made their decision and the citizen decides to file a complaint against the public authorities' decision. However, Danish legal aid offices have argued that vulnerable citizens with claims against or claims processed by public authorities and cases processed by boards of appeal are often in need of legal aid, because they consider public authorities to be untrustworthy advice-givers and struggle to understand the advice they are given. The Council of the Danish Bar and Law Society has furthermore problematized the public authorities' superiority toward citizens in claims handling situations.[28] In addition, legal aid is no longer provided in small-claims cases. Aiming at ensuring simpler, more efficient, and less expensive court operations, a small-claims court procedure based on citizens' self-representation was introduced in 2008 as a comprehensive reform of the Danish police and court system.[29]

Meanwhile, the legal aid field becomes still more absorbed by conflicting interests. The reconfiguration of the Danish legal aid scheme led to a more formalized collaboration with and responsibility to the third sector, that is, to membership organizations and not-for-profit organizations, some of which rely on the volunteer work of law students.[30] This, in turn, has resulted in a shift in the role of lawyers in providing access to justice. First, they now provide limited services for low or no payment and in circumstances that are administratively burdensome; and, second, they now share the legal aid field with other providers who are not supported by the Department of Civil Affairs and therefore are not constrained by the government's bureaucratic and restrictive subsidy eligibility requirements.

The Danish government has not made an explicit link between less investment in lawyers offering legal aid and more voluntary legal aid work. Nevertheless, the Danish government has explicitly encouraged collaboration between the public and third sector (including volunteer organizations) to relieve the public sector of some of its traditional welfare responsibilities.[31] This encouragement, of course, also goes to legal professionals. To serve as an example, the National Council for Volunteering held a conference in 2006 where it was discussed how the third sector in collaboration with the corporate sector could undertake welfare responsibilities. One way to assume responsibility was discussed by the manager of LawWorks, who illustrated how UK lawyers conducted pro bono work in different settings for the benefit of society.[32] The take-home message concerning the importance of pro bono awareness and encouragement was passed on to most Danish lawyers via the Danish Bar and Law Society's trade magazine *The Lawyer* (*Advokaten*). The fundamental challenges caused by the reduced legal aid scheme have nevertheless been left unstated, and Danish citizens are facing a new reality where they must rely to a greater extent on either insurance or voluntariness from legal professionals and law students to ensure their access to justice. The need for legal aid should be related to the following discussion about how legal expertise via pro bono programs is increasingly allocated to other areas and "purchasers." Pro bono has become a supplement to the legal aid scheme.

MATERIAL AND METHOD

Legal voluntary work in Denmark has received very little academic attention. Several studies have, however, examined the need for legal aid in Scandinavian welfare societies and the legal profession's role in providing legal aid.[33] Recent studies from Denmark and Norway have further discussed legal aid in relation to the welfare state.[34] Yet, these studies do not address pro bono legal work. Because of the research gap regarding lawyers' pro bono work and because only sporadic data on the subject exists, we include relevant data from Norway and Sweden. Considered as "the Nordic legal family,"[35] the development of the Danish, Norwegian, and Swedish legal professions and their historical relationship to the state and the law had similar characteristics and has since the 1980s developed interdependently toward marketization and internationalization.[36] Data of Scandinavian bars and legal institutions (and states in general) can be related because their legal professions in relation to the reconfiguration of the welfare states have undergone comparable and historically interlinked developments.

The core of the following analysis is based on two original data sources: first, a qualitative document analysis of 632 issues of the Danish Bar and Law Society's trade magazine *The Lawyer* was conducted for the period from 1976 to 2018. The period was selected in order to cover developments leading up to the important initiative Lawyers on Call, which was launched in 1978. *The Lawyer* is today printed in eight thousand copies, ten times annually.[37] All lawyers in Denmark are obligated to register as a member of the Danish Bar and Law Society, which makes *The Lawyer* the only trade magazine to reach all lawyers while also addressing relevant stakeholders, journalists, etc. The magazine consists of articles covering topical themes written by external experts and specialized lawyers in various legal fields, the disciplinary boards' most essential decisions regarding complaints against lawyers, and general information from the Danish Bar and Law Society to their members. Each magazine was manually examined to identify the content and contextual setting of discussions about and invitations to do any form of legal voluntary work. No predefinition of legal voluntary work was used. Sections about legal voluntary work were recorded by document title, author(s)/year, keywords, and a summary of the specific discussion based on a who–what–when–where–why–how template.[38] The template facilitated a deeper understanding of the context in which legal voluntary work was discussed. Based on the structured summaries, data was both chronologically and thematically organized and analyzed. The aim was to develop empirical knowledge about the structures and rationale that have dominated and defined the trajectory of lawyers' voluntary work over the last forty-two years. The chronological and thematic structure of the document analysis substantiates the following findings, and references will thus be made only when direct statements from a specific magazine are included.

The second data source consists of an interview study, conducted to strengthen the validity of the document analysis and to make a stronger argument for the interpretation of the diversification of voluntary legal work.[39] Thus, after having emphasized the structures that historically have constituted the framework for lawyers' voluntary work, we conducted semistructured interviews with legal professionals and law students to provide thorough, firsthand knowledge about the changing phenomenon of legal voluntary work. We conducted sixteen interviews in total with legal professionals who represented different positions in the field in terms of different career stages as well as size and location of firms and organizations. The interviewees are divided as follows: four managers from lawyers' organizations, three heads of legal aid offices, one solo practitioner in Copenhagen, one from a small law office in Stockholm, two from a small midsize law firm located in a midsize Danish town, and five practitioners from the top five law firms in Copenhagen, Stockholm, and Oslo. The interviews had a retrospective focus aiming to outline how trends, structures, and rationales of legal practice and culture had emerged and how these developments had framed legal voluntary work in Denmark. The majority of the interviewees had many years of experience, and two interviewees had even been with their firms since the beginning of the mergers and were now retired but still counseling. The data collection's retrospective focus nevertheless did not support an analysis identifying specific agents and intermediaries crucial to the development and import of pro bono programs. Furthermore, we conducted ten interviews with law students with practical experience in the field of legal voluntary work. The interviews were carried out in 2017–18 in Denmark, Norway, and Sweden. They lasted between half an hour to 2 hours and were digitally recorded, transcribed for analyses, and translated from Danish, Norwegian, and Swedish to English when quoted. The names of the interviewees and the involved law firms and organizations are anonymous.

LAWYERS' VOLUNTARY WORK

Legal voluntary work is not a new phenomenon in Denmark. In 1638, the Danish king Christian IV required attorneys to take cases for widows, the insane, the poor, and defenseless people without a fee. The first attempt to systematize voluntary legal aid work may be the establishment of *Studentersamfundets Retshjælp for Ubemidlede* (The Student Association for Securing Legal Aid for the Poor) in 1885, which was related to the University of Copenhagen. In this organization, which later was renamed Copenhagen Legal Aid, publicly employed legal professionals, private lawyers, and law students offered voluntary legal assistance to citizens without means.[40] In 1906, this legal aid initiative was followed by legal requirements that prescribed appointed lawyers outside Copenhagen to provide legal aid to necessitous citizens against a remuneration from the state. The second legal aid office was founded in 1936 in Denmark's second largest city, Aarhus, following the establishment of a legal degree at the University of Aarhus.[41] The budding of lawyers' different voluntary initiatives started to gain momentum in the 1960s when another eight legal aid offices were established in cities scattered across Denmark.

In this section we will examine the development of voluntary legal work in Denmark and discuss lawyers' previous tacit and unsystematic approach to voluntary work. The discussion will be followed by our analysis of how branches of legal voluntary work over time have become more strategic and systematized.

A Tacit and Unsystematic Approach to Legal Voluntary Work

Even though the legal aid field blossomed in the 1960s, legal voluntary work independent from government intrusion and support was still undertaken tacitly without any systematizing or professionalizing efforts. The body of lawyers grew continuously over the years (see Table 11.1), which provided a supply side that needed new counseling markets.[42]

Unlike today, where two-thirds of the Danish bar is situated in the two largest cities and larger law firms occupy a significant proportion of the lawyers, the bar until the 1980s was made up of smaller firms and solo practitioners' offices situated across the country with relatively close relations to the community. However, since the 1980s mergers between law firms have taken place with the effect of creating a division of labor, where solo practitioners and small law firms mainly counsel individuals and small businesses, while the few large law firms counsel the corporate sector and large institutions. Thus, in 1998 no law firms had more than one hundred employees, whereas eight law firms had more than one hundred employees in 2017.[43]

TABLE 11.1 Number of lawyers and assistant attorneys-at-law 1928–2014

Year	1928	1952	1985	2000	2014
Lawyers and assistant attorneys-at-law	1,304	2,170	3,400	4,153	5,337

Source: Hammerslev, Lawyers in Denmark, Sweden & Norway: Liberalisation, Differentiation and the Emergence of a Market for Legal Services, 2020.

The data concerning this geographic dispersal of the lawyers and their roots in the local community suggested that local lawyers were thoroughly versed in their clients' living conditions and familiar with their unique needs, which may involve sensitive legal matters. Legal voluntary work was therefore often provided because lawyers recognized the issue faced by the client or acquaintance and the aid was customized to deal with that exact issue and carried out as a private affair between the local lawyer and the client or acquaintance.[44] In line with lawyers' multifaceted approaches to voluntary work, a knowing senior lawyer from one of the largest Danish law firms expressed how, back in the 1970s, he had experienced an unspoken code of ethics permeating the bar and local lawyers' approach to low-income clients:

> You may say that running a law firm was previously more like running a Robin Hood business . . . you did not charge too much. You would charge the important clients in the big cases, so you could keep the prices down, thus Mr. and Mrs. Sørensen could afford to draw up a will. What I am saying is that everybody should be able to afford a lawyer, to draw up a will, and they would not be able to afford that if you charged them your hourly wage. So, in that sense there has always been a sort of pro bono element in it.

Among many different aid measures, one way to contribute to "charity" was through an unsystematic and unspoken "low bono," that is, a redistribution of lawyers' fees benefiting those in need and to the detriment of the well-off – not the lawyers themselves. Thus, legal voluntary work was in this period closely linked with the local community, dependent on personal relations, and permeated with irregularity.

Lawyers on Call

During the 1970s, the bar gained a tarnished reputation for poor lawyering and was accused of being "unable to speak to ordinary people, being greedy and only think of money."[45] This occurred simultaneously with the Danish welfare state facing economic pressure, which challenged the distribution of welfare services. Ordinary people's need for legal assistance was furthermore identified in several studies during this period,[46] and unmet need for legal aid turned out to be the pivot to improve the bar's reputation. A group of progressive lawyers and the Danish Bar and Law Society each developed their own respective initiatives to improve the bar's low reputation and ensure access to justice for people in need. The Danish Bar and Law Society's proposal focused on reforming and systematizing legal aid. In 1978, they put forward a legal aid model developed with support from the Ministry of Justice, which was based on lawyers providing basic oral legal aid for a fixed fee (three-fourths state-funded, one-fourth client copayment). Contrary to this, a group of lawyers wanted to position Danish lawyers and law offices as independent, qualified, and progressive counselors and protectors of the rule of law who cared for all citizens' access to justice without demanding payment for basic oral legal advice. As a result, Lawyers on Call was launched in 1978. This initiative added a new systematization to legal voluntary work independent from the government's interference and subsidy,[47] and independent of the Danish Bar and Law Society. The first Lawyers on Call was established in Copenhagen, and more than fifty lawyers volunteered for the project. The idea was that lawyers and assistant attorneys-at-law should be at the disposal of any citizen who personally sought aid. The aid should be provided without payment, and lawyers should be available for a few hours weekly in which they assisted citizens in all legal matters with basic oral legal advice.[48] Our data shows how the initiative gained a foothold during the 1980s and became a lawyers' grassroots movement in the rest of the country, as it extended to local practicing lawyers who met citizens at public libraries, in court buildings, and occasionally at law offices around the country. Annually, however, basic financial public support to Lawyers on Call has been allocated since the 1980s to cover equitable operating costs. One of the founders of the initiative stated the following when interviewed on the occasion of the twenty-fifth anniversary of Lawyers on Call:

> Not only did my colleagues turn up and offered help without payment. The first six months, each lawyer also paid 100 DKK [approx. 15 USD] monthly to cover the offices' expenses for light, heath, and cleaning until the Ministry of Justice started paying the operating costs . . . . The

> initiative had nothing to do with party policy. It was the grassroots that rose and established this initiative without asking permission from the Danish Bar and Law Society. It was people driven by public spirit.

She went on to recall how the volunteer lawyers during the first years – in the spirit of the time – met up after counseling and had a beer and went out to dinner while discussing the inquiries of the day and the legal issues of the time. Today, twenty-five years later, volunteer lawyers no longer hang out after having finished counseling, and the beer crate at the back of the office is long gone. "Today young lawyers hurry back to their family or they have to go back to the office. They are extremely purposeful [or goal-oriented rational acting, to use Weber's notion]."[49]

Since Lawyers on Call was not providing extended legal assistance but offered only basic oral advice and fragmentary information, the initiative has been referred to as a "legal emergency room" that provided "legal first aid" but did not cope with citizens' legal problems in detail. Regardless of certain limitations, our data shows that the services provided by Lawyers on Call were the pivot of the legal voluntary work debate in the 1980s and 1990s.

THE COMMENCING OF PRO BONO WORK

In the early 2000s, new trends reshaped the legal industry and the way large law firms interpreted and undertook voluntary work. A good example of the transformation of voluntary work and how lawyers and law firms reconsidered the potential thereof is the Swedish bar's approach to the tsunami catastrophe in southeast Asia in 2004, where more than five hundred Swedish citizens died or went missing. The Swedish Bar Association established a project that helped the victims and their families. The project became the largest Swedish legal pro bono project ever, with 275 law firms of all sizes participating and collaborating. The lawyers spent 24,400 pro bono hours on cases related to different fields of law, such as foundation law, corporate law, family law, estate law, and insurance law.[50] After the catastrophe, Swedish lawyers (re)defined their social responsibility and slowly raised their pro bono awareness. A lawyer from a top five firm noted:

> After the tsunami [in 2004] the Bar Association urged law firms to spend hours in a form of time bank. We wanted to take part in that [project] just like many other firms did. Subsequently, I think that many firms,

> instead of giving Christmas presents and the like, have started to spend not only money but also time and engagement and the like ... on sustainable efforts.

The term "pro bono" was entered in the Danish vocabulary at the beginning of the 2000s,[51] and our analysis of *The Lawyer* shows how the pro bono concept, like in the Swedish case, slowly seized a prominent position in the large Danish law firms' reestablishment and in their branding profiles. Until the 2000s, Denmark and the other Scandinavian countries had limited experiences with systematized legal pro bono work.[52] However, the large law firms had slowly gained a foothold, and they adopted the pro bono concept. According to our document analysis, the inspiration came primarily from global Anglo-American law firms, through American experts who supervised the industry and via Danish lawyers who had spent time in the United States.

Large law firms began to systematize and professionalize their pro bono work, which has resulted in specific lawyers being heads of pro bono programs.[53] A senior lawyer from one of the Danish top five law firms elaborates:

> Our company has an arrangement; we assist a number of charitable associations with aid without payment. I do not know the scale of it, but it is definitely quite a few [associations] and according to my knowledge, it is quite a lot of effort we are putting into it .... I think it [pro bono work] has always been there. It is not unusual for our industry. It has just become more systematized.

The systematization of pro bono work mentioned by the senior lawyer recurs in the interviews with lawyers from the large law firms several times. It reflects why a company policy is necessary, as market considerations permeate the largest law firms and call for consistent invoicing and time recording in order for lawyers to justify their actions and to make sure that the tasks they have spent their time on stand out distinctly. When the individual lawyer undertakes pro bono work, it requires understanding from the employer, who should be able to see that pro bono work also benefits the firm. In that connection, another senior lawyer stresses that it is of vital importance "to undertake pro bono work in orderly conditions" when the firm's business model is founded on profit sharing and "true partnership."[54] As an example, another top five law firm places pro bono hours as equal with debiting hours when it comes to paying bonuses to lawyers and assistant attorneys-at-law. The firms' organization of pro bono work can thus take different forms and have different impact. In 2011, for example, the first Danish law firm became affiliated with TrustLaw Connect, which helps nongovernmental organizations (NGOs) transnationally, while other firms have worked pro bono for transnational NGOs without the affiliation of transnational intermediary organizations.

Differentiated Pro Bono Work

There is no statistical data on the amount of pro bono work in Denmark, but two Norwegian business surveys of lawyers and law firms indicate that employees' awareness about the firms' pro bono activities has grown from approximately 65 percent to 90 percent between 2013 and 2015, and with the surge in awareness an increase in pro bono hours simultaneously occurred. Of the Norwegian law firms with more than 50 lawyers, 25 percent undertook pro bono work in 2013, which on average amounted to 150 pro bono hours annually. Two years later, 92 percent of firms with more than 50 lawyers worked pro bono and had increased their average annual pro bono hours to 850.[55] However, the surveys neither establish a precise definition of pro bono work nor clarify what kind of pro bono work the Norwegian lawyers undertake. The development of Norwegian law firms' amount of pro bono work is most likely comparable to the situation in Denmark. Thus, a 2018 CSR report from one of the top five law firms in Denmark reported that more than fifty assistant attorneys-at-law, lawyers, and partners spent more than 1,000 working hours on their pro bono programs.[56] The increased awareness and undertaking of pro bono work coincided with an enhanced focus in *The Lawyer* on pro bono work and a discussion about whether law firms should be required to do pro bono work.

Like in the Norwegian surveys, no clear definition of pro bono work exists in Denmark. Nevertheless, according to the Association of Danish Law Firms' code of social responsibility, pro bono work may consist of a range of different services supporting, for example, disadvantaged groups in society with individual legal aid, national or international organizations and associations, and local communities.[57] For example, pro bono work can consist of providing legal advice to sports associations, cultural and religious institutions, or to teach or disseminate professional knowledge.[58] The diverse understanding of pro bono work is also reflected in our interviews in which the lawyers included various forms of voluntary work as pro bono work, such as collegial work in the bar association, disciplinary councils, teaching, and legal advice to national and international organizations. The interviews also showed how pro bono work was considered in relation to – or at the same level as – giving grants to specific communities or purposes. As a senior partner in one of the top five Swedish law firms noted,

> We receive a lot of applications from individuals, organizations and local communities who want money or legal advice .... We meet young students in disadvantaged areas to tell them about how it is to work in the judicial system ... we have internships, we give money to those schools.

Even though "pro bono work" as a term has taken precedence over "legal voluntary work" in the legal field's vocabulary, our data suggests that the field's differentiated positions of lawyers from the elite law firms on the one hand, and solo practitioners or lawyers from small law offices on the other, understood and approached their commitment to volunteering very differently.[59] Lawyers in smaller law offices did not have the financial capacity to carry out highly systematized programs and therefore favored a more flexible approach that focused on supporting individuals and local communities, which included Lawyers on Call work. When smaller law firms occasionally organized their voluntary involvement, the limited amount of inquiries to support community-based activities meant that they did not have to target their initiatives and make sure they reflected the company's policy and core values.

Pro Bono Strategies Included in CSR Programs

The elasticity of the pro bono concept was further illustrated in its combination with law firms' corporate social responsibility (CSR) programs.[60] The first law firms included pro bono work in their CSR in 2009, and other large law firms have followed suit. The merging of CSR and pro bono programs emphasized how earnings, recruitment, branding, and charity are interknitted elements strategically contemplated through a "win-win perspective." In that regard, a senior partner notes that "it [pro bono work] is important .... When we have meetings with clients, they also ask which type of pro bono work we do. We find it very important; it is important for us just like it is very important for society."

The Scandinavian bar associations have regularly encouraged law firms to incorporate social justice values into their practices and strategies since it strengthens the law firm's relationship with its clients, its reputation, recruitment, and retention.[61] The largest law firms' pro bono work has deemphasized legal advice to individuals including traditional Lawyers on Call work at the expense of collaborations or even partnerships with NGOs, local communities, educational institutions, etc. The largest law firms' systematization of pro bono work is equally important when it comes to graduate and client recruitment, that is, a form of business case for pro bono work.[62] The newest tendencies are that some of the largest law firms have joined the UN Global Compact's governance framework and, in accordance with this, publish their CSR program yearly. The Association of Danish Law Firms has recently implemented a specific code of conduct, which includes social responsibility and pro bono work to demarcate lawyers' work from other professions and counselors. They not only give online advice, provide examples of CSR and pro bono work, and discuss ethical and societal issues relevant to lawyers; they also give step-by-step guidance on how to conduct pro bono work.[63]

Competitive or on the Prowl?

Our data illustrates that there are two sides of the coin when it comes to the reformed legal industry with its intensified competition and the new requirements of CSR. On the one hand, large law firms managed to engage with specific third-sector organizations and local communities that assist various people with different needs. On the other hand, law firms started to compete with one another to attract the most beneficial organizations to support. As a solo practitioner who is strongly engaged in pro bono work noted: "Suddenly it became mightily modern to do pro bono work. The large law firms had entire branches of pro bono work. And they went on the prowl in our territories." This statement suggests that with the enhanced focus on CSR, law firms increasingly competed for the most relevant and significant organizations and initiatives to offer their legal assistance as pro bono.

Large Danish law firms' enhanced focus on CSR reflects the reconfiguration of the legal industry. The Danish legal industry competes in a new market structure with critical, less loyal clients and strategic competitors. At the same time, the welfare state has withdrawn from a number of social areas that were previously considered a state responsibility. This abdication left room for third-sector organizations and civil society to take on more social responsibility. The shift in social welfare providers also influenced the legal industry and expanded its areas of responsibility. However, the competition to find the most suitable organizations to support has also been met with skepticism among more traditional lawyers with exhaustive experience in work on a voluntary basis. These lawyers criticized the knowledge profile that had slowly developed since the early 2000s and had led to specialized lawyers employed at large law firms with legal skills relevant for organizations and companies, compared with generalist lawyers from smaller law offices or solo practitioners to work with counseling of individuals. As the large firms still groped for a clear strategy for their pro bono work, a few unfortunate misfits between law firms and organizations did not help the organizations as intended, if at all. A lawyer stressed such a view by noting that "it is obvious that the statutes in an ecclesiastical organization are different than the statutes in Novo Nordisk. The law firm had advised the organization wrongly, so the organization ended up paying a fortune on lawyers' fees. So, then I said, 'That is not pro bono.'"

After the preliminaries and after having committed slip-ups when assuming the role of "pro bono command" of some attractive organizations, law firms started to focus their efforts and target their competence profiles strategically to benefit the collaborating organizations, NGOs, etc. Thus, lawyers with a specialized profile often argued that their daily training and orientation toward business law and global markets hindered them in adopting a legal generalist perspective and in handling citizens' ordinary cases. As a lawyer from a top firm noted on a question about giving legal advice directly to citizens:

> If you work in one of the largest firms, you are good at business law, but not good at family law, criminal law, or asylum law. You do not know anything about that. Therefore, if you want to give advice to the really needy, it has to be in an indirect way. To start to devote time to asylum law as a lawyer would be too difficult and do no good.

Acknowledging the limitations of specialized profiles, the strategic approach to pro bono work was even further strengthened in the large firms. Thus, they focused on helping mainly organizations and associations that to a certain extent corresponded in size and profile to the firms' paying client groups. In that way, the firms utilized their specific knowledge profile.

Lawyers on Call Facing Hardships

As a part of the reconfiguration of the welfare state and its focus on effectiveness, the judicial system was also reformed in order to make large and more professional entities. This led to a reform of the Danish judicial system from 2007, merging eighty-two jurisdictions into twenty-four larger district courts. This structural change gave rise to a large relocation of law firms, and lawyers moved from provinces to cities where district courts were now situated and furthermore contributed to closure threats or shutdowns of a large number of Lawyers on Call in peripheral regions.[64] The availability of initial legal assistance has thus dropped dramatically, as Lawyers on Call were only located in sixty-three places in Denmark in 2017 compared to one hundred in 2004.[65] Statistical data on enquiries to Lawyers on Call from 1985 to 2001 likewise show that the number of inquiries increased until the mid-1990s, after which it dropped and returned to roughly twenty thousand inquiries annually, which is comparable to the number of inquiries in 1985,[66] despite the fact that citizens still have unmet legal needs.[67]

A senior lawyer from a midsize law firm implicitly touched upon the downturn of Lawyers on Call when, during an interview, he recalled memories from his activities as a lawyer in the 1980s. On these grounds he emphasized: "What is interesting is that ... back in the day, all lawyers took their share, you agreed on providing voluntary legal work .... Today, I presume that 95 percent of the lawyers in this country have never offered legal assistance without payment." This critical statement from a senior lawyer should be considered in the light of the technical and geographical distances between lawyers and the local population that have slowly taken shape and challenged the grassroots tradition of Lawyers on Call. Moreover, new working conditions and procedures following the marketization characterizing the bar have influenced the understanding and performance of volunteering commitments.

A head of a Lawyers on Call working group under the Danish Bar and Law Society's Council emphasizes that "it is the same lawyers who are doing the hard [Lawyers on Call] work and when they get older there is a need for the next generation to take over."[68] One of the main barriers to maintaining the grassroots tradition, however, is that young lawyers are driven away from idealistic, voluntary work, which challenges the recruitment of lawyers and attorneys-at-law to Lawyers on Call. To cope with the recruitment challenge, the Danish Bar and Law Society formed a committee in 2011 to promote that Lawyers on Call are competitive and among the opportunities that lawyers and law firms prioritize when determining a pro bono program. The committee's intention was, among others, to draw attention to lawyers' responsibility to society in providing legal aid to marginalized groups that otherwise were deprived of free legal advice. Moreover, the committee stressed that Lawyers on Call experiences are rewarding and of great personal and professional value to the lawyers who offer this service. Nevertheless, when the committee asked lawyers with Lawyers on Call experience whether there were any measures that could be put in place to support their voluntary work, the lawyers' common suggestions did not focus on the moral obligation of lawyers to serve society. On the contrary, they advocated for structuring Lawyers on Call work so that they could brand themselves as committed members of the community through, for example, a specific Lawyers on Call labeling solution. In addition, they suggested Lawyers on Call work to be included in their (private) businesses' CSR program, and they would furthermore like to use the opportunity for drawing in new clients when providing voluntary work.[69] Another working group under the Association of Danish Law Firms[70] and the Danish Bar and Law Society came up with recommendations about how to attract more lawyers to Lawyers on Call.[71] The working group suggested that the Association of Danish Law Firms and the Danish Bar and Law Society should offer free-of-charge courses relevant for assistant attorneys-at-law and lawyers, who should get credit for taking these courses as a part of mandatory postgraduate training. Another suggestion was to endorse voluntary work in Lawyers on Call as a postgraduate course. Thus, the working groups' strategies serve as an example of how the nature of traditional voluntary legal work is transformed and commoditized. To recruit lawyers to take part in Lawyers on Call work, the working group recommendations focused on how lawyers could benefit financially or educationally from working pro bono rather than relying on a moral ethos of social responsibility to facilitate and enhance access to justice. Regardless of these points of criticism, Lawyers on Call work is still of great importance in providing basic oral legal advice to people in need.

LAW STUDENTS' PERSONAL BRANDING

It is not only among law firms that competition has increased over the years, and strategic branding cannot only be attributed to lawyers. A comparable development (on a smaller scale) has also taken place among law students.

The reconfiguration of the welfare state and the marketization of the legal industry have influenced the way law students approach and take part in voluntary work. First, law firms and other employers of law students have professionalized their recruitment processes to get the best graduates, which, among other places, is emphasized at universities' career fairs.[72] Second, the students' scramble for higher grades is today combined with so-called individual branding strategies. Social ethos and moral engagement of lawyers is not (yet) highly promoted in the universities' curricula and approaches.[73] Instead, university career counselors and law school recruitment panels urge students to market themselves and to consider student-related activities that can provide them with practical experience, a network, and a compelling CV. In short, the students are encouraged to strategically consider whether and how activities can contribute to a personal and academic profile that may help them land their dream job after graduation. Third, the welfare state's reconfigurations have made it possible for legal aid offices and third-sector organizations to expand their domains of legal advice. Law students are therefore recruited to these volunteer positions. Voluntary work and entrepreneurship may provide a positive impact on students' personal brand, strengthen their CV, and arouse interest in their LinkedIn profile. Our data suggests that voluntary tasks, including legal aid work, is not only run by students with a predominant desire to ensure effective access to justice for people in need but also driven by the students' objectives of providing key components in order to land a future job. Legal aid offices are dependent on law students working on a voluntary basis, but many law students' professional approach to personal branding and short-lived interest in voluntary work, combined with the law firms' early recruitment of the most talented students, challenged the offices' day-to-day management. As the head of a legal aid office explained:

> We need to recruit the students as early as possible to be able to keep them as long as possible, but they still need some legal knowledge. When they have worked here [at the legal aid office] for a while and they start their master's degree, the law firms recruit them and we can start training new candidates all over again. And that demands considerable resources, which we do not have. But we have no other choice.

Thus, competitive vibes and professional approaches to CSR and pro bono programs related to branding strategies not only permeate the legal industry but also, to a great extent, characterize the culture of law students and their self-image.

FINAL REMARKS

For more than a century, Danish lawyers have been engaged in voluntary work. Our empirical findings concerning the structures and rationales that have dominated and defined the trajectory of lawyers' voluntary work for the last four decades suggests that carrying out voluntary work targeted at those most in need has always been included in Danish lawyers' narratives. Lawyers have further compared their working methods with a "Robin Hood approach" – or low bono – when redistributing the billing to the richest clients and leaving the financially unprivileged with cheaper counseling. Lawyers have, furthermore, fought to maintain a reputation as heralds of the rule of law and defenders of access to justice.

In the late 1970s, the reputation of lawyers was challenged. Simultaneously, the welfare state struggled with being incapable of fully meeting the obligations of the universalist paradigm. The devaluation of the profession's status and the fact that citizens in need were unable to claim their rights, despite a strong welfare state, influenced progressive lawyers to establish a grassroots movement that launched the Lawyers on Call initiative during the late 1970s and 1980s. While the volunteer work of this period (and before) can be characterized as unsystematic and carried out tacitly as private affairs between local lawyers and clients or acquaintances, voluntary work slowly transformed into an enterprise with a relatively clear division of labor between lawyers from the large law firms and lawyers from smaller offices or solo practitioners.

Heavily inspired by Anglo-American law firms, a long-term restructuring of the legal industry slowly began in the 1980s with mergers of law offices. In parallel with the changing lawyers' market, the universal welfare state also reconfigured. The Danish welfare state abdicated from several welfare areas, which placed a greater responsibility on the third sector. These developments encouraged the large Danish law firms to reconsider how to comprehend, structure, and perform voluntary work. Based on these new trends and changing market conditions, the form and content of legal counseling transformed; slowly, voluntary work and voluntariness was translated into pro bono work and became an important aspect in the way the largest law firms organized and performed voluntary work in close relation to the firms' branding strategies and CSR programs. Large law firms therefore tailored pro bono work toward organizations, communities, and the like at the expense of individual citizens, a strategy reflecting the firms' specialized knowledge and market segments in the form of companies and large organizations. These organizations may (or may not) give individual legal advice to their members and/or nonmembers, but the larger law firms mainly gave advice to organizations. Thus, the very change in how large law firms addressed work for a small consideration or free of charge – whether they call it voluntary or pro bono work – has further changed the connotations, audiences, and forms of practice, and it has been strategically developed by systematically considering a firm's brand, values, and expertise. The changing division of voluntary labor indirectly placed the responsibility of performing Lawyers on Call work upon lawyers from the other side of the hemisphere, namely, lawyers from smaller law offices and solo practitioners who had a more generalized legal profile and mainly focused on private clients. Yet, it became increasingly difficult to recruit lawyers and assistant attorneys-at-law to Lawyers on Call.

One question that remains unanswered is whether or not the narrative among lawyers concerning their so-called Robin Hood enterprise and their undertaking of pro bono work is solely based on a social ethos. Our study illustrates that lawyers adopt a win–win approach to voluntary work. The Lawyers on Call initiative was launched in 1978 to improve on the reputation of the legal industry, which was poor at the time. This and the recruitment strategies that were introduced in 2011 to maintain this endangered service not only echo a social ethos but are also permeated by financial and educational concerns. Meanwhile, large law firms prefer to interlink branding, social responsibility, and "charity" and direct this service to partners with similar profiles to the firms' paying clientele; all supported by the Association of Danish Law Firms. One good turn deserves another seems to be the Danish legal industry's approach to voluntary work – throughout history as well.

NOTES

1. We want to thank Tue Schmidt Schack for great assistance with data collection.
2. Ole Hammerslev, *Lawyers in Denmark, Sweden and Norway: Liberalisation, Differentiation and the Emergence of a Market for Legal Services*, *in* LAWYERS IN 21ST-CENTURY SOCIETIES, VOL. 1: NATIONAL REPORTS 175 (Richard L. Abel, Ole Hammerslev, Ulrike Schultz & Hilary Sommerlad eds., 2020).
3. GØSTA ESPING-ANDERSEN, THE THREE WORLDS OF WELFARE CAPITALISM (1990).
4. MADS BRYDE ANDERSEN, ADVOKATRETTEN (2005).
5. ROBERT ERIKSON, THE SCANDINAVIAN MODEL: WELFARE STATES AND WELFARE RESEARCH (1987); THE NORDIC MODEL

OF WELFARE: A HISTORICAL REAPPRAISAL (Niels Finn Christiansen et al. eds., 2006).

6. GIULIANO BONOLI & DAVID NATALI, THE POLITICS OF THE NEW WELFARE STATE (2012).
7. CHRISTOFFER GREEN-PEDERSEN, THE POLITICS OF JUSTIFICATION: PARTY COMPETITION AND WELFARE-STATE RETRENCHMENT IN DENMARK AND THE NETHERLANDS FROM 1982 TO 1998 (2002).
8. Ole Hammerslev & Olaf Halvorsen Rønning, *Outsourcing Legal Aid in the Nordic Welfare States*, *in* OUTSOURCING LEGAL AID IN THE NORDIC WELFARE STATES 311 (Ole Hammerslev & Olaf Halvorsen Rønning eds., 2018); Rosemary Hunter, Annette Olesen & Rebecca L. Sandefur, *Lawyers and Access to Justice*, *in* LAWYERS IN 21ST-CENTURY SOCIETIES: COMPARISONS AND THEORIES (Richard L. Abel, Ole Hammerslev, Ulrike Schultz & Hilary Sommerlad eds., forthcoming).
9. LUC BOLTANSKI & EVE CHIAPELLO, THE NEW SPIRIT OF CAPITALISM (2007).
10. JOHN P. HEINZ & EDWARD O. LAUMANN, CHICAGO LAWYERS: THE SOCIAL STRUCTURE OF THE BAR (1994).
11. Hammerslev, *supra* note 2.
12. We acknowledge that the pro bono concept in many circumstances has replaced the term "legal voluntary work" in the Danish language; however, we retain the two concepts for analytical purposes.
13. BERETNING OM TILSKUD TIL RETSHJÆLPSINSTITUTIONER (2016).
14. DANSKE ADVOKATER & ADVOKATSAMFUNDET, RETSHJÆLPEN I NØD? EN ANALYSE AF UDVIKLINGEN SIDEN 2007 OG DENS KONSEKVENSER (2012).
15. Ch. 66, LBK nr. 1069 af 06.11.2008 om bekendtgørelse af lov om rettens pleje [The Danish Administration of Justice Act].
16. ADVOKATEN, 1976, at 226.
17. *Id.*
18. DANSKE ADVOKATER & ADVOKATSAMFUNDET, RAPPORT OM RETSHJÆLP (2016).
19. SCANDINAVIAN STUDIES IN LAW, STOCKHOLM INSTITUTE FOR SCANDINAVIAN LAW, THE DANISH BAR AND LAW SOCIETY 4 (2009).
20. Sys Rovsing Koch, *Adgangen til Domstolene – Hvis Ansvar er Det?*, ADVOKATEN, 2004.
21. KATRINE ELLERSGAARD, NIELSEN FREDERIK HARHOFF, CLAUS KASTBERG NIELSEN & THOMAS WESTERGAARD-KABELMANN, DANSKE ADVOKATER OG ADVOKATSAMFUNDET, RETSHJÆLPEN I NØD? EN ANALYSE AF UDVIKLINGEN SIDEN 2007 OG DENS KONSEKVENSER (2012); Birgitte Arent Eiriksson, *Den Danske Retshjælpsmodel – er der Lige Adgang til Hjælp?*, JUSTITIA (July 12, 2017), http://justitia-int.org/den-danske-retshjaelpsmodel/#:~:text=8.,ende%20f%C3%A5%20pr%C3%B8vet%20deres%20ret. (last visited Sept. 23, 2020).

22. Marie Krogsgaard Pedersen, *Fri Proces – har Danskerne Reelt Adgang til Domstolene?*, JUSTITIA (May 28, 2016), http://justitia-int.org/analyse-fri-proces-har-danskerne-reelt-adgang-til-domstolene/ (last visited Sept. 23, 2020).
23. DANSKE ADVOKATER & ADVOKATSAMFUNDET, *supra* note 18.
24. Birgitte Arent Eirikkson, *Retshjælpsforsikringer – En Social Skæv Tryghed?*, JUSTITIA (Nov. 27, 2017), http://justitia-int.org/rapport-retshjaelpsforsikring-social-skaev-tryghed/ (last visited Sept. 23, 2020).
25. Association of Danish Law Firms and the Danish Bar and Law Society (2011).
26. Hammerslev & Rønning, *supra* note 8; Bettina Lehmann Kristiansen, *Legal Aid in Denmark*, *in* OUTSOURCING LEGAL AID IN THE NORDIC WELFARE STATES, *supra* note 8, at 99.
27. White Paper 1436/2004.
28. ADVOKATRÅDET 2015, RETSSIKKERHED I FORVALTNINGEN (2015).
29. DANSKE ADVOKATER & ADVOKATSAMFUNDET, *supra* note 14.
30. Hammerslev & Rønning, *supra* note 8; Annette Olesen & Ole Hammerslev, *Nye Udbydere af Retshjælp i Danmark*, *in* FESTSKRIFT TIL HÅKAN HYDÉN (Reza Banakar, Karl Dahlstrand & Lotte Ryberg Welander eds., 2018).
31. SOCIAL OG INDENRIGSMINISTERIET, NATIONAL CIVILSAMFUNDS STRATEGI: EN STYRKET INDDRAGELSE AF CIVILSAMFUNDET OG FRIVILLIGE ORGANISATIONER I DEN SOCIALE INDSATS (2010).
32. Pia Møller, *Pro Bono Batter*, ADVOKATEN, 2004.
33. ARILD EIDESEN, STÅLE ESKELAND & THOMAS MATHIESEN, *RETTSHJELP* OG *SAMFUNNSSTRUKTUR* (1975); STÅLE ESKELAND & JUST FINNE, RETTSHJELP (1973); RETSHJÆLP I ET LOKALOMRÅDE (Lis Sejr ed., 1977); Jørgen Dalberg-Larsen, *Retshjælpsproblemer i et Historisk Perspektiv. Om Behovet for Retshjælp og om Ideologi, Praksis og Forsning på Retshjælpsområdet*, *in* RETSHJÆLP I ET LOKALOMRÅDE, *supra*; Thomas Mathiesen, *Noen Konklusjoner om Rettshjelp, Rettspolitikk og Samfunnsstruktur*, *in* RETTSHJELP OG SAMFUNNSSTRUKTUR, *supra*.
34. JON T. JOHNSEN, RETTEN TIL JURIDISK BISTAND (1987); BØRRE LID, FANGERS RETTSHJELPSBEHOV (1981); CAMILLA LIED, GATEJURISTER: OPPSØKENDE RETTSHJELP TIL FOLK MED RUSRELATERTE PROBLEMER (2013); Ole Hammerslev, *Retshjælpsforskning*, *in* JURIDISKE *EMNER* VED SYDDANSK UNIVERSITET 2015 (Hans Viggo Godsk Pedersen ed., 2016); Ole Hammerslev, Annette Olesen & Stine Piilgaard Porner Nielsen, *Gadejura – Kunsten at Fremelske Gadefolkets Oplevelse af at Bære Rettigheder*, *in* FESTSKRIFT TIL HANS VIGGO GODSK PEDERSEN (Nis Jul Clausen ed., 2017); Hammerslev & Rønning, *supra* note 8; Hunter et al., *supra* note 8; Bettina Lehmann Kristiansen, *Retshjælp – Fortsat et Udækket Behov?*, *in* PROTECTING THE RIGHTS OF OTHERS: FESTSKRIFT TIL JENS VEDSTED-HANSEN (Thomas Gammeltoft-

Hansen, Ida Elisabeth Koch, Bettina Lemann Kristiansen & Sten Schaumburg-Müller eds., 2013).

35. KONRAD ZWEIGERT & HEIN KÖTZ, AN INTRODUCTION TO COMPARATIVE LAW (1998).

36. MARGARETA BERTILSSON, RÄTTEN I FÖRVANDLING. JURISTER MELLAN STAT OCH MARKNAD (1995); OLE HAMMERSLEV, DANISH JUDGES IN THE 20TH CENTURY: A SOCIO-LEGAL STUDY (2003); Vilhelm Aubert, *The Changing Role of Law and Lawyers in Nineteenth- and Twentieth-Century Norwegian Society*, *in* LAWYERS IN THEIR SOCIAL SETTING (Donald Niel MacCormick ed., 1976); Ole Hammerslev, *Convergence and Conflict Perspectives in Scandinavian Studies of the Legal Profession*, 17 INT'L J. LEG. PROF. 135 (2010); Hammerslev, *supra* note 2.

37. The publication tradition has, however, varied significantly over the years: In the period 1976–90 *The Lawyer* was published twenty-four times annually; in 1991 it was published seventeen times; in 1992 it was published eleven times; from 1993 to 2007 it was published twelve times; and from 2008 until today it has been published ten times annually.

38. Nigel King, *Using Templates in the Thematic Analysis of Texts*, *in* ESSENTIAL GUIDE TO QUALITATIVE METHODS IN ORGANIZATIONAL RESEARCH (Catherine Cassell & Gillian Symon eds., 2004).

39. Glenn A. Bowen, *Document Analysis as a Qualitative Research Method*, 9 QUALITATIVE RES. J. 27 (2009).

40. Copenhagen Legal Aid was a source of inspiration for legal clinical work in the United States. Richard J. Wilson, *Legal Aid and Clinical Legal Education in Europe and the USA: Are They Compatible?*, *in* OUTSOURCING LEGAL AID IN THE NORDIC WELFARE STATES, *supra* note 8, at 263. Law students from the University of Copenhagen have been crucial in running the Copenhagen Legal Aid.

41. Thus, setting up legal aid offices and institutions dependent on a certain volume of voluntary work, which was and is still to some extent today dependent on the location of universities offering legal degrees. Birgitte Arent Eiriksson, *Den Danske Retshjælpsmodel – er der Lige Adgang til Hjælp?*, JUSTITIA (July 12, 2017), http://justitia-int.org/den-danske-retshjaelpsmodel/#:~:text=8.,ende%20f%C3%A5%20pr%C3%B8vet%20deres%20ret (last visited Sept. 23, 2020).

42. On lawyers' constructions of new markets, see, for example, RICHARD L. ABEL, AMERICAN LAWYERS (1989).

43. Hammerslev, *supra* note 2.

44. Scott L. Cummings, *The Politics of Pro Bono*, 52 UCLA L. REV. 1 (2004).

45. ADVOKATEN, 1978, at 149.

46. *See, e.g.*, EIDESEN, STÅLE ESKELAND & THOMAS MATHIESEN, *supra* note 33; ESKELAND & FINNE, *supra* note 33; RETSHJÆLP I ET LOKALOMRÅDE, *supra* note 33.

47. BEK nr. 637 af 11.06.2014 om tilskud til retshjælpskontorer og advokatvagter [Executive Order on subsidies for legal aid offices and law firms].
48. ADVOKATSAMFUNDET, RAPPORT OM ADVOKATVAGTER I DANMARK (2011).
49. Anne Meiniche, *Her er Gode Råd Gratis*, BERLINGSKE (Aug. 16, 2003), www.berlingske.dk/samfund/her-er-gode-raad-gratis (last visited Sept. 23, 2020); *see also* MAX WEBER , ECONOMY AND SOCIETY (1978).
50. *Advokater i det Godas Tjänst*, ADVOKATEN, no. 3, 2012, www.advokaten.se/Tidningsnummer/2012/Nr-3–2012-Argang-78/Advokater-i-det-godas-tjanst/ (last visited Sept. 2, 2018).
51. An Infomedia (i.e., a media monitoring company) search of the term "pro bono" underlined a precipitous rise in the use of the term. The search included 17 national, 85 regional, and 457 local newspapers; 587 magazines; 13 news agencies; 1,548 web sources; 31 television features; 46 radio features; and 3 other Danish media sources. It showed that pro bono had not been used as term in 1980–89; it appeared 26 times in 1990–99, 167 times in 2000–09, and 860 times in 2010–18 (Sept. 1, 2018).
52. Ulrika Brandberg & Tom Knutson, *Fokus Pro Bono på Svenska*, ADVOKATEN, 2012.
53. Scott L. Cummings & Deborah L. Rhode, *Managing Pro Bono: Doing Well by Doing Better*, 78 FORDHAM L. REV. 2357 (2010).
54. True partnership means that every assignment is treated as an assignment for the firm, not as an individual assignment, and the firm's earnings are divided equally with the basis of distribution determined by level of experience.
55. RAPPORT FRA BRANSJEUNDERSØKELSEN 2016 (2016), www.advokatforeningen.no/globalassets/3387/bransjeundersokelsen_2016.pdf (last visited Sept. 23, 2020); RAPPORT FRA BRANSJEUNDERSØKELSEN 2014 (2014), www.advokatforeningen.no/globalassets/rapport-2014.pdf (last visited Sept. 23, 2020).
56. LÆS MERE OM PLESNERS PRO BONO POLITIK, UN GLOBAL COMPACT COMMUNICATION ON PROGRESS 2018, http://epaper.dantryk.dk/Plesner/Plesner_CSR_2018/mobile/index.html#p=1 (last visited Sept. 27, 2018).
57. *Socialt Ansvar*, ADVOKAT KODEKS, http://advokatkodeks.dk/cases/socialt-ansvar/ (last visited Sept. 1, 2018).
58. *Dedikeret tid til Frivilligt og Pro Bono Arbejde*, ADVOKAT KODEKS, http://advokatkodeks.dk/cases/socialt-ansvar/dedikeret-tid-til-frivilligt-og-pro-bono-arbejde/ (last visited Sept. 1, 2018).
59. *See* Scott L. Cummings & Rebecca L. Sandefur, *Beyond the Numbers: What We Know – and Should Know – About American Pro Bono*, 7 HARV. L. & POL'Y REV. 83 (2013); Cummings, *supra* 44.
60. *See* Thomas Linden, Steven Vaughan & Alastair Young, *Symbolism over Substance? Large Law Firms and Corporate Social Responsibility*, 18 LEG. ETHICS 138 (2015).

61. DANSKE ADVOKATER, VIRKSOMHEDERS PRO BONO ARBEJDE (2013); Brandberg & Knutson, *supra* note 52.
62. Cummings, *supra* note 44.
63. *See* ADVOKAT KODEKS, http://advokatkodeks.dk/ (last visited Sept. 15, 2018).
64. ADVOKATRÅDET [THE COUNCIL OF THE DANISH BAR AND LAW SOCIETY], RETSSIKKERHED I FORVALTNINGEN (2015).
65. DANSKE ADVOKATER & ADVOKATSAMFUNDET, *supra* note 18; Pedersen, *supra* note 22.
66. DANSKE ADVOKATER & ADVOKATSAMFUNDET, *supra* note 14.
67. LEHMANN KRISTIANSEN, LEGAL AID IN DENMARK (2018).
68. ADVOKATEN, Aug. 16, 2011.
69. ADVOKATRÅDET, *supra* note 64.
70. The Association of Danish Law Firms (*Danske Advokater*) is a trade organization established in 2008. They represent three-quarters of all lawyers and attorneys-at-law in Denmark and aim to further the interests of Danish law firms by, for example, promoting the practice of law and the use of lawyers in society. *See* Hammerslev, *supra* note 2.
71. DANSKE ADVOKATER & ADVOKATSAMFUNDET, *supra* note 18.
72. Hammerslev, *supra* note 2.
73. OLE HAMMERSLEV, OTILIA PACURARI & DANIELA PIANA, LEGAL AND JUDICIAL TRAINING IN EUROPE (2013); Håkan Hydén & Eva Anderberg, *Rätten i Förvandling*, *in* RÄTTEN I FÖRVANDLING: JURISTER MELLAN STAT OCH MARKNAD (Margareta Bertilsson ed., 1995).

PART THREE

OCEANIA

CHAPTER TWELVE

THE TRIPARTITE EFFECT OF PRO BONO: THE AUSTRALIAN EXPERIENCE

Fiona McLeay and Lucy Adams

> *I think what's happened over the past 18 years is we've really developed a good collegial approach to pro bono, and it's markedly different to anywhere in the world .... At some point, we'll look back on how remarkable a thing it is that we've achieved. But in the meantime, we're getting on with doing it.*
>
> David Hillard, Pro Bono Partner, Clayton Utz[1]

This chapter is dedicated to Anton Hermann, a champion of social justice and a true mensch. Anton remains an inspiration to us all and his legacy will endure.[2]

INTRODUCTION

Over the last thirty years, government funding for legal services in Australia has declined and legal need has increased.[3] At the same time, pro bono legal work by private lawyers has increased and now plays a small but important role in the delivery of free legal help for people and communities experiencing disadvantage in Australia. Various models have developed to enable lawyers in the private profession to do this work. Some firms employ lawyers solely to undertake free work or establish in-house pro bono teams to coordinate pro bono work. Others work via pro bono "clearing-houses," which employ their own multidisciplinary teams and match pro bono lawyers with clients.[4] These clients may be nongovernmental organizations (NGOs) that work with people and communities experiencing disadvantage, or they may be the people directly. Some firms use a blend of these approaches to pro bono.

The small but strategically important role of pro bono in assisting people experiencing disadvantage in Australia includes services for traditionally underserved clients such as Aboriginal and Torres Strait Islander people, refugees, young people, and people experiencing homelessness. This work is done in partnership with community legal centers, legal aid commissions, and Aboriginal community controlled organizations, as well as other social services and health services.[5]

There are many positives from these developments. There are also some important public policy questions that should be examined. This chapter will consider these questions in the context of the recent history of pro bono legal work in Australia. First, it briefly describes the legal services landscape in which pro bono exists in Australia. It then reflects on what "pro bono" is in Australia (and why this definition matters), before setting out a history of the development of structured or institutionalized pro bono in Australia. The origins of structured or institutionalized pro bono in Australia – through the cross-pollination of activist grassroots movements in community legal centers and lawyers in large law firms – is posited in this chapter as being central to Australia's pro bono culture today. The chapter next looks at the policy settings that have helped build, sustain, and strengthen pro bono in Australia. Finally, it explores what we call the "tripartite effect" of pro bono in Australia: the primary effect being the direct impact of legal services for the individuals, NGOs, and communities assisted; the secondary effect being the contribution to systemic change and reform; and the tertiary effect being the impact on legal culture that has been informed by the exposure of lawyers to social justice work through institutionalized pro bono.[6]

Using this framework, this chapter suggests that pro bono culture in Australia has a "robustness" that might not otherwise be present in jurisdictions where the genesis of structured pro bono has been driven more heavily by market motivations such as recruitment and competition. It is argued that this is due to a combination of the progressive sociopolitical movements that helped shape the emergence of structured pro bono in Australia, the ongoing commitment to providing legal assistance to individual clients (rather than solely to nonprofits), the authentic partnerships with the government-funded legal assistance sector and community organizations, and the exposure to injustice that each of these provided. It also suggests that comparisons of the role and impact of pro bono across jurisdictions require a nuanced understanding of history and context and that this should be taken into consideration by both those who want to see pro bono work expand and those who seek to critique it.

THE LEGAL ASSISTANCE LANDSCAPE IN AUSTRALIA

The Australian government established the Legal Service Bureaux (LSB) in 1942 in response to new and unmet need for legal help experienced by members of the armed services and their families.[7] Fleming and Regan explain:

> During WWII and in the immediate post-war years the LSB was a significant social presence. Thereafter its role and functions steadily contracted due to lack of support from the Menzies Government, and the restoration of social stability and prosperity. When the LSB was finally absorbed into the Australian Legal Aid Office in 1973 it was a mere shadow of its original self. Nevertheless it remains the most long-lasting Commonwealth institutional response towards citizens' legal aid. The life of the [Australian Legal Aid Office] was brief in comparison, and the legal aid scene since the 1970s is littered with various institutional transformations of Commonwealth participation in the inter-governmental agreements with the States and Territories.[8]

As Fleming and Regan allude to, Australia's jurisdictional context is as a common-law legal system, and federal system of government, comprising Commonwealth and state and territory governments.[9]

Prior to 1973, in addition to the LSB, there existed state-based "judicare" systems run by the private legal profession and some salaried services in New South Wales, Victoria, and Queensland.[10] In 1973, the Commonwealth Labor Government established a national system of legal aid, the Australian Legal Aid Office. The attorney general at the time, Senator the Honorable Lionel Murphy AO QC, said in his announcement:

> One of the basic causes of the inequality of citizens before the law is the absence of adequate and comprehensive legal aid arrangements throughout Australia .... The ultimate object of the Government is that legal aid be readily and equally available to citizens everywhere in Australia and that aid be extended for advice and assistance of litigation as well as for litigation in all legal categories and in all courts.[11]

With the election of a conservative Commonwealth government in 1975, although funding continued to be shared by the states and the Commonwealth governments, the states were given responsibility for provision of legal aid. The mechanics of this included the legislative establishment of legal aid commissions in each of the states and territories (eight in total).[12]

The 1970s and 1980s saw the establishment of community legal centers and specialist legal services for Aboriginal and Torres Strait Islander people. The late 1990s saw substantial cuts to Commonwealth funding for legal aid. These developments – and their relevance to pro bono in Australia – are discussed more fully below.

The resulting legal landscape is that Australia has a diversified model of legal assistance for people experiencing disadvantage, including four categories of government-funded legal assistance providers.[13]

1. Legal aid commissions (LACs) are the largest provider of publicly funded legal assistance in Australia, including receiving the most funding from government and serving the highest number of Australians. The LACs are independent statutory authorities, established under the legislation of each state or territory.[14] They have offices in metropolitan, regional, and remote areas and provide legal assistance services in criminal cases[15] and (depending on the jurisdiction) some family and other civil law matters. Funding is provided by Commonwealth and state and territory governments under the National Partnership Agreement on Legal Assistance Services, and is administered by state and territory governments.[16] LACs provide a range of services, including information, legal advice, and representation in courts and tribunals. Information and telephone advice are free of charge. To be eligible for representation through a grant of aid, applicants' legal problems and financial circumstances must meet certain criteria set by the LAC.[17] LACs use a "mixed model" to deliver legal representation services; a grant of assistance for legal representation may be made to either an in-house lawyer employed by a LAC or to a private legal practitioner.[18] In 2017–18, the eight LACs in Australia provided approximately 1,258,880 client services (phone or in-person advice and information, duty lawyer representation at courts and tribunals, and non-legal support); 149,730 grants of aid for legal representation; and 1,061,850 information and referral services (including community legal education sessions).[19]

2. Community legal centers (CLCs) are independent community-based not-for-profit organizations, located in all states and territories. There are around two hundred CLCs across Australia that "play a distinct role assisting Australians who cannot afford a private lawyer but who are unable to obtain a grant of legal aid."[20] CLCs are typically embedded in local communities and focus primarily on provision of legal information, advice, casework, and community legal education in areas of civil law. Some CLCs specialize in particular areas of law or target clients, such as consumer protection, tenancy, social security, women, or young people, but the majority are general in their coverage. CLCs draw on volunteers and pro bono services (as will be discussed throughout this chapter) and funding for CLCs primarily comes from state and federal governments and is largely administered by the LACs.[21] CLCs provide advice and legal information and support self-help, as well as taking on a small number of cases for full representation. In 2016–17, CLCs provided assistance to 211,991 people.[22]
3. Aboriginal and Torres Strait Islander legal services (ATSILSs) deliver culturally tailored legal assistance and related services, including community legal education, to Aboriginal and Torres Strait Islander people. There are eight ATSILSs across Australian states and territories, with most offices located in regional and remote areas, and their work covers both criminal and civil matters. The Commonwealth government also funds ATSILSs.[23] In 2016–17, under the federally funded Indigenous Legal Assistance Program, ATSILSs provided assistance to Aboriginal and Torres Strait Islander people in 209,844 matters (92,914 advices, 90,805 case files, and 26,125 duty lawyer services).[24]
4. Family violence prevention legal services (FVPLSs) provide culturally tailored legal services and assistance to Aboriginal and Torres Strait Islander victims of family violence and sexual assault. There are 14 FVPLSs across all states and territories, except the Australian Capital Territory and Tasmania. FVPLSs specialize in family violence matters and, like ATSILSs, are funded by the Commonwealth government.[25] In 2014–15, FVPLSs provided approximately 3,050 legal advices and 11,000 nonlegal advices (including casework, counseling, and court support).[26] FVPLSs support an average of approximately 2,284 clients per year, and 90 percent are Aboriginal and Torres Strait Islander women and children.[27]

In addition to publicly funded legal help, the private profession also provides access to legal help via deferred fee options, such as "no win, no fee," where a client is not required to pay professional costs unless their case is successful. This is commonly utilized in compensation cases, such as personal injury and workplace accidents. Advice and self-help is also available to a larger subset of low-income people (for example, working people living in poverty), which is often provided by CLCs, community organizations, and increasingly via online information and self-help tools and low-cost online legal services.[28]

Pro bono can thus be understood as sitting on a legal assistance continuum, with government-funded legal assistance at one end and full fee-paying legal assistance at the other. In this landscape, the eligibility policies of pro bono services provided by clearinghouses or law firms limit pro bono help to those on very low incomes (usually government benefits) and aim to supplement – but not supplant – other sources of legal help. This approach to eligibility is underpinned by a strongly held position that if a person is eligible for help via any of these other sources, they should receive that assistance first.[29] This rule of application is essential to pro bono's position in this legal assistance ecosystem. It avoids, on the one hand, undermining public funding and, on the other, corroding the good will of the legal profession if pro bono is perceived to be undercutting the work of sole practitioners and small firms by drawing clients who can pay away from these lawyers to free services. In 2014, the Australian Productivity Commission reported:

> Pro bono plays a small but important role in bridging the gap [in free legal assistance to individuals] . . . . Expressed as a measure of the number of lawyers, pro bono from larger firms equates to around 3 per cent of the capacity of the legal assistance sector, and less than 1 per cent of the entire legal market.[30]

The following section discusses the way pro bono is defined in Australia and the role this plays in maintaining pro bono's place in a diversified legal services landscape. We then discuss the way in which growth, retraction, and change in other arms of Australia's legal assistance sector have shaped pro bono in Australia.

DEFINING PRO BONO IN AUSTRALIA

The definition of pro bono in Australia is consistent with that being used throughout this publication: the provision of legal services on a free or significantly reduced fee basis, with no expectation of a commercial return.[31] The development of Australia's definition, and the debates around this, were influenced and informed by early US pro bono influencers. In explaining its definition, the Australian Pro Bono Centre (APBC),[32] Australia's center of excellence on pro bono legal services refers to the paper presented by the late Esther Lardent, founder and former president and chief executive officer of the US Pro Bono Institute, at Australia's Second National Pro Bono Conference in October 2003 for "a useful discussion of the pros and cons of broad and narrow definitions of 'pro bono.'"[33] The Pro Bono Institute and its definition of pro bono were influential in the early delineation of pro bono in Australia for both law firms and the APBC.

The APBC's definition of "pro bono legal services" is:

1. Giving legal assistance for free or at a substantially reduced fee to:
    a. individuals who can demonstrate a need for legal assistance but cannot obtain legal aid or otherwise access the legal system without incurring significant financial hardship; or
    b. individuals or organisations whose matter raises an issue of public interest which would not otherwise be pursued; or
    c. charities, other not-for-profit organisations or social enterprises, in each case where their sole or primary purpose is to work in the interests of low income or disadvantaged members of the community, or for the public good;
2. Conducting law reform and policy work on issues affecting low income or disadvantaged members of the community, or on issues of public interest;
3. Participating in the provision of free community legal education on issues affecting low income or disadvantaged members of the community or on issues of public interest; or
4. Providing a lawyer on secondment at a community organisation (including a community legal organisation) or at a referral service provider such as a Public Interest Law Clearing House.[34]

The APBC explains that it has worked to create a definition that "is specific about certain activities that were previously considered 'grey areas.'"[35] The APBC considered it necessary to be specific about these issues to enhance measurement of pro bono in Australia and "provide leadership on 'definitional fringe' issues such as: community service work by lawyers; sitting on boards; work for sporting organizations;

[and] work done without any reference to the capacity of a pro bono client to pay for pro bono services."[36]

The first limb of the eligibility definition refers to "individuals who can demonstrate a need for legal assistance but cannot obtain Legal Aid or otherwise access the legal system without incurring significant financial hardship." These are typically people who are on low incomes or in receipt of government benefits, including traditionally underserved clients such as Aboriginal and Torres Strait Islander people, refugees, young people, and people experiencing homelessness.

In attempting to clearly address the "definitional fringe" issues, the APBC definition also articulates what is *not* regarded as pro bono work in Australia:

1. giving legal assistance to any person for free or at a reduced fee without reference to whether he/she can afford to pay for that legal assistance or whether his/her case raises an issue of public interest;
2. free first consultations with clients who are otherwise billed at a firm's normal rates;
3. legal assistance provided under a grant of legal assistance from Legal Aid;
4. contingency fee arrangements or other speculative work which is undertaken with a commercial expectation of a fee;
5. the sponsorship of cultural and sporting events, work undertaken for business development and other marketing opportunities; or
6. time spent by lawyers sitting on the board of a community organisation (including a community legal organisation) or a charity.[37]

The definition is important in two key respects. First, it has focused the attention of pro bono lawyers on areas where the unmet legal need is greatest, that is, for people or organizations that have no capacity to pay and in areas of law where there is no other service. In Australia this is particularly the case in civil law matters, which receive limited or no government funding, and is thus where the majority of pro bono work is done. Second, the definition focuses on legal assistance rather than the other sorts of nonlegal help that lawyers can render. This is seen as being crucial because it prioritizes the utilization of the "special" legal skills of a lawyer over charitable or corporate social responsibility (CSR) activities (for example, general board service, painting a school, or gardening at a child care center).[38] Pro bono leaders in Australia have maintained that "pro bono springs from a different source" than charity.[39] Reiterating Esther Lardent's guiding ideas, the APBC has sought to avoid a definition that:

> blurs the distinction between "good citizen/neighbor" activities hopefully undertaken by many individuals in our society and the ethical obligations specifically targeted to lawyers in light of their skills, access to the justice system, and enjoyment of a monopolistic capacity to practice law.[40]

A combination of strong leadership from within a small number of large pro bono firms and the efforts of the APBC in sharing and promoting the definition to firms that were developing new pro bono programs has seen the APBC definition become the standard definition of pro bono in Australia.[41] In addition, in 2007, the APBC launched the National Pro Bono Target, where firms publicly commit to a voluntary aspirational target of performing a minimum of 35 hours of pro bono per lawyer per year. The APBC definition of pro bono was the one that firms were required to commit to. It became the definition that is used in the annual reporting by signatories to the Target, and then by the Commonwealth government as part of its contract tender conditions (discussed further below). The APBC notes that 95 percent of respondents to its National Law Firm Pro Bono Survey in 2014 (a biennial survey of law firms with fifty or more full-time equivalent lawyers) indicated that they use this definition.[42]

The definitional clarity of pro bono legal services – including the articulation of both what is in and what is out – has provided a foundation for strategy, prioritization, and accountability when planning, undertaking, talking about, and considering the impact of pro bono in Australia.

THE EMERGENCE OF STRUCTURED PRO BONO IN AUSTRALIA

Pro bono culture as it exists in Australia today has been shaped by two key developments: changes to the structure of the legal profession, and evolution in the way free legal assistance is provided to low-income Australians, including levels of public funding for legal assistance. This part provides a brief history of these developments through discussion of changing legal environments, social movements, and community lawyering, as well as the emergence of pro bono clearinghouses in Australia.

Changing Legal Environments, Social Movements, and Community Lawyers

Like lawyers elsewhere, some Australian lawyers have always undertaken pro bono work.[43] Until the 1990s, however, it was likely to be individualized, ad hoc, delivered informally, and, at times, unclear in its parameters and definition.[44]

The Honorable Michael Kirby AO QC, former justice of the High Court of Australia, reminisced about his pro bono work as a junior lawyer in the late 1960s and early 1970s in an address at the Australian Law Awards in 2002. He discussed pro bono work coming via his connections with the Council of Civil Liberties. He referred to this era as:

> The days of highly personalized involvement with a wide mix of clients of modest means. The days when every lawyer did a range of work and *pro bono* were unknown words because fee waiver was such a common fact of life. The days of modest premises before marble and glass became the norm.[45]

Allowing for the nostalgic glow, Kirby's comments illustrate the changes to the profession and to the way pro bono work is performed in Australia, as firms grew in size, to cross state boundaries and become national firms removed from the "High Street" practices of Kirby's early years.[46] The liberalization of the Australian economy began in the early 1980s, and Australian law firms changed their way of conducting business to take advantage of the boom in commercial activities. Law firms that traditionally engaged in professional partnerships were gradually adopting a more managerial approach to the business.[47] By the end of the 1980s, many top Australian firms engaged in international work, and a number of them had established offices in Asia. From 2000 to 2010, large global law firms from the United States and United Kingdom entered the legal market in Australia and transformed legal services "top down" through internationalization.[48] In response, local firms formed alliances with one another against the established international players and actively honed their Australian service propositions.[49]

In the early stages of these changes, separated from "a wide mix of clients of modest means," lawyers who wanted to do pro bono work needed to look outside their four walls.[50] Some did this by helping to establish and then volunteering at their local community legal center,[51] which emerged on the Australian legal landscape in the

1970s. As will be discussed below, some of these lawyers went on to play important roles in the development of pro bono in Australia.

As an aside, it is interesting to note that the relationship between LACs and pro bono lawyers has been much weaker than that existing between CLCs and pro bono. LACs are far greater in size and receive the lion's share of government funding for free legal services. There has thus not been a strong incentive for pro bono lawyers to partner with LACs. There is also underlying concern that government may have used increasing pro bono activity by the private profession as an excuse to reduce funding for legal aid.[52]

CLCs in Australia emerged out of grassroots advocacy and a concern about inequality, injustice, and limited access to legal help for low-income and marginalized people. The first, the Fitzroy Legal Service, was established in Melbourne, Victoria, in 1972, and Redfern Legal Service was New South Wales's first in 1977.[53] The development of CLCs coincided with, and was located within, the broader social movements of the time, both transnational (for example, the fight against apartheid in South Africa and conflict and displacement in southeast Asia) and domestic civil rights (for example, abuse of police powers and discrimination against Aboriginal and Torres Strait Islander people).[54] For these activists, law was viewed as a tool for social change, not merely a procedural tool. As Basten, Graycar, and Neal discuss:

> The political events of the early 1970s and the legal aid system at that time provide the background from which the legal centres movement emerged. These events had politicised a number of lawyers and convinced them of the possibility of significant social change through the legal system and the possibility of significant change in the legal system itself, especially in the way in which it operated in relation to the poor.[55]

In this changing legal and political context, lawyers, often from commercial firms, were motivated to volunteer their time out of hours to support this work.[56] Some of these lawyers also began to do pro bono work from their law firm desk during work hours, often helping people whom the CLC did not have the time, resources, or expertise to assist. As the mandate of CLCs expanded to become the key "shopfront" for legal help for Australians living in poverty,[57] the range of issues they addressed grew and so too did the types of legal problems their pro bono volunteers helped with. This helped broaden the understanding of what pro bono lawyers could do and also sowed the seeds for the commitment of Australian pro bono lawyers to providing legal help directly to individuals experiencing disadvantage.[58]

The impact of this thinking is illustrated by the reflections of pioneers of the establishment of structured pro bono. A founder of this movement in Australia is Andrea Durbach, professor of law at the University of New South Wales and former director of the Australian Human Rights Centre (now Institute). She joined the Public Interest Advocacy Centre (PIAC) in 1991 and was instrumental in establishing Australia's first pro bono clearinghouse, the Public Interest Law Clearing House in New South Wales (PILCH NSW), in 1992. PILCH NSW was a program of PIAC and funded by PIAC and the participating law firms, which contributed a "membership fee" to cover the costs of the pro bono matching. PIAC itself was (and is) a charity, funded by a mix of private and philanthropic donations, government grants, and income from legal training programs.[59]

In a 2017 interview (undertaken by Justice Connect), Durbach recounted her story:

> I had come from South Africa and was working as a lawyer at [a large corporate law firm] Freehills in Sydney. I was aware that some of my friends in private practice would leave work for the day saying they were going to play sport, but in fact they were going to do volunteer work at community legal centers. I found it very odd that this [volunteering at CLCs] wasn't something that was encouraged or celebrated in their law firms. It wasn't given visibility or formalized. When I was later offered a position at the Public Interest Advocacy Centre (PIAC) I did work that very much resonated with the work I had done in South Africa except I was struck by the lack of the connection between the organization and private law firms.
>
> PIAC's policy director at the time, Betty Hounslow, had just spent a year looking at public interest organisations in the US such as New York Lawyers for the Public Interest. This model was similar to the one I knew from South Africa where there was a public interest litigation organization doing human rights based work with very strong relationships with the private sector. I started speaking to private law firms [in Sydney] to gauge their interest in joining a pro bono scheme and when I mentioned some of the very significant Wall Street law firms in the US that were doing public interest work that made the law firms here think "we really need to lift our game."[60]

Similar threads of a desire to leverage large firm resources to assist people experiencing marginalization and disadvantage can also be seen in the story of Mitzi Gilligan, the principal and founder of the Melbourne law firm Hive Legal. Gilligan was a lawyer and partner at large Australian law firm, Minter Ellison, for over twenty years and was on the board of Victoria's Public Interest Law Clearing House (PILCH Victoria) (which merged with PILCH NSW and became Justice Connect in 2013) from 2006 to 2017. In a 2017 interview, Gilligan provided insights into the interaction between CLC volunteering and pro bono:

> [When I was a university student], I volunteered at the Nunawading Legal Service, which was a very long bus ride from where I was living. I got a bit of a taste then for the kinds of services that lawyers could provide to disadvantaged people. I also ended up being their cleaner because I needed the money. So I used to go up there every week and clean the toilets and then do the legal work. They gave me my own files, which was pretty good. That was where the interest came from originally.
>
> When I did articles at [law firm] Minter Ellison in 1990, I carried with me that real interest in pro bono and found that – as was the case for most firms – the pro bono opportunities were not very well organized and it was hard for junior lawyers to find out about where you might be able to participate. The way that the firms dealt with pro bono was significantly more ad hoc then. It was a strong part of individual lawyer's culture and way of thinking, but it wasn't necessarily a part of culture at a firm level or an organizational level, or even really in the thinking within government I don't think – other than the fact that a lot of people did volunteer at community legal services . . . . When I came back [from overseas] in 1997, I went back to Minter Ellison, and Justice Connect [then PILCH Victoria] was in the process of being established . . . . I put up my hand straight away and got a couple of really interesting referrals quite early on . . . . And then in the early 2000s . . . [Justice Connect] was looking into setting up the Homeless Persons' Legal Clinic, as it was then known. And the call went out at the firm . . . . I was a fairly new partner I think, and so I stuck up my hand and said yes that would be great, that sounds fantastic. We got some really good training, went up to [homelessness service] Ozanam House, and had the first orientation sessions, and got into going to the clinics. So I was doing that, and matters afterwards, and was part of the Homeless Persons' Legal Clinic team from when it very first started right through to until when I left Minters in 2014.[61]

These personal accounts provide some insight into the motivations of Australian lawyers at the time. There was a commitment to justice and equality from individuals – located within their personal values and sociopolitical environment – who went on to be pioneers and leaders in the pro bono sector. The motivations of these leaders are largely consistent with early surveys of the legal profession, which sought to understand "why do firms do pro bono work?" In 1999, Voluntas, the Victorian Pro Bono Secretariat, a project of the Victoria Law Foundation, undertook a survey of Victorian law firms. Of 459 law firm respondents, by far the most significant motivations identified for undertaking pro bono work were: "social conscience, social responsibilities, sense of duty and professional obligation" (142 responses); "to provide a service not otherwise available; if we didn't who would? And to meet a need" (140 responses); and "justice" (40 responses). "Goodwill, public relations and marketing" received 25 responses.[62]

State bar associations have also had some influence in encouraging pro bono work. While no state bar association has mandated pro bono work, most state bars have sought to encourage pro bono work. A detailed examination of the role of bar associations in the development of Australian pro bono is outside the scope of this paper. However, a quick survey of the activities of bar associations shows that the pro bono engagement of lawyers during the 1990s and early 2000s was mirrored by their member bodies. The New South Wales Law Society developed a pro bono policy in 1991, and in 1994 the New South Wales Bar Association established its pro bono legal assistance reference scheme, which continues today. The Western Australian Law Society established its "Law Access" pro bono referral scheme in 1992. The Victorian Bar Association established a similar pro bono program a few years later, and the Law Institute of Victorian established its pro bono legal assistance scheme in 2000. Justice Connect now administers both Victorian association programs on behalf of the associations.

Community and Law Firm Lawyers Join Forces for Australia's First Pro Bono Clearinghouses

The push for a more structured response to unmet legal need via pro bono during the 1990s was heightened when funding cuts forced most Australian LACs to wind back the provision of services in civil law. As discussed above, Australia, like a number of developed countries, established publicly funded legal aid schemes in the post–World War II era as part of the development of the welfare state. The aim was equality before the law and equal access to justice for all. However, these schemes received limited funding and struggled with "ambivalent" support among the Commonwealth/state structure of Australian government.[63] Disputes about which level of government should pay for what services have been a feature, culminating in significant cuts by a conservative federal government in 1996 and, in 1997, the Commonwealth's withdrawal from funding anything other than matters that come within the federal jurisdiction (e.g., family, social security, and migration), leaving states to cover the rest.[64] A senate inquiry conducted in 1996–98 found that "legal aid is available to an increasingly restricted and exceptionally small group of Australian citizens."[65]

Levels of funding for legal assistance have never returned to the levels of the early 1990s in real terms.[66] The legal aid cuts in the mid-1990s helped prompt leaders at a handful of Australian law firms to appoint dedicated pro bono lawyers who could help to focus their firm's pro bono work and increase the amount of work being performed for vulnerable people unable to obtain legal aid.[67]

More broadly for the profession, these cuts to legal aid took place at a time of emerging criticism about the elitism and exclusivity of the legal profession and its increasingly commercial focus.[68] These phenomena led to private firms, law societies, bar associations, and CLCs working together for a coordinated, structured approach to pro bono, of which the clearinghouses are the most obvious example.[69]

Australia's first pro bono clearinghouses were founded and run by a unique coalition of CLC and law firm lawyers.[70] As pro bono began to take hold, these pioneers could see the need to both nurture this movement and also manage the risks of fragmentation, duplication, lack of coordination, and difficulty of consumers finding pro bono when needed.[71] As outlined above by Andrea Durbach, in 1992, the Public Interest Law Clearing House (PILCH) was established in New South Wales as the first formal pro bono referral program in Australia.[72] In 1994, PILCH Victoria was established.[73] Both organizations were initially established to connect individuals and organizations with lawyers who were willing to assist them on a pro bono basis, where the case had a "public interest" element. The State of Queensland followed in 2001, and South Australia in 2009. The Law Access service established by the Western Australian Law Society in 1992 became a registered charity in 2014. In 2013, PILCH NSW and PILCH Victoria merged and formed Justice Connect. All these organizations are charities, funded by a mix of law firm membership fees or donations, individual and philanthropic donations, and government grants.

These independent nonprofits now provide a focal point for the coordination of a wide range of social justice activities.[74] Their remit has expanded beyond only "public interest" matters. They now develop and manage programs for a diverse range of clients including people experiencing homelessness, older people, refugees, Aboriginal and Torres Strait Islander people, young people, and community organizations that work with these groups.[75] They give advice and undertake ongoing representation using staff lawyers, as well as drawing on pro bono lawyers. They also undertake training and capacity building, and do law and policy reform work aimed at generating changes informed by their direct casework and the work of pro bono lawyers. These clearinghouses helped to nurture and lead the development of pro bono work, enabled lawyers and firms to find pro bono clients, helped CLCs better access pro bono, championed best practice, and led pro bono into new areas.[76]

POLICY SETTINGS THAT HAVE HELPED EMBED A PRO BONO CULTURE

Since the early 1990s, a series of initiatives have been introduced that have supported the embedding of a pro bono culture in Australia. These have included: the emergence of pro bono legal "professionals" to structure, coordinate, and champion pro bono within firms, and as part of the access-to-justice landscape; the establishment of a law firm "aspirational target" commitment to achieving a certain number of pro bono hours each year; government encouragement and incentives for law firm pro bono, including requirements to be eligible for government legal service contracts; proactive approaches to resolving so-called commercial or positional conflicts of interest that would otherwise hinder pro bono work done against government or other large corporate clients; and the role of leadership bodies, including law societies and a center of excellence.[77]

Many of these initiatives emerged first in the United States – a leader in institutionalized pro bono – and were adapted for the Australian context.[78] As discussed above, the nature of this adaptation to Australia's sociopolitical context – including the progressive, activist, client-centered experiences at CLCs that informed the development of structured pro bono in Australia – is key to the nature and form of pro bono in Australia today.

Pro Bono Professionals and a Pro Bono Target

In August 2000, the first National Pro Bono Conference was held in Australia's capital city, Canberra. The conference was the brainchild of Kathy Laster, then CEO of the Victoria Law Foundation and Fiona McLeay, at that time pro bono coordinator at Clayton Utz in Melbourne. Under Laster's leadership, the Victoria Law Foundation had established a "secretariat" to connect emerging pro bono lawyers. Known as Voluntas, it undertook some of the earliest research into the drivers of law firm pro bono work in Australia. Laster persuaded the federal attorney general, Daryl Williams, to find funds to underwrite the conference from the Commonwealth Attorney-General's Department. The conference was very successful, with more than three hundred delegates, including members of the judiciary, academics, and representatives from major law firms, barristers' associations, law societies, community legal centers, and other community organizations attending.[79] A key outcome of the conference was the delegates' recommendation that a national task force be established to examine pro bono and develop priorities to help grow pro bono, and a further conference. Both recommendations were actively and successfully progressed; the second National Pro Bono Conference took place in 2003 (and has continued biannually since), and the National Pro Bono Resource Centre (now the Australian Pro Bono Centre) was established in August 2002.[80]

At the time of the first Pro Bono Conference in 2000, a number of large law firms already had dedicated pro bono roles, and these staff worked part- or full-time managing pro bono work, sometimes with a paying client caseload and sometimes entirely doing and managing pro bono work.[81] The leadership by these professionals, the momentum generated by the early pro bono conferences, and the establishment of the APBC helped to establish pro bono as a feature of most midtier and large law firms (defined by the Australian Pro Bono Centre as firms with more than fifty full-time equivalent lawyers) by the mid-2000s.[82] This in turn contributed to the "normalization" of pro bono work – that it should be treated as part of the regular work of lawyers, managed and supervised to the same standards as other work, and with credit given for its performance.[83]

One of the distinguishing features of law firm pro bono culture in Australia from the beginning has been its collegiality, with firms with more established programs sharing resources and tactics with emerging programs. Firms have also often collaborated on larger cases or formed teams of lawyers serving clinics (for example, the Justice Connect Homeless Law program is supported by lawyers from six firms). David Hillard, who has led the pro bono practice at large Australian law firm Clayton Utz since 1997 and was appointed as the firm's first pro bono partner in 2005, explains it in this way:

> The at-first relatively small pro bono lawyer community within firms worked closely together from the late 1990s, sharing policy ideas, sharing precedents, speaking together with community legal centers, with Legal Aid policy makers and even with decision makers at other firms. There was a joint interest in "professionalizing" pro bono work and helping to create best practice together. There was a general agreement about what was and was not pro bono work, and a common view that pro bono was about providing access to justice for vulnerable clients, rather than providing opportunities for law firm self-promotion. Awards were eschewed, media was largely avoided, and public league tables of law firm pro bono credentials were dismissed as inappropriate.
>
> Instead, what developed was support for a voluntary pro bono target, which might set a benchmark for the whole profession and lift performance across the board. Rather than celebrate a "best pro bono law firm," the target would be seen as a way of celebrating the common cause which all lawyers have to undertake pro bono work.[84]

Hillard addressed the second National Pro Bono Conference in 2003 about the merits of establishing a voluntary minimum pro bono target for Australian lawyers:

> [A voluntary minimum target] will send a powerful message to the legal profession that the conduct of pro bono work is a fundamental professional responsibility of all lawyers, regardless of their seniority or the nature of their practice. Without such a target, the legal profession has no benchmark by which it is able to judge itself and its performance in relation to its pro bono responsibilities. Leadership from within the profession itself would remove any suggestion that encouraging the conduct of pro bono work is a ploy by government to further reduce funding for legal aid and community legal centres. It will also provide the profession with greater authority to convey to government that pro bono assistance cannot be a substitute for a properly funded system of legal aid, and that the private profession is unable to fill many of the gaps left by the present legal aid arrangements.[85]

In 2007, informed and influenced by US models[86] but with a distinctly Australian edge, pro bono leaders and the Australian Pro Bono Centre (then the National Pro Bono Resource Centre) established the

National Pro Bono Aspirational Target (Target), where firms committed to aim for 35 hours of pro bono legal services per lawyer per year.[87] Firms began to record and compare metrics of pro bono, most commonly the number of pro bono hours done per lawyer per year.[88] It also became increasingly common for firms to count pro bono work as part of billable hours.[89] Unlike the United States, however, no system of ranking of pro bono work by reference to hours has ever been established in Australia. As the comments by Hillard above illustrate, such a move is likely to be strenuously resisted by pro bono professionals and it has never been pursued by the APBC. At the time of its introduction, the APBC explained the aims of the Target: "To raise the profile of the professional commitment to conduct pro bono work across the profession by providing a benchmark for the conduct of pro bono work. The Target confirms the shared professional responsibility of lawyers to provide pro bono assistance."[90] As of June 2018, approximately 12,000 full-time equivalent lawyers[91] work at firms that have signed up to the Target, including 102 law firms as well as 29 individual solicitors and 9 barristers.[92]

In 2008, the APBC commenced a biannual survey of pro bono work at firms with more than fifty full-time equivalent lawyers. In the first National Law Firm Pro Bono Survey: Australian Law Firms with Fifty or More Lawyers, 21 firms recorded an average of 21 hours per lawyer. In 2016, the average (from 41 firms) was 34.8 hours. The larger firms (450–1,000 full-time equivalent lawyers) averaged close to 40 hours (39.4), with some firms recording 50 hours.[93] The average lawyer participation rate was 57 percent, up from 50 percent in 2014.[94] The number of firms meeting the Target of 35 hours per lawyer per annum increased to 17 firms in 2016 from 12 in 2014.[95]

Recent figures released by the APBC, reflecting on the ten-year life of the National Pro Bono Target, found that since 2007 Australian lawyers have reported doing over 2.86 million hours of pro bono legal work, "helping disadvantaged people and the organizations that support them."[96] It reported that in 2016–17, 11,795 Australian lawyers provided a total of 420,195 hours of pro bono legal services, which equates to 233 lawyers working pro bono full-time for one year.[97] The APBC also found that, of the forty-one firms with over fifty full-time equivalent lawyers who participated in the 2016 National Law Firm Pro Bono Survey, "signatories to the Target performed better against key pro bono metrics" than nonsignatories. Although participation rates were similar (58 percent and 56 percent respectively), the average hours of legal work per lawyer were significantly higher, with signatories reporting 34.8 hours per lawyer and nonsignatories 12.5 hours.[98]

Government Service Contracts and Approaches to Commercial Conflicts of Interest

There is almost no support in Australia for pro bono work to be mandated by courts or professional bodies and, as noted above, no Australian state, territory, or national legal professional association has implemented a target (mandatory or voluntary) within their professional conduct rules.[99] However, there is support for the view that purchasers of legal services, particularly government, can encourage the development of pro bono by including requirements to perform pro bono work in the conditions of its service contracts with its preferred law firms. The first example of this occurred in 2002, when the Victorian government[100] required firms that tendered for government work to do a minimum amount of pro bono work, pegged to the value of the paid work they did for government. These tender requirements also included a commitment to briefing women barristers and other diversity and inclusion goals. This initiative had a significant influence on the development of pro bono in Victoria.[101] It spurred many firms to move toward a more strategic approach to planning, undertaking, and measuring pro bono work.[102] For the period 2009–15, the Victorian panel arrangements resulted in pro bono services with a value of AUD $114 million being performed by panel firms;[103] and the value of pro bono legal services performed under panel arrangements in Victoria increased from $5.2 million in 2005–06 to $22.08 million in 2010–11.[104]

In 2012, the Commonwealth government introduced a new *Legal Services Multi-Use Deed* by which it manages the use of private lawyers undertaking government legal work. Firms who apply for inclusion on this list are assessed on their capacity to meet the requirements of the Legal Services Directions, which include a commitment to pro bono legal work (as well as other diversity and inclusion metrics).[105] This is demonstrated by a firm becoming a signatory to the National Pro Bono Target to undertake 35 hours of pro bono legal services per lawyer per year.[106] The firms are required to report their hours, and these are publicly released, although firms are not sanctioned for failing to meet the Target or required to demonstrate progress toward meeting it.[107] The Victorian government has also taken proactive steps to overcome a persistent barrier to pro bono, which is the "commercial conflict," sometimes called an "indirect" or "positional" conflict. The commercial conflict arises when there is a perception of conflict because "presentation of a legal argument on behalf of one client that is directly contrary to, or has a detrimental impact on, the position advanced on behalf of a second client in a different case or matter."[108] It is distinct from an actual professional conflict of interest in that the law firm is not acting for the client in the particular matter and there is no risk of confidential information being held or disclosed. Instead, the concern on the part of the firm is "that past, existing or potential clients will question a law firm's allegiances."[109] Common scenarios in which commercial conflicts can be perceived – and present a risk that pro bono will be avoided – include defending evictions by the state-run public housing provider; challenging fines issued by state bodies such as the police or department of transport; and representing clients in immigration matters where the Commonwealth government is the other party.[110]

In 2001, Wentworth discussed the way in which the emergence of an increasingly competitive market for government legal services provision, which included tenders and reduced reliance on government solicitors, created a risk of an "unintended side effect" in the form of "a reluctance on the part of law firms with existing or developing government practices to put the relationship at risk by undertaking pro bono work against government even where there is no real conflict of interest."[111] To help minimize the deterrent of a concern about adverse treatment in the allocation of legal work by government, and the potentially deleterious effect on pro bono, the Victorian government has established a pro bono coordinator to help deal with any concerns about a conflict of interest that might arise when a panel firm is considering acting for a client that has a dispute with a government agency. Both the Productivity Commission and Victoria's Access to Justice Review recognized that "a pro bono co-ordinator can 'potentially increase pro bono services' by 'dispelling adverse perceptions' that firms that act pro bono against government agencies will not be favoured for government work."[112] There is no research on the efficacy or otherwise of these attempts to avoid the impact of commercial conflicts. Anecdotally, the existence of a pro bono coordinator, and policy statements by government that firms will not be disadvantaged by undertaking pro bono work against government, have a generally positive effect. However, there are still stories of government officials expressing displeasure about a firm taking on a particular case, or of law firm partners who are unwilling to risk possible reputational damage by even making contact with the coordinator. Notwithstanding this, in Victoria, this practical, coordinated government approach has made a positive contribution to a robust and healthy pro bono culture and the Productivity Commission recommended that other jurisdictions establish a coordinator role based on the Victorian model.[113]

Law Societies and a Center of Excellence

Two other components that have helped build, sustain, and strengthen pro bono in Australia are, first, the role of law societies, especially the Victorian bar, Law Institute of Victoria, New South Wales Law Society, and Western Australian Law Society, which, as noted above, were all early adopters of policies to encourage pro bono.[114] The Victorian bar and Law Institute of Victoria have also provided significant funding for over fifteen years for pro bono referral services, run by Justice Connect.[115]

Secondly, as discussed throughout this chapter, the Australian Pro Bono Centre, formerly the National Pro Bono Resource Centre, has played a key role in identifying and sharing best practice, encouraging and reporting on growth, and influencing regulation and policy to support pro bono and access to justice.

THE PRIMARY ROLE OF PRO BONO: DIRECT IMPACT AND THE "BEST USE" OF PRO BONO

This part contemplates the "primary" role of pro bono – defined in this chapter as the direct impacts in terms of provision of legal assistance as part of a diversified legal assistance sector. In doing so, it discusses debates that have been had in Australia regarding the "best use" of pro bono, including: What is the "proper" role for pro bono and will pro bono undermine other forms of assistance? Are there certain legal issues that are best dealt with via pro bono and are there areas where other actors (including government) should take responsibility? Who is best placed to provide this assistance? Private lawyers and barristers, or lawyers from the government-funded legal assistance sector?

The Proper Role for Pro Bono: Government Funding and the Risk of "Displacement"

A common caution about the growth of pro bono is that it will provide "cover" for reductions in government funding for legal assistance.[116] At the first National Pro Bono Conference in 2000, the then Attorney General Daryl Williams directly addressed these concerns:

> I want to tell you what this conference is not about. Contrary to the suspicions of some, it is not about asking lawyers to make up for a shortfall in legal aid .... The issues of equity and access to legal representation and support cannot be solved by any single approach .... What is needed is a range of responses that are tailored to address the range and complexity of legal problems faced by the community. Governments have never been in a position to manage that alone .... I know there is a view that the Government considered pro bono some sort of substitute for legal aid – that we want to encourage pro bono work so that we can scale back legal aid. It is important that I make it clear that this view is wrong.[117]

Despite this, concerns persisted about the risk of displacement. Writing about the relationship between pro bono and legal aid in the late 1990s, Cornwall stated: "Some people argue that *pro bono* actively undermines political support for legal aid, pointing to the USA as evidence that *pro bono* flourishes where legal aid is absent."[118] She cited examples where the emergence of pro bono was used to justify cuts to legal aid, including the New South Wales Legal Aid Commission in 1992, which referred to the establishment of pro bono schemes by the Law Society and the Public Interest Advocacy Centre in justifying cuts to legal aid in civil matters; and the legal aid commission in Victoria, which in 1991 called upon all members of the private profession to undertake at least one case per year free of charge for people who had become ineligible for legal aid as a result of cuts.[119]

These statements by LACs were not accompanied by any analysis of whether and how pro bono could make up the shortfall in legal assistance funding. While there may be some correlation between reductions in legal aid funding and increases in pro bono, there is no evidence of a causal effect. In fact, rather than accepting any role as a substitute or competitor, these comments served instead to mobilize the private legal profession in Australia as an ally in the ongoing battle for adequate government funding of the legal assistance sector. For example, in response to the statements by the NSW Legal Aid Commission in 1992, the president of PIAC (a partner in a private firm) wrote to the Commission saying it was "erroneous for Commissioners to conclude that the Clearing House was designed to, or would have the capacity to, replace the provision of legal aid," noting that "legal aid is an obligation attaching to the state which cannot be shifted to the private profession."[120]

More recently, in response to the Commonwealth government's 2015 announcement of a 25 percent cut to legal assistance funding, which was due to commence from July 1, 2017, a coalition of senior leaders and pro bono partners from ten pro bono practices in Australian law firms published an open letter in support of an adequately funded legal assistance sector. It states in part:

> Pro bono legal assistance cannot be a substitute for government-funded Legal Assistance Services in Australia. This is much more than a statement of fundamental principle. Not just philosophically, but also as a matter of practical reality, pro bono assistance by private lawyers could not possibly fill the gap which exists. Australia has a pro bono culture stronger than almost every other country, and yet pro bono work at large firms might amount to less than 3% of the capacity of Legal Assistance Services to assist low-income and disadvantaged clients.
>
> We have little or no pro bono capacity to assist with family law, criminal law, immigration or with clients in regional Australia. We cannot come close to meeting the level of unmet legal need which will be created by a reduction of CLC capacity....
>
> We cannot provide effective pro bono assistance without an effective Legal Assistance Sector. Virtually none of our pro bono work for low-income and disadvantaged people could be performed without partnerships and relationships with Legal Assistance Services, including with CLCs.
>
> The individual clients we assist on a pro bono basis usually are referred to us by a Legal Assistance Service or attend one of the outreach clinics we conduct with a Legal Assistance Service. The delivery of many pro bono services by the private legal profession requires a partnership or collaboration with effectively-functioning Legal Assistance Services.[121]

In 2017, after a sustained campaign from the legal profession, including the private profession, it was announced that these Commonwealth government funding cuts would not go ahead.[122]

Apart from the two comments by LACs in the early 1990s, a search of the literature has not revealed any other occasion where private pro bono was called upon to fill the gap in publicly funded legal services. While there has still been significant downward pressure on legal assistance funding in Australia, the private sector has been a voice of opposition to, rather than complicity with, government in its ongoing failure to adequately fund the legal assistance sector.

The Best Use of Pro Bono

Although without the acquiescence of the private sector, it is true the growth in structured pro bono in Australia has coincided with increasing levels of unmet legal need, often driven by cuts to legal assistance funding and changes in government policy in other areas.[123] Anderson and Renouf described the "tension between advocacy for the state to fulfill these obligations and responding to the consequences of the reality that it does not currently do so."[124] It is in this context that the Australian legal sector has contemplated how "best" to use pro bono, and "best use" now generally entails working in partnership and an emphasis on assisting individuals who would otherwise miss out. While there has also been a commitment to responding to unmet need, the extent to which this has happened in practice – or can happen – continues to be contemplated in Australia.

In the Australian experience, and as emphasized in the open letter quoted above, pro bono is seen as working best when it is done in partnership with the other arms of the legal assistance sector – legal aid commissions, community legal centers, Aboriginal and Torres Strait Islander legal services, and family violence prevention legal services – as well as NGOs and frontline services in, for example, the housing, health, homelessness, and family violence sectors.[125] These community and legal assistance sector partners help pro bono lawyers identify the most pressing areas of unmet need, design effective outreach programs that find the right clients and deliver the service in the most appropriate way, evaluate effectiveness and impact, and drive long-term systemic change.[126] Through these partnerships, pro bono can complement publicly funded legal services, as part of Australia's legal assistance architecture to meet the needs of low-income and disadvantaged people and the organizations that assist them.[127]

This commitment to assisting individuals based on need was identified at Australia's first National Pro Bono Conference in 2000 and documented by the subsequently established National Pro Bono Task Force:

> There was also a strong view that *the provision of pro bono services should not be driven entirely on the basis of what lawyers were prepared to offer.* Rather, there is an urgent need to "map client needs" – and if corresponding legal resources are not available, then there should be a concerted effort to recruit and/or equip lawyers with the necessary skills and expertise, and provide the necessary back-up support.[128]

This commitment to meeting the needs of individuals, including an openness to mechanisms and partnerships that allow pro bono lawyers to provide high-quality legal help to individuals with legal needs that sit outside commercial lawyers' traditional areas of expertise, has remained a feature of pro bono in Australia. For example, the Homeless Persons' Legal Clinic, established by PILCH Victoria in 2001 (inspired by a trip to the United States by the then executive director of PILCH Victoria, Caitlin English), was the first outreach-based clinic on a "secondary specialization" model, where specialists at the legal clearinghouse trained and supervised law firm lawyers.[129] Now called Homeless Law and run by Justice Connect, it is replicated in adapted forms in most Australian states and territories.[130] The Victorian service now employs a combination of civil lawyers, a criminal lawyer, social workers, and paralegals, and draws on over five hundred pro bono lawyers from six large law firms.

As the Homeless Law model has evolved, it has come to focus on the provision of ongoing legal representation (rather than one-off advice or on-the-day "duty lawyer" representation at court), combined with social work support. It focuses on areas of legal need that disproportionately affect people experiencing or at risk of homelessness, including evictions and public space offenses.[131] All pro bono lawyers are given 10 hours of induction training, supported by detailed online resources and overseen by Homeless Law's multidisciplinary in-house team (including supervision, consultation, and file review via an online case management database). Like its counterparts in other states and territories, Homeless Law converts the evidence from this casework and the insights of their clients into sustained work toward law reform and systemic change.[132]

There is an ongoing role for pro bono in Australia as the legal assistance sector grapples with how best to respond to unmet legal need, and a key part of this is understanding the nature and extent of unmet legal need. As discussed throughout this chapter, pro bono generally relies on community legal center partners to help identify unmet legal need through observation and practice.

Until recently, there was not a substantial analysis of unmet legal need in Australia. In 2012, the Law and Justice Foundation of New South Wales published the largest survey of legal need in Australia, the Legal Australia-Wide Survey (LAW Survey).[133] The LAW Survey identified that 50 percent of Australians have a legal problem, but only 16 percent seek legal help.[134] The findings also showed clear links between unmet legal need and other measures of social and economic disadvantage. In most states and territories, the four most prevalent legal problem groups in Australia were consumer (20.6 percent of all respondents), crime (14.3 percent), housing (11.8 percent), and government (10.7 percent).[135]

The LAW Survey also showed that legal problems often have considerable adverse impacts on a broad range of life circumstances, including health, financial, and social circumstances,[136] and that people often do not take action to resolve their legal problems:

> A sizeable proportion of people take no action to resolve their legal problems and consequently achieve poor outcomes .... Most people who seek advice do not consult legal advisers and resolve their legal problems outside the formal justice system.... Cost is likely to be a major barrier for many of the legal problems for which people wish to obtain expert legal advice.[137]

The impact of this unmet legal need is increasingly well recognized, with a recent Access to Justice Review by the Victorian state government finding:

> Increasingly ... unresolved civil legal problems, such as those related to a community member's housing, mental health, employment or family, are recognised as having far reaching consequences for both the individuals involved and the state. For individuals, unresolved legal problems can lead to diminishing health and restrict social and economic participation, as well as triggering further legal problems, including possible criminal legal issues. These consequences for individuals often generate costs that must be borne by the state, whether in the justice system or in other publicly funded systems. Just as government has a role in providing access to healthcare and education, it has a role in supporting all Victorians, especially the disadvantaged and vulnerable, to gain access to justice.[138]

Pro bono in Australia has displayed some movement in response to emerging research on the nature and extent of legal need and the impact of unaddressed legal problems. For example, while continuing to advocate for adequate government funding for the legal assistance sector, the private legal profession is becoming involved in more integrated models of providing legal services to Australians experiencing disadvantage and poverty. A notable example is the role of pro bono in Health Justice Partnerships, including through partnerships with CLCs and LACs, and through supporting the establishment of Health Justice Australia, Australia's national center for partnerships between health and justice services.[139]

There is also evidence of a shift over the last eight years (as evidenced by data in the 2018 APBC triennial pro bono survey) that firms have increased the amount of pro bono work they do in the area of employment law. In 2010 and 2012, around 40 percent of firms indicated that they did this work. In the most recent surveys, more than 50 percent of firms nominated employment law, and it became the area of law most nominated by pro bono firms.

Despite this, there are still significant areas of unmet legal need, which pro bono in Australia has not addressed. One example is the so-called missing middle. The 2014 Productivity Commission Inquiry Report into Access to Justice Arrangements noted that "only 8 per cent of households would likely meet income and assets tests for legal aid, leaving the majority of low and middle income earners with limited capacity for managing large and unexpected legal costs."[140] The then president of the Law Council of Australia, Morry Bailes, described this group in a March 2018 speech to the National Press Club as "the ordinary working people who cannot afford legal representation for everyday legal concerns such as commercial matters, family law, injury compensation ... [they] would never able to qualify for legal assistance, so they fall through the cracks in our justice system."[141] And there is open recognition that pro bono will never be the appropriate response to some areas of legal need. The 2018 APBC survey notes: "In every Survey since 2008, Family law and Criminal law have been the two most rejected areas of law. The 2018 Survey was no exception."[142] The Australian experience has shown that its contribution to the provision of legal assistance to people and communities can be both in areas of law where pro bono lawyers already have skills and expertise, or, with the right resourcing, training, and support, in unfamiliar areas of law. It has also shown that pro bono must continue to grapple with how it responds to unmet legal need as the extent and nature of that unmet legal need grows and changes. There are areas of legal need that seem highly unlikely to ever receive the help of pro bono lawyers. This underscores the importance of proper government funding for legal services. It also highlights the need for a rethink of the costing model of legal services for the missing middle with some capacity to pay (and where pro bono may not be an appropriate response).

THE SECONDARY AND TERTIARY EFFECTS OF PRO BONO IN AUSTRALIA

Having analyzed the sociopolitical context in which structured pro bono was developed in Australia, the policy settings that have helped embed it, and the primary role of pro bono in providing direct legal help to individuals experiencing disadvantage and the NGOs that support them, we now turn to what this chapter has identified as the secondary and tertiary effects of pro bono in Australia.

In a diversified model of legal assistance, we suggest that pro bono has also had:

- a secondary effect, being the contribution to systemic change and reform; and
- a tertiary effect, being the changes in career paths and legal culture that have been informed by the exposure of lawyers to social justice work through institutionalized pro bono.[143]

The Secondary Effect of Pro Bono in Australia: Reform and Systemic Change

In 2003, when PILCH Victoria was in its ninth year, its co-executive directors, Samantha Burchell and Emma Hunt, published an article titled "From Conservatism to Activism," which reflected:

> Almost a decade ago, the involvement of lawyers in private practice in public interest work was an innovative and curious idea. Until then, the practice of public interest law had generally been confined to lawyers working in legal aid services and community legal centres (CLCs).
>
> In 1994, even the most visionary could not have foreseen the role PILCH would ultimately play in galvanising the private legal profession, which had traditionally been characterised by conservatism, to become involved in public interest pro bono work. Then it would have been unrealistic to envisage that lawyers in private practice, particularly in commercial law firms or even corporate legal departments, would regularly involve themselves, without expectation of fee, in legal matters that were political, controversial, unpopular and which have the

> potential to divide the community. Nor would it have been contemplated that through involvement in public interest work a number of private legal practitioners would be seen in some quarters as "agitators," "activists" or even, in the words of the current Federal Attorney General, "promoting unlawful activity."[144]

Fifteen years on from this reflection, we suggest that this commitment to social change and reform continues to have a strong place in the culture and practice of pro bono in Australia. In this way, beyond the outcomes for individual people and NGOs, pro bono has played a role in promoting executive accountability and in using the legal system to try to remedy, rather than reinforce, injustice.

Burchell and Hunt described these responses as becoming "progressively more creative and courageous, with [law firm] members demonstrating a preparedness to work on social justice or human rights matters, unpopular causes or issues of a politicised nature."[145] Two examples are briefly explored below.

First, commencing with what has become known as the "Tampa affair" in 2001, pro bono lawyers and barristers partnered with the legal assistance sector to challenge the Australian government's policies in relation to people seeking asylum in Australia who arrived by boat. In August 2001, a boatload of asylum seekers, primarily from Afghanistan and Iraq, sank en route to Australia. The 433 asylum seekers were rescued by a Norwegian merchant vessel, the MV *Tampa*, which sought to disembark the passengers in Australia, as the first port of safety. The Australian government intercepted the MV *Tampa* using the Australian Defence Force and refused to allow the ship to enter Australian waters, thus preventing the asylum seekers from seeking refuge and protection in Australia. The legal community quickly mobilized in response to the Australian government's disregard for its international humanitarian obligations. With coordination from PILCH Victoria and PILCH NSW, pro bono lawyers and barristers, with Liberty Victoria as the applicant because instructions could not be obtained from asylum seekers on the vessel, commenced urgent proceedings in the Federal Court of Australia. The applicants were seeking orders of *habeas corpus* and *mandamus* to compel the release and delivery onto Australian soil of the 433 asylum seekers. The applicants were successful at first instance, but lost on appeal in the full court.[146]

A decade later, in 2011, as the deeply politicized approach to asylum seekers and refugees continued in Australia, pro bono lawyers and barristers assisted to challenge in the High Court of

Australia the Labor government's proposed deal to send eight hundred asylum seekers to Malaysia in exchange for four thousand already processed refugees. The high court struck down the so-called Malaysia solution.[147] The government subsequently amended the Migration Act 1958 (Cth) to allow the minister to designate a country as a regional processing country. Pro bono lawyers and barristers again mobilized to challenge this law and its application, but this time were unsuccessful.[148] Since that time, teams of pro bono lawyers and barristers have combined with specialist lawyers from legal aid commissions and community legal centers, to persistently run cases that seek to improve accountability of the Australian government and uphold the rights of asylum seekers and refugees.[149]

In terms of analyzing impact and the secondary effect of pro bono in this area, some of the cases were successful and some were not. The Tampa case, for example, did not positively impact the Australian government's laws or policies in relation to asylum seekers. In fact, it contributed to the hasty introduction of the so-called Pacific solution, which was the genesis of Australia's current offshore detention and processing of asylum seekers. Despite this, the founder and former director of Australia's Human Rights Law Centre, and current executive director of the International Service for Human Rights in Geneva, Phil Lynch, articulated what this work did achieve. In relation to the change brought about by the Tampa litigation, Lynch, who was seconded from a large law firm to PILCH Victoria at the time of the Tampa affair, said:

> The case I think was very significant in sending a strong signal to the government that where it undertook those kinds of actions it would be subject to scrutiny, that it would be subject to judicial oversight. And the case I think was historically very significant in that it brought together and really galvanised a cohort of pro bono lawyers and barristers prepared to stand up for human rights, access to justice and the rule of law.[150]

Perhaps as testament to the impact of this work in frustrating the government's willingness to "[ride] roughshod over people's rights and liberties,"[151] in 2017, federal Minister for Immigration and Border Protection Peter Dutton described lawyers representing asylum seekers as "un-Australian" and "politically correct," noting:

> It extends to some of our major law firms where part of their social justice agenda is for pro bono work to be provided .... So there are lawyers across the country who are providing pro bono support to people in this situation. And they lodge their papers in the High Court and it costs taxpayers tens of millions of dollars to defend these actions.[152]

Dutton's comments were met with immediate criticism from the legal profession, including a statement of the Australian Pro Bono Centre:

> Major law firms (those with more than 50 lawyers) undertook a total of over 370,000 hours of pro bono legal work last financial year, averaging 35 hours per lawyer .... This is without charge to the public or the taxpayer. The federal government has actively supported this voluntary effort for many years and formally encourages major law firms to undertake pro bono work through its legal purchasing arrangements .... This context makes Minister Dutton's comment attacking the pro bono work of these firms all the more regrettable.[153]

In Australia, the contribution of pro bono firms and barristers to the divided, politically fraught, challenging work defending the rights of asylum seekers and refugees – alongside the work of lawyers in community legal centers and legal aid commissions who do this work day after day – is the type of courageous, committed, intensive work that contributes to change beyond the individual clients being assisted. It plays a crucial role in promoting the accountability of government where power might otherwise go unchecked and, in doing so, contributes to maintaining the health of Australia's democracy.

The second example of the secondary effect of pro bono has a more positive trajectory of social change, as documented by the Australian Pro Bono Centre in "Advancing LGBTIQ Rights through Pro Bono: A Chronology."[154] This publication profiles the pro bono contribution to the rights of the lesbian, gay, bisexual, transgender, intersex, and queer (LGBTIQ) community starting in the early 2000s with law firm Gilbert + Tobin's successful petition to the United Nations Human Rights Committee regarding the denial of a "veteran's dependent pension" to a same-sex partner.[155] This work escalated from 2004 when Prime Minister John Howard amended the Marriage Act 1961 (Cth) to define marriage as a "union of a man and a woman to the exclusion of all others" and the advocacy group, Australian Marriage Equality, was established. The APBC discusses the breadth of pro bono contributions, again alongside leaders in LGBTIQ organizations and the legal assistance sector, and describes its impact as "strengthen[ing] civil society by pursuing equality . . . [and having] a positive transformative effect on society as a whole."[156]

The contributions of pro bono lawyers and counsel included:

- Strategic litigation, for example, unsuccessfully defending the validity of the Australian Capital Territory's legislation legalizing same-sex marriage, but obtaining confirmation from the High Court of Australia that the federal parliament had the constitutional power to legislate for marriage equality; prompting recognition of gender outside the male and female binary;[157] challenging discrimination;[158] and unsuccessfully challenging the legality of the 2017 "postal survey" or plebiscite on marriage equality, again in the High Court of Australia[159]
- Legal advice and assistance to establish and strengthen community groups and organizations, including Australia's first LGBTI Legal Service in Queensland and the YES campaign in support of marriage equality
- Legal representation for transgender and gender-diverse young people seeking access to cross-sex hormone treatment approved by their medical practitioners[160]
- Publicly affirming support for marriage equality, including joining leading Australian companies in a full-page advertisement in a national newspaper in 2015 and in 2017 publicly affirming Australian Marriage Equality's open letter to Prime Minister Malcolm Turnbull, advocating against the proposed plebiscite on antidiscrimination and human rights grounds[161]

In addition to upholding and advancing the rights of LGBTIQ people, in December 2017, after a multisector and community campaign, the Marriage Amendment (Definition and Religious Freedoms) Act 2017 (Cth) commenced, enshrining marriage equality in Australia.

Consistent with discussions of the importance of partnerships to pro bono in Australia above, this advocacy was led by community organizations, including the strategy for change and reform. The collaborative effort across the community, business, and legal sectors is one of Australia's strongest examples of pro bono contributing to impact beyond individual clients or NGOs and playing an active role in a progressive movement for social, political, and legal change.

The Tertiary Effect of Pro Bono in Australia: A Network of Public Interest Influence and Cultural Change

Aside from direct assistance and advocacy and law reform, we argue that pro bono engagement in Australia has a further "tertiary" effect. By exposing lawyers to the injustices faced by individual clients, communities, and NGOs, and giving them experience in using law for systemic change and reform, pro bono has played a role in shaping the careers of leaders in the human rights and justice sectors in a way that has arguably altered Australia's legal culture.

As noted above, in an address to the Australian Law Awards in 2002, former justice of the High Court of Australia, the Honorable Michael Kirby AO QC, reflected on his work and the work of his fellow justices of the high court in the 1960s and 1970s before saying:

> Self-evidently it is desirable that Australian law firms should include in their services a sizeable pro bono component. The advantages of doing so go far beyond salving the "social conscience" of lawyers. It affords a variety of challenges to the highly talented young lawyers who need occasional rotation from a six trolley commercial dispute. *It reminds them of the imperative demand for justice that may originally have sparked their interest in the profession of law. The righting of wrongs. The redress of discrimination. The protection of the underdog. Upholding the law against the strong and powerful. Is this not why we were all, one day long ago, attracted to the law? We must make sure that we do not lose our direction and forget that original impulse.*[162]

Whether or not it was "protection of the underdog" that initially attracted legal professionals to the law, in an Australian context, it is arguable that direct involvement in "righting of wrongs" and "upholding the law against the powerful" embeds in many lawyers an appetite for continuing to do so – in various ways – throughout lengthy and influential legal careers.

Julian Burnside AO QC provides some insight into the tertiary effect of pro bono work in an address on "ethical choices":

> With one possible exception, I have not had to make such profound existential choices .... The exception was the choice to take on the Howard Government in 2001 over the Tampa episode, and then over the issue of the treatment of asylum seekers generally. For a person who had never been politically engaged, it was a strange choice, but an easy one. It was made easier by the fact that my naïveté prevented me from

> foreseeing the personal cost of doing what I did. But even if I had been smart enough to predict the death threats, the hate mail and the vilification by government acolytes .... I would have made the same choice.
>
> If I had thought it through, it was a collision of principle (which said it is essential to do something) and pragmatism (which said "this is a bad career move.")[163]

Burnside was – and still is – one of Australia's most highly regarded commercial barristers when, in 2001, he was approached to act pro bono in the Tampa litigation. He has since become one of Australia's most high-profile advocates for the rights of refugees and asylum seekers. He explains his transformation in this way:

> If you do a pro bono case in any area, soon enough you get asked to do lots of pro bono cases in the same area. So I ended up discovering, case after case, how dreadful things were, just how awful we were being to frightened people.[164]

A reflection on the trajectories of staff and board members involved in the development of structured pro bono and the early stages of the clearinghouse model in Australia also illustrates that involvement in the primary and secondary aspects of pro bono work generates a tertiary effect through shaping careers in a way that, in turn, shapes the legal culture of Australia.[165] By way of example, Phil Lynch, who was seconded to PILCH Victoria in 2001 from Allens Linklaters, said:

> I owe my career in many ways to Justice Connect. I had, prior to working with Justice Connect, commenced volunteering with Community Legal Centres and involvement with the likes of Amnesty International. But it was with Justice Connect that I was for the first time really able to combine passion and profession and start to pursue a career in public interest and human rights law. I was set on that path in 2001, and it's one that I have pursued for almost two decades since.[166]

Lynch helped establish Victoria's Homeless Persons' Legal Clinic in 2001, before founding the Human Rights Law Centre in 2006. Both have changed the access-to-justice and human rights landscape in Australia.

Kristen Hilton, the current Victorian equal opportunity and human rights commissioner, started her legal career at law firm

Blake Dawson Waldron (now Ashurst), where she was seconded to the specialist community legal center, Youth Law, before commencing at PILCH Victoria in 2004. She worked at PILCH Victoria for five years, including two as the executive director. In relation to this path, she says:

> I was working at Blake Dawson Waldron and I went on secondment to Youth Law and was there for about a year .... I was only the second secondee to a community legal center with Blakes, and now they're very much part and parcel of life in a law firm. Young graduates go in and ask firms, "What's your pro bono program? What opportunities will there be for me?" But it was very different twenty years ago. ... When I went to Youth Law and worked with clients, even just on the first day, I realized that this is what you can use a law degree for, and so that really piqued my interest in social justice and human rights advocacy.
>
> There was no going back for me, but having said that, I think having started at Blakes and having the relationships that I still have really put me in very good stead to do the work at Justice Connect because I understood the corporate environment and I also understood the desire for lawyers there to tap into something beyond billable hours and use their law degree for a range of different purposes.
>
> It is two parts of the community coming together in pursuit of a fairer society. Community and business coming together in a place where they understand each other about issues that need to change, I think that's the beauty of the model ... [it's a] social model that created this community of interests around the work that it did.[167]

In providing an opportunity to work directly with people and organizations experiencing injustice, pro bono in Australia provides a perspective and insight that is hard to forget as careers progress.[168] For participants in this culture – including as barristers acting pro bono, lawyers in firms, and staff in clearinghouses – this work can be transformational. And, in transforming the motivations and understanding of influential legal professionals, pro bono arguably has a tertiary effect of shaping the legal culture and justice system in Australia.

CONCLUSION

The chapter has demonstrated that in Australia, pro bono has contributed to direct legal services and systemic change. It has also impacted on the career paths and culture of leaders in the legal profession, many of whom undertake their influential roles with their experience of pro bono as a shaping and guiding experience. This tripartite effect has emerged out of a particular historical and sociopolitical context.

For countries with emerging or changing pro bono cultures, leaders should consider casting their thinking beyond the primary impacts of pro bono to building the infrastructure that also fosters the secondary and tertiary effects. In the Australian experience, these effects have stemmed from strong partnerships with frontline NGOs and the government-funded legal assistance sector that, together, have reached the right clients to deploy pro bono strategically and for maximum impact both for individuals and systemically.

The secondary and tertiary benefits have arguably been stronger because of the commitment to the provision of direct legal help to disadvantaged people and communities. Through direct exposure to injustice, the voices for change – in current and future roles – have been louder.

NOTES

1. Sophie Schroder, *Aussie Pro Bono Culture Reflects Absence of Civil Assistance, Says Partner*, AUSTRALASIAN LAW (June 6, 2014), www.australasianlawyer.com.au/news/aussie-pro-bono-culture-reflects-absence-of-civil-assistance-says-partner-188405.aspx (last visited Sept. 22, 2020) (citing David Hillard, Pro Bono Partner, Clayton Utz).
2. Anton Hermann was director of pro bono and community investment at Minter Ellison from 1998 until his untimely death in 2019.
3. *See, e.g.*, CHRISTINE COUMARELOS ET AL., LAW AND JUSTICE FOUNDATION OF NEW SOUTH WALES, LEGAL AUSTRALIA-WIDE SURVEY: LEGAL NEED IN AUSTRALIA (2012); *see also* AUSTRALIAN GOVERNMENT PRODUCTIVITY COMMISSION, ACCESS TO JUSTICE ARRANGEMENTS, PRODUCTIVITY COMMISSION INQUIRY REPORT (OVERVIEW) NO. 72, 29 (2014).
4. See, for example, *Pro Bono Referral Schemes and Organisations*, AUSTRALIAN PRO BONO CENTRE, www.probonocentre.org.au/legal-help/pro-bono-referral-schemes-and-organisations (last visited Sept. 22, 2020), which lists: ACT Pro Bono Clearing House (Australian Capital Territory), Justice Connect (New South Wales and Victoria), Northern Territory Pro Bono Clearing House (Northern Territory), LawRight (Queensland), JusticeNet SA (South Australia), Law Society of Tasmania's Pro Bono Clearing House (Tasmania), and Law Access (Western Australia).
5. See AUSTRALIAN PRO BONO CENTRE, THE AUSTRALIAN PRO BONO MANUAL: A PRACTICAL GUIDE AND RESOURCE KIT FOR

LAW FIRMS (3d ed. 2016) for examples of pro bono work undertaken in Australia.

6. Between May–October 2017, thirteen people were interviewed to help understand the history of pro bono in Australia as part of the twenty-fifth anniversary of Justice Connect (which commenced as the Public Interest Law Clearing House NSW [PILCH NSW] in 1992). Transcripts of these interviews have been reviewed and relied on in drafting this chapter. The people interviewed included former staff and board members of PILCH NSW and PILCH Victoria, and representatives from pro bono firms and partner organizations. Since their involvement with PILCH NSW and PILCH Victoria, the interviewees have gone on to be academics, law firm partners, magistrates, coroners, CEOs and directors, international human rights professionals, and human rights commissioners. These interviews do not purport to be exhaustive accounts of the history of pro bono in Australia. They were carried out with a small number of people involved in Melbourne and Sydney. The perspectives provided are enlightening while inevitably being subjective and limited in scope by the interviewees' experiences.
7. *See, e.g.*, Francis Regan, *Assessing Pro Bono Legal Aid Schemes*, 73 LAW INST. J. 30, 30 (1999) ("The publicly funded legal aid schemes were established in the post-war era because the legal profession's pro bono efforts were insufficient to meet the demand for legal assistance for the high volume, routine but not necessarily uncomplicated cases"); *see also* Don Fleming & Francis Regan, *"Evatt's Bastard Child": The Commonwealth Legal Service Bureaux 1942–51*, 7 AUST. L. LEG. HIST. 15 (2003).
8. Fleming & Regan, *supra* note 7, at 15.
9. *See* AUSTRALIAN GOVERNMENT PRODUCTIVITY COMMISSION, *supra* note 3, at 29.
10. Mary Anne Noone, *The State of Australian Legal Aid*, 29 F. L. REV. 37, 38 (2001) (citing RONALD SACKVILLE, LEGAL AID IN AUSTRALIA: A REPORT (1975)); *see also* John Basten, Regina Gravcar & David Neal, *Legal Centres in Australia*, 6 UNSW L.J. 163 (1983).
11. Commonwealth, *Parliamentary Debates*, Senate, 13 Dec. 1978, 2800 (Lionel Murphy, Attorney General).
12. *See* Noone, *supra* note 10 (citing *Legal Aid Ordinance 1977* (ACTLR); *Legal Services Commission Act 1977* (SASR); *Legal Aid Commission Act 1977* (WAR); *Legal Aid Act 1978* (Qd R); *Legal Aid Act 1978* (VR); *Legal Aid Commission Act 1979* (NSWLR); and noting that it was ten more years before the Northern Territory and Tasmania formed commissions: *Northern Territory Legal Aid Act 1990* (NTLR) and *Legal Aid Commission Act 1990* (Tas R); *see also* LATHAM & WATKINS LLP, A SURVEY OF PRO BONO PRACTICES AND OPPORTUNITIES IN 71 JURISDICTIONS 8–10 (Aug. 2012), www.lw.com/admin/Upload/Documents/PBI-2012-survey-Germany.pdf (last visited Sept. 22, 2020).

13. Australian Government Productivity Commission, *supra* note 3, at 25.
14. *See* Noone *supra* note 10, at 38; *see also* Basten, Gravcar & Neal, *supra* note 10, at 181.
15. In *Dietrich* v. *The Queen* (1992) 177 CLR 292, the High Court of Australia held that there is no absolute right to legal representation in Australia. However, legal representation should be provided in most trials for serious criminal offices. In cases where the lack of legal representation would undermine the accused's right to a fair trial, the court has the discretionary power to adjourn a trial until legal representation is provided.
16. Australian Government Productivity Commission, *supra* note 3, at 25–26.
17. *See, e.g.*, *Get a Lawyer to Run Your Case*, Victoria Legal Aid, www.legalaid.vic.gov.au/get-legal-services-and-advice/get-lawyer-to-run-your-case (last visited Sept. 22, 2020).
18. *See, e.g.*, Australian Pro Bono Centre, *supra* note 5, at § 3.1.
19. *See* Legal Aid Act, Annual Report 2017–2018 (2018), www.legalaidact.org.au/sites/default/files/files/publications/annualreport_2017–2018.pdf (last visited Sept. 22, 2020); Legal Aid New South Wales, Annual Report 2017–2018 (2018), www.legalaid.nsw.gov.au/__data/assets/pdf_file/0011/29954/Annual-Report-2017–2018.pdf (last visited Sept. 22, 2020); Legal Aid Queensland, Annual Report 2017–18 (2018), www.legalaid.qld.gov.au/files/assets/public/publications/about-us/corporate-publications/annual-reports/2017–18/laq-annual-report-2018-web.pdf (last visited Sept. 22, 2020); Legal Services Commission of South Australia, 40th Annual Report 2017–18 (2018), https://lsc.sa.gov.au/resources/Full_40th_MASTER_AR_2018.pdf (last visited Sept. 22, 2020); Legal Aid Commission of Tasmania, Annual Report 2017–2018 (2018), www.legalaid.tas.gov.au/wp-content/uploads/2018/11/LACTAnnualReport2017-2018.pdf (last visited Sept. 22, 2020); Legal Aid Western Australia, Annual Report 2017–2018 (2018), www.legalaid.wa.gov.au/sites/default/files/inline-files/79069-Legal-Aid-WA-AR-2018%5FDIGITAL%5F0.pdf (last visited Sept. 22, 2020); Northern Territory Legal Aid Commission, Annual Report 2017/2018 (2018), www.legalaid.nt.gov.au/wp-content/uploads/2018/12/NTLAC-Annual-Report-2017–18.pdf (last visited Sept. 22, 2020); Victoria Legal Aid, Annual Report 2017–18 (2018), www.legalaid.vic.gov.au/sites/www.legalaid.vic.gov.au/files/vla-annual-report-2017–18.pdf (last visited Sept. 22, 2020). We note that not all LACs report on the number of "unique clients," and many people will receive multiple episodes and types of assistance. Also, the categorizations of assistance provided vary between states and territories, so the categories provided are indicative only.

20. Australian Government Productivity Commission, *supra* note 3, at 26.
21. *Id.* at 25. The exceptions are South Australia, where it is administered by the Attorney-General's Department, and the territories, where it is administered by the Commonwealth government.
22. National Association of Community Legal Centres, National Census of Community Legal Centres: 2017 National Report (2018), https://clcs.org.au/index.php/publications (last visited Sept. 22, 2020).
23. The first Aboriginal Legal Service was founded in the inner Sydney suburb of Redfern in 1971. See Basten, Graycar & Neal, *supra* note 10, who note and we echo: "The story of Aboriginal people's struggle in Australia, and their particular relationship with the legal system warrants separate detailed treatment, beyond what is possible here." In 1991, the Royal Commission into Aboriginal Deaths in Custody identified indicators of disadvantage that contributed to disproportionate representation, including that "Aboriginal people were dispossessed of their land without benefit of treaty, agreement or compensation." *See* Coumarelos et al., *supra* note 3, at 349; *see also* Australian Law Reform Commission, Pathways to Justice–Inquiry into the Incarceration Rate of Aboriginal and Torres Strait Islander Peoples, ALRC 133 Summary 12 (Mar. 28, 2018), www.alrc.gov.au/publications/pathways-justice-summary (last visited Sept. 22, 2020). The ARLC provides a picture of the impact of the social determinants of incarceration on Aboriginal and Torres Strait Islander peoples, including education and employment, health and disability, housing and homelessness, and child protection and youth justice.
24. National Aboriginal and Torres Strait Islander Legal Services, Submission to the Review of the Indigenous Legal Assistance Programme (Oct. 2018), www.natsils.org.au/portals/natsils/submission/NATSILS%20ILAP%20Submission%20For%20Website5a22.pdf?ver=2018-10-29-161426-540 (last visited Sept. 22, 2020). For 2016–17, 82 percent were criminal matters, 11 percent civil matters, 5 percent family law matters, and 2 percent violence protection. This figure does not include death in custody inquests, custody notification services, the number of Community Legal Education services, or community justice programs and some other services provided.
25. Australian Government Productivity Commission, *supra* note 3, at 25. In 2012–13 the funding for each of these agencies within the legal assistance sector was: LACs (Commonwealth $212.6 million; state and territory $366.5 million; self-generated income $30.4 million) (total of $609.5); CLCs (Commonwealth $36.7 million; state and territory $30.9 million; fees, philanthropic donations, and other sources $22 million) (total of $89.6); ATSILS (Commonwealth $68.2 million); and FVPLSs (Commonwealth $19.1 million).

26. *What We Do*, NATIONAL FAMILY VIOLENCE PREVENTION LEGAL SERVICES, www.nationalfvpls.org/What-We-Do.php (last visited Sept. 6, 2020).
27. *Id.*
28. *Self-Help Legal Information*, AUSTRALIAN PRO BONO CENTRE (2017), www.probonocentre.org.au/legal-help/diy (last visited Sept. 6, 2020).
29. See, for example, eligibility policies for pro bono clearinghouses: *Get Legal Help*, LAWRIGHT, www.lawright.org.au/cms/page.asp?ID=60731 (last visited Sept. 6, 2020) ("LawRight cannot assist with ... Clients who could afford to pay a lawyer, get Legal Aid, or obtain 'no win, no fee' assistance"); *Legal Assistance*, JUSTICENET, www.justicenet.org.au/get-help (last visited Sept. 22, 2020) ("JusticeNet helps individuals who cannot afford a lawyer or get the help they need from other services. To ensure that pro bono resources are directed to those most in need, we apply eligibility criteria and guidelines to all applications. We are unlikely to be able to assist with: Family law or criminal law matters, except in exceptional circumstances; Complex commercial or building disputes; People who we consider can afford to pay a lawyer, obtain legal aid, or obtain 'no win, no fee' assistance (such as in personal injury claims)"); *Referring to Justice Connect*, JUSTICE CONNECT, https://justiceconnect.org.au/refer/public-interest-referral/ (last visited Sept. 22, 2020) ("Our eligibility criteria includes the following: Can the person afford a lawyer? We consider the expenses likely to be involved in the case, along with the individual's assets and income to help determine an answer to this question. If a person can afford a lawyer, generally the Public Interest Law Service will not assist. Is the person eligible for Legal Aid? If they are, they are unlikely to be eligible for assistance through the Public Interest Law Service").
30. AUSTRALIAN GOVERNMENT PRODUCTIVITY COMMISSION, *supra* note 3, at 32.
31. *What Is Pro Bono?*, AUSTRALIAN PRO BONO CENTRE (2017), www.probonocentre.org.au/information-on-pro-bono/definition (last visited Sept. 22, 2020) [hereinafter *APBC Pro Bono Definition*].
32. See *infra* "Pro-Bono Professionals and a Pro Bono Target" regarding the genesis of the Australian Pro Bono Centre.
33. Esther F. Lardent, *Workshop 3A: Aiming High: Goals, Targets, Definitions and Quantifying Pro Bono: The Pros and Cons*, PRO BONO CENTRE (2003), https://probonocentre.org.au/wp-content/uploads/2015/05/ProBono-EstherLardent.pdf (last visited Sept. 22, 2020).
34. AUSTRALIAN PRO BONO CENTRE, FOURTH NATIONAL LAW FIRM PRO BONO SURVEY: AUSTRALIAN FIRMS WITH FIFTY OR MORE LAWYERS – FINAL REPORT 21 (2014), https://probonocentre.org.au/wp-content/uploads/2015/09/4th_National_Law_Firm_Pro_Bono_Survey_2014_Final_Report.pdf (last visited Sept. 22, 2020) [hereinafter NATIONAL LAW FIRM PRO BONO SURVEY 2014]; *see also* Maria Twomey & John Corker, *Pro Bono at Work: Report on the Pro*

Bono Legal Work of 25 Large Australian Law Firms, 11 LEGAL ETHS. 255, 256–57 (2008), which sets out the substantially similar definition that was used in the first national pro bono survey of the legal profession undertaken by the National Pro Bono Resource Centre (now the Australian Pro Bono Centre) in May 2008. Clause 1c of the definition was amended from July 1, 2018. Prior to this it was "charities or other non-profit organisations which work on behalf of low income or disadvantaged members of the community or for the public good" (i.e., it did not include social enterprises).

35. *APBC Pro Bono Definition*, *supra* note 31.
36. *Id.*; *see also supra* note 34. The Australian Pro Bono Centre (APBC) notes that 95 percent of respondents to its National Law Firm Pro Bono Survey in 2014 (biennial survey of law firms with fifty or more full-time equivalent lawyers) indicated that they use this definition. This definition was developed by the APBC (formerly the National Pro Bono Resource Centre) in 2006. For discussion and contestation over the definition of "pro bono legal services," see AUSTRALIAN PRO BONO CENTRE, NATIONAL PRO BONO ASPIRATIONAL TARGET: THE TARGET AT TEN YEARS (2017), www.probonocentre.org.au/wp-content/uploads/2017/09/the-target-at-10-years-public-discussion-paper-FINAL-260917.pdf (last visited Sept. 22, 2020).
37. NATIONAL LAW FIRM PRO BONO SURVEY 2014, *supra* note 34, at 22. See Lardent, *supra* note 33, regarding the disadvantages of including this work in the definition of pro bono: "The inclusion of legal assistance to a broad range of non-profit groups could, potentially, draw resources away from poverty law and public interest matters to 'white glove' pro bono, such as serving as a general counsel to the local museum or symphony."
38. *See* Fiona McLeay, *The Legal Profession's Beautiful Myth: Surveying the Justifications for the Lawyer's Obligation to Perform Pro Bono Work*, 15 INT'L J. LEGAL PROF. 249 (2008).
39. *Id.* at 255.
40. Lardent, *supra* note 33.
41. For early discussion of the definition of pro bono in Australia, see CHRISTOPHER ARUP, DEFINING PRO BONO: MODELS AND CONSIDERATIONS. BRIEFING PAPER FOR FIRST NATIONAL PRO BONO CONFERENCE (Aug. 4, 2000), www.probonocentre.org.au/information-on-pro-bono/conference/npbc-2000/ (last visited Sept. 22, 2020).
42. NATIONAL LAW FIRM PRO BONO SURVEY 2014, *supra* note 34, at 21.
43. *See, e.g.*, Scott L. Cummings, *The Politics of Pro Bono*, 52 UCLA L. Rev. 1, 4 (2004) (referring to pro bono in the United States before the 1990s, "pro bono had traditionally been provided informally – frequently by solo and small firm practitioners who conferred free services as a matter of individual largesse").

44. *See, e.g.*, Amanda Cornwall, *Lawyers Doing Good Works: Pro Bono Legal Services*, *in* LEGAL AID IN VICTORIA AT THE CROSSROADS AGAIN 111, 112 (JEFF GIDDINGS ed., 1998) (citing Richard Evans, *Will the Real Pro Bono Please Stand Up?*, 68 LAW INST. J. 1128 (1994), which refers to a 1994 survey of the fifty largest law firms in Victoria, in which many lawyers indicated that they regarded any work done for free or at a reduced fee – including favors for friends, relatives, and clients, work done to attract new clients, and time spent on committees of professional bodies or community groups – to be pro bono).
45. Honorable Justice Michael Kirby AC, Address at the Australian Law Awards at Westin Hotel Sydney (Mar. 7, 2002).
46. *See, e.g.*, Twomey & Corker, *supra* note 34. In reporting on the May 2008 survey by the Australian Pro Bono Centre (then the National Pro Bono Resource Centre), Twomey and Corker described the twenty-five firms with more than twenty partners that had responded to the survey: The twenty-five firms included eight with twenty to thirty-nine partners, and seventeen with more than forty partners; ten of the firms that responded to the survey had more than 300 lawyers each and together had a total of 10,215 fee earners, representing approximately 20 percent of the total legal profession.
47. Ashly H. Pinnington & John T. Gray, *The Global Restructuring of Legal Services Work? A Study of the Internationalisation of Australian Law Firms*, 14 INT'L J. LEGAL PROF. 147, 150–51 (2007).
48. *Building the Law Firm of the Future*, MACQUARIE GROUP LIMITED, www.macquarie.com/au/business-banking/marketing-networking/expertise/building-the-law-firm-of-the-future/ (last visited Sept. 22, 2020).
49. *Id.*
50. *See, e.g.*, Jill Anderson & Gordon Renouf, *Legal Services "For the Public Good"* 28 ALTERNATIVE L.J. 14 (2003) (noting that by 2003, "pro bono legal services are increasingly provided at locations other than solicitors' offices or the courts. Locations include community legal centres (by secondees from firms as well as volunteers), on the premises of non-legal community service providers and in outreach premises established by a firm for the purposes of providing a shopfront legal service").
51. See, for example, Cornwall, *supra* note 44, at 116, which discusses CLCs in Australia using the voluntary services of private lawyers since their beginnings in the 1970s and notes: "Historically, many CLCs were staffed by pro bono lawyers providing their time free of charge in shop-front legal centres in their local community. Most CLCs rely on volunteer solicitors and barristers to provide part of their core operations."
52. See, for example, Esther Lardent, *Post-Conference Observations and Trends: Pro Bono Down Under*, *in* TRANSFORMING ACCESS TO JUSTICE: 2ND NATIONAL PRO BONO CONFERENCE 25 (2003) [hereinafter *Pro Bono Down Under*], in which Lardent observed:

"Unlike in the United States, a substantial portion of government funding is used to pay private lawyers, at below-market rates, to provide representation. There is serious concern, in an era of declining funding for legal aid and clinics, that pro bono will be used as an excuse to further reduce funding levels. That worry creates some antipathy towards pro bono."

53. Basten, Graycar & Neal, *supra* note 10.
54. *See, e.g.*, Twomey & Corker, *supra* note 34, at 255 ("The first documented organised law firm pro bono initiative was sparked by apartheid protests in New South Wales in 1967, with Dawson Waldron organising a roster of its solicitors attending the local court to represent protestors"); *see also* Basten, Graycar & Neal, *supra* note 10, at 186, who note that the formation of the Aboriginal Legal Service in Sydney in 1971 arose largely in direct response to police harassment in the streets of Redfern. For other sources, see *History of Pro Bono in Australia*, AUSTRALIAN PRO BONO CENTRE, www.probonocentre.org.au/information-on-pro-bono/history-of-pro-bono/ (last visited Sept. 22, 2020).
55. Basten, Graycar & Neal, *supra* note 10, at 170.
56. *Id.* at 172 (noting that during the establishment of the Fitzroy Legal Service "the primary case work was done … by seventy rostered volunteers, lawyers and non-lawyers, who saw clients in the evenings between 6 p.m. and 10 p.m." and stating "this reliance on volunteers continues to be a distinguishing characteristic of legal centre operations").
57. *See* Mark Rix, *Community Legal Centres and Pro Bono Work: For the Public Good?*, 28 ALTERNATIVE L.J. 238, 241 (2003) ("many of the matters on which CLCs provide advice and support are constitutive of what has come to be known as 'community law'. At present, CLCs are the only specialists in this area of the law in Australia. Community law matters represent most people's experience of the law and account for many people's dealings with government and its agencies. In taking up such matters, CLCs play a pivotal advice and advocacy role for their clients").
58. *See, e.g.*, Anderson & Renouf, *supra* note 50; *see also* AUSTRALIAN LAW REFORM COMMISSION, NATIONAL PRO BONO TASK FORCE, NATIONAL PRO BONO TASK FORCE: RECOMMENDED ACTION PLAN FOR NATIONAL CO-ORDINATION AND DEVELOPMENT OF PRO BONO LEGAL SERVICES 26 (2001), https://probonocentre.org.au/wp-content/uploads/2015/05/NPBRCActionPlan.pdf (last visited Sept. 28, 2020). The National Law Firm Pro Bono Survey 2016 identified that an average of 56 percent of pro bono was provided to organizations and 44 percent to individuals. AUSTRALIAN PRO BONO CENTRE, REPORT ON THE FIFTH NATIONAL LAW FIRM PRO BONO SURVEY: AUSTRALIAN LAW FIRMS WITH FIFTY OR MORE LAWYERS (2017), www.probonocentre.org.au/information-on-pro-bono/our-publications/survey/ (last visited Sept. 22, 2020) [hereinafter

NATIONAL LAW FIRM PRO BONO SURVEY 2016]. The Report is based on data collected from forty-one of the fifty-eight firms in Australia with fifty or more full-time equivalent (FTE) lawyers as of June 30, 2016, including nineteen of the twenty largest firms. Most data relate to the 2015/2016 financial year.

59. For a detailed account of the establishment of PILCH NSW, including the people involved, governance, members, and funding arrangements, see NATIONAL PRO BONO RESOURCE CENTRE (NOW THE AUSTRALIAN PRO BONO CENTRE), PRO BONO REFERRAL SCHEMES IN AUSTRALIA: A HISTORY OF PROFESSIONAL ASSOCIATION & LAW FIRM SCHEMES 22–27 (2006), https://probonocentre.org.au/wp-content/uploads/2015/09/ReferralSchemesHistoryReport.pdf (last visited Sept. 28, 2020) [hereinafter HISTORY OF PRO BONO REFERRAL SCHEMES IN AUSTRALIA].

60. Interview with Andrea Durbach, Law Professor, University of New South Wales, in Sydney, Australia (Sept. 4, 2017).

61. Interview with Mitzi Gilligan, Chairperson, Justice Connect, in Melbourne, Australia (June 5, 2017).

62. Noelene Gration, Pro Bono Secretariat, Voluntas, Pro Bono Survey Report (1999) (on file with author).

63. *See* Noone, *supra* note 10, at 40, noting that in the attorney general's 1996–97 budget press release, he stated that the Commonwealth would "no longer provide funds to support the growing demand for legal aid matters arising under State or Territory laws" and further: "That a proper apportionment of responsibility between the Commonwealth and the States and Territories for legal aid will lead to a reduced requirement for Commonwealth funding: accordingly, the Commonwealth outlays will be reduced by $33.16 million from 1997/98" (citing Press Release, Daryl Williams, Law and Justice for Australians – 1997–98 Budget No. 20 Attachment 3 (Aug. 1996)); *see also The Joint Pro Bono Protocol for Legal Work* cl. 1.3, LAW SOCIETY OF ENGLAND AND WALES (2018), www.lawsociety.org.uk/Support-services/Practice-management/Pro-bono/The-pro-bono-protocol (last visited Sept. 28, 2020) ("Pro Bono Legal Work is always only an adjunct to, and not a substitute for, a proper system of publicly funded legal services"). The legal aid system in England and Wales was traditionally robust, and available for both criminal and civil matters and to people on low incomes, people receiving social security, and people who met other requirements. Demand for civil legal aid rose sharply after the global economic crisis, and significant cuts to legal aid were announced in 2013.

64. *See, e.g.*, Carrie Chan & Chris Cunneen, *Federal Programs for Access to Justice Under a Conservative Australian Government*, 10 CURR. ISSUES CRIM. JUSTICE 15, 20 (1998); *see also* Rix, *supra* note 57, at 239 (citing Francis Regan, *Rolls Royce or Rundown 1970s Kingswood: Australia's Legal Aid in Comparative Perspective*, 22 ALTERNATIVE L.J. 225, 225 (1997): "It is common knowledge that in the 1996 budget

the Commonwealth cut $33 million from its legal aid budget for each of the following three years. This represented a cut of approximately 20% to the Commonwealth's legal aid expenditure").

65. SENATE STANDING COMMITTEES ON LEGAL AND CONSTITUTIONAL AFFAIRS, COMMONWEALTH PARLIAMENT OF AUSTRALIA, INQUIRY INTO THE AUSTRALIAN LEGAL AID SYSTEM (THIRD REPORT) (1998), www.aph.gov.au/Parliamentary_Business/Committees/Senate/Legal_and_Constitutional_Affairs/Completed_inquiries/1996-99/legal/report/contents (last visited Sept. 22, 2020) (cited in Rix, *supra* note 57, at 239).
66. *See, e.g.*, Mark Richardson, *Contemporary Comments: A Background to the Current Legal Aid Funding Issues*, 9 CURR. ISSUES CRIM. JUSTICE 153, 157 (1997). In March 2019, the Law Council of Australia stated: "Commonwealth legal aid funding is at its lowest in decades. In 1997 the Federal Government spent $11.22 per capita. Today, it is spending less than $8 per capita. Many living under the poverty line are ineligible." *See* "'Lives Are Being Destroyed' – Legal Assistance Funding Needs Urgent Review, Huge Budget Boost," LAW COUNCIL OF AUSTRALIA (Mar. 7, 2019), www.lawcouncil.asn.au/media/media-releases/lives-are-being-destroyed-legal-assistance-funding-needs-urgent-review-huge-budget-boost (last visited Sept. 22, 2020).
67. Gilbert + Tobin and Clayton Utz appointed Australia's first in-house law firm pro bono roles in 1997.
68. *See, e.g.*, Cornwall, *supra* note 44 (citing *Legal Aid "For Rich and For Poorer," Cost of Legal Services and Litigation* (Senate Standing Committee on Legal and Constitutional Affairs, Discussion Paper No. 7, 1992); *see also* Mary Anne Noone & Stephen Tomsen, *Service Beyond Self-Interest? Australian Lawyers, Legal Aid and Professionalism*, 8 INT'L J. LEGAL PROF. 251, 262 (2001).
69. Cornwall, *supra* note 44 (citing SENATE STANDING COMMITTEES ON LEGAL AND CONSTITUTIONAL AFFAIRS, *supra* note 65).
70. *See, e.g.*, Cornwall, *supra* note 44, at 117, 122 (noting that the Public Interest Law Clearing House (Vic) Committee was primarily constituted by member law firms, but also included representatives of Fitzroy Legal Service, Consumer Law Centre, and an academic representing associate members).
71. *See* Noone, *supra* note 10.
72. *See History of Pro Bono in Australia*, *supra* note 54.
73. *Id.* at 44: "PILCH was an initiative of Denis Nelthorpe, Director of [Consumer Law Centre Victoria], and Greg Connellan at Fitzroy Legal Service. Initially they met with representatives from various law firms in Victoria and the Victorian Bar to garner support for PILCH in Victoria. They then submitted an application to the Victoria Law Foundation (VLF) for seed funding. One of the law firms provided advice about the most suitable legal structure for PILCH and also assisted with drafting its Constitution. Once PILCH was established

and funded, other firms were approached on a systematic basis to join PILCH."

74. JUSTICE CONNECT, www.justiceconnect.org.au/ (last visited Sept. 22, 2020) (New South Wales and Victoria); JUSTICENET SA, www.justicenet.org.au/ (last visited Sept. 22, 2020) (South Australia); LAW ACCESS, www.lawsocietywa.asn.au/law-access/ (last visited Sept. 22, 2020) (Western Australia); LAWRIGHT, www.lawright.org.au/ (last visited Sept. 22, 2020) (Queensland); *ACT Pro Bono Clearing House*, ACT LAW SOCIETY, www.actlawsociety.asn.au/for-the-public/legal-help/clearing-house#:~:text=What%20is%20the%20Pro%20Bono,able%20to%20provide%20that%20assistance (last visited Sept. 22, 2020) (Australian Capital Territory); *Northern Territory Pro Bono Clearing House*, LAW SOCIETY NT, https://lawsocietynt.asn.au/for-the-community/pro-bono-clearing-house-2.html (last visited Sept. 22, 2020) (Northern Territory); *Pro Bono Information*, LAW SOCIETY OF TASMANIA, https://lst.org.au/public-info/pro-bono/pro-bono-information-guide/ (last visited Sept. 22, 2020) (Tasmania).
75. For example, Justice Connect (New South Wales and Victoria) provides specialist programs, including multidisciplinary services and health justice partnerships for people experiencing homelessness, victims of elder abuse, and trans and gender-diverse young people; LawRight (Queensland) offers targeted programs for people experiencing homelessness, Aboriginal and Torres Strait Islander people, young people, and people experiencing mental health issues. *Get Legal Help*, LAWRIGHT, www.lawright.org.au/cms/page.asp?ID=60731 (last visited Sept. 22, 2020).
76. For discussion of the formation and leadership of pro bono clearinghouses in Australia, see, for example, NATIONAL PRO BONO RESOURCE CENTRE (NOW THE AUSTRALIAN PRO BONO CENTRE), PRO BONO REFERRAL SCHEMES IN AUSTRALIA: A HISTORY OF PROFESSIONAL ASSOCIATION & LAW FIRM SCHEMES (2006); *see also* LAWRIGHT, 15 YEARS OF LAW FIRM PRO BONO IN QUEENSLAND 2001–2016 (2001–16 QPILCH MILESTONES), www.lawright.org.au/_dbase_upl/15_years_pro_bono PREVIEW.pdf (last visited Sept. 22, 2020); Samantha Burchell & Emma Hunt, *From Conservatism to Activism: The Evolution of the Public Interest Law Clearing House in Victoria*, 28 ALTERNATIVE L.J. 8 (2003).
77. Regarding the impact of some of these initiatives, see LAW FIRM PRO BONO SURVEY 2016, *supra* note 58, at 71–77 ("What has an impact on our pro bono program?").
78. *See, e.g.*, AUSTRALIAN LAW REFORM COMMISSION, *supra* note 58 (which contains a number of references to models in the United States in formulating its recommendations for national coordination and development of pro bono legal services in Australia).

79. *See, e.g.*, Melinda Brown, *Historic Conference Examines Pro Bono*, 74 LAW INST. J 29 (2000); Emily Di Cesare & Jo Pride, *Pro Bono: An Australia Perspective, Public Good for Goodness' Sake*, BULLETIN (LAW SOCIETY OF SOUTH AUSTRALIA), Oct. 2000.
80. *See* FOR THE PUBLIC GOOD: PRO BONO AND THE LEGAL PROFESSION IN AUSTRALIA (CHRISTOPHER ARUP & KATHY LASTER eds., 2001); *see also* AUSTRALIAN LAW REFORM COMMISSION, *supra* note 58, at 30–31.
81. *See, e.g.*, Twomey & Corker, *supra* note 34, at 257 (reporting on the results of the May 2008 national survey of 25 firms with more than 20 partners, which identified that 20 firms (80 percent) employed a pro bono co-ordinator, 11 of whom worked full-time; four firms had a designated pro bono partner (with three being appointed between 2005–2008); and six firms had a designated pro bono solicitor).
82. *See, e.g.*, Twomey & Corker, *supra* note 34, at 255 ("Today, all large Australian law firms contribute to providing access to justice through *pro bono* legal services.").
83. *See, e.g.*, *id.* at 257 (reporting on the results of the May 2008 national survey of 25 firms with more than 20 partners, which identified that 24 firms (96 percent) had formal/written pro bono policy; 10 firms (40 percent) had a pro bono committee; and 24 firms (96 percent) kept written records of pro bono work. Contrast this with the results of a 1999 Law Institute of Victoria survey sent to Victorian firms, which received 500 responses (25 percent of the sample) and revealed that only 25 percent of respondents reported that they had a pro bono policy. Of these, 11 percent had a written policy); *see also* Voluntas Pro Bono Secretariat, *Building a Pro Bono Culture*, 73 LAW INST. J 49 (1999).
84. David Hillard, quote provided to the authors on March 22, 2019, Sydney, Australia. Regarding the collegiality of the Australian pro bono sector, see, for example, *Q&A with Jo Renkin, Lander and Rogers*, AUSTRALIAN PRO BONO CENTRE (Mar. 2018), www.probonocentre.org.au/apbn/video-lander-and-rogers-qanda/ (last visited Sept. 22, 2020).
85. David Hillard, *Establishing a Voluntary Minimum Pro Bono Target for Australian Lawyers*, *Transforming Access to Justice*, *in* 2nd National Pro Bono Conference (2003), www.nationalprobono.org.au/conference/pdf/2003_papers/3a_hillard.pdf (last visited Sept. 22, 2020).
86. Lardent, *supra* note 33 (whose work is quoted on the APBC site: "establishing an ambitious, but feasible, target for pro bono service is an effective means to create appropriate expectations regarding pro bono performance … and to create a national norm of appropriate and acceptable pro bono performance at a time when local pro bono norms (and pro bono numbers) varied widely").
87. *See* Twomey & Corker, *supra* note 34, at 259.
88. *See* Cornwall, *supra* note 44, at 111, 118 (citing Evans, *supra* note 44 (stating that this was in contrast to the practices identified in a 1994

Law Institute of Victoria survey of the fifty largest law firms in Victoria, which revealed that just under half of the firms surveyed kept no records of the work they performed for free)).

89. Contrast this with the results of a 1999 Law Institute of Victoria survey sent to Victorian firms, which received 500 responses (25 percent of the sample) and revealed that 87 percent of respondents said pro bono was not counted as part of billable hours. *See* Voluntas Pro Bono Secretariat, *supra* note 83.
90. *Id.*
91. *Media Release: National Pro Bono Target Remains at 35 Hours Per Lawyer Per Annum But Now Includes Work for Social Enterprises*, AUSTRALIAN PRO BONO CENTRE (June 27, 2018), www.probonocentre.org.au/media/media-release-national-pro-bono-target-remains-at-35-hours-per-lawyer-per-annum-but-now-includes-work-for-social-enterprises/ (last visited Sept. 22, 2020).
92. AUSTRALIAN PRO BONO CENTRE, NATIONAL PRO BONO ASPIRATIONAL TARGET: THE TARGET AT TEN YEARS – FINAL REPORT 16 (2018), www.probonocentre.org.au/wp-content/uploads/2018/06/The-Target-at-10-Years_FINAL_Report-250618-1.pdf (last visited Sept. 22, 2020).
93. NATIONAL LAW FIRM PRO BONO SURVEY 2016, *supra* note 58.
94. *Id.* at 9, 17: "The 41 firms that responded to the 2016 Survey employed 10,745 lawyers in Australia. This represents 22.6 percent of all lawyers in private practice in Australia" (citing LAW SOCIETY OF NEW SOUTH WALES, 2014 LAW SOCIETY NATIONAL PROFILE FINAL REPORT (2015), which surveyed all Australian state and territory law societies and found that there were 66,211 practicing solicitors in Australia at October 2014, with 47,569 in private practice).
95. *Id.*
96. AUSTRALIAN PRO BONO CENTRE, 10TH ANNUAL PERFORMANCE REPORT OF THE NATIONAL PRO BONO ASPIRATIONAL TARGET (2017), www.probonocentre.org.au/wp-content/uploads/2017/09/Aspirational-Target-2017-V11-FINAL.pdf (last visited Sept. 22, 2020).
97. *Id.*
98. NATIONAL LAW FIRM PRO BONO SURVEY 2016, *supra* note 58, at 71–72.
99. *Development of the National Pro Bono Target*, AUSTRALIAN PRO BONO CENTRE, www.probonocentre.org.au/provide-pro-bono/target/development/ (last visited Sept. 22, 2020); *see also* AUSTRALIAN LAW REFORM COMMISSION, *supra* note 58, at 13; Rowena Maguire, Gail Shearer & Rachael Field, *Reconsidering Pro Bono: A Comparative Analysis of Protocols in Australia, the United States, the United Kingdom and Singapore*, 37 UNSW L.J. 1164, 1178–79.
100. *See* Anderson & Renouf, *supra* note 50 ("Law firms tendering to provide legal services to government were recently required to commit to providing pro bono legal services to the value of between 5% and 14% of the value of the tender. Ultimately 33 law firms were

successful."); *see also* Victorian Government Solicitor's Office, *Government Legal Services Panel: Deed of Standing Offer for the Provision of Legal Services* cl. 11, BUYING FOR VICTORIA, www.procurement.vic.gov.au/State-Purchase-Contracts/Legal-Services-Panel (last visited Sept. 22, 2020). In 2015, the Victorian government lifted the minimum pro bono requirement from 5 percent to 10 percent of professional costs earned from panel arrangements.

101. Anderson & Renouf, *supra* note 50; *see also Comparison of Government Pro Bono Provisions*, AUSTRALIAN PRO BONO CENTRE, www.probonocentre.org.au/provide-pro-bono/government-tender-arrangements/ (last visited Sept. 22, 2020).

102. *Pro Bono Requirements in Government Tender Arrangements for Legal Services*, AUSTRALIAN PRO BONO CENTRE (2017), www.probonocentre.org.au/provide-pro-bono/government-tender-arrangements/ (last visited Sept. 22, 2020). The value of pro bono legal services performed under panel arrangements in Victoria increased from $5.2 million in 2005–06, to $22.08 million in 2010–11.

103. VICTORIA STATE GOVERNMENT, ACCESS TO JUSTICE REVIEW: REPORT AND RECOMMENDATIONS 442 (2016), https://myviews.justice.vic.gov.au/accesstojustice (last visited Sept. 22, 2020).

104. *Pro Bono Requirements in Government Tender Arrangements for Legal Services*, AUSTRALIAN PRO BONO CENTRE (2017), www.probonocentre.org.au/provide-pro-bono/government-tender-arrangements/ (last visited Sept. 22, 2020).

105. *See* Twomey & Corker, *supra* note 34, at 255, 259.

106. *See* ATTORNEY-GENERAL'S DEPARTMENT, AUSTRALIAN GOVERNMENT, LEGAL SERVICES MULTI-USE DEED: PART 1 – IMPORTANT INFORMATION AND GUIDANCE FOR APPLICANTS 16.

107. *See Purchasing Legal Services*, AUSTRALIAN GOVERNMENT ATTORNEY-GENERAL'S DEPARTMENT (2018), www.ag.gov.au/LegalSystem/LegalServicesCoordination/Pages/purchasing-legal-services.aspx (last visited Sept. 22, 2020). Recent changes to the Commonwealth government's tendering process mean that from July 1, 2018, onwards, the Legal Services Multi-Use List requirements have been replaced with the Commonwealth procurement framework.

108. Elisabeth Wentworth, *Barriers to Pro Bono: Commercial Conflicts of Interest Reconsidered*, 19 LAW IN CONT. 166, 167 (2001) (citing Esther Lardent, *Positional Conflicts in the Pro Bono Context: Ethical Considerations and Market Forces*, 67 FORDHAM L. REV. 2279, 2279 (1999)).

109. *See* Wentworth, *supra* note 108, at 167. Note also that in May 2012, the Legal Profession and Public Notaries Amendment Act 2012 (Vic) commenced operation in Victoria, which allows in-house lawyers to undertake pro bono legal work. Prior to this, Victoria's in-house lawyers were permitted to provide legal advice only to their employers.

Queensland and New South Wales have also already lifted similar restrictions.

110. *See, e.g.*, AUSTRALIAN LAW REFORM COMMISSION, *supra* note 58, at 18 ("Issues also were raised within the Task Force about the difficulty some times in securing pro bono legal assistance in actions involving Government departments and agencies that retain large numbers of private lawyers and law firms (or a significant portion of experts in an area of specialist legal expertise) – and thus cast a large shadow of real and perceived conflict of interest. The Task Force believes that the [Australian Pro Bono] Centre would be well placed to work with the Office of Legal Services Coordination in the federal Attorney-General's Department (the office which provides advice to government agencies in relation to the supply and procurement of legal services to the Commonwealth, and oversees compliance with the Attorney's legal services directions) to develop a protocol aimed at minimising this obstacle to the delivery of pro bono services. Similar initiatives should be pursued in relation to State and Territory governments").

111. *Id.* at 170.

112. VICTORIA STATE GOVERNMENT, ACCESS TO JUSTICE REVIEW: REPORT AND RECOMMENDATIONS 441 (2016), *citing* AUSTRALIAN GOVERNMENT PRODUCTIVITY COMMISSION, *supra* note 3, at 833.

113. *Id.*

114. *See, e.g.*, HISTORY OF PRO BONO REFERRAL SCHEMES IN AUSTRALIA, *supra* note 59.

115. *See, e.g.*, Burchell & Hunt, *supra* note 76.

116. *See, e.g.*, Rix, *supra* note 57 (stating that the growth in pro bono in the late 1990s and early 2000s, "while this growth has been far from adequate in terms of the ability to meet increased client demand, it is part of the Commonwealth Government's agenda of outsourcing legal service delivery to the private sector. For hopelessly inadequate funding for legal aid and CLCs and the rapid but stunted growth in pro bono work are two sides of the [new public management] coin").

117. Daryl Williams, Attorney-General, Address at the National Pro Bono Conference in Canberra, Australia (August 4–5, 2000), *cited in* Brown, *supra* 79, at 29.

118. Cornwall, *supra* note 44, at 115; *see also* Rowena Maguire, Gail Shearer & Rachael Field, *Reconsidering Pro Bono: A Comparative Analysis of Protocols in Australia, the United States, the United Kingdom and Singapore*, 37 UNSW L.J. 1164, 1176 (2014) ("The legal profession in the US is arguably a leader in the provision of pro bono services. This, in part, stems from public sector funding for access to justice being one of the lowest per capita rates of any developed nation, coupled with a strong demand for low cost legal services … virtually all civil legal aid is provided on a pro bono basis").

119. *Id.* (citing Report from the Public Interest Advocacy Centre to the Board of Directors, Public Interest Law Clearing House, July

1992–March 1993 (1993); *President's Page*, LAW INST. J., July 1991; LEGAL AID COMMISSION OF VICTORIA, 13TH STATUTORY ANNUAL REPORT 1991/92 6 (1992)).

120. Cornwall, *supra* note 44, at 115.

121. Pro Bono Leaders, *Open letter from Pro Bono Practices in Australian Law Firms*, AUSTRALIAN, June 24, 2016, www.theaustralian.com.au/business/legal-affairs/funded-legal-assistance-sector-crucial-to-pro-bono-work/news-story/e5fbfcccff90d10e39fe36139ac79a87?nk=1001324f2d2745b8e176a304147ff6ec-1531891641 (last visited Sept. 22, 2020). In addition, see the 2015 letter from leaders of pro bono practices at Australian law firms to the attorneys general in all Australian governments, which advocated that the renewal of the National Partnership Agreement on Legal Assistance Services be guided by the relevant findings made by the Productivity Commission in its Report into Access to Justice Arrangements. Australian law firms also supported the Law Council of Australia's Legal Aid Matters campaign and Community Law Australia's Fund Equal Justice campaign.

122. Henry Belot & Louise Yaxley, *Federal Government to Reverse Community Legal Funding Cuts in May Budget*, ABC NEWS, Apr. 24, 2017, www.abc.net.au/news/2017-04-24/federal-government-to-reverse-community-legal-funding-cuts/8465420 (last visited Sept. 22, 2020).

123. *See, e.g.*, COUMARELOS ET AL., *supra* note 3; PRODUCTIVITY COMMISSION, ACCESS TO JUSTICE ARRANGEMENTS: INQUIRY REPORT, *supra* note 3.

124. Anderson & Renouf, *supra* note 50.

125. *See, e.g.*, Andrea Durbach, *Pro Bono: Challenging the Definitions*, LAW SOC. J., Oct. 2000, at 64; *see also* Jane Farnsworth, *Examples from Practice – Mallesons Stephen Jaques*; Bill Mitchell, *Opposites Attract, but Can They Last?*; Peter Seidel, *Example from Practice – Arnold Bloch Leibler*, *in* 2nd National Pro Bono Conference (2003).

126. See, for example, Lardent, *Pro Bono Down Under*, *supra* note 52, at 27, for Esther Lardent's observations in 2003 of the strength of Australian pro bono partnerships: "As public interest organisations, law firms, and corporate legal departments in the United States and elsewhere begin to explore creation of long-term, multi-layered relationships – by identifying appropriate and workable structures, areas of focus, and respective roles – they have much to learn from their colleagues in Australia. For a number of years, many of that nation's largest law firms have established in-depth, complex, and extremely successful partnerships with a wide range of public interest and community organisations – partnerships that not only generate satisfying and effective pro bono work, but also substantially advance the objectives and goals of the public interest partner."

127. *See, e.g.*, Anderson & Renouf, *supra* note 50, at 13 (referring to pro bono legal services as "an adjunct to publicly funded legal services"). Nicky Friedman, head of pro bono at Allens (then as Arthur Robinson

Hedderwicks), won the pro bono award at the first Australian Law Awards ceremony in 2001 for its partnership with the Fitzroy Legal Service in Melbourne. Fourteen years on, Friedman reflected: "partnerships remain at the core of Allens' pro bono practice. … Working closely with different community organisations, particularly community legal centre organisations, allows us to rely on those expert organisations to understand what community needs are. … Our day-to-day work doesn't see us at the grassroots unless we're doing that in partnership with other organisations. Alone, we're not able to reach that client base." Stefanie Garber, *Fifteen Years On: Allens Pro Bono Sticks to Winning Strategy*, LAWYERS WEEKLY, July 15, 2015.

128. AUSTRALIAN LAW REFORM COMMISSION, *supra* note 58, at 26.

129. *See* Anderson & Renouf, *supra* note 50, at 13 (regarding the establishment of the PILCH Homeless Persons' Legal Clinic in 2001).

130. *Homeless Law*, JUSTICE CONNECT, https://justiceconnect.org.au/how-we-help/homeless-law/ (last visited Sept. 22, 2020) (Victoria); *Homeless Persons' Legal Clinic*, LAWRIGHT, www.lawright.org.au/cms/page.asp?ID=60736 (last visited Sept. 22, 2020) (Queensland); *Homeless Persons' Legal Service*, PUBLIC INTEREST ADVOCACY CENTRE, www.piac.asn.au/projects/homelessness/ (last visited Sept. 22, 2020); *Homelessness Legal Service*, DARWIN COMMUNITY LEGAL SERVICE, www.dcls.org.au/wp-content/uploads/2015/08/homeless_-brochure-2012.pdf (last visited Sept. 29, 2020) (Northern Territory); *Housing Legal Clinic*, Welfare Rights Centre SA, South Australia, http://wrcsa.org.au/ (last visited July 16, 2018) (South Australia); *Street Law*, CANBERRA COMMUNITY LAW, www.canberracommunitylaw.org.au/street-law.html (last visited Sept. 22, 2020) (Australian Capital Territory); *see also* STREET LAW CENTRE, https://streetlawcentre.org.au/ (last visited Sept. 22, 2020) (Western Australia).

131. *See, e.g.*, *Keeping Women and Children Housed: Two Years, Ten Client Stories and Ten Calls for Change*, JUSTICE CONNECT (2017), https://justiceconnect.org.au/how-we-help/homeless-law/homeless-law-reports-and-submissions/ (last visited Sept. 22, 2020).

132. *See* JUSTICE PROJECT, LAW COUNCIL OF AUSTRALIA, FINAL REPORT 37–38 (2017), www.lawcouncil.asn.au/justice-project/final-report (last visited Sept. 22, 2020); *see also* TAMARA WALSH ET AL., SUBMISSION TO THE LAW COUNCIL OF AUSTRALIA IN RESPONSE TO THE "HOMELESS PERSONS" CONSULTATION PAPER 4 (2017), https://opus.lib.uts.edu.au/bitstream/10453/118497/1/Law%20Council%206%20oct%202017%20SUBMISSION.pdf (last visited Sept. 22, 2020) (noting that Australia's specialist homelessness legal services assist over three thousand clients per year, and provide legal advice and assistance with a commercial value of millions of dollars. Homeless people in Australia often experience multiple legal problems simultaneously and interact with the legal system as both defendants and

victims of crime – in addition to the myriad of social problems they face. Nevertheless, most specialist homelessness legal services in Australia are chronically underfunded and rely on volunteer lawyers to deliver legal services on a pro bono basis).

133. COUMARELOS ET AL., *supra* note 3.
134. *Id.*
135. *Id.* at 76.
136. *Id.*
137. *Id.*; *see also* VICTORIA STATE GOVERNMENT, ACCESS TO JUSTICE REVIEW: SUMMARY REPORT 4 (2016), https://myviews.justice.vic.gov.au/accesstojustice (last visited July 16, 2018).
138. VICTORIA STATE GOVERNMENT, *supra* note 137, at 4; *see also* JUSTICE CONNECT, A JUSTICE LIFE: THE ROLE FOR LEGAL HELP IN BUILDING FAIRER, SAFER AND HEALTHIER COMMUNITIES 11 (2018), https://justiceconnect.org.au/wp-content/uploads/2018/06/AJustLifeReport.pdf (last visited Sept. 22, 2020).
139. HEALTH JUSTICE AUSTRALIA, www.healthjustice.org.au (last visited Sept. 22, 2020).
140. AUSTRALIAN GOVERNMENT PRODUCTIVITY COMMISSION, *supra* note 3, at 20.
141. Morrie Bailes & Fiona McLeod, Justice State of the Nation at the Law Council of Australia (Mar. 14, 2018).
142. AUSTRALIAN PRO BONO CENTRE, REPORT ON THE SIXTH NATIONAL LAW FIRM PRO BONO SURVEY: AUSTRALIAN LAW FIRMS WITH FIFTY OR MORE LAWYERS 44 (2019), www.probonocentre.org.au/wp-content/uploads/2019/02/Report-of-the-Sixth-National-Pro-Bono-Survey-2018.pdf (last visited Sept. 22, 2020).
143. See interviews with Andrea Durbach and Mitzi Gilligan, *supra* notes 60 and 61.
144. Burchell & Hunt, *supra* note 76.
145. *Id.*
146. *Victorian Council for Civil Liberties v. Minister for Immigration and Multicultural Affairs* [2001] FCA 1297; *Ruddock v. Vadarlis* [2001] FCA 1329.
147. *Plaintiff M70/2011 v. Minister for Immigration and Citizenship* [2011] HCA 32; *Plaintiff M61 v. The Commonwealth* [2010] HCA 41. The High Court of Australia found that, under the Migration Act 1958 (Cth) as it then stood, the minister for immigration and citizenship did not have the power to declare Malaysia a country to which Australia could send asylum seekers, including because it did not have international or domestic legal obligations to protect asylum seekers. *See M70 – The End of Off-Shore Processing?*, LAW INSTITUTE OF VICTORIA: PRESIDENT'S BLOG (Sept. 2, 2011). The legal teams involved in this work included barristers Julian Burnside AO QC, Matthew Albert, Deborah Mortimer SC (now a judge with the Federal Court of Australia), and Richard Niall SC and law firm Allens Arthur Robinson (now Allens Linklaters), together with

specialist community legal center, the Refugee and Immigration Legal Centre (now Refugee Legal).

148. *Plaintiff S156/2013 v. Minister for Immigration and Border Protection* [2014] HCA 22.

149. Other examples include work with King & Wood Mallesons, Russell Kennedy, Maurice Blackburn, and Lander and Rogers. *See* NATIONAL LAW FIRM PRO BONO SURVEY 2016, *supra* note 58, at 5 ("In 2016, immigration was third overall in the list of areas of law in which the most pro bono work was done, moving up from twelfth in 2014. Forty per cent of firms also nominated Immigration as one of their top five areas of law and pro bono practice"); Amanda Copp, *Demand for Legal Help from Asylum Seekers Driving Rise in Pro Bono Work*, SBS NEWS (Apr. 13, 2017), www.sbs.com.au/news/demand-for-legal-help-from-asylum-seekers-driving-rise-in-pro-bono-work (last visited Sept. 22, 2020) (noting that immigration significantly increased as an area of pro bono work, between the APBC Pro Bono Surveys in 2014 (when the Australian government cut funding for immigration advice and assistance) and 2016).

150. Interview with Phil Lynch, Director, International Service for Human Rights, in Geneva, Switzerland (May 5, 2017).

151. Burchell & Hunt, *supra* note 76.

152. Rashida Yosufzai, *"Extraordinary Attack": Lawyers Angry at Peter Dutton's "Un-Australian" Remark*, SBS NEWS, Aug. 29, 2017; *see also* Bianca Hall, *Lawyers Representing Asylum Seekers Are "Un-Australian": Peter Dutton*, SYDNEY MORNING HERALD, Aug. 28, 2017, www.smh.com.au/politics/federal/lawyers-representing-asylum-seekers-are-unaustralian-peter-dutton-20170828-gy5ci7.html (last visited Sept. 22, 2020).

153. Tom Lodewyke, *Pro Bono Centre Defends "Highest Tradition" of Legal Profession*, LAWYERS WEEKLY, Aug. 31, 2017, www.lawyersweekly.com.au/wig-chamber/21779-pro-bono-centre-defends-highest-tradition-of-legal-profession (last visited Sept. 22, 2020) (citing the Australian Pro Bono Centre).

154. *Advancing LGBTIQ Rights Through Pro Bono: A Chronology*, AUSTRALIAN PRO BONO CENTRE (Dec. 2017), www.probonocentre.org.au/apbn/advancing-lgbtiq-rights-through-pro-bono/ (last visited Sept. 22, 2020). Note the extensive collection of law firms, barristers, legal aid commissions, community legal centers, and NGOs identified as contributing to this work and the change it generated.

155. U.N. Human Rights Committee, *International Covenant on Civil and Political Rights*, U.N. Doc. CCPR/C/78/D/941/2000 (Sept. 18, 2003).

156. *Advancing LGBTIQ Rights Through Pro Bono*, *supra* note 154.

157. *NSW Registrar of Births, Deaths and Marriages v. Norrie* [2014] HCA 11.

158. *Christian Youth Camps Limited v. Cobaw Community Health Services Limited* [2014] VSCA 75.

159. *Wilkie v. The Commonwealth of Australia; Australian Marriage Equality v. Minister for Finance* [2017] HCA 40 (run by the Public Interest

Advocacy Centre and Human Rights Law Centre respectively, with pro bono with legal teams led by prominent barristers Ron Merkel QC and Kate Richardson SC).

160. *Re Kelvin* [2016] Fam CAFC 258 (Kelvin's father was represented pro bono by the Inner City Legal Centre; the Human Rights Law Centre and Lander & Rogers assisted community organization A Gender Agenda to intervene in the proceeding in support of Kelvin and to represent the broader interests of trans and gender-diverse young people); *see also Re Isaac* [2014] FamCA 1134 (run by Victoria Legal Aid).

161. *Id.*; *see also Allens Supports Marriage Equality*, ALLENS LINKLATERS (May 15, 2015), www.allens.com.au/insights-news/news/2015/05/allens-supports-marriage-equality/ (last visited Sept. 22, 2020). In 2015, Gilbert + Tobin joined Google, Qantas, Optus, the ANZ and Commonwealth banks, and the Football Federation of Australia publicly supporting marriage equality; and in 2017 the ten law firms were Allens, Ashurst, Baker McKenzie, Corrs Chambers Westgarth, Dentons, Dowson Turco Lawyers, Gilbert + Tobin, Henry Davis York, Herbert Smith Freehills, K&L Gates, Lander & Rogers, Slater & Gordon, and Squire Patton Boggs.

162. Kirby, *supra* note 45 (emphasis added).

163. Julian Burnside, *Unenlightened Self-Interest*, 5 VIC. U. L. JUST. J. 3 (2015).

164. Mark Dapin, *Julian Burnside: Fighting from the Bar*, SYDNEY MORNING HERALD, Nov. 8, 2014, www.smh.com.au/national/julian-burnside-fighting-from-the-bar-20141106-11hudf.html (last visited Sept. 22, 2020).

165. Interviews with Durbach, *supra* note 60; Gilligan, *supra* note 61; Lynch, *supra* note 150.

166. Interview with Lynch, *supra* note 150.

167. Interview with Kristen Hilton, Victorian Equal Opportunity and Human Rights Commissioners, in Melbourne, Australia (Aug. 7, 2017).

168. *See* ADRIAN EVANS ET AL., OFFICE FOR LEARNING AND TEACHING, BEST PRACTICES: AUSTRALIAN CLINICAL LEGAL EDUCATION: THE FINAL REPORT OF THE PROJECT STRENGTHENING AUSTRALIAN LEGAL EDUCATION BY INTEGRATING CLINICAL EXPERIENCES: IDENTIFYING AND SUPPORTING EFFECTIVE PRACTICES 20 (2013) (describing an analogous concept of clinical legal education in Australia providing a "learning methodology for law students that compels them, through a constant reality check, to integrate their learning of substantive law with the justice or otherwise of its practical operation").

PART FOUR

AFRICA

CHAPTER THIRTEEN

PRO BONO IN SOUTH AFRICA

Thabang M. Pooe, Alice L. Brown, and Jonathan Klaaren

THE SOUTH AFRICAN CONTEXT

Located at the southernmost tip of Africa, South Africa is characterized by a history of racial discrimination and racialized inequality that goes back centuries. It was in 1948, however, that the all-white National Party came into power and the policy of "apartheid" – from the Afrikaans language meaning "apartness" – was systemically and rigidly institutionalized throughout the legal system. Apartheid mandated the separate development of different racial groups, and various pieces of legislation were enacted in furtherance of this mission including, among others, the Prohibition of Mixed Marriages Act of 1949, the Population Registration Act of 1950, the Group Areas Act of 1950, and the Immorality Amendment Act of 1950.[1] Later, the Nationalist government enacted the Pass Laws Act of 1952, the Bantu Education Act of 1953, and the Promotion of Bantu Self-Government Act of 1959.[2] These discriminatory laws were reinforced by security legislation that resulted in detention without trial, restrictions, the banning of individuals and organizations, torture, maimings, assassinations, and related human rights abuses against those who purposefully challenged the regime and any others who inadvertently got in the way of the apartheid machinery.

This barrage of laws and regulations led to the perpetuation of an extremely unequal and deeply divided society. Moreover, they fueled a deep resentment of the legal system[3] on the part of its victims and those who believed in equality, human rights, and social justice. In the

1990s, after decades of petitions, appeals, protests, armed resistance, unrest, boycotts, international sanctions, and negotiations,[4] a transition from the apartheid state to a democratic one was embarked upon, culminating in the first democratic election in 1994 and the adoption of a new Constitution. The aim of that document was to (1) establish a society based on equality, democratic values, social justice, and fundamental human rights, and (2) improve the quality of life of all citizens.[5] Part of the task ahead involved working to ensure that the relationship between the law and the vast majority of the citizenry was mended and that moving forward, the law could be seen as a tool to combat injustice and unfairness as opposed to an instrument of oppression.

The Constitution was adopted with an entrenched bill of fundamental rights meant not only to avoid a repetition of, and to redress, South Africa's past injustices,[6] but also to establish a new society based on dignity, equality, and freedom.[7] It further aimed to heal the divisions of the past and improve the quality of life of all citizens, seeking to eradicate social and economic disadvantages. This was confirmed in 1997 by the Constitutional Court in the *Soobramoney* judgment,[8] in which it highlighted the socioeconomic and historical conditions prevailing in South Africa. The Court stated that:

> We live in a society in which there are great disparities in wealth. Millions of people are living in deplorable conditions and in great poverty. There is a high level of unemployment, inadequate social security and many do not have access to clean water or adequate health services. These conditions already existed when the Constitution was adopted and a commitment to address them, and to transform our society into one in which there will be human dignity, freedom and equality lies at the heart of our new constitutional order. For as long as these conditions continue to exist that aspiration will have a hollow ring.[9]

Since the advent of democracy, the government, civil society, and other sectors of South African society have worked diligently to disassemble the old legal framework and to implement the aspirations of the Constitution. It is generally accepted, however, that this process has not been as efficacious as expected. Nor has it resulted in widespread societal trust in the law and its institutions or in sufficient access to justice. According to a study conducted by the Institute for Justice and Reconciliation in 2016, 43 percent of the South Africans surveyed indicated that they did not trust courts of law.[10] Moreover, access to courts and related institutions is largely unobtainable to the vast majority of South Africans. The primary reasons for this are the high levels of poverty and marginalization, a dearth of affordable legal services in poor communities, and a lack of governmental will, resources, and capacity to provide such services.

The authors of this chapter submit that to address past injustices, heal divisions, and provide remedies for current violations of rights, access to legal services is essential and at the cornerstone of South Africa's young democracy. At a 2002 conference titled "Pro Bono: The Responsibility of Lawyers to Undertake Pro Bono Publico and Public Interest Work," Judge Mahomed Navsa observed that "there is a growing perception that in spite of South Africa's having one of the best Constitutions in the world, its legal practitioners are losing their social consciences. Whereas the Constitution has created many opportunities for the use of law to promote social justice and democracy, there are probably fewer lawyers practicing in this area than was the case under apartheid."[11] Is this an accurate reflection of current circumstances? This chapter will explore this and other issues related to the state of pro bono legal services in South Africa.

Defining Pro Bono and Access to Justice

As is made clear in this book, what is referred to as "pro bono" comes from the Latin *pro bono publico*, meaning "for the public good." It describes legal work undertaken by legal practitioners without remuneration or at significantly below-market rates as a public service for individuals or organizations who cannot afford to pay. In the South African context, the concept of pro bono must be understood alongside specific constitutional provisions as well as against the structure of the legal profession.

The South African Constitution of 1996

Section 9 of the Constitution provides that everyone is equal before the law and has the right to equal protection and benefit of the law.[12] Further along, Section 34 provides that everyone has a right to have a dispute resolved by the application of law decided in a fair public hearing before a court.[13] Lastly, Section 35 also establishes the right of every arrested, detained, and accused person in a criminal matter to have access to a fair trial and legal representation.[14] These provisions, read in conjunction with the Bill of Rights in its entirety, give rise to a mandate to provide access to justice.

"Access to justice" in the South African context is understood to mean far more than access to legal rights, processes, and procedures. In the narrow sense, it denotes the situation where state legal systems are organized "to ensure that every person is able to invoke the legal processes for legal redress irrespective of social or economic capacity" and "that every person should receive a just and fair treatment within the legal system."[15] In the broad sense, it refers to social justice that encompasses the fair distribution of socioeconomic rights (health, housing, and education, for example), promoting redress for past injustice and discrimination through the utilization of affirmative action measures and related interventions.[16] The implementation of this vision is, of course, a further step.

Effect of the Constitution on the South African Understanding of Pro Bono
The South African Constitution contemplates the transformation of South Africa from a society characterized by racial injustice, inequality, and a disregard for fundamental freedoms to a new nation that is based on social justice, equality, dignity, and respect for fundamental human rights and freedoms. This transformation was initially introduced by the Interim Constitution in 1994 and was formalized with the adoption of the new Constitution in 1996. To facilitate the transformation of South African society, the Constitution contains a Bill of Rights that protects both civil and political rights and, to alleviate socioeconomic conditions brought about by past discrimination, this provision contains justiciable socioeconomic rights.

The Constitution also introduced a new legal order predicated on constitutionalism and constitutional supremacy. Its justiciable Bill of Rights guarantees the enforcement and protection of the fundamental rights of the individuals of the state. Bills of rights have been conceived as a mechanism for the enforcement of fundamental human rights against the state and protection from the abuse of state authority.[17] Such an application has been typified as the vertical application of the Bill of Rights. During the drafting process of the Interim Constitution, the Technical Committees commissioned by the Multi-Party Negotiating Process were preoccupied with the question as to whether the South African Bill of Rights should apply in the private sphere between private persons acting *inter se*, such an application being typified as the horizontal application.[18]

The result was an ambiguous text in which two provisions in particular speak to the application of the Bill of Rights and obligations it gives rise to in relation to private actors. Section 8 provides:

(1) The Bill of Rights applies to all law, and binds the legislature, the executive, the judiciary and all organs of state.
(2) A provision of the Bill of Rights binds a natural or a juristic person if, and to the extent that, it is applicable, taking into account the nature of the right and the nature of any duty imposed by the right.
(3) When applying a provision of the Bill of Rights to a natural or juristic person in terms of subsection (2), a court –
   (a) in order to give effect to a right in the Bill, must apply, or if necessary develop, the common law to the extent that legislation does not give effect to that right; and
   (b) may develop rules of the common law to limit the right, provided that the limitation is in accordance with section 36(1).

It must be noted that Subsection 1 explicitly states that the Bill of Rights applies to all law and binds the legislature, the executive, the judiciary, and all organs of state. Subsection 2 explicitly states that the Bill of Rights binds a natural or legal person to the extent that it is applicable, depending on the right and nature of duties involved. In the case *In Re: Certification of the Constitution of the Republic of South Africa* (1996),[19] the Court certified that Section 8 (2) of chapter 3 unequivocally provided for the horizontal application of the Bill of Rights.

Section 8 must be read in conjunction with Section 39 of the Constitution. Section 39(2) provides as follows: "When interpreting any legislation, and when developing the common law or customary law, every court, tribunal or forum must promote the spirit, purport and objects of the Bill of Rights." Hence, this section is one of the primary tools through which the Constitution does its revolutionary work, by requiring that all legislation, common law, and customary law be interpreted and developed in accordance with the spirit, purpose, and objects of the Bill of Rights. As a result of the Constitutional Court's interpretation of that section, the Constitution has had and will continue to have an extensive and transformative impact on the law governing relations between private persons.

With this in mind, our understanding of pro bono includes aspirations of access to justice with the legal profession playing a part in its realization. This can only be made real for all people living in South Africa if they have access to legal representation, and much of the private legal profession understands and acknowledges that it has an obligation in this regard. Pro bono practice is therefore a necessary institution for addressing access to justice. It is not, however, sufficient. As will be discussed below, pro bono practice must be augmented by the work of paralegals and extended to the particular South African vision of community service, which itself does aspire to implement and achieve access to justice.

The Origins and Development of Pro Bono in South Africa

The Early Years

There are a number of factors that helped to shape the extent and nature of the institutional development of pro bono in South Africa, and many of these emerged out of the race-based repression and discrimination promulgated by the apartheid state. Indeed, much of the origins of pro bono was a response to the dire circumstances of Black South Africans who were marginalized, dispossessed, disenfranchised, and discriminated against under the laws and regulations of apartheid.

Although they do not fall within the traditional definition of pro bono – that is, legal services provided by lawyers for free or at significantly below-market rates for individuals or organizations who cannot afford to pay – advice offices and paralegals played, and continue to play, a crucial role in providing legal services and access to justice in the context of South Africa. Indeed, in this country, there is a long history of legal work provided by nonlawyers including staff of nongovernmental organizations (NGOs) and community-based volunteers. The role of these actors, and their connection to the development of pro bono, cannot be ignored or discounted.

Since 1937, when the Legal Aid Bureau was established in Johannesburg, advice offices and paralegals have offered free legal advice, information, and support to impoverished and underprivileged South Africans.[20] Prior to 1994, advice offices, advice office workers, and paralegals[21] provided legal aid, advocacy, and public education; they mediated disputes and provided rights literacy. Moreover, when required, they sought help from pro bono legal practitioners who provided legal assistance and litigated when necessary.

By way of illustration, in the early 1950s, when the South African Institute of Race Relations was conducting research on racial problems, housing, juvenile delinquency, and education, it also provided free legal assistance to the "African, Asian and Coloured populations,"[22] who were being subjected to the brutality and violence of apartheid.

During the same era, another NGO that saw the necessity of legal advice work was the Black Sash. Founded in 1955 by six white South African women in response to the Nationalist government's continued encroachment on the rights and dignity of Black South Africans, Black Sash established its first advice center in Cape Town in 1958. The initial focus was on assisting Black women who had been snagged by the influx control regulations under the Group Areas Act.[23] Mary Burton, a member, former national leader and chronicler of the history of Black Sash, noted that:

> From the start, the advice and pro bono services of lawyers were of inestimable value. Donald Molteno, a prominent member of the Cape Bar and liberal politician, gave the founding members of the Black Sash his support and advice, and encouraged them in the formation of the advice office. A valued early supporter was the lawyer Ian Dichmont . . . . He drew in a legal colleague, David Dallas . . . and over the years there were others who gave their services. Several legal firms agreed to make one of their staff available on a daily roster basis. Many newly qualified lawyers were thus exposed to the pass laws through this experience.[24]

Burton also notes that in 1963, when Black Sash opened its next advice office in Johannesburg, a number of lawyers there provided services to persons who were being prosecuted under the pass laws and those accused of political crimes. Moreover, "in later years a significant further number of lawyers became members and provided advice and support."[25]

Over the next three decades, Black Sash and other NGOs and community-based organizations (CBOs) established advice offices in various locations around the country. In addition to offering much-needed assistance to thousands of people in peril, the paralegals and interpreters who staffed those facilities developed extensive knowledge and expertise with regard to relevant legislation and regulations. Beyond matters involving pass law challenges, advice office workers dealt with issues related to unfair labor practices, forced removals, and political charges, among others. Given their proximity and grassroots connections, they were often the first to see patterns and practices that could be challenged and loopholes that could be exploited in the courts, and they brought these to the attention of attorneys in the private sector who provided pro bono services and those in the public interest law organizations[26] that came into being in the late 1970s and early 1980s. Although many of these cases involved individual claims, favorable judgments could establish legal precedents that would result in relief and remedies for a multitude of people in similar situations.[27] During this period, an increasing number of legal practitioners became involved in pro bono legal activities and public interest law.

Accordingly, the advice office movement and paralegals played a crucial role in engaging and guiding lawyers in rights-related matters on behalf of marginalized and persecuted South Africans. As a consequence, they were essential to the development and expansion of pro bono specifically and in improving access to justice generally.

In the late 1970s and early 1980s, a number of public interest law organizations were established: the Centre for Applied Legal Studies at the University of the Witwatersrand ("Wits"), the Legal Resources Centre, Lawyers for Human Rights, and the Black Lawyers Association with its affiliated Legal Education Centre. The Carnegie Corporation of New York, the Ford Foundation, and the Rockefeller Brothers Foundation were among the first private philanthropies to support these types of efforts.[28]

University Law Clinics

Student activism on the law clinic/legal aid model began as early as 1969, and university law clinics were first established in South Africa during the early 1970s.[29] One model was an initial non-credit-bearing program established at the University of Cape Town (UCT) in 1971. Another was the more integrated practical legal studies model of the Wits. At UCT, law students were supervised by volunteer lawyers from the profession. This model was then popularized by David McQuoid-Mason at the University of Natal with the subsequent establishment of eleven university-based clinics by 1981. Peggy Maisel argues that the most important factors in this development were: (1) the desire of law students and key members of the faculty and administration to be involved in the struggle for social justice, (2) private bar support, (3) exposure to clinical education in other countries, and (4) international assistance.[30]

In the 1970s and 1980s, university law clinics had as their primary mission to supply free legal advice and assistance to indigent persons under the supervision of legal practitioner staff members. By the 2000s, a major change had occurred and university law clinics understood their primary mission as the experiential learning of law students through clinical legal education.[31] Despite a long-standing advocacy effort dating back to the 1970s, South African university law clinics have not yet succeeded in establishing student practice rules, such as in the United States.[32]

As prefigured by their establishment, the actual relationship of these clinics to their universities varied considerably from the 1970s to the present, where nearly all the nineteen university law faculties have clinics of some sort.[33] The Association of University Legal Aid Institutes was established in the mid-1980s with the primary objective of promoting clinical legal education programs at South African universities. Many university law clinics operate through coordination of volunteer activities, though some law faculties have mainstreamed the program through the establishment of permanent staff positions in the law faculty.

In the 1990s and early 2000s, university law clinics received support from philanthropic sources, such as the International Commission of Jurists–Sweden and the Ford Foundation, which were primarily interested in promoting access to justice and exposing law students to the practice of public interest law. State funding for university law clinics has gone through several phases. From the 1970s, there was no state support. Then, in 1994, Legal Aid SA began to fund university law clinics in part to provide representation in civil matters, complementing the criminal representation provided by legal aid.[34] This was then phased out as Legal Aid SA restructured into an organization able to coordinate both criminal and civil legal representation. At present, the university law deans are pushing for law clinics to be recognized by the state in terms of the experiential learning mission and funded as legal learning clinics through the state subsidy for higher education.

As a consequence of the variable donor, university, and state support, the reach of these university law clinics has always been and remains limited. The volume of their operations was linked to the fluctuating availability of law students who needed to take exams and enjoyed long and frequent holidays. As a rule, the impact of clinics was felt largely in urban locations. Moreover, where clinics were situated within the campus, the universities often wished to restrict the access of poor persons to university grounds.[35]

Law Students in Legal Literacy and Awareness Programs

University students and others have participated in legal literacy and rights awareness programs in South Africa from at least the 1980s. One commonly used term for these programs is "Street Law." The formal development of these programs in South Africa is yet another example of external influences; it was exposure to the Street Law program created in 1972 by Georgetown University law students that led to its establishment in South Africa, initially in what is now the KwaZulu-Natal province. Street Law was distinct from the establishment and operation of university law clinics.[36] In these programs, students facilitated access to legal information largely through a teaching philosophy fused with one of access to justice.[37] The teaching philosophy overlapped significantly with the concept of legal empowerment: unless ordinary people know that they have certain legal rights and where to obtain the services of lawyers, they will not be able to access justice. In this tradition, this concept of legal empowerment was taught regardless of whether people would be able to afford the services of lawyers, the concept at the heart of most access-to-justice initiatives.

Post-1994

There are numerous postapartheid factors that have helped to shape the extent and nature of the institutional development of pro bono in South Africa, and they include the manner in which the framers of the first democratic Constitution purposefully and intentionally laid down a mandate to move light-years away from the race-based repression and exclusion of the apartheid state.

Specifically, as noted earlier, Section 34 of the Constitution gives everyone the right to have any dispute resolved by the application of law decided in a fair public hearing before a court, or another independent and impartial tribunal or forum. This provision would have no meaning if the vast majority of South Africans, who are poor and underresourced, could not access legal representation, and the potential role of pro bono services in this context has been acknowledged by a number of respected members of the South African legal profession. For instance, in 2002, during his opening address at the conference titled *The Responsibility of Lawyers to Undertake Pro Bono Publico and Public Interest Work*, 10–11 May, the then deputy chief justice of the Constitutional Court Pius Langa stressed the necessity of access to justice in making constitutional rights a reality. He stated, "access to justice is key to our Constitutional democracy, but becomes an empty gesture and makes a mockery of the Constitution, if it is not backed by mechanisms that are adequate for the enforcement of the right," while acknowledging that "it is primarily the duty of the state to deliver justice." Langa, who prior to his appointment to the bench had been a human rights legal practitioner who represented political prisoners and other victims of apartheid, added that "pro bono work provides the niche which the legal community should claim for itself in the construction and development of a South Africa that is as close to our ideals as possible. The consequence of this access to justice would be to facilitate the enjoyment of other fundamental human rights by the greatest number of people in our country." Furthermore, he noted that "voluntary pro bono work provides the legal community with an opportunity to make the Constitution work and develop confidence in the courts. Underlying pro bono is the notion of community service."[38]

Geoff Budlender, a prominent long-serving human rights advocate, stated at the same conference that "[m]y own view is that pro bono is essential because it is essential for the development and entrenchment of our new constitutional order, which is still quite fragile."[39]

The South African Legal Profession

The profession in South Africa has historically been divided into two sets of legal practitioners: attorneys (solicitors) and advocates (barristers), with no dual practice permitted.

An attorney is the practitioner with whom a client would first make contact with when seeking legal advice or legal representation. The admission requirements for attorneys in South Africa were previously prescribed by the Attorneys Act[40] and now are governed by the Legal Practice Act. To qualify as an attorney, a law graduate is required to serve as a candidate attorney for a two-year apprenticeship or training period known as articles of clerkship. Such "articles" must be served under a qualified attorney.

Attorneys comprise the majority of the legal profession in South Africa. As of July 2017, there were 25,854 practicing attorneys and 6,669 candidate attorneys in South Africa.[41] The large majority of attorneys practice either as sole practitioners or in firms with a small number of practitioners. This group of legal practitioners mainly practices in lower courts and is a first point of entry for people seeking legal services. When required, attorneys brief advocates to take on litigation in the higher courts. Attorneys are regulated by the Law Society of South Africa (LSSA),[42] which is an umbrella body composed of constituent members including the Black Lawyers Association, the National Association of Democratic Lawyers, the Law Society of the Northern Provinces, the Cape Law Society, the Kwa Zulu Law Society, and the Law Society of the Free State.

A significant and growing number of attorneys practice in larger commercially oriented firms. In 2016, fifteen South African firms were reported to have between twenty and forty-nine partners, and seventeen firms had fifty partners or more. The large commercial firms can charge on the order of US $300 per hour for a partner's time, but the top attorneys in the country can charge more. For the lowest-ranked qualified attorney, the hourly rate is approximately US $125 per hour, and candidate attorneys are charged out at an hourly rate of just under US $80. Even at small and medium firms, a client should expect to pay in the region of US $75 per hour.

As mentioned above, the advocates' profession in South Africa is a referral profession. This means that a client approaches an attorney who, in turn, instructs or briefs an advocate. The requirements for admission as an advocate were laid out in the Admission of Advocates Act,[43] and are now prescribed by the Legal Practice Act. Interested persons may be admitted into practice if they possess an LLB degree, have served a year of unpaid pupilage under an experienced advocate, and have passed the bar examination. Advocates constitute approximately 10 percent of the profession.

Advocates have historically self-regulated through joining locally based associations – such as the Johannesburg bar – affiliated under the umbrella General Council of the Bar (GCB) and working only with other associated advocates. As of April 2017, there were 2,915 advocates who were members of the GCB,[44] which is composed of fourteen societies located at the seat of every provincial and local division of the High Court of South Africa. Increasing numbers of advocates have remained independent of these associations and advocates' governance has become more fractured and complex since 1994.

In Johannesburg, the largest city in the country, members of the bar typically charge from US $400 to $550 per day immediately after pupillage. Contrast this with the latest statistics indicating that the average monthly household income in South Africa is around US $780,[45] while the average household income of a Black family is about US $395, and that of households headed by a woman, Black or white, roughly US $350.[46] Hence, in reality, the services of an advocate are inaccessible to the majority of people living in South Africa.

CURRENT PROVISION OF PRO BONO LEGAL SERVICES

At both a local and international level, there has been much debate with regard to mandatory pro bono services. Considerations have included the question of whether pro bono work is or should be an individual, ethical decision to be undertaken voluntarily or whether it should be a professional obligation imposed upon each member of the profession.

We argue, as is generally accepted by the South African profession, that the duty to transform society and eradicate past inequality is a duty that both the state and the legal profession (among others) has to bear. It is important to note that, with the establishment of the Legal Aid Board in 1969,[47] this obligation was recognized by the state even prior to the establishment of a democratically elected government in 1994.

In terms of the profession, of relevance is the Legal Services Sector Charter of 2007,[48] which provides that "the legal profession undertakes to recognise the ethical obligation to carry out pro bono work and develop and enhance the pro bono system with a view to making it compulsory for all practitioners." The Charter, however, did not introduce mandatory pro bono services for the legal profession – the legal profession was to devote at least 5 percent of its total billing hours per month to pro bono work.

In the context of advocates, the General Council of the Bar asserts in its mission statement that "[t]he Bar is committed to: ... providing greater access to justice by the expansion of legal services to all who require them, while maintaining the high standards, professional integrity and independence which are established hallmarks of the Bar."[49]

We expand on both the public and private sector pro bono initiatives below.

Public Sector Initiatives

Legal Aid South Africa

The Legal Aid Board is the primary means for the delivery of tax-funded legal assistance in South Africa. The aim of Legal Aid South Africa (Legal Aid SA) is to make legal aid available to indigent persons, within its financial means, so as to give content to the rights to legal representation at state expense. Initially, the Board was given complete discretion as to how it would offer legal assistance to indigent persons, and to this end it established a set of working rules that are incorporated in the Legal Aid Guide.[50] In 1994, after the first democratic government took office and enacted an interim Constitution, the Board became responsible[51] for providing legal aid in criminal cases where accused persons could not afford lawyers and "a substantial injustice would otherwise result" if they were not represented.[52] Thus, Legal Aid

SA obtains its mandate from the Constitution, the Legal Aid Act[53] as read with the current Legal Aid Guide, which will be replaced by the Legal Aid Regulations (Policy Provisions) and Legal Aid Manual (Procedural Provisions), as well as other national legislation that gives content to the rights and obligations enshrined in the Constitution.

Legal Aid SA uses a combination of justice centers and satellite offices to provide a full range of legal and paralegal services to indigent clients in the larger cities and towns. The justice centers are one-stop state-funded law firms that are fully staffed to provide comprehensive legal services to legal aid clients. To qualify for assistance, Legal Aid SA requires that a household must show that it has a net monthly income of about US $430 per month or less to be considered for fully subsidized legal aid.

In the 2016–17 financial year, Legal Aid SA had a budget of roughly US $131 million, which covered the legal costs of over 767,656 people, 87 percent of whom were facing criminal charges. That works out to approximately US $164 per client, without taking into account other costs related to the operations of Legal Aid SA.

As stated above, Legal Aid SA dedicates most of its resources to criminal matters, thus leaving a lacuna in the provision of legal services in civil matters. Budgetary constraints prevent Legal Aid SA from significantly expanding its assistance in civil matters and, to close this gap, the Board entered into cooperation agreements with legal service providers such as public interest law firms and the independent university law clinics. It also established its own impact litigation division.[54] When the justice centers or impact litigation divisions are unable to handle cases, they are referred to private lawyers.

Beyond Legal Aid SA, state-funded provision of legal services has also been mandated for farmworkers and generally in the area of land tenure reform.[55]

Collaboration between Legal Aid South Africa and Public Interest Law Organizations

Legal Aid SA has increasingly embraced the idea of state-funded impact litigation.[56] The primary vehicle through which this is implemented is the Impact Litigation Unit. By working with partners in the NGO sector, the Impact Litigation Unit has funded and litigated matters in all areas of the Bill of Rights – children's rights, housing rights, women's rights, access to education, and environmental rights, among others.

An example of this kind of collaboration is in the Silicosis Class Action litigation.[57] Legal Aid SA, through its Cooperation Agreement with the Legal Resources Centre (LRC), has funded this action since 2004. The LRC, assisted by Leigh Day and Associates of the United Kingdom, is representing a group of former gold miners who were employed at the President Steyn Gold Mine in the Free State Province. These former mine workers contracted silicosis, a lung disease that is untreatable and predisposes the sufferer to tuberculosis infection.[58]

Private Sector

Attorneys

As described earlier, pro bono work had been carried out by legal practitioners on an informal basis for decades. Yet, a formal initiative in respect of pro bono practice was only developed in South Africa in 2003. At that time, the Cape Law Society, one of the regional law societies regulating attorneys, instituted a mandatory pro bono rule for its members. The Society's initiative was prompted by the recognition that the government's legal aid system was inadequate to address the South African public's legal needs – particularly those of the poorest members of society.

Each of the regional law societies has, since then, required its members to perform pro bono services; today the LSSA mandates attorneys to provide 24 hours per year of free legal advice to members of the public who qualify for this service in terms of a means test. In most cases, refusing to perform pro bono services without good cause amounts to unprofessional conduct, although sanctions have never been imposed. Some law societies publish a list of services that, when performed by attorneys at no charge for those who cannot afford to pay, are recognized as pro bono services capable of being delivered in compliance with the provisions of the societies' pro bono rules.

Currently, Rule 25 of the Rules for the Attorneys' Profession promulgated in 2016 regulates pro bono among attorneys.[59] This rule is similar to the various provincial law society rules that had been adopted by the KwaZulu-Natal Law Society, Free State Law Society, Law Society of the Northern Provinces, and Cape Law Society from around 2010 onwards. In addition to the efforts of the law societies, individual legal practitioners and firms in South Africa provide pro bono services on a voluntary basis through both formal and informal structures.

As discussed earlier, in South Africa, pro bono legal services developed largely in response to the plights of Black South Africans who were marginalized, dispossessed, disenfranchised, and discriminated against under the laws and regulations of apartheid. Today, in many instances, pro bono aims to be responsive to the needs of indigent and vulnerable individuals and groups, the majority of whom are poor and Black. And, it would be accurate to state that pro bono efforts are generally supported by the private legal sector with assistance being provided by large, medium, and small firms in addition to solo practitioners.

Moreover, intermediary organizations such as ProBono.Org have also helped to develop and expand pro bono work. Established in 2006 with an initial infusion of funds from the Atlantic Philanthropies, ProBono.Org is an NGO that works with the South African private legal profession to provide pro bono legal services to those who are unable to afford legal representation. It links private practitioners to cases and clients that it identifies with the goal of creating sufficient free legal representation for all who need it.[60] In connecting the public interest legal needs of the poor with the private legal sector, ProBono.Org helps to facilitate both individual legal assistance and strategic impact litigation. It operates a legal clearinghouse in which it services clients on a daily basis and refers cases to its panel of pro bono attorneys where necessary. ProBono.Org also organizes legal clinics on matters relating to wills and deceased estates, refugees, labor law, housing, domestic violence, family law, and consumer law. In addition, it conducts workshops and seminars for both attorneys and communities and works with NGOs and CBOs that refer cases to it.[61]

Large Firms

Most of the country's large commercial law firms have adopted policies and programs in support of pro bono. For instance, all of the five large firms known informally as the "Big Five" have formal pro bono programs or activities: Bowman Gilfillian, Cliffe Dekker Hofmeyr, ENSafrica, Norton Rose Fulbright South Africa, and Webber Wentzel in alliance with Linklaters. Werksmans Attorneys and smaller firms, such as Fluxmans Attorneys, or South African branch offices of international law firms, such as Hogan Lovells, also have formal pro bono programs. There is, however, a variety in the different models and approaches utilized. As a rule, these formal programs facilitate either the provision of pro bono legal services through (1) an individual attorney, (2) a general services pro bono unit, or (3) programs linked to specific specializations (such as wills and estates or family law or insolvency). What follows is a description of some of these models and approaches; this list is illustrative and not exhaustive.

Following the adoption of the pro bono rule by the Cape Law Society in 2003, Webber Wentzel recruited an attorney with extensive experience in public interest litigation to set up its in-house pro bono practice.[62] The work of this practice "is guided by the recognised need to narrow the divide between the advantaged and disadvantaged members of South African society and the obligation to play a role as a good citizen in promoting the transformative goals of the [South African Constitution]." It represents the firm's "commitment to contributing to these processes through equal justice for all."[63] Over the years, Webber Wentzel has taken on matters involving vulnerable groups including women, children, LGBTI persons, people with mental and physical disabilities, refugees, and people living with HIV. Among others, it has dealt with issues involving crimes against humanity, rule of law, land reform, housing and service delivery, traditional authorities and customary law, sexual harassment, the rights of refugees, and discrimination based on HIV status. Through its pro bono practice, Webber Wentzel has worked with numerous public interest law centers including Section27, the LRC, and the Southern Africa Legal Centre along with governmental bodies such as Legal Aid SA and the South African National AIDS Conference, and international entities like the International Labour Organization.

Through its pro bono and corporate social responsibility (CSR) programs, the firm of Bowman Gilfillian ("Bowmans") provides legal services to various clinics focused on labor, housing, refugees, and domestic violence located in NGOs, courts, and administrative offices. It also litigates individual and public interest matters in courts.[64]

In 2011, Cliffe Dekker Hofmeyr (CDH) established a dedicated pro bono and human rights practice that offers a range of free legal services to individuals, nonprofit organizations, and other institutions engaged in public interest or human rights matters. With specialized expertise in constitutional law, access to information, disability law, and refugee law, this practice provides 1000 of hours of pro bono assistance annually. It regularly assists in staffing the ProBono.Org Refugee Legal Clinic, the Inner City Housing Clinic, and help desks in several courts. CDH offers services and litigation for both individuals and impact litigation. The latter is often in concert with NGOs such as the South African History Archive Trust, the Right to Know Campaign, and Corruption Watch. Moreover, each lawyer in the firm is encouraged to participate in pro bono activities and human rights–focused initiatives and special projects.[65]

ENSafrica established two dedicated offices located within the underserved and poor communities of Mitchells Plain near Cape Town and Alexandria Township in Johannesburg. The services offered at these locations include legal advice and rights education programs.

All the attorneys at Norton Rose Fulbright South Africa are required to perform, at minimum, the 24 hours of pro bono services annually as mandated by the Law Society of South Africa. These services include free legal counseling and assistance to victims of domestic violence and operating a help desk at one of the magistrate's courts on a weekly basis and every day during the internationally recognized Sixteen Days of Activism for No Violence Against Women and Children that takes place annually from November 25 to December 10. Moreover, in addition to working with individual clients, Norton Rose Fulbright SA also represents institutions and organizations. For instance, it successfully represented a museum seeking to uphold the provisions of the National Heritage Resources Act and prevent unlawful alluvial diamond mining on a declared heritage site. It also supported the South African Commission for Gender Equality in its role as an amicus curiae in a matter involving forty Thai women who had been detained by the South African Department of Home Affairs for two months in violation of the Immigration Act of 2015. In this instance, the Court found that the South African Police Service and the Department of Home Affairs acted unconstitutionally and ordered the immediate release of these detainees into a place of safety.

Werksmans Attorneys maintains a dedicated public interest law team of three full-time staff who coordinate the pro bono activities of the firm. The pro bono strategy of this firm is multifaceted and aligned to the firm's areas of specialties including consumer rights, children's rights, disability rights, environmental rights, rights related to labor, access to health care, access to justice, and corporate governance for nonprofits. Specifically, the Werksmans Consumer Law Clinic operates in partnership with the NGO Afrika Tikkun in Diepsloot Township north of Johannesburg, and the firm collaborates with ProBono.Org and its legal advice clinics focused on consumer, housing, and environmental issues. It also provides ad hoc legal support to over fifty organizations that are involved with various matters such as education, mentoring, and fundraising for victims of domestic violence. Werksmans further provides support and advice to public interest law firms such as Section27, the Centre for Applied Legal Studies, and Lawyers Against Abuse in addition to entities like the Treatment Action Campaign.[66]

In some instances, these large firm-based pro bono providers interact with social movements, usually through an intermediary public interest law center. For example, in 2017, acting on instructions from the Socio-Economic Rights Institute (SERI), the law firm of Bowman Gilfillan represented *Abahlali baseMjondolo* (a shack dwellers' movement) and 241 families in an action seeking interim interdicts against a local municipality in the city of Durban following illegal evictions and the demolition of homes by the municipality. Interim relief was granted resulting in approximately 650 individuals who had been evicted from their homes obtaining court-sanctioned approval to rebuild their dwellings.[67]

While attempting to be responsive to the needs of the most disadvantaged and vulnerable individuals and groups, some large South African firms have added a component to their pro bono work that seeks to assist and promote business development and newly established entrepreneurs. For instance, Norton Rose Fulbright partners with Shanduka Black Umbrellas, a project focused on Black economic empowerment. The firm conducts a legal education program for the clients of Shanduka, which incubates small Black businesses with the aim of helping them to become sustainable large enterprises. Topics covered in the course include commercial leases, credit legislation, competition law, corporate governance, and fraud and money laundering, among others. From this partnership, Norton Rose Fulbright has developed what it calls a "commercial pro bono initiative" in which it assists qualifying small businesses with commercial contracts and governance issues.[68]

In a similar vein, Bowmans established the *Ishishini Lethu* (Our Business) Project in 2013 to address the legal requirements of entrepreneurs, nonprofit entities, and micro and small enterprises. The intention is to provide short-term legal assistance combined with education to enable entrepreneurs and small enterprises to participate more effectively in the South African legal and economic environments. In doing so, Bowmans works with nonprofit organizations that identify and refer start-up clients and small businesses to the firm and, in turn, the internal pro bono team refers these requests for support to attorneys who have expertise in the particular area. As of the beginning of 2018, Bowmans had assisted 170 small businesses through this program.[69]

Small and Medium Firms

According to Erica Emdon, former national director of ProBono.Org, small firms in South Africa are engaged in a great deal of pro bono work with many of them focusing on assisting individuals with issues pertaining to family law, wills, and deceased estates, for example. Over her years with ProBono.Org, Emdon witnessed a supportive and positive attitude toward pro bono from practitioners in small firms, and she observed that this assistance to individuals is "very important work" that places these attorneys "at the coal face" of the problems and issues encountered by underresourced and vulnerable persons.[70]

Interestingly, Emdon pointed to a "gap" in the pro bono arena. Large firms and small practitioners provide pro bono services but, in her opinion, midsize firms (in the South African context, these are practices with ten to twenty partners) as a rule do not have dedicated pro bono departments, and the pro bono work they perform can be "very ad hoc." Yet, when a midsize firm does engage, its pro bono work can be "impressive," with Emdon citing Fluxmans Attorneys as an exemplar in this regard.[71]

Hybrids

Another model of specialized pro bono delivery operates under the auspices of the South African Society for Labour Law (SASLAW),[72] which, in 2011, established the SASLAW Pro Bono Project, a nonprofit company that administers pro bono services in four labor courts in Johannesburg, Durban, Cape Town, and Port Elizabeth. The SASLAW Pro Bono Project and its volunteers assist unrepresented and indigent litigants by providing advice on their labor matters from specialist legal practitioners. By doing so, the project also assists the Labor Court in addressing the backlog in its caseload and facilitating the efficient operations of the various labor courts. As of 2018, over 18,500 clients have been assisted since the inception of the Project.[73]

This model of pro bono delivery is especially interesting in the way in which it brings together legal practitioners from various firms within its collaborative structure. Since 2015, over thirty South African law firms – large, medium, and small – in addition to several advocates, have partnered with the SASLAW Pro Bono Project in its provision of free legal services. Cheadle Thompson & Haysom Inc. Attorneys, Cowan–Harper Attorneys, and Hlatshwayo Du Plessis Van Der Merwe Nkaiseng Attorneys are among the smaller firms in this collective, and all of the Big Five (NRF, CDH, Bowmans, Webber Wentzel, ENS) in addition to Werksmans work with the Project.[74]

Whether utilized by large, medium, or small firms or solo practices, the manner and extent of these models of pro bono delivery in South Africa are not without challenges.

- The first challenge relates to the enforcement, or lack thereof, of the LSSA 24 hours per year of pro bono services requirement. There is little enforcement of this requirement, and to date there has been no report of an attorney having been disciplined for failing to undertake pro bono work.
- The second relates to the amount of time an attorney is required to spend on these cases. In many instances, the allocation of 24 hours is insufficient to finish a matter, resulting in cases not being completed. In addition, there may be a lack of quality control over services provided.
- The third challenge, as we see it, is the use of dedicated pro bono units in some large law firms. In firms that have established units that conduct all of the firm's pro bono work, this can result in a lack of pro bono services being rendered by the majority of the attorneys in that firm who are not members to those units.
- Fourth, as a rule, these services are not available in areas with the most destitute and vulnerable populations. Many firms are located in urban centers, and very few have outreach in poor, rural districts of South Africa. Many of the people living in these districts do not know about the availability of the pro bono services, and where they do, they do not have the means to access them.
- Lastly, and this happens on many occasions, particularly when an indigent person wants to bring a claim against a corporate institution, a law firm has to decline a pro bono instruction referred to it

because of a conflict of interest. Entities that litigate often, such as banks, have numerous firms on their panels. That immediately excludes all of these attorneys in those firms from assisting in, for instance, foreclosure matters, which is a commonplace issue in pro bono work in South Africa.

Advocates

The General Council of the Bar Constitution is silent on the duty to render pro bono services, as are most, if not all, of the constitutions of the local bars. In its mission statement, however, the GCB does assert that "[t]he Bar is committed to: . . . providing greater access to justice by the expansion of legal services to all who require them."[75] Only in 2002 was there a reference to the duty to do pro bono work included in the Uniform Rules of Ethics. According to the "cab rank" rule, advocates are required to take on all legal work they are briefed on.[76]

Under the South African cab rank rule (following the global norm), although advocates are permitted to reject cases for a number of functional reasons, including lack of expertise, overcommitment, or conflicts of interest with other clients, cases cannot be rejected because the advocate dislikes the client or the case. For example, in the proposed code of conduct that will apply under the Legal Practice Act, Rule 18.2 forms part of the broader Rule 18 entitled "Acceptance of Briefs and Cab Rank Rule" that provides: "Counsel shall not refuse to accept briefs in an area of practice in which they profess to practise or in a court which they profess to practise on the grounds that they disapprove of the client or of the client's opinions or alleged conduct or because of any disregard in which such person might be held."[77]

Today, the General Council of the Bar, Johannesburg Bar Council, Pretoria Bar Council, Cape Bar Council, and Eastern Cape Society of Advocates all have pro bono rules that apply to advocates. Advocates are required to commit a minimum of 20 hours a year pro bono. But the definition of pro bono is broad, and many get around this not by representing poor people but by allocating their pro bono time to committee activities they would have done anyway.[78] There is an incidental mention in Section 21.1 of the February 10, 2017, Draft Code of Conduct in its section on legal practitioners appointed as advocates: "Counsel shall not refuse to accept a *pro bono* brief in counsel's professed area of practice solely on the grounds that the brief is *pro bono*, except for good cause."[79]

Insofar as challenges with the provision of pro bono legal services by advocates are concerned, the profession's model makes provision a complicated matter. One such challenge borne from the structure is matching the need for legal services with willing and able practitioners. It is clear that there is a discord between the areas where the greatest need exists and the areas of the law in which most practitioners earn a living. The majority of pro bono matters pertain to family law, women's and children's rights, estates, housing and residential property rights, labor disputes, refugees and migrants, access to social grants, and pensions and other social security–related issues. This puts a disproportionate burden on members practicing in these areas. Thus, an advocate can avoid rendering pro bono services on the grounds that the advanced or complicated nature of the work does not accord with a member's experience, or that the skills required fall outside of a member's area of specialization.

Another challenge, though one could argue that it is more of a double-edged sword, is the willingness of most junior members to do pro bono work. For junior members, this type of work can be a good opportunity to learn. For the client, however, receiving services from a practitioner who lacks the experience to deal confidently with the matter can be detrimental and result in the most vulnerable being serviced by the least experienced. Some argue that one way to remedy this is through the combination of two counsel on one brief, with the more senior member serving as adviser and mentor to the more junior colleague over the period of execution of the brief. In this way, more people can obtain effective legal assistance, junior members with available time can gain experience under the guidance of an experienced practitioner, and more senior members will be able to render pro bono services effectively.

For many years in South African civil cases, free legal aid has been provided in the high court under the *informa pauperis* procedures in the Rules of the High Court. These proceedings may be brought in terms of the Rules of the High Court, whereby the Registrar of the High Court refers poor people – people with assets of less than approximately US $700 – to private practitioners (attorneys who brief advocates) for assistance.[80] The private practitioners must take the cases without compensation, but may recover their fees and disbursements at ordinary tariff rates if the litigant is awarded costs.

It can be argued that these various rules do not go far enough to protect the rights of the indigent to have access to pro bono legal services. The various rules adopted by the South African legal profession in its own professional bodies must be strengthened, and the best way to do so is through legislation. Thus the Legal Practice Act is important in this regard.

The Regulation of Legal Practice and Its Relevance to Pro Bono in South Africa

Pro bono practice in South Africa is likely to influence as well as be significantly affected by contemporary developments in how the legal profession is regulated. After a nearly two-decade gestation process, the passage of the Legal Practice Act (LPA or Act) of 2014 repealed and replaced the apartheid-era legislation governing advocates as well as the law governing attorneys. In the works since 1995, the LPA creates a single category of legal practitioner that encompasses both attorneys and advocates, thus regulating both historically separate subprofessions in one comprehensive law. It will, for instance, create "a consolidated database of all legal practitioners – attorneys and advocates" that will comprise the rolls of the new governing body.[81] It provides authority to establish a single South African Legal Practice Council with regulatory and disciplinary powers as well as a legal services ombud. The LPA may fruitfully be seen against the background of the UK Legal Services Act of 2007, providing for a single external oversight regulator in legal services with consistent oversight regulation of professional bodies, which would retain day-to-day regulatory functions.[82] Paralegals are not covered in the Act, an agreement having been reached that a separate legislative process will cover such practitioners.

The legislation does not, however, do all its work at one go. Instead, it establishes interim and transitional structures to discuss the structures and details of the Act's implementation. Set up in terms of the Act, the National Forum on the Legal Profession began meeting in 2015 and will terminate at the end of October 2018. From that time, a new Legal Practice Council will begin to govern the legal profession.

Of major import is the fact that the Act does not itself use the term "pro bono." Instead, its key term is "community service." One of the purposes of the Act, stated in Section 3(b)(ii), is to "broaden access to justice by putting into place . . . measures to provide for the rendering of community service by candidate legal practitioners and practising legal practitioners." Defining what is meant by community service has become a matter of much debate in the profession. And because there is no express provision for pro bono services in the LPA, it is generally accepted that community service will encompass voluntaristic notions of pro bono.

Not surprisingly, the particular place of pro bono within the LPA has been a subject of contestation. As the legitimate and comprehensive statute governing the entirety of the legal profession, the Act and its implementation process have changed many of the parameters of professional politics. In particular, it has provided one single framework within which most – though not all, especially in view of the work of paralegals – traditions and policies regarding pro bono legal services in South Africa must be governed and performed. While the contestation continues, as of writing, some points about its passage and effects appear clear.

First, the LPA is the first to prescribe mandatory pro bono services for all legal practitioners. While various segments of the professions had adopted internal rules and policies to this effect, the principle of mandating pro bono legal services had not previously been adopted as a matter of legislation (or even subordinate legislation). As described earlier in this chapter, pro bono service in South Africa has deep and significant roots in a voluntaristic ethos in the private sector. We would claim that this is one of the sources (with access to justice and community service) of the particularly South African style and institution of pro bono, which is distinct from the model spread globally, in particular from large American corporate law firms and their clients.

Second, it may be equally significant that the principle of pro bono services is now mandated for all members of the legal profession. This legislative innovation recognizes and elevates the provision of pro bono services to one of the core elements of the legal profession. To be a legal practitioner in postapartheid South Africa means, in part, to provide pro bono legal services. Indeed, this extends even to the provision of pro bono services by candidate attorneys – to train to be a lawyer also means providing pro bono legal services.

The above said, there have been very different approaches to the understandings within segments of the legal profession as to meanings of pro bono and the implications for its practice and its incorporation within the LPA. For example, some have differed in their understandings of whether pro bono should even be within the Act. Some have reflected the radical voluntaristic understanding and argued it should not be included. Others have claimed not only that the Act embraces pro bono but that it entrenches the maximalist interpretation of community service in so doing.

Further in Section 6 of the LPA, the Council (which is to begin operation on November 1, 2018) has the power in relation to law students to "advise the Council on Higher Education established in terms of the Higher Education Act, 1997, regarding matters relevant to education in law, including the desirability of including in the LLB curriculum a form of community service to be undertaken by all law students." Thus, there is the future prospect of "a form of community service" to be determined for law students. The debate here is between those who strongly support community service as a vehicle to advancing access to justice and those who raise and address the concern of vulnerability that has often surfaced in relation to student practice rules. This concern is usually stated as one querying whether having the least-qualified legal professionals (students or law graduates in training) representing the most vulnerable is fair or just or ethical.

The debate over the proper understanding of community service for practitioners entering the profession must, however, also be read with Section 29 of the Act, "Community Service," which applies to all practitioners and states:

29. (1) The Minister must, after consultation with the Council, prescribe the requirements for community service from a date to be determined by the Minister, and such requirements may include –
- (a) community service as a component of practical vocational training by candidate legal practitioners; or
- (b) a minimum period of recurring community service by practising legal practitioners upon which continued enrolment as a legal practitioner is dependent.

(2) Community service for the purposes of this section may include, but is not limited, to the following:
- (a) service in the State, approved by the Minister, in consultation with the Council;
- (b) service at the South African Human Rights Commission;
- (c) service, without any remuneration, as a judicial officer in the case of legal practitioners, including as a commissioner in the small claims courts;
- (c) the provision of legal education and training on behalf of the Council, or on behalf of an academic institution or nongovernmental organisation; or

(d) any other service which the candidate legal practitioner or the legal practitioner may want to perform, with the approval of the Minister.

(3) The Council may, on application and on good cause shown, exempt any candidate legal practitioner or legal practitioner from performing community service, as set out in the rules.

This "adult" community service provision is also contested. Indeed, one difficulty of interpretation is that the concept of community service is defined differently or at least employed in different senses in different parts of the legislation. In regard to candidate attorneys, community service must be "a component of practical vocational training." In regard to licensed professionals, there must be "a minimum period of recurring community service by practising legal practitioners upon which continued enrolment as a legal practitioner is dependent." The qualification of "a form of" is used in referring to community service for law students.

Community service was not a topic included in the draft regulations that the National Forum sent to the minister as it terminated its work. Instead, the Forum noted that for "Community service: This Regulation can only be drafted after the Minister has consulted with the Council to identify the types of appropriate community service."

The profession has recognized and to some extent structured this contestation. Since 2016, the Law Society of South Africa together with its constituent members and the support of the Foundation for Human Rights has undertaken a dialogue project aimed at investigating relevant models for the implementation of a national model for the delivery of pro bono/community services by the South African legal profession.[83] As mentioned above, one of the intended purposes of the LPA is to broaden access to justice by putting in place measures to provide for the rendering of community service by candidate legal practitioners and community service for practicing legal practitioners.

Defining what is meant by community service has become a matter of much debate in the profession. And because there is no express provision for pro bono services in the LPA, it is generally accepted that community service will encompass voluntaristic notions of pro bono.

The former director of ProBono.Org has placed on record its organizational stance on what community service should mean for legal professionals, adopting a position that falls in between the two identified above. She explains that:

> Regarding community service for professionals, ProBono.Org believes that the purpose of undertaking pro bono service is to make access to justice available to the most impoverished members of our society. For this reason we believe that the paltry 24 hours required per annum should be skewed towards casework for impoverished clients, as this is where the need is greatest. We believe that while options, such as providing training, service to the state, acting as a commissioner at a small claims court and so forth are options to be considered, there should be an imperative in the regulations requiring that a substantial majority of the 24 hours should be devoted to case work and direct legal assistance to people unable to afford private legal fees.[84]

This stance was supported by Judge Taswell Papier of the Western Cape Division of the High Court in Cape Town: "The enactment of the community service provision in the Act is timeous and offers an enormous opportunity to the profession to take the *pro bono* project to its next level with vigour, innovation and commitment. We must always be mindful that community service must not be rendered at a lesser quality. The time has come to revisit the establishment of a clearing house for *pro bono*,"[85] said Judge Papier.

Similarly, in a recent article titled "How Legal Practice Act Overlooks the Spirit of Pro Bono Work," Melody Emmet argues that the LPA does not clearly address the critical question of access to justice through pro bono services.[86] The Cliffe Dekker Hofmeyr director of pro bono and human rights practice, Jacquie Cassette, was quoted as saying that depending on how community service is defined, Section 29 of the act might divert resources away from the provision of traditional pro bono services to the poor:[87]

> This will all depend on the regulations made by the minister, who is given a wide discretion to determine whether community service is to be imposed on practitioners and, if so, what will constitute community service and what will be its requirements. There are concerns about the constitutionality of vesting such wide and uncircumscribed power in the minister.

The regulations are yet to be published. The legal profession is waiting in anticipation so that the debate can continue based on framing provided by the minister.

CONCLUSION

Increasing access to justice for the poor, marginalized, and indigent individuals and communities should be seen by members of the South

African legal community as an essential component to fulfilling not only their civic duty but also their constitutional obligations. For this to occur, legal practitioners must continue to recognize and embrace the important role they can play by deploying their expertise and skills on behalf of the multitudes that are unable to pay for the prohibitive cost of legal services. Furthermore, individual attorneys and advocates along with firms, bars, and professional associations must be willing to go beyond the mere minimum requirements. If indeed the aspirations articulated in the Constitution are to be made more real, if indeed South African society is to accelerate the rate of meaningful transformation for the majority of its inhabitants, then legal practitioners and the profession, along with numerous other individuals and institutions, will need to look beyond personal gain and individual achievement toward the greater good.

The Legal Practice Act gives us an opportunity to reimagine and define community service in ways that would fulfill our constitutional aspirations. Given that there is no clear reference to pro bono legal services, the question arises as to whether we can read the concept of pro bono legal services into the community service provisions of Section 29. Section 29(1)(b) of the LPA provides for recurring community service rendered by legal practitioners every year. Utilizing this reading, the words "recurring community service by practising legal practitioners" could mean something similar to what we currently know as pro bono services covered by various rules of law societies. What is more is that we can now argue for a construction of provision of legal services that increases hours of required service, or even sets a different requirement altogether, including a requirement to take one or two cases without remuneration in a lawyer's area of expertise, as well as other exciting ways of establishing a system that truly encompasses the spirit and ethos of the Constitution.

NOTES

1. The Prohibition of Mixed Marriages Act 55 of 1949 prohibited marriages between "Europeans" and "non-Europeans"; the Population Registration Act 30 of 1950 required each inhabitant of South Africa to register as a member of one of four officially defined racial groups (Black, White, Coloured, and Indian); the Group Areas Act 41 of 1950 formally segregated races by assigning racial groups to different residential and business sections in urban areas and led to the forced removal of

Blacks located in areas designated for Whites; and the Immorality Amendment Act 21 of 1950 amended the original Immorality Act 5 of 1927 by extending the existing ban on interracial sex between "Europeans" and "natives" to disallow all sex between "Europeans" and "non-Europeans," thus including Coloured and Indian South Africans within the scope of this law.

2. The Abolition of Passes and Co-Ordination of Documents Act 67 1952 (commonly known as the Pass Laws Act) repealed the numerous regional pass laws that had been in place and enacted one national law with the purpose of segregating the population, managing urbanization and allocating migrant labor. All this to benefit the apartheid state while the humanity, dignity, and rights of Black South Africans, who were required to carry "pass books" at all times within White areas, were nullified. The Bantu Education Act 47 of 1953 enforced racially separated and highly unequal educational facilities by bringing African education under the control of the state with funding for Black schools becoming conditional on the acceptance of a racially discriminatory curriculum. The Promotion of Bantu Self-Government Act 46 of 1959 established "Bantustans," or fully independent states that, in theory, allowed for self-determination for Black ethnic groups who were expected to exercise their political rights in these homelands and not in South Africa. In reality, under this law, millions of Black South Africans were stripped of their South African citizenship and forcibly removed to underdeveloped and underresourced locations.
3. Michael Robertson & Megan Seneque, Human Rights for South Africans 21 (1990).
4. The Congress for a Democratic South Africa was convened in late 1991 as a body of major political formations in South Africa that was tasked with the drafting of the interim Constitution. In 1992, the Congress was replaced by the Multi-Party Negotiating Forum. *See* South African Constitutional Law in Context 19 (Danie Brand, Pierre De Vos & Warren Freedman eds., 2014).
5. S. Afr. Const., 1996 preamble.
6. S. Afr. Const., 1996.
7. Linda Jansen van Rensburg, Jabulani Francisco Khoza, Elsabe Klinck & Marius Paul Olivier, *Constitutional Issues*, *in* Social Security: A Legal Analysis 52 (Evance Kalula, Marius Paul Olivier & Nicola Smit eds., 2003).
8. *Soobramoney v. Minister of Health (KwaZulu Natal)* 1997 (12) BCLR 1696 (CC).
9. *Id.* at ¶ 8.
10. Anyway Chingwete, *South Africa, Citizens' Trust in President, Political Institutions Drops Sharply*, The Institute for Justice and Reconciliation, Afro Barometer (May 17, 2016), http://afrobarometer.org/sites/default/files/publications/Dispatches/ab_r6_dispatchno90_south_africa_trust_in_officials.pdf (last visited Sept. 24, 2020).

11. Pro Bono: The Responsibility of Lawyers to Undertake Pro Bono Publico and Public Interest Work (2002), a conference organized by Lawyers for Human Rights and funded by the Ford Foundation; *see also* Jeremy Sarkin, *Promoting Access to Justice in South Africa: Should the Legal Profession Have a Voluntary or Mandatory Role in Providing Legal Services to the Poor?*, 18 S. Afr. J. Hum. Rts. 630 (2002).
12. S. Afr. Const., 1996 § 9.
13. S. Afr. Const., 1996 § 34.
14. S. Afr. Const., 1996 § 35. There is no equivalent automatic right to legal representation afforded to civil litigants.
15. S. Murlidhar, Law, Poverty and Legal Aid – Access to Criminal Justice 1 (2004).
16. David McQuoid-Mason , *Teaching Social Justice to Law Students Through Community Service – The South African Experience*, *in* Transforming South African Universities: Capacity Building for Historically Black Universities: Challenges and Strategies for the Next Millennium (J. Baloro et al. eds., 2000).
17. Chetty Karun, The Horizontal Application of the South African Bill of Rights 3 (1998) (unpublished LL.M. study), https://researchspace.ukznt.ac.za/bitstream/handle/10413/5240/Chetty_Karun_D_1998.pdf?sequence=1&isAllowed=y (last visited Sept. 22, 2020).
18. *Id.* at 4.
19. *In Re Certification of the Constitution of the Republic of South Africa* 1996 (10) BCLR 1253 (CC).
20. Saranel Benjamin, *Case Study: Joining Forces for the Poor: Alliance Building for Social Justice in South Africa and the Story of the National Alliance for the Development of Community Advice Offices*, Atlantic Philanthropies 8 (Sept. 2012), www.atlanticphilanthropies.org/wp-content/uploads/2015/09/Joining-forces-for-the-poor.pdf (last visited Sept. 22, 2020).
21. Initially, the term "paralegal" was not part of the South African terminology. In 1974, a leader of the Black Sash visited the United States and met with groups engaged in similar work. When she returned to South Africa, she introduced Black Sash to the term "paralegal" and compared the advice office work with the "paralegal clinics" she had visited. *See* Mary Burton, The Black Sash, Women for Justice and Peace 95 (2015). For purposes of this chapter, the terms "advice office worker" and "paralegal" are used interchangeably and we rely on the definition of paralegal provided in *Many Roads to Justice*: "paralegals are persons with specialized training who provide legal assistance to disadvantaged groups and who often [but not exclusively] are themselves members of those groups. *See* Mary E. MacClymont & Stephen Golub , Many Roads to Justice: The Law Related Work of Ford Foundation Grantees Around the World 297 (2000).
22. In 1952, this work was supported by the first grant made in South Africa by the Ford Foundation. *See* Patricia Rosenfield & Rachel Wimpee,

Continuity Amidst Change: The History of the Ford Foundation in South Africa, 1952–1993 2 (unpublished memorandum) (on file with the Rockefeller Archive Center Ford Foundation History Project).

23. BURTON, *supra* note 21, at 37, 79.
24. *Id.* at 81.
25. *Id.*
26. These included the Centre for Applied Legal Studies at the University of the Witwatersrand (1978), Lawyers for Human Rights and the Legal Resources Centre (1979), and the Black Lawyers Association and its affiliated Legal Education Centre (early to mid-1980s).
27. BURTON, *supra* note 21, at 86, 96.
28. Heather S. McKay, Patricia L. Rosenfield & Courtenay C. Sprague, *Ethical Dimensions of International Grantmaking: Drawing the Line in a Borderless World*, 11 J. LEADERSHIP ORG. STUD. 48, 57 (2004).
29. *Id.*; *see also* BURTON, *supra* note 21.
30. Peggy Maisel, *Expanding and Sustaining Clinical Legal Education in Developing Countries: What We Can Learn from South Africa Symposium: Global Alliance for Justice Education (GAJE) North American Regional Conference*, 30 FORDHAM INT'L L.J. 374 (2006).
31. Willem De Klerk, *University Law Clinics in South Africa*, 122 S. AFR. L. J. 929 (2005).
32. David McQuoid-Mason, *Whatever Happened to the Proposed South African Student Practice Rules?*, 41 DE JURE 580 (2008).
33. Shaheda Hassim Mahomed, Critical Evaluation of the Practical Legal Studies Programme at the University of the Witwatersrand (Oct. 22, 2014) (unpublished Ph.D. thesis, University of Witwatersrand), http://wiredspace.wits.ac.za/handle/10539/15786 (last visited Sept. 24, 2020); A. M. Du Plessis, Assessment Methods in Clinical Legal Education (Jan. 30, 2015) (unpublished Ph.D. thesis, University of Witwatersrand), http://wiredspace.wits.ac.za/handle/10539/16834 (last visited Sept. 24, 2020).
34. TESSA MURRAY, LEGAL AID BOARD: BALANCING THE SCALES OF JUSTICE 1–7 (2008).
35. Willem De Klerk, *University Law Clinics in South Africa*, 122 S. AFR. L. J. 929 (2005).
36. Maisel, *supra* note 30, at 384; David McQuoid-Mason, *Street Law as a Clinical Program*, 17 GRIFFITH L. REV. 27 (2008).
37. David McQuoid-Mason, *Methods of Teaching Human Rights: Some Examples from Street Law Legal Literacy Programmes*, 5 J. COMMONWEALTH L. & LEGAL EDUC. 127 (2007).
38. *See Welcome Report of the Conference*, *in* Pro Bono: The Responsibility of Lawyers to Undertake Pro Bono Publico and Public Interest Work (2012), www.internationalprobono.com/resources/attachment.162333 (last visited Sept. 24, 2020).
39. *Id.*
40. Attorneys Act 53 of 1979.

41. *Statistics for the Attorneys' Profession*, LAW SOCIETY OF SOUTH AFRICA, www.lssa.org.za/about-us/about-the-attorneys–profession/statistics-for-the-attorneys–profession (last visited Sept. 24, 2020).
42. *See* LAW SOCIETY OF SOUTH AFRICA, www.lssa.org.za (last visited Sept. 24, 2020).
43. Admission of Advocates Act 74 of 1964. These are:

> Subject to the provisions of any other law, any division shall admit to practice and authorize to be enrolled as an advocate any person who upon application made by him/her satisfies the court:
>
> a. that he/she is over the age of twenty-one years and is a fit and proper person to be so admitted and authorized;
>
> b. that he/she is duly qualified;
>
> c. that he/she is a South African citizen or that he/she has been lawfully admitted to the Republic for permanent residence therein and is ordinarily resident in the Republic;
>
> d. in the case of any person who has at any time been admitted to practice as an attorney in any court in the Republic or elsewhere, that his/her name has been removed from the roll of attorneys on his/her own application.

44. L.E.A.D. STATISTICS FOR LEGAL PROFESSION 2016/2017.
45. *Living Conditions of Households in South Africa: An Analysis of Household Expenditure and Income Data Using the LCS 2014/2015*, STATISTICS SOUTH AFRICA, www.statssa.gov.za/publications/P0310/P03102014.pdf (last visited Sept. 24, 2020).
46. *Id.*
47. Legal Aid Act 22 of 1969 § 2.
48. Legal Services Sector Charter, DEPARTMENT OF JUSTICE & CONSTITUTIONAL DEVELOPMENT SOUTH AFRICA, www.justice.gov.za/LSC/LSSC_Dec%2007.pdf (last visited Sept. 24, 2020).
49. *About the General Council of the Bar (the GCB)*, GENERAL COUNCIL OF THE BAR OF SOUTH AFRICA, https://gcbsa.co.za/about/ (last visited Sept. 24, 2020).
50. LEGAL AID BOARD, LEGAL AID GUIDE (2002). Amendments to the *Guide* must be put before Parliament. Legal Aid Act § 3A(2).
51. Legal Aid Amendment Act 20 of 1996 § 1.
52. S. AFR. CONST., 1996 § 35(2)(c) and § (3)(g).
53. Legal Aid South Africa Act 39 of 2014.
54. David J. McQuoid-Mason, *The Delivery of Civil Legal Aid Services in South Africa*, 24 FORDHAM INT'L L.J. S111 (2000).
55. SERI REPORT 112 (2016).
56. The concept of a state-funded public litigation strategy has been employed in a number of countries as a means to ensure that unconstitutional laws can be challenged by those who otherwise could not afford it (for example, Canada established the Court Challenges

Programme in 1985 to ensure that the government abided by the terms of the newly enacted Canadian Charter of Rights and Freedoms).

57. *Nkala v. Harmony Gold Mining Company Limited (Treatment Action Campaign NPC and Sonke Gender Justice NPC Amicus Curiae)* ("*Nkala*") 2016 (7) BCLR 881 (GJ). The applicants sought an order for the certification of one consolidated class action comprising two classes. The applicants proposed a bifurcated process through which the single class action would proceed in two stages: stage one, during which issues common to both classes shall be determined, and stage two, during which individual issues shall be determined with the court sanctioning the adoption of a bifurcated process. The potential class members may range from between seventeen thousand and five hundred thousand, the bulk of which belong to the silicosis class.
58. *Legal Aid South Africa Pleased with Historic Ruling on Silicosis Class Action*, LEGAL AID SOUTH AFRICA, https://legal-aid.co.za/3d-flip-book/13-may-legal-aid-sa-pleased-with-historic-ruling-on-silicosis-class-action-115-kb-pdf/ (last visited Sept. 24, 2020).
59. The Cape Law Society has its own rule. *See* Rules for the Attorneys' Profession, GN 2 of GG39740 (26 Feb. 2016), at 41.
60. PROBONO.ORG, www.probono.org.za/ (last visited Sept. 24, 2020).
61. *Id.*
62. Tom Lebert, *Giving Hope and Dignity to the Poor: The Story of ProBono.Org.*, ATLANTIC PHILANTHROPIES, www.atlanticphilanthropies.org/case-studies/giving-hope-and-dignity-poor-story-probonoorg (last visited Sept. 22, 2020).
63. *ProBono Overview*, WEBBERWENTZEL.COM, www.webberwentzel.com/Expertise/Services/Pro-Bono/Pages/default.aspx (last visited Sept. 24, 2020).
64. BOWMANS, PRO BONO & CSR ANNUAL REPORT 2017/18 4, www.bowmanslaw.com/wp-content/uploads/2018/04/Pro-Bono-Report-2018.pdf (last visited Sept. 24, 2020).
65. *See Pro Bono and Human Rights Brochure*, CDH, www.cliffedekkerhofmeyr.com/export/sites/cdh/en/practice-areas/downloads/Pro-Bono-and-Human-Rights-Brochure.PDF (last visited Sept. 24, 2020).
66. *Pro Bono*, WERKSMANS ATTORNEYS, www.werksmans.com/who-we-are/pro-bono/ (last visited Sept. 24, 2020).
67. *See* BOWMANS, *supra* note 64, at 15. Note: The interim interdicts were granted in July 2017. A few months later, Bowmans had to return to court in contempt of court proceedings against the municipality and other parties who demolished the rebuilt dwellings.
68. *See* NORTON ROSE FULBRIGHT, www.nortonrosefulbright.com/en-za (last visited Sept. 24, 2020).
69. *See* BOWMANS, *supra* note 64.
70. Interview with Erica Emdon (Jan. 2018).
71. *Id.*

72. The South African Society for Labour Law was established in 1997 as a membership association for those involved in all aspects of labor law in South Africa. With chapters in five of South Africa's nine provinces, the Society's 1,400 members include judges, advocates, attorneys, human resource and IR managers, trade unions, and employers' organizations, among others.
73. SASLAW Pro Bono NPC, www.saslawprobono.co.za (last visited Sept. 22, 2020).
74. *Id.*
75. *See About the General Council of the Bar, supra* note 49, at *Mission Statement*.
76. General Council of the Bar of South Africa, Uniform Rules of Professional Ethics F3 (2017).
77. *See* National Forum on the Legal Profession Code of Conduct, made under the authority of Legal Practice Act 28 of 2014 § 97(1)(b).
78. Nathan Geffen, *South Africa, a Country of Chequebook Justice*, Daily Maverick (Sept. 5, 2013), www.dailymaverick.co.za/opinionista/2013-09-05-south-africa-a-country-of-chequebook-justice/ (last visited Sept. 24, 2020).
79. National Forum on the Legal Profession, *Code of Conduct for Legal Practitioners, Candidate Legal Practitioners and Juristic Entities*, Government Gazette (Feb. 10, 2017), www.justice.gov.za/legislation/notices/2017/20170210-gg40610-no81-NFLP-CodeOfConduct.pdf (last visited Sept. 24, 2020).
80. Rule 40 of the Uniform Rules of the Court, as provided by Supreme Court Act 59 of 1959.
81. Barbara Whittle, *National Forum Starts Shaping the New Dispensation*, 18 De Rebus 155 (2015).
82. Andrew Boon, *Professionalism under the Legal Services Act 2007*, Int'l J. Legal Prof. 17, 195 (2010).
83. Law Society of South Africa, *Join the Discussion on Community Service and Pro Bono*, Go Legal, www.golegal.co.za/community-service-pro-bono/ (last visited Sept. 24, 2020).
84. Erica Emdon, *The Legal Practice Act and Community Service*, ProBono.Org (Apr. 29, 2016), www.probono.org.za/the-legal-practice-act-and-community-service/ (last visited Sept. 24, 2020).
85. Ricardo Wyngaard, *Pro Bono Work under the Legal Practice Act*, De Rebus, Dec. 1, 2017, www.derebus.org.za/pro-bono-work-legal-practice-act/ (last visited Sept. 24, 2020).
86. Melody Emmett, *How Legal Practice Act Overlooks the Spirit of Pro Bono Work*, Business Day, Nov. 2, 2017, www.businesslive.co.za/bd/opinion/2017-11-02-how-legal-practice-act-overlooks-the-spirit-of-pro-bono-work/ (last visited Sept. 24, 2020).
87. *Id.*

CHAPTER FOURTEEN

THE EVOLUTION OF PRO BONO LEGAL SERVICES IN NIGERIA

Jayanth K. Krishnan and Kunle Ajagbe

INTRODUCTION

Since becoming free from British colonialism in 1960, Nigeria has experienced, in total, nearly thirty years of military rule: 1966 to 1979 and then again from 1983 to 1999.[1] While the years from 1960 to 1966 and from 1979 to 1983 might be seen as periods of Nigerian democracy, they were nonetheless fractured times. Only since 1999 has democracy in Nigeria sustainably taken hold, and even then, the last eighteen years have not been easy. There is an insurgency ongoing in the northeast against the Boko Haram network, and the Delta region of the country also continues to witness instability.[2] Given these conditions, it is not surprising that the current government has faced enormous challenges. A lack of resources and perpetual bureaucratic inefficiency have impaired state institutions, as has corruption – which the current president, Muhummadu Buhari (himself the head of state of a military regime during the 1980s), has identified as Nigeria's most pressing problem.[3]

Against this backdrop, is there an opportunity for most Nigerians to avail themselves of legal services, and have they been able to use the law and lawyers to access their legal rights in the postcolonial era? Or more specifically relating to this chapter, does Nigeria have a culture of pro bono activism where those in need receive legal assistance for free or at rates significantly below market value?

As we will argue, in spite of the above obstacles, Nigeria, perhaps somewhat unexpectedly, has had episodes where pro bono legal services have not just emerged but thrived as well. Particularly telling is that these developments have occurred both during periods of democracy and during military eras.

Yet, to fully understand the manifestation of pro bono legal services in Nigeria, it is also important to be familiar with what the broader concept of legal aid means within the country. In the American context, Scott Cummings' landmark piece "The Politics of Pro Bono"[4] discusses in detail how in the early 1900s "legal aid societies were structured as charitable organizations located in poor neighborhoods, relied on staff attorneys to provide free services to specific categories of poor clients, and were subsidized, usually very meagerly, by philanthropic contributions."[5] As Cummings describes, the US bar initially kept its distance from these activities. Only in the 1960s, with the assistance of funding by the federal government, which provided "an undeniable shift in tone as well as strategy,"[6] did American legal aid move from its conservative approach to one that sought to help the needy in a more structural, systematic manner. However, as funding declined toward the last two decades of the twentieth century, the result was "the organized bar play[ing] a central role in building the institutional structures of pro bono . . . investing heavily in organizing nonprofit pro bono programs and promoting private-sector volunteerism in large law firms."[7]

The story of Nigeria, though, is different. Pro bono legal services have long been tied directly (rather than inversely) to government legal aid. It is important to remember that predating independence, and continuing to this day, most lawyers in Nigeria have been (and remain) solo practitioners. They work as courtroom advocates, many struggling to eke out an existence. Also, these lawyers tend to be generalists; the cases they take on range from civil to criminal, with most being in the petty form. With rare exception, then, these private-sector solo practitioners lack the time and resources to take cases on a pro bono basis. The only way they have historically been able to do so is through support from the state, through the various legal aid programs that it has sought to implement. Otherwise put, where state support for legal aid has been active, pro bono lawyering by private sector practitioners has tended to be active as well.

However, there have been exceptions. As this chapter will show, private sector lawyers, particularly during the military periods, have occasionally engaged in pro bono practice to assist those who were being oppressed – working in coordination with either the Nigeria Bar Association or with local civil society groups. Yet, such pro bono lawyering has had mixed results and has also tended to be ad hoc and atomistic rather than sustained and transformative. There is, though, a hopeful sign: since 1999, when Nigeria transitioned to democracy, there have been broader efforts to embed a deeper sense of pro bono culture into the way lawyers operate on a daily basis.

This narrative of Nigerian lawyers attempting to work as pro bono advocates over the years needs also to be understood within the larger literature of social justice lawyering in authoritarian and transitioning environments.[8] Most relevant for this study is Okechukwo Oko's research on "lawyers [living] under the military regimes of Nigeria,"[9] where he finds that the legal profession "face[d] an intractable dilemma."[10] Lawyers were seen as a threat because of their promotion of democracy and rule of law; at the same time, military leaders saw them as coercible and a possible legitimizing force for their authoritarian hold on power. Additionally, lawyers were viewed as potential defenders of the persecuted; yet if they veered too far in the human rights direction, they risked their careers and personal safety. But to not do enough was also a betrayal to their dignity and professional oath to uphold the rule of law.[11]

The analysis here on pro bono lawyering draws on this important scholarship. The latest moment in Nigeria's postindependence history offers the best opportunity to go beyond episodic instances of assistance and toward a longer-term, sustained movement of aid for those most in need. Indeed, the efforts of today build upon the struggles, and at times, achievements, of past pro bono activists – many of whom worked under arduous, and often authoritarian, circumstances.

CONSTITUTIONALISM, LEGAL AID, AND PRO BONO LAWYERING: 1963–1979

Following independence, the 1963 Republican Constitution of Nigeria sought to facilitate the provision of legal services to ordinary citizens. Former attorney general of Nigeria's Akwa Ibom State and legal commentator Uwemedimo Nwoko have argued that this constitution has been Nigeria's most significant document in the postcolonial era, because it carefully set forth the parameters of a fair, functioning democratic system of governance.[12]

Just three years into its tenure, however, it was superseded by a military coup, which itself was followed by a series of military governments that lasted for the next thirteen years.[13] Constitutional democracy went dark. Yet before it was dismantled, the 1963 constitution did provide certain legal aid protections for the needy, at least on paper. For example, it guaranteed all people charged with criminal offenses the right to have legal representation, to be presumed innocent, and to be protected against double jeopardy and self-incrimination.[14] In addition, "[a supplemental] legal aid bill was introduced by T. O. Elias, the Attorney-General in the civilian government immediately prior to the 1966 military coup."[15] Due process for defendants *was* a priority for these Nigerian democrats.

Still, both the constitution and the bill remained silent on how defendants were to actualize these entitlements – and for noncriminal matters, no reference was made on how to access legal aid. The 1963 legal framework thus offered initial steps for promoting a culture of serving those in need, but given the ensuing set of military governments that followed, it never had a chance to fulfill these promises.

At the same time, as Osagha argues, a counterintuitive phenomenon emerged during this era. Because it held power, the military could not simply be seen as one-dimensional autocrats.[16] The military sought to portray itself as both the "saviour and guardian of the nation . . . [and even was] invited to play this role by various sections of the aggrieved public."[17]

Enter the formation of the Legal Aid Council. This body came into existence as a result of the passage of the Legal Aid Act (1976), which was pushed for by a group of civically minded lawyers. One leader in this movement was Chimezie Ikeazor, who was frequently referred to as the "Poor Man's Lawyer" and "Father of Legal Aid in Nigeria."[18] During this time, Ikeazor was famed, for example, for engaging in "many pro-bono cases for people who didn't have the means to be represented at courts or pay legal fees . . . . [He also] campaigned from university to university, organising seminars and conferences to justify why the poor who could not afford to pay for legal services should be assisted," and together with other activists, he carefully, but forcefully, agitated for a statute that empowered the Council to grant representation to certain classes of criminal defendants.[19] Furthermore, to safeguard against the potential for abuse by patrons of the state (who did not need the assistance), the process provided such legal aid only to those who lived below a prescribed income.[20]

And more comprehensively, legal aid, under the Act, did not simply equate to litigation, but it included the range of nonlitigation activities in which lawyers regularly engaged.[21] It could mean, for instance, providing ordinary transactional assistance on property law, family law, or employment-related matters for the indigent, setting up legal awareness seminars, or visiting prisons to advise the incarcerated. Moreover, while the Council was staffed by lawyers who were paid by the state, it relied heavily on the pro bono efforts of those within the bar. There was thus a mutually enforcing relationship between the state's first major legal aid initiative and pro bono activism among private sector lawyers.

Nevertheless, the sheer presence of the military dictatorship hobbled the enforcement of the Act. Members of the Council and private sector lawyers were understandably wary of how far they could challenge the government. Additionally, there was always the issue of funding – there were simply never enough resources to assist state and nonstate lawyers to help all those with legal needs.[22] There was also discontent and cynicism among many within civil society toward both these sets of lawyers, namely because in exchange for the passage of the Act, military leaders were promised immunity upon their eventual relinquishing of power to civilian control.[23]

Finally, it was difficult to populate the Council with sufficient numbers of skilled, passionate lawyers who were needed to ensure that the Act would be properly executed.[24] In his work, David McQuoid-Mason found that in addition to the Council relying on lawyers doing work on a pro bono basis, it tried desperately to recruit private lawyers whom it would pay "a nominal fee,"[25] as well as young lawyers who were part of the National Youth Service Corps.[26] Yet, these efforts failed to provide structured, continuous, or systematic legal assistance[27] and rendered such aid atomistic or ad hoc at best.[28]

DEMOCRACY IN NIGERIA: 1979–83 – HOPE FOR REAL PRO BONO AID

In 1976, the regime's leader, Murtala Muhammed, was assassinated. Facing intense domestic and international pressure and reeling from an unstable economy, the military relinquished power and ceded control of the government to civilian rule in October 1979.[29] To the delight of many, a new constitution emerged that year. Legal aid, in particular, was formally incorporated within the Fundamental Rights section of the Constitution. Influenced by the Legal Aid Act of 1976, subsection 42 of the 1979 document required that the federal legislature ensure that "indigent"[30] Nigerians be entitled to receive legal aid whenever claiming a violation or needing protection of their fundamental rights.

Rights advocates also believed that reforming legal education within the country had to be a priority. If Nigeria was to become a respected power, it needed to develop a strong bar whose members were committed to volunteering part of their time to help the most vulnerable within society. Legal education had suffered significantly during the military era, so in order to train the next generation of lawyers skilled in a range of legal services – including on how best to engage in pro bono activism – law schools in the country had to be revamped.

This argument harkened back to a project that had operated immediately in the years following independence. Beginning in 1962, the government had invited the American-based philanthropic organization, the Ford Foundation, to come to Nigeria to work with local academics to strengthen the quality of legal training for students. Ford labeled this program "SAILER" – Staffing of African Institutions of Legal Education and Research. It focused on three key educational institutions: the Lagos Law Faculty, the Ife Law Faculty, and Zaria-Ahmadu Bello University's Institute of Administration.[31]

The SAILER project involved hiring mainly recent American law school graduates who, upon invitation by different anglophone African governments (including Nigeria), traveled to these respective countries' law schools. Upon arriving, they helped create legal courses, prepare treatises, teach research and writing classes, and establish clinics and programs supporting access to justice – all with the purpose of developing well-rounded lawyers sensitive to grassroots causes. A major goal of this project was that even if these students went into private practice, they would recognize the importance of allocating a percentage of their time toward pro bono matters.[32] (With the military coup in 1966, the SAILER project came to an end in Nigeria shortly thereafter.)

With the end of military rule in 1979, optimists hoped that the new civilian government would support a state-led initiative similar to Ford's SAILER program of the 1960s. Instead, however, a different approach was taken.[33] Rather than focusing on legal education and building a cohort of "bottom-up" lawyers who valued pro bono, the 1979 government believed that the best way Nigerians could enjoy the fundamental rights guaranteed to them was if legal aid came from the top down – mainly from the courts. Because the state possessed and had control over the distribution of the greatest amount of resources, these leaders believed that a systematic state-led approach provided the best opportunity for macro-level change.[34]

Unfortunately, this plan of judicial-led, rights-based protection never really took hold. The main reason was because of how weak the central government was. Eventually, the bar, the press, and religious organizations, among others, demanded that the president step down, and although he proceeded to win the 1983 election, the boisterous, widespread calls against his corrupt administration persuaded the military to depose him in December of that year.[35]

Nigeria subsequently endured military rule for the next sixteen years. This period was among the harshest in Nigeria's tumultuous history. But significantly, issues of legal aid and pro bono activism – working hand in hand – did not disappear.

1983–99: REVERSION TO MILITARY RULE AND THE IMPACT ON PRO BONO

The sordid saga of the military period between 1983 and 1999 has been previously documented.[36] Predictably, with all the political tumult occurring during this time, access to justice and concerns for individual rights were low priorities for state institutions. Nevertheless, as O. C. Okafor has written, rights activism was energized in 1987 with the birth of the prominent Civil Liberties Organization (CLO).[37] Other rights-based nongovernmental organizations (NGOs) soon followed. Funded by underground donations that had to be kept secret because of the military presence, these groups operated as a domestic response to widespread human rights abuses that were occurring in the country. Okafor also details how great efforts by Nigerian lawyers, working in a pro bono manner, served as the main advocates in trying to promote access to justice for all Nigerians – for which there were some wins.[38]

For example, the CLO, together with civically minded, public-spirited lawyers from the private bar, sought to represent those tormented by the military regime.[39] In fact, this coalition implemented a range of tactics that went beyond litigation, such as street protests, public awareness campaigns, educational seminars, and the publication of provocative literature – including two widely distributed circulars highlighting the various human rights abuses being committed by the military.[40] They even lobbied government officials and civil servants and, quite surprisingly, persuaded the military to update the Legal Aid Act in 1990.[41]

It perhaps should not be surprising that the CLO and its pro bono legal partners engaged in these other tactics, given that the domestic courts were in the hands of the military. But litigation was not completely ignored. In fact, during the 1990s, this coalition frequently appeared in a continental judicial forum: the African Commission on Human and People's Rights. The typical manner in which this pro bono relationship operated in front of the Commission was as follows: the CLO would cooperatively work with socially conscious solo practitioners – at times systematically but in other instances in a more ad hoc fashion – to bring forth cases on behalf of claimants suing African governments alleged to be in violation of the African Charter on Human and People's Rights.[42]

For example, one landmark case involved the Nigerian military's detention of political opponents in 1991. The opponents were eventually released the following year, and the military argued that this decision relieved it from any financial liability to the petitioners. Pro bono lawyers and the CLO argued otherwise, and the Commission held that the military was not insulated from owing damages.[43] In another case, the Commission ruled that individuals who had been held for three years in custody by the military without a trial were deprived of their due process rights under Article 6 of the African Charter.[44] And a few years later, during the dictatorship of Sani Abacha, the Commission was asked by the CLO and its partner lawyers to review a case involving a group of defendants who had received the death penalty.[45] The Commission held that Articles 7(1)(a) and (c) of the Charter – which require the right to appeal, sufficient time to mount a defense, and allowing defendants the right to choose their legal representatives – all had been ignored by the military regime.[46]

There were other noteworthy victories by this CLO/pro bono lawyers' coalition. In one matter, for example, involving Article 10 of the Charter, the Commission ruled that government opponents were entitled to associate with one another, collectively congregate, and seek redress in the domestic courts when they had legal grievances against the state.[47] In another case, the Commission held that the military could not unilaterally declare that the Charter did not apply in the Nigerian domestic context, nor could judicial review be removed from the Nigerian courts, nor could political parties be banned from challenging the government in court. According to the Commission, if the military wished to extract itself from its human rights obligations, it had to adhere to specific principles set forth in the Charter, such as providing timely notice to the other member states.[48] And in two other decisions, the Commission ruled that an opposition newspaper was deemed to have the right under the Charter to stay open,[49] and that, separately, the military could not stack the Nigerian Bar Association with over three-quarters of its own appointees.[50]

Yet, arguably no case was as high profile for the coalition than when it represented the brilliant writer and environmental activist from the Niger Delta region, Kenule B. Saro-Wiwa. His story is discussed next.

The Saro-Wiwa Case: More NGO and Pro Bono Lawyering Cooperation

The Niger Delta region has long been the epicenter for debate, discord, and uprisings.[51] Okafor explains that the combination of long-standing discrimination against the indigenous Ogoni people, coupled with the oil and natural resources exploitation by multinational conglomerates, has fueled the disharmony.[52] In 1990, an organization known as the Movement for the Survival of Ogoni People (MOSOP) was founded by Ken Saro-Wiwa.[53]

From its inception, MOSOP argued that international companies had failed to address the Ogoni people's needs. Saro-Wiwa distrusted the military and saw the regime as only concerned with financially lining its pockets from the profits these companies produced. Saro-Wiwa sought to undermine the alliance between these companies and the military and to champion environmental and socioeconomic justice for those living in this area.[54]

Saro-Wiwa's strategic populism earned the ire of the military. He was imprisoned for a period of time in 1992 and detained again the following year. The turning point came in 1994 after four Ogoni men – who had been opponents of MOSOP – were murdered. Sani Abacha, who was in power, accused Saro-Wiwa and eight others of the killings and prosecuted them in a military tribunal. An interesting and powerful alliance came to the aid of the "Ogoni nine."[55] Two prominent international organizations, International Pen and Interights (both based out of Europe), together with two Nigerian NGOs, the Constitutional Rights Project, and the CLO, worked with a range of members from the private bar (perhaps most notably, Gani Fawehinmi) on this case.[56]

On the other side of the aisle, the government tapped as its main prosecutor a lawyer from the private bar itself, Joseph Daudu. As the proceedings went on, it became clear that the trial was a sham. Witnesses who testified against the defendants had been bribed, and the military judges were clearly aligned with the government's interests.

In fact, midway through the process, several of Saro-Wiwa's private lawyers (including Fawehinmi) resigned in protest, with Saro-Wiwa himself refusing to actively participate in his defense.[57] Unremarkably, he and his fellow defendants lost their case. The Ogoni nine were convicted, and in 1995 they were executed, resulting in domestic and international outrage.[58] (As for Daudu, he was elevated by the government to the designation of a SAN, or senior advocate of Nigeria. Since 1975, SANs have held a position equivalent to that of a Queen's Council in the United Kingdom or a senior advocate in India. At the time of the trial, Fawehinmi was not a SAN and only achieved that rank in 2000.)

In their new book on Saro-Wiwa's life, Roy Doron and Toyin Falola show that the Shell Corporation – the major extractive industry in this region at the time – was also complicit in this miscarriage of justice.[59] Shell, according to the authors, sought the protection of the military, which it knew engaged in human rights abuses.[60] In fact, the authors examine the civil case brought by Saro-Wiwa's son and other plaintiffs in US federal court (under the Alien Tort Claims Act) against Shell for collusion with the government in the execution of the Ogoni nine.[61] This matter ultimately settled with Shell paying the plaintiffs $15.5 million in what it called a "humanitarian gesture."[62] Even though an American nonprofit, the Center for Constitutional Rights, brought the case against Shell in the United States,[63] we believe that had it not been for the efforts of the international and Nigerian NGOs as well as the pro bono lawyering by the private bar, which all jointly shined a light on this tragedy, this settlement would never have occurred.[64]

This last point is important to remember in light of a broad set of critiques made against NGO lawyers and pro bono lawyers in Nigeria over the years. These observers have expressed concern about the operations, agenda, leadership, and transparency of these actors. There are the frequently made derisive comments that these lawyers are too urban or Lagos-based; that they are more focused on issues tied to cities rather than the countryside; and that too often they are interested in gaining access to publicity, which they believe will result in enhanced resources from paying clients or other funders, than on alleviating the plight of those most in need.[65]

Prominent evidence for this argument, according to critics, is the unholy partnership that emerged between the private bar, the NGO sector, and the military in 1995. That year, the Nigerian National Human Rights Commission (NHRC) was established. The NHRC was supposed to be the government's main agency ostensibly in charge of monitoring and eliminating human rights abuses within the country. Sani Abacha, true to his conniving reputation, sought to portray to the world that he cared about this issue and that he was willing to oblige the bar with its request to set up this institution. In reality, however, there was no illusion among skeptical civil society activists as to who controlled the NHRC and how much independence it would have. Recall that it was during this period when Saro-Wiwa was being tried and then subsequently executed. That elite, solo practice pro bono lawyers (who came primarily from the upper echelons of the Lagos bar) and rights-based NGOs, such as the CLO, would cooperate with the military regime placed into great question, for these critics, the motives of these actors in creating the NHRC.[66]

Yet, this portrayal of pro bono lawyering and civil society activism does not paint a complete picture of what transpired in Nigeria during the military years. In fact, it ignores the various ways that members of the private bar, through their volunteerism, helped shape the resistance and brought about the transition to democracy that occurred in 1999. That discussion is next.

PRIVATE LAWYERING VOLUNTEERISM DURING THE TRANSITIONING YEARS

Even among the skeptics described above, there is a concession that pro bono lawyering, together with the wider legal and political actions by "NGOs were at the forefront of the campaign to end military rule"[67] by 1999. As Okafor demonstrates, between 1987 and 2001, there were nearly two dozen active groups (most prominently the CLO) operating in the country that relied, in good measure, on the volunteerism of lawyers to engage not just in litigation but also in legislative monitoring and drafting, international outreach, awareness initiatives, educational efforts, and grassroots mobilization – all to increase the public's ability to better access their rights.[68] Indeed, the CLO worked with private pro bono lawyers to publish "a groundbreaking book-length report . . . that captured the dehumanizing conditions in Nigerian prisons"[69] during the height of the Babangida-led military regime.

Finally, in 1999, Olusegun Obasanjo (a former military ruler of the country from 1976 to 1979) returned to power in what was a relatively peaceful election that, while not error-free, was deemed acceptable given Nigeria's history.[70] Prior to this transition, the brutal reign of

Sani Abachi, which began in 1993, ended with his surprising death in 1998.[71] His successor, General Abdulsalami Abubakar, took power but quickly realized that the demands for democracy by civil society activists were too strong. He thus helped facilitate the national elections that occurred less than a year later.[72]

During the first two years of Nigeria's new democratic Fourth Republic, the CLO and a team of civically minded solo practice lawyers (primarily from Lagos) opted to work voluntarily with the state in two key ways. First, they helped with the education, training, and professionalization of judges who would serve in the rejuvenated court system.[73] And second, they sought to strengthen the NHRC, to make it more legitimate and more aware of the range of past and ongoing human rights abuses.[74]

But in those immediate years of the transition, the CLO and its pro bono legal partners also worked to counter state action. For example, they were able to lobby (successfully) the democratic government to commute the life sentences of a number of prisoners convicted by the aforementioned military tribunals.[75] In addition, they litigated cases on behalf of women, criminal defendants, and prisoners. This litigation concentrated on the civil and political rights of those in need, and their efforts did produce a certain amount of success.[76]

At the same time, these accomplishments had limits. For example, NGOs and private sector pro bono lawyers teamed up to champion the cause of laborers' rights in the courts. While there were some victories, overall this litigation did not translate into major transformation, as these campaigns failed to provide widespread change for those at the grassroots level.[77]

There was also the immense amount of time invested by NGOs and volunteer private-sector lawyers relating to the "truth commission" established by the democratic government in 1999. The commission had different names, but it soon came to be called the "Oputa Panel," named for its chair, Chukwudifu Oputa, who was a retired justice of the Nigerian Supreme Court. The Oputa Panel was charged with investigating all of the human rights abuses that had occurred within the country between 1966 and 1999. It had investigative powers, such as the ability to call and cross-examine witnesses, find on issues of fact and law, and issue recommendations to the different branches of government. The Panel's members also saw themselves as serving on a cathartic body – one that would emotionally help heal the wounds for those who had suffered so unjustly under the previous regimes.

Additionally, they were to issue both legal and moral judgments on past actions by the state, and to ensure that these abuses would never occur again.[78]

Unfortunately, reality fell short of aspirations. Although NGOs and volunteer private-sector lawyers helped aggrieved claimants submit the vast majority of the over 10,000 petitions to the Panel, only 1–2 percent of these cases were ever heard.[79] To its credit, the Panel did write a voluminous report that contained policy recommendations and judgments – largely in part because it could not simply ignore all of the claims that had come before it. But before it was released, the Panel was sued by members of the former military junta. They argued that the federal government had no jurisdiction to impose the Panel's recommendations on the states, because the states had not been involved in the Panel's establishment nor had consented to its powers. The case was heard in the Nigerian Supreme Court, which agreed with this argument and ruled that the Panel had acted unconstitutionally.[80] Soon thereafter, in January 2003, the government dismantled the Panel and prohibited the public release of its report.[81]

For many, the government's creation of the Oputa Panel was nothing more than a pretext, and so the disassembling of it was not a surprise. In fact, the Court's ruling gave the government the perfect excuse to do away with all of the Panel's work. Sadly, however, the justices had failed to recognize the extraordinary efforts of the NGO sector and pro bono lawyers, and the Court lost the chance "to contribute to the developing jurisprudence on the right to truth for victims of gross human rights violations."[82]

Still, it is worth noting that after the *Oputa Panel* case, Nigeria did not revert to military rule. It has remained a democracy, albeit a fragile one, that continues to wrestle with how best to address and respond to different access-to-justice issues in recent years.

The NBA's Involvement in Pro Bono Lawyering

The struggles of pro bono lawyering, and of NGO legal activism more broadly, continue to this day. The country's primary organization representing the legal profession, the Nigerian Bar Association (NBA), is at a crossroads. The NBA predates Nigeria's independence by nearly three decades.[83] During the colonial period, NBA members, many of whom were trained under the English legal education model, banded loosely together for professional purposes, including networking, sharing referrals, developing business connections, and engaging in volunteer advocacy.[84] And as past research has shown, such professionals were instrumental in the independence movement.[85]

At points in the postcolonial era, the NBA has served as the preserver of the bar's reputation and integrity, the defender of individual rights and liberties, and an opponent of state oppression. It has done so by having its members work through formal and grassroots means without remuneration and on a volunteer basis. For example, consider a famous 1984 episode when the military regime was in charge. The government instituted several draconian decrees, including establishing military tribunals where formal rules of evidence and procedure were not in effect. A subsequent order went so far as to suspend the rights and liberties established by the 1979 Constitution.[86]

The NBA decried these measures and staged boycotts and demonstrations. Its moves galvanized the public, and soon thereafter there were other mass protests. The military cracked down on these activists, but the protestors, including the NBA, were undeterred. By August of the following year, that military government relinquished power to a subsequent regime. In the process, the NBA gained enormous political capital through its defiant confrontation.[87]

Additionally, the NBA was an important player in the passage of the first two postindependence statutes regulating the legal profession – the 1962 Legal Practitioners Act (LPA), and then its replacement, a 1975 version under the same name.[88] The 1975 LPA remains the signature piece of legislation governing lawyers in Nigeria to this day. Specifically, it establishes the process for who can become a lawyer; it provides the parameters of how lawyers can be disciplined; and it is accompanied by an administrative set of "Rules of Professional Conduct"[89] passed by the bar in 2007.

Unfortunately, neither the LPA nor the Rules have explicit provisions requiring private practitioners to engage in pro bono legal services. The closest is what is found in the latter, where, under Section D, Rule 38, the regulation states that: "A lawyer assigned to defend an indigent prisoner shall not ask to be excused except for substantial reason, but shall exert his best effort in the defence of the accused."[90]

However, there is one document that has demonstrated the bar's commitment to pro bono work that was passed in 2009. That year, the NBA issued its "Pro Bono Declaration," which was a three-page memorandum urging all of its members to remember that "access to justice and legal representation are essential to democratic societies."[91] The memo further committed to have its members "provide, on a pro bono basis, more than 20 hours or three days of legal services per individual lawyer per annum, or in the case of law firms, institutions or other groups of lawyers, an average of more than 20 hours per lawyer per annum."[92]

It is difficult to determine specifically the causal roots of this declaration and why the NBA adopted it in 2009. We suspect that, in part, globalization played a role. Throughout the first decade of the new millennium, the Nigerian government aggressively promoted itself as an essential market within the Global South – alongside the "BRICS." Concurrently, the NBA also sought to project to the world that it was a competitive and sophisticated organization that understood the norms of the global legal labor marketplace. Seeing that other bar associations proudly displayed their commitment to pro bono work, the NBA was eager not to be left behind. Furthermore, international donor agencies, which entered Nigeria after 1999 and prioritized aiding the marginalized, we believe, also influenced the NBA in its decision to emphasize pro bono work. And although foreign law firms are prohibited from establishing offices in Nigeria, there is a presence of foreign lawyers (particularly in Lagos and Abuja) who regularly visit, and the sharing of ideas and norms about what law practice entails today is undeniable.

That said, it would be inaccurate to infer that the transnational component has been the sole driving force behind the recent emphasis of doing pro bono work in Nigeria. The 2009 Declaration was a reiteration of a principle that has been long present within the NBA's Constitution – namely, the goal of creating a framework of legal aid for the socially and economically disadvantaged.[93] To that end, the NBA has established its Law Reform and Human Rights Committee, which is in charge of ensuring that there be an avenue for the poor to receive free legal representation.[94] It has also become a requirement for lawyers seeking to qualify as SANs to "have been involved in the provision of at least 3 *pro bono* legal services [to] indigent clients or some form of community services."[95] And recently, in June 2017, the NBA entered into a formal partnership with the government's Legal Aid Council (discussed in the first section) to provide pro bono assistance to inmates who have been languishing in Nigeria's overcrowded prisoners.[96] A month after this compact was signed, the partnership expanded to include an international component, as the United Nations Office on Drugs and Crime joined to lend legal services to indigent defendants facing prosecution for narcotics offenses.[97] The current vice president of Nigeria, Professor Yemi Osinbajo, is a former law professor, and he has been committed to supporting a strong relationship between the LAC and the NBA that focuses on pro bono activity.

One other pro bono development of note has been the emergence of the NBA's Section on Business Law (SBL). Begun in 2004, the SBL was "set up primarily to engender the professional development of Nigerian commercial lawyers, thereby raising the level of business law practice in Nigeria."[98] Admittedly, the number of members in this section is relatively small (roughly 2 percent) compared with the overall population of lawyers in the country (120,000). (The vast majority of these constituents are urban-based, solo practice courtroom litigators, many of whom struggle to earn even a modest standard of living.) Furthermore, the number of Nigerian business law firms that do what might be seen as "Big Law" corporate work is no more than thirty in the entire country, with the largest law firm having approximately seventy to eighty lawyers. (Foreign firms are prohibited from entry into Nigeria.) Nevertheless, over the years, the SBL leadership has tirelessly devoted time to encouraging its members to engage in pro bono work, as prior to its establishment, such a culture among law firms has been all but absent. Particularly through its annual conference, SBL speakers over the years have impassionedly discussed how the corporate bar has a responsibility to help those who cannot help themselves.[99] The SBL's hope is that such a shift in the mindset of law firm lawyers will eventually materialize in the years ahead.

Interestingly, though, certain members of the NBA still argue that the organization can and must do much more pro bono work – especially beyond offering representation in the courts. For example, in 2016, a prominent human rights lawyer, Ebun-Olu Adegboruwa, urged the NBA to engage in strikes and boycotts after the Department of State Services conducted raids on the homes of several judges presiding over cases involving government officials.[100] Harkening back to 1984, he declared that the Nigerian government was returning to a "jackboot system of intolerance."[101] That the NBA vacillated on Adegboruwa's suggestion drew noticeable criticism from him and his supporters.

The Association then felt added pressure that same year from human rights activist Femi Falana. Falana believed that the NBA was not encouraging enough of its members to volunteer their time and energy to fight actual, known corruption in the judiciary.[102] In addition, Chidi Odinkalu, a noted human rights activist, led a committee that published a blistering account of how the NBA was besieged by inefficiency and internal strife, with the result being that many of its various outreach efforts, including its volunteer work, were ineffective and did not reach enough people in need.[103]

The story of the NBA, therefore, is a complicated one. As one of the country's longest-standing civil society organizations, the NBA has been at the forefront of key rights-based moments. At the same time, there have been problems – indeed, significant ones. The NBA thus epitomizes a group that is conflicted, a reality that is perhaps not surprising given the environment in which it operates.

Pro Bono Work and the Clinical Legal Education Movement

In 2003, the First All-Africa Colloquium on Legal Education was held in Durban, South Africa.[104] Sponsored by three different organizations, the conference brought in educators skilled in clinical practice from around the continent. Although formal clinical education had not yet then been incorporated into Nigerian law schools, representatives from the country's newly created Network of University Legal Aid Institutions (NULAI) attended. The most studied portion of this conference was on how South Africa's legal aid clinics interacted with civil society and government agencies to deliver services to the poor.

This example highlights a key argument of this chapter. Namely, that in Nigeria as well, private sector pro bono lawyers have often worked in tandem with NGOs and the state. NULAI officials were particularly interested in such cooperation, and the following year they sponsored a conference in the capital, Abuja. Since then, NULAI has been actively engaging in national and continental seminars, and it has sought to press law faculties throughout Nigeria – forty-nine in total – to incorporate skills education into their curriculums so that, in part, graduates can be ready to deliver pro bono services after being called to the bar.[105]

NULAI's efforts have not been in vain. In less than a decade (2005–14), NULAI helped found seventeen clinics across the country. It also established a clinical program at the Nigerian Law School. In addition, in 2011, the group successfully lobbied the federal government to amend the Legal Aid Act to include a new provision that provided NULAI-established law clinics with the opportunity to receive government certification. Although there is no accompanying funding from the state, this was still an important step because potential clients looking for credentialed, bona fide assistance could now feel more assured that these legal aid providers were government certified. And critical to this development was that private practitioners have been dedicating their time, albeit typically in a nonsystematic ad hoc fashion, to work with students in these educational clinics.[106]

As for how these legal aid clinics are performing, the empirical evidence is modest but hopeful. For example, clinical law students at Ambrose Alli University receive training from faculty and private sector lawyers on how to assist fellow students who cannot afford legal representation to address different civil claims they encounter. The University of Ibadan Women's Law Clinic offers students the chance to work with rural women on issues relating to health rights, as faculty and private sector lawyers provide close supervision. The students here also use "the mobile clinic approach" – where vehicles take them and their supervisors to villages to educate women on their rights.[107] In sum, these efforts highlight how legal education clinics are helping to enhance volunteerism in present-day Nigeria.

CONCLUSION

This chapter has attempted to provide a comprehensive review of the state of pro bono legal services in Nigeria since 1960. The instability of Nigerian politics over the last six decades has made the delivery of legal assistance to those in need a monumental challenge. Still, as this study has shown, even in the bleakest of times, brave lawyers and organizations have asserted themselves, standing up to military dictators and defending the rights of the powerless. There are also other recent examples that provide hope. In 2000, Lagos State opened its Office of the Public Defender (OPD),[108] with the mission of focusing on the "rights of the disadvantaged"[109] and providing "free representation in court and legal advice"[110] for the indigent. In 2015, the NBA agreed to devote greater resources and personnel toward assisting the OPD so that more people might be served.[111]

Additionally, since 1999, Lagos State has operated the Citizen Mediation Centre (CMC), which has been intended to help parties – regardless of background or financial status – resolve disputes in a timely and just manner.[112] The CMC proudly reports that its most recent figures show that "within the period of January to December 2015, a total number of 34,511 new cases were received; 20,966 [m]ediated; [and] 19,464 matters were resolved."[113]

The CMC also notes that in 2015 it helped parties recover over $52 million.[114] Once again, private sector lawyers have volunteered their time to help the state with this initiative.

But perhaps the most well-known attempt to provide enhanced access to justice is the Lagos Multi-Door Courthouse (LMDC) project, which was established in 2002 in Lagos State. Drawing upon Frank Sander's work, Oyeniyi Ajiboye has written about this initiative and how the objective behind the LMDC was to allow the courts to determine whether a case should proceed to litigation or instead be diverted to an alternative dispute forum.[115] As the first "court connected" dispute resolution institution on the continent, the LMDC has brought together the Lagos judiciary, the American Embassy, an NGO (Negotiation and Conflict Management Group), and private sector pro bono lawyers to work on streamlining the way civil cases enter local courts. Over the years, Ajiboye notes that this project has had qualified success. Cases that otherwise might have gone through the lengthy process of litigation have been resolved using alternative means;[116] this model has been replicated in other states.

And what these examples, as well as the entire discussion above, show is that pro bono in the Nigerian context has to be imagined in a two-dimensional way. First, the efforts today to assist those with legal needs have not manifested in a vacuum. The lawyers who are currently working in various pro bono capacities have built upon past initiatives. Whether it was the NBA's promotion of pro bono both before and shortly after independence, or the SAILER program that trained lawyers to reflect on ways to give back to their community, or the many different grassroots attempts by solo practice lawyers (working with NGOs) to represent the persecuted during the military years, pro bono in the present moment indeed has historical roots. Second, it is not possible to discuss pro bono activism in Nigeria without considering how legal aid by the state has developed. In the Nigerian context, the two often have worked hand in hand, although as we have seen, at times – especially when the state has tried to co-opt legal aid programs and institutions – there can be resistance by pro bono activists from the private bar.

So, for now, this is how our discussion concludes on the state of pro bono in Nigeria. The above narrative shows that there have been numerous challenges, but also some successes, since 1960. And while clearly more must be done, recent steps in particular offer glimmers of hope that efforts will continue and ultimately improve the country's access-to-justice sector.

NOTES

1. *See generally* OMOLADE ADUNBI, OIL, WEALTH AND INSURGENCY IN NIGERIA (2015); MAX SIOLLUN, OIL, POLITICS, AND VIOLENCE: NIGERIA'S MILITARY COUP CULTURE (1966–1976) (2009). This chapter extracts from a larger article that was published in 2018. *See* Jayanth K. Krishnan & Kunle Ajagbe, *Legal Activism in the Face of Political Challenges: The Nigerian Case*, 42 J. LEGAL PROF. 197 (2018). For the sake of space, please see detailed citations in that article where needed.
2. *See* ADUNBI, *supra* note 1; SIOLLUN, *supra* note 1; MIKE SMITH, BOKO HARAM: INSIDE NIGERIA'S UNHOLY WAR (2015). See also the comments from lawyer, academic, and widely respected intellectual Dr. Aminu Gamawa: Aljazeera, *Aminu Gamawa on Boko Haram and Bring Back Our Girls Campaign*, YOUTUBE (June 18, 2014), www.youtube.com/watch?v=i_7n1SRU7fk&t=63s (last visited Sept. 15, 2020).
3. *See Corruption Is Nigeria's Worst Problem – Buhari*, PREMIUM TIMES, Jan. 12. 2017, www.premiumtimesng.com/news/top-news/220324-corruption-nigerias-worst-problem-buhari.html (last visited Sept. 15, 2020).
4. *See* Scott L. Cummings, *The Politics of Pro Bono*, 52 UCLA L. REV. 1 (2004).
5. *See id.* at 11.
6. *See id.* at 16.
7. *See id.* at 18.
8. *See, e.g.*, YVES DEZALAY & BRYANT GARTH, THE INTERNATIONALIZATION OF PALACE WARS: LAWYERS, ECONOMISTS, AND THE CONTEST TO TRANSFORM LATIN AMERICAN STATES (2002); Richard Cullen & Hualing Fu, *Weiquan (Rights Protection) Lawyering in an Authoritarian State: Building a Culture of Public-Interest Lawyering*, 59 CHINA J. 111 (2008); Yves Dezalay & Bryant Garth, *Investing in Human Rights as an Alternative Political Strategy*, *in* CAUSE LAWYERING AND THE STATE IN A GLOBAL ERA 354 (Austin Sarat & Stuart Scheingold eds., 2001); Stephen Meili, *Latin American Cause-Lawyering Networks*, *in* CAUSE LAWYERING AND THE STATE IN A GLOBAL ERA, *supra*, at 307; Ethan Michelson, *Lawyers, Political Embeddedness, and Institutional Continuity in China's Transition from Socialism*, 115 AM. J. SOC. 352 (2007); *see also* SIDA LIU & TERENCE C. HALLIDAY , CRIMINAL DEFENSE IN CHINA: THE POLITICS OF LAWYERS AT WORK (2016).
9. *See* OKECHUKWU OKO, PROBLEMS AND CHALLENGES FOR LAWYERS IN AFRICA: LESSONS FROM NIGERIA 217–22 (2007).

10. *Id.* at 221. Richard Abel and Philip C. S. Lewis have a multivolume set of classics on the roles of lawyers who face various types of quandaries. *See, e.g.*, LAWYERS IN SOCIETY: THE COMMON LAW WORLD (Richard L. Abel & Philip C.S. Lewis eds., 1988); LAWYERS IN SOCIETY: COMPARATIVE THEORIES (Richard L. Abel & Philip C. S. Lewis eds., 1989).
11. OKO, *supra* note 9, at 217–57.
12. *See Nigeria Has to Adopt the 1963 Constitution*, THE LEARNED FRIENDS (Nov. 24, 2016), http://thelearnedfriends.com/2016/11/24/nigeria-adopt-1963-constitution/ (last visited Sept. 15, 2020). Also, note that Nigeria is a federation of thirty-six states and with Abuja as a Federal Capital Territory.
13. *Id.*; *see also* TOYIN FALOLA & MATTHEW M. HEATON, A HISTORY OF NIGERIA 158–209 (2008).
14. *See* CONSTITUTION OF NIGERIA (1999), § 22, subsections 5–10.
15. *See* Adrian Collett, *Legal Care in Nigeria: Beginnings II: Remaking Land Law and Local Administration*, 24 J. AFR. L. 220, 223 (1980).
16. *See* EGHOSA E. OSAGHE , THE CRIPPLED GIANT: NIGERIA SINCE INDEPENDENCE 54–90 (1998).
17. *Id.* at 54.
18. *See* Ojama Akor, *Developing Legal Aid Strategies for Poor Nigerians*, DAILY TRUST (Aug. 19, 2004), www.pressreader.com/nigeria/daily-trust/20140819/282325383136021 (last visited Sept. 30, 2020); Uju Ikeazor, *"The Poor Man's Lawyer" and "The Father of Legal Aid in Nigeria," Chief Dr. Chimezie Ikeazor, SAN*, THIS DAY (Nov. 6, 2016), www.pressreader.com/nigeria/thisday/20161108/281878707942078 (last visited Sept. 24, 2020).
19. *See* Ikeazor, *supra* note 18. The phrase that is quoted in this sentence describing his work during this era is also from *id.*, although it is unclear whether the words "pro bono" were actually used during this time or whether they were a descriptor provided by the author (his widow) when she wrote her piece in 2016. *See* LATHAM & WATKINS, PRO BONO PRACTICES AND OPPORTUNITIES IN NIGERIA. EXCERPT FROM: A SURVEY OF PRO BONO PRACTICES AND OPPORTUNITIES IN SELECTED JURISDICTIONS (2010), https://www.probonoinst.org/wpps/wp-content/uploads/nigeria.pdf (last visited Sept. 30, 2020); David McQuoid-Mason, *Legal Aid in Nigeria: Using National Youth Services Corps Public Defenders to Expand the Services of the Legal Aid Council*, 47 J. AFR. L. 107, 111 (2003). As McQuoid-Mason writes, in citing Schedule 2 of the Act, the "Legal Aid Council may provide legal aid for the following offences under the Criminal Code: (i) murder of any degree; (ii) manslaughter; (iii) maliciously or willfully wounding or inflicting grievous bodily harm; (iv) assault occasioning actual bodily harm; (v) common assault; (vi) affray; (vii) stealing; and (viii) rape." *Id.* at 111–12.
20. *See* LATHAM & WATKINS, *supra* note 19, at 3; McQuoid-Mason, *supra* note 19, at 110–11.

21. *See* LATHAM & WATKINS, *supra* note 19, at 4.
22. *See* OKO, *supra* note 9, at 207.
23. For this point on how military officials were granted immunity from prosecution upon leaving office, see Gabriel Omoshemime Arishe, *Reconsidering Executive Immunity under the Nigeria Constitution*, NIGERIAN CURRENT L. REV. 2007–2010 274, 280–83 (2010).
24. *See* OKO, *supra* note 9, at 207.
25. *See* McQuoid-Mason, *supra* note 19, at 113.
26. *Id.* at 112–14. The National Youth Service Corps (NYSC) has been seen by some as one of the only other positive aspects that came out of the military period. Started in 1973, the NYSC is a mandatory program that requires university graduates to spend their first year after graduation working on cultural and social service projects to benefit the needy. Young lawyers who participate in the NYSC also can engage in legal aid services under the Act, but scholars such as McQuoid-Mason argue that they are underutilized (*id.*, at 113–14). There has also been criticism that the program does not protect its service workers adequately and exploits them, and that NYSC leaders (dating back to the time of the military) have not overseen the program as meticulously as necessary.
27. *See* Jill Cottrell, *The New Nigerian Legal Aid Decree*, 22 J. AFR. L. 78, 79 (1978).
28. *Id.* For a discussion of this point more broadly in Africa, see OKO, *supra* note 9, at 408–10.
29. *See* FALOLA & HEATON, *supra* note 13, at xvii, 201.
30. CONSTITUTION OF NIGERIA, 1979, (4)(b)(i-ii).
31. *See generally* Jayanth K. Krishnan, *Academic SAILERS: The Ford Foundation and the Efforts to Shape Legal Education in Africa, 1957–1977*, 52 AM. J. L. HISTORY 261 (2012).
32. *See id.* at 272–91, 306–12.
33. *See* F. OLISA AWOGU, THE JUDICIARY IN THE SECOND REPUBLIC OF NIGERIA, 1979–1983 (1984).
34. *Id.* at 109–19. Extensive treatment of these cases is given in the article from which this chapter is extracted. *See* Krishnan & Ajagbe, *supra* note 1.
35. This paragraph draws upon FALOLA & HEATON, *supra* note 13, at 181–209, 205–09.
36. *See id.* at 209–35. For an outline of the various leaders who ruled during this time, see Krishnan & Ajagbe, *supra* note 1.
37. *See* OBIORA CHINEDU OKAFOR, LEGITIMIZING HUMAN RIGHTS NGOS: LESSONS FROM NIGERIA 8 (2006).
38. *Id.* at 151–209, 239–45.
39. *Id.* at 15–18, 52–54.
40. *See* CIVIL LIBERTIES ORGANISATION, ANNUAL REPORT ON HUMAN RIGHTS IN NIGERIA – 1990, 41–47 (1990); CIVIL LIBERTIES ORGANISATION, EXECUTIVE LAWLESSNESS IN THE BABANGIDA REGIME – A REPORT OF THE CIVIL LIBERTIES ORGANIZATION, NIGERIA (1991).

41. *See* OKAFOR, *supra* note 37, at 15–18; Muiz Adeyemi Banire , *Legal Aid in the Administration of Justice in Nigeria*, *in* CURRENT THEMES IN NIGERIAN LAW 6 (I. O. Agbede & E. O. Akanki eds., 1997), http://mabandassociates.com/pool/Legal_Aid_in_the_admin_of_justice_Nigeria.pdf (last visited Sept. 30, 2020). It is important to keep in mind that the military regime did not see much political cost in terms of updating the Act. For one thing, it knew that it controlled how much aid would actually be distributed, and for another, it saw this move as a way to mollify those who wanted the change – at least in the short term.
42. Note, procedurally the typical manner in which a party could appear before the Commission would be to exhaust all domestic court appearances first. The Commission reaffirmed this principle, coincidentally, in a case involving the CLO. *See Civil Liberties Org. v. Nigeria* (Communication No. 45/90) [1994] ACHPR 2. Also note, the cases discussed here were brought by this coalition made up of the CLO, other previously mentioned NGOs, and private solo practitioners. The private bar lawyers worked on a pro bono basis, and the NGOs pursued these cases as part of their mission to serve those on the margins.
43. *See Civil Liberties Organisation v. Nigeria* (Communication No. 67/91) [1995] ACHPR 5, adopted at the 14th Ordinary Session of the Commission, Addis Ababa, Ethiopia, Dec. 1993; *see also* Chidi A. Odinkalu, *The Individual Complaints Procedures of the African Commission on Human and People's Rights: A Preliminary Assessment*, 8 TRANSNAT'L L. & CONTEMP. PROBS. 359, n.95 (1998).
44. *See Constitutional Rights Project & Civil Liberties Organization v. Nigeria* (Communication No. 102/93) [1998] ACHPR 2; *see also* the Commission's decision in *Constitutional Rights Project v. The President of the Federal Republic of Nigeria and 5 Others* [1993] Unreported Suit No. M/102/93 (originating in the High Court of Lagos State of Nigeria). As Odinkalu described in his account of the case, the defendants were released by the military in 1996 – years after the Commission's ruling. *See* Odinkalu, *supra* note 43, at 402–03.
45. *Civil Liberties Organisation, Legal Defence Centre, Legal Defence and Assistance Project v. Nigeria* (Communication No. 218/98) [2001] ACHPR 30.
46. *Id.*
47. *Civil Liberties Org. v. Nigeria* (Communication No. 101/93) [1995] ACHPR 1, www.worldcourts.com/achpr/eng/decisions/1995.03_Civil_Liberties_Organisation_v_Nigeria_AR08.htm (last visited Sept. 24, 2020).
48. *Civil Liberties Organization v. Nigeria* (Communication No. 129/94) [1995] ACHPR 4, *available at* www.worldcourts.com/achpr/eng/decisions/1995.03_Civil_Liberties_Organisation_v_Nigeria_AR09.htm (last visited Sept. 30, 2020).
49. *Civil Liberties Organisation and Media Rights Agenda v. Nigeria* (Communication No. 140/94, 141/94, 145/95) [1999] ACHPR 6,

http://hrlibrary.umn.edu/africa/comcases/140-94.html (last visited Sept. 30, 2020).

50. *Civil Liberties Organization in Respect of the Nigerian Bar Association v. Nigeria* (Communication No. 101/93) [1995] ACHPR 1.
51. *See* OKAFOR, *supra* note 37, at 39–41.
52. *Id.*
53. *Id.*
54. *Id.* at 40; *see also* FALOLA & HEATON, *supra* note 13, at xxxi, 231–32, 239.
55. *See* OKAFOR, *supra* note 37, at 102.
56. For this paragraph, see *id.* at 40; *see also* FALOLA & HEATON, *supra* note 13, at xxxi, 231–32; Jon Henley, *Nigerian Activist Ken Saro-Wiwa's Daughter Remembers Her Father*, GUARDIAN, Dec. 30, 2011, https://www.theguardian.com/lifeandstyle/2011/dec/31/noo-saro-wiwa-kens-daughter-nigeria (last visited Sept. 24, 2020). Several of the private bar lawyers who worked on this case pro bono were noted opponents of the military regimes during the 1980s and 1990s. Fawehinmi was arguably the most famous. He was a prominent member of the Nigerian Bar Association who had been jailed multiple times for his outspoken opposition. Other private lawyers who helped on this case were similar in character, although it was Fawehinmi who, as stated, was perhaps the most well-known.
57. *See* Kaye Whiteman, *Gani Fawehinmi: Nigerian Lawyer and Politician, He Strove to Protect Human Rights*, GUARDIAN (Sept. 8, 2009), www.theguardian.com/world/2009/sep/08/gani-fawehinmi-obituary (last visited Sept. 24, 2020).
58. *See* FALOLA & HEATON, *supra* note 13, at 231–32; OKAFOR, *supra* note 37, at 40.
59. *See* ROY DORON & TOYIN FALOLA, KEN SARO-WIWA 79–98 (2016).
60. *Id.*
61. *See* Jad Mouawad, *Shell to Pay $15.5 Million to Settle Nigerian Case*, N.Y. TIMES, June 8, 2009; *see also* DORON & FALOLA, *supra* note 59, at 155.
62. *See* Mouawad, *supra* note 61.
63. *Id.*
64. *Id.*; see also, more directly, the background information on the Ogoni Nine published by the CCR, which describes the events that took place in Nigeria before the case made its way into the American federal judiciary, including a discussion of the civil society activism of MOSOP. *See Wiwa et al v. Royal Dutch Petroleum et al*, CENTER FOR CONSTITUTIONAL RIGHTS, https://ccrjustice.org/home/what-we-do/our-cases/wiwa-et-al-v-royal-dutch-petroleum-et-al (last visited Sept. 24, 2020).
65. It is important to note that how NGOs were funded during the military years has been difficult to ascertain. The reason is simple: these groups guarded this information for fear of retribution from the ruling regimes.

In recent years, information on funding has been more open. For example, the CLO receives funds from membership dues and international donors, along with philanthropic support from other domestic backers. For critiques of these actors, see OKAFOR, *supra* note 37, at 77–150; Shedrack Gutto, *Non-Governmental Organizations, People's Participation and the African Commission on Human and Peoples' Rights: Emerging Challenges to Regional Protection of Human Rights*, *in* HUMAN RIGHTS IN DEVELOPING COUNTRIES YEARBOOK: 1991 (Bård Anders Andreassen & Theresa Swineheart eds., 1992); Makau Mutua, *A Discussion on the Legitimacy of Human Rights NGOs in Africa*, AFR. LEGAL AID Q., Oct–Dec. 1997, at 28; Makau Mutua, *Domestic Human Rights Organizations in Africa: Problems and Perspectives*, 22 ISSUE: J. OPINION 30 (1994); Makau Mutua, *Human Rights and Politics in Africa: Democratizing the Rights Discourse*, 1 EAST AFR. J. PEACE HUM. RTS. 250 (1993); Chidi A. Odinkalu, *Why More Africans Don't Use Human Rights Language*, 2 HUM. RTS. DIALOGUE 3 (2000); Alex de Waal, *Human Rights Organizations and the Political Imagination: How the West and Africa Have Diverged*, J. HUM. RTS. 475 (2003); *see also* Joe Oloka-Onyango, *Beyond the Rhetoric: Reinvigorating the Struggle for Economic and Social Rights in Africa*, 26 CAL. W. INT'L L.J. 1 (1995).

66. *See* OKAFOR, *supra* note 37, at 183; OKO, *supra* note 9, at 227.
67. OKAFOR, *supra* note 37, at 185.
68. *Id.* at 13–123.
69. *Id.* at 80. See another report that it published in 1996, as noted by OKAFOR, *supra* note 37, at 90.
70. *See* FALOLA & HEATON, *supra* note 13, at 234–35.
71. *Id.* at 234 (noting that Abacha died of "apparent heart attack").
72. *Id.*
73. OKAFOR, *supra* note 37.
74. *Id.* at 183.
75. *Id.* at 180.
76. For this paragraph, see Shedrack Agbakwa & Obiora Chinedu Okafor, *Social Action Litigation and Access-to-Justice in Nigeria: A Critical Case Study*, *in* JUSTICE FOR THE POOR: PERSPECTIVES ON ACCELERATING ACCESS 221 (Ayesha Dias & Gita Honwana-Welch eds. 2009).
77. *See, e.g.*, Obiora Chinedu Okafor, *Irrigating the Famished Fields: The Impact of Labour-Led Struggles on Policy and Action in Nigeria (1999–2007)*, 27 J. CONTEMP. AFR. STUD. 159 (2009); Obiora Chinedu Okafor, *Remarkable Returns: The Influence of Labour-Led Socio-Economic Rights Movement on Legislative Reasoning, Process and Action in Nigeria, 1999–2007*, 47 J. MOD. AFR. STUD. 241 (2009).
78. For this paragraph, see UNITED STATES INSTITUTE FOR PEACE, TRUTH COMMISSION: NIGERIA (June 14, 1999), www.usip.org/publications/1999/06/truth-commission-nigeria (last visited Sept. 24, 2020); Hakeem O. Yusuf, *Human Rights Violations Investigation*

Commission, the Oputa Panel (Nigeria), *in* ENCYCLOPEDIA OF TRANSITIONAL JUSTICE 161 (Lavinia Stan & Nadia Nedelsky eds., 2013) [hereinafter *Human Rights*]; Hakeem O. Yusuf, *The Judiciary and Political Change in Africa: Developing Transitional Jurisprudence in Nigeria*, 7 INT'L.J. CONST. L. 654 (2009) [hereinafter *Judiciary*]; Hakeem O. Yusuf, *Travails of Truth: Achieving Justice for Victims of Impunity in Nigeria*, INT'L J. CONST. L. 268 (2007) [hereinafter *Travails*]; *see also* ELISABETH GUAKER, A STUDY OF THE NIGERIAN TRUTH COMMISSION AND WHY IT FAILED (2009); OKAFOR, *supra* note 37, at 183.

79. The numbers seem to vary depending on the sources. *See* GUAKER, *supra* note 78 (stating that about 200 cases were chosen); UNITED STATES INSTITUTE FOR PEACE, *supra* note 78 (stating that about 150 cases were selected); *Travails*, *supra* note 78 (stating that about 200 cases were chosen).

80. *See Gani Fawehinmi, Justice Chukwudifu Oputa (Rtd.) and Human Rights Violations Investigation Commission v. General Ibrahim Babangida, Brigadier Halilu Akilu and Brigadier Kunle Togun* [2003], MJSC 63.

81. GUAKER, *supra* note 78; OKAFOR, *supra* note 37, at 183; *Human Rights*, *supra* note 78; UNITED STATES INSTITUTE FOR PEACE, *supra* note 78; *Judiciary*, *supra* note 78; *Travails*, *supra* note 78.

82. *Judiciary*, *supra* note 78, at 679.

83. *See, e.g.*, Nicholas Ibekwe, *Inside the Rot Called the Nigerian Bar Association*, PREMIUM TIMES, June 15, 2013, www.premiumtimesng.com/news/138802-exclusive-inside-the-rot-called-nigerian-bar-association.html (last visited Sept. 24, 2020) (showing that incorporated within the skepticism of the bar are similar sentiments, by some, toward the judiciary). The NBA is the "non-profit, umbrella professional association of all lawyers admitted to the Bar in Nigeria and a member of all statutory bodies that regulate the Nigerian Bar and Bench. The NBA is Nigeria's foremost and oldest professional membership organisation and Africa's most influential network of legal practitioners, with over 120,000 lawyers on its roll in 125 active branches across the 36 States and the Federal Capital Territory of Nigeria. It is organised into three practise Sections, eleven Fora, and two Institutes, all supported by one National Secretariat. The NBA is engaged in the promotion and protection of human rights, the rule of law and good governance in Nigeria. It has an observer status with the African Commission on Human and People's Rights, and a working partnership with many national and international governmental and non-governmental organisations concerned with human rights, the rule of law and good governance in Nigeria and across the world. The NBA offers a unique National platform that is not available to any other Civil or professional organization in Nigeria. The NBA renews its leadership every two years when it elects a new President and other officials. The tenure of elected officials of the NBA runs for two years and is

non-renewable." *See About Us*, NBA, https://nigerianbar.org.ng/about-us (last visited Sept. 24, 2020).

84. *See The History of the Nigerian Bar Association, Port Harcourt Branch*, NIGERIAN BAR ASSOCIATION, http://nbaph.org.ng/history.php (last visited Dec. 30, 2016); *see also* OKO, *supra* note 9, at 99–103.
85. *See* Okechukwu Oko, *Consolidating Democracy on a Troubled Continent: A Challenge for Lawyers in Africa*, 33 VAND. J. TRANSNAT'L L. 573, 635–36 (2000) ("The Nigerian legal profession that admirably served as a vital piece of the struggle for independence has undergone a tremendous transformation").
86. FALOLA & HEATON, *supra* note 13, at 212–16; *see also* OKO, *supra* note 9, at 230–39, 243–50.
87. FALOLA & HEATON, *supra* note 13.
88. The 1975 Act has had amendments added to it over the years as well, including in 1990, 1994, and 2004.
89. *See* Michael C. Ogwezzy, *The Legal Practitioners Act: A Code for Regulating the Conduct of Lawyers in Nigeria*, 3 AGORA INT'L J. JURIDIC. SCI. 108, 109 (2013).
90. *See Rules of Professional Conduct for Legal Practitioners 2007*, LAWYARD, www.lawyard.ng/wp-content/uploads/2015/11/RULES-OF-PROFESSIONAL-CONDUCT-FOR-LEGAL-PRACTITIONERS-2007-lawyard.ng_.pdf (last visited Sept. 24, 2020).
91. NIGERIAN BAR ASSOCIATION, PRO BONO DECLARATION (2015), www.nigeriabar.com/2015/05/pro-bono-declaration-for-members-of-the-nigerian-bar-association#.X20ejZNKgW- (last visited Sept. 24, 2020).
92. *Id.* Note in 2015, the declaration was amended to encourage law firm lawyers to engage in pro bono by representing at least five socioeconomically disadvantaged clients per year. *See* LATHAM & WATKINS, PRO BONO PRACTICES AND OPPORTUNITIES IN NIGERIA 455, www.lw.com/admin/Upload/Documents/Global%20Pro%20Bono%20Survey/pro-bono-in-nigeria.pdf (last visited Sept. 24, 2020); *see also* NIGERIAN BAR ASSOCIATION, *supra* note 91.
93. Above, it has been discussed how the Nigerian Bar Association dates back to colonial times. Even then, there was a spirit of assisting those in need, who lacked resources to pay for their own representation. The most recent version of this principle has been adopted by the NBA in its constitution, and it states that "the Aims and Objectives of the Association shall be the … establishment, maintenance and operation of a system of prompt and efficient legal aid and assistance for those in need but who are unable to pay for same." *See* NIGERIAN BAR ASSOCIATION, NIGERIAN BAR ASSOCIATION CONSTITUTION 4 (2015), https://nigerianbar.org.ng/sites/default/files/2020-02/NBA%20Constitution.pdf (last visited Sept. 24, 2020).
94. *Id.* at 21, 44 (noting in the constitution that each respective committee "shall provide free legal aid services in suitable circumstances").

95. *See* Legal Practitioners Act (2004) Cap. (L11), § 19(7)(c). Since 1975, when the category was created, there have been 479 SANs appointed. Unfortunately, the number of women who have been selected to this position in the history of this category has been under 5 percent.
96. Bukar Waziri, *NBA Gives a Major Boost to Pro Bono Legal Services in Nigeria*, NIGERIA BAR ASSOCIATION (July 18, 2017), www.prawa.org/nba-gives-a-major-boost-to-pro-bono-legal-services-in-nigeria/ (last visited Sept. 24, 2020).
97. *See* Adelanwa Bamboye, *Legal Aid, NBA, UNODC on Free Services*, DAILY TRUST (July 25, 2017), https://dailytrust.com/legal-aid-nba-unodc-on-free-services (last visited Sept. 24, 2020).
98. *See About the NBA-SBL*, NIGERIA BAR ASSOCIATION SECTION ON BUSINESS LAW, http://nbasbl.org/about-the-sbl/ (last visited Sept. 24, 2020).
99. The information comes from the second author who has played an important leadership role within the SBL.
100. *See* Dyepkazaha Shibayan, *Adegboruwa: Buhari Has Taken Us Back to the 1984 Jackboot Era of Intolerance*, CABLE (Oct. 8, 2016), https://www.thecable.ng/adegboruwa-buhari-has-taken-us-back-to-the-1984-jackboot-era-of-intolerance (last visited Sept. 24, 2020).
101. *Id.*
102. *See Femi Falana Blasts Nigerian Bar Association*, EASTWIND NEWSPAPER, Oct. 10, 2016, https://eastwindnewz.wordpress.com/2016/10/10/femi-falana-blasts-nigeria-bar-association/ (last visited Sept. 24, 2020).
103. NIGERIAN BAR ASSOCIATION COMMITTEE ON PROFESSIONALIZATION OF THE NBA SECRETARIAT, FINAL REPORT 4 (2013), www.premiumtimesng.com/wp-content/files/2013/06/NBA-Secretariat-Prof-Cmmttee-.pdf (last visited Sept. 24, 2020).
104. COMBINING LEARNING AND LEGAL AID: CLINICS IN AFRICA: REPORT ON THE FIRST ALL-AFRICA COLLOQUIUM ON CLINICAL LEGAL EDUCATION, 23–28 JUNE 2003, 1–2 (2003), www.opensocietyfoundations.org/sites/default/files/southafrica_20030628.pdf (last visited Sept. 24, 2020).
105. The specific activities in which these lawyers engage include working on legal education reform proposals, planning of conferences and CLEs, client counseling services, and freedom of information act cases. *See Clinical Law Programs*, NULAI, www.nulai.org/index.php/partners/clinical-law-programs, last visited Sept. 24, 2020. For this paragraph, see *id.*; *see also Combining Learning and Legal Aid: Clinical Legal Education in Africa*, OPEN SOCIETY FOUNDATIONS (June 28, 2003), www.opensocietyfoundations.org/reports/combining-learning-and-legal-aid-clinical-legal-education-africa (last visited Sept. 24, 2020); *The Network of Clinical Legal Education*, NULAI, www.nulai.org/index.php/blog/83-cle (last visited Feb. 9, 2018) [hereinafter *The Network*]. Note, as of 2016, there are fifteen federally based law faculties, nineteen state-based law faculties, and fifteen private law faculties in Nigeria. *See*

Updated: List of Accredited/Approved Faculties of Law in Nigeria, NIGERIAN LAWYER (Sept. 21, 2016), http://thenigerialawyer.com/updated-list-of-accreditedapproved-faculties-of-law-in-nigeria/ (last visited Sept. 24, 2020).

106. For this paragraph, see *The Network*, *supra* note 105; *see also* Oluyemisi Bamgbose, *Access to Justice Through Clinical Legal Education: A Way Forward for Good Governance and Development*, 14 AFR. HUM. RTS. J. 378, 379–81 (2015). Also, according to the NULAI, the local clinics that are currently ongoing within the country are: ABSU Law Clinic, Abia State University; AKUNGBA Law Clinic, Adekunle Ajasin University, Akoko Akungba Ondo State; Maiduguri Law Clinic, University of Maiduguri; UNIUYO Law Clinic, University of Uyo; EBSU Law Clinic, Ebonyi State University; AAU Law Clinic, Ambrose Alli University, Ekpoma Edo State; Women's Law Clinic, University of Ibadan; UniAbuja Law Clinic, University of Abuja, Legal Advice Center and Law Clinic Nigerian Law School, Augustine Nnamani Campus, Abgani Enugu; UNN Legal Aid Clinic, University of Nigeria Nsukka, Enugu Campus; ABU Law Clinic, Ahmadu Bello University, Zaria; Legal Aid Clinic, University of Ilorin; NSUK Law Clinic, Nasarawa State University; OOU Law Clinic, Olabisi Onabanjo University; Nigerian Law School Yola Campus Law Clinic; Nigerian Law School Abuja Campus Law Clinic; Bagauda Law Clinic, Nigerian Law School Kano Campus; Nigerian Law School Lagos Law Clinic, Lagos Campus.

107. For further readings, see Afolasade A. Adewumi & Oluyemisi A. Bamgbose, *Attitude of Students to Clinical Legal Education: A Case Study of Faculty of Law, University of Ibadan*, 3 ASIAN J. LEGAL EDUC. 106 (2016); Bamgbose, *supra* note 106, at 394; Ibijoke Patricia Byron, *The Relationship Between Social Justice and Clinical Legal Education: A Case Study of the Women's Law Clinic, Faculty of Law, University of Ibadan, Nigeria*, 20 INT'L J. CLINICAL LEGAL EDUC. 563, 571–73 (2014); Simon K. Mokidi & Cordelia A. Agbebaku, *Legal Clinics and Professional Skills Development in Nigeria*, 17 INT'L J. CLINICAL LEGAL EDUC. 38, 44–45 (2012); Kevwe Omoragbon, *Interface of Law and Medicine: Success Story of Clinical Legal Education in Improving Health of Women and Ensuring Women's Access to Justice*, 17 INT'L J. CLINICAL LEGAL EDUC. 49, 54 (2009).

108. *See Office of the Public Defender*, LAGOS STATE GOVERNMENT, http://opd.lagosstate.gov.ng/ (last visited Sept. 24, 2020).

109. *Id.*

110. *Id.*

111. *See* Akinwunmi Ambode, *Lagos Moves to Boost Office of Public Defender*, AKINWUNMIAMBODE.COM (Nov. 29, 2015), http://akinwunmiambode.com/lagos-moves-to-boost-office-of-public-defender/ (last visited Sept. 30, 2020).

112. *See Citizen's Mediation Centre Gains Government Support*, BRITISH COUNCIL (Nov. 10, 2014), www.britishcouncil.org.ng/about/press/citizen%E2%80%99s-mediation-centre-gains-government-support (last visited Sept. 30, 2020); *see also Citizen Mediation Centre*, LAGOS STATE MINISTRY OF JUSTICE, http://lagosministryofjustice.org/offices/citizens-mediation-centre/ (last visited Sept. 30, 2020).
113. *Citizen Mediation Centre*, *supra* note 112 (noting that "3,622 matters were adjourned while 1,351 matters were unresolved").
114. *Id.*
115. *See* Oyeniyi Ajigboye, *The Concept of Multi-Door Courthouse in Nigeria: Rethinking Frank Sander's Concept*, 1 AJAYI CROWTHER U. L.J. 10 (2014).
116. *See id.* It should be noted that the second author's first job, after law school, was at Aina, Blankson & Co, which founded the NCMG (with a board composed of retired senior judges, businessmen, retired diplomats, and a retired general). The NCMG in turn established the LMDC. At this point, it was entirely pro bono and private sector driven. Only later did the Lagos state government see the promise of the multidoor concept. The state subsequently took over the LMDC, and it is now a statutory body.

PART FIVE

ASIA

CHAPTER FIFTEEN

THE EVOLVING CONTOURS OF PRIVATE PRO BONO POLICY AND PRACTICE IN INDIA: LOCAL AND GLOBAL CONTEXTS

Arpita Gupta

INTRODUCTION

The projection of India as the fastest growing large economy in the world from 2018 to 2021[1] stands in stark juxtaposition with the fact that it also houses the largest number of the world's poor.[2] The primary approach being favored by international development organizations as well as the Indian state to address the issue of large-scale poverty in general and legal poverty[3] in particular has been to facilitate legal empowerment of the poor through the promotion of access to justice and rule of law among the underprivileged sections of the population.[4] Following the widespread dissemination of the rights discourse, providing free legal assistance to the poor has emerged as the cornerstone of access-to-justice efforts globally.

The three important providers of free pro bono legal assistance are the state, civil society organizations, and private lawyers. Owing to specific political and historical factors, different providers are dominant in different jurisdictions. In India, in terms of overall reach and scope, the state has historically been the largest provider of free legal services,[5] followed by nongovernmental/civil society organizations[6] and private lawyers respectively. It is the pro bono practice of this third category of service providers that is the primary subject of this study.

With the launch of the Pro Bono Legal Services Initiative by the Ministry of Law and Justice, the year 2017 can be seen to mark the beginning of a shift in the Indian government's predominantly state-centric approach to providing free legal assistance. Under this Initiative, the state has for the first time officially urged private lawyers to volunteer for providing pro bono legal services to underprivileged litigants. The launch of the initiative was soon followed by the Supreme Court of India's guidelines on designation of senior advocates in the country's higher courts, making pro bono work a compulsory criterion for such appointments. But, even though the pro bono landscape in the country is evolving rapidly, and the concept of free private legal services is gaining popularity within policy and lay circles, it has not yet been systematically studied. This chapter fills this gap by analyzing the pro bono practices of two important components of the legal profession – corporate law firms and individual/solo lawyers – and situating them at the intersection of the domestic context and global influences.

As an initial point of reference, this chapter uses the term "pro bono" in its commonly and broadly understood sense, particularly among global actors involved in the practice and active promotion of pro bono: the provision of legal assistance by private lawyers to those in need for free or at reduced rates. This definition provides a flexible frame of reference to initiate an inquiry into the different contours of the rapidly evolving practice of private pro bono in India.

Since the term "pro bono" has gained traction in the Indian popular vocabulary only very recently, but the practice of providing free legal services and the traditions of doing good in general are preexisting, flexibility of definitional parameters is crucial so as not to miss significant local nuances. As the chapter progresses in its analysis of the practical specificities of pro bono as a function of the relevant local and global contexts, a substantive definition of pro bono emerges that in its details both departs from and convergences with pro bono as conventionally defined.

As the United States is a major source of influence on promoting pro bono globally through various US-based foundations, intermediary organizations, and international law firms, where relevant, this chapter compares and contrasts the Indian context with pro bono practices prevalent in the United States. This exercise serves two important purposes. First, it brings out the distinctive traits of pro bono in India more clearly. Second, it sheds light on the important question of transplantation from the West that especially arises when dealing with globalization of practices even if they are state-mediated.

The data on corporate law firms is based on the pro bono practices of eleven of the top twenty law firms in India (see Appendix).[7] Six firms shared their pro bono/CSR documents with the author, and the information on the other five firms is derived from their websites and the intermediary organizations that they work with. The information on the pro bono practice of solo practitioners is assessed from some of the prominent public interest law (PIL) cases in which these lawyers appeared on a pro bono basis and from the databases of intermediary organizations. This information is supplemented by news archives, case study databases of intermediary organizations such as iProbono, research reports, and email correspondence with some of the key stakeholders.

BACKGROUND CONTEXT

This section delineates in detail two sets of factors, the tension and interaction between which define and shape the specific form that the concept and practice of private pro bono has acquired in India. The first set of factors brings out the uniqueness of Indian context, divergences from the global context (particularly the American context), and challenges to the practice of private pro bono in general. These are met by a second set of factors that include the similarities between the Indian and global contexts, convergences between the factors facilitating global pro bono including transnational pro bono networks, and opportunities for the growth of private pro bono in the country.

Narrative I: Difference, Divergence, and Challenges

Constitutional and Regulatory Context

As a matter of constitutional mandate, judicial interpretation, and political choice, the Indian government has traditionally focused on state legal aid as the primary instrument for providing legal services to facilitate access to justice among the weaker sections of society, as opposed to private pro bono. The first government-appointed committees to study the problem of access to justice were established for the states of Bombay and West Bengal in 1949, a mere two years after the country's independence.[8] Since then, a number of reports on this issue have been prepared by government-appointed committees either independently or in collaboration with international organizations like the United Nations Development Program (UNDP).[9] Thus, starting from a few states and sections of the society, the ambit of state-led legal aid machinery has gradually expanded to cover the entire country and has been systematically institutionalized.[10]

This is reflective of the welfare nature of the Indian state as is apparent from the preamble to the Constitution of India, which declares India as a "socialist" republic, and the Directive Principles of State Policy (DPSP), which direct the state to strive toward establishing a just society in the country. With respect to legal aid in particular, Article 39A, which was inserted into the Constitution through the Forty-Second Amendment in 1976 as part of the DPSP, directs the state and state agencies to "provide *free legal aid*, by suitable legislation or schemes or in any other way, to ensure that opportunities for securing justice are not denied to any citizen by reason of economic or other disabilities."

As per this constitutional mandate, the National Legal Services Authorities Act was enacted in 1987. The Act provides for the establishment of the National Legal Services Authority and various state, district, and *taluk*-level legal services authorities throughout the country for the provision of free legal services to disadvantaged sections of society. In addition, it provides for the establishment of legal services committees for the courts (supreme court, high court, and district courts), village legal aid clinics, and *lok adalats* (people's courts), one of the alternative dispute redressal mechanisms in India. The free legal services are available to all sections of the population facing socioeconomic vulnerability[11] for all sorts of legal matters, including criminal matters.[12] Additionally, there are special legal aid schemes for groups such as the mentally ill, victims of disasters, sex workers, and children. In accordance with its policy of increased digitalization, the government is making unprecedented use of technology to deliver its legal aid services.[13]

This comprehensive framework for state-led pro bono services, the constitutional promise of free legal aid to all weaker sections of society, and the fundamental right to state–supplied legal aid in criminal cases guaranteed by Article 21 of the Constitution of India are the most significant factors underlying the traditionally low emphasis being placed on private pro bono in the country.[14] This stands in stark contrast to the US pro bono model that is primarily private pro bono–centric. The Legal Services Corporation is the largest funder of independent nonprofit legal aid programs in the United States. It has been established to provide free legal assistance to low- and middle-income people, but unlike India, its scope of assistance is confined only to civil law matters. Even in civil law matters, due to resource constraints, more than 50 percent of those below the poverty line who apply for legal help are denied assistance.[15]

Challenges of Fighting the State

Although the state legal aid machinery is institutionalized throughout the country, it often breaks down in areas that are affected by internal conflicts, especially where the state and the military have special powers. Many of these regions have the highest rates of poverty and illiteracy in the country and are predominantly inhabited by the Scheduled Tribes. With the largest concentration of land, environmental, and human rights conflicts in the country, these are the areas where pro bono legal assistance is needed the most but is most challenging to provide. Pro bono lawyers face hostility not just from the administration but in some cases also from the local bar, as is evident from a recent instance where a local bar passed a resolution banning outside lawyers from practicing in the local courts, effectively targeting the human rights lawyers providing free legal assistance to those affected by police violence and unlawful detention.[16]

Structure of the Indian Legal Profession and Economic Differentiation

Home to over 1.3 million lawyers, India has the largest number of lawyers in the world.[17] However, the legal profession in the country is very different in its internal organization and distribution of income as compared with the United States. These two factors have a great bearing on the capacity of large numbers of lawyers in India to provide pro bono services. Unlike the United States, where the majority of lawyers are part of law firms, which makes it easier to design, fund, and institutionalize pro bono policy at the firm level, the organization of the Indian legal profession is such that law firms employ less than 0.1 percent of the total lawyers in India,[18] and the vast majority of lawyers are solo practitioners with very limited and irregular earning opportunities.

Even in terms of economic leverage, the Indian legal profession is highly fragmented. Most of the earnings of the legal profession as a whole are concentrated among a few supreme court, high court, and district court-level senior lawyers ("Grand Advocates")[19] and a handful of corporate law firms in large cities, which do report doing regular pro bono work.[20] For the rest of the lawyers who primarily practice in the various courts and tribunals of the country, average income has traditionally been very low. In fact, when state legal aid was initially sought to be introduced on a large scale in India, it was mistakenly understood to imply "aid to indigent lawyers"![21] This disparity within the legal profession remains largely true to this day as well. The honorarium paid by the state to lawyers for participating in state legal aid committees is paltry, especially in comparison with the amount charged by the elite advocates for each court appearance.[22] These facts shed light on the economic and practical challenges that the majority of solo lawyers, especially those practicing in the lower courts of the country, are likely to encounter in conducting regular and quality pro bono work.[23]

In comparison with individual lawyers (both private and public), the large corporate law firms that emerged in the wake of India's economic liberalization in the early 1990s are moving toward greater institutionalization and systematization of pro bono work.[24] Yet, in comparison with US law firms, their economic and institutional capacity to do pro bono work seems minuscule. This is primarily because of the differences between the Indian corporate law firms and their American counterparts with respect to parameters such as size, resources, and revenue. The largest law firm in India (Cyril Amarchand Mangaldas) has 630 lawyers, and only 19 Indian firms have more than 100 lawyers,[25] whereas the largest American law firm (Baker McKenzie) has over 5,700 lawyers, and over 50 American law firms have more than 1,000 lawyers.[26] In terms of annual revenue, for FY2016, Baker McKenzie reported global revenue of $2.62 billion,[27] which is more than double the combined estimated revenue of the top 40 Indian law firms in FY2017.[28] These differences can partly be attributed to the comparatively recent establishment of Indian corporate law firms in 1990s and 2000s, whereas on average most of the largest American law firms were established long ago, mostly around the mid-1900s. Thus, owing to their significantly larger size, resources, revenue, and age, the American law firms have a considerably greater pro bono capacity than their Indian counterparts.

Institutional Context: Judicial Institutions in India

The fourth set of factors particular to India that are likely to deter lawyers from engaging in pro bono matters relates to the on-the-ground workings of judicial institutions in India, such as delays in case disposal, case backlogs, and low per-capita availability of judges. With over 27 million cases still pending in the country's courts,[29] an average time of ten to fifteen years to decide cases in the country's top courts, and a low judge-to-population ratio of 19.66 judges per million people[30] (whereas in the United States this ratio is 107 judges per million people), litigation in the country turns out to be a particularly challenging engagement, deterring potential litigants and their pro bono advocates. This is also the reason for the considerable emphasis that is placed on alternative dispute redressal mechanisms like *lok adalats*[31] and on enacting and enforcing ex ante preventive laws as compared with ex post dispute resolution mechanisms such as litigation.[32]

It must be noted that these factors delineating the differences, divergences, and challenges to private pro bono in the Indian context are not static and are themselves evolving both organically and through their interaction with the second set of factors discussed in the next section.

Narrative II: Similarity, Convergence and Opportunities

Bar Council Rules and Cultural-Historical Norms of Doing Good

Though the use of the term "pro bono" has gained popularity only very recently in India, the fundamental essence underlying the concept of pro bono legal services is preexisting in the country, as is evident from the Bar Council of India Rules in particular,[33] and the cultural-historical norms of doing good prevalent in the Indian subcontinent in general.

Rule 46 of the Bar Council of India Rules clearly lays down the lawyer's duty toward those who are "genuinely in need of a lawyer," stating that providing "free legal assistance to the indigent and oppressed is one of the highest obligations an advocate owes to society."[34] The fact that this duty to do pro bono for those in need is incorporated in the chapter on Standards of Professional Conduct and Etiquette alludes to the presence of an implicit shared understanding of the linkage between professionalism and pro bono in India as well.[35]

At a more nuanced level, the core idea underlying pro bono – giving legal services for free or at a nominal price – deeply resonates with the popular cultural-historical notions of doing good through giving that are embodied in both the religious and secular philanthropic traditions prevalent in the country. While the commonly practiced forms of giving in the Indian subcontinental traditions, such as Hinduism, Islam, Sikhism, Christianity, Jainism, Buddhism, and Gandhian philosophy, vary in their finer details, the notion of every individual's duty to give back to society constitutes an important cross-cutting theme.[36] The primary foci of these traditions have mostly been individuals, but professional organizations too have traditionally participated in such practices of giving, implying that the structure for both individual and institutional forms of pro bono has long existed in the country.[37] Though pro bono and philanthropy are generally distinguished as two separate concepts, especially in the United States, this chapter argues in favor of seeing the two as fundamentally similar; the practice of altruistic giving to those in need constitutes the common core of the two concepts. The only difference between them is that in the case of pro bono there is the provision of legal services, whereas in the case of philanthropy there is the giving of money or goods. A practical instance of this can be seen in the intersection between the corporate social responsibility (CSR) and pro bono practices of most of the large corporate law firms in India, discussed below.

Economic Liberalization and Emergence of the Corporate Legal Sector

The rise and expansion of a globally conscious corporate legal sector in India in the wake of the country's first phase of economic liberalization is of special relevance for the institutionalization of law firm–centric private pro bono in the country. In response to the 1991 balance-of-payment crisis, the Indian government initiated the process of liberalization and privatization of the Indian economy. The ensuing complex multiparty business transactions created an unprecedented demand for sophisticated legal services, paving the way for the rise of multispecialty corporate law firms in the country. The fact that these firms regularly advise multinational clients, work closely with foreign law firms on cross-border transactions, and are amply staffed with American- and British-educated lawyers is increasingly exposing Indian law firms to global influences, as is apparent from the range of global best practices being adopted by these firms.[38] This is true for their pro bono and CSR practices too. Most of the top-tier law firms in India are moving toward a greater institutionalization of their pro bono practices through measures such as drafting pro bono policies for the firm, counting pro bono work as billable work, and having a partner in charge of overseeing the firm's pro bono work.[39]

Another important contributing factor toward institutionalization of pro bono among Indian law firms is the establishment of the Society of Indian Law Firms (SILF) in 2000. With a membership of over one hundred firms, it is the apex body of Indian law firms. Its aims include promotion of the public interest through the use of law, promotion of the welfare of Indian law firms, and promotion of Indian law firms' relations with the Indian bar, bench, and public, as well as with foreign lawyers.[40]

In line with its objective of promoting the public interest, SILF places particular emphasis on private pro bono by encouraging its member firms to undertake pro bono work on a regular basis and organizing activities like panel discussions on pro bono.[41] There appears to be both intrinsic and extrinsic motivations for SILF's emphasis on pro bono, including its participation in programs like TrustLaw (Thomas Reuters Foundation's global pro bono program) and garnering good publicity for the Indian corporate legal sector both domestically and internationally.[42]

Intermediary/Matchmaking Organizations

The emergence of intermediary organizations, also commonly referred to as matchmaking organizations, has played an important role in promoting private pro bono in India. These organizations are of recent origin and have been visible in the country's pro bono landscape since the late 2000s. The core function of these organizations is to connect lawyers and law firms willing to provide free legal services with individuals in need or nongovernmental organizations (NGOs) working with vulnerable groups of the population. Many of these organizations are based outside India, such as iProbono, TrustLaw Connect, and the Lex Mundi Pro Bono Foundation, while others such as ProBono India are based within India. These are nonprofit organizations that receive donations of finances, services, and facilities from a range of sources including individual and institutional philanthropists, international organizations, and law firms.[43]

With the recent launch of the Pro Bono Legal Services Initiative (discussed in detail below), a smartphone-based application designed to connect pro bono lawyers with indigent clients, even the Indian state has assumed the role of an intermediary organization. The intermediary organizations differ in their modus operandi. For instance, Lex Mundi and TrustLaw Connect limit their role to matching pro bono lawyers with clients, whereas iProbono takes a more engaged approach that goes beyond matching lawyers with clients. When needed, iProbono also facilitates the collection of donations for affected persons and helps them find suitable employment.[44]

Decision to Liberalize the Corporate Legal Sector

The impending opening up of the Indian legal market to foreign law firms is likely to push Indian law firms to further institutionalize their pro bono policy. Though numerous proposals to liberalize the Indian legal market have been made over time, the year 2017 marks an important juncture in this regard.[45] In July 2017, the government organized a meeting on "the issue of entry of foreign lawyers/law firms in India," where it conveyed its decision to liberalize the Indian legal market.[46] In the wake of this decision, the government asked the Supreme Court of India to expedite its decision on two pending cases on the operation of foreign law firms in India.[47] The minister of law and justice clearly stated that since the government has unequivocally decided to liberalize the legal sector, the only matters that remain open to discussion are the finer details through which the process of liberalization would be given effect, and asked the attendees, which included the presidents of SILF and BCI, to make recommendations on the matter.[48]

The recommendations on this issue favor opening up the Indian legal market in phases, where the first phase would entail making domestic reforms to help bring Indian law firms up to par with their foreign counterparts in certain key aspects.[49] Though the proposed reforms include measures such as removing restrictions on lawyers and firms from advertising and marketing their services by amending the Advocates Act, they do not include any explicit guidelines on mandatory pro bono requirements for lawyers. Nevertheless, these reforms are likely to influence law firm pro bono in India. For instance, the permission to set up websites and advertise lawyers' services and achievements would give them an avenue to publicize their socially oriented activities like pro bono and CSR.

The proposed liberalization is likely to have a more direct and pronounced impact on large corporate law firm pro bono in comparison with the pro bono practices of other constituents of the Indian legal profession, because it is the nonlitigious transactional legal services, the primary work of such law firms, that would be opened up to foreign lawyers and firms rather than the litigation services that the majority of Indian lawyers engage in. The Indian corporate legal sector is likely to move toward even greater harmonization with global legal best practices, including pro bono practices. A particular instance demonstrating that pro bono practices of foreign law firms have had a visible impact in India was the defense filed by the respondents in the case of *A. K. Balaji* v. *Government of India & Others*.[50] In this writ petition, the petitioners alleged that foreign lawyers and law firms should not be allowed to practice law in India because they regard the legal profession as a business, whereas in India it is regarded as a noble profession. In response to this allegation, the law firms (US-based law firms in particular) provided detailed information on their pro bono work, which far exceeded their Indian counterparts. Thus, it can be observed that the international law firms' systematic and quantifiable pro bono record has contributed to diluting and diffusing domestic resistance to the opening up of the legal market in India.[51]

Even though the litigation sector in India is not the object of focus of the impending liberalization of the legal market and the consequent pressure to increase its pro bono engagement, litigation sector pro bono has begun to receive active encouragement from another source: the government of India, as is evident from the launch of the Pro Bono Legal Services Initiative.

Pro Bono Legal Services Initiative

Taking a step beyond its mandate of publicly funded state-led legal aid, the Indian government launched the Pro Bono Legal Services Initiative (PBLSI) in April 2017 to actively involve private lawyers in providing free legal aid to underprivileged litigants. Recognizing the population's increasing legal needs, the access-to-justice gap in the country, and the limitations of the state-led legal aid program with respect to outreach and resources, the Department of Justice (Ministry of Law and Justice) in collaboration with the UNDP launched a mobile application to connect lawyers with those in need of legal help.[52]

Through this mobile application, lawyers willing to provide their services for free can register themselves. As of February 2019, more than two hundred lawyers had registered themselves to provide pro bono services.[53] The Department of Justice has also directed the state bar councils[54] to provide the names of lawyers who engage in pro bono activities. This would lead to the creation of a comprehensive and centralized database of lawyers undertaking pro bono work, and this list of lawyers can be accessed by those in need through an interface provided by the UNDP. Under this initiative, there are no mandatory pro bono requirements for lawyers. Instead, to incentivize lawyers to register on the platform, the government has "proposed to include and recognize pro bono legal assistance provided by lawyers as a yardstick to be considered for appointment to appropriate positions."[55] Though the Department of Justice has not yet provided any further information on the details of the proposed appointments (referred to as "appropriate positions"), they are most likely to be judicial appointments to the courts and tribunals, similar to the October 2017 guidelines issued by the Supreme Court of India for designating senior advocates in the Supreme Court and the twenty-six high courts of the country.[56]

These guidelines mention pro bono work done by lawyers as one of the criteria for assessing the candidature of applicants for their designation as senior advocates. Notably, this provision of the Supreme Court guidelines is based on the Nigerian guidelines for awarding senior advocate status, which require the applicant advocate to have provided assistance in at least three pro bono matters or to have been involved in some other form of community service.[57] This instance of "horizontal learning"[58] shows that the country is experiencing cross-border influences on its pro bono policy from multiple sources, including international developmental organizations, western countries, as well as other developing countries of the Global South.

This inclusion of the criterion of pro bono work for judicial appointments and promotion in PBLSI and the Supreme Court guidelines has to be seen in light of the general political debate on judicial appointments in the country, and the ensuing back-and-forth between the government and the judiciary. Through the National Judicial Appointments Commission (NJAC) Act 2014, the government sought to replace the all-judges collegium system of judicial appointments to the higher courts of the country with a body consisting of nonjudicial members as well.[59] While the Supreme Court of India struck down the NJAC Act in 2015 as unconstitutional on the grounds of undue executive interference with the independence of judiciary, the Court also acknowledged the defects in the collegium system.[60] The Court welcomed suggestions to improve the collegium system with respect to transparency, accountability, and eligibility, and in a subsequent order directed the government to finalize a new Memorandum of Procedure in consultation with the chief justice of India. Thus, the recent emphasis on pro bono can be seen as part of a larger effort at making the eligibility criteria for judicial appointments more transparent and accountable.

The PBLSI represents a conscious effort on the part of the Indian government to institutionalize private pro bono in India along the lines of countries like the United States and South Korea, as has been expressed by the Union Law Minister at the launch of the initiative.[61] The official note on the initiative states that in India "many lawyers provide poor and underprivileged clients with valuable legal advice and support without seeking any professional fee"; nevertheless, this tradition "remains more of an ad hoc, individualized practice lacking an institutional structure."[62] Striking an aspirational tone, the note further remarks that in a number of other countries, private pro bono is "the dominant means of dispensing free representation to poor and underserved clients."[63]

The Indian government's move toward institutionalization of pro bono along the lines of countries like the United States can be seen as an outcome of a combination of factors. The nudge toward private pro bono from UNDP (India's long-term partner in its access-to-justice endeavors) and the impact of judicial accountability and transparency debates on the legal profession in general are two such factors. The government's emphasis on private pro bono also seems to be an indication of its intention of sharing the responsibility of providing free legal aid with private advocates and law firms. This move toward supplementing state-led legal aid with private pro bono is another illustration of the practice of public-private partnership that is gaining traction in the country, and the general proliberalization and proprivatization trend in India.[64]

The difference–similarity, divergence–convergence, challenges–opportunities, and local–global narratives explored in this section form the larger backdrop against which private pro bono practice has evolved and is evolving in India. The following section discusses and analyzes the significant contours of private pro bono practice in the country.

AN OVERVIEW OF PRIVATE PRO BONO PRACTICE IN INDIA

A perusal of the historical timeline of private pro bono in India depicts three significant moments that stand out: 1981, 1991, and 2017. Significantly, these moments also coincide with important changes in the composition of the Indian legal profession. The year 1981 ushered in the PIL revolution in the country, resulting in dilution of *locus standi* requirements. It allowed any publicly spirited individual to file a writ petition against the government on behalf of an individual or group facing a violation of fundamental rights. This led to the emergence of a new category of lawyers often referred to as "sociolegal entrepreneurs" who represented a range of vulnerable groups including prisoners on trial and bonded laborers on a pro bono basis.[65] The year 1991 marked the rise of corporate lawyers and the beginning of a corporate legal culture in the country. The establishment of corporate law firms gave rise to a different kind of pro bono in India, that is, an institutionalized and transaction work-focused pro bono. The year 2017 is significant because of the launch of the Pro Bono Legal Services Initiative by the Indian government, the Supreme Court's guidelines on the designation of senior advocates, and the clear expression of intent to open up the Indian legal market to foreign lawyers.

As per the available data, there are three broad categories of nonstate legal services providers doing pro bono work on a regular basis in the country: large corporate law firms,[66] independent lawyers (including networks of lawyers consisting of progressive lawyers), and law students through their law schools' legal aid clinics.[67] The pro bono work done by these primary actors is facilitated by another set of actors, namely the government, the higher judiciary, intermediary organizations connecting the legal service providers with those in need of legal assistance, NGOs, right-to-information activists, international development organizations, private funders promoting access to justice for vulnerable sections of the society, and, more recently, foreign law schools and foreign law firms as well. Apart from the occasional overlaps and some general points of commonality, the pro bono work done by these actors varies broadly in terms of the primary mode(s) of doing pro bono, clients/beneficiaries, and the nature of the impact of their work. The following two subsections focus on the pro bono practice of the first two categories of legal services providers, top-tier corporate law firms, and independent lawyers.

Large Corporate Law Firms

Primary Mechanisms for Conducting Pro Bono Work

The predominant mechanism for conducting pro bono[68] among Indian law firms is transactional work. Firm lawyers also prepare research reports and memoranda, advise the government,[69] and participate in legal awareness and literacy campaigns. In some instances, a firm's lawyers also participate in litigation matters. The most important modes of doing pro bono work are described and illustrated below.

Transactional work: The most common kind of transactional work that firms engage in includes preparing contracts and deeds;[70] advising clients (mostly nonprofit entities) on incorporation, structuring, tax, and compliance requirements;[71] and advising on domestic legislation such as labor law, environmental law, and laws on cross-border funding such as the Foreign Contribution (Regulation) Act 2010. Since most of these firms specialize in providing legal transactional services rather than litigation, it seems natural for them to prefer doing transactional work when it comes to pro bono work as well. This way they can efficiently provide pro bono services while doing their routine work.

Research reports: As conducting legal research is considered to be one of the core skills of lawyers generally, firms regularly engage in preparing research reports for domestic and international nonprofit organizations, as well as governments, on a range of social issues including those that are cross-border in nature. For instance, Jyoti Sagar Associates (JSA) has reported preparing research reports on acid violence–related law in India for Acid Survivors Trust International (ASTI), on laws and policies related to age of consent in India for the South Africa AIDS Trust, and on Indian laws related to intellectual disability for Operation Ghana to campaign for legal reform in Ghana. It also prepared a research memorandum for the Bangladesh Legal Aid Service Trust (BLAST) on changes in Indian law on the use of character evidence in rape trials. At the request of the International Centre for Missing and Exploited Children, the Trilegal firm prepared a detailed report on legal provisions related to issues like exploitation of children, human trafficking, cybercrime, and data protection.

At the behest of the government, firms often make recommendations on legislative and regulatory changes in socially relevant areas on a pro bono basis. For instance, the Securities and Exchange Commission has accepted the recommendations of firms like AZB & Partners and Nishith Desai Associates for the creation of a social venture fund to raise funding for social ventures by including it in Alternative Investment Funds–Category 1.[72]

Primary Clients/Beneficiaries

The primary clients of law firm pro bono in India are nonprofit organizations and social enterprises. The social enterprises assisted by these firms are mostly start-ups or start-up incubators, which are primarily focused on alleviating poverty through innovations and grassroots engagement with farmers and small-business owners by providing services like microloans, procurement services at fair prices, supply chain assistance, and business training.[73] Many of the social businesses that law firms assist on a pro bono basis combine poverty alleviation with other causes like gender equality, waste management, and environmental conservation.[74]

Firms also provide regular transactional services to foundations working in diverse areas such as health care, poverty alleviation, child welfare, housing, and education.[75] They also work with a number of organizations engaged in human rights protection.[76]

Impact

The impact of law firm pro bono depends on the lens through which it is viewed. For instance, if direct impact is considered, then the nonprofits, social enterprises, and other entities that they provide pro bono services to can be seen as the immediate beneficiaries. Also, since most of these firms are located in big cities, their impact seems largely confined to metropolitan urban areas. However, if one views pro bono in wider context, then the indirect impact of law firms on various societal causes espoused by the organizations they assist and in the geographic areas they work in can be gauged to be far-reaching.[77]

A second dimension of the impact of law firm pro bono is its transnational dimension, as is apparent from the firms' research reports: for instance, Trilegal's report for the International Centre for Missing and Exploited Children, and JSA's research memorandum on character evidence in rape trials that was used by the Bangladesh Legal Aid Service Trust to advocate for change in the legal position of the courts in Bangladesh.

Third, the impetus given by law firm pro bono to Silicon Valley–inspired social entrepreneurs makes these firms facilitators of the US-style entrepreneurship model of development for addressing social, economic, and environmental challengess.[78]

Facilitators

Intermediary organizations have started playing an important role in facilitating Indian law firms in their pro bono practice since they first appeared on the scene around 2010. For instance, iProbono not only connects law firms to civil society organizations, social enterprises, and people in need, but also organizes conferences and workshops to promote pro bono around the country.[79] Awards by intermediary organizations, such as the Annual Lex Mundi Pro Bono Foundation Award and Trustlaw Global Impact Award, also contribute toward the promotion of pro bono among law firms.[80]

Institutionalization

Corporate legal sector pro bono is moving toward greater institutionalization. The process of institutionalization is more visible in six of the top ten law firms studied in this chapter. Though there is no mandatory requirement to do pro bono in any of the firms, they count pro bono work as billable work.[81] In most of the firms, pro bono work is supervised by the partner heading the social sector practice of the firm. JSA also has a full-time pro bono coordinator and a formal pro bono policy.[82] A perusal of the pro bono practices of these firms shows that the process of institutionalization of pro bono among Indian law firms is developing in large part along the lines of CSR.

Distinctive Characteristic: Pro Bono and CSR Overlap

In the case of Indian corporate law firms, pro bono is closely linked with their CSR.[83] The two concepts are regarded as essentially similar, and understood as being two variants of the duty to give back to society, one being in the form of services, while the other being in the form of goods and finances. It is argued here that the relationship between the two concepts is deeply intertwined. The firms have dual identities, one as a constituent of the legal profession and the other as a corporate entity, thus making it difficult to separate their pro bono and CSR duties. In fact, both pro bono and CSR are construed as integral elements for "designing a socially responsible law firm."[84]

Both CSR and pro bono are the private counterparts to state social welfare and state legal aid efforts respectively. An analysis of the way in which pro bono culture among Indian corporate law firms is evolving shows that it is largely developing along the lines of the more developed practice of CSR and philanthropy in the country. This is particularly evident from the similarity of debates, modes, and methodologies that the two concepts have come to share.

For instance, the question of whether pro bono efforts should be led by individuals or institutions is relevant for both philanthropy and pro bono. Further, with respect to pro bono, there is a recent emergence of intermediary/matchmaking organizations in the country, similar to those existing in the field of philanthropy, such as GiveIndia. The significant issue of impact assessment with respect to CSR is being raised in the case of corporate bro bono as well. Also, along the lines of the mandatory 2 percent CSR expenditure requirements for corporations with annual revenues above a certain limit in India,[85] a law firm partner proposed a similar rule with respect to law firm pro bono, expressing that "the Bar council can require firms crossing certain revenue thresholds to contribute in local legal aid committees and other pro bono efforts or to adopt a formal policy."[86]

The linkage between law firm CSR and pro bono and the importance of the former for the promotion of the latter is also apparent from an innovative proposal made by the late N. R. Madhav Menon, according to which large urban corporate law firms can promote pro bono for meeting the justice needs of vulnerable communities living in remote areas by funding specialized rural law firms with their CSR funds.[87] The importance of CSR for corporations in general and not just corporate law firms is also evident from pro bono programs like Bharti Enterprises' Nyaya Bharti, aimed at protecting the rights of thousands of under-trial prisoners languishing in jails in the Delhi NCR region.[88]

Given this linkage, the division between pro bono and CSR does not appear to be watertight. Donations made by law firm associates through intermediaries such as the EdelGive Foundation and GiveIndia to legal aid and legal rights organizations for causes that they cannot directly do pro bono work for owing to constraints such as distance, lack of expertise, and institutional limitations can be regarded as indirect or "proxy pro bono."[89] Even in the United States, where pro bono and CSR have traditionally been regarded as clearly distinct practices, there is an emerging trend to evaluate the overall impact of a lawyer or firm on society by looking holistically at the various forms of giving back they engage in, including pro bono, charity, and community service.[90]

Independent Lawyers

As mentioned earlier, independent lawyers constitute over 99 percent of Indian lawyers. There is a hierarchy among the independent lawyers depending upon the court(s) where they practice. Among the lawyers practicing in the higher courts there is a further subdivision between senior advocates and other advocates, where less than 1 percent of all enrolled advocates in India are senior advocates. All categories of independent advocates are known to engage in some kind of pro bono work. However, as the majority of independent advocates are dispersed throughout the country and there has been no district, state, or national level database to record their pro bono work, estimates on the extent, reach, and scope of pro bono work they do are difficult to make. However, this is set to change with the PBLSI, which seeks to create the first-ever centralized database of independent lawyers engaging in pro bono work throughout the country.

Primary Mechanisms for Conducting Pro Bono Work

As opposed to corporate law firms, the primary mechanism through which solo practitioners conduct pro bono work is litigation, including PIL. They also often engage in legal awareness and literacy programs, and accept *amicus curiae* appointments.

The most common mechanism that solo lawyers engage in conducting pro bono work is litigation, which includes advising, drafting, and representing clients in court. Advocates in the lower courts and junior advocates in the higher courts usually assist with advising and drafting, and if the matter is in a higher court, a senior advocate can volunteer to argue the case. Many of the senior advocates in the country are known to take up pro bono cases on a regular basis.[91]

Primary Clients/Beneficiaries

The primary clients or beneficiaries of independent lawyers' pro bono work can be the particular individuals whom the lawyers are assisting or representing, or entire groups of people facing injustice and vulnerability such as migrant laborers, refugees, prisoners, and human trafficking victims who are often represented by rights-based organizations that approach lawyers for assistance on behalf of these groups. Some of the landmark decisions involving these groups are described in the next section.

Impact

The impact of lawyers' pro bono assistance varies, depending upon who and what cause is being represented. The impact can be in the form of immediate relief for petitioners, as is illustrated by a recent stay order obtained by the pro bono advocate Siddharth Aggarwal from the Delhi High Court on the demolition of a slum by local law enforcement authorities without first rehabilitating or resettling the residents who would have been affected by the demolition.[92]

The impact can also be very far-reaching, being both domestic and transnational in nature. An excellent example of a pro bono matter that impacted millions of people in India is the "Right to Food" case,[93] where Colin Gonsalves brought to the Supreme Court of India's attention the fact that although thousands of people in India were dying of hunger and malnutrition, massive amounts of food grains were rotting in government granaries. This led the Supreme Court to interpret the right to food as part of the right to life, the fundamental right enshrined in Article 21 of the Constitution of India. This ultimately led the

Indian government to enact the National Food Security Act 2013, entitling around two-thirds of India's population to subsidized food grains. The transnational impact of pro bono can be illustrated through the Supreme Court's stay on the deportation of Rohingya refugees due to the pro bono petitions filed in the Supreme Court against the government's decision to deport over forty thousand Rohingya refugees escaping ethnic violence and persecution in Myanmar.[94]

Facilitators

Individual lawyers are primarily facilitated in their pro bono endeavors by higher courts, the state, and intermediary organizations. The Supreme Court's guidelines on designating senior advocates[95] and the PBLSI[96] are the two most significant measures. Both measures have built-in incentives for doing pro bono work by promising seniority and government appointments respectively. The rationale for this becomes obvious from a note on the measures recognizing the prevalence of the practice of giving free legal services among lawyers, and stating that "unfortunately, this laudable tradition of public service has not received any deserving recognition."[97]

The role of intermediary organizations and NGOs that approach individual advocates and match them with pro bono clients is particularly relevant for promoting pro bono work among solo practitioners throughout the country, not only in domestic matters but also in transnational cases. For instance, iProbono linked an Indian lawyer with an International Justice Mission (IJM) project to assist a victim of cross-border sex trafficking from Bangladesh to India.[98]

The biggest contribution of these intermediary organizations is to provide a ready database of organizations in need of pro bono assistance that can be easily accessed by lawyers and law students interested in doing pro bono work in their areas of interest and expertise. With the creation of a centralized database of lawyers and those needing legal services under the PBLSI, the government too is set to play an important intermediary role.[99]

Institutionalization

Unlike law firms, individual lawyers' pro bono practice has been lacking in institutional structure. However, this is set to change with the Supreme Court of India's guidelines for designating senior advocates, and the PBLSI. The former is relevant for lawyers practicing in the Supreme Court and the high courts, while the latter is of special relevance for lawyers working in the smaller courts throughout the country. Taken together, the two measures would cover the entire litigation sector in India.

Distinctive Characteristic: PIL

The uniquely Indian mechanism of PIL[100] is the most important tool used for cause lawyering in the country.[101] The widening of the scope of *locus standi* requirements has empowered socially inclined lawyers to perform pro bono services. This has the potential of impacting large sections of the population positively.[102] The higher courts of the country, cause lawyers, and common citizens have often collaborated to promote the cause of justice in the face of legislative shortcomings and executive inaction or excesses. Through a series of rulings, the Supreme Court has made decisions seeking to protect the interests of vulnerable sections such as bonded laborers,[103] persons on trial and prisoners,[104] women at the workplace,[105] and people in custody.[106] The impact of PIL judgments of Indian courts has not just been confined to the domestic arena but has also spread transnationally, as is evident from their influence on foreign courts.[107]

In response to the growing visibility of the unmet legal demands of disadvantaged sections of the population, the differences in the primary mechanisms, beneficiaries, institutionalization, and impact between law firm and independent advocate pro bono that are brought forth in this section show a growing specialization and expansion of private pro bono in India. The rise in the need for legal assistance can partly be attributed to the proliferation of the language of rights, and the expression of socioeconomic problems in legal terminology. For instance, the issue of poverty, which was earlier regarded as primarily a socioeconomic issue, is now being expressed as a legal problem, and access to justice (through mechanisms like pro bono) has come to be regarded as an essential tool to address it.[108]

CONCLUSION

An analysis of the two main kinds of private pro bono in India – that is, law firm and independent lawyers' pro bono (delineated in light of the difference–similarity, divergence–convergence, and challenges–opportunities matrix outlined above) – provides significant insights with respect to the following five aspects of pro bono in India.

Particular Traits and Scope

There are three distinctive traits of private pro bono in India: the division between transaction-based and litigation-based pro bono, a more holistic approach toward doing good that regards practices like philanthropy/CSR and pro bono as essentially similar and interlinked, and the wide usage of PIL for providing redress to disadvantaged groups. Further, due to encouragement from the state in the form of infrastructural support (including technological support and the national, state, and district legal services authorities networks) and incentives, litigation-based private pro bono in India seems to be developing along the lines of its preexisting and well-institutionalized public counterpart, that is, state legal aid. Since state legal aid is available not only to the economically disadvantaged but to a wide range of other vulnerable groups as well, the ambit of private pro bono in India is also set to similarly expand.

Global Convergences

To get a holistic picture of private pro bono in India, the particular traits of private pro bono have to be seen in relation to the convergence of the Indian private pro bono model with those of other countries. Depending upon the type of pro bono practices, convergences can be seen flowing from North to South, South to South, and South to North. In addition to the practices of Western countries, the Indian private pro bono model also has influences from other developing countries. For instance, the Supreme Court of India's guidelines on designation of senior advocates is based on the Nigerian guidelines. Another notable instance of an unconventional convergence is the close connection between CSR and pro bono that has been widely acknowledged in India, which is now gaining traction in the United States as well.

Motivations/Politics of Pro Bono

The recent emphasis on private pro bono in India is also reflective of underlying motivations of some of the key internal and external actors. For instance, the tussle between the government and the judiciary over judicial appointments, eligibility, and transparency is likely to have contributed to the inclusion of pro bono work as an important criterion in the Supreme Court of India's guidelines on designation of senior advocates, and the government of India's PBLSI. With respect to corporate law firm pro bono in particular, the impetus for institutionalization can be seen in part as a consequence of the pressure from domestic and foreign investors toward corporate governance reforms in general.

Transnational Elements

Although most of the pro bono work in India is domestically focused, significant transnational linkages have emerged in the form of cases involving multiple jurisdictions, such as the IJM's efforts at curbing cross-border sex trafficking, and preparation of research reports and memoranda by Indian pro bono lawyers using Indian laws and judgments as templates for law reform in other developing countries. Intermediary organizations, international development organizations, and pro bono–focused international foundations have come to play a major role in facilitating transnational pro bono.

Future Trends

Although the large-scale quantitative impact of private pro bono on the access-to-justice cause in India is not very significant at the moment, it is nevertheless growing. There is considerable scope for pro bono to supplement the state in its efforts to meet the rising need for legal assistance among the underserved. Web and mobile-based technologies, as well as innovations in service delivery including collaborations between various actors such as the state, law firms, independent lawyers, law schools, and civil society organizations are set to play a decisive role in its expansion. The overall impact of the legal assistance provided through private pro bono can be further augmented by combining it with other forms of assistance to form an integrated solution to meet the substantive justice needs of the society.

APPENDIX

List of Law Firms

1. AZB & Partners
2. J. Sagar Associates (JSA)
3. Trilegal
4. Shardul Amarchand Mangaldas & Co. (SAM)
5. Cyril Amarchand Mangaldas (CAM)
6. Khaitan & Co.
7. Luthra & Luthra Law Offices

8. Nishith Desai Associates
9. Talwar Thakore & Associates
10. Platinum Partners
11. Fox Mandal

NOTES

1. *World Economic Outlook Update*, International Monetary Fund (Jan. 2018), www.imf.org/en/Publications/WEO/Issues/2018/01/11/world-economic-outlook-update-january-2018 (last visited Oct. 4, 2020).
2. World Bank, Poverty and Shared Prosperity 2016: Taking on Inequality 40 (2016), https://openknowledge.worldbank.org/bitstream/handle/10986/25078/9781464809583.pdf (last visited Oct. 4, 2020).
3. The term "legal poverty" essentially implies legal marginalization or a lack of effective access to avenues of justice (including formal legal institutions) that is generally experienced by economically and socially marginalized groups. *See* George F. R. Ellis, *The Dimensions of Poverty*, 15 Soc. Indicators Res. 229, 245 (1984); Guillermo O'Donnell, *Reflections on Contemporary South American Democracies*, 33 J. Latin Am. Stud. 599, 601(2001).
4. *See, e.g.*, UNDP, Making the Law Work for Everyone (Vol. I), Report of the Commission on Legal Empowerment of the Poor (2008).
5. Since the early years of India's independence, the Indian government has focused on state-funded free legal aid as the primary tool to address the vast magnitude of legal poverty prevalent in the country and has since established an extensive network of state legal aid institutions throughout the length and breadth of the country.
6. *See* Dasra, Tipping the Scales: Strengthening Systems for Access to Justice in India 17 (2017), www.dasra.org/assets/uploads/resources/Tipping%20the%20Scales%20-%20Strengthening%20Systems%20for%20Access%20to%20Justice%20in%20India.pdf (last visited Oct. 4, 2020) (report analyzing the role of one hundred nonprofit organizations in promoting access to justice in India).
7. This categorization of Indian law firms is based on the rankings assigned by the RSG India Law Center, a legal strategy and research business. *See Top 40 Indian Law Firms*, RSG India Law Center, http://rsg-india.com/rankings (last visited Feb. 28, 2019) [hereinafter *RSG Ranking 2017*].
8. International Commission of Jurists, *For the Rule of the Law*, 10 ICJ Bull. 25 (1960).

9. *See, e.g.*, UNDP-GOI, ACCESS TO JUSTICE FOR MARGINALIZED PEOPLE (2018), http://doj.gov.in/other-programmes/access-justice-marginalized/access-justice-marginalized (last visited Feb. 28, 2019).
10. For an overview of the scope, eligibility criteria, and institutional structure for providing free state-sponsored legal services in India, see *Legal Aid*, NATIONAL PORTAL OF INDIA, https://archive.india.gov.in/citizen/lawnorder.php?id=10 (last visited Feb. 28, 2019).
11. *Id.* Free state legal aid in India is made available to a wide range of vulnerable groups in the country including women and children; members of Scheduled Caste/Scheduled Tribe; industrial workmen; victims of mass disaster (violence, flood, drought, earthquake, industrial disaster); disabled persons; persons in custody; persons whose annual income does not exceed INR 50,000; and victims of trafficking in human beings.
12. Legal Services Authorities Act § 12, 1987, No. 39, Acts of Parliament, 1987 (India).
13. *See* TNN, *Tele-Law Launched to Mainstream Legal Aid in Rural India*, TIMES INDIA, June 9, 2017.
14. The National Legal Services Authority regularly publishes state-wise statistics on the number of people belonging to the various vulnerable groups including victims of mass disaster, disabled persons, and human trafficking victims that have received free legal aid from the state. *See, e.g.*, NATIONAL LEGAL SERVICES AUTHORITY, NUMBER OF PERSONS BENEFITED THROUGH LEGAL SERVICES PROVIDED UNDER LEGAL SERVICES AUTHORITIES ACT 1987 APRIL 2017 TO MARCH 2018 (2018), https://nalsa.gov.in/sites/default/files/document/Legal_Service_Beneficiaries,April_2017_to_March_2018.pdf (last visited Feb. 28, 2019).
15. *Civil Legal Aid 101*, UNITED STATES DEPARTMENT OF JUSTICE, www.justice.gov/atj/civil-legal-aid-101 (last visited Feb. 28, 2019).
16. *See* Megha Bahl & Sharmila Purkayastha, *Condemn Continuing Attacks on Lawyers and Journalists in Bastar, Chhattisgarh*, PEOPLES UNION FOR DEMOCRATIC RIGHTS (Oct. 9, 2015), http://pudr.org/condemn-continuing-attacks-lawyers-and-journalists-bastar-chhattisgarh (last visited Oct. 4, 2020); Max Bearak, *Shoestring Legal Aid Group Helps Poor in Rural India*, N.Y. TIMES, Mar. 1, 2015.
17. Kian Ganz, *RTI Reveals: 1.3m Advocates; 1 in 300 Delhi-ites a Lawyer; Maharashtra Lawyers 'Richest'; Jharkand, Assam, J&K Fastest*, LEGALLYINDIA: BAR, BENCH & LITIGATION (Feb. 18, 2013), www.legallyindia.com/201302183448/Bar-Bench-Litigation/rti-reveals-number-of-lawyers-india (last visited Oct. 4, 2020).

18. For instance, in 2017 the total number of lawyers employed by the top forty law firms was slightly over six thousand. *See RSG Ranking 2017*, *supra* note 7.
19. *See generally* Marc Galanter & Nick Robinson, *Grand Advocates: The Traditional Elite Lawyers*, *in* THE INDIAN LEGAL PROFESSION IN THE AGE OF GLOBALIZATION: THE RISE OF THE CORPORATE LEGAL SECTOR AND ITS IMPACT ON LAWYERS AND SOCIETY 455 (Vikramaditya Khanna, David M. Trubek & David B. Wilkins eds., 2017) (delineating and explaining the role and significance of the elite litigators or the "Grand Advocates" in the Indian judicial system).
20. *See generally* Arpita Gupta, *Pro Bono and the Corporate Legal Sector in India*, *in* THE INDIAN LEGAL PROFESSION IN THE AGE OF GLOBALIZATION, *supra* note 19, at 275 (a qualitative empirical study of the pro bono practices of the top-tier law firms in India).
21. G. Oliver Koppell, *The Indian Lawyer as Social Innovator – Legal Aid in India*, 3 LAW & SOC'Y REV. 299, 299–300 (1969).
22. One of the key reasons attributed to the inadequacy of the quality of state legal aid services is the low remuneration paid to the lawyers serving on legal aid panels. *See* COMMONWEALTH HUMAN RIGHTS INITIATIVE (CHRI), HOPE BEHIND BARS? STATUS REPORT ON LEGAL AID FOR PERSONS IN CUSTODY, VOL. 1, at 5 (2018); *see also* Sharmeen Hakim, *Judge Hikes Lawyer's Fee from Rs 900 to Rs 10,000*, MUMBAI MIRROR, Mar. 22, 2017.
23. *See* COMMONWEALTH HUMAN RIGHTS INITIATIVE, *supra* note 22.
24. *See generally* Gupta, *supra* note 20.
25. *See RSG Ranking 2017*, *supra* note 7.
26. *America's Largest 350 Law Firms*, INTERNET LEGAL RESEARCH GROUP, www.ilrg.com/nlj250 (last visited Feb. 28, 2019).
27. *Baker McKenzie Announces Global Revenues of US$2.62 Billion*, BAKER MCKENZIE (AUG. 2016), www.bakermckenzie.com/en/newsroom/2016/08/global-revenue-results-fy16/ (last visited Feb. 28, 2019).
28. The potential size of the corporate legal market for FY 2017–18 is estimated to be around $1.3 billion. *See* Deepali Gupta, *Foreign Law Firms Averse to India Entry, Finds Study*, ECON. TIMES, Nov. 25, 2017.
29. Satya Prakash, Bhadra Sinha & Soibam Rocky Singh, *Waiting for Justice: 27 Million Cases Pending in Courts, 4500 Benches Empty*, HINDUSTAN TIMES, Nov. 15, 2016.
30. Press Trust of India, *India's Judge-Population Ratio Goes up Marginally*, ECON. TIMES, Jan. 7, 2018, https://economictimes.indiatimes.com/news/politics-and-nation/indias-judge-population-ratio-goes-up-marginally/articleshow/62400461.cms.
31. *Lok adalat* (the "people's court") is a kind of alternative dispute redressal mechanism through which disputes and cases pending in a court of law or at the prelitigation stage are sought to be settled

amicably. As per the Legal Services Authorities Act, *supra* note 12, *lok adalats* have statutory status, and "the award (decision) made by the lok adalats is deemed to be a decree of a civil court and is final and binding on all parties and no appeal against such an award lies before any court of law." *Lok Adalat*, NATIONAL LEGAL SERVICES AUTHORITY (NALSA), https://nalsa.gov.in/lok-adalat (last visited Oct. 4, 2020).

32. *See* NAINA KAPUR, UNITED NATIONS, SEXUAL HARASSMENT AND LAW REFORM IN INDIA 7 (2008).

33. Chapter II of the Bar Council of India rules are laid down in accordance with Section 49(1)(c) of the Advocates Act, 1961, No. 25, Acts of Parliament, 1961. The Indian legal system is based on British common law and the duty to provide free services to the poor as a professional norm for the lawyers can be traced back to the early fifteenth century. *See generally* PAUL BRAND, THE ORIGINS OF THE ENGLISH LEGAL PROFESSION (1992); *History of the Legal Profession*, BAR COUNCIL OF INDIA, www.barcouncilofindia.org (last visited Feb. 28, 2019).

34. Bar Council of India Rules pt. VI ch. II, 1975, Gazette of India, p. III sec. 4 (Sept. 6, 1975).

35. Professionalism is considered to be essentially intertwined with pro bono and to be an important element of the understanding and practice of pro bono in the United States. *See generally* Paul Kilpatrick Jr., *Professionalism and Pro Bono: A Natural and Necessary Partnership*, 28 GA. ST. B.J. 123 (1991); Lorne Sossin, *Public Interest, Professionalism and Pro Bono Publico*, 46 OSGOODE HALL L.J. 131 (2008).

36. *See generally* SANJAY AGARWAL, DAAN AND OTHER GIVING TRADITIONS IN INDIA (2010) (describing the various kinds of philanthropic practices traditionally prevalent in the Indian sub-continent); Elizabeth Branigan, John Godfrey & Sabith Khan, *Old and New Forms of Giving: Understanding Corporate Philanthropy in India*, 28 VOLUNTAS 672 (2017) (explaining the distinctive character of corporate philanthropy in India as an outcome of the interaction between historically prevalent philanthropic traditions and contemporary global business and philanthropic practices).

37. *See* Jane Buckingham, *Guilds and Governance in Ancient India: Historical Practices of Corporate Social Responsibility*, *in* MANAGING RESPONSIBLY: ALTERNATIVE APPROACHES TO CORPORATE MANAGEMENT AND GOVERNANCE 93 (2012).

38. This is evident from the large number of referral agreements between the Indian law firms and their foreign counterparts. *See generally* Christine Garg, *Affiliations: Foreign Law Firms' Path into India*, 56 N.Y.L. SCH. L. REV. 1162 (2012) (concluding that in the current regulatory environment where foreign lawyers are not allowed to practice law in India, the referral agreements between Indian and foreign law firms are the most viable options available to foreign

firms for conducting business in India, and out of the three kinds of affiliations between Indian and foreign law firms – ad hoc, surrogate, and "best friends" – best friends agreements are the most effective ones).

39. Gupta, *supra* note 20, at 281–83.
40. *Introduction*, SILF, www.silf.org.in/Introduction.php (last visited Oct. 4, 2020).
41. As a starting point, SILF issued pro bono guidelines for its member firms, asking them to perform at least 10 hours of pro bono work per week, which, according to SILF president Lalit Bhasin, most of the firms comply with. Gupta, *supra* note 20, at 282–83. In July 2016, SILF coorganized a panel discussion with the Thomas Reuters Foundation on "Law for Social Change: Advancing Pro Bono in India." *Law for Social Change: Advancing Pro Bono in India*, SILF, www.silf.org.in/events/97/Law-for-Social-Change–Advancing-Pro-Bono-in-India.htm (last visited Feb. 28, 2019).
42. Rebecca Furtado, *Advertising Policies of Law Firms in India*, iPLEADERS (Oct. 29, 2016), https://blog.ipleaders.in/advertising-policies-law-firms-india/ (last visited Oct. 4, 2020).
43. iProbono is a nonprofit organization registered with the UK Charity Commission and incorporated as an s.25 company (nonprofit company) in India. It is primarily a South Asia–focused organization and has field offices in London, New Delhi, Dhaka, Colombo, and Islamabad. Its core objective is to connect marginalized people in need of legal assistance with its network of lawyers (law firms and independent lawyers). *About Us*, iPROBONO, www.i-probono.com/about-us (last visited Feb. 28, 2019). TrustLaw is the global pro bono program of the Thomson Reuters Foundation, an independent charity registered in the United States and United Kingdom. It connects lawyers with NGOs and social enterprises in need of legal assistance. The program operates in over 170 countries, including India. Some of the largest Indian law firms like AZB & Partners, Luthra & Luthra, and JSA Advocates & Solicitors are its members. *About Us*, TRUSTLAW, www.trust.org/trustlaw/ (last visited Oct. 4, 2020). LexMundi Pro Bono Foundation is a US-based nonprofit corporation that connects its member law firms with social entrepreneurs in need of pro bono legal assistance. Shardul Amarchand Mangaldas & Co is LexMundi's Indian member firm. *About Us*, LEXMUNDI PRO BONO FOUNDATION, www.lexmundiprobono.org/lexmundiprobono/About_Us.asp (last visited Oct. 4, 2020). ProBono India is a nonprofit organization based in Surat, Gujarat. It collaborates with legal aid clinics of law schools in India, lawyers/firms, NGOs, and national and state legal aid societies in India for the purposes of promoting the outreach and depth of legal aid in India. *See About Us*, PROBONO INDIA, http://probono-india.in/about-probono-india.php (last visited Oct. 4, 2020).

44. *Compensation for Akash: Bringing Hope for Male Child Survivors of Sexual Assault*, IPROBONO (Oct. 2016), https://iProbono.com/case-study-detail?id=106 (last visited Feb. 28, 2019).
45. Apart from the pressure from global law firms seeking to do business in the growing economy of India, foreign bars like the American Bar Association (ABA), and the portion of the Indian bar that stands to benefit from it, this push to liberalize the corporate legal sector in India is largely an outcome of the incumbent government's reliance on incoming foreign direct investment (FDI) as a crucial mechanism for sustaining and accelerating the country's growth. The decision to allow foreign lawyers and law firms to operate in India is based on the belief that the presence of foreign firms in the country will boost foreign investors' confidence, and this will in turn significantly increase FDI in India. *See* MINISTRY OF LAW AND JUSTICE, GOVERNMENT OF INDIA, LIBERALISATION MEET MINUTES, http://s3.documentcloud.org/documents/3954287/Law-Ministry-Liberalisation-Meet-Minutes-August.pdf (last visited Oct. 4, 2020) [hereinafter LIBERALISATION MEET MINUTES].
46. LIBERALISATION MEET MINUTES, *supra* note 45.
47. *Id.*; *see also* Samawaya Rautray, *Foreign Law Firms Case: Will Step in if BCI Fails to Frame Rules, Says Center*, ECON. TIMES, Jan. 11, 2018.
48. LIBERALISATION MEET MINUTES, *supra* note 45.
49. *Liberalisation: SILF Submits 52-Page Vision About How Legal Market Should Open in Phases*, LEGALLYINDIA (Aug. 24, 2016), www.legallyindia.com/law-firms/liberalisation-silf-submits-52-page-vision-about-how-legal-market-should-open-in-phases (last visited Oct. 4, 2020). The proposed phased approach toward liberalization of the Indian legal market draws heavily from the Chinese and Singaporean models. The recommendation to permit the foreign law firms to operate only in the special economic zones (SEZs) of the country in the initial phase is based upon the former, and the proposal to permit collaboration between the foreign law firms and their Indian counterparts only during the subsequent phases of liberalization is based upon the latter. *See* LIBERALISATION MEET MINUTES, *supra* note 45; *see also* Huang Liyue, *The Legal Service Market in China: Implementation of China's GATS Commitments and Foreign Legal Services in China*, 5 TSINGHUA CHINA L. REV. 29 (2012) (examining the opening up of the legal services market in China to foreign legal services providers in light of China's commitments to WTO GATS).
50. A.K. Balaji v. Government of India, AIR 2012 Mad. 124.
51. *See 31 Foreign Law Firms Deny All Allegations Made by AK Balaji*, BAR & BENCH (Aug. 1, 2011), https://barandbench.com/31-foreign-law-firms-deny-all-allegations-made-ak-balaji/ (last visited Oct. 4, 2020).
52. *See Pro Bono Legal Services Initiative*, DEPARTMENT OF JUSTICE (MINISTRY OF LAW AND JUSTICE), http://doj.gov.in/page/about-pr

o-bono (last visited Oct. 4, 2020) [hereinafter PBLSI]. The PBLSI is an outcome of the long-term collaboration between the Indian government and the UNDP. Over the years, the UNDP has worked closely with the Indian government in formulating and implementing a number of state-led access-to-justice initiatives and programs under the aegis of the National Legal Services Authority. *See* GOI-UNDP, INCREASING ACCESS TO JUSTICE FOR MARGINALIZED PEOPLE PROJECT (2017), www.in.undp.org/content/india/en/home/operations/projects/democratic_governance/access_to_justice.html (last visited Oct. 4, 2020).

53. *See List of Registered Lawyers in Pro Bono Legal Services as on 29.06.2018*, DEPARTMENT OF JUSTICE (MINISTRY OF LAW AND JUSTICE), http://doj.gov.in/page/list-registered-lawyers-pro-bono-legal-services-29062018 (last visited Oct. 4, 2020).
54. The Advocates Act, *supra* note 33, provides for the establishment of the Bar Council of India under § 4, the apex body that regulates legal practice and legal education in the country, as well as the individual state bar councils under § 3 for different states that enroll advocates on their rolls.
55. *See Encouraging Pro Bono Legal Services*, DEPARTMENT OF JUSTICE (MINISTRY OF LAW AND JUSTICE), http://doj.gov.in/page/about-pro-bono (last visited Oct. 4, 2020).
56. These guidelines are a part of the Supreme Court of India's judgment on Indira Jaising v. Supreme Court of India (2017) 9 SCC 766, alleging that the process for designating senior advocate status in India was flawed and arbitrary, and petitioning the court to intervene to make the process more transparent and fair. The court in its judgment perused the senior advocate selection criteria prevalent in other jurisdictions, such as the United Kingdom, Nigeria, and Australia, and issued a detailed set of guidelines to be uniformly applicable in the Supreme Court and the high courts with respect to the appointment of senior advocates. SUPREME COURT OF INDIA, JUDGMENT 12 OCT. 2017 (2017), https://main.sci.gov.in/supremecourt/2015/21817/21817_2015_Judgement_12-Oct-2017.pdf (last visited Oct. 4, 2020).
57. *Id.* at 23.
58. *See* David M. Trubek, *Scan Globally, Reinvent Locally: Can We Overcome the Barriers to Using the Horizontal Learning Method in Law and Development?*, 258 NAGOYA UNIV. J.L. POL. 11 (2014) (explaining the importance of horizontal learning, i.e., learning from their peers, for developing countries and the ways in which this process can be further fostered).
59. In the two cases of Supreme Court Advocates on Record Association and another v. Union of India, AIR 1994 SC 268, and In re Presidential Reference, AIR 1999 SC 1, the Court underscored judicial independence as an essential feature of the Constitution of

India and created the Collegium System under which the chief justice of India along with the four senior-most judges of the Supreme Court appoint/elevate judges and lawyers to the Supreme Court and transfer judges of the Supreme Court and high courts. The "judge appoints judge" or the Collegium System was sought to be replaced by the National Judicial Appointments Commission Act 2014, whereby a constitutional body consisting of judicial and non-judicial members (minister of law and justice and two eminent persons) was sought to be created for recommending appointments and transfers in the higher judiciary (Supreme Court and the high courts). *See* National Judicial Appointments Commission Bill, 2014, No. 96-C, Acts of Parliament, 2014, www.prsindia.org/sites/default/files/bill_files/National_Judicial_bill_as_passed_by_LS.pdf (last visited Oct. 4, 2020).

60. Supreme Court Advocates-on-Record Assn. v. Union of India (2016) 5 SCC 1.

61. Sanjeev K. Ahuja, *Poor to Get Free-of-Cost Legal Aid, Govt Urges Lawyers to Offer Pro Bono Service*, HINDUSTAN TIMES, Apr. 21, 2017, www.hindustantimes.com/india-news/poor-to-get-free-of-cost-legal-aid-govt-urges-lawyers-to-offer-pro-bono-service/story-Szq2i16wd8eo9L8s789IRL.html (last visited Oct. 4, 2020).

62. PBLSI, *supra* note 52.

63. *Id.*

64. *See generally* INDIA TRANSFORMED: 25 YEARS OF ECONOMIC REFORMS (Rakesh Mohan ed., 2017) (providing a comprehensive overview of economic reforms in India since 1990); *see also* Alka Sapat, *Privatization Strategies Adopted for Public Sector Reform in India: Determinants and Constraints*, *in* ADMINISTRATIVE REFORM AND NATIONAL ECONOMIC DEVELOPMENT (2017) (analyzing India's economic liberalization reforms as an outcome of various internal and external factors and arguing that strategies like green-field privatization and marketization have been particularly favored).

65. *See* Upendra Baxi, *Taking Suffering Seriously: Social Action Litigation in the Supreme Court of India*, 4 THIRD WORLD LEGAL STUD. 107 (1985).

66. The lawyers at medium and small law firms also engage in pro bono and other forms of public service. This engagement lacks structure, unlike with their larger counterparts, and it is difficult to make generalizable statements about their pro bono practice as a group. However, as is evident from iProbono case studies, intermediary organizations are playing an important role in increasing their involvement in the country's pro bono movement by matching them with clients they can service on a pro bono basis. *See, e.g.*, *Right to Housing: 14 Homeless Families Get Relief*, IPROBONO (Aug. 2017), www.iProbono.com/case-study-detail?id=126 (last visited Feb. 28, 2019) (noting that iProbono

engaged Robin Dua, a partner at Dua Associates, in a housing rights matter).

67. The BCI circular of 1997 makes it mandatory for all law schools in India to have compulsory courses on clinical legal education. Bar Council of India, Circular No. 4/1997 (Oct. 21, 1997). Although a practical component in these courses is not mandatory, a number of law schools have started legal aid clinics. These clinics mostly undertake activities like legal literacy and awareness camps, legislative advocacy, and organizing clinical workshops. Recognizing the potential of law students in furthering the access to justice cause in India, the National Legal Services Authority envisaged an important role for legal aid clinics. NATIONAL LEGAL SERVICES AUTHORITY, NALSA – A QUINQUENNIAL VISION AND STRATEGY (2009). In some of the states, such as Rajasthan, the state legal services authority has issued directives asking the district legal services authorities to collaborate with legal aid clinics in the law schools. Yet, the ground-level functioning of these clinics leaves much to be desired. For instance, unlike the United States, law students in India are not authorized to represent clients in court even under the supervision of faculty or lawyers. Therefore, their legal aid work in these clinics is mostly confined to undertaking legal awareness projects. Although, with the rise of National Law Schools and private law schools, law school legal aid is receiving greater impetus, studies show that in the majority of the remaining law schools in the country, legal aid clinics are not functioning well. *See* GOI & UNDP, A STUDY OF LAW SCHOOL BASED LEGAL SERVICES CLINICS (2011), www.undp.org/content/dam/india/docs/a_study_of_law_school_based_legal_services_clinics.pdf (last visited Oct. 4, 2020).

68. This includes both pro bono and low bono work. For instance, AZB & Partners report doing a large amount of work for free or "deeply discounted rates for not-for-profits and for-profits working in socially relevant areas."

69. Indian law firms usually consider giving advice to the government, such as advice on WTO matters where India is a party to a dispute, as pro bono work. It might be contested that the government does not fall under the category of poor or underserved, and thus, the advice given to the government should not be counted as pro bono. However, in the Indian context where the government is the largest welfare provider of food, education, and health, this might be considered as pro bono so long as the costs of incurring expensive legal advice is saved and limited state resources are diverted toward welfare activities. *See* Gupta, *supra* note 20, at 286–87.

70. Contract drafting is the most common kind of transactional work that law firms perform. Examples of contracts that law firms reported preparing for their pro bono clients include employment contracts (JSA's assistance to Noora Health), standardized forms (Trilegal prepared for

Operation Smile to be used for the surgical operations carried out by the organization in their camps), and trust deeds (Trilegal assisted the World Resources Institute with formation and registration of the India Resources Trust).

71. The major pro bono clients for these kinds of services are nonprofit foundations and social enterprises. Depending on the client's needs and the advising firm's specialization, the advice can vary from a single matter such as choice of incorporation to a range of matters. For instance, Nishith Desai Associates, with its specialty in tax law, mention providing comprehensive advice to nonprofits on setup, structuring, architectural design, and tax advice, such as income tax exemptions, FCRA compliance, and leveraging international tax treaties.

72. Providing pro bono legal services to the socially oriented businesses and start-ups also has future fee-generating prospects for the firm. Gupta, *supra* note 20, at 285.

73. Social businesses or enterprises are organizations that seek to balance profit motive with social impact. According to the Social Enterprise Alliance, they are "organizations that address a basic unmet need or solve a social problem through a market-driven approach." These social enterprises are primarily inspired by the Silicon Valley innovation-focused entrepreneurship model. Innovations in areas like technology, procurement, production, and finance form the basis of these social enterprises. The most well-known examples of social enterprises are microfinance institutions. *What Is Social Enterprise?*, SOCIAL ENTERPRISE ALLIANCE, https://socialenterprise.us/about/social-enterprise/ (last visited Oct. 4, 2020).

74. For instance, AZB & Partners is known for its social sector practice, especially in the area of microfinance. It works closely with the Grameen Foundation, and the firm's role is acknowledged in the Foundation's annual reports. It has advised not only large microfinance institutions like Grameen but also small nonprofits like Cashpor Microfinance Company and Friends of Women's World Banking. Trilegal reported assisting social enterprises like the Aavishkar India Micro Venture Capital Fund, which provides micro equity funds to low-income businesses to become commercially successful. JSA reported providing legal assistance to enterprises like Plastics for Change and Krishi Star (which works to tackle poverty among small farmers by giving them access to larger margins through direct purchase).

75. The following illustrative list of law firms and the foundations they have advised on a pro bono basis shows the variety of social and economic causes that the law firms contribute to indirectly: Trilegal: eGovernments Foundation (works for promoting democracy), Akshara Foundation (educating underprivileged children), Drishtee Foundation (involved in livelihood development in rural

areas), JSA: Genesis Foundation (providing critical medical intervention for children from orphanages and from underprivileged families), The/Nudge Foundation (providing entrepreneurial guidance to combat poverty), Noora Health (disseminating high-impact health skills to patients and their families), Luthra & Luthra SRIMS Free Ambulance Service, Advanced Nursing Foundation (promoting nursing education, training, and research), Lotus Flower Trust (engaged in providing assistance to the underprivileged for establishing shelters, skill centers, and schools in remote villages of India), Shardul Amarchand & Mangaldas: Gram Vaani (a rural empowerment initiative), Ashoka Foundation (encouraging social entrepreneurship), and Digital Greens (global development organization working to combat poverty and malnourishment among small farmers).

76. For instance, AZB & Partners reports assisting Amnesty International and South East Asia Investigations into Social and Humanitarian Activities (SISHA); Trilegal-assisted organizations like International Federation of the Red Cross and Red Crescent Societies (IFRC); and JSA-assisted organizations like Justice Ventures International (JVI), Missing Links Trust, and Inclusion Ghana.

77. It must be noted that it is difficult to assess the social impact even of organizations engaged in various social causes. Though a number of impact assessment tools have been developed, there is no consensus as yet on their efficacy. *See generally* OECD, POLICY BRIEF ON SOCIAL IMPACT MEASUREMENT FOR SOCIAL ENTERPRISES – POLICIES FOR SOCIAL ENTREPRENEURSHIP (2010).

78. The social enterprise sector in India is receiving impetus and support not only from big law firms but from other venues as well. For instance, there is a recent rise of boutique firms like Impact Law Ventures–Blue Dot Law that charge very low rates (low bono) for their legal services to start-ups in the social sector. Another notable example is the entrepreneurship cell at the Jindal Global University that seeks to provide professional law firm–quality pro bono legal support to start-ups and individual grassroots entrepreneurs who are not in a position to afford such services.

79. *See Ashoka India: A Roundtable Pro Bono Legal Workshop*, IPROBONO (May 2016), https://i-probono.com/case-study-detail?id=99 (last visited Feb. 28, 2019).

80. Shardul Amarchand Mangaldas & Co was honored at the Seventh Annual Lex Mundi Pro Bono Foundation Awards 2016 for its role in supporting social entrepreneurs. JSA has been nominated for various categories of awards such as the Domestic Law Firm of the Year (2016) and the Impact Award (2017) by TrustLaw.

81. *See* Gupta, *supra* note 20, at 282.

82. JSA, Corporate Social Responsibility & Pro Bono Document (on file with author).

83. It must be noted that CSR in India too has both historical-domestic and modern-transnational dimensions. *See, e.g.*, Buckingham, *supra* note 37 (discussing practices akin to the modern-day concept of CSR by *srenis*, the merchant guilds, in early India).
84. Some of the key characteristics generally associated with a socially responsible law firm include an inclusive work environment, sustainability, community outreach including pro bono and CSR, and ethical criteria such as professional conduct. *See generally* JUSTICE ADDA, CAMBRIDGE PRO BONO PROJECT, THE HANDBOOK ON DESIGNING SOCIALLY RESPONSIBLE LAW FIRMS IN INDIA (2018).
85. The mandatory CSR requirement in India is part of the broader corporate governance reforms that have been underway since the country's economic liberalization in the 1990s. The corporate governance reforms are considered to be crucial for expanding the country's domestic and foreign investor base. *See* Afra Afsharipour & Shruti Rana, *The Emergence of New Corporate Social Responsibility Regimes in China and India*, 14 UC DAVIS BUS. L.J. 175, 209 (2014). Apart from the corporate governance angle, the government's emphasis on CSR is also reflective of its intention to make the private sector share with it the responsibility of facilitating more equitable development in the country, *see* MINISTRY OF CORPORATE AFFAIRS, GOVERNMENT OF INDIA, CORPORATE SOCIAL RESPONSIBILITY VOLUNTARY GUIDELINES 2009 5 (2009), www.mca.gov.in/Ministry/latestnews/CSRVoluntaryGuidelines24dec2009.pdf (last visited Feb. 28, 2019).
86. Email correspondence with JSA representative.
87. N. R. Madhava Menon, *Serving the Justice Needs of the Poor*, HINDU, Dec. 3, 2013, www.thehindu.com/opinion/lead/serving-the-justice-needs-of-the-poor/article5415018.ece (last visited Oct. 4, 2020). The CSR funds are funds that certain corporations in India are required to invest in CSR activities (such as environmental protection and social welfare) under s. 135(1) of the Companies Act 2013.
88. Danish Khan, *Bharti Enterprises' Philanthropic Arm Facilitates Release of Undertrials on Bail from Jails in Delhi–NCR*, ECON. TIMES, May 23, 2016, https://economictimes.indiatimes.com/news/politics-and-nation/bharti-enterprises-philanthropic-arm-facilitates-release-of-undertrials-on-bail-from-jails-in-delhincr/articleshow/52397186.cms (last visited Oct. 4, 2020).
89. Gupta, *supra* note 20, at 287–89.
90. Julianne Hill, *For More Good: Law Firms Find Other Ways to Provide Service to Society*, ABA J. (2017), www.abajournal.com/magazine/article/law_firm_pro_bono_alternatives?icn=most_read (last visited Oct. 4, 2020).
91. Well-known senior advocates such as Dushyant Dave, Salman Khurshid, Ram Jethmalani, Kapil Sibal, Mukul Rohatgi, K. K. Venugopal, and C. A. Sundaram regularly appear in pro bono cases.

See Prachi Shrivastava, *Which 9 Top Lawyers Easily Charge Rs 15+ Lakh per Hearing? 42 Delhi Seniors' Fees Revealed*, LEGALLY INDIA: BAR, BENCH & LITIGATION (Sept. 8, 2015), www.legallyindia.com/the-bench-and-the-bar/revealed-delhi-rsquo-s-top-advocates-won-rsquo-t-even-touch-your-case-for-less-than-rs-5-lakh-20150908-6555 (last visited Oct. 4, 2020). The number or percentage of pro bono cases that each senior advocate appears in varies. PIL-focused lawyers like Colin Gonsalves, M. C. Mehta, and Prashant Bhushan take a majority of their cases on a pro bono basis. For instance, Bhushan stated in an interview that, on average, he appears in 75 percent of cases on a pro bono basis, and for the other 25 percent he charges merely 5 percent of the regular charges (low bono). Rashmee Roshan Lall, *Citizen Anna and Agent Prashant*, TIMES INDIA, Apr. 10, 2011, https://timesofindia.indiatimes.com/home/sunday-toi/special-report/Citizen-Anna-and-agent-Prashant/articleshow/7931100.cms?referral=PM (last visited Oct. 4, 2020).

92. *Safeguarding the Right to Shelter for East Kidwai Nagar Residents*, IPROBONO (May 2017), www.i-probono.com/case-study-detail?id=117 (last visited Feb. 28, 2019).
93. PUCL v. Union of India and Others (2003) 2 SCR 1136.
94. *See Meet the Top Lawyers Fighting for Rohingyas in Supreme Court: A Myanmar-Born Padma Awardee, an IIT-Bombay Grad*, INDIA TODAY, Sept. 21, 2017, www.indiatoday.in/india/story/meet-the-top-lawyers-fighting-for-rohingya-muslims-in-supreme-court-1049624-2017-09-21 (last visited Oct. 4, 2020).
95. *See* SUPREME COURT OF INDIA, JUDGMENT 12 OCT. 2017 (2017), *supra* note 56, at 23. Notably, the Supreme Court of India can also use pro bono as a tool to punish advocates for contempt of court by requiring them to do mandatory pro bono for a certain period of time. *See* LAW COMMISSION OF INDIA, REPORT NO. 266 25–26 (2017) (In R. K. Anand v. Registrar, Delhi High Court, AIR 2013 SC 670, the Supreme Court directed the contemnor to do only pro bono work for those in need for one year and prohibited him from doing any paid work for this time).
96. PBLSI, *supra* note 52.
97. *Id.*
98. *International Justice Mission, India: Rescuing and Rehabilitating Victims of Sex Trafficking*, IPROBONO (Jan. 2014), www.i-probono.com/case-study-detail?id=25 (last visited Feb. 28, 2019).
99. *Nyaya Bandhu Mobile Application*, PRO BONO LEGAL SERVICES, DEPARTMENT OF JUSTICE, MINISTRY OF LAW AND JUSTICE, GOVERNMENT OF INDIA, www.probono-doj.in/home/index (last visited Oct. 4, 2020).
100. The PIL movement that began in India in 1981 differs from its American counterpart on a number of grounds, including the *locus*

standi requirements. Delineating the significant differences between the two, Baxi coined the term "social action litigation" for the Indian version. *See* Baxi, *supra* note 65.

101. For a detailed distinction between the two strata of cause lawyers in India, see Jayanth K. Krishnan, *Transgressive Cause Lawyering in the Developing World: The Case of India*, *in* THE WORLDS CAUSE LAWYERS MAKE 349 (Austin Sarat & Stuart Scheingold eds., 2005).

102. It must be noted that PIL in India is a deeply contested topic, particularly with respect to its merits versus drawbacks. *See generally* Surya Deva, *Public Interest Litigation in India: A Critical Review*, 1 CIVIL J.Q. 19 (2009). Criticizing the motivations of the elite lawyers who engage in PIL, Dezalay and Garth see the use of PIL by these lawyers as a tool for gaining social and professional credibility. *See* Yves Dezalay & Bryant G. Garth, *Lawyers as Political Champions against Authoritarianism-Relative Successes Exemplified by the Philippines and India*, *in* ASIAN LEGAL REVIVALS: LAWYERS IN SHADOW OF EMPIRE 188 (2014).

103. Bandhua Mukti Morcha v. Union of India and others, AIR 1984 SC 802.

104. Sunil Batra (II) v. Delhi Administration, AIR 1980 SC 1579.

105. Vishakha v. State of Rajasthan, AIR 1997 SC 3011.

106. Nilabati Behera v. State of Orissa, AIR 1993 SC 1960.

107. Decisions of the Indian Supreme Court (especially PIL cases) are routinely cited in many other foreign courts, including courts in other South Asian and African countries. For instance, Indian Supreme Court judgments are often cited by South African courts, including the Constitutional Court of South Africa. *See* Andrea Lollini, *The South African Constitutional Court Experience: Reasoning Patterns Based on Foreign Law*, 8 UTRECHT L. REV. 55, 79 (2012); *see also* Malathi Nayak, *Indian Case Law sets Precedent for Commonwealth Countries*, LIVEMINT (Dec. 12, 2008), www.livemint.com/Politics/SS2mCO9tbaCJLUMqxR3uRO/Indian-case-law-sets-precedent-for-Commonwealth-countries.html (last visited Oct. 4, 2020). For an analysis of the importance of the Indian PIL model for providing recourse to disadvantaged groups in other developing countries, see generally Zachary Holladay, *Public Interest Litigation in India as a Paradigm for Developing Nations*, 19 IND. J. GLOBAL LEGAL STUD. 555 (2012); Wouter Vandenhole, *Human Rights Law, Development and Social Action Litigation in India*, 2 ASIA-PACIFIC J. HUM. RTS. L. 136 (2002).

108. *See, e.g.*, MAGDALENA SEPÚLVEDA CARMONA & KATE DONALD, ACCESS TO JUSTICE FOR PERSONS LIVING IN POVERTY: A HUMAN RIGHTS APPROACH (2014).

CHAPTER SIXTEEN

"PRO BONO" IN SINGAPORE: IMPORTING, ADOPTING, TRANSFORMING

Helena Whalen-Bridge and Robert Granfield

INTRODUCTION

Singapore is a common-law country in Southeast Asia known for its impressive economic development, the presence of government in many aspects of daily life, and its no-nonsense approach to crime and criminal procedure.[1] Lawyers, referred to as advocates and solicitors,[2] are not self-regulated, although they carry out most stages of the disciplinary process. The Law Society advocates for lawyers' interests, and it has statutory duties such as maintaining and improving standards of conduct and learning, and assisting the public in matters related to law.[3] Admission of domestic lawyers to the Singapore bar is overseen by the Supreme Court, and the main subsidiary legislation for professional conduct, the Legal Profession (Professional Conduct) Rules 2015, is overseen by a multistakeholder body known as the Professional Conduct Council (PCC).[4] In Singapore, the government is prominent in the law landscape,[5] and it plays a major role in access to justice by funding legal aid, and together with Singapore organizations such as the Law Society Pro Bono Services,[6] promoting and encouraging pro bono.

This chapter addresses the emergence and development of Singapore pro bono, understood to mean the provision of free legal services to poor or vulnerable persons in which the cost is assumed by lawyers or law firms. Although not referred to as "pro bono," lawyer-organized legal services have been provided to poor litigants in civil and criminal matters, for example, when lawyers organized the Criminal Legal Aid

Scheme (CLAS) in 1985. Building on this foundation, pro bono was at first an imported concept in the early 2000s, but it became an enthusiastic adoption that ultimately transformed how many law firms view legal services to poor or vulnerable persons. Using data from media sources including newspapers and legal periodicals, as well as statements from and interviews with representative stakeholders within the Singaporean legal community, we review key historical developments in the organization and practice of pro bono, and then address current practices. The interviews undertaken for this chapter were conducted by the first coauthor in 2018, and while the smallness of the interview set means it is not a representative sample, the interviews highlight aspects of how pro bono is currently viewed and practiced in Singapore.

"Pro Bono": The Concept and the Phrase

Prior research by the first coauthor regarding use of the term "pro bono" in Singapore suggests that, broadly speaking, public discussion of indigent representation developed in three stages.[7] The first stage, prior to the passage of the seminal Legal Aid and Advice Ordinance in 1956, was characterized by introduction of the then-novel idea of government-funded indigent representation, coupled with a charitable provision of legal services by lawyers. The second stage was the passing of the Legal Aid and Advice Ordinance in 1956 and the subsequent failure to implement broad-based criminal legal aid. During this stage, non-state-funded indigent representation continued to be discussed as if it were a voluntary, charitable act, and the concepts of access to justice and pro bono were not referred to. The third stage, the rise of pro bono terminology and conceptualization of a professional obligation, followed amendments to the Legal Aid and Advice Act that removed the possibility of criminal legal aid from the regulatory scheme. This stage was characterized first by increasing discussions of access to justice, initially in connection with the courts, and then pro bono and access to justice, in connection with lawyers.

Prior to the 2000s, the main phrases used to describe representation of indigent persons in Singapore were "legal aid,"[8] "free,"[9] and "voluntary lawyer."[10] After decades of this usage, public discourse in Singapore shifted to "pro bono," at first preceded by and then coupled with "access to justice." As reflected in the main Singapore newspaper, *The Straits Times*, the term "pro bono" appears to have been a direct import from the United States. "Pro bono" had been used in Singapore to indicate the provision of free services of a nonlegal sort, but the first

The Straits Times article to use the term in connection with indigent legal services appears to have been in 1978.[11] The content of the article suggests the large degree to which the phrase was imported, as the article did not report on activity in Singapore but rather on the state of legal practice in the United States. The article noted that the US legal profession had been "taking it on the chin" because of criticism of lawyerly greed and erosion of protective regulation such as advertising bans. The article also reported on a *Washington Post* survey of large law firms indicating that they did fewer pro bono cases than in the 1960s and 1970s.

After 1978, *The Straits Times* did not use "pro bono" in connection with lawyers until 1990, and again it described activities in the United States – but this time pro bono was getting closer to home. The article noted that a Singapore lawyer practicing in the United States had won an award for work with the underprivileged in the state of North Carolina.[12] The lawyer, Madam Maureen Chee Man Lin, credited her "soft heart" to her father, a doctor who used to treat poor people for free. Referring to the basis for pro bono, she stated that "lawyers should first serve justice and not think of the fees."[13]

In 1995, pro bono made another sporadic appearance, in comments made by then Malaysia Deputy Prime Minister Datuk Seri Anwar Ibrahim to the ASEAN Law Association General Assembly. The prime minister noted that lawyers should do more pro bono work and make legal services more accessible to less affluent persons.[14]

Pro bono did not appear again in *The Straits Times* until 2000, but this time it was applied directly to Singapore lawyers as well as access to justice. Speaking at the Opening of the Legal Year, then newly elected Law Society President R. Palakrishnan highlighted recent Law Society programs, including a new scheme in the Law Society to connect younger lawyers with more experienced lawyers, a panel of mediators and arbitrators to complement the services offered by the Singapore International Arbitration Centre and Singapore Mediation Centre, and expansion of CLAS.[15] He stated that the legal profession had been "unique" in its willingness to engage in pro bono work for the less privileged, and they "shall continue to do so in our mission to ensure that access to justice is not denied to the poor."[16] Palakrishnan specialized in criminal litigation and in fact had been appointed senior counsel on January 6, 2001,[17] the first criminal defense specialist to receive this recognition.[18] Like other criminal litigators, Palakrishnan would have been familiar with the number of unrepresented criminal defendants in Singapore courts.[19]

This use of the term "pro bono" is significant because it was the first time pro bono was applied to the Singapore context. Because the phrase appeared together with "access to justice," this signaled that pro bono was connected to the legal profession's obligations regarding poor and vulnerable clients, a change from the previous conception of charitable activity undertaken purely by choice.

The next article to address pro bono was published in July 2003, and it addressed a senior counsel's representation of a former nominated member of Parliament in order to assist him with appealing a bankruptcy judgment.[20] The lawyer, Jimmy Yim, viewed the move as a good public cause, stating that the client "is one of the icons of the industry, a public figure who had done so much but has now fallen on hard times."[21] Starting in 2003, the term "pro bono" was invoked on a yearly basis, in ever increasing numbers.[22]

The concept of pro bono thus appears to have been imported from the United States, but outside forces have not played a major role in pro bono development. Unlike some other jurisdictions,[23] international law firms have not had a substantial impact on domestic pro bono. International and some Singapore law firms formed the Joint International Pro Bono Committee, an informal group that acts as a clearinghouse for legal advice and representation for international community organizations based in Singapore, but matchups are geared toward corporate and transactional matters.[24] Persons interviewed for this chapter noted that some nongovernmental organizations, such as Humanitarian Organisation for Migration Economics (HOME)[25] and Transient Workers Count Too (TWC2),[26] were instrumental in connecting them with pro bono clients and relevant information, but these organizations are primarily local in nature.[27] Foreign lawyers make considerable contributions to Law Society Pro Bono Services projects, and they are allowed to assist the Legal Aid Bureau with certain out-of-court matters,[28] but they are not able to appear in Singapore courts or practice in the domestic law areas of criminal law and family law[29] that poorer clients need assistance with,[30] although these restrictions do not necessarily distinguish Singapore from other jurisdictions. In 2013, the minister for law promulgated rules which allowed a "solicitor" without a current practicing certificate to provide certain "permitted pro bono legal services" that otherwise would have violated the Legal Profession Act,[31] but this permission does not extend to persons other than this kind of solicitor.[32] Fluency in languages other than English can also be a limiting factor for foreign lawyers.[33] These restrictions do not mean that foreign law firms cannot support access to justice in ways other than direct representation,[34] and some law firms, a few of which had a license to practice limited areas of Singapore law that would expire in a period of years,[35] have contributed financial support for pro bono, for example, in donations to Law Society Pro Bono Services[36] and to the Asia Pro Bono Conference when held in Singapore in 2014.[37] In Singapore, however, pro bono has developed primarily as a local phenomenon.

Pro Bono and Legal Aid in Singapore

Pro bono in Singapore is very much tied to the country's approach to legal aid. The main legislative vehicle for legal aid in Singapore was and continues to be the Legal Aid and Advice Act.[38] Originally passed in 1956 as the Legal Aid and Advice Ordinance while Singapore was still a Crown colony,[39] the Ordinance provided for legal aid in civil cases[40] and criminal cases,[41] as well as legal advice.[42] Per normal procedure, the Act was to be implemented on dates to be publicized in the *Gazette*.[43] Parts I, III, IV, and V were brought into effect between 1957 and 1958, but Part II on criminal legal aid was never implemented.[44] After independence in 1965, Singapore maintained that the survival of the nation had to take precedence over all other issues.[45] In 1983, then acting minister for social affairs, Dr. Ahmad Mattar, stated that "all available resources were needed to build the nation during the late 50s and 60s,"[46] although that does not explain why civil legal aid was implemented but criminal legal aid was not. Earlier on there were concerns about the pace of legal aid implementation and associated costs,[47] but after those were no longer relevant, the primary reason articulated for nonimplementation of criminal legal aid was the perceived conflict between expending considerable public funds to investigate crime and prosecute a criminal defendant, while simultaneously providing the defendant with the means to avoid prosecution.

This perceived conflict was discussed in the most detail in 1995, when the Legal Aid and Advice Act underwent substantial amendment, including the deletion of criminal legal aid. The Legal Aid and Advice Act 1995 repealed the 1985 version of the Legal Aid and Advice Act, which contained provisions on criminal legal aid,[48] and the Legal Aid and Advice Act that replaced it did not include criminal legal aid.[49] During the Second Reading of the Legal Aid and Advice Bill in 1995, then minister for law, Professor S. Jayakumar, stated that Part II of the existing Act was never brought into operation and was being deleted "because the policy of the Government is not to grant legal aid in criminal cases except for cases involving capital punishment."[50]

Speaking in support of the Bill, then-nominated member of parliament, Associate Professor Walter Woon, questioned the position on criminal legal aid. He stated in part:

> In the old Legal Aid and Advice Act, Part II, as the Minister has said, was never brought into force. It is well and good to give legal aid to civil litigants .... But in the case of criminal prosecutions, very often, a poor person cannot afford a lawyer. Here, it is not just money at stake. The person could go to jail. In capital cases, we have assigned counsel. But in all other cases, the only legal aid that poor people can get for criminal cases is the Criminal Legal Aid Scheme run by the Law Society of Singapore. This is financed entirely, I think, out of the generosity of members of the legal profession. It seems paradoxical that in something like civil legal aid, the Government should provide funds. But in matters where a person could actually lose his livelihood, lose his freedom, there is no such provision of funds.[51]

In response to questions about the Bill, Professor Jayakumar stated:

> Assoc. Prof. Walter Woon's point can be argued with some persuasion. But as I said, the Government's policy is to provide legal aid to criminal cases only in capital offences .... To elaborate, the State spends a lot of resources in maintaining as best as possible a first class, top-rate law enforcement machinery – the Police, the Central Narcotics Bureau, the Commercial Affairs Department and so on. It also invests heavily in an excellent legal service with very good legal officers handling prosecutions, who sieve and vet all the police investigation papers. Their job is to investigate offences when there is evidence to prosecute, when accused persons are brought to book, only after thorough and careful process. Why are they prosecuted? They are prosecuted in the public interest and the State expends these monies in the public interest and in order to protect the law abiding majority .... It is incongruous and inconsistent that public funds should be used to defend an accused person which the State has decided ought to be charged in court and use public funds at the same time to get him off. The exception is where life is involved and for capital cases, counsel is assigned.[52]

In the absence of state funding for noncapital offenses, who would provide criminal defense for poor, unrepresented criminal defendants in these areas? Professor Jayakumar suggested that the Law Society should step in:

> I also agree that the legal profession itself has a role to play here. The legal profession has grown since the days the Legal Aid Act was enacted in the 1950s. It is larger today than what it was in the 1950s. The Legal Profession Act states that one of the purposes of the Law Society is: "to make provision for or assist in the promotion of a scheme whereby impecunious persons on non-capital charges are represented by advocates." So Parliament's intent is, to some extent, very clear that the legal profession must fulfil this social and public role through the Law Society.
>
> I would like to take this opportunity really to commend the Law Society for running a very well established criminal legal aid system since 1985. I know many lawyers who give of their time voluntarily and I want to congratulate the Law Society on its programme which is in the right direction. I have told the President of the Law Society that I will do my best to give support to him and his council in their commendable efforts on the Criminal Legal Aid System, provided it does not involve State funds. I will discuss with the Attorney-General how best we can give such support.[53]

As noted in this parliamentary debate, all criminal defendants in Singapore facing a capital offense have access to legal representation by the government upon request, whether they are indigent or not, under the Legal Assistance Scheme for Capital Offences (LASCO).[54] Under the scheme, which is still in place today, persons "charged with capital offenses . . . are assigned free counsel" and there is no "means test to pass or eligibility criteria to satisfy."[55] The main challenge in Singapore regarding indigent criminal defense has therefore been representation in noncapital offenses.

It is clear that the lack of broad-based criminal legal aid and the presence of unrepresented criminal defendants motivated lawyers to contribute representation and to form CLAS in 1985.[56] A short history of CLAS written in 1988 noted that the 1980 census was an important turning point. The census stated that four hundred thousand Singaporeans lived on "a combined family income of less than S$500 per month," meaning that they "waged a daily battle to make ends meet"; this was a "sobering, if not shocking discovery."[57] In addition to this realization, there was a shift in attitude at that time among younger members of the bar, who felt that the managing

Council of the Law Society were too placid and out of touch with the general public, and who wanted to engage in more service to the public.[58] These younger members and lawyers in smaller firms practiced in the then subordinate courts,[59] where many accused went to trial without any representation.[60] In 1981, local academic Stanley Yeo carried out a study demonstrating that defendants without representation faired consistently worse than defendants with representation,[61] empirical findings that confirmed what criminal lawyers had known for some time.[62] Opinion grew that something needed to be done, and in 1983 the Law Society's Council established a small committee that canvased views and collected information regarding unrepresented criminal defendants.[63] In January 1984, the Law Society announced its intention to make free legal services available to poor criminal defendants.[64] CLAS was formally launched on September 2, 1985.[65]

In addition to CLAS, the Association of Criminal Lawyers of Singapore (ACLS), formally founded in 2004,[66] and other groups have provided pro bono representation in criminal matters. Identifying the need for representation and assisting in arranging representation is also supported by the judicial system.[67] In 2010, former Chief Justice Chan Sek Keong noted that in criminal matters, "the Subordinate Courts have instituted a centralised referral system to facilitate the referral by the Community Court of undefended cases involving young, mentally ill and intellectually challenged offenders for pro bono representation."[68] The system referred remandees in the community court to Law Society Pro Bono Services, which decided whether to refer the cases to CLAS or to ACLS. The chief justice also noted the existence of a dock brief system for an indigent party *in forma pauperis*, which had been "put in place with ACLS to activate lawyers to act for unrepresented accused persons."[69]

In civil matters, civil legal aid had been provided in Singapore since before independence, but in 2006 the low cut-offs in place prompted the Law Society to appoint a committee to undertake a review of the needs of the poor in what appears to be the first comprehensive review of legal services for the poor in Singapore.[70] The Legal Aid Review Report evaluated the state of civil legal assistance, provided primarily via the government-funded Legal Aid Bureau but supplemented by voluntary schemes, and criminal legal assistance.

As a requirement for civil legal aid, the Legal Aid and Advice Act imposed a means and a merits test. At the time of the Legal Aid Review Report, applicants were required to have reasonable grounds for the legal position asserted, and not be in possession of more than the capital and disposable income limitations of S$7,000 and S$10,000 respectively.[71] The Committee noted that although the bottom 10 percent of the population were covered by this means test, some applicants were not able to access services because they could not afford the obligatory copayment; others failed the income or capital assets tests but were still unable to afford needed legal services.[72] The Legal Aid Review Report noted that legal aid was restricted to the bottom 10 percent of the population, which meant that significant portions of the population, including the lower middle class or "sandwich" class, were excluded from legal aid but still could not afford legal services.[73]

The Committee reviewed how different sources of civil legal aid were funded. The Legal Aid Bureau (LAB) was the main provider of civil legal services for the poor,[74] pursuant to the Legal Aid and Advice Act,[75] and it was funded primarily by the government.[76] LAB handed 75 percent of its cases with its legal services office and support staff, while the remaining 25 percent were handled by a panel of volunteer lawyers.[77] Statistics indicated that in 2005 these external lawyers received an average of S$647 as an honorarium per case. Feedback from lawyers indicated that the sum was "inadequate in view of the amount of time spent in each case,"[78] and in some divorce cases the costs incurred by a volunteer lawyer would be three times the amount received.[79] The Legal Aid Review Report therefore noted that in addition to the copayment from the applicant, lawyers also contributed "to the cost of legal aid by way of accepting reduced fees."[80]

The Committee also reviewed the system for defense in capital cases, LASCO. The Legal Aid Review Report noted that no records indicated exactly when the scheme was set up, but that it was organized in its current form sometime in 1992–93.[81] The practice of providing defense counsel for capital offenses had been in existence for some time and probably originated under British rule. LASCO did not administer a means test, and volunteer lawyers on the scheme were paid an honorarium, which in 2005 averaged S$836.03 per hearing day for lead counsel and S$262.27 for assisting counsel.[82] The Legal Aid Review Report did not specifically address the degree to which the payment reimbursed counsel for the time expended but it is fairly clear that, like volunteer lawyers assisting with civil legal aid, the honorarium was not intended to compensate at market rates. Unlike civil legal aid, however, government-paid employees did not provide defense representation. The structure of indigent capital defense was based on the honorarium model, in which the government provided a minimum payment to the lawyer and the lawyer donated a portion of the legal services.

The Legal Aid Review Report recommended that the Law Society address the needs of the population via an increased means test and other financial adjustments.[83] In order to implement the suggestions, the Legal Aid Review Report recommended that each law firm pledge 25 pro bono hours for its lawyers per year, together with a tax deduction for pro bono hours.[84] Regarding the tax incentive, the Legal Aid Review Report suggested that a tax incentive could function as incentive to perform pro bono work. Law firms could assign a value of S$200 per hour for work done by their attorneys and claim the amount as a deduction since that work would be "in every sense a charitable contribution."[85] This recommendation was not pursued. The Legal Aid Review Report also recommended that starter funding from the government and other sources be provided for a new office of Pro Bono Services,[86] which would function within the Law Society and allocate and administer pro bono work.[87] The majority of the Legal Aid Review Report's recommendations were adopted, and Law Society Pro Bono Services in particular has been instrumental in identifying legal need and organizing effective pro bono services.

In recent years, both civil and criminal assistance for indigent litigants have experienced considerable change. For decades, CLAS was funded primarily by contributions raised at a charity golf tournament.[88] In 2013, in "a significant departure from its long-held stance towards legal aid for those accused of non-capital crimes," the Singapore government announced it would provide direct legal assistance and support to defendants in criminal cases.[89] In view of the major changes to legal aid and pro bono in Singapore in recent years, we focus on the forms pro bono takes in Singapore today and the challenges currently posed.

SINGAPORE PRO BONO TODAY

Singapore targets three different kinds of legal need: legal information, legal advice, and legal representation. These distinctions are important in Singapore because of the perceived need to manage the diverse needs of the public in a sustainable manner. Legal information is supplied by courts[90] and organizations such as the Law Society Pro Bono Services[91] and the Community Justice Center,[92] and lawyers participate in the provision of legal information by assisting with guides to the law[93] and talks targeted on particular subjects.[94] As pro bono is primarily understood to cover legal advice and representation, we address these legal services in the different contexts of civil and criminal matters. In part due to the history of legal aid in Singapore, pro bono services for indigent persons take clearly bifurcated paths depending on whether the matter is civil or criminal.

Civil Pro Bono

Indigent persons with a civil legal issue immediately fall within one of two categories. If they meet the requirements of the Legal Aid Bureau, they are fully covered under that system and they are assisted by either a Legal Aid employee or an assigned solicitor. If they do not meet legal aid requirements and cut-offs, they would need to pursue assistance from other sources such as pro bono schemes. The divided architecture created by the civil legal aid scheme is such that there is no general *in forma pauperis* filing status in Singapore, and while legally aided persons are entitled to fee waivers, others are required to request them.

Persons who do not come within legal aid cut-offs can first attend a legal clinic to determine whether the issue can be handled with legal advice. Like many jurisdictions, the staffing and focus of legal clinics is spread over different organizations[95] and is not necessarily coordinated.

One of the major expansions in civil pro bono came via the development of multiple community legal clinics (CLCs)[96] and their staffing by law firms.[97] Prior to the launch of Law Society Pro Bono Services, pro bono work was undertaken by individual lawyers and law firms.[98] One of the many programs launched by Law Society Pro Bono Services were the CLCs. These legal clinics are staffed by voluntary lawyers, who provide free basic legal advice to needy citizens and permanent residents.[99] CLCs had their venue in community development councils, which in Singapore are "umbrella grassroots bodies created to coordinate and lead smaller grassroots organizations" that encourage "bonding and enhance social cohesion within local communities."[100] The activities and persons using community development councils made them a natural choice for a legal clinic. Law Society Pro Bono Services, via its CEO Lim Tanguy, organized two CLCs as a pilot project in 2007, and they were launched at the North-West and South-East community development councils.[101] In 2014, CLCs were established at all five community development councils.[102]

The CLCs rotate among different community development council locations, and they serve as a "first contact point for people wondering whether a dispute or grievance they have could stand up to scrutiny in court."[103] Applicants are provided with an advice session, which if they paid a lawyer, would cost between S$300–S$1,000.[104] Currently, Singaporeans or permanent residents living in Singapore may have a free session in a CLC with a lawyer on a personal matter; investment, business, and professional matters are not covered.[105] The clinics are open on different days of the week, Mondays to Thursdays, and prior registration is required. The advice is limited to one session and it is not available if the applicant has sought legal advice on that issue before.[106] If approved, applicants see a lawyer on a one-to-one basis for a limited time period of twenty minutes.[107]

At the time the CLCs were launched, there were other one-off clinics functioning in Singapore, but the regularity of the CLCs was a major step forward.[108] More lawyers were needed to staff the CLCs,[109] and seventeen law firms contributed lawyers to provide assistance.[110] Historically, solo practitioner and small law firms have provided pro bono in Singapore,[111] so larger firms' undertaking of legal clinics was an important factor in CLC development. One interviewee who has observed Singapore pro bono practices for many years suggested that a few factors likely contributed to this commitment. Once one or two larger law firms made this arrangement, other law firms were prompted to volunteer. The interviewee also noted the influence of law students, who began to ask larger law firms about pro bono policy in interviews for associate positions.

In addition to the CLCs, other legal clinics are offered in Singapore. In the state courts, there is a civil legal clinic and a family legal clinic that function one or two days a week.[112] The Community Justice Centre (CJC), an independent charity that works to support access to justice for litigants in person, organizes the On-site Legal Advice Scheme, which provides immediate basic legal advice and directions to litigants in person at no cost.[113] The CJC also organizes the Primary Justice Project, which offers "affordable and effective solutions by exploring possibilities of dispute resolutions to [litigant] legal issues while eliminating the need for resorting to the courts to adjudicate their disputes as first option"; fixed fees are charged and listed on the CJC website.[114] Clinics are also run by groups, such as the Singapore Council of Women's Organisations[115] and the Association of Women for Action and Research.[116] Some of these clinics take walk-ins, such as

CJC's On-site Legal Advice Scheme, which is available every weekday morning and afternoon.[117]

Sessions with a lawyer in this kind of legal clinic are not intended to establish a continuing lawyer–client relationship. Previously, rules applicable to similar sessions prohibited lawyers from even sharing their name or identifying information.[118] The clinics are intended to meet the kind of legal need that can be addressed by a lawyer in a relatively short span of time. Structuring pro bono in this way allows limited legal needs to be meet with appropriate levels of resources, and it allows lawyers and law firms to contribute in a way that controls and limits the relationship. This structure appears to be a well-organized, effective method of handling this kind of legal question, but some clients will need ongoing advice and representation.

Ongoing civil representation for indigent parties who do not meet legal aid cut-offs presents a substantial challenge in Singapore. In its 2009 Annual Report, the subordinate courts of Singapore stated there was a "sizeable number" of litigants without representation, including "about one third of criminal cases . . . [and] more than 90% of maintenance and family violence cases."[119] Lawyers interviewed in connection with this chapter reported concerns about taking on pro bono civil cases because of liability issues and the need to contain the number of hours taken away from profit-generating activity. These concerns are present in many jurisdictions, although they are exacerbated where the law firm itself has an equivocal relationship to pro bono.

Interviewees reported somewhat different views about the distribution of law firm approaches to pro bono in Singapore, but their observations suggest three main approaches to pro bono, which can be categorized as malign, neutral, and benign. In the malign categories, some law firms keep lawyers entirely engaged with paying work and do not discuss pro bono. In these firms, where lawyers work long hours already, taking on a pro bono case indicates that the lawyer has spare time, which should be filled with paying work. There are indications in Singapore that while historically the majority of law firms might have been in this category, recent shifts in attitudes mean this is no longer the case. A second law firm approach is neutral. These law firms tolerate a limited amount of pro bono if it does not interfere with the lawyer's ability to meet minimum earning requirements or other job expectations. Interview subjects reported that many law firms now tolerate pro bono efforts to some degree. A third category of law firm is benign or encouraging. This kind of law firm takes active steps to support or encourage its lawyers in their pro bono activities.

An important example of benign law firm pro bono is the "ownership" taken by some law firms of a certain number of CLAS cases or a commitment to staff CLCs on specified days of the week. Some law firms send a junior as well as senior lawyer to the clinic, an investment in associate training that is not lost on law students who assist in the clinics.[120] This shift of position toward encouraging pro bono is consistent with the qualities now required for senior counsel, which include public service.[121]

There are two other approaches to law firm pro bono in Singapore that could be understood as falling within the benign category, which merit separate discussion owing to the greater degree of law firm commitment. These law firms are not statistically significant but they offer distinctly different alternatives to the majority of law firms, by either making pro bono mandatory for law firm lawyers or adopting an intentional low bono approach.

A small number of law firms in Singapore require their lawyers to do pro bono. Two interviewees had former associate and current partner-level experience with the same firm that had adopted this approach. The law firm policy was not written, and while the partner agreed that the approach was mandatory, both the partner and the associate characterized pro bono as "strongly encouraged." Both the associate and the partner observed that the requirement applied across the board to lawyers at all levels, although the partner described the policy as primarily reflecting the character of the firm, for example, with partners in leadership positions in the Law Society and various pro bono programs. The associate reported knowing about the policy upon the start of employment, and the partner noted that either the policy is mentioned at associate interviews or associates know about it when they join the firm.

In terms of logistics, this law firm would normally roster lawyers for pro bono programs run by Law Society Pro Bono Services; associates prepped the cases beforehand and partners accompanied associates. There was also discretion to undertake other kinds of pro bono cases. In addition to ensuring that lawyers had opportunities to serve poorer clients, there are indications that associates appreciated the mandatory pro bono because it gave them an opportunity to exercise leadership in cases earlier in their career.

One issue mentioned by the associate and the partner interviewees was the potentially negative effect of pro bono hours on the earnings of the lawyer doing pro bono. This firm did not use a strict minimum billing requirement, and the associate and partner confirmed that partners had made adjustments in earnings to compensate for the nonbilled hours, for example, by sharing a portion of the partner's billings. Neither the associate nor the partner interviewees characterized earnings as a drawback of the mandatory policy.

The other law firm approach to pro bono in Singapore is an intentional low bono scheme. Compared with pro bono, which is the provision of free legal services, low bono is understood as "practices of offering reduced legal fees" to clients who cannot afford a full fee.[122] Like many jurisdictions, low bono in Singapore would likely be pervasive if it included all the down billing and discounts provided by law firms to clients who request lower fees.[123] Some law firms in Singapore, though, are "consciously positioned" and structured to offer low bono services.[124] Firms in this category have full-fee clients, but these clients are used in part as one source of funding for low bono and pro bono work. A key proponent of the low bono law firm in Singapore is Eden Law, which was started in 2014 by an NUS law graduate, June Lim.[125] Lim went to law school with the clear aim of serving the underprivileged.[126] After five years working at Singapore law firms, she realized that pro bono would always take a backseat to other obligations.[127] Having received litigation training in matrimonial and criminal cases, she started the firm based on the belief that serving the community and having a successful practice did not have to be mutually exclusive.[128] This law firm takes an explicit low bono approach, and instead of using contingency fees, which historically have not been allowed in contentious matters,[129] or low hourly rates, they use fixed-fee payment arrangements.[130] For needy clients, the firm determines the amount payable based on the client's monthly salary and for some clients the fee is waived entirely.[131] Clients include members of the "sandwich class," who are just above legal aid cut-offs but cannot afford legal fees typically charged.[132] In order to keep fees low, the firm has also worked to reduce costs with legal technology. The practice is largely paperless, lowering costs for rent and support staff,[133] and allowing lawyers to work at a hospital, a shelter, or even overseas.[134] The firm does pro bono as well as low bono, and Lim noted that lawyers in her firm average the recommended 25 pro bono hours a year.[135]

Over the course of its development, Eden Law has been profitable.[136] In terms of lawyer compensation, law firm lawyers have not had to suffer financially.[137] At the time of writing, the firm had five lawyers and showed steady growth,[138] suggesting that the model is financially sustainable. Despite its survival in the Singapore legal market, the low bono model does appear to be limited to a small number of firms. This model may also be limited to firms doing primarily civil work because, as one interviewee observed, the criminal defendant population does not contain the same percentage of clients able to pay the fees that could support nonpaying clients.[139]

Criminal Pro Bono

As in civil matters, indigent criminal defense is split into two categories, determined by historical patterns of government funding; instead of the categories of civil legal aid and other civil matters, criminal defense falls into the categories of capital defense and other criminal matters. As noted above, defendants in capital cases are entitled to free representation via the Legal Assistance Scheme for Capital Offenses. Capital defense has been provided for defendants in Singapore since prior to independence, although LASCO was institutionalized in its present form in 1992.[140] Under the scheme, all persons facing capital charges in the high court are eligible for legal representation, and it has been reported that 90 percent of all capital cases are defended by LASCO counsel.[141] Applicants are eligible for assigned counsel by the state free of charge and no means test or other eligibility criteria is imposed.[142] Generally, two counsel are assigned, one to lead and one to assist, and as of March 2018, the scheme had two hundred lawyers.[143]

Advocates and solicitors who participate in LASCO receive an honorarium, so technically the activity is low bono as opposed to pro bono, but the honorarium is low enough that it is regularly discussed as pro bono. In 2010, then Chief Justice Chan Sek Keong observed that "participating in LASCO may be regarded as a moral obligation on the part of any member of the legal profession, especially those who practice at the Criminal Bar, to advance and promote criminal justice, and prevent or reduce any miscarriage of justice."[144] There have been concerns about the quality of representation in this scheme, which have led to plans for monitoring and improvement.[145]

The bulk of noncapital criminal advice and representation is still primarily handled by CLAS,[146] as supplemented by the Association of Criminal Lawyers of Singapore[147] and by the CJC's Guidance for Plea Scheme.[148] Representation by a CLAS lawyer has always been limited to a particular set of statutes.[149] Organized in 1985, the scheme was traditionally funded primarily with donations, which led to some difficult choices regarding representation, such as no representation where there was a guilty plea[150] and the defendant only needed assistance with mitigation.

CLAS began before the concept of pro bono was introduced in Singapore, although as volunteer legal services to poor and vulnerable clients, this activity clearly fits the definition of pro bono. As explained previously, CLAS was organized because Singapore did not have a broad-based approach to criminal legal aid. However, this arrangement changed in 2013, when in "a significant departure from its long-held stance towards legal aid for those accused of non-capital crimes," the Singapore government announced it would provide direct legal assistance and support to defendants in criminal cases.[151] As described by the minister for foreign affairs and law, K. Shanmugam, the funding represented "a clear shift in policy and philosophy for the Government."[152] The minister acknowledged that lawyers did "a bulk of the heavy lifting, volunteering their services through 'CLAS,' and various Community Legal Clinics."[153] The envisioned program was large but not intended to cover all criminal defendants.

The new scheme is referred to as Enhanced CLAS,[154] in recognition of the nonpaid CLAS representation in which lawyers had provided the majority of noncapital criminal defense since 1985. The steering committee in charge of Enhanced CLAS, comprising representatives from the Law Society, the criminal bar, the courts, Singapore Academy of Law, and the ministry of law,[155] considered various approaches. The UK approach with its open-ended budget is now arguably understood as financially unsustainable, although the steering committee took the need to sustain the criminal bar into serious consideration.[156] The Law Society opted for a hybrid staffing model with two prongs: CLAS Fellows, a few full-time lawyers who were seconded or whose salary was sponsored by law firms for a period of one or two years,[157] together with the volunteer pool, now paid via an honorarium, which per interview reports is roughly 10–15 percent of the market rate. Volunteer lawyer payments are funded by the government, but an independent group determines the details of cases and payment amounts.

Enhanced CLAS was soft-launched in January 2015[158] and officially launched on May 18, 2015.[159] As originally envisioned, the scheme anticipated four tiers of legal assistance, ranging from tier 1 to tier 4.[160] Tier 1 would provide all accused persons awareness of channels for legal advice and representation as well as relevant social service agency assistance; tier 2 would offer basic legal advice for accused persons facing charges that may attract a custodial sentence; tier 3 would offer legal assistance not involving court attendance by a lawyer, such as preparing a mitigation plea; and tier 4 would offer full representation.[161] All CLAS applicants receive legal advice during the means/merits testing process, whether or not they eventually qualify for legal aid. Some applicants who pass the means test may not pass the merits test and therefore not receive CLAS defense counsel, e.g., where an applicant is pleading guilty to an offense with a mandatory minimum sentence. As implemented, it also appears that tiers 3 and 4 may be combined, and if an applicant is approved for CLAS counsel, applicants receive full representation.

As described by Senior Minister of State for Law Indranee Rajah, the "significant shift in Government philosophy" was made in order "to provide greater access to justice for genuine cases of need."[162] Prior to the provision of government funding, CLAS applicants had increased over the years, but "only a fraction could be helped due to limited resources. In 2014, there were 1,780 applications out of which only 431 were granted."[163] In the new program, the government provided "the bulk of funding, comprising S$800,000 for start-up costs and an annual commitment of S$3.5 m."[164] The state courts estimated that there were approximately twelve thousand litigants-in-person per year, "of which half could benefit from some form of legal representation. Enhanced CLAS aims to help up to 6,000 accused persons per year, a tenfold increase from the number previously helped."[165]

Government funding allowed considerable expansion of CLAS coverage. A relaxed means test, of disposable income of not more than S$10,000 per annum and disposable capital of not more than S$10,000, also allowed more applicants to qualify for criminal legal aid.[166] CLAS assistance was further extended to the Moneylenders Act, resulting in coverage for offenses under a total of sixteen statues.[167] Finally, under the previous scheme, only those claiming trial were allowed full representation, with the exception of young offenders and those with mental illnesses. Enhanced CLAS now covers criminal defendants pleading guilty to charges,[168] so legal assistance with mitigation can be provided. A copayment was required "to ensure that applicants also contribute towards their defense, and do not abuse the system."[169]

Under Enhanced CLAS, Law Society Pro Bono Services would continue to run the CLAS program and legal services would still be done primarily by volunteer lawyers, but the funding was intended to cover "operational costs, honoraria and disbursements" to lawyers.[170] The senior minister of state for law noted that it is "called pro bono but in fairness, it would not be right to ask volunteer lawyers to do this regularly on a long term basis all for free. Hence, volunteer lawyers will be paid honoraria. . . . While not the same as market rate, the honoraria will go some way towards defraying their legal fees. Disbursements will continue to be covered so volunteer lawyers need not incur out-of-pocket expenses."[171]

Like the Law Society Pro Bono Services' launch of CLCs, Enhanced CLAS required lawyers and law firms to take on the additional cases. Law firms entered into agreements with Law Society Pro Bono Services to do this, such as the Memorandum of Understanding (MOU) signed by local law firm Eversheds Harry Elias Partnership and Law Society Pro Bono Services in 2014. This MOU obligated the law firm to take twenty-five CLAS cases a year.[172] Files are assigned to junior lawyers with supervision from senior lawyers, and the law firm keeps track of "the time they spend on such files and this is also taken into consideration in assessing performance and contribution to the firm."[173]

Quality control in criminal defense for LASCO has been raised as an issue, and quality control is a key concern in CLAS as well. CLAS Fellows go through an extensive training regime,[174] deemed to be a highlight of participating in the program.[175] Interview subjects reported the use of formal and informal methods of feedback on performance, including review by fellow CLAS volunteers and feedback from judges.

A recent development in indigent criminal defense is the position of CLAS Advocates, full-time advocates paid for with even more additional Enhanced CLAS monies provided by the government.[176] When asked what prompted the government to directly sponsor CLAS lawyers, a MinLaw spokesperson said that "the Government made a philosophical shift in 2013 to directly fund non-capital criminal legal aid, as we decided we should do more to provide criminal legal aid to accused persons who cannot afford legal representation . . . (The CLAS Advocates) will help strengthen the scheme by working alongside existing volunteer lawyers and CLAS Fellows."[177]

Enhanced CLAS has only been functioning for a few years, so analysis of how it has affected pro bono is necessarily limited. It can be observed that while representation for extremely needy criminal defendants has been greatly expanded, persons of low or moderate income who are over the cut-off still have considerable difficulty paying lawyer fees. These criminal defendants will either be unrepresented or attempt to secure pro bono representation. One potential difficulty is that if Enhanced CLAS has absorbed available attorneys to do the increased honorarium work available under the program, pro bono representation could be even more difficult to find. The other fly in the ointment is potential corrections in the private practitioner market arising out of government funding of Enhanced CLAS. Interviewees noted that some criminal practitioners felt their earnings were reduced after Enhanced CLAS implementation, although if these observations are accurate, they do not necessarily spring from Enhanced CLAS and could be caused by other factors, such as a tough market or the impact of legal technologies.

CONCLUSION

The Enhanced CLAS scheme has put in place a greatly expanded, government-funded program for criminal defense of indigent persons, which by most accounts had been missing in Singapore. Now that the government is contributing funding to noncapital indigent criminal defense, the numbers of represented defendants have grown and access to justice has increased. Volunteer CLAS lawyers technically do not perform pro bono because they receive an honorarium, but the rate of pay is relatively low, which means that lawyers assisting indigent criminal defendants still make a substantial contribution. There remains, however, a need for criminal pro bono with no honorarium, as the current program does not cover all criminal defendants who cannot afford a lawyer. One question in Singapore will be the viability of this criminal pro bono, as lawyers practicing criminal law may be engaged in honorarium work. Another related question in civil matters is how to meet the substantial needs for civil representation beyond legal advice.[178]

Law firm support for Enhanced CLAS and CLCs demonstrate that many law firms in Singapore have undergone a change in orientation toward pro bono, a view confirmed by interviewees as well. There were impressive examples of indigent representation in civil and criminal matters before the concept of pro bono appeared in Singapore, but it was not until this activity was linked to access to justice as a professional obligation and enthusiastically promoted by the government and the Law Society that practices changed on a wider scale. There are still different law firm approaches to pro bono, and as noted by Lim Tanguy, the CEO of Law Society Pro Bono Services, "the reality is such that even if a lawyer wants to do pro bono work, unless he or she is with a firm that is pro-pro bono, it would be very difficult for them to do so and by getting the managing partners to commit their firm, it becomes about their firm branding, their firm's reputation and you have firm alignment from top to bottom as well."[179] However, a number of firms have determined that for various reasons, such as commitment to access to justice, branding, or training, a certain amount of pro bono is worthy of consideration and resources.

Given the pro bono development that has already occurred in Singapore, what lies in the future? With encouragement and organization from Law Society Pro Bono Services, important contributions to pro bono continue to develop, e.g., regarding in-house counsel,[180] but Singapore has also taken two different kinds of steps. Regarding education, Singapore launched a third law school, Singapore University of Social Sciences, with the explicit goal of producing lawyers who will practice "community law" including criminal and family law.[181] Singapore also implemented a mandatory pro bono program for law students, intended to raise awareness of legal need.[182] These are early days for these educational programs,[183] but assuming modest success, the practitioner's need for a viable way of making a living remains. Clients with income above criminal and civil legal aid cut-offs pose considerable challenges if they need representation beyond legal advice. It appears as though pro bono will ultimately be making room for something else, and that remaining challenges will be partially addressed through a second step: developing programs in low bono.[184]

NOTES

1. *See* Michael Hor, *Singapore's Innovations to Due Process*, 12 CRIMINAL L.F. 25 SCM 152 (2001); Ho Hock Lai, *The Privilege Against Self-Incrimination and the Right of Access to a Lawyer – A Comparative Assessment*, 25 SINGAPORE ACAD. L.J. 826 (2013) (Special issue on Constitutionalism and Criminal Justice); Jack Tsen-Ta Lee, *Reforming the Right to Legal Counsel in Singapore*, RES. COLLECTION SCH. L. (2012), http://ink.library.smu.edu.sg/sol_research/1101 (last visited June 26, 2018).

2. Legal Profession Act 2009 Rev. Ed. (version in force from April 18, 2018), c. 161, § 12(1).
3. *Id.* at § 38(1).
4. Alvin Chen & Helena Whalen-Bridge, *Singapore: Regulating Domestic and Foreign Lawyers – Singapore's Unified Approach*, *in* INTERNATIONAL PERSPECTIVES ON THE REGULATION OF LAWYERS AND LEGAL SERVICES 45 (Andrew Boon ed., 2017).
5. *See* JOTHIE RAJAH, AUTHORITARIAN RULE OF LAW: LEGISLATION, DISCOURSE, AND LEGITIMACY IN SINGAPORE (2012).
6. The Pro Bono Services Office of the Law Society of Singapore, an Institution of a Public Character, was established on September 10, 2007; the Pro Bono Services Office was corporatized on April 1, 2017, when it commenced operations as Law Society Pro Bono Services, a registered charity and Institution of a Public Character (IPC) incorporated as a Company Limited by Guarantee, www.lawsocprobono.org/Pages/default.aspx (last visited Sept. 26, 2020). In this chapter, the organization is referred using the current name, Law Society Pro Bono Services.
7. Helena Whalen-Bridge, *The Conceptualisation of Pro Bono in Singapore*, ASIAN J. COMP. L. 97, 117 (2014).
8. *Id.* tbl.3.
9. *Id.* at 114–15.
10. *Id.* at 126–29.
11. Milton Chase, *Battle for Survival for Lawyers in United States*, STRAITS TIMES, July 17, 1978, at 31.
12. *Singaporean Lawyer Wins US Award for Helping Underprivileged*, STRAITS TIMES, Aug. 13, 1990.
13. *Id.*
14. *Judges and Lawyers Must Be Above Suspicion: Anwar*, STRAITS TIMES, Dec. 8, 1995, at 38.
15. *New Mentor Scheme Launched for Young Lawyers*, STRAITS TIMES, Jan. 11, 2000.
16. *Id* .
17. Directory of Senior Counsel, SINGAPORE ACADEMY OF LAW, www.sal.org.sg/Services/Appointments/Senior-Counsel/Directory (last visited June 27, 2018).
18. Abdul Rashid Gani, *A Tribute to Pala*, 02 LAWLINK 22 (2003), https://law.nus.edu.sg/alumni/pdfs/lawlinkv2n2.pdf (last visited June 27, 2018).
19. *See* Monica Kotwani, *The Lawyers Who Take Cases for No Fee: Pro Bono Movement Now Seen As a 'Golden Crown'*, CHANNEL NEWS ASIA (Oct. 15, 2017), www.channelnewsasia.com/news/singapore/pro-bono-movement-lawyers-9300718 (last visited June 27, 2018); *see also* CRIMINAL LEGAL AID SCHEME, CRIMINAL LEGAL AID SCHEME: COMMEMORATIVE ISSUE 1985–1988, at 10 (1988).

20. Kelvin Wong, *Lawyer Fights for Ex-NMP – for Free*, STRAITS TIMES, July 30, 2003.
21. *Id.*
22. Whalen-Bridge, *supra* note 7, at tbl.3.
23. Regarding the United Kingdom and international law firms, see Andrew Boon & Avis Whyte, *"Charity and Beating Begins at Home": The Aetiology of the New Culture of Pro Bono Publico*, 2 LEGAL ETHICS 169 (1999).
24. *See* Law Society of Singapore, Joint International Pro Bono Committee, www.lawsocprobono.org/Pages/Joint-International-ProBonoCommittee.aspx (last visited Sept. 26, 2020).
25. HOME, www.home.org.sg/ (last visited Sept. 26, 2020).
26. TWC2, http://twc2.org.sg/ (last visited Sept. 26, 2020).
27. *See* Latham & Watkins LLP, A Survey of Pro Bono Practices and Opportunities in 84 Jurisdictions 581–582 (Mar. 2016).
28. *See id.* at 579.
29. *See* Chen & Whalen-Bridge, *supra* note 4.
30. TrustLaw, TrustLaw Index of Pro Bono 2016, at H13.
31. Legal Profession Act 2009 Rev. Ed., c. 161, Legal Profession (Pro Bono Legal Services) Rules 2013 (No. S 658/2013).
32. See Legal Profession Act 2009 Rev. Ed., c. 161, § 2(1), which states that "'advocate' and 'solicitor' mean an advocate and solicitor of the Supreme Court."
33. Latham & Watkins, *supra* note 27, at 583.
34. *See* Law Society Pro Bono Services, "I'm a Foreign Qualified* lawyer. Can I participate in pro bono work?," www.lawsocprobono.org/Pages/volunteer-Schemes-Supportforourvolunteers.aspx (last visited Sept. 26, 2020).
35. For a brief review of the Qualifying Foreign Law Practice (QFLP) scheme, see Update on Qualifying Foreign Law Practice Licences Awarded in 2013, MINISTRY OF LAW (2017), www.mlaw.gov.sg/content/minlaw/en/news/press-releases/update-on-qualifying-foreign-law-practice-licences-awarded-in-20.html (last visited June 27, 2018) ("The QFLP licences allow Foreign Law Practices (FLPs) to practice Singapore law, except in domestic areas of litigation and general practice, for example, criminal law, retail conveyancing, family law and administrative law. The QFLPs can practice the permitted areas of Singapore law through Singapore-qualified lawyers with practising certificates or foreign lawyers holding the foreign practitioner certificate.")
36. Michelle Quah, *Foreign Law Firms Top List of Pro Bono Work Donors*, BUSINESS TIMES, July 12, 2013.
37. *See* 3RD ANNUAL ASIA PRO BONO CONFERENCE 2014 FINAL REPORT, 3RD ANNUAL ASIA PRO BONO CONFERENCE 2014 FINAL REPORT (2014), https://law.nus.edu.sg/pdfs/cals/events/asiaprobonoconference2014.pdf (last visited June 27, 2018).
38. Legal Aid and Advice Act 2014 Rev. Ed., c. 160.

39. H. Y. Yeo, *Assessing the State of Civil Legal Aid in Singapore*, 41 I.C.L. Q. 875, 876 (1992).
40. Legal Aid and Advice Ordinance 1956, No. 19 of 1956, Part III.
41. *Id.*, Part II.
42. *Id.*, Part IV.
43. *Id.*, Part IV, § 1.
44. *See* Yeo Hwee Ying, *Provision of Legal Aid in Singapore*, *in* THE SINGAPORE LEGAL SYSTEM 446, 449, n.17 (Kevin Y. L. Tan ed., 2d ed. 1999).
45. Yeo, *supra* note 39, at 875, n.2.
46. Remarks of then acting minister for social affairs, Dr. Ahmad Mattar, noted in Ivan Fernandez & Ng Weng Hoong, *Lawyers for the Needy ...*, STRAITS TIMES, Apr. 24, 1983, at 1.
47. *See* Christine Sim & Tan Zhi Feng, *The Paradox of Legal Aid in Singapore: Civil Legal Aid Without Criminal Legal Aid*, 30 SINGAPORE L. REV. 165, 169-70 (2012).
48. Legal Aid and Advice Act 1985 Rev. Ed.
49. Legal Aid and Advice Act 1995 (Bill No. 15/95 published on 16 March 1995).
50. SINGAPORE PARLIAMENTARY REPORTS, Second Reading, Legal Aid and Advice Bill (7 July 1995), at col. 1345.
51. *Id.* col. 1346–47.
52. *Id.* col. 1349–50.
53. *Id.*
54. Supreme Court of Singapore, "Help for Those Charged with Capital Offences," https:/www.supremecourt.gov.sg/services/self-help-services/legal-assistance-for-capital-offences (last visited Sept. 26, 2020).
55. *Id.*
56. LEGAL AID REVIEW COMMITTEE OF THE LAW SOCIETY OF SINGAPORE, REPORT 11 (Oct. 2006).
57. CRIMINAL LEGAL AID SCHEME, *supra* note 19, at 10.
58. KEVIN Y. L. TAN, FIAT JUSTITIA – FIFTY YEARS OF THE LAW SOCIETY OF SINGAPORE 64 (2017).
59. The subordinate courts, the lower of the two tiers of Singapore courts, were renamed the state courts in 2014 via the Subordinate Courts (Amendment) Act 2014, Act 5 of 2014; *see* State Courts Act, 2007 Rev. Ed., c. 321, § 3.
60. Tan, *supra* note 58, at 65.
61. Stanley Yeo Meng Heong, *Unrepresented Defendants in the Subordinate Criminal Courts of Singapore*, 23 MALAYA L. REV. 41 (1981); *see also* Stanley Yeo Meng Heong, *Re-Opening the Case for Criminal Legal Aid in Singapore*, MALAYAN L.J. cxxiv (Nov. 1983); Whalen-Bridge, *supra* note 7, at 110, n.89.
62. Tan, *supra* note 58, at 65.
63. *Id.*; *see also* LEGAL AID SUB-COMMITTEE OF THE LAW SOCIETY OF SINGAPORE, REPORT TO THE COUNCIL OF THE CRIMINAL LEGAL AID SCHEME (May 20, 1985).

64. TAN, *supra* note 58, at 65.
65. CRIMINAL LEGAL AID SCHEME, *supra* note 19, at 11.
66. Association of Criminal Lawyers of Singapore, www.facebook.com/pg/ACLS-802897269743245/about/ (last visited June 27, 2018).
67. *See* Gary Chan Kok Yew, *Access to Justice for the Poor: The Singapore Judiciary at Work* 17 PACIFIC RIM L. & POL'Y J. 595 (2008).
68. *See* Honourable Chief Justice Chan Sek Keong, *Access to Quality Justice for All*, SUBORDINATE COURTS WORKPLAN 2010, at ¶ 2 (Feb. 26, 2010), www.statecourts.gov.sg/Resources/Documents/Resources_2010_Annual%20WP_Keynote%20Address_by%20CJ.pdf (last visited Sept. 15, 2018).
69. *Id.*
70. Legal Aid Review Report, at 1 (copy on file with author).
71. *Id.* at 6.
72. *Id.* at 27.
73. *Id.* at 28–29.
74. *Id.* at 5.
75. Legal Aid and Advice Act 2014 Rev. Ed., c. 160.
76. Legal Aid Review Report, *supra* note 70, at 6.
77. *Id.*
78. *Id.* at 10.
79. *Id.*
80. *Id.*
81. *Id.* at 14.
82. *Id.* at 15.
83. *Id.* at 54–56.
84. *Id.* at 53.
85. *Id.*
86. The Pro Bono Services Office of the Law Society of Singapore, a charity and Institution of a Public Character, was established in 2007 and corporatized as a company limited by guarantee in 2017 under the name Law Society Pro Bono Services. For ease of reference, this organization is referred to throughout by the current name, the Law Society Pro Bono Services.
87. *Id.*
88. *See* Michael Hwang, President, The Law Society of Singapore, *A Conversation with the Chief Justice of Russia*, SINGAPORE LAW GAZETTE (May 2010), http://v1.lawgazette.com.sg/2010–05/news2.htm (last visited June 28, 2018).
89. Amir Hussain & Amanda Lee, *Govt Will Provide Direct Legal Aid to Defendants in Criminal Cases*, TODAY (December 7, 2013), www.todayonline.com/singapore/govt-will-provide-direct-legal-aid-defendants-criminal-cases?singlepage¼true (last visited June 28, 2018); *see also* S. Ramesh, *Govt to Enhance Criminal Legal Aid Scheme*, CHANNEL NEWS ASIA (Dec. 6, 2013), www.channelnewsasia.com/news/singapore/shanmugam-announces-new/912780.html (last visited June 28, 2018); Thian Yee Sze, Director-General, Ministry

of Law, *The Four Principles That Anchor Singapore's Criminal Justice System*, SINGAPORE LAW GAZETTE (Feb. 2014), http://v1.lawgazette.com.sg/2014–02/964.htm (last visited June 27, 2018) (from 2014, "the Government will enhance the funding to the Law Society for the operation of its pro bono criminal legal aid efforts").

90. In the state courts, see, for example, "Self-Represented in a Criminal Matter" and "Self-Represented in a Civil Matter" at www.statecourts.gov.sg/Pages/default.aspx (last visited Oct. 13, 2019), and the Community Justice Centre, www.cjc.org.sg/ (last visited Oct. 13, 2019).

91. *See* LAW SOCIETY PRO BONO SERVICES, COMMUNITY LEGAL EDUCATION, www.lawsocprobono.org/Pages/Help-for-Public.aspx (last visited Oct. 13, 2019).

92. Community Justice Centre, "Information," https://cjc.org.sg/services/ (last visited Oct. 13, 2019).

93. *See, e.g.*, THE LAW SOCIETY OF SINGAPORE, KNOW THE LAW NOW! (2015), http://probono.lawsociety.org.sg/Documents/Know the Law NOW-FINAL.pdf (last visited June 28, 2018); THE LAW SOCIETY OF SINGAPORE, LEGALESE: A LEGAL TOOLKIT FOR COMMUNITY ORGANISATIONS, http://probono.lawsociety.org.sg/Pages/LegaleSE.aspx (last visited June 28, 2018).

94. *See, e.g.*, Law Awareness Weeks @ CDC 2017, LAW AWARENESS WEEK (LAW) @CDC 2017 – LAW SOCIETY PRO BONO SERVICES, www.lawawarenessweek2017.com/ (last visited June 27, 2018); About Law Awareness Week (LAW) @CDC 2016, LAW AWARENESS WEEK @CDC 2016, www.lawsociety.org.sg/event/LawAwareness2016/overview.aspx (last visited June 28, 2018).

95. *See* Singapore Free Legal Clinics, SINGAPORE FREE LEGAL CLINICS, http://legalclinics.sg/ (last visited June 28, 2018).

96. *See* Laura Philomin, *More Legal Clinics Islandwide*, TODAY (Sept. 13, 2014), www.todayonline.com/singapore/more-legal-clinics-islandwide (last visited June 28, 2018); Indranee Rajah, *Speech by Senior Minister of State for Law, Indranee Rajah, at the Launch of Law Awareness Week @ CDC*, LAUNCH OF LAW AWARENESS WEEK @ CDC, www.mlaw.gov.sg/content/minlaw/en/news/speeches/speech-by-senior-minister-of-state-for-law–indranee-rajah–at-t0.html (last visited June 28, 2018).

97. *See, e.g.*, TSMP LAW CORPORATION, www.tsmplaw.com/community.html (last visited June 28, 2018); WMH Law Corporation, Navin Sregantan, *Playing a Part in Making Legal Aid Accessible to All*, BUSINESS TIMES (Sept. 26, 2017), www.businesstimes.com.sg/life-culture/company-of-good/playing-a-part-in-making-legal-aid-accessible-to-all (last visited June 28, 2018).

98. Tan Dawn Wei, *Want Free Legal Advice? Get in Line*, STRAITS TIMES, Sept. 9, 2007.

99. The Law Society of Singapore, Pro Bono Guide, https://www.lawsociety.org.sg/probono/pdf/probonoguide.pdf (last visited June 28, 2018).
100. *Community Development Councils Are Envisaged: 17 August 1996*, Singapore separates from Malaysia and Becomes Independent – Singapore History, http://eresources.nlb.gov.sg/history/events/27e53f92-2b03-4e63-9b0b-4dbf127008ed (last visited June 28, 2018).
101. Wei, *supra* note 98.
102. Kotwani, *supra* note 19.
103. Radha Basu, *Clients Throng Law Society's Free Clinic*, Straits Times, Feb. 9, 2008.
104. *Id.*
105. The Law Society of Singapore, Community Legal Clinic, http://probono.lawsociety.org.sg/Pages/Community-Legal-Clinic.aspx (last visited June 28, 2018).
106. *Id.*
107. *Id.*
108. Radha Basu, *Clients Throng Law Society's Free Clinic*, Straits Times, Feb. 9, 2008.
109. Kotwani, *supra* note 19.
110. Basu, *supra* note 108.
111. *Message from the Chief Justice*, Supreme Court of Singapore Annual Report 2012, at 8–9, www.supremecourt.gov.sg/docs/default-source/default-document-library/annual-report-2012.pdf (last visited June 28, 2018).
112. *See Legal Clinics*, Community Legal Clinic, http://probono.lawsociety.org.sg/Pages/Volunteer-Schemes-Legal-Clinics.aspx (last visited June 28, 2018).
113. The Community Justice Center, https://cjc.org.sg/services/legal-services/on-site-legal-clinic-oslas/.
114. *Primary Justice Project*, Community Justice Center, https://cjc.org.sg/services/legal-services/primary-justice-project/ (last visited Sept. 26, 2020).
115. *See Legal Clinics – Free Legal Advice*, Singapore Council of Women's Organisations, www.scwo.org.sg/what-we-do/services/legal-clinics/ (last visited June 28, 2018).
116. *See Free Legal Clinic*, AWARE (2018), www.aware.org.sg/support-services/legal-services/ (last visited June 28, 2018).
117. *See Community Justice Centre*, Community Justice Centre, https://www.cjc.org.sg (last visited Mar. 31, 2019).
118. Alvin Chen & Helena Whalen-Bridge, Understanding Lawyers Ethics in Singapore 9.32 (2016).
119. Subordinate Courts of Singapore, Annual Report 2009, at 50.
120. Helena Whalen-Bridge, Pro Bono in Singapore: The PBG Story 27 (2016).

121. *See* K. C. Vijayan, *Senior Counsel Not Just a Title*, STRAITS TIMES, Jan. 13, 2016 (per the chief justice, key considerations are "outstanding advocacy skills over time and proven track records in public service or pro bono work").
122. Luz E. Herrera, *Encouraging the Development of Low Bono Law Practices*, 14 U. MD. L.J. RACE, RELIGION, GENDER & CLASS 1, 3 (2014).
123. *See, e.g.*, CARROLL SERON, THE BUSINESS OF PRACTICING LAW: THE WORK LIVES OF SOLO AND SMALL-FIRM ATTORNEYS (1996); Herrera, *supra* note 122.
124. Leslie C. Levin, *Pro Bono Publico in a Parallel Universe: The Meaning of Pro Bono in Solo and Small Law Firms*, 37 HOFSTRA L. REV. 722 (2009).
125. Letters of the Law, *June Lim, Founder, Eden Law Corporation* (Feb. 21, 2017), www.lettersofthelaw.org/read-all/2017/2/21/june-lim-founder-eden-law-corporation (last visited Sept. 26, 2020).
126. *Id.*
127. Hoi I Yune, *Super She-Ro #2: This Woman Provides Legal Help for the Underprivileged* (17 August 2017), HER WORLD, www.herworld.com/features/women-now/how-lawyer-woman-provides-legal-help-needy (last visited Sept. 26, 2020).
128. Letters of the Law, *supra* note 125.
129. Civil Law Act, s 5B; Legal Profession Act, s 107(1)(b), and Legal Profession (Professional Conduct) Rules 2015, No. S 706, Rule 18; but as of 2019, a change was being considered. *See* Singapore Ministry of Law, *Public Consultation on Conditional Fee Agreements in Singapore*, https://app.mlaw.gov.sg/news/public-consultations/public-consultation-on-conditional-fee-agreements-in-singapore (last visited Oct. 13, 2019).
130. Letters of the Law, *supra* note 125.
131. Yune, *supra* note 127.
132. *Id.*
133. K. C. Vijavan, *Honing Competitive Edge of Legal Profession* (Feb. 2, 2017), STRAITS TIMES, www.straitstimes.com/singapore/honing-competitive-edge-of-legal-profession (last visited Sept. 26, 2020).
134. Yune, *supra* note 127; *see also* Art Daryanani & Vanessa Phang, *CLIO: Making Lawyers Efficient, Paperless and Mobile* (Oct. 2017), SINGAPORE LAW GAZETTE, https://lawgazette.com.sg/practice/tech-talk/clio-making-lawyers-efficient-paperless-and-mobile/ (last visited Sept. 26, 2020).
135. Letters of the Law, *supra* note 125.
136. Yune, *supra* note 127.
137. Letters of the Law, *supra* note 125.
138. Eden Law Corporation, http://edenlaw.com.sg/ (last visited Sept. 26, 2020).
139. Interview in Singapore (Aug. 2018).
140. Supreme Court Launches Inaugural Award for the Legal Assistance Scheme for Capital Offences (LASCO) (2010) www.supremecourt.g

ov.sg/news/media-releases/supreme-court-launches-inaugural-award-for-the-legal-assistance-scheme-for-capital-offences-lasco (last visited June 28, 2018).

141. Latham & Watkins LLP, *supra* note 27, at 579.

142. *Id.*

143. *Legal Assistance for Capital Offences (LASCO)*, SUPREME COURT (2018), www.supremecourt.gov.sg/services/self-help-services/legal-assistance-for-capital-offences (last visited June 27, 2018).

144. *Speech of the Chief Justice of Singapore, Chan Sek Keong*, LEGAL ASSISTANCE SCHEME FOR CAPITAL OFFENCES (LASCO) INAUGURAL LASCO AWARD DINNER (2010), http://v1.lawgazette.com.sg/2011–05/105.htm (last visited June 28, 2018).

145. *Supreme Court Launches New Initiatives for the Legal Assistance Scheme for Capital Offences (LASCO) Enhancing the Standards of the Criminal Bar and Providing Greater Support for LASCO Counsel*, SUPREME COURT (2011), www.supremecourt.gov.sg/docs/default-source/default-document-library/rules/lasco-media-release_20-may-2011.pdf (last visited June 28, 2018).

146. *Criminal Legal Aid Scheme*, THE LAW SOCIETY OF SINGAPORE, http://probono.lawsociety.org.sg/Pages/Criminal-Legal-Aid-Scheme.aspx (last visited June 27, 2018).

147. Association of Criminal Lawyers of Singapore, *supra* note 66.

148. Community Justice Centre, Guidance for Plea Scheme, https://cjc.org.sg/services/legal-services/guidance-for-plea-scheme-gps/ (last visited Sept. 26, 2020).

149. *Id.*

150. *Enhanced Criminal Legal Aid Scheme Set to Provide Greater Access to Justice*, MINISTRY OF LAW (2015), www.mlaw.gov.sg/content/minlaw/en/news/press-releases/Enhanced-CLAS-to-provide-greater-access-to-justice.html (last visited June 28, 2018).

151. 7 Dec. 2013, www.todayonline.com/singapore/govt-will-provide-direct-legal-aid-defendants-criminal-cases?singlepage¼true (last visited June 28, 2018); *see also* S. Ramesh, *Govt to Enhance Criminal Legal Aid Scheme*, CHANNEL NEWS ASIA (Dec. 6, 2013), www.channelnewsasia.com/news/singapore/shanmugam-announces-new/912780.html (last visited June 28, 2018); Thian Yee Sze, Director-General, Ministry of Law, *The Four Principles That Anchor Singapore's Criminal Justice System*, SINGAPORE LAW GAZETTE (Feb. 2014) http://v1.lawgazette.com.sg/2014–02/964.htm (last visited June 28, 2018) (from 2014, "the Government will enhance the funding to the Law Society for the operation of its pro bono criminal legal aid efforts").

152. *Speech by Minister for Foreign Affairs and Law, K Shanmugam, at the Association of Muslim Lawyers' Inaugural Lecture*, ASSOCIATION OF MUSLIM LAWYERS' INAUGURAL LECTURE ¶ 33 (2013).

153. *Id.* at ¶ 16.

154. *See Ministry of Law*, ENHANCED CRIMINAL LEGAL AID SCHEME, www.mlaw.gov.sg/content/dam/minlaw/corp/News/AnnexA.pdf (last visited June 28, 2018).
155. On May 19, 2015, it was reported that the committee included Senior Minister of State for Education and Law Indranee Rajah, as adviser to the steering committee, along with Judge of Appeal Justice Chao Hick Tin, and that the chairman of the committee was presiding judge of the state courts, Judicial Commissioner See Kee Oon, the vice-chairman was then president of the Law Society, Thio Shen Yi, SC. *See Enhanced Criminal Legal Aid Scheme Set to Provide Greater Access to Justice*, *supra* note 150, at ¶ 5(II).
156. *Id.*
157. Kelly Ng, *Five Full-Time Lawyers Help Boost Legal Aid Scheme*, TODAY (May 19, 2015), www.todayonline.com/singapore/five-full-time-lawyers-help-boost-legal-aid-scheme (last visited June 28, 2018).
158. Enhanced Criminal Legal Aid Scheme Set to Provide Greater Access to Justice, *supra* note 150, at ¶ 5(II).
159. Lim Yi Han & Amos Lee, *Enhanced Criminal Legal Aid Scheme officially Launched*, STRAITS TIMES, May 19, 2015.
160. Enhanced Access to Justice through Enhanced CLAS: A Note from Indranee Rajah SC, Senior Minister of State for Law (May 26, 2015), https://www.mlaw.gov.sg/files/NotebySMSonEnhancedCLAS.pdf/ (last visited June 28, 2018) [hereinafter Enhanced Access to Justice through Enhanced CLAS].
161. Amanda Lee, *Govt to Enhance Criminal Legal Aid*, TODAY (Dec. 6, 2013), www.todayonline.com/singapore/govt-enhance-criminal-legal-aid (last visited June 28, 2018).
162. Enhanced Access to Justice Through Enhanced CLAS, *supra* note 160.
163. *Id.*
164. *Id.*
165. *Id.*
166. Sara Grosse, *Enhanced Criminal Legal Aid Scheme to Benefit up to 6,000 People Yearly*, CHANNEL NEWS ASIA (May 18, 2015), www.channelnewsasia.com/news/singapore/enhanced-criminal-legal-aid-scheme-to-benefit-up-to-6–000-people-8261448 (last visited June 28, 2018).
167. *Id.*
168. *Id.*
169. *Enhanced Criminal Legal Aid Scheme Set to Provide Greater Access to Justice*, *supra* note 150, at ¶ 5(II).
170. Enhanced Access to Justice Through Enhanced CLAS, *supra* note 160.
171. *Id.*
172. Kotwani, *supra* note 19.
173. *Id.*
174. *See* Enhanced Access to Justice Through Enhanced CLAS, *supra* note 160, at 3 and Annex B.

175. *See* Eoin Ó Muimhneacháin & Dinisha Thadani, *Keeping It CLASy*, SINGAPORE LAW GAZETTE, Jan. 2015; Sujatha Selvakumar, CLAS Fellow, *CLAS 2015: Breaking New Ground*, SINGAPORE LAW GAZETTE, Mar. 2015; *see also* JusNewSG, CLAS FELLOWSHIP PROGRAMME FOR CRIMINAL LEGAL AID, Nov. 2016, https:/www.lawsociety.org.sg/jusnewsg/newsletter/201611/news03.html (last visited June 28, 2018).
176. Kelly Ng, *More Help for Those Who Can't Afford Lawyers in "High Stakes" Court Cases*, TODAY (Dec. 27, 2016), www.todayonline.com/singapore/more-help-those-who-cant-afford-lawyers-high-stakes-court-cases (last visited June 28, 2018).
177. *Id.*
178. See the discussion of low bono in Opening of the Legal Year 2018, Response by Chief Justice Sundaresh Menon ¶¶ 32, 60 (Jan. 8, 2018), www.supremecourt.gov.sg/Data/Editor/Documents/Response%20by%20Chief%20Justice%20%20(Checked%20against%20Delivery%20version%20-%20080118).pdf (last visited Sept. 26, 2020).
179. Kotwani, *supra* note 19.
180. *See* Association of Corporate Counsel, "ACC Singapore Introduces Pro Bono Committee" (Jan. 13, 2020), DOCKET, www.accdocket.com/articles/acc-singapore-introduces-pro-bono-committee.cfm (last visited Sept. 26, 2020).
181. SIM University to Start Full-Time Programmes in 2014 and to Set Up Third Law School in Singapore, SUSS, Oct. 16, 2013, https://www.unisim.edu.sg/Happenings/Latest-Highlights/Pages/H2013_16Oct.aspx (last visited June 28, 2018).
182. See *Pro Bono Programme*, SINGAPORE INSTITUTE OF LEGAL EDUCATION (2017), www.sile.edu.sg/pro-bono-programme (last visited June 28, 2018), where the SILE acknowledged the role of the 2007 Report: "In the 2007 Report of the Committee to Develop the Singapore Legal Sector, one of the recommendations made by the committee was that measures should be taken to foster idealism and community bonding amongst lawyers, in particular, through the promotion of pro bono work. Building on the committee's recommendation, the SILE has initiated a pro bono programme for law students from the National University of Singapore (NUS) Faculty of Law and the Singapore Management University (SMU) School of Law ('Pro Bono Programme')."
183. Helena Whalen-Bridge, *Student "Pro Bono" and the NUS Faculty of Law*, SINGAPORE J. LEGAL STUD. 1 (2017).
184. In the family justice courts, see the Family Justice Support Scheme, in Response by Chief Justice Sundaresh Menon, Opening of the Legal Year 2018 8 January 2018, ¶¶ 32 & 60(b); Report of the Committee to Review and Enhance Reforms in the Family Justice System 3, 36-37 (Sept. 13, 2019); and Gregory Vijayendran, *President's Message*, LAW GAZETTE (Sept. 2019).

CHAPTER SEVENTEEN

THE RISE OF PRIVATE PUBLIC INTEREST LAWYERS IN CHINA

Jin Dong and Qian Cheng

INTRODUCTION

Although it is hard to give a unified and standardized definition to pro bono, this practice has become increasingly institutionalized worldwide.[1] Driven by transnational legal practice, the global market for legal services, and international rule of law campaigns, pro bono work has taken place not only in developed countries (e.g., the United States, Ireland, Canada, and Austria) but also in developing countries and so-called emerging economies, such as China, India, and Brazil.[2] The International Bar Association (IBA) has done a great deal of work to facilitate pro bono practice throughout the world. An unprecedented international pro bono initiative by the DLA Piper law firm has yielded pro bono lawyers who donated over two hundred thousand hours in 2017.[3] Law schools also participate in this social movement.[4] Law students who take international public interest courses in the United States apply their knowledge in a global setting. Graduates of American law schools have even begun to practice public interest law in other counties.[5] Therefore, pro bono has become a globalized social movement accompanying legal globalization.[6]

Beginning at the end of the 1990s, Chinese lawyering began to boom following the rapid development of the Chinese economy. In this process, the Chinese legal profession was increasingly "professionalized."[7] Private lawyers and law firms emerged and multiplied, new qualification examinations for legal professionals were introduced, legal education was transformed, and many lawyers and law firms gained global exposure. According to the latest statistical data from March 2018, the number of lawyers practicing law is over 360,000.[8] Categorized by size, Yingke Law Firm, the largest law firm with its headquarters in China, now has more than 8,000 lawyers and forty-seven officers globally.[9] Moreover, a top Chinese law firm, King & Woods, merged with Mallesons, a leading Australian law firm, in 2013, giving rise to a transnational super law firm headquartered in China.[10]

Following this boom of the legal profession in China, pro bono practice and values have been increasingly institutionalized among Chinese legal professionals.[11] In 2017, Chinese lawyers took over 3.2 million pro bono legal cases. Of these cases, 578,000 cases were legal aid cases designated by local governments, and 987,000 cases were for disadvantaged claimants. Approximately 2.3 million involved free legal consultation in rural areas, covering over 553,000 Chinese villages. Currently, the Chinese government states that the state-run legal aid system covers the whole of China. More importantly, any criminal defendant can apply for free state legal aid under the new legal aid regulation, which became effective in 2016. The budget for state-run legal aid has significantly increased since 2012.[12] Since the Chinese government is expected to honor law firms' pro bono work, large Chinese firms like to declare their pro bono contributions through their websites. Annual pro bono awards are set up by local bar associations to cite lawyers who do well in pro bono work.[13]

Also, pro bono education has expanded in Chinese law schools. Based on the US legal clinic training model, Chinese law schools (departments of law) began to develop legal clinic training programs in 2000, funded by the Ford Foundation. Currently, there are over two hundred such training programs in Chinese law schools or departments of law.[14] Law students can receive pro bono training and practice through these programs in schools, accompanied by outside pro bono training programs run by the Committee of Chinese Legal Clinic Training. Several Chinese law schools (e.g., Wuhan University, Chinese University of Law and Politics) have established pro bono centers, which provide pro bono training for professional lawyers. Also, they are devoted to organizing a pro bono network to help low-income and disadvantaged people in China.[15]

Previous research has demonstrated that global processes and forces have driven the development of pro bono work in China considerably.[16] The Global Pro Bono Association has honored Chinese lawyers' pro bono efforts. Jianmei Guo, recipient of the International Women of Courage Award in 2011 from the US

Department of State, has been devoted to representing family violence and women's rights cases without financial compensation for over ten years. In 2013, the IBA announced that Lihua Tong, a well-known Chinese pro bono lawyer, had won the 2012 IBA Pro Bono Award.[17] The global pro bono network PILnet established a Beijing office in 2008.[18] Currently, Chinese PILnet fellows consistently advocate for Chinese pro bono and related work and development throughout China. Partnering with Columbia University Law School, PILnet has sent over twenty Chinese lawyers and scholars to train on public interest legal issues in New York City since 2003.[19]

In this research, we focus on a certain group of lawyers that has (re)emerged in this context: Chinese private public interest lawyers. Although these lawyers might not be in the mainstream of the Chinese legal profession, their pro bono work and related public interest law service is very meaningful for the way pro bono work or lawyers' work for the public good can be performed in the Chinese context, and for how Chinese professional lawyers understand pro bono under the current political structure of Chinese society. Our claim is that, due to these special circumstances under which pro bono has been institutionalized in China, the meaning of pro bono shared by Chinese legal professionals may not match the meaning emanating from global frameworks.

We use multiple research methods to offer a preliminary picture of this group. Our research methods include archival research on documents from the Chinese Republican era, public data from websites, data from newspapers, and a small number of qualitative telephone interviews (of fifteen lawyers) using the widely used social networking site WeChat.

Such breadth in our research methods is important and necessary. Based on historical documents, we notice that private public interest lawyers are not newcomers to China. The practice of private public interest law in China began in the Republican age (1911–49). Many private public interest lawyers played an important role in promoting social change and providing access to justice at this time.[20] After that, they disappeared due to the huge transformation of the Chinese political structure. Legal professionals ceased to exist in Chinese society for a long time.[21] But because, in the 1980s, the Chinese government launched a profound movement called "Reform and Open Up," the Chinese legal profession, including these private public interest lawyers, revived and has received more attention from Chinese social media and the community.[22]

Our research has focused on this group of private public interest lawyers, and it offers a good opportunity for scholars to describe a distinctive picture of professional legal practice in which Chinese lawyers take account of the issues of lawyering for the public good or good lawyering. In particular, Chinese lawyers have rapidly taken over a large portion of the global legal service market in recent years, although the Chinese legal profession is still in a stage of formation.[23] It is important to examine the meaning of pro bono for Chinese private public interest lawyers closely and to compare them with global ideas.

THE FORMATION OF PRO BONO IN THE CHINESE CONTEXT[24]

Although pro bono's institutionalization in twenty-first-century China definitely owes much to global forces[25] and Chinese integration into the world economy, the process is also heavily shaped by the Chinese political structure.

To begin with, in the Chinese context, pro bono practice involves many nonlegal public services as well as state-run legal assistance programs.[26] Perhaps most importantly, the development of pro bono work in China has been highly dependent on political power. Previous studies have demonstrated that legal globalization involves the diffusion of legal knowledge and institutional models from core Western countries, such as the United States or Germany, which push for global convergence.[27] In the case of China, this process was more intricate. Starting in the 1990s, the government launched a top-to-bottom movement that came to be known as "rule by law." The goal was to import legal institutions from Western counties to build up a more modern country.[28] But the process was controlled by the government and, therefore, attached to the Chinese political structure. For example, the rule by law movement has not authorized lawyers' independence in the legal market until recently. Political institutions in China would like to resist or suppress this change and not allow for lawyers' professional independence.[29] Hence, a remarkable characteristic of the contemporary Chinese legal system is its political embeddedness.

Chinese lawyers' pro bono work emerged in this period.[30] The All Chinese Lawyer Association (ACLA), a Chinese nationwide bar association, and the Chinese government made great efforts to promote a well-established system of pro bono work. But in doing so, they also made pro bono a tool to control lawyers' work.

Unlike the American Bar Association, which is run independently, China's organized bar association was established and is fully controlled by the Ministry of Justice (MOJ), that is, the government. By underscoring lawyers' social responsibility and commitment to the public interest, the ACLA introduces a professional duty of Chinese lawyers to perform pro bono work. As Junfeng Wang, the current president and deputy general secretary of the Chinese Communist Party (CCP) committee of the ACLA, said in 2012, public interest service is an inherent professional norm, and lawyers should have the heart to provide any service for the public good.[31]

There are similarities between Chinese and US lawyering practices in that pro bono is a principle instilled into Chinese lawyers through the Chinese Bar Association's regulations and through other efforts. Taking effect in 2004 and revised in 2009 by the ACLA, the Code of Practice on the Conduct of Lawyers states that local lawyer associations should be responsible for encouraging and directing lawyers' public interest service (Article 10). The ACLA also created the Committee of Public Interests and Social Responsibility to improve lawyers' public interest service. In addition to the efforts from the ACLA, local bars have enacted related regulations or set up special committees to promote and manage lawyers' public interest service. For example, the Beijing Lawyers Association's Code of Practice for Lawyers states that lawyers should participate in public interest service. The Shanghai Bar Association set up the Legal Aid and Community Service Committee, which is responsible for organizing public interest service in Shanghai.

The ACLA also began to release Chinese lawyers' reports of their social responsibility work in 2013. It claimed that lawyers' associations at the provincial level should annually report law firms' activities on legal aid, free legal service, and other public interest affairs. The aim of the initiative was to create a routine report system for lawyers' broad public service participation. This report summarized individual lawyers' pro bono work and the operation of pro bono organizations from 2010 to 2012.[32] Since then, local bar associations (e.g., Shanghai, Hangzhou, and Hefei) have released several social responsibility reports. These reports have included diverse public services, and they have been generalized as lawyers' inherent social responsibility.[33]

Besides enacting conduct codes, building pro bono committees, and releasing related public service reports, the bar honors lawyers' and law firms' pro bono efforts. As early as 2003, the ACLA enacted the Code of Methods for Awarding Lawyers. Under Article 7, individual lawyers who are enthusiastic about public interest service and who have been praised by their local communities should be rewarded. Although the ACLA has not yet established a nationwide award for lawyers' public service, local lawyers' associations have set up annual awards for lawyers who have made great contributions to the public interest. For instance, the Beijing Lawyers Association has given out an annual lawyer's award for pro bono practice since 2010.[34]

In the code of bar associations, it is notable that neither the ACLA nor the government gives an official definition of pro bono. In practice, it has been understood as a broad service to the public interest, including civic engagement, community service, political participation, CCP party-building activities, social charity, and state-run legal aid instead of pro bono legal service as lawyers in the United States understand it.

Following up on these developments, Chinese law firms and lawyers began to report on their social responsibility activities. For example, a leading corporate law firm, Grandall, has been releasing its lawyers' social responsibility report since 2013.[35] They also began to use the term "pro bono" to describe such activities. On many well-known Chinese law firms' websites (e.g., Dacheng, Allbright), varieties of public service (e.g., civic engagement, community service, party building, and charity service) have been listed in the pro bono column of services.[36]

Lawyers practicing law in small firms or solo practitioners can deliver their public interest service through state-run channels, such as local bar associations and government-owned social media. For example, the Guangxi Bar Association, accompanied by the *Nanguo Morning News*, a government-owned newspaper, hosts a free legal consultation hotline. Every Tuesday, volunteer lawyers on duty provide free legal assistance through this hotline.[37] The Shanghai Bar Association also conducts jumble sales for physically or mentally challenged children.[38] Consequently, social responsibility and public interest service have become the professional norm among Chinese lawyers and law firms as well as bar associations, and this has been recognized by the Chinese legal market as well.

On the other hand, local state-run legal aid systems have been rapidly developed by the Chinese local governments. In 2017, the MOJ enacted "Opinions on Legal Aid for Lawyers" to request

Chinese lawyers to participate in government-run legal aid, delivering free or substantive fee reduction legal advice.[39] Those systems have become an important part of pro bono work among Chinese legal professionals. In China, there are 474 legal aid administration institutions, 3,263 legal aid agencies, and 68,225 legal aid workstations. In terms of the 294 prefecture-level cities throughout the country (excluding Hong Kong, Macao, and Taiwan), the average city has 1.6 legal aid administration institutions, 11 legal aid agencies, and 232 legal aid workstations, which basically has produced a depth of coverage of legal aid organizations throughout the country. Local governments around China have put legal aid funds into their local financial budgets.

In 2017, local finance departments invested legal aid funds of RMB 2,350,000,000.[40] However, the number of government legal aid lawyers is very limited in relation to the needs of Chinese citizens. According to the latest data, only 6,600 government legal aid lawyers provide legal aid services in China. To fill this gap, the Chinese government thus encourages professional lawyers to take their cases for a government stipend.[41] These services have been looked at as pro bono among Chinese legal professionals.

Due to the work conducted by the Chinese government and its agencies, the original meaning of pro bono has been altered. Unlike the meaning of pro bono in the United States, which focuses on free legal services or substantive service fee reductions, it is more likely to be understood as a broad service for the public good in the Chinese context.[42] More specifically, pro bono activities that are conducted through the government along with the CCP will obtain priority among Chinese law firms, lawyers, and bar associations. Chinese lawyers and firms want to perform their pro bono commitments under the framework of the CCP and its related institutions, such as bar associations, the CCP branch or committees in communities, and the state bureaucracy system. Despite the fact that Chinese legal professionals have recently come to use the term "pro bono" widely, pro bono in China has a global outlook, but it embodies local meanings.[43] The work of private public interest lawyers makes this interplay visible.

THE DEFINITION OF PRIVATE PUBLIC INTEREST LAWYER

It is hard to offer a global, unified, and standardized definition of the term "private public interest lawyer." It can have a mixed meaning that might include the public good as well as the private interest, as argued in previous US research.[44] On one side, lawyers in this group like to seek a social justice or social change mission beyond their legal business. Most of their services are totally free, or they receive a small stipend. Through working with nongovernmental organizations (NGOs) and other charity or community service groups, private public interest lawyers donate their billable hours frequently, and they like to believe that serving the public good is a lawyer's responsibility. However, they are not full-time public interest lawyers or human right lawyers. They are practicing law in professional law firms rather than public interest law firms relying on financial support from international NGOs. Their income from for-fee cases helps them to provide free services to the public consistently.[45]

How to distinguish between private public interest lawyers and their counterparts is certainly a key issue. By nature, professional lawyers focus on business and profit making.[46] According to previous research in the United States, lawyers' pro bono work is becoming increasingly institutionalized. For most lawyers and law firms, pro bono work is a tool for them to pursue business interests in the legal service market. Therefore, pro bono work among private lawyers and law firms can be understood as a mode of market reliance.[47] However, private public interest lawyers challenge this bottom line. They practice law for business reasons, but they like to participate frequently in various types of public interest work through different channels. Their daily work mixes pro bono and legal practice for business, and this blurs the boundary between the public good and commercial purposes, which are two competing aspects in the legal profession.

Research conducted in the United States[48] shows that private public interest lawyers devote a large proportion of their work time to social reform, in areas like environmental rights, women's rights, food safety, land rights, consumer rights, and others. However, considering today's Chinese context, social reform–oriented pro bono service that might be politically sensitive and funded by international NGOs is heavily monitored or even forbidden by the government. For example, Jianmei Guo, recipient of the International Women of Courage Award in 2011, has practiced pro bono law for over ten years in Beijing, running a public interest law firm focused on women's rights. Besides her brilliant work on public interest legal service, she is also a legal activist. Through her longtime work, a network for women's rights composed of dozens of law firms and more than one hundred volunteer lawyers has become well established. Nevertheless, her social justice research institute, the Center for Women's Law Studies and Legal Services of Peking University, was kicked out of Peking University because of the sensitive nature of the cases it represented. The board of Peking University thus closed down her research institution without warning. Even worse, in January 2016, Guo declared that her public interest law firm, Zhongze Women Legal Aid Center, had been closed down because it applied for US financial aid for sensitive cases.[49]

There have also been an increasing number of cases where Chinese public interest lawyers have been prosecuted and had their licenses revoked. They have frequently been intimidated and even abruptly stopped in their public interest legal service by local bureaucracy. In addition to directly constraining public interest lawyers' legal service, the Chinese government may take charge of public interest law firms and lawyers by limiting their international financial support.[50] Currently, a considerable number of NGOs and public interest law firms rely on international funding. Chinese NGOs face many difficulties in receiving international funding, since the Chinese government has introduced harsh restrictions on currency exchange for NGOs and public interest law firms. While their pro bono work is investigated and constrained by the Chinese government, such firms still have the opportunity to make social change and to expand social justice.[51]

According to this discussion, private public interest lawyers may be defined as professional lawyers working in commercial legal practice, but who voluntarily provide various types of public interest service, frequently including nonprofit legal services, and who like to declare the value of public interest to the public and to their colleagues. Their status as professional lawyers is commercially oriented, but advancing the public good is one of their core missions rather than a secondary concern. However, the Chinese political structure is a key factor influencing these lawyers' pro bono preferences and the extent of their pro bono work, as we demonstrate in the remainder of this chapter.

THE HISTORY OF PRIVATE PUBLIC INTEREST LAWYERS IN CHINA

China's feudal dynasties did not have lawyers. There were legal practitioners called litigation masters (*songshis*), who had an unsavory reputation. In imperial China, due to the influence of Confucianism, common people traditionally resisted lawsuits and legal representatives, and thus the public always showed distrust toward this group.[52] At the beginning of China's modern era from 1911, people usually made no distinction between lawyers and *songshis*.[53]

China's first generation of private public interest lawyers made great efforts to redeem their image by advocating for social causes and delivering public interest service to the people. These private public interest lawyers worked in tough social conditions. However, they worked hard to bring social justice to the public. As a result, they led the movement for social reform and the institutionalization of pro bono work in that period.

The rise of lawyers in China is traceable to the Republican era (1911–49), when China's social structure underwent a revolutionary transformation. In 1911, Chinese society entered a new age in the country's history. The last feudal dynasty vanished, and the Kuomintang (KMT) established the Republic of China (ROC). China then began modernization, which was a top-to-bottom movement, to erode the Chinese legal tradition of feudalism. The government, although unstable, tried to adopt a Western style of politics, as well as emphasizing the value of rule by law. The government expected to offer people more liberality than the traditional feudal society. Following this transformation, lawyers become an independent professional group.

In 1911, just after Jiangsu Province declared its independence during the revolution, it enacted the Interim Act of Lawyers within its territory, and it established the Bar Association of Jiangsu under its high court.[54] Later, fourteen graduates who studied law in Japan petitioned the governor of Shanghai to establish the Bar Association of the Republic of China.[55] During the revolution, many bar associations were founded either by local governments or by lawyers, but there was no official network among them. Even though there were no national regulations regarding lawyering, lawyers participated in the development of China's modern judicial system. In February 1912, the former mayor of Shanyang, Yao Rongze, was prosecuted for murdering two leaders of a local revolutionary force. Wu Tingfang, minister of justice and a British barrister, wrote a letter to Sun Yat-sen, the provisional president, stating that "as the Republic was recently established, we should adopt civilized judicial procedures in all the litigations. This case [against Yao] was important. We must try it carefully to show our respect for the laws. I will appoint legal officials who have profound knowledge of Chinese and Western laws to hear this case . . . . We also should allow lawyers to represent each party to advocate before the judges."[56]

In September 1912, the Department of Justice issued the Interim Act of Lawyers of China. It demonstrated that the central government had set up a nationwide, modern system of lawyers in China. The number of lawyers increased rapidly after the Interim Act was adopted. By the end of 1912, there were only 297 lawyers registered with the Department of Justice, while just a year later there were 2,716 registered lawyers in China.[57] The legal profession was granted remarkable autonomy under the Interim Act of Lawyers. The president was in charge of the daily management of the bar association, and the standing committee's members met regularly to decide major issues. Both the president and the standing committee were directly elected by the members of the bar association. The bar association had the power to decide their election procedures, to regulate professional responsibilities, to set standards for lawyers' fees, and to punish their member lawyers. Many first-generation Chinese lawyers were trained in Western law schools and were highly influenced by Western lawyering culture. They were concerned with protecting the autonomy of the bar associations, and they constantly resisted interference by the government. Due to the autonomy of bar associations, lawyers in the ROC became an independent force involved in shaping the judicial system and delivering justice. They provided legal services for many of the government's opponents, and usually for free.

Western legal education heavily affected Chinese lawyering culture in its early stages. In the Republican era, a large portion of Chinese lawyers received their law degrees in Japan, the United States, the United Kingdom, or Germany. Even though some lawyers were trained in China, Chinese law schools were based on models from the United States and France. Since China did not have any tradition of legal education, law schools in China had to learn from the West. The textbooks, professors, and curriculum design came from Western countries.[58] In this regard, Christian universities were deeply involved, because they contributed a lot to orient the newborn Chinese society toward Western civilization, including Western-style education. Some of China's leading law schools were run by Western churches. Fourteen Christian universities recruited Chinese students. Three of these universities (Soochow University, Yenching University, and Aurora

University) had internationally known law schools.[59] The Republican government was less likely to interfere in the operation of schools. Global legal value for the public good and political liberalism could diffuse directly into Chinese local law schools and legal professionals at that time.[60] The value of pro bono and political liberalism greatly affected these lawyers' behavior and attitudes. For example, the Soochow Law School introduced a model of a Legal Aid Society from the United States.[61]

Chinese lawyers in the ROC also shared the value of serving the public good from the very beginning. A letter issued by the Bar Association of Shanghai to its members stated that "lawyers practice according to law, and [they] share equal judicial power with judges and prosecutors. In the society, lawyer is one of the most honorable professions. No other profession can compare with it."[62] Shen Junru, a leading lawyer in the ROC, said that "the purpose of lawyers is to aid the disadvantaged groups, and to protect the rights of people."[63] He also often encouraged younger lawyers to fulfill the duty of "protecting human rights."[64]

In this context, these private public interest lawyers were too important for Chinese society to overlook. According to historical documents, Chinese private public interest lawyers suggested that lawyers' top mission was social justice rather than business. They believed that they had a professional obligation to serve the public, unlike US lawyers, who had blurred the line between profits and principle. Chinese private public interest lawyers have always focused on public interest legal service. Although they were legal practitioners seeking profits, they often voluntarily offered their billable hours in legal service for the advancement of social causes. For instance, Shi Liang, who lived in Shanghai, frequently offered free legal aid to individual women who belonged to lower social strata.[65]

While Chinese private public interest lawyers provided public interest legal service for individual social justice cases, they also campaigned as legal activists working to promote social change through their social reputation and networks. They often organized NGOs to advance social movements for the public good. Many Chinese private public interest lawyers were socially prominent, and they could afford to charge the highest fees for commercial work while also doing pro bono work. Their strong social networks made it possible for them to promote social change. Their legal work was thus related to their progressive political missions to promote the rule of law. However, contemporary Chinese lawyers are embedded into CCP politics, so it is hard for them to practice law independently. Chinese private public interest lawyers in the Republican era had the independence to practice law and to focus on social causes. Lawyers in the ROC often advanced social change through their public lectures and publications. They liked offering free legal service to Chinese NGOs, including women's rights organizations and labor rights organizations. Well-known private public interest lawyers stood at the frontier of social change as human rights fighters. For example, Shi Yang organized a range of strikes to seek equal pay and labor rights for Chinese railroad workers, and he was eventually killed by a local warlord.[66] Zheng Yuxiu, the first woman in China to earn a PhD in law, ran a liberal and feminist newspaper in Tianjin to emphasize the value of Chinese women's liberation.[67]

Chinese private public interest lawyers at that moment resembled elite politicians. Many of them became congressmen, and they advanced legal reform through legislative activities. Chinese private public interest lawyers fought against arbitrary state power in the legislature, judiciary, and civil society. When Chinese society came onto the global map because of the invasion of Western military forces and political pressure at the end of the nineteenth century, the Chinese social structure was not well established. Private public interest lawyers were active in building constitutionalism and political liberalism. Therefore, they hoped to establish a liberal government and civil society in China. These lawyers launched the compensation for wrongful detentions and executions movement in the 1930s. Chinese lawyers submitted an official proposal to the KMT government, asking it to pass a special law offering financial compensation to people who had been wrongly convicted. After five years, the government passed the Act of Compensation for Wrongful Detentions and Executions, and finally, compensation for people who had been wrongly convicted was added to the first amendment of the Republican constitution.[68]

Besides their work on victims' human rights, the first generation of Chinese private public interest lawyers shaped China's first legal aid system. By using their personal resources and knowledge, they institutionalized pro bono work. The Chinese free legal aid system is based on the Interim Acts of Trial in Tianjin jurisdiction. It was the first written government regulation in China that allowed the poor to obtain substantive fee reductions for their litigation.[69] However, although the government enacted the Act for Appointment of Legal

Representatives to request lawyers to provide free legal service to the poor in criminal cases in 1914, the scope of legal aid was very limited. Hence, lawyers started to initiate and promote legal aid programs to provide pro bono service to the poor. As early as 1924, a private public interest lawyer, Wang Fengying, published an academic article titled "Lawyers' Role in Judiciary Reform." In this article, he argued that Chinese lawyers must voluntarily run legal aid societies.[70] This was the first time in Chinese history that providing pro bono work received public attention. Wang also explored the lawyers' pro bono system and introduced US legal aid practices by citing the publications of American lawyers, including "The Training of Lawyers" and "Case and Comment."[71] Zhang Weiran also published the article "An Overview of Legal Aid in Europe," introducing the practice and experience of legal aid in Europe.[72]

On April 20, 1924, Song Shixiang, Wang Yanguan, Wu Bing, and several other lawyers established the Shanghai Legal Aid Society.[73] A year later, the Chongqing Legal Aid Society and the Minhou Legal Aid Society were established.[74] It became necessary for lawyers' pro bono work to be officially recognized. On December 24, 1933, the managing committee of the Chinese Bar Association proposed that all local bar associations establish a uniform Legal Aid Society.[75] The Ministry of Judicial Administration approved this proposal, and it promptly passed the Temporary Regulations on the Society of Legal Aid for the Poor, providing that local bar associations could establish societies of legal aid to provide free legal service for the afflicted poor.[76] However, the local bar associations were only encouraged, not required, to establish such societies. Thus, not every city had its own legal aid organization.

In 1941, the KMT government enacted a new law formally regulating legal aid services. According to the KMT government's revision, bar associations could assign pro bono work. The new law also provided that standing committee members of the bar associations should routinely work on the duty to handle legal aid affairs and lawyers must submit monthly reports about their pro bono work to the standing committee for review. The local bar associations were also required to submit pro bono briefs to the provincial chief prosecutors, who would then submit them to the Ministry of Judicial Administration. The KMT government penalized local bar associations that were slow to implement this policy.[77] Since the government worked hard to promote lawyers' pro bono value and practice, it was eventually institutionalized.

In the Republican era, because of private public interest lawyers' long-term hard work, public trust in Chinese lawyers began to improve. Unlike today's Chinese lawyers, who have a bad reputation, under the Republic, people liked having public interest lawyers assist them with obtaining social justice. All these developments in pro bono value and work contributed to the work of private public interest lawyers at that moment. They believed that lawyers had a professional responsibility to deliver free legal service to all those who needed legal assistance.

Private public interest lawyers indeed emerged and rapidly expanded in the Republican era, though they were not very numerous. Their privileged social standing enabled them to engage in public interest service. Many Chinese first-generation public interest lawyers came from affluent families with prominent social backgrounds and social networks. They thus had many opportunities to participate in globalization. A Western-style system of legal aid was established in China. It was run by practicing lawyers in regular law firms. Their efforts to bring social change and access to justice were driven by global forces. In this process, Chinese private public interest lawyers, as brokers between different forms of legal/political culture, acquired their knowledge, values, and legal practice from Western cultures, and they made efforts to apply these in the construction of modern Chinese society. Besides professional responsibility for pro bono work, one important issue that should receive more attention is the Chinese political structure of the time. The government was less likely to get involved with the legal profession. Therefore, Chinese lawyers and bar associations had greater professional autonomy in the legal services market.

CONTEMPORARY CHINESE PRIVATE PUBLIC INTEREST LAWYERS

In the twenty-first century, China has become the second-largest national economy in the world. There are more than 360,000 professional lawyers practicing in China at present, more than 100 times the number in 1937. The ACLA and the Chinese government encourage lawyers to perform pro bono services. There are thus lawyers and firms that provide nonlegal public services and that participate in state-run legal aid activities to fulfill their pro bono commitments. Sensitive cases, the outcomes or progress of which may be inconsistent with the politics of the CCP, are heavily monitored and access to them is restricted by the government.[78]

The CCP has been the only significant political power in China since 1949, and the CCP government has retained little legal tradition or culture from the Republican era. For example, the Christian universities that taught law were closed when the CCP took control of the higher educational system, and some were restructured as state-owned universities.[79] Many lawyers licensed by foreign bars were charged as traitors during the Anti-Rightism Campaign from 1957 to 1959.[80] Western-style legal education was abandoned and replaced by Soviet-style education until the 1990s.[81] Even worse, the public began to believe that lawyers damage social stability.[82] However, things are changing, and Chinese private public interest lawyers are developing in a new direction in the twenty-first century.

As the number of professional lawyers in China has boomed, the number of private public interest lawyers has also grown, as have their practice areas and geographic diversity, although there is no centralized resource tracking exactly how many are now working in China. They widely recognize pro bono work as a social responsibility. One lawyer working for environmental protection for the ocean stated that "these environmental protection services I am doing should be done by every citizen instead of only professional lawyers."[83] Previous research has shown that many Chinese lawyers dislike pro bono work because of their already large workloads.[84] Private public interest lawyers have some characteristics in common. No matter what their social background, work environment, or political status, they are devoted to voluntarily donating their billable hours to all kinds of public service, often encouraging their colleagues to perform public service for their communities as well.

Moreover, many of these lawyers are leaders or they play an active role in promoting pro bono work.[85] They believe that the number of Chinese lawyers doing pro bono work can be increased through sustained attention to this issue.[86] They do not believe that practicing law for the public good and for commercial interests are in conflict. They strike a balance between their legal work and their pro bono service.[87] Although they are working for the public good, they have sharply different attitudes toward the political structure and culture in China.

As noted previously, Chinese lawyering is an important force in the global legal market. Local Chinese legal services are becoming highly globalized. Current data show that 242 foreign law firms have offices in China.[88] However, the legal work environment in China is closely controlled by the government. At the CCP's 19th National Congress in Beijing in October 2017, President Xi Jinping declared that the Chinese government must constantly work to strengthen the CCP's leadership. Its authority has priority in social structures, and even the movement to pursue the rule of law should be conducted under the guidance of the political power of the CCP, according to the report.[89] As a direct result, Chinese lawyers and law firms have become involved in CCP politics. Current statistical data show that the number of lawyers who are also members of the CCP is increasing every year. Currently, over 30 percent of lawyers are CCP members. Politics appears in the management of law firms: over 50 percent of Chinese firms have a CCP committee or branch.[90]

Unlike ordinary public interest lawyers in China, who rely on financial support from international foundations like the Ford Foundation, private public interest lawyers are less likely to be internationally funded. As the Chinese government is investigating the work of international foundations in China, public interest lawyers may receive added scrutiny.[91] Therefore, private public interest lawyers are doing pro bono work in a very special situation.

To explore the work of Chinese private public interest lawyers, we used content analysis and telephone interviews. We collected content data from various media: websites, newsletters, public blogs, and lawyers' WeChat circles. We also interviewed fifteen private public interest lawyers via telephone.[92] These data allowed us to determine the substantive work and the understanding of pro bono among this group of lawyers precisely. Chinese private lawyers serving the public interest vary in their political identity. Previous research has demonstrated that the lawyers' politics, in the Chinese context, can be divided into two types.[93] The first is political liberalism, in which lawyers challenge state power and pursue social justice and social change in favor of civil rights and improved legal procedures. The second is political embeddedness, in which lawyers choose to practice law following government policy and to be attached to the CCP political structure.[94] They will not get involved in cases that might have political implications. We thus call these two modes the challenger mode and the safe mode, respectively.

Generally speaking, Chinese lawyers must support CCP politics if they expect to practice law in China unmolested. Our sharp distinction between differentiated modes of practice among private public interest lawyers in China should be used, instead of trying to understand them based on their work environments, social backgrounds, education, or experience. Mode of practice drives the difference between the two types of private public interest lawyers.

The Safe Mode

The private public interest lawyers working in the safe mode perform their pro bono commitment in a controlled way. Their pro bono work centers around state-run legal assistance, legal training, civic engagement, and community service. Their financial resources come from state-owned NGOs, approved charity groups, and government-run associations. For example, Ms. Z, who practices finance law in Shenzhen, is invited each month by the state-run consumer rights protection association to provide free legal services on consumer rights. The Shenzhen consumer rights protection association pays a certain transportation stipend for this service.[95] Mr. J and Ms. Y, who are both lawyers and environmental advocates, present environmental films in association with Better Blue, an environmental protection NGO. Every week, volunteers conduct public sessions in local communities to discuss the value of environmental protection and to present information about the topic to the public in the city of K, with no financial support.[96] Ms. L, a professional lawyer, has run a special school serving disadvantaged children in the city of N for over ten years, supported by a charitable group. Hundreds of disadvantaged children obtain education at this institution.[97] Mr. F provides legal training coursework, supported by bar associations.[98]

All of these lawyers believe that their practices are the right pathway for Chinese lawyers to follow in performing their social responsibilities.[99] These lawyers term their work "volunteering": "My primary status in my pro bono work is that of a community volunteer instead of as a professional lawyer."[100] This work meets with support from communities, bar associations, and law firms, and it does not face political intervention. The Chinese government and the bar associations both need pro bono work from lawyers to maintain community stability.[101] Law firms, for their part, need pro bono work to advertise their social responsibility. For this reason, they allow lawyers to structure pro bono work. Once an agreement to do pro bono has been made with a firm, lawyers no longer have to worry about daily legal duties. Then, they feel that pro bono practice is valued for its contribution to the public good in general. For example, Ms. O, a private public interest lawyer and member in good standing of the China Council of X Clubs, one of the largest charitable groups in the world, often voluntarily participates in and manages varieties of nonlegal public service in Shanghai. She believes that doing pro bono work as community service helps children and increases the rate of pro bono participation among lawyers.[102]

Although lawyers freely admit that their pro bono work might not directly bring in clients, it does benefit them by allowing them to establish a good social image within their social network or by improving legal skills in certain areas.[103] The motivation for doing pro bono varies among these lawyers. Some prefer work that aligns with their ideals, but others have different reasons, including personal and market benefits, such as networking.[104]

For this group of lawyers, conforming to governmental demands and directives is the highest priority in practicing law. Therefore, lawyers tend to offer pro bono services through or to certain institutions as long as they are recognized or approved by the government or bar associations, but they avoid issues with political overtones or any association with ideas of political liberalism.[105] To their minds, such practices related to liberalism are complex and sensitive. They do not consider working on any case that might be seen to challenge the government or to violate political agreements or understandings. One private public interest lawyer describes this attitude in the following way:

> Personally, I am a little conservative, politically. The first priority in doing pro bono work is safety. No matter what lawyers do, they should consider their family, daily work, and public interest service. All these should be done under safe conditions .... If lawyers insist on taking these [social cause] cases, it will hurt [their] families and children. I think this work does not deserve to be done at all.[106]

Other private public interest lawyers are filling the gaps their colleagues have left in professional lawyering. Although they are in the minority of Chinese legal professionals by number and geographical distribution, their pro bono legal practice embodies political liberalism, and it supports the well-being of civil society.[107] This is the challenger mode.

The Challenger Mode

Unlike private public interest lawyers, who are dedicated to delivering Chinese-style pro bono, challengers focus on cases relating to important social causes. Their work helps to check arbitrary state power, supports legal proceduralism, and affirms judicial independence.[108] The scope of the pro bono work of this group is thus relatively narrow compared with that of its counterparts. The cases challengers take, in large part, challenge the authority of the state bureaucracy system, which is led by the CCP. Evidence from interviews shows their legal cases focusing on environmental protection, labor rights, women's rights, children's rights, lawyers' rights, victims' rights, and wrongful conviction.[109] Their pro bono work flourishes under the following conditions: (1) the local government has arbitrarily used political power to infringe on human rights; (2) the *gongjianfa* (the police, the procuracy, and the courts) system has violated the principle of due process; or (3) a local courtroom has issued a wrongful conviction.

When the government abuses political power in an administrative decision violating human rights, such as environmental protections or labor rights, Chinese private public interest lawyers may come forward to question or even challenge the legality of the government's decision in order to protect human rights, with the goal of preserving the well-being of civil society. In such cases, the local government and its affiliates are defendants.[110] For example, when local bureaucracy and its affiliates unlawfully refuse to employ people with disabilities, someone like Mr. R, who pursues labor rights for disabled people in N Province, may provide free legal assistance to those whose labor rights are infringed by this action.[111] Mr. S, a private public interest lawyer focusing on public environmental litigation, describes how the local government unlawfully impedes social justice in a case involving pollution:

> The government expresses extreme repugnance toward lawyers' efforts to file environmental protection lawsuits on behalf of NGOs .... I am currently representing a case involving pollution in which the government's affiliate is the defendant. The director of a local environmental bureau directly ordered me to withdraw the suit [because this case will negatively influence the local government's social image].[112]

When the local *gongjianfa* system violates the principles of legal proceduralism and impedes social justice, private public interest lawyers may challenge decisions based on legal procedure. For instance, attorneys believe a court in the city of G violated Chinese criminal procedure and made an array of unlawful decisions in a criminal trial. During the trial, judges limited the defense lawyers' legal rights, and the attorneys were not even allowed to meet the defendants.[113] After the news spread throughout Chinese legal circles, several private public interest lawyers specializing in criminal law organized a large volunteer group of legal professionals, including lawyers, left-wing reporters, and legal scholars, to protect the defendants' rights and lawyers' rights to combat judicial power using their in-depth knowledge and experience of Chinese criminal procedure. They paid all fees and related expenses themselves.[114] Ultimately, the court reversed some of its decisions, and the defendants' rights were partially protected.[115]

Beyond efforts similar to this, Chinese lawyers are increasingly participating in projects to rescue the innocent. Since the rise of the use of social media among Chinese civil society (e.g., South Weekend, The Paper, Ifeng), many wrongful decisions have been uncovered. Networks to rescue innocent people from wrongful judicial decisions have taken shape in China. Chinese lawyers, scholars, law firms, and participants on social media have closely worked together to challenge abuses of judicial power to obtain social justice for victims of wrongful decisions: "I am doing pro bono [work] to bring blessings to victims of wrongful convictions."[116]

For example, in May 2014, the Shangquan Law Office, a well-known Beijing firm specializing in criminal defense, established an innocence assistance project together with the Chinese University of Politics and Law. The firm offers financial support to volunteer lawyers who appeal cases where a conviction has been wrongfully obtained.[117] Another well-known network for innocent, wrongfully convicted defendants is called the Rescuing Innocents Project (*Xiyuan Wang*). This project takes as its model organizations in Western countries (the United Kingdom, the United States, and Canada). This project covers every Chinese province, like similar organizations that work in every US state. To accomplish this mission, the manager of the project recruits professional lawyers throughout China to volunteer. Currently, eighty-three volunteer lawyers from different geographical areas who can deliver legal services have listed their names and contact information on the official website of the project. The project provides financial support to the volunteers when they are providing legal services. Moreover, the project provides a free training program to guide volunteer lawyers in helping wrongfully convicted innocents and their families. Many high-profile cases have been opened by volunteer lawyers, according to newsletters published by the project.[118]

As the pro bono work they value tends to be liberal and oriented toward social causes, most challengers distrust the Chinese *gongjianfa* system and its officers. These lawyers believe that unprofessional relationships (*guanxi*) among lawyers and the *gongjianfa* may injure social justice. Local state-run legal aid centers and their lawyers do not, in general, take cases that attract challengers: "Because of conflicts of interest, the state-owned legal aid system and lawyers might support local government to maintain community stability."[119] The mainstream media generally espouse a critical view of the challengers, saying that they threaten community stability and have a political agenda to disturb the public order in Chinese society.[120] This small group of Chinese lawyers has thus become known as troublemakers who like to challenge the decisions of local courts using legal proceduralism and trumpeting the value of the rule of law. These lawyers themselves, however, believe that they are helping to generate a modern country with the rule of law: "When laws are effective, they are not a symbol.... We work to implement them properly.... We must believe that Chinese laws can be trusted by the public through our long-term hard work."[121]

Private public interest lawyers marked as challengers are in an ambiguous position. Their social cause–oriented work is entirely free, or it is financed by charity or NGOs. Funds are very limited, according to our investigation. Generally, the money available covers only basic expenses for transportation and lodging. Although their pro bono work is liberal, their daily legal work, which does not have the same aim, is their main financial resource. The challengers' law firms and managing partners also express themselves negatively toward their pro bono practices, warning such lawyers to reduce their levels of pro bono exposure.[122] This is a difficult environment in which to persevere. Striking a balance between their main business and their pro bono work is an important concern. Unlike full-time public interest lawyers, private public interest lawyers must practice law in a professional law firm to support themselves. To achieve balance here, private public interest lawyers have created a unique strategy to advance their pro bono work. They each have a legal specialization, such as real property, contract disputes, or commercial legal counseling. They are known to practice in that area. However, to avoid trouble in their ordinary legal work, they distinguish their pro bono and earning work based on geographical area. A lawyer explains this strategy in the following way:

> I only pursue pro bono cases outside the province where I regularly practice law with my business clients. This helps me avoid conflict [between pro bono and business clients]. I know that my practice of pro bono work could hurt my other clients [due to political embeddedness]. I try to distinguish them through geographical areas.[123]

THEORETICAL DISCUSSION

This chapter gives an overview of the landscape of China's private public interest lawyers. Our findings demonstrate that they do not embrace "a singular ideology of professionalism operating across the legal profession."[124] Rather, differences related to the local political structure and culture in which these lawyers practice deeply divide them.

Although all private public interest lawyers believe that their practice is for the public good, their understandings of pro bono are complicated by their understandings of politics. Lawyers who prefer the safe mode are distinguished by their attitudes on market reliance and political reality, and they tend to have a conservative ideology. In contrast with professional lawyers who are less supportive of pro bono work, private public interest lawyers who prefer safety nevertheless practice pro bono more frequently than their counterparts. They believe that pro bono should be understood to have a broad meaning.

Lawyers who do pro bono work in the safe mode have two main characteristics. First, their service does not merely focus on pro bono legal work, as that of their US colleagues does. Rather, they have an understanding of pro bono work that is linked to broader volunteerism.[125] Second, they are politically conservative. They engage in public service to establish a social image as good citizens. Their service is attached to the political system. Because the CCP has great power and authority, their work for the public good should follow CCP policy and orders if they want to practice law in the market smoothly.

Safe mode lawyers' norms and consciousness can be explained using a theoretical framework of challenge–reconstruction. Previous study has shown that local Chinese lawyers play the role of institution builders to bring forward legal globalization. As global forces challenge the Chinese legal system and the operation of its legal profession, Chinese lawyers will not resist the diffusion of global elements into the field of the legal profession. Rather, lawyers reconstruct themselves as an outward-looking profession.[126] It should be noted that the safe practice mode of Chinese private public interest lawyers partially supports this theory. Although professional lawyers in China recognize that pro bono certainly should be looked at as an inherent responsibility, following global norms, the meaning of pro bono has been reconstructed to mean good citizenship more than lawyering for the public good. Pro bono work related to social volunteerism allows lawyers to present a positive image in the legal market. Their motivation for doing pro bono resembles that of US legal professionals. Because the pro bono work of Chinese lawyers appears to be market oriented, they tend to embed themselves with corporate clients through pro bono work. Law firms tend to screen out cases that might cause conflicts of interest with business clients.[127]

The lawyers who work as challengers, however, use their legal skills and professional status to challenge arbitrary power and to seek social justice. Their financial support comes mainly from small amounts of funding made available by liberal NGOs, social charity donations, and their own personal income from their main work. They are motivated to do pro bono to advance social reform, strengthen legal proceduralism, and pursue social justice related to the mission of the rule of law. As was the case during the Republican era, the norms and consciousness of private public interest lawyers are consistent with those of US private public interest lawyers.[128]

Challengers believe that the Chinese government and the judicial system are unreliable. To protect human rights, they reject the dichotomy between the private interest and public interest by practicing law for paying clients during their regular hours. Challengers organize themselves into teams to file cases resisting abuses of power by the government and the courts when they have reliable information. Taking such cases, so the reasoning goes, could spur policymakers to move social reform in China forward, promoting Chinese civil society and leading the country toward the rule of law.

Private public interest lawyers performing pro bono in the challenger mode reflect the globalized concept of pro bono. Following a wave of legal globalization, the value of political liberalism has diffused into the practice of law in China through the formation of Chinese civil society. Chinese professional lawyers have realized the importance of advancing social cause work, as Chinese civil society has consolidated. The values of rule of law and political liberalism have developed and spread in China through the third sphere: civil society.

However, current practices and understandings of Chinese private public interest law have also been shaped by local forces. As discussed earlier, the first generation of Chinese private public interest lawyers can be traced back to the 1910s. During the Republican era, Chinese private public interest lawyers routinely provided legal services for social causes. This practice has a deep historical background, reflecting the transformation of Chinese society. Private public interest lawyers came from privileged and affluent families, which brought them greater opportunities to be in contact with Western cultures and to learn from them. Thus, they had the human and social capital to take pro bono cases and to advance legal reform without having to worry about earning an income. Some of them were educated in Western countries, where they learned the value of pro bono work and social causes. The government of China was not very highly developed at this time, so pro bono practice may have encountered fewer obstacles from political structures. These lawyers fulfilled their pro bono commitments mainly from a sense of *noblesse oblige*.[129]

Most importantly, the Chinese political structure tended to be liberal in this earlier period. Although many warlords wished to establish autocracy, the forces promoting political liberalism were very strong. The Chinese government followed a Western-style rule of law that shaped lawyers' professional autonomy and independence. This context was an ideal environment for civil society to develop. NGOs formed a new public sphere for civil liberties. Chinese private public interest lawyers worked with NGOs to fight for human rights. The broader movement in favor of political liberalism therefore supported Chinese private public interest lawyers in focusing their legal services on social causes.

In contrast, today's Chinese lawyers simply do not have the social status that lawyers did in the ROC. In fact, they have a poor social image, as previous research has shown.[130] Most lawyers are involved in politics and they practice law for profit in the market. Although the concept of pro bono does appear at present to be spreading among Chinese law schools, it is very hard to avoid political embeddedness, because the government is entirely in charge of the system of legal education. Most private public interest lawyers do not fight for social causes. Doing Chinese-style pro bono work, these lawyers network and attract clients by establishing a reputation for good citizenship. Only a few private public interest lawyers attempt work for social causes. This evidence suggests that political structure affects lawyers' norms and actions. Although the species of private public interest lawyers appears to have been reborn, the meaning of private public interest law has changed in China due to lawyers' distinctive responses to the political structure.

CONCLUSION

According to our theoretical discussion, the distinct styles of Chinese private public interest lawyering highlight how political structure shapes lawyers' norms, behaviors, values, and consciousness. Influenced by the Chinese political structure, the meaning of pro bono in the Chinese context can only be understood in relation to political embeddedness and political liberalism.

It is thus notable that Chinese pro bono service takes place in a complex environment in which global knowledge and indigenous practice coexist in one social structure. According to our investigation, it is unclear which of these – global or local – is more powerful. Influenced by legal globalization, Chinese lawyers' commitment to serving the public good has also been shaped by the government, professional associations, the legal market, and civil society. In this way, both global and local institutions are showing their power to impact the meaning and practice of pro bono in China. It is especially notable that private public interest lawyering in China has been profoundly shaped by the local sovereign power of the Chinese government, thereby distinguishing it from its US counterpart.

Although Chinese lawyering has grown as a major force in the global market, the local political structure is strong enough to resist global convergence and instead to mold Chinese lawyering into a cultural hybrid. Pro bono, which is not taken for granted, has been localized due to a Chinese political structure that is deeply attached to CCP values and culture. Our research thus supports the idea that legal globalization is not a simple process of exporting and building a new order of transnational law.[131] Although pro bono is increasingly being institutionalized in both developing and developed countries, this does not mean that the meaning and practice of pro bono is entirely dictated by global sponsors or Western countries. Particularly with respect to Chinese private public interest lawyers, local professional traditions and political systems also profoundly impact their ideology and practice.

NOTES

1. Harvard Law School held a wide-ranging discussion on this subject at the Global Pro Bono Conference on April 18, 2014. For an analysis of pro bono, see PRIVATE LAWYERS AND THE PUBLIC INTEREST: THE EVOLVING ROLE OF PRO BONO IN THE LEGAL PROFESSION (Robert Granfield & Lynn Mather eds., 2009).
2. *See* Fabio de Sa e Silva, *Doing Well and Doing Good in an Emerging Economy: The Social Organization of Pro Bono Among Corporate Lawyers and Law Firms in São Paulo, Brazil, in* THE BRAZILIAN LEGAL PROFESSION IN THE AGE OF GLOBALIZATION: THE RISE OF THE CORPORATE LEGAL SECTOR AND ITS IMPACT ON LAWYERS AND SOCIETY 210 (Luciana Gross Cunha et al. eds., 2018); *see also* Arpita Gupta, *Pro Bono and Corporate Legal Sector in India, in* THE INDIAN LEGAL PROFESSION IN THE AGE OF GLOBALIZATION: THE RISE OF THE CORPORATE LEGAL SECTOR AND ITS IMPACT ON LAWYERS AND SOCIETY 275 (David B. Wilkins, Vikramaditya S. Khanna & David M. Trubek eds., 2017).
3. See the official site of the DLA Piper law firm: www.dlapiper.com/en/us/focus/probono/pro-bono/ (last visited Mar. 15, 2018).
4. *See* Richard Wilson, *Training for Justice: The Global Reach of Clinical Legal Education*, 22 PENN. STATE INT'L L. REV. 421 (2004).
5. *See* Louise Trubek, *Crossing Boundaries: Legal Education and the Challenge of the New Public Interest Law*, 16 WIS. L. REV. 455–76 (2005).
6. *See* Scott Cummings & Louise Trubek, *Globalizing Public Interest Law*, 13 UCLA J. INT'L L. & FOR. AFF. 1 (2008).
7. *See* Ethan Michelson, Unhooking from the State: Chinese Lawyers in Transition (2003) (unpublished doctoral dissertation, University of Chicago) (on file with the Department of Sociology, University of Chicago).
8. The data are available at http://mini.eastday.com/a/180313094549900.html (last visited Mar. 4, 2018).
9. See the official site of the Yingke Law Firm at www.yingkelawyer.com/YKJS/YKJS.aspx (last visited June 4, 2017).
10. See the comments at www.law360.com/articles/293811/king-wood-mallesons-merge-to-create-asian-superfirm (last visited May 11, 2018).
11. *See* Jin Dong, The Institutionalization of Pro Bono in China, paper presented at the third conference of the Eastern Asia Law and Society Association, Shanghai (Mar. 27, 2013).

12. The data are drawn from the report of the Chinese Ministry of Justice (MOJ). *See* www.sohu.com/a/227194962_441498 (last visited Apr. 11, 2018).
13. *See* Jin Dong, How Do Chinese Lawyers View Pro Bono? A Sociological Analysis (2016) (unpublished doctoral dissertation, University at Buffalo) (on file with the Department of Sociology, University of Buffalo).
14. The data are available at https://cliniclaw.cn/hylm.asp (last visited Apr. 12, 2018).
15. The first pro bono (legal aid) center affiliated with a Chinese law school was established in 1992. It is officially financed by Wuhan University Law School. See the introduction at https://cprdc.org/web/ (last visited June 20, 2018). Both provide professional training programs for professional lawyers.
16. *See* Dong, *supra* note 13, at 238.
17. *See 2012 IBA Pro Bono Winner - Tong Lihua*, International Bar Association (Oct. 3, 2012), https://ibanet.org/Article/Detail.aspx?ArticleUid=FF0446C9-B3DD-4698-A4C7-8FEE975E22E7 (last visited May 10, 2018).
18. *See* information at https://2009-2017.state.gov/s/gwi/iwoc/2011/bio/index.htm (last visited June 2, 2018).
19. *See* https://law.columbia.edu/chinese-legal-studies/china-public-interest-law/public-interest-fellows-from-china (last visited June 6, 2018).
20. *See* Qian Cheng, The History of Chinese Lawyers: Chinese Lawyers' Spirit and the Republic of China (2015).
21. *See* Deborah L. Rhode, Pro Bono in Principle and in Practice: Public Service and the Professions 114 (2005).
22. *See* Ethan Michelson, *Lawyers, Political Embeddedness, and Institutional Continuity in China's Transition from Socialism*, 113 Am. J. Soc. 352–414 (2007); *see also* Michelson, *supra* note 7, at 86.
23. *See* Sida Liu, *Globalization as Boundary-Blurring: International and Local Law Firms in China's Corporate Law Market*, 42 Law & Soc. Rev. 771 (2008).
24. See more discussion at Dong, *supra* note 13, chapter 3.
25. *See* Scott L. Cummings, *The Politics of Pro Bono*, 52 UCLA L. Rev. 1 (2004); *see also* Cummings & Trubek, *supra* note 6, at 1.
26. See the comprehensive review in Dong, *supra* note 13, at 48–95.
27. *See* Terrence Halliday, *Lawyers as Institution Builders: Constructing Markets, States, Civil Society and Community*, *in* Crossing Boundaries: Traditions and Transformations in Law and Society Research 242 (Austin Sarat et al. eds., 2004). Also, *see* Sida Liu, *Beyond Global Convergence: Conflicts of Legitimacy in a Chinese Lower Court*, 31 Law & Soc. Inquiry 75 (2006).
28. *See id.*
29. *See* Michelson, *supra* note 7, at 357.
30. *See* Dong, *supra* note 13, at 42.

31. *See* Junfeng Wang's speech at http://news.sina.com.cn/c/2012-03-15/105924119884.shtml (last visited May 4, 2018).
32. See the report at https://360doc.com/content/14/0306/21/2543594_358338180.shtml (last visited Mar. 3, 2018).
33. See the introductions of these reports at https://lawyers.org.cn/info/40837d94543040ad8c705aa5d392a827 (last visited Apr. 3, 2018); https://hangzhou.gov.cn/art/2016/12/29/art_812270_4795626.html (last visited Apr. 4, 2018); http://ssfj.hefei.gov.cn/9601/9603/201806/t20180626_2593681.html (last visited Apr. 5, 2018).
34. *See* https://beijinglawyers.org.cn/cac/1436497766380.htm (last visited June 29, 2018).
35. These annual reports are available at https://grandall.com.cn/social-responsibility/social-responsibility-report/ (last visited May 1, 2018).
36. See the introduction to pro bono on law firms' official websites: https://dachengnet.com/en/responsibility/charity and https://allbrightlaw.com/en/generalview/utility (last visited June 4, 2018).
37. *See* https://ngzb.com.cn/forum.php?mod=viewthread&tid=451493&extra=page&page=1 (last visited May 5, 2018).
38. *See* https://lawyers.org.cn/info/30c42c73f5b84c97b835e5ac42037593 (last visited Apr. 3, 2018).
39. *See* https://moj.gov.cn/index/content/2017-03/10/content_7084542.htm?node=86542 (last visited Apr. 30, 2018); *see also* remarks by Zhao Dacheng, deputy minister of MOJ, at https://sohu.com/a/128384593_119038 (last visited May 1, 2018).
40. The data are drawn from the 2017 legal aid report, https://ahxb.cn/c/3/2018-01-26/4860.html (last visited May 9, 2018), and Chongyi Fan, *The Construction and Prospect of China's Legal Aid System*, 18 CHINA L. REV. 192 (2017).
41. *See id.*
42. *See* Shenjian Xu, *Promoting Pro Bono Service in China*, http://newspaper.jcrb.com/html/2013-03/13/content_122051.htm (last visited June 29, 2018).
43. *See* Dong, *supra* note 13, at 220.
44. *See* Scott Cummings & Ann Southworth, *Between Profit and Principle: The Private Public Interest Law Firm*, *in* PRIVATE LAWYERS AND THE PUBLIC INTEREST: THE EVOLVING ROLE OF PRO BONO IN THE LEGAL PROFESSION, *supra* note 1, at 183.
45. In total, we interviewed fifteen lawyers. They all stated that their main incomes came from business legal practice.
46. *See* MAX WEBER, THE PROTESTANT ETHIC AND THE SPIRIT OF CAPITALISM (T. Parsons, trans., 1992).
47. *See* Rebecca Sandefur, *Lawyers' Pro Bono Service and American-Style Civil Legal Assistance*, 41 LAW & SOC. REV. 79 (2007).
48. *See* Cummings & Southworth, *supra* note 44, at 183–211.
49. *See* Didi Kirsten Tatlow, *China Is Said to Force Closing of Women's Legal Aid Center*, N.Y. TIMES, Jan. 29, 2016, https://nytimes.com/2016/01/

30/world/asia/beijing-women-legal-aid-guo-jianmei.html (last visited June 20, 2017).

50. This is drawn from the Chinese Human Rights Report (2014) released by the US Department of State.
51. *See* http://finance.sina.com.cn/stock/t/20110805/230010270950.shtml (last visited Mar. 1, 2018).
52. *See* Dong Li, *The Reputation of Songshi in the Ming and Qing and An Explanation*, 2 CHINA LEGAL SCIENCES 117 (2013); *see also* Michelson, *supra* note 7, at 20.
53. In a conversation between the first president of the ROC, Yuan Shikai, and the first registered lawyer in the ROC, Cao Rulin, in the early 1910s, President Yuan asked Cao, "Why do you work as a lawyer? Lawyer is just like *songshi*, isn't it?" Cao replied, "Lawyers are totally different from *songshi*. Lawyers protect human rights in accordance with the law; however, *songshis* seek profits by distorting the facts." *See* CAO RULIN, A MEMOIR OF THE LIFE OF CAO RULIN 109 (2009).
54. *See* Yancheng Li, A Study of the Bar Association in the Republic of China (1911–1936) (2006) (unpublished doctoral dissertation, Central China Normal University) (on file with the Central China Normal University).
55. *See The Discovery of the Bar Association*, MIN LI NEWS (MIN LI BAO), Jan. 7, 1912.
56. *See* Wu Tingfang, Telegram to Sun Yat-sen (No. 2, Feb. 18, 1911).
57. *See* Xiutao Han, A *Brief Discussion on the Development of Justice of the Beiyang Period*, 2 ANHUI U. L. REV. 59 (2002).
58. *See* Xinyi Hou, *Research on Legal Education in the Republic of China*, ht tp://new.qq.com/cmsn/20140302/20140302003637 (last visited Apr. 9, 2018).
59. Among them, Soochow University was run by the US Christian church system. Aurora University was affiliated with the Society of Jesus (France). Yenching University was jointly run by US and UK Christian forces. *See* Hou, *supra* note 58.
60. *See* Cheng *supra* note 20; *see also* QIANG HOU, RESEARCH ON THE TRANSITION OF LEGAL EDUCATION AND SOCIAL TRANSFORMATION IN THE REPUBLICAN ERA (2008).
61. *See* Alison W. Conner, *The Comparative Law School of China*, *in* UNDERSTANDING CHINA'S LEGAL SYSTEM 210 (C. Stephen Hsu ed., 2003).
62. Bar Association of Shanghai, A *Letter to All the Members* (1935).
63. SHEN WANG, THE CHINESE MODERN LAWYER SYSTEM AND LAWYERS 166 (1994).
64. ZHUGE JIEMING, MR. SHENJUNRU: THE OLD MAN WHO SAVES OUR COUNTRY (Guang Ming Bao, 1945) (New 15).
65. *See* SHI LIANG, AN AUTOBIOGRAPHY OF SHILIANG 10 (1987).
66. *See* Yunan Lin, A *Biography of Shi Yang*, *in* COLLECTED WORKS TO COMMEMORATE SHI YANG 127 (1988).

67. *See* Yuguang Zhang, A *Female Hero: Zheng Yuxiu*, 4 LITERATURE & HISTORY (2006).
68. *See* Yanjing Tang, A *Brief Discussion on the Functions of Lawyers in the Compensation for Wrongful Detentions and Executions Movement in 1930s*, 10 LAW & ECON. 15 (2008).
69. *See* Lizhi Xu, *The History and Development of the Contemporary Legal Aid System in China*, 4 LEGAL HIST. F. 452 (2006).
70. *See* Wang Fengying, *Lawyer's Role in Judicial Reform*, 31 LAW REVIEW (BEIJING) (1924).
71. *Id.*; *see also* Wang Fengying, *The Organization of Legal Aid Societies*, 41 LAW REVIEW (BEIJING) (1924). He cited *The Training of Lawyers*, 4 AMERICAN LAW SCHOOL REVIEW and *Case and Comment, Charities and Legal Aid Number*, May 1917.
72. *See* Zhang Weiran, *An Overview of Legal Aid in Europe*, 7 LAW REVIEW (BEIJING) (1933).
73. *See Shanghai Lawyers Organized a Legal Aid Society*, 46 LAW REVIEW (BEIJING) (1924).
74. *See Chongqing Lawyers Organized a Legal Aid Society*, 20 LAW REVIEW (BEIJING) (1924); *Minhou Lawyers Organized a Legal Aid Society*, 14 LAW REVIEW (BEIJING).
75. *See* Report of Judicial Administration 104-06 (1934) (released by the ROC Ministry of Judicial Administration).
76. *See Society of Legal Aid for the Poor*, 3 JIAO YU YI WEN LU (1934).
77. *See The Implementing Framework of Bar Association Society of Legal Aid for People*, REPORT OF JUSTICE 484–89 (1941).
78. *See* Dong, *supra* note 13, at 184.
79. *See* https://sohu.com/a/113996654_481652 (last visited May 9, 2018); *see also* https://360doc.com/content/16/0318/11/102310_543282404.shtml (last visited June 10, 2018).
80. *See* RHODE, *supra* note 21, at 115.
81. *See* Dong, *supra* note 13, at 53; *see also* Xiangde Yi, *Chinese Mode of Legal Education*, https://chinalegaleducation.com/jyyj/ShowArticle.asp?ArticleID=44447 (last visited June 19, 2018).
82. *See* Michelson, *supra* note 7, at 16.
83. Telephone interview with Lawyer 3 (Feb. 15, 2018).
84. *See* Dong, *supra* note 13, at 161.
85. Telephone interview with Lawyer 1 (Feb. 6, 2018), Lawyer 2 (Feb. 9, 2018), and Lawyer 14 (May 18, 2018).
86. Telephone interview with Lawyer 1 (Feb. 6, 2018), Lawyer 2 (Feb. 9, 2018), and Lawyer 15 (May 19, 2018).
87. *See id.*
88. The data come from the MOJ, https://sohu.com/a/227194962_441498 (last visited May 18, 2018).
89. This was generalized from the official report of the 19th National Congress of the CCP. *See* http://cpc.people.com.cn/19th/n1/2017/1023/c414305-29603299.html (last visited June 13, 2018).

90. The data was generalized from the news report of the ACLA and the MOJ. *See* https://legaldaily.com.cn/index/content/2017-10/31/content_7373794.htm?node=20908 and https://huxiu.com/article/291115.html (last visited Mar. 20, 2020).
91. *See* Dong, *supra* note 13, at 184.
92. For the purpose of privacy, they have been coded as Lawyers 1 to 15. Our telephone interviews ran from February 2018 to May 2018. No personal information will be released in our research.
93. *See* Sida Liu & Terence C. Halliday, *Political Liberalism and Political Embeddedness: Understanding Politics in the Work of Chinese Criminal Defense Lawyers*, 45 LAW & SOC. REV. 831 (2011).
94. *See id.* at 833.
95. Telephone interview with Lawyer 8 (May 14, 2018).
96. Telephone interview with Lawyer 3 (Feb. 15, 2018), and Lawyer 6 (May 10, 2018).
97. Telephone interview with Lawyer 2 (Feb. 9, 2018).
98. Telephone interview with Lawyer 13 (May 17, 2018).
99. Telephone interview with Lawyer 1 (Feb. 6, 2018), Lawyer 2 (Feb. 9, 2018), Lawyer 6 (May 10, 2018), and Lawyer 13 (May 17, 2018).
100. Telephone interview with Lawyer 6 (May 10, 2018).
101. *See* Dong, *supra* note 13, at 71.
102. Telephone interview with Lawyer 1 (Feb. 6, 2018).
103. Telephone interview with Lawyer 2 (Feb. 9, 2018), Lawyer 3 (Feb. 15, 2018), and Lawyer 6 (May 10, 2018).
104. *Id.*
105. Telephone interview with Lawyer 1 (Feb. 6, 2018) and Lawyer 2 (Feb. 9, 2018).
106. Telephone interview with Lawyer 1 (Feb. 6, 2018).
107. Telephone interview with Lawyer 5 (Apr. 27, 2018).
108. Telephone interview with Lawyer 4 (Mar. 11, 2018), Lawyer 7 (Apr. 28, 2018), Lawyer 10 (May 15, 2018), Lawyer 11 (May 15, 2018), and Lawyer 15 (May 19, 2018).
109. Telephone interview with Lawyer 4 (Mar. 11, 2018), Lawyer 10 (May 15, 2018), Lawyer 11 (May 15, 2018), and Lawyer 15 (May 19, 2018).
110. Telephone interview with Lawyer 4 (Mar. 11, 2018) and Lawyer 15 (May 19, 2018).
111. Telephone interview with Lawyer 15 (May 19, 2018).
112. Telephone interview with Lawyer 11 (May 15, 2018).
113. *See* https://xiyuanwang.net/html/xhae_1295_1819.html (last visited June 20, 2018).
114. *See* https://360doc.com/content/12/0814/09/9742787_230075757.shtml (last visited Mar. 1, 2018).
115. These volunteers provide free services. *See* https://360doc.com/content/17/0822/07/34433067_681131261.shtml (last visited Jan. 3, 2018).
116. Telephone interview with Lawyer 10 (May 15, 2018).

117. See the introduction to the project on Shangquan Law Office's official website: https://sqxb.com/swrong.php (last visited Feb. 3, 2018).
118. See the introduction on its official website: https://xiyuanwang.net/html/wzjj_1276_1769.html (last visited May 17, 2018).
119. Telephone interview with Lawyer 4 (Mar. 11, 2018).
120. *See* https://xinhuanet.com/legal/2016-01/14/c_128626255.htm (last visited Apr. 5, 2018).
121. Telephone interview with Lawyer 11 (May 15, 2018).
122. Telephone interview with Lawyer 11 (May 15, 2018), and Lawyer 15 (May 19, 2018).
123. Telephone interview with Lawyer 11 (May 15, 2018).
124. *See* Robert Granfield, *The Meaning of Pro Bono: Institutional Variations in Professional Obligations Among Lawyers*, 41 LAW & SOC. REV. 120 (2007).
125. *See* John Wilson, *Volunteering*, 26 ANN. REV. SOC. 215 (2000).
126. *See* Dong, *supra* note 13, at 219.
127. *See* Cummings & Southworth, *supra* note 44, at 198.
128. *Id.* at 200.
129. *See* Bryant Garth, *Noblesse Oblige as an Alternative Career Strategy*, 41 HOUSTON L. REV. 93 (2004).
130. *See* Michelson, *supra* note 7, at 56.
131. *See* GLOBAL PRESCRIPTIONS: THE PRODUCTION, EXPORTATION, AND IMPORTATION OF A NEW LEGAL ORTHODOXY (Yves Dezalay & Bryant G. Garth eds., 2002).

INDEX

CAMBRIDGE STUDIES IN LAW AND SOCIETY

Books in the Series

Diseases of the Will: Alcohol and the Dilemmas of Freedom
Mariana Valverde

The Politics of Truth and Reconciliation in South Africa: Legitimizing the Post-Apartheid State
Richard A. Wilson

Modernism and the Grounds of Law
Peter Fitzpatrick

Unemployment and Government: Genealogies of the Social
William Walters

Autonomy and Ethnicity: Negotiating Competing Claims in Multi-Ethnic States
Yash Ghai

Constituting Democracy: Law, Globalism and South Africa's Political Reconstruction
Heinz Klug

The Ritual of Rights in Japan: Law, Society, and Health Policy
Eric A. Feldman

Governing Morals: A Social History of Moral Regulation
Alan Hunt

The Colonies of Law: Colonialism, Zionism and Law in Early Mandate Palestine
Ronen Shamir

Law and Nature
David Delaney

Social Citizenship and Workfare in the United States and Western Europe: The Paradox of Inclusion
Joel F. Handler

Law, Anthropology, and the Constitution of the Social: Making Persons and Things
Edited by Alain Pottage and Martha Mundy

Judicial Review and Bureaucratic Impact: International and Interdisciplinary Perspectives
Edited by Marc Hertogh and Simon Halliday

Immigrants at the Margins: Law, Race, and Exclusion in Southern Europe
Kitty Calavita

Lawyers and Regulation: The Politics of the Administrative Process
Patrick Schmidt

Law and Globalization from Below: Toward a Cosmopolitan Legality
Edited by Boaventura de Sousa Santos and Cesar A. Rodriguez-Garavito

Public Accountability: Designs, Dilemmas and Experiences
Edited by Michael W. Dowdle

Law, Violence and Sovereignty among West Bank Palestinians
Tobias Kelly

Legal Reform and Administrative Detention Powers in China
Sarah Biddulph

The Practice of Human Rights: Tracking Law between the Global and the Local
Edited by Mark Goodale and Sally Engle Merry

Judges beyond Politics in Democracy and Dictatorship: Lessons from Chile
Lisa Hilbink

Paths to International Justice: Social and Legal Perspectives
Edited by Marie-Bénédicte Dembour and Tobias Kelly

Law and Society in Vietnam: The Transition from Socialism in Comparative Perspective
Mark Sidel

Constitutionalizing Economic Globalization: Investment Rules and Democracy's Promise
David Schneiderman

The New World Trade Organization Knowledge Agreements: 2nd Edition
Christopher Arup

Justice and Reconciliation in Post-Apartheid South Africa
Edited by François du Bois and Antje du Bois-Pedain

Militarization and Violence against Women in Conflict Zones in the Middle East: A Palestinian Case-Study
Nadera Shalhoub-Kevorkian

Child Pornography and Sexual Grooming: Legal and Societal Responses
Suzanne Ost

Darfur and the Crime of Genocide
John Hagan and Wenona Rymond-Richmond

Fictions of Justice: The International Criminal Court and the Challenge of Legal Pluralism in Sub-Saharan Africa
Kamari Maxine Clarke

Conducting Law and Society Research: Reflections on Methods and Practices
Simon Halliday and Patrick Schmidt

Planted Flags: Trees, Land, and Law in Israel/Palestine
Irus Braverman

Culture under Cross-Examination: International Justice and the Special Court for Sierra Leone
Tim Kelsall

Cultures of Legality: Judicialization and Political Activism in Latin America
Javier Couso, Alexandra Huneeus, and Rachel Sieder

Courting Democracy in Bosnia and Herzegovina: The Hague Tribunal's Impact in a Postwar State
Lara J. Nettelfield

The Gacaca Courts, Post-Genocide Justice and Reconciliation in Rwanda: Justice without Lawyers
Phil Clark

Law, Society, and History: Themes in the Legal Sociology and Legal History of Lawrence M. Friedman
Edited by Robert W. Gordon and Morton J. Horwitz

After Abu Ghraib: Exploring Human Rights in America and the Middle East
Shadi Mokhtari

Adjudication in Religious Family Laws: Cultural Accommodation, Legal Pluralism, and Gender Equality in India
Gopika Solanki

Water on Tap: Rights and Regulation in the Transnational Governance of Urban Water Services
Bronwen Morgan

Elements of Moral Cognition: Rawls' Linguistic Analogy and the Cognitive Science of Moral and Legal Judgment
John Mikhail

Mitigation and Aggravation at Sentencing
Edited by Julian V. Roberts

Institutional Inequality and the Mobilization of the Family and Medical Leave Act: Rights on Leave
Catherine R. Albiston

Authoritarian Rule of Law: Legislation, Discourse and Legitimacy in Singapore
Jothie Rajah

Law and Development and the Global Discourses of Legal Transfers
Edited by John Gillespie and Pip Nicholson

Law against the State: Ethnographic Forays into Law's Transformations
Edited by Julia Eckert, Brian Donahoe, Christian Strümpell and Zerrin Özlem Biner

Transnational Legal Ordering and State Change
Edited by Gregory C. Shaffer

Legal Mobilization under Authoritarianism: The Case of Post-Colonial Hong Kong
Waikeung Tam

Complementarity in the Line of Fire: The Catalysing Effect of the International Criminal Court in Uganda and Sudan
Sarah M. H. Nouwen

Political and Legal Transformations of an Indonesian Polity: The Nagari from Colonisation to Decentralisation
Franz von Benda-Beckmann and Keebet von Benda-Beckmann

Pakistan's Experience with Formal Law: An Alien Justice
Osama Siddique

Human Rights under State-Enforced Religious Family Laws in Israel, Egypt, and India
Yüksel Sezgin

Why Prison?
Edited by David Scott

Law's Fragile State: Colonial, Authoritarian, and Humanitarian Legacies in Sudan
Mark Fathi Massoud

Rights for Others: The Slow Home-Coming of Human Rights in the Netherlands
Barbara Oomen

European States and Their Muslim Citizens: The Impact of Institutions on Perceptions and Boundaries
Edited by John R. Bowen, Christophe Bertossi, Jan Willem Duyvendak, and Mona Lena Krook

Environmental Litigation in China: A Study in Political Ambivalence
Rachel E. Stern

Indigeneity and Legal Pluralism in India: Claims, Histories, Meanings
Pooja Parmar

Paper Tiger: Law, Bureaucracy and the Developmental State in Himalayan India
Nayanika Mathur

Religion, Law and Society
Russell Sandberg

The Experiences of Face Veil Wearers in Europe and the Law
Edited by Eva Brems

The Contentious History of the International Bill of Human Rights
Christopher N. J. Roberts

Transnational Legal Orders
Edited by Terence C. Halliday and Gregory Shaffer

Lost in China? Law, Culture and Society in Post-1997 Hong Kong
Carol A. G. Jones

Security Theology, Surveillance and the Politics of Fear
Nadera Shalhoub-Kevorkian

Opposing the Rule of Law: How Myanmar's Courts Make Law and Order
Nick Cheesman

The Ironies of Colonial Governance: Law, Custom and Justice in Colonial India
James Jaffe

The Clinic and the Court: Law, Medicine and Anthropology
Edited by Ian Harper, Tobias Kelly, and Akshay Khanna

A World of Indicators: The Making of Government Knowledge through Quantification
Edited by Richard Rottenburg, Sally Engle Merry, Sung-Joon Park, and Johanna Mugler

Contesting Immigration Policy in Court: Legal Activism and Its Radiating Effects in the United States and France
Leila Kawar

The Quiet Power of Indicators: Measuring Governance, Corruption, and Rule of Law
Edited by Sally Engle Merry, Kevin Davis, and Benedict Kingsbury

Investing in Authoritarian Rule: Punishment and Patronage in Rwanda's Gacaca Courts for Genocide Crimes
Anuradha Chakravarty

Contractual Knowledge: One Hundred Years of Legal Experimentation in Global Markets
Edited by Grégoire Mallard and Jérôme Sgard

Iraq and the Crimes of Aggressive War: The Legal Cynicism of Criminal Militarism
John Hagan, Joshua Kaiser, and Anna Hanson

Culture in the Domains of Law
Edited by René Provost

China and Islam: The Prophet, the Party, and Law
Matthew S. Erie

Diversity in Practice: Race, Gender, and Class in Legal and Professional Careers
Edited by Spencer Headworth and Robert Nelson

A Sociology of Constitutions: Constitutions and State Legitimacy in Historical-Sociological Perspective
Chris Thornhill

A Sociology of Transnational Constitutions: Social Foundations of the Post-National Legal Structure
Chris Thornhill

Shifting Legal Visions: Judicial Change and Human Rights Trials in Latin America
Ezequiel A. González Ocantos

The Demographic Transformations of Citizenship
Heli Askola

Criminal Defense in China: The Politics of Lawyers at Work
Sida Liu and Terence C. Halliday

Contesting Economic and Social Rights in Ireland: Constitution, State and Society, 1848–2016
Thomas Murray

Buried in the Heart: Women, Complex Victimhood and the War in Northern Uganda
Erin Baines

Palaces of Hope: The Anthropology of Global Organizations
Edited by Ronald Niezen and Maria Sapignoli

The Politics of Bureaucratic Corruption in Post-Transitional Eastern Europe
Marina Zaloznaya

Revisiting the Law and Governance of Trafficking, Forced Labor and Modern Slavery
Edited by Prabha Kotiswaran

Incitement on Trial: Prosecuting International Speech Crimes
Richard Ashby Wilson

Criminalizing Children: Welfare and the State in Australia
David McCallum

Global Lawmakers: International Organizations in the Crafting of World Markets
Susan Block-Lieb and Terence C. Halliday

Duties to Care: Dementia, Relationality and Law
Rosie Harding

Insiders, Outsiders, Injuries, and Law: Revisiting "The Oven Bird's Song"
Edited by Mary Nell Trautner

Hunting Justice: Displacement, Law, and Activism in the Kalahari
Maria Sapignoli

Injury and Injustice: The Cultural Politics of Harm and Redress
Edited by Anne Bloom, David M. Engel, and Michael McCann

Ruling Before the Law: The Politics of Legal Regimes in China and Indonesia
William Hurst

The Powers of Law: A Comparative Analysis of Sociopolitical Legal Studies
Mauricio García-Villegas

A Sociology of Justice in Russia
Edited by Marina Kurkchiyan and Agnieszka Kubal

Constituting Religion: Islam, Liberal Rights, and the Malaysian State
Tamir Moustafa

The Invention of the Passport: Surveillance, Citizenship and the State, Second Edition
John C. Torpey

Law's Trials: The Performance of Legal Institutions in the US "War on Terror"
Richard L. Abel

Law's Wars: The Fate of the Rule of Law in the US "War on Terror"
Richard L. Abel

Transforming Gender Citizenship: The Irresistible Rise of Gender Quotas in Europe
Edited by Eléonore Lépinard and Ruth Rubio-Marín

Muslim Women's Quest for Justice: Gender, Law and Activism in India
Mengia Hong Tschalaer

Children as 'Risk': Sexual Exploitation and Abuse by Children and Young People
Anne-Marie McAlinden

The Legal Process and the Promise of Justice: Studies Inspired by the Work of Malcolm Feeley
Jonathan Simon, Rosann Greenspan, Hadar Aviram

Sovereign Exchanges: Gifts, Trusts, Reparations, and Other Fetishes of International Solidarity
Grégoire Mallard

Measuring Justice: Quantitative Accountability and the National Prosecuting Authority in South Africa
Johanna Mugler

Negotiating the Power of NGOs: Women's Legal Rights in South Africa
Reem Wael

Indigenous Water Rights in Law and Regulation: Lessons from Comparative Experience
Elizabeth Jane Macpherson

The Edge of Law: Legal Geographies of a War Crimes Court
Alex Jeffrey

Everyday Justice: Law, Ethnography, and Injustice
Sandra Brunnegger

The Uncounted: Politics of Data in Global Health
Sara L. M. Davis

Transnational Legal Ordering of Criminal Justice
Gregory Shaffer and Ely Aaronson

www.ingramcontent.com/pod-product-compliance
Lightning Source LLC
LaVergne TN
LVHW052012200926
848481LV00005B/1468
* 9 7 8 1 1 0 8 4 6 9 9 2 0 *